Praise for Hal Roth

"Roth writes with grace, humor, and poetic insight about the vastness and beauty of the ocean."
—*Library Journal*

"Roth's books about his life at sea, including *Two on a Big Ocean* and *Two Against Cape Horn*, are universally listed among the most influential sailing books ever published."—*SpinSheet*

Two on a Big Ocean

"A valuable addition to the literature of the sea."
—H. W. Tilman

"By all means read all of Hal Roth you can find."
—*Practical Sailor*

"A first-class outing for the armchair adventurer."
—*Library Journal*

"A fine personal account. A unique voyage."—*SAIL*

"A first-rate account of a great adventure."—*Yachting*

"Roth's Polynesian sequences are the best Pacific Island reporting in years."
—William Hogan, *San Francisco Chronicle*

"A seaman's yarn *par excellence*, and ever so much more."— Don Greame Kelly, *Oceans*

Two Against Cape Horn

"A wonderful book."—Eric Hiscock

"A great story and a great accomplishment. It left me dumbfounded. [The voyage] is almost impossible for the imagination to grasp."—Irving Johnson

"An extraordinary book."—William F. Buckley, Jr.

"Absorbing reading. Roth has managed to escape the confines of a pure sea story."—Ernest K. Gann

"Roth can charm you out of your armchair."—*Kirkus*

"Enthralling . . . Roth makes it clear why sailors risk the dangerous Horn passage: for the sailor it is the equivalent of Everest to the mountaineer."
—*John Barkham Reviews*

"This exciting book is a celebration of survival against all odds."—Book of the Month Club

"Will stir your blood."—Joe Brown, *San Diego Union*

"It becomes impossible for the reader to put the book down."—Miles Smeeton

"Stands out among many great tales."—*SAIL*

"The Horn. Shipwreck. Adventure at the end of the earth. Roth at his best and cruising at its limits. Read it."—*Cruising World*

"This book is a classic."—*Practical Sailor*

"A nautical saga so tense and exciting as to make the *Whisper*'s eventual rounding of the Horn almost an anticlimax."—*Publishers Weekly*

The Longest Race

"As a tale of high adventure of a kind which rarely happens and usually few survive, Hal Roth's account of the race is as good as any nautical yarn ever written."
—*Alan Cameron Reviews*

"Far beyond the other books that were rather superficial, and had not got their facts right."—Robin Knox-Johnston

"An epic in the annals of sailing [and] high adventure."
—Herb McCormick, *Cruising World*

"Only a superb seaman who is also a fine writer could weave a narrative as evocative and seamless."
—John Rousmaniere, *Dolphin Book Club*

"Proof indeed that truth can be stranger—and more rewarding—than fiction."—Noland Norgaard, *Club Ties*

THE HAL ROTH

SEAFARING
TRILOGY

Three True Stories of Adventure Under Sail

Books by Hal Roth

Pathway in the Sky
Two on a Big Ocean
After 50,000 Miles
Two Against Cape Horn
The Longest Race
Always a Distant Anchorage
Chasing the Long Rainbow
Chasing the Wind
We Followed Odysseus
How To Sail Around the World

THE HAL ROTH
SEAFARING TRILOGY

Three True Stories of Adventure Under Sail

TWO ON A BIG OCEAN | TWO AGAINST CAPE HORN | THE LONGEST RACE

HAL ROTH

International Marine / McGraw-Hill

Camden, Maine • New York • Chicago • San Francisco • Lisbon • London • Madrid •
Mexico City • Milan • New Delhi • San Juan • Seoul • Singapore • Sydney • Toronto

The McGraw·Hill Companies

1 2 3 4 5 6 7 8 9 DOC DOC 0 9 8 7 6

Library of Congress Cataloging-in-Publication Data
Roth, Hal, 1927–
  The Hal Roth seafaring trilogy : three true stories of adventure under sail
/ Hal Roth.
      p.   cm.
  Summary: This is three books published by other publishers. The
longest race, Two on a big ocean, and Two against Cape Horn.
  Includes bibliographical references.
  ISBN 0-07-146133-7 (hardcover : alk. paper)
  1. Sailing. 2. Sailboat racing. 3. Voyages and travels. I. Title: Seafaring
trilogy. II. Roth, Hal, 1927– Longest Race. III. Roth, Hal, 1927– Two
against Cape Horn. IV. Roth, Hal, 1927– Two on a big ocean. V. Title.
  GV811.R588 2006
    797.124—dc22   2005019340

Two on a Big Ocean first published in 1972 by Macmillan. Maps by John
Armstrong.

Two Against Cape Horn first published in 1978 by W. W. Norton. Maps by
Sam F. Manning.

An earlier version of *The Longest Race* was published by W. W. Norton in
1983. The manuscript was revised and new material added in 2005.

Two on a Big Ocean

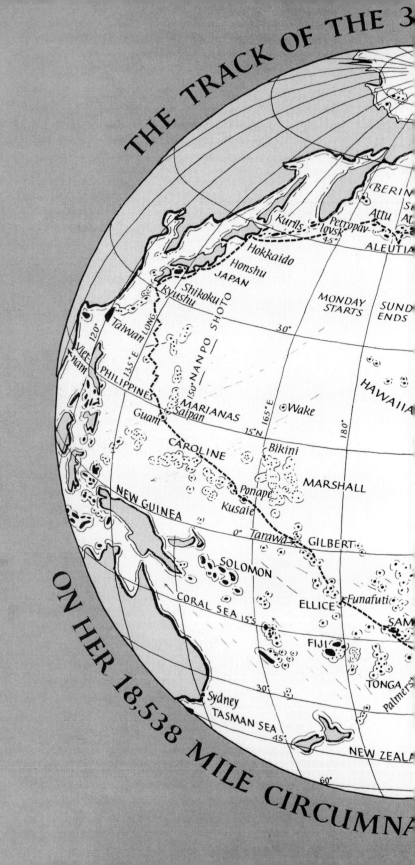

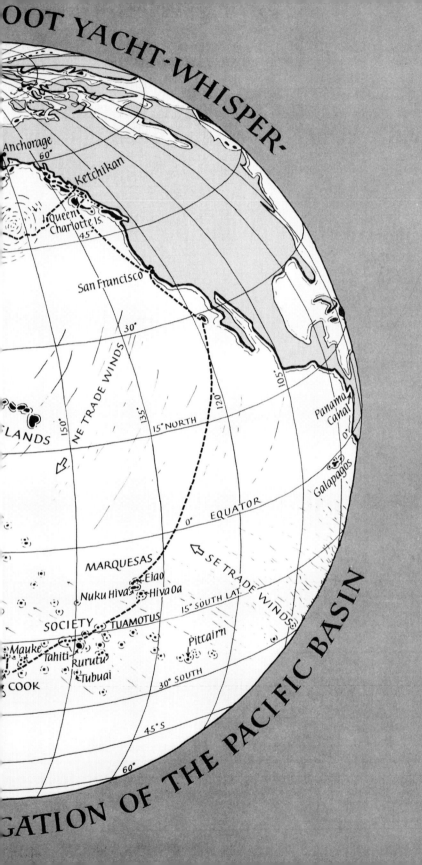

Anchorage
60°

Ketchikan

Queen
Charlotte Is.
45°

San Francisco

30°

NE TRADE WINDS

ISLANDS

150°

135°

15° NORTH

120°

105°

Panama
Canal
0°

Galapagos

0°   EQUATOR

MARQUESAS

Eiao

Nuku Hiva   Hiva Oa

SE TRADE WINDS

15° SOUTH LAT.

SOCIETY   TUAMOTUS

Mauke

Tahiti

Rurutu

Pitcairn

COOK

Tubuai

30° SOUTH

45° S

60°

HAL ROTH

Two on a Big Ocean

The story of the first circumnavigation of

the Pacific basin in a small sailing ship

Maps by John Armstrong

ACKNOWLEDGMENTS

I would like to thank Joe Brown the editor of *Oceans*, Hans Strepp of *Die Yacht*, Bill Robinson of *Yachting*, Gerry Kidd of *Pacific Yachting*, and Bernard Hayman of *Yachting World* for their kind permission to use some of the material which appeared originally in these magazines. The Gilbert Island song is from *We Chose The Islands* by Arthur Grimble, New York, William Morrow, 1952, and is used by permission.

This book is dedicated to
Bobby Uriburu, the veteran
sailor from Argentina, whose
constant encouragement, assistance,
common sense, and good humor
might well be copied by men
everywhere.

CONTENTS

Even in a little thing
(A leaf, a child's hand, a star's flicker)
I shall find a song worth singing
If my eyes are wide, and sleep not.

Even in a laughable thing
(Oh hark! The children are laughing!)
There is that which fills the heart to overflowing,
And makes dreams wistful.

Small is the life of a man
(Not too sad, not too happy):
I shall find my songs in a man's small life.
                    Behold them soaring!

Very low on earth are the frigate-birds hatched,
Yet they soar as high as the sun.

—SONG FROM THE GILBERT ISLANDS

1 / An Idea

As with most grand schemes our plan was simple. We wanted to sail a small yacht from our home in San Francisco to Japan via the islands of the South Pacific, and then to return to the United States on the great circle northern route by way of the Aleutian Islands, Alaska, and finally the Queen Charlotte Islands on the west coast of Canada. The proposal called for 19,000 miles of sailing on a roughly oval-shaped course that followed the sweep of the major surface currents of the Pacific. During the nineteen-month trip we would call at some seventy-five ports and sail in both warm and cold waters. In the South Pacific our biggest hazard would be coral reefs. In the North Pacific our difficulty would be fog.

We were two. Margaret and I decided after examining the records of many small-yacht trips that crew problems were often more severe than the trips themselves. We would man the ship ourselves, although we realized that meant watch and watch in turn, not so easy sometimes, especially when the going was difficult. However, we weren't worried about the troublesome moments. What we thought of were lovely anchorages in turquoise lagoons, weeks of splendid sailing with the warm trade winds behind us, getting to know such places as Samoa, Moorea, Rarotonga, Kusaie . . . and the fun of meeting Polynesians and Micronesians. I was anxious to hear Tahitian music at first hand. Margaret was keen to see a coral atoll. Japan and the northern islands were unknown mysteries.

1

We planned to stay entirely in the Pacific and to begin with French Polynesia, the Cook Islands, and Samoa. Then we would shape our course to the northwest and sail to the Ellice, Gilbert, and Eastern Caroline islands, before stopping at Guam and crossing the Philippine Sea on the way to Japan.

It all seemed a long way and a big undertaking. Could we do it?

I learned long ago that travel is more worthwhile if you spend a little time reading about where you are going. There was certainly no lack of writing about most of our goals in the Pacific. The shelves in the libraries bulged with reports of exploration, memoirs of English and French navigators, dusty histories, reminiscences of early travelers, surveys of modern governments, and various long-haired studies. The books about Japan and the Far East often filled a whole room—even in small libraries.

However, when we tried to find out something about the Ellice and Gilbert islands the librarians shook their heads.

"Not much on those places," they said. "Hardly anyone goes there. No steamship or air service. In fact the Ellice and Gilbert islands are not even on most maps."

"Just the islands for me," said Margaret eagerly. "I want to discover some new places. I want to sing and dance with strange people. I want to sit in the kitchens of the women and see how they cook. I want to find out how their clothes are made and I would like to look at their houses. But I guess the only way we can visit such forgotten islands is in our own ship."

Our own ship! Our own ship! The phrase sounded nice, but it was only talk. At that time we didn't own a ship or even know what to buy, though we had been getting plenty of ideas from the splendid shelf of sailing books we had found in the library. More suggestions came from yachting magazines. But most of the advice was from our acquaintances on the docks of Sausalito, a small community just north of the Golden Gate Bridge inside San Francisco Bay.

"What kind of a ship shall I get?" I asked my expert sailing friends.

"A ketch with a powerful engine," said one.

"By all means buy a schooner," said another. "It's the traditional ship of America and the best for going anywhere."

"A cutter is the only yacht to have," said a third. "The two headsail rig is easy to handle and . . ."

Ralph Holloway, my neighbor in Sausalito, owned a trim blue-and-white gaff yawl. "It's just the sail plan you need," he said enthusiastically, unrolling the blueprints on his living-room floor. "Everybody knows that a gaff rig is the best for offshore work. A yawl sail plan is perfect."

Four answers to the same question. I should have known better, but like a fool I held out my burned hand toward the flame.

"What is the best material for a ship?" I asked.

"Wood is the only thing for small ships," said Bill Hauselt, who owned a ten-ton schooner and who spoke with authority. "You can always fix wood yourself and the repairs are simple and quick."

Nipper Riddell, a veteran of a long Pacific cruise, had other ideas. "Bah! Wood is the worst choice you can make for a cruising yacht," he said menacingly. "Forget wood. It's only a homestead for worms. Get yourself a good steel ship. You want strength in case you hit anything. *Steel* is best."

I mentioned Nipper's suggestion to Bob Van Blaricom, an expert sailor who was a civil engineer.

"Steel! Wood! Are you mad?" said Bob. "Do you want to spend the rest of your life replacing rotten planks and soft frames? Or scraping rust and painting steel? Forget woodies and tin boats. Get with the times. Buy a fiberglass ship. Plastic is the best choice these days."

My head was spinning from all these opinions, each of which seemed to go off on a different point of the compass. Only one thing was certain. Small sailing-ship owners were an outspoken, fiercely independent lot who delighted in expressing forceful, earnestly argued views.

The yacht brokers had more ideas. In fact once they started talking they never stopped. They sounded like violin players entranced by the sound of their own fiddling. The brokers never asked us what *we* wanted; they only tried to sell us what *they* wanted. They kept telling us what we should have. The brokers asked nosy questions about our finances and suggested schemes for buying harbor-type, cocktail-hour yachts that would have had us in debt forever. Margaret and I fled in horror.

We began to read newspaper advertisements and to tramp the San Francisco Bay docks seeking FOR SALE signs. We shopped diligently for months and inspected several dozen yachts. A ship we could afford was generally too small, too old, in bad condition, or perhaps all three. The cost of big, handsome yachts was beyond us. One ship had a splendid hull but we didn't like the interior. A Hong Kong-built cutter seemed a good choice until an expert told us the frames and deck beams were too light for offshore cruising. We were shown a forty-two-foot cutter named *Helaine* that had been constructed by a famous Alameda shipyard. We looked, we liked it, we hesitated . . . and a friend bought it.

We drove to the Pacific Northwest to see what yachts were for sale. One Sunday morning in October at the Shilshole Bay Marina in Seattle we saw a sleek black-hulled sloop about to go out for a race. The yacht seemed much larger than her thirty-five feet. We liked the ship right away but sighed at the probable cost of a fiberglass hull.

The craft turned out to be a Spencer 35, a design with a good racing record that was built in Canada, just across the border. We traveled to Vancouver and looked up the tiny boat works on Mitchell Island, where we met the builder and later the naval architect, John Brandlmayr. The price was more than we had planned, but we were thrilled at the prospect of a sleek new yacht beautifully finished in teak below decks. I outlined the Pacific trip proposal to Brandlmayr and he thought the ship could do it. We had barely enough money, so I agreed to do a little of the interior finishing and to shop for the Diesel engine, rigging fittings, ground tackle, and the sails myself.

We decided on the name *Whisper* for our new ship. The builder started construction in November 1965, and she was launched the following February. We spent March fitting her out and installing a Hasler wind vane automatic steering gear which we hoped would reduce tedious watches. In April we sailed *Whisper* south to San Francisco, covering the 1,000 miles in eleven days.

We soon learned that a new ship needs many modifications, refinements, and a continuing supply of equipment. We threw out an expensive Diesel cooking and heating stove because the depth of the ship made a proper draft impossible. The ship lacked conventional bilge drainage, so we ran a hose from the chain locker to the engine bilge. The floor of the head compartment had no drainage and had to be rebuilt. We put the hand bilge pump in three places before it found a permanent home. We installed larger outlet pipes and valves in the self-draining cockpit. We had trouble with deck leaks around the chain plates and in the after section of the forepeak. A friend, Doug Duane, a magician with metal, made us a dozen special stainless-steel fittings, including a fifteen-gallon kerosene tank that we needed to hold the fuel for lamps, a new cooking stove, and a cabin heater from England.

Margaret and I both kept our regular jobs, but we spent every spare hour of 1966 working on *Whisper*. Our problems fell into two classes:

(1) Instead of stockpiling money for the trip we found we were spending large sums outfitting the ship ($55 to Paris for charts of French Polynesia, $14 for two mushroom ventilators, $9 for fire-extinguisher refills, $150 for a spare sextant, etc.).

(2) For every job we scratched off our project list we found two more to do. For example, on April 30 I had a list with thirty-eight projects (drill locker ventilation holes, improve cockpit locker drainage, install windlass spring, make dinghy chocks, and so forth). That day I completed four jobs but found six new ones, so the list increased to forty!

The following March we began to lay in stores. One evening at dusk a driver from a wholesale grocer unloaded most of his truck on the dock. We almost fainted when we saw the mountain of canned goods ("Opening a grocery?" inquired a man walking his dog). However, little by little we tucked away the thirty cases of canned meats, vegetables, and fruits, a sack of rice, long skinny boxes of spaghetti, and giant cans of onion flakes, instant potatoes, and dried eggs. Fang, the ship's cat, was mystified by all the containers, and while we were putting the stores away she liked to hide behind the boxes and to jump among the cans.

By now we had both given up our jobs and were living and working full time on *Whisper*. There was so much to do that even day and night weren't long enough. We constructed shelves underneath the cockpit and strapped in such items as eight gallons of bottom paint, varnish, fiberglassing chemicals, and various solvents and sealants. We tucked away a dozen lamp chimneys, extra winch handles, spares for the Primus stoves, and a large box of engine parts. We slipped 130 charts beneath the forepeak bunks, which began to rise alarmingly. Doctors whom we knew loaded us down with enough drugs to start a pharmacy.

"I don't approve of your trip particularly," said Dr. Hank Turkell, the Coroner of San Francisco, who owned a nearby motor-sailer, "but if you're really going you had better take these antibiotics along," he said, generously handing me a small box.

A dentist, Jerry Williams, who had the ship next to us obligingly fitted out a kit for emergency tooth fillings.

We hired an expert to adjust the compass.

We had both shorts and swimming suits for the tropics, and heavy sweaters, thermal underwear, sea boots, and oilskins for the North Pacific. We had light bulbs, nose drops, Stillson wrenches, birthday candles, metric taps, ukulele strings . . .

We had thousands of items on board, so many that Margaret was obliged to keep lists in order to find things. For foodstuffs she kept one notebook with locations and a second that listed the quantity. We got visas in our passports for the countries we planned to visit. We went to the doctor for various traveler's injections and booster shots. It seemed that we were working twice as hard and twice as long as we did when we had regular jobs.

But sometimes we stopped work to go sailing, which after all was what the ship was for. San Francisco is a lovely place to sail, for the winds are good and the seas slight. At dawn the sky above the bay was often a delicate garden of daffodil yellow and wild rose. In the afternoon, tongues of cottony white fog would slip in from the Pacific and gently drift past the massive towers of the Golden Gate Bridge. At dusk the lights of San Francisco spun a web of silver that floated above the strong, silent water. In our little ship we would glide along and marvel at it all.

The word had gotten around that we were soon to leave on a long trip. The number of curious visitors on weekends became a problem. Although we had many jobs we were glad to see people and to explain the working of the automatic wind vane steering gear which was a novelty. However, on some Sundays twenty-five or thirty people would appear, some expecting to be fed, given drinks, and generally entertained. Hardly anyone took off his shoes, and by Sunday night the decks and cabin sole would be black with tracked-on dirt.

Sometimes we solved the weekend problem by slipping out for a sail and anchoring in a cove somewhere, often with our friends, Bob and Jane Van Blaricom, who helped us immensely. They had a new baby, Anne, who Bob carried on board in a basket. Bob and Jane had purchased a forty-foot cutter in England and had sailed it across the Atlantic, through the Panama Canal, and up to San Francisco, where they had sold it at a big profit.

"And hated ourselves ever since," said Bob wistfully, wishing that he still owned *Armorel*. "Cruising in small boats is the real life. We certainly wish we were going with you. What fools we were to sell *Armorel*."

"Some of our friends think us quite adventurous and brave," I said. "Others think us quite mad. One thing is certain. We'll be entirely on our own when we're out there. We'll have to be self-sufficient and to look out for ourselves. Of course the first question most people ask when they hear about the trip is: 'How powerful is your radio transmitter?' I tell them that we have no transmitter and that even if we did there would be no one to call far out in the Pacific, certainly no U.S. Coast Guard. Many people profess to like boating but they have a genuine fear of the sea—or maybe it's a fear of the unknown. I don't wish to sound cocky, but I am supremely confident."

"You won't have any problems at all," replied Bob. "The biggest problem for adventurers is to get away from home. The world is full of talkers and dreamers. Not many people do anything."

Neither Margaret nor I had ever visited the South Pacific or the Far East. Although we had sailed a little in the West Indies, in Greece, in Scotland, and up and down the west coast of the United States, we had never undertaken a major ocean crossing by ourselves. There was much talk about the Pacific being too large for a small yacht. We would have to find out. . . .

We were ready to go. We had a good ship, hopefully were well prepared, and had an exciting itinerary.

The table was set. The meal was in front of us.

The Long Crossing

ON OUR TWELFTH DAY AT SEA, MAY 15, WE WERE HALF-way between California and the Marquesas, the northernmost islands of French Polynesia. We had forgotten about land. Civilization seemed remote and unbelievable. Our position that day was 15° 15′ north of the equator and 125° west of Greenwich. San Francisco was 1,560 miles to the north. Hilo, Hawaii, lay 1,740 miles in a direction a little north of west, and my chart showed that El Salvador, in Central America, was 2,340 miles to the east.

When I stood in the companionway and looked around I saw only the ocean, the sky, and the trade wind clouds—small rabbit tails of cotton that lay stacked overhead like puffs from a giant pipe. We had seen no ships since leaving California, and we were emphatically alone—alone in a world of blue. A feathery turquoise glowed in the sky; around me as I turned I could see a hard rim of ink-bottle blue where the sky stopped and the sea began. The etched line of the horizon was firm and definitive and it almost seemed to enclose a private world. It was a delight to be by ourselves, and how free we were! Our lives lay in our hands alone—no one knew where we were—and the independence was a good feeling. I felt exuberant and reassured somehow. I knew that I was in charge of the ship and what we did, but I also had the notion that I was in control of the sea that I could see around me—a foolish idea, I suppose, for it is manifest that the sea knows no master. Yet as long as we paid proper respect to the might of the ocean I felt sure that our tiny ship would be safe.

On that sun-drenched day *Whisper* flew along with the strong northeast trade wind blowing hard on her port quarter. We had eased the mainsail to starboard so the wind blew directly against the big sail, which we balanced with a jib held out to port on a long pole set at right angles to the following wind. In general we had found the northeast trades stronger than we had reckoned. The arrows on the Pilot charts indicated winds of Force 4, eleven to sixteen knots, but we often experienced Force 6, twenty-two to twenty-seven knots, and sometimes more. However, the winds were fair and behind us.

The trade wind sailing was glorious. *Whisper* seemed totally alive and as responsive as a lady in love. How we rushed along! With the sails full and straining we would ride up on a big swell and whoosh forward as a white-topped crest raced past. The air was fresh and you took in great lungfuls of the clean stuff. The sun felt hot on my bare shoulders, and Margaret and I often sat on the side decks and let our feet hang over the edge into the 75° water. When I looked aloft the sun glinted on the warm brown of the spruce mast and sparkled on bits of the rigging. *Whisper* rolled steadily from side to side, and I looked up through half-closed eyes to see the white sails dancing beneath the blue of the sky. Was the ship moving and the sky steady or was it the other way? The white embraced the blue and waltzed around and around. The white pirouetted. The blue bowed. It was a dream; it was heaven!

We steered *Whisper* largely with an automatic mechanism, a Hasler wind vane steering gear. The device was a valuable crewman who was always alert and working, never grumbled, never got hungry, and was particularly good on long night watches. As time went on we found the steering gear more and more useful. It gave Margaret and me time to navigate, do odd jobs, read, and get plenty of sleep. Steering hour after hour at sea is a bore; we had plenty of other things to do.

The wind vane gear was similar to the devices used to steer model yachts—the trim little ships I remember so well in San Francisco's Golden Gate Park on Sunday afternoons. You put the model ship on the course you wanted and trimmed the sails for the wind. Then if the ship changed direction for any reason when sailing across the pond a small wind blade near the stern turned and its corrective movements were linked to the rudder, which put the ship back on its proper course. On a model yacht the wind blade was coupled directly to the rudder, but on a larger ship the force of the wind blade was not strong enough to move the tiller. On *Whisper* we had a clever mechanism invented by Blondie Hasler, the English sailing expert, which mechanically amplified the movements of a wind blade and exerted a powerful steering force on the tiller.

Our automatic steering gear meant we were relieved of the slavery of steering most of the time. We had to know what the wind was doing, of course, and adjust the setting of the steering vane from time to time, but sometimes we didn't touch it for hours or days. Without a hand on the tiller we could keep a better lookout because you could stand up and move around. In the neighborhood of ships it was easier to keep track of steamers, and along a coastline the person on watch could navigate instead of going cross-eyed watching the compass. Around land or near shipping lanes where there was a risk of collision, Margaret and I kept watches twenty-four hours a day, generally four hours on and four hours off. But when we were a thousand miles from shore and far from shipping lanes I eased the rigid watch schedule. At night one of us would sleep deeply while the other read or dozed below, going on deck every twenty or thirty minutes for a look around. You got used to the creaking of the ship and the water gurgling along the hull, and like a mother with a new baby you were instantly alerted by any unusual sound.

There was a different dimension to nighttime sailing. The log for May 9, read:

2045. Tearing along with the sails unchanged for over 24 hours. Margaret and the cat sound asleep. The night is so black that only after I look around for a few minutes do my eyes become aware of faint stars through a thin layer of cloud. The wind has picked up to 20 knots or so. Although we're only traveling at something like six miles an hour, the illusion of speed is tremendous; we hurtle along through the black night like an express train in a tunnel. Rivers of phosphorescence stream from the stern and our wake is a luminous, glowing ribbon of milky froth that is pure magic. The wind has veered a trifle and I have lowered our course to put us back on 175°M. The barometer has been reading low and unchanged for over two weeks and I am sure it is broken. Better forget about it. No one can predict weather anyway.

When the winds blew stronger our little ship churned through the seas. On one day our sleek hull knifed through 151 miles in twenty-four hours, a record run for us and good time for a ship only twenty-five feet on the waterline. But we paid for the speed by rolling heavily. With winds from astern we had trimmed the sails for running, and with little fore and aft canvas effectively set, *Whisper* rolled a good deal. The faster we sailed the more we rolled. We had to hold on grimly when below, and on deck we crawled around. The endurance of the crew became the limiting factor. We got exhausted. The ordinary acts of living became perilous adventures. It was time to slow down.

We reduced the area of the mainsail by rolling up half a dozen turns around the main boom. We replaced the jib with one only 75 percent as big. With the drive of less horsepower we slowed from six knots to five knots or a little less. The small reduction in speed caused a big reduction in the violent motion; no longer were we dolls controlled by a palsied puppeteer, but human beings on a peaceful trip.

A few days later the wind increased to Force 7, twenty-eight to thirty-three knots, a moderate gale, and though it was behind us we found the sea conditions too rough for us to continue. We hove to— that is, we headed into the wind and arranged the sails and tiller so the ship almost stopped. I went on deck a little after midnight, hauled down the working jib, and hanked on the storm jib. However, *Whisper* lay so smoothly under the triple reefed mainsail alone that I left her without any headsail. As I turned to go below I looked around. The clouds were gone and overhead the world was all sky and stars. Deep in the darkness of the southern sky I saw a small cluster of stars. It was a new constellation, the Southern Cross, one I had never seen before. I was enthralled. I thumbed through a star chart and added Acrux, Gacrux, Hadar, and Rigil Kent to my friends up there.

The next morning we dropped the mainsail, hoisted the storm jib, and bent on and raised the trysail, a small boomless storm sail used in place of the mainsail in bad weather. We squared away before the northeast wind again, and with only the two small scraps of sails flying we logged runs of 107 and 108 miles during the next forty-eight hours. The wind then moderated to fifteen knots and we hoisted our regular canvas.

Mariners, especially sailing people, plan their routes and try to minimize adverse currents and headwinds by studying Pilot charts. These special weather maps cover the world in various sheets and are prepared for each month or every other month. The information is based on thousands and thousands of observations and dates back to the pioneering work of Matthew Fontaine Maury, a lieutenant in the U.S. Navy, who provided nineteenth century sailing-ship masters with special logbooks in which to record the weather they found. On Pilot charts every ten-degree square of latitude and longitude is broken into four smaller squares, each with a blue wind quadrant that tells the percentage of time and force the wind has been observed to blow from a certain direction. You can read about the weather generally and inspect diagrams that detail barometric pressure and the chances of gales. The Pilot charts show the air temperature in dotted red, magnetic variation in gray, ocean currents in small blue arrows, storm tracks in solid red, fog in dotted blue, and the type and limits of ice in patterned red lines.

On our passage to French Polynesia we were concerned with the trade winds and doldrums. A straight-line course between San Francisco and the Marquesas measured about 3,000 miles. We picked up the northeast trades roughly 250 miles south of the United States–Mexican border when we were an equal distance west of the mainland. According to the Pilot chart for May, we could expect to stay in the fair northeast trades to about 8° N. and 132° W., or some 1,140 miles. But after passing through the doldrums and into the southeast trades we would have wind forward of the beam. We could improve this prospect by keeping farther east in the northeast trades so that when we finally struck the southeast trades we would have a fair wind. We also wished to cross from one trade wind belt to the other through an area where the doldrums, the place of fickle winds and prolonged calms, were narrow. Further complications were the equatorial surface currents. After studying the Pilot charts and reading accounts of other voyages, we headed for 125° W. and 10° N., a reasonable compromise that made our route some 200 miles longer but augured better winds.

"Time!" shouted Margaret from on deck. I was below with a second-setting watch in my hand. I wrote down 09:28:57.

"I read 42° 41'," called Margaret. I noted the angle in the workbook and repeated it aloud. Margaret handed down the sextant and I stowed it away in its box.

We navigated in turn. I would find our position one day. Margaret would do it the next. This way both of us kept in practice, and if one of us were sick or busy, the other could carry on. It was exciting to cross one position line with a second and to find where we were to within a mile or two. Sometimes I would be so anxious for the final cross that my hands would shake with excitement.

I think the difficulties of celestial navigation are highly overrated. We learned it ourselves, mainly from Eric Hiscock's *Voyaging Under*

Sail. You have an almanac—issued yearly—which gives the position of each navigational body for every second of time for each day. You measure the angle between the horizon and a heavenly body—generally the sun—with an angle-measuring device called a sextant. You make three slight corrections to the sextant angle, extract two figures from the almanac, and enter a second book—H.O. 249—from which in effect you take out half of your position. Observations of two heavenly bodies at the same time or of one heavenly body at different hours of the day give you two position lines and a precise fix.

Margaret and I generally made a sun sight between 0900 and 1000 and a second around noon. Or if the moon was up and we could find it we used it. (My favorite sights were simultaneous observations of the sun and moon.) Sometimes we shot stars, three of which gave a precise position. We found the main difficulty with celestial navigation was not the calculations but the observations. It was important to see the horizon sharply at the instant of measurement when no intervening waves were in the way. You waited until the ship lifted on a wave, the horizon was clear, and then turned the micrometer screw on the sextant until the reflected sun just met the horizon. At this instant you noted the exact time. Of course when the weather was rough and the ship was rolling heavily it was hard to get a good sight, but, like everything else on earth, practice was the answer.

In the old days a sailing-ship master had trouble knowing his exact position because he lacked the precise time needed to find his longitude. Chronometers helped greatly, but the invention of radio solved the problem. On *Whisper* we tuned our Zenith transistor radio to WWV and WWVH, powerful U.S. stations that broadcast special time signals. In the Western Pacific we got a time signal sent out before news broadcasts from Radio Australia. Later we got time checks from Guam and Tokyo before returning to the range of U.S. stations. On no day during our nineteen-month trip did we fail to receive time signals on one of our two receivers. In addition we carried two rated timepieces.

Shortly after we had left California we had had trouble with deck leaks, supposedly an impossibility in a fiberglass yacht. We didn't mind a few drops of water, but a steady drip from the shelves along both sides of the forepeak soon turned the books, bedding, and a hundred other things into a soggy mess. South of San Francisco we had hit contrary winds which had resulted in a lot of water over the foredeck. So much water had gotten below that I began to fear for the safety of the ship. We had two bilge pumps that drew from beneath the engine compartment, but the rest of the bottom of the hull was partitioned off into tanks and sections without conventional fore and aft drainage beneath them. Water from forward couldn't drain aft to be pumped out until it collected to the point where it flooded over the cabin floor. We mopped up the water with sponges and buckets. I was alarmed ("Would the leaks get worse?") and put back into Southern California from several hundred miles offshore. Once in port Margaret hosed off the wet things and hung them out to dry. I called on experts to help me with the leak.

We pulled off the port toerail and found that the hull-deck joint underneath, though strong, had been fabricated in such a way that water could work down inside the joint and get below through the toerail bolt holes. We sealed the top of the hull-deck joint as best we could, put plenty of bedding compound underneath the toerail, and bolted it back in place. We also caulked a leak in the front hatch coaming.

"If you'll take my advice you'll seal that front hatch with heavy tape all around the outside," counseled an old sailor. "Then she'll never leak."

We followed his suggestion, filled our water tanks, and headed out to sea determined to carry on. *Whisper* sailed beautifully with her magnificent hull, but at that moment I had a poisonous opinion of naval architects and yacht builders after a week of expensive, difficult, inconclusive, frustrating, and time-wasting leak-hunting. I formulated a thought I was to recall many times in the months ahead: "If only the naval architect and the builder had to sail their creation across an ocean!"

Now many days later and far to the south the leaks were largely forgotten. The warm northeast trade wind blew behind us. The sun was hot, all the ports were open, and the decks were dry. The cat slept stretched out under the shade of the dinghy, and I stood on the foredeck dumping buckets of sea water over my head to cool off. All the blankets and heavy clothes and shoes had been tucked away. We slept under one sheet. Our uniforms were sun hats, shorts, and bare feet.

Margaret cooked on a two-burner Primus stove that used kerosene

under pressure from a three-gallon tank. We had taken twelve dozen freshly laid eggs (which kept perfectly when coated with Vaseline) and generally had eggs and tea and toast for breakfast. Sometimes we ate cold cereal with milk made from powdered whole milk, which became a creamy, rich liquid when stirred with a little water. We often lunched on soup or bouillon and sandwiches made with tinned meat. We started off with eight loaves of bread, which kept reasonably well for several weeks. Margaret then trimmed off the moldy bits and made toast. When the bread got beyond salvage we heaved the remains over the side and changed to ship's biscuit.

We always had a hot meal for dinner: spaghetti with tinned meat, salmon or tuna in a white sauce, roast beef and rice, corned beef and cabbage. . . . We had a large box of fruits and vegetables in the forepeak, and just before we left, a friend, Mabel Rolley, gave us an enormous bag of big, tree-ripened oranges. How we enjoyed those oranges on the long crossing! How many times I blessed Mabel. When the sun beat down and the ship had rolled away your appetite the sweet juicy segments were cool and refreshing and almost seemed to pour energy into your bones.

Margaret's cooking was first-rate. She would open a can or two, ask me for a few potatoes or carrots from the vegetable bin, rattle around in the galley, and shortly afterward hand me a warm and savory plate of buttered diced beets, fluffy steaming rice, and spicy chicken curry. Or maybe creamed carrots, roast beef braised with wine, and sautéed potatoes. You always find corned beef at sea because it is cheap, keeps well, and is wholesome and solid. But you get tired of it. Margaret was a wizard at disguising corned beef. Sometimes she would dip slices of the meat into beaten egg, roll them in coarse brown flour, and fry them crispy and golden. She made a special chile con carne with corned beef. Sometimes we ate it on crackers together with white-hot mustard and pickles. Her steamed dumplings gave corned beef and cabbage a new dimension.

I saw clever work in the galley. With no refrigeration we couldn't keep leftovers long, but we hated to waste food. Margaret often stuffed the remains of the evening meal into an omelet the next morning. A little peppery spaghetti and meat did wonders to the eggs. My favorite meal was beef stroganoff made with canned button mushrooms, thick canned cream, and tinned roast beef from Colorado.

The last few paragraphs may give the idea that we dined on starched linen with gold knives and forks after consulting menus chiseled in marble. Hardly! We ate well. Margaret was a wonder with modest ingredients, but there were plenty of days when the weather was bad and we had stew, or macaroni and cheese served in bowls. Then we ate wedged in somewhere, generally with our backs pushed firmly against the corner formed by a bulkhead and a settee and our feet jammed against the opposite settee.

Whisper continued to leak a little forward, which was disappointing after our repair efforts in California. There wasn't much we could do except to move things out of the way, try to dry them out a little, and to mop up.

One night when we were hurrying along with a strong following wind, a small jib, and a deep reef in the main, there was a terrible crash and *bang! bang!* I rushed outside to find that the roller reefing gear had slipped somehow and the reefed mainsail had unrolled from the boom. Without the support of the sail, the end of the boom had dropped, and with every roll of the ship the eighteen-foot boom crashed into the dinghy, which was stowed upside down on the coachroof. Already there was a dent in the aluminum skiff, and I felt splinters from the spruce boom under my bare feet as I stood on deck. I raised the boom end with the topping lift and inspected the expensive roller reefing gear with a flashlight. Unintentional unwinding was supposed to have been impossible; clearly the roller reefing gear was faulty, which meant that every time I reefed the mainsail I had to leave the handle in place and lash it to prevent the boom from unrolling. I cursed the makers and the builder who installed such unrepairable junk. Every time I used the roller reefing gear on the trip thereafter—several hundred times—I had to tie the handle in place.

On May 15 the log read:

1500. Very hot as we sail on and on toward the equator. Temperature of 86° in the cabin and we are dressed only in shorts. Three squalls today—the first at 0500— and a lovely refreshing shower with each. The rain pelts down and feels like needles at first but the soothing effect is marvelous. Noon position of 9° 44′ N. and 126° 20′ W. We have traveled 1,698 miles from San Francisco. Eiao in the Marquesas is 1,372 miles away. Good star sights of Sirius and Dubhe and the moon at dusk yesterday. Complicated to plot because the star fixes need to be moved for precession before the position line of the moon is drawn. I have never heard this problem discussed. 138 miles noon to noon.

The next day the strong northeast winds fell away as we worked south into the doldrums, the area of calms and variables that I had reckoned would last for 175 miles before we got into the southeast trades. I wondered what was going to happen? Would we be becalmed for weeks and finally run out of food? *Whisper's* light weight and easily driven hull were advantages now, and with the full main and a big genoa headsail we glided along on a calm blue sea. Tall banks of cumulus clouds towered into the hot reddish sky around us, and I counted eight rain squalls spaced around the horizon. The clouds were all tints of green, blue, and gray whose shades changed as fast as you turned your head. To describe such a scene was hopeless. While I was wondering how to do it a squall providentially erased my problem in a flood of rain and darkness.

I learned that squalls were short-lived heavy gusts of wind and rain (or snow) that could occur anywhere but appeared more often in the tropics and especially in the doldrums, where the air was particularly hot and moist. During the day you would see a bank of clouds, well worried with slashes of gray, advancing toward you. Sometimes you would realize that a squall was coming when you saw the sea under a low cloud suddenly kicked up into short whitecaps that danced beneath the wind. At night you learned to recognize an unreal quiet before a squall struck. When a squall hit the ship Margaret or I would race up on the foredeck and let the jib halyard fly to lower the headsail to ease the wind pressure on *Whisper*. Heavy rain would pour down for perhaps ten minutes (a good time for a freshwater shower) and the squall would pass. Then up with the sail again and back on course. Sometimes the squalls were bigger, as I found out on May 16:

Last night at 0300 I heard the wind coming. The ship heeled, the rain started, and I eased off to the west with the wind behind me. But the rain! It began lightly and soon increased. It poured. Then the volume doubled and doubled again! The rain fell so heavily that it blotted out the sails, the ship, the cabin—everything. I began to wonder where I was and what I was doing out in the middle of the Pacific in such a deluge. Then the rain increased again! Were we caught under a waterspout? I couldn't even see the kerosene cabin light only a few feet away.

The water beat down on my head and back and sloshed on the floor of the cockpit which filled faster than the drains could empty it. Suddenly there was a big crash next to me as the cat's box filled to the top and tipped off the cockpit seat. I was aware that the rain had eased a little when lightning jerked across the sky, igniting the low clouds with blue fire. I began to count one-one-thousandth, two-one-thousandth, etc., to work out how far the lightning was

from the ship by the number of seconds later the accompanying
thunder roared, but I had forgotten how to do it and gave up such
useless calculations of doom. There was so much thunder that
I would have mixed up the various peals anyway.

I was dressed only in shorts and a cotton T-shirt and I got very
cold. I finally called to Margaret to pass me an oilskin jacket.
I had no idea whether the squall had lasted ten minutes or half an
hour. I clicked on a flashlight and wiped the water from my watch.
The storm had lasted two hours.

We had good luck getting through the doldrums and began to pick
up southeast winds only thirty-six hours after leaving the northeast
trades. On the two days in the doldrums we made daily runs of 120
and 97 miles, remarkable times in such an area, but *Whisper* was at
her best in light going.

Sometimes we saw flying fish, silvery bluish creatures eight or ten
or twelve inches long that would suddenly appear a few feet out of
the water and soar parallel to the waves for perhaps a quarter or
half a mile. Once in a while Fang would find one of the fish on deck.
She then became a wild animal. Growling hoarsely, she would seize
the fish in her mouth and rush off to a secluded corner to work on her
victim, first playing with the poor creature until it was a bloody mess
before she ate it. For some reason Fang liked to drag the fish into the
toilet compartment. She soon had blood and fish scales all over the
floor. I couldn't stand this and banished the cat and her blasted fish
to the cockpit. For a while she tried to sneak the fish below, but she
gave herself away because she always growled when she had a fish.
She finally got the idea: *no fish below.*

One morning when we were 570 miles from Eiao and below eating breakfast we heard a ship's whistle alongside. We jumped up to
see the U.S.N.S. *Richfield*, a large gray military vessel with yellow
rings painted on her stack. She was the first ship we had seen since
California more than three weeks before. The whole crew appeared
to be on deck and everyone was waving and smiling. We couldn't
imagine where the ship was going or why she was in such an isolated
part of the Pacific. From her heading she seemed outbound from
Panama. Her speed was easily two or three times that of our five
knots, and as we waved she was already pulling ahead. In a little
while she was out of sight and we were alone again. What excitement to see a ship!

On May 24 I got an excellent five-star fix from Arcturus, Spica,

Acrux, Canopus, and Sirius. We were now south of the equator and 310 miles from the Marquesas. At the time I knew it was ridiculous, but after I had plotted our position I went on deck and looked for land.

The sea voyage was long, perhaps too long. After three weeks I was impatient for land. The 64,000,000 square miles of the Pacific were too much. I took a pair of scissors and a map of the world and cut out the North Atlantic and laid its pattern over the Pacific. It took four North Atlantics to fill the Pacific. The distance from Ecuador to the Philippines along the equator measured 9,300 miles!

"Just as I thought," I said to Margaret when I showed her my paper dolls. "The blasted Pacific is endless."

Yet it was beautiful out there, and after a time you learned a rhythm from the sea. The day would break, the sun would rise in the eastern sky, the sun would beat down from overhead, and then the light would fall away to the west and the day was gone. Your life was measured in pulse beats of the sun, ticks on a colossal clock whose pendulum had its pivot among the stars and its weight on the wave tops.

The sea was calm. The sea was stormy. The sea was always there, regular and sure, swelling up and down, massive and huge. You were in its embrace and its arms were strong. Sometimes my breath came in

gasps when I felt its throbbing presence so closely. But what am I talking about? The relationship between the sea and a man is the same sort of stuff as between a man and a woman. The best parts of it are unspoken matters of the senses and the guts. You can't talk about it because no one is skilled enough. The words don't exist. It is personal and private and if you know it you feel it. If you don't you don't. There is no nonsense with mere words. That's how it was between the might of the sea and me.

Strange birds sometimes circled around and around the ship. We would get out our bird books and the binoculars and spend hours trying to identify them. One morning a beautiful red-billed tropicbird flew around *Whisper*, perhaps attracted by the white sails. When he got near the cockpit he fluttered his wings and slowed down, almost treading air, so he could have a close look at the peculiar creatures beneath him. He saw two sunburned human beings dressed in bits of cotton cloth and straw hats.

We looked up at the tropicbird and saw a slender white bird about two and a half feet in length, with two extremely long central tail feathers that extended behind him in a graceful arc perhaps eighteen inches long. He had a thick, heavy, orange-reddish bill and a long black patch on each cheek. His wing tips on top were black and his white back had fine crosswise dark lines. He was a powerful flier, and the curious bird stopped in mid-air again and again only a few feet from us. He seemed to say: "Just who are you anyway? What are you doing here?" It was a thrill to see him so near, a completely wild and uninhibited creature.

Long ago, sailors gave the tropicbird the nickname bosun bird because of the marlinspike—the long feathers—he carried in his tail.

At 0700 on May 25 I figured that we were 167 miles from land. I began to spend more time with the sextant and navigation books, and we made a big effort to steer a good course. I had no cause to doubt our position, but I was nervous nevertheless, since the distance from California to the Marquesas was more than 3,000 miles. What if I had made a constant error in navigation? To ease my mind I calculated *Whisper*'s position with H.O. 211, an alternate scheme of celestial navigation. I checked the time with the radio anew and took separate observations with the sextant. Our position appeared to be accurate.

That afternoon I replaced a chafed line from the steering vane to the tiller, but while I was tucking an eye splice in the 3/8″ line I kept peering ahead. We had seen a few land birds and the excitement at being close began to grow.

"O.K., mighty navigator," Margaret shouted a few hours later. "Wake up. It's star time."

I rubbed my eyes, got up from the starboard berth, grabbed the sextant, and climbed sleepily on deck. The sun was down in the west, and the sky was just dark enough to see the first stars. The warm southeast wind blew about fifteen knots and we galloped along at between five and six knots under the full main and the working jib.

"I've got Canopus, Sirius, and Arcturus in sight," said Margaret. "And Venus and Mars. You'd better hurry before the clouds cover them."

I braced myself on deck and shot sights of the stars and planets while Margaret used a small flashlight to read the watch and to write down the time and sextant angles. The 1900 star fix put us sixty-two miles east-northeast of Hatutu; the position lines from Mars and Venus crossed at a point fifty-five miles from land, or seven miles closer. Eiao, our destination, was a few miles farther. The wind had eased a little, and I thought we wouldn't see the islands until the next day.

One thing in our favor was that the land we were headed toward was high and mountainous and had no coral reefs. With deep water all around except for a shoal to the north, I wasn't afraid to stand in closely at night. A partial moon would give us enough light to see the islands. Surely we would see and hear breakers if we got too close.

As I sat in the cockpit and looked at the inky night I wondered how many other navigators had pondered their calculations and worried about landfalls. I thought how fortunate I was to have a good sextant, precise time, and advice on their use from generations of seamen. A small bird fluttered around the ship, the fourth I had seen since noon. I kept *Whisper* on a heading of 235° and peered ahead until midnight, when Margaret took over.

At 0300 Margaret called me. "There's something ahead," she said. I scrambled topsides and we both stared into the darkness. The light from the waning moon filtered through the trade wind clouds and cast a weak glow on the sea in front of us.

"Look a little to starboard," said Margaret excitedly. "I see two long mountainous islands."

3 / So Lofty and Green

HISTORIANS OF THE WESTERN WORLD TELL US THAT THE Marquesas Islands were discovered by Alvaro de Mendaña y Castro in 1595. A captain during the golden age of Spain, Mendaña was in charge of four ships carrying settlers from Peru to the Solomon Islands far to the west. Halfway to his goal and 3,700 miles from Peru, Mendaña blundered onto four volcanic islands whose mountains were tall and dark and whose valleys grew lush and green. The navigation in those days was so shaky that at first the Spaniards thought they had reached the Solomons, but instead of being greeted by natives who were short and black, the people who came out to the ships were tall, fair, clear-skinned, and had long, loose hair. The natives brought gifts of coconuts, plantains, and water in bamboo joints.

Quiros, the chief pilot, wrote of the excellent water, the luxuriant trees, and the splendid climate. He noted the thirty or forty paddlers in the great canoes carved from a single trunk, the houses of wood and cane that were roofed with leaves, and the regal women, graceful and nearly white, who seemed more lovely than even the beautiful women of Lima.

Mendaña solemnly bestowed the name Las Islas Marquesas de Don Garcia Hurtado de Mendoza de Cañete on the tropical islands, naming them for the viceroy of Peru. The friars on the ships zealously thought of new souls to save from purgatory, but as usual the Spanish needed little provocation to demonstrate their skill in musketry—especially on pagans—and the soldiers freely killed the friendly

Marquesans. As soon as it became certain that the all-important gold and jewels were not to be found, the islands were declared useless. After two weeks Mendaña sailed, leaving at least 200 dead Marquesans and three crosses erected to the glory of God.[1]

The islands lay undisturbed for 179 years. Then in 1774 Captain James Cook arrived in the *Resolution*. "The Inhabitents of these Isles are without exceptions as fine a race of people as any in this Sea or perhaps in any whatever," wrote the famous explorer.[2]

One of Cook's artists made engravings of Marquesan chiefs that showed elaborate facial tattooing and ornate headdresses. Under the steep cliffs of Vaitahu Bay on Tahuata the artist sketched slender outrigger canoes with delicately upcurved prows and decorated sterns that were driven by lofty spritsails of pandanus thatch. The muscular Marquesan paddlers sported extensive body tattoos of blue, and high, plumed headwear. The scientists of the expedition collected plants, studied the language, and worked on many useful projects, but in the end Cook and the natives came to blows. Again the Marquesans were killed.

Both Mendaña and Cook had looked at a Polynesian society near the peak of its development.

In the Marquesas the deep, isolated, high-walled valleys encouraged self-sufficient, independent tribes, some of whom were fierce, warring cannibals. Hereditary chiefs, often distinguished by feather headdresses, complete body tattooing, and whale tooth necklaces, ruled the tribes. The chiefs held all the tribal lands and parceled them out in return for a share of the chickens, yams, taro, etc., that was raised on them. With this income the chiefs supported extensive temples and ceremonial plazas. The Marquesan homes were built on elevated stone platforms, and the chiefs, who surrounded themselves with tough warriors, lived in large houses and had beautiful wives renowned for their sexuality. Below the chief but often on a par with him in authority stood the inspirational priest who controlled all religious affairs.

The houses, cooking sheds, and storage huts were clustered in hamlets along streams on the valley floors. Quantities of fermenting bread paste from the breadfruit, a Marquesan staple, were stored in deep holes. Other pits served as earth ovens, cooking arrangements that used hot rocks covered with leaves to steam food. The people ate pigs, chickens, dogs, taro, sweet potatoes, yams, coconuts, bananas, and breadfruit. From the sea came shellfish, tuna, octopus, manta rays, sharks, and lobsters.

The Marquesan society had many specialists and craftsmen. Fishing masters managed complicated net systems, tattoo artists decorated the skins of the people, and canoe builders produced graceful, high-prowed sailing outriggers. Wood carvers engraved superb primitive sculpture on bowls, war clubs, and statues. Officer warriors spent their time planning raids on neighboring tribes and perfecting fortifications for the home valley.

The Marquesans worshiped dozens of Polynesian and local deities, and the people erected splendid temples to various gods and placed offerings before elaborate images. The ceremonial area of each chief was a stone terrace several hundred feet long, with the corpses and the heads of recent victims displayed at one end. Dances were impressive affairs. Dozens of plumed and painted partakers danced, sang, chanted, drank, and ate. Troops of naked girls whirled through involved routines, and the feasting and dancing were uninhibited and sensuous.

The complex life of the Marquesans was taught from infancy. Not only did children learn to take care of their younger brothers and

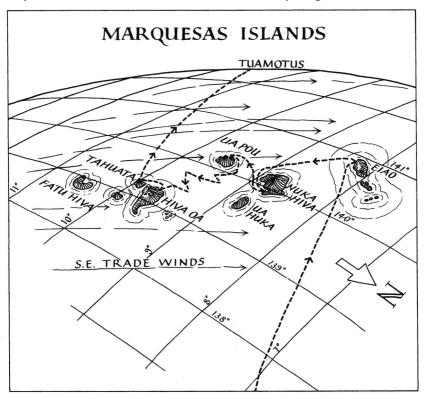

sisters but the boys were taught fishing, canoeing, navigation, and farming. The girls learned mat weaving, basketmaking, cooking, medicinal arts, and clothmaking.

This was the society the early explorers had found, but now the influence of the Western world speeded up. After 1790 Yankee traders and whalers began to round Cape Horn and to stop at the islands. Since sperm whales were caught near the equator it was natural that ships would call at the excellent Marquesan harbors for supplies and rest.

During the War of 1812, Captain David Porter of the U.S. Navy used Taiohae Bay in Nuka Hiva as headquarters for his two ships. Porter's job was to sink British shipping, but he soon got involved in intertribal Marquesan conflicts. However, when his men weren't fighting they were busy making eyes at the shapely Marquesan women. "With the common sailors and their girls, all was helter-skelter," wrote Porter.[3]

The American sailors, their British prisoners, the earlier explorers, the whalers—all had consorted with the native women. Venereal diseases became widespread. By now the Marquesan men had rifles, and the whalers not only passed on dreadful diseases but taught the natives how to distill alcohol.

The Marquesan society was wounded but still quite alive when Herman Melville visited Taipivai Valley on Nuka Hiva in 1842. A new menace, however, was the missionaries. The first Protestants failed and left, but the French Catholics who followed were tough, energetic, and practical as nails. Beginning in 1838 in Tahuata, they soon learned the language, mastered the customs, and gained the respect and friendship of the natives. By 1842, when Admiral Dupetit-Thouars claimed the islands for France, the work of the missionaries had created a favorable native attitude toward the new rulers. However, the understanding and tactful early missionaries were withdrawn and replaced with hard-core Catholics who under the shadow of French musketry severely repressed the Marquesan culture.

The power of the native leaders was diluted by intrigue, and the men in black robes fought against all native arts. Singing and dancing were forbidden. New churches were erected everywhere, but a dull Christian theology could scarcely replace the vibrant culture of the islanders. The natives were confused and frightened by the contradictions of the alien religion.

"Tattooing, a matter of great pride to both male and female, next fell under the ban," wrote Robert C. Suggs in *The Hidden Worlds of Polynesia*. "Tattooed adults would not be allowed to take the communion!"[4]

Even blackbirding, the worst of all offenses, was practiced. Unsuspecting Marquesan men would be lured on board ships, seized, and spirited away to South America to become slaves in Chilean mines. In 1863 a shipload of islanders contracted smallpox from the crew. The demonic captain dumped the infected natives on the beach at Taiohae. In a short time whole families and villages were infected. Large valleys became silent, inhabited only by the ghosts of hundreds and hundreds of rotting bodies. The culture had been tottering; disease pushed out the bottom block; the birth rate plummeted.[5]

In 1774 Captain Cook had estimated the Marquesan population to be between 50,000 and 100,000 for the five southern islands, half of the group. In the 1830s the French gave the population as 20,000 to 25,000 for all ten islands. A missionary wrote in 1838 of the infrequent birth of a child because of the excess of debauchery. Fifty years later the Marquesans were still declining. Their fine villages were deserted, their splendid canoes rotten and forgotten, and their temples tumbled and overgrown. Now charged with European alcohol and doped with opium supplied by Chinese traders, the shattered remnants of the people lost all respect for themselves and often spent their days in marathon orgies. Tuberculosis flamed among the weakened islanders, and by 1936, the low point, only 1,300 natives were left, pathetic remnants of the fierce and proud thousands that Mendaña had seen some 300 years earlier.[6]

With this melancholy history behind us we approached the lovely islands—so lofty and green—with misgivings. We brought no dogma, suffered no contagion, and wanted no jewels. We came only to look and to sample the islands for a little while.

In the yellowish light of early morning on May 26, we rounded the squarish volcanic cliffs on the southern side of Eiao. Dozens of birds spiraled above our mast, their high-pitched calls knifing through the warm air. We saw a large bird new to us, a black, swift-flying giant with a seven-foot wing span that we identified as a frigate bird from its angular profile, enormous beak, and scissorslike tail. After so long at sea and thinking about the islands so much we could scarcely believe what we saw. Eiao burst out of the ocean in front of us, a crenelated, oval-shaped plum about six and a half miles long, with mountains up to 2,000 feet. I knew the island was uninhabited, but I looked for smoke and houses anyway. Our chart, the best in existence, was poor and had a scale of about one million to one; on it Eiao measured less than an inch in length. The water was deep all around, however, and we sailed close to the shore for a good look.

We anchored in Vaitahu Bay on the northwest side. Since we had no chart of the bay we stopped a long way from shore. Margaret took the dinghy and the lead line and sounded the depths. I moved *Whisper* closer to shore as she waved me in. After I had veered lots of chain I put Fang, who was meowing loudly, in the dinghy, jumped in, and we all went ashore. The beach was stony, the swells were larger than I realized, and in maneuvering to get ashore I got crosswise to the swells. Before I knew what had happened, the dinghy was upside down, we were in the water, and Fang had disappeared.

We were only a few feet from shore and easily got to the beach, but we couldn't find Fang. We called and called, but the poor cat probably got frightened and ran into the woods. We looked a long time and finally went back to *Whisper*. I was a bit chastened at my poor dinghy handling. Margaret had sprained her ankle, I had wrenched my shoulder, and we had lost the rowlocks that I had neglected to tie to the dinghy.

Back on the ship, we found that the swells set up a steady, monotonous rolling, but our stomachs were well used to the motion and we were reasonably comfortable. I caught several red snappers for supper and we turned in early. The next day we searched everywhere for Fang and even left a dish of food on the beach. We walked through a grove of handsome gray-barked pisonia trees with large, light-green leaves and ate our lunch in the shade while in the treetops above us dozens of fairy terns fluttered about like butterflies. In the afternoon we walked up on a high ridge to the north. Wild goats clattered on the rocks ahead of us, and we soon got exhausted climbing up the forty degree slopes in the tropical heat. No wonder each tribe was isolated in the old days! On top we had a fresh breeze and we sat and rested while the clouds from the trade winds streamed seaward over our heads. About four miles to the northeast we could see the brown profile of the island of Hatutu.

On Sunday, May 28, after hours and hours of hunting for Fang, and sad at losing our dear little mascot, we headed for Taiohae Bay on Nuka Hiva. We arrived the next day at noon, the eighty miles taking twenty-six hours. Nuka Hiva, the principal island of the group, measured about ten by fourteen miles with mountains that ranged up to 3,890 feet. The cliffs of the island were high and green—a heavy green that seemed powerful and strong, perhaps from the contrast with the dark volcanic rock that was everywhere. As we slipped past the two rock sentinels guarding the entrance to Taiohae Bay we could see several small ships at the head.

"Good heavens," said Margaret, handing me the binoculars. "I do think one of the masts has a blue top. And only one ship has a mast with a blue top."

"*Escapee*," I said. "But she can't be here. Raith and Vivienne Sykes were bound for the West Indies when we last saw them in San Francisco."

"I know," said Margaret. "But the mast top is blue."

The bay was deep and calm, but a swell pushed in from the south. As we edged deeper into the long bay we got closer to the spurs of the mountains, which came right down to the water. Everything was green, too green, garish almost, and the impressions on my eye were as intense as a spray of colors from a prism. A native was fishing along the western shore, and I found myself looking at my first Marquesan. He smiled and waved. A puff of wind pushed us faster and suddenly we were next to the ship with the blue-topped mast, our friends from Canada, the Sykes in their heavy forty-foot cutter. Our anchor rattled down and we swung near them.

"How many days?" chorused the crew.

"Twenty-five days from California," we shouted.

We were soon aboard *Escapee* exchanging gossip. The Sykes, with two men and two women for crew, had come to Nuka Hiva from Mexico.

"We decided to follow the trade winds," said Raith, tall and handsome as always. "We had a wonderful crossing. But six people eat a phenomenal quantity of food in a month. I thought we had put enough on board in Acapulco for a small army, but we ate everything except the rice husks and the spinach."

The swells rumbled and smashed to spray on the beach near us, and when *Whisper* got parallel to the incoming rollers the motion flung the dishes off the saloon table. We noticed that the one other ship, a blue-green trimaran from Seattle, had a second anchor laid out from the stern to hold the hull at right angles to the swells. We did the same and life on board became easier.

We inflated our Avon rubber dinghy—which wouldn't capsize—and rowed ashore, hopping out on the small stone pier between waves. On the front of the warehouse was lettered KAOHANUI, the Marquesan greeting. Half a dozen boats were pulled up on the beach and others were stored in boathouses of native thatch. About 150 people, mostly Marquesan, lived in Taiohae, the main settlement in the islands, and many of their small houses paralleled the beach, fronting on a short road that I later found out was the only road in the Marquesas. The government buildings had roofs of red sheet iron and the style was early nineteenth-century colonial.[7]

When I walked around I thought I was looking at faded prints in an old history book. The post office, for example, was quartered in one corner of a large, squarish, two-story building with enormous shuttered windows, surrounded with wide outside porches with white railings. French and Marquesan were the languages. There was no air transport (no airfields, no business) and people and goods came and left on schooners that arrived from Tahiti once or twice a month. In 1967 the population of the Marquesas was 6,000.

We called on the local gendarme and showed him our passports, French visas, and ship's papers. We told him that we planned a brief visit in the Marquesas and a short cruise through the southeast Tuamotus before heading for Tahiti, where we hoped to be on July 14, Bastille Day.

"Ah yes, monsieur," nodded the French official courteously, "I will radio Papeete of your plans and we will hear tomorrow."

During our interview the daylight faded and the office grew dark. The gendarme called to a woman somewhere. A moment later a small engine chugged into life. A tiny bulb over the desk flickered and began to cast a feeble, yellowish light. The official smiled with pride. We smiled too, but I realized how far from home we were and how remote in time were these islands. I looked around and saw the mustachioed Frenchman, the fading horse prints on the wall, the tropical foliage through the window, the ancient typewriter, and the carafe of wine on the lace tablecloth. Was I seeing this scene or had I taken it from Paul Gauguin?

The next day we found the baker and for ten francs (11 cents U.S.) bought delicious-smelling batards, long slim loaves of freshly baked bread that tasted wonderful with butter (canned, from Australia, at 55 francs) and coffee early in the morning. We got papayas from a Chinese-Marquesan family and took quiet walks along the shore and up the valley. Next to the warehouse near the pier was a shower. You soaped up and then danced under the single pipe while the icy water rinsed you off.

We met Bob MacKetterick, a white-haired Englishman from Liverpool who had been a trader and a storekeeper among the islands for much of this century. A seaman on sailing ships in his youth, Bob was now old, half blind, and ailing, but his love of yarning was undimmed. We sat on his peaceful veranda, which looked south across the bay, and drank a glass of wine while his mind trailed back over a hundred subjects. But one subject he never mentioned was his son Maurice, now the main trader with his store and house only a little way down the road. Many years ago they had had an argument, and Maurice, who had been helping his father, had left to open his own store. From that day the father and son have not spoken.

In Maurice's store we saw our friends from *Escapee*. They were buying heavily. Maurice, cheerfully rushing around and chatting in three languages, sold everything: rice and sugar, globes for pressure kerosene lamps, Diesel oil, Hinano beer, soft drinks, cloth, sewing thread, canned goods. . . .

We walked to the end of the pier, one of the social centers of Taiohae, where people were always fishing. The fishing was in two parts. First the islanders caught silvery bait fish six or seven inches long on dry flies, two of which were pulled behind a short piece of bamboo dragged crosswise to the water. A bait fish was then hooked through the tail with a big hook and tossed out in hope of getting a big fish for dinner.

In the Marquesas there was no electricity for cold storage, so you could buy fresh meat only when an animal was slaughtered locally. Occasionally a beef was brought down from one of the plateaus and led out on the rocks along the shore. The animal was killed and the meat sold at so many francs per kilo. The butcher spoke only Marquesan, but from what we could make out, all parts of the animal cost the same, whether you got filet mignon or scraps for the cat. If a piece of meat was too big, you gestured to have it cut in half; you could have either part for the same price, no notice being made that one side was prime meat and the other side mostly gristle and bone.

If you wanted the best meat you had to get out on the rocks early and stand at the butcher's elbow while he hacked away. (If you were late, all that would be left would be hoofs, horns, and hide.) The butcher had no paper or bags and most people simply carried their bits of meat—bloody and dripping—away in their hands. All told it was a grisly scene, too much for my weak stomach, and though I enjoy a steak once in a while I preferred to eat from a tin rather than witness the slaughtering. Ugh!

The next morning the gendarme sent a message to come to his office.

"It is difficult now with the atomic affairs for us to give permission for you to travel to Hao," explained the official. "The trip would be dangerous. The southern Tuamotus are not possible these days."

We spent the afternoon rearranging our itinerary to visit the northern Tuamotus. The change turned out to be wise. So far as we had known, the last foreign sailors to have seen Hao were aboard the three-masted barkentine *Cap Pilar* in 1937 and the Brixham trawler *Arthur Rogers* in 1952. The crews of both ships had found the island primitive and unspoiled. Now we were told that the atoll had a long airstrip for jet aircraft, innumerable military facilities, and hundreds of French military men. For Hao the old ways were finished. For us the interest was gone.

In the afternoon we were surprised to see a small sailboat with a Japanese flag tacking up the bay. The ship was the *Pioneer*, a twenty-one-foot sloop with three excited fellows on board. They had come from Panama and were the first Japanese yachtsmen to visit the Marquesas. The skipper was Susumu Amao, an enthusiastic twenty-four-year-old navigator who wore a wristwatch chronometer large enough to be a sundial. We wondered about the language problems between Japanese and Marquesan, but the three fellows soon returned from shore holding up a fish and a stalk of bananas, trophies of smiles and gestures.

In company with *Escapee* we sailed to Taioa Bay, five miles to the west, where we found a perfectly sheltered anchorage, splendid in every way except for microscopic no-no flies, pestiferous insects that combined the qualities of biting ants with the cunning of mosquitoes.

Daniel and Antoinette Tikitohe paddled out to see us in a small canoe and brought us bananas and limes. They were glad to have visitors in their quiet valley, once peopled with perhaps a thousand human beings, and we showed them *Whisper* and told about our trip. Daniel took us and the crew from *Escapee* up the canyon through groves of coconut palms to a wonderful ribbon waterfall that poured down from the green mountains almost overhead. Daniel was an excellent woodcarver, and I bought a ceremonial lance incised with traditional Marquesan carving that we put up in *Whisper*'s saloon. Margaret made lunch and everyone sat around eating, except Daniel, who finally admitted that he had a toothache.

"There are no dentists in the islands," he said. "The French doctor at Taiohae will pull bad teeth but he is often away on rounds to isolated places. Sometimes he is short of local anesthetic."

I got out my dental kit and put a temporary filling in Daniel's tooth after explaining that it would be good for only one or two months. The next morning I found two freshly caught fish wrapped in a banana leaf in the cockpit.

A little before noon we headed for Ua Pu, whose warm gray skyline cut high above the horizon with a forest of stony peaks, spires, and pinnacles. The island would have been right at home in the Swiss Alps, and from twenty miles away you were certain the misty silhouette was a fanciful illustration in a book of fairy tales. But closer at hand the mirage firmed into reality, and we anchored near a rocky ledge in Hakahetau Bay on the northwest side of the island. While I did a few jobs on board, Margaret went ashore. Later I read her journal:

June 11. Yesterday I went ashore in the Avon dinghy with my washing. A group of young girls helped me land and lift the dinghy up on the rocks. I walked up the stream and was about to begin when some of the local women who were washing beckoned to me. They found me a nice place with running water, no leaves, and a good stone to pound on. "Do you know how to pound?" one asked. I nodded vaguely and slyly imitated the movements of the women. We chatted as we worked and pounded. "How old are you?" they asked. "How many children?" "Where was your boat built?" "How long did it take to get here?" "From what country do you come?"

I said that I was English but had lived in France and America. We talked about the nasty no-no flies that bit so viciously. "Do you have no-nos in America?" asked one of the women.

On the way home I picked up two loaves of bread that I had ordered from the baker. When I passed the store I saw half a dozen tipsy, red-eyed men outside and I was invited to have a drink with them. Red wine and beer seem big stuff here.

Too bad the men spend all their money on drink. God knows the women and children and houses are poor enough. I saw the Catholic priest with his prayer book pacing back and forth underneath a breadfruit tree outside the church. His hour of meditation,

I suppose. Prayer, however, is not enough. What these people
need is less booze and something constructive to do.[8]

Sometimes in the afternoons a few natives paddled out to *Whisper*
in a pirogue, tied astern, and climbed aboard for a look. Often they
brought fruit or coconuts. In return they were happy with a few
cigarettes and were delighted to look below, to inspect the compass,
to finger the sails, and to handle the tiller, when they always smiled
and got faraway looks in their brown eyes. For the Marquesans, however, the days of sail were finished except for an occasional yacht and
a few inter-island schooners. The horsepower of the islands was calculated not in terms of sail area but in Johnson and Evinrude outboard
motors, which the men always ran at full throttle. The natives often
went between the islands in outboard-powered runabouts, not a small
undertaking, and they liked to boast about their fast times.

Everyone we met was a good singer and enjoyed nothing better
than to play the ukulele or guitar. Their tunes had simplified chord
structures, but any lack of harmonic variations was compensated for
by fast-paced strumming. Some evenings we had a dozen people in
the cockpit strumming and singing and laughing. It was good fun for
all.

One Saturday morning at dawn we lay becalmed five miles off the
northwest coast of Hiva Oa. The leeward side of the island was
brown, and the parched volcanic tableland climbed slowly toward
distant clouds. It took four hours to sail five miles, but finally we
slipped past Grosse Tour, a 735-foot thumb of black rock, and into
the eastern bight of Hanamenu Bay, the prettiest small anchorage
that we had ever seen. Open to the north, the bay was about one
fourth of a mile wide and three fourths of a mile long, with high cliffs
of brown jutting up hundreds of feet almost from the water's edge on
the east and west.

But the head of the bay was its heart. Immediately above a long
beach of white sand rose a splendid grove of young and old coconut
palms whose bare trunks arched skyward into thick masses of bright
green foliage (I thought of a giraffe wearing an Easter bonnet). Our
eyes traveled to two huts above the beach and to several outrigger
canoes drawn up beyond the reach of high tide. In back somewhere
smoke puffed up from a cooking fire, and in the distance we were
vaguely aware of dun-colored cliffs. The warm sun beamed down and
I got a whiff of sweet scent. The only sound was the surf running up

on the beach as the small waves lapped on the white sand. Suddenly we were in the South Seas, the tropical islands of one's dreams.

As we looked, scarcely believing our eyes, one of the outriggers set out from the beach and three men waved to us as they paddled north to fish. We anchored in six fathoms near the other ship in the bay, a blue, thirty-three-foot Belgian cutter named *Procax.* We jumped into our dinghy and splashed ashore, where we found a fine stream of sparkling water at the end of the beach. Along the stream were lush growths of tropical foliage, dozens of small and large plants, and we saw a human hand in the cultivation of enormous shield-shaped leaves of taro, the serrated green of *épinard*, and the tall swordlike bunches of sugar cane. As the water tinkled along it sometimes bore petals of red from hibiscus flowers. We sat in the stream with only our noses showing and let the wonderful water run over us.

The outrigger returned and the three men ran the canoe up on the beach and covered it with palm fronds. They waved us nearer. The youngest climbed a coconut palm and threw down drinking nuts, which the others husked, chopped open, and handed us. The liquid was cool, sweet, and refreshing.

We introduced ourselves to Lucien Rohi, his teenage son Ozanne, and to the old man, gray-haired Tuo Kaimuko, who was seventy-two. Lucien's father was French; his mother was Marquesan. He owned much of the land around Hanamenu and lived there with his Tahitian wife, Louise, and his son. The fourth resident of the valley was the old man. A bearded European appeared with a smiling, round-faced blonde woman, and we met Guy and Viviane Cappeliez, the owners of the Belgian yacht.

Suddenly we heard the snort of a motorboat and shortly were introduced to the French doctor from Atuona, his male nurse, and the driver of the launch. Lucien had planned a luncheon for the doctor and we were all invited.

"*Faîtes comme chez vous,*" said Lucien. "My home is yours." He stood smiling as he welcomed us when we arrived at his small dining house up the valley. He led us to a table heaped with fresh *poisson cru* (raw fish marinated in lime juice), steaming bits of pork, savory fried goat, tart *épinard* (spinach) picked that morning, still-warm home-baked bread, large red plantains, and breadfruit that had been baked, sliced, and fried. After lunch a guitar and ukulele were soon going full blast. The launch driver was fat and toothless, but when he smiled his eyes laughed; his right hand was a blur on the guitar strings and he played song after song, each faster than the last, and soon everyone had a foot tapping to the Marquesan and Tahitian tunes. Dancing was inevitable, and we were soon all out under a big tree, clapping and shouting and trying new steps. It was a wonderful day.

The next morning we saw Lucien and Ozanne disappear around the corner of the bay in their canoe. A little later they appeared with the outrigger loaded with bananas and papayas, which they presented to us and the Belgian couple. Another morning we watched the men lay out a long gill net from shore and catch several dozen small fish; just before lunchtime we were given some of the fish, neatly cleaned. We walked up a mountain with the Rohi family on a coffee-picking expedition and on the weekend were invited to two meals and singing that lasted eight hours. We didn't know what hospitality was until we met Lucien. "I think the old Polynesian way," he said. "Everyone is my friend. If you're nice to people, they're good to you."

The old man, Tuo, lived by himself in one of the huts on the beach. Sometimes at night it was chilly and one morning he asked

Margaret for a blanket. "In the dark it is cold and I am so old," he said sadly. Tuo appeared to have only a ragged old cotton blanket, so we gave him a good woolen one. Not that it was an extra blanket, but Tuo seemed to need it more than we did.

When Lucien found out about the blanket he was furious. "That confounded old man has demons in his head," he snorted. "Tuo keeps asking for things he doesn't need. He already has seven blankets from seven yachts!"

The people at Hanamenu had been good to us. What could we do for them? I thought and thought and finally decided to ask them to lunch on *Whisper* and then to go for a little sail. From our supply of California foodstuffs Margaret fixed a meal of things the Rohis normally didn't get. Afterward we went out for a sail and we let each of our guests take the tiller for a bit. They loved it and told us that although yachts occasionally called at Hanamenu, no one had ever taken them sailing.

On the day we said goodbye we had real tears in our eyes. Lucien handed us a big sack of ripe mangoes and Tuo, still chuckling about the blanket, passed along a basket of oranges. A breeze ruffled the placid water of the bay, our sails billowed out, and we glided away from our friends.

4

~~~~~~~~~~~~~
~~~~~~~~~~~~~~~
~~~~~~~~~~

The People of the Sea

AT 1745 ON JUNE 20 WE SAID GOODBYE TO THE MAR-
quesas and set a course to the west-southwest toward the Tuamotus,
500 miles away. As we sailed out from the lee of Tahuata the wind
freshened and I soon rolled a small reef in the mainsail. Astern the
scene was savage. The dark mountains were all mixed up with heavy
clouds that swirled upward in the brooding dusk. I wondered
whether the gloomy prospect had something to do with the tragic history of the place.

Our visit to the Marquesas had been crammed with interest, but
it was good to be at sea again. Heavy squalls hove *Whisper*'s rail
down to the sea, and I steered the ship with the tiller between my
knees while I played the mainsheet like a fisherman with a big catch
on his line. We had a fair wind, twenty knots from the southeast, and
as the islands slipped into the darkness behind us the squalls eased
and we were able to get the ship to steer herself.

Our destination was the Tuamotus, or the Dangerous Archipelago,
a name often found on charts. And a proper descriptive name it is,
for no appellation strikes more terror into the hearts of navigators than
these seventy-eight low islands spread across half a million square
miles of ocean. All but one of the islands are flat and low-lying atolls,
irregular rings of coral thirty feet above the sea at maximum and often
only ten or fifteen feet higher than the waves. Coconut palms increase
the height a little; however, from the deck of a small ship you can't

see the islands until you are within five or six miles—even when the conditions are ideal. Many of the reefs are hardly awash and extend a few feet below the surface for miles, especially on the southeast sides of the atolls. The coral is hard and unyielding, and a pinnacle of the flintlike stone can puncture a ship's bottom as easy as a hammer can smash a light bulb. Charts and surveys are imperfect, and unpredictable and often reversing currents flow strongly. It is easy to run onto an island at night or during thick weather, and many hundreds of ships have collided with reefs in this geographical jigsaw puzzle.

The combination of restricted visibility, treacherous currents, and poor charts are enough to give fainting spells to any navigator, especially when he reflects on the miserable history of ships among the Tuamotus. Marine insurance agents turn white at the mere mention of the name. A few navigational aids would help immensely, but the French government—which has spent billions of francs on its nuclear program in the southern Tuamotus—has failed totally to help the surface navigator. There are no buoys, no beacons, no lightships, no radio stations, no electronic aids—nothing. It is up to you. In the Tuamotus the captain of a ship *must* keep track of where he is.

On *Whisper* we relied on celestial navigation, and as we neared the Dangerous Archipelago we were up each dawn and dusk taking star sights. During the day we implemented the star sights with observations of the sun and moon. In fact we shot the sun so much I thought it would fall out of the sky.

On the morning of Wednesday, June 21, we were running hard, rolling along the tops of big waves, and had logged ninety miles in fifteen hours. The swells had increased from the southeast and at 0900 two heavy seas thundered over the port quarter and slammed on board. To slow the yacht we handed the mainsail and continued under the working jib alone. The motion was fairly severe, and the cooking stove got to swinging so violently in its gimbals that I had to lash it in place. That night we listened to some wonderful Latin jazz music and to a superb woman singer—with a voice like Sarah Vaughan—from Havana, Cuba, of all places. I always marveled at the short-wave reception on the Zenith radio.

The deck leaks were worse than ever. Everything in the forepeak was soaked again. In disgust I grabbed an armful of ruined sailing books and flung them over the side. Margaret held up a blanket saturated with salt water. "Ah, the joys of cruising," she said, shaking her head sadly.

After lunch the following day we bent on the storm trysail, which helped to steady us a bit. Later the wind veered to the east and increased to twenty-five knots, not so windy really, but the seas were large and lumpy. During the past two days we had seen some monsters. By noon on Saturday—the fourth day—we had logged 478 miles and the island of Ahe should have been in sight. At dawn that morning I thought I had a whiff of land—"some sort of sweet smell," I noted—and birds flew around the ship. The sky was overcast, half a dozen dark patches of rain were scattered around the horizon, and visibility was poor. We saw no land.

"According to the moon and sun sights we should be four miles from Ahe," I told Margaret at 1100. "I am sure the island is east of us and the easterly wind should continue to set us away. However, I don't want to be around here in the dark. I'm going to head for Rangiroa, which is about seventy miles away. We'll carry on for forty miles and then heave to until daylight. We should see the atoll tomorrow."

The wind was now behind us and the jib flogged and banged. It was held out with a pole to balance the mainsail, but when the ship yawed on a big sea the sail would get backwinded. Then when *Whisper* went the other way the sail would suddenly fill with wind and belly out with a tremendous bang. To keep the sail from blowing to pieces we replaced it with a smaller storm jib, which set much better for the sea conditions.

At 2100, an estimated thirty miles from Rangiroa, we hove to until 0400 the next morning, when we got under way with a bright moon lighting the sea. The wind had eased a little and we wanted plenty of sailing power in case we had to claw off land, so we put up the reefed mainsail in place of the trysail and hoisted the working jib. I sharpened the course up to windward to compensate for leeway and current and steered by hand since the vane couldn't cope with the big seas coming up on our port beam.

Shortly after lunch, as we rose on top of a swell, I saw something ahead. I rubbed my eyes and looked again. It was an atoll. What a thrill to see a long strip of green and a glistening ribbon of white coral stretching across the horizon. We were about five miles away and soon ran near enough to see the blue waves bursting into white spray on the barrier reef. How exciting it was to see the white sand and the palms close up!

Now a new game began. We were at an atoll—but which one?

They all looked the same, and with no navigational aids it was hard to identify particular islands. I was certain from my daily sights that the land in front of us was Rangiroa. The next question was which part of the island lay before us? The atoll was forty-four miles long and fourteen miles wide at one point and made up of a continuous reef about one half mile wide that went around in an oval to form a large lagoon. What we saw was only one section and all parts looked roughly identical. Of course my sights should have told me where I was located along the reef, but under the seas that had been running I didn't trust my position closer than ten or fifteen miles.

From our direction of approach I assumed that we had closed the northeast side of the atoll and that a distant point to port was the eastern corner of the island. Therefore we turned to starboard and ran in the lee of Rangiroa, reaching along at high speed in the calm water. The scenery was gorgeous. Close in we could see the reddish lip of the barrier reef that pushed above the surface. Generally the water was deep, but in a few places close in where the water shoaled over coral sand the color of the sea changed from purple to lighter blues. We could distinguish separate islets and groups of palms on the land and occasionally we passed large blocks of coral that had been thrown up on the beach. We saw no people.

Our course paralleled the land and we should have been steering 315 degrees; instead, our course was 200 degrees. I began to take bearings of different points of land with the hand-bearing compass. Nothing checked, and I soon realized that we had come upon the northwest side of the island instead of the northeast. We were going away from the passes instead of toward them! Now that I had a notion where we were we hove to in the calm water and I climbed the ratlines and sat on the spreaders. With the binoculars I looked carefully toward the west. Staring as hard as I could, I was just able to pick out the smudge of Tikehau atoll, ten miles away. This confirmed our position. The strong southeast current had set us northwest about twenty-five miles since the previous evening.

We retraced our steps quickly, for the sun was low. However, by the time we got to the northern tip of Rangiroa it was late in the afternoon, and around the corner of the island the seas, wind, and current were totally against us. We had eight miles to go before dark to locate one of the passes and finally to enter the lagoon. It was impossible.

We returned to the lee of Rangiroa and found a patch of coral sand about one fourth of a mile from the reef and anchored in six and a half fathoms. The anchorage was perfect as long as the winds continued south or east, for they held us away from the barrier reef. The anchorage outside the lagoon was not worryfree certainly, but it was calm and sheltered and gave us a place to spend the night. I put a blanket and pillow on the cockpit seat and stretched out, ready to put to sea at the first shift of wind. But the trades remained steady and I dozed through the night, wakening from time to time to see the black outline of the palms against the starry sky.

The next morning we sailed around the northeast corner of the atoll to Avatoru Pass, which we identified by the village on the southeast side toward the lagoon. We had calculated the time of slack water, and sure enough the water was calm in the pass. It was just before noon, the sun was high and in the east, and the light conditions were excellent for coral pilotage. I put on Polaroid sunglasses, climbed the ratlines, and waved Margaret ahead. She eased the sheets and we headed in.

It was my first passage through coral and I had a bit of stage fright. However, with the sun over my shoulder I found it easy to direct the ship from up the mast. Whenever the water shoaled over coral sand the color of the water changed to increasingly lighter shades of blue and finally to greens and whites. It was simple to watch for the heavy brown coral heads beneath the surface and to signal the helmsman accordingly. The pass was noisy from the roar of water, so I directed Margaret with hand signals that we had worked out beforehand.

In a minute we were at the pass, and the ship was even with the ends of the barrier reef which ran away on each side of us like great barricades of dull-red iron. As far as I could see on both sides the force of the ocean rose and fell on the reef, and I wondered how mere stone could stand such pounding. A big swell would hesitate for a moment, shudder, and then boom into fragments of white, sending thousands of tons of water cannonading against the reef. No ship, no mere structure of man, could stand *those* breaking waves for long!

We slipped inside the pass and into smoother water. The deep purple of the ocean depths was behind us. Now we saw lighter blues and greens and fish darting away from the yacht. The *U.S. Pilot* book had suggested anchoring behind Avatoru village, but as we neared a small concrete wharf where a group of people stood watching, an outrigger canoe came out and a man motioned us to stay in the pass and to anchor about 150 yards off the village. The man, a stocky, muscular Tuamotuan, paddled alongside, tied up, and hopped on board.

"My name is Rita Maruhi," he said in broken French. "Best to anchor in the shelter of the pass. Strong winds in the lagoon. Put one anchor out in front and one in back."

We tacked, sailed back to the place Rita indicated, and dropped the bower anchor in five fathoms. Rita carried out a stern anchor in his pirogue and then dived overboard to check it after I had hauled in on the warp. He climbed back aboard smiling.

"O.K. now," he said. "The current normally runs two to five knots in the pass. We find that two anchors keep a ship from swinging and fouling her ground tackle on patches of coral."

I gave Rita a cigarette and Margaret handed him a glass of lime drink. He was intrigued with our fiberglass hull and with a chart that showed our trip. He told us that he had worked as a deckhand on a large schooner and was madly in love with all sailing ships. He stayed a little while and then went to check his fish traps.

We rowed ashore and pulled the dinghy up on the white coral. Sometimes it was sandy, sometimes fine gravel or small lumps, and sometimes large blocks. But regardless of the form the coral was always underfoot and always hard and brilliantly white in the sun.

The village of Avatoru, one of two on Rangiroa, boasted 300 residents, several churches, half a dozen small stores, a light-generating plant, and a tiny refrigerated fish storage warehouse. The houses were mostly small, one-story clapboard homes with porches, glass windows, and tin roofs. Many were painted startling shades of pink and green and yellow. The doors and windows stood open, and bright, boldly patterned cotton curtains flapped in the wind. Inside we noticed strongly colored covers on the beds and chairs—often large flowered prints in heavy blues and reds. A few houses were old native style of plaited palm leaves over thin wooden frameworks. The streets were neatly laid out, and several children were busy raking yards and walks. Around a few of the larger houses a little stringy plant that served as grass was cultivated. The women with these "lawns" carefully raked them and we were amazed to see one woman pushing a lawn mower. Palms grew here and there along with a few hardy shade trees and shrubs. We stopped to admire some large hibiscus blossoms.

"*Ia ora na*," said a stout, elderly woman sitting crosslegged on a porch near the road. "*Ia ora na*." This was the melodious Polynesian greeting that we were to hear often. The lady was drilling tiny holes in a pile of small shells she had collected on the reef. She then strung the shells on a length of fishline. The woman beckoned to Margaret and put a shell necklace around her neck and kissed her gently on each cheek. She gave me a necklace also. It was a pleasant, friendly gesture, and the lady's smile showed that she enjoyed giving the necklaces as much as we liked getting them.

We saw children lugging pails of drinking and washing water from the cistern behind the main church, whose large metal roof was the principal catchment of rainwater for the village. In front of several houses small papaya trees grew in old gasoline drums that held a few precious bits of soil that were carefully covered with old leaves to make humus. When we passed the school we heard shrill shouts of a phrase we were soon to know well: "*Uatae mai te popaa*," which meant "Here come the white people." The youngsters scampered around us, laughing and shouting. Some were flying kites. We were startled by a battered truck that rattled past us on the hard coral road. We crossed to a Chinese store, where we bought stout pandanus sun hats, and we finished our long walk by circling back to the dinghy, where we met Rita, who gave us a fish for dinner.

In the three weeks we stayed at Rangiroa we found the Tuamotuans completely generous, fun-loving, remarkably gentle with children, hopeless drinkers, and totally unconcerned with money and possessions. Their lives and language reflected the openness of their sea environment, their attachment to the atoll, and their dependence on fish and the coconut palm.

The Tuamotuans required no clocks and calendars. A native only had to look up, and we heard a moon or sun or star name that defined the very minute. In some mysterious way Rita always knew the exact state of the ingoing and outgoing tidal stream in the pass; he could instantly tell me the time of the next period of slack water, which I could approximate only after calculations with the tide tables. The men would cock their heads and listen to the roar on the reef for a moment and let you know whether the sea was angry or troubled or sleeping and whether the reef was dry or swept by foaming seas. You had to sing an American song to them only once and they could sing it back to you.

The men were masters at fishing and could quickly catch what they wanted from the bountiful lagoon, along the reef, or in the open sea. Every fish had three or four names, depending on its stage of development and its suitability for eating. Before going out the men

would earnestly talk over not only which fish to catch but how many and at what stage of growth.

Our English word *coconut* meant nothing in the South Pacific. The Polynesians recognized at least five stages of nut growth and three types of nut coloration that combined to make fifteen or more names in everyday use. For example, the common drinking nut was called *viavia kekeho*. *Viavia* was the third stage of nut growth, a full-size nut with thin coconut meat and nicely flavored water. *Kekeho* referred to the color of the nut—light yellowish brown—and denoted certain aspects of taste and quality. To have asked a Tuamotuan for a *coconut* would have been as puzzling to him as for an American to have asked a New York automobile salesman for a *vehicle* instead of a Ford convertible or a Chevrolet station wagon.

The main method of earning hard cash in the South Pacific is from the sale of copra, the meat of mature *ngora* coconuts, split away from the shells and dried, and sent away for its oil, which is used in soap, lard, and glycerine. But generally the natives make only enough copra to satisfy their whims for luxury goods. On the average a man might cut copra four or five days a month. Why do more? There are always fish and coconuts. The house is already there and one can play with the children, sing with friends, or just sleep—in the shadow of the coconut palms, of course.

Not only did the palms supply the wonderful coconut—eaten in a dozen ways—but the trees were used for everything. Palm trunks made good house posts. The hard outer part of the trunk was excellent for furniture and canoe paddles. Palm leaves were plaited into mats for wall coverings, roofs, sleeping mats, handbags, and fans. Split leaves could be woven into hats and slippers. The women could plait a small basket to carry food or goods in one or two minutes. Coconut shells served as cups, boat bailers, dishes, scrapers, and made excellent buckles, buttons, and first-rate charcoal. Coconut fiber was burned in cooking fires, stuffed into pillows and bed sacking, and the fiber could be rolled into stout lashing twine. Three tough green strips could be ripped from a central leaf stalk and braided together for a canoe anchor line. Coir fibers made first-class floating rope, and fine dance skirts were fashioned from dry root fiber. Yes, the coconut palm was wonderful![9]

During our visit we sailed across the big lagoon to see the wreck of the ninety-eight-foot San Francisco schooner *Wanderer* that had piled up on the southern tip of the atoll in November 1964 while trying to sail between Arutua and Rangiroa at night. We stumbled through the deserted village of Otepipi, once a busy place; now we saw only old stone foundations and a few huts used by fishermen. In the middle of the dead village we walked through a large Catholic church in perfect condition. It looked ready for a Sunday service and was neat and tidy with a deep-blue ceiling and pretty panes of colored glass. It needed only a pastor and people, but no one was there. It was spooky.

We crossed to the northeast shore and anchored seventy-five yards from tall coconut palms in the perfect calm of the lagoon, dozens of miles from any human beings. The trade wind blew in our faces and the tops of the palms rustled and swayed. A half mile across the narrow islet we could see whitecaps curling up on a nervous ocean, but we were sheltered and safe.

The lagoon shoaled over clear white sand and we sat over the shadow of the ship and watched the colors of the pellucid water change from cobalt blue to milky green. The colors were so real and strong that I almost felt the *texture* of the blue water. What words could I use? Viridian? Agate? Turquoise? Emerald? Amethystine? Indigo? I was at the blue and green ribbon counter in a Paris silk shop and all the ribbons were unwound in front of me. I saw a blue rainbow with a hundred separate colors of sheeted flame all intensified by the searing rays of the sun that bounced up from the floor of white sand. *Whisper* seemed to float on a dream of color, a shining essence of bottled sunlight.

At night I looked out and saw the same scene under the quiet light of the full moon. The blues had softened to delicate purples; the greens had been drawn out to gentle grays. The glare of the noon light had eased to a whisper and a touch. Maybe the whole thing was a dream. . . .

A big advantage of cruising in a small ship was that we had our home with us, lots to eat, comfortable beds, and plenty of reading. We had letters to write and a dozen small jobs to do on the yacht. We took long walks on the beaches and out on the reef. We put on face masks and swam a dozen times a day, paddling around the coral heads to watch the tropical fish. At one place we saw hundreds of tiny blue fish with yellow tails and big white eyes. Margaret pointed to an orange diamond-shaped fish marked on its sides with black cones underlined with white. We saw angel fish, both black with white stripes and white with black stripes. But as soon as you would exclaim at the coloration or shape of one fish, it would get topped by another fish that darted in front of your mask.

Rita had invited us to go fishing with him, so we sailed back to

Avatoru and went out in his canoe. We anchored in a depth of thirty feet near a small islet or motu. The current was racing out of the pass and when we got into the water we needed to hold onto the anchor line. We all wore face masks and could look down through the clear water to the bottom, where there were gray sharks three to five feet long and dozens of fat blue-gray fish with wavy blue-striped fins. Rita smacked the water with the flat of his hand several times and then quickly dove down to the bottom with his spear gun. He never missed, and in fifteen minutes he had a dozen meaty eighteen-inch fish in the canoe.

"The sharks won't harm you as long as you can see them," Rita explained to us later. "We don't like to swim at night, though."

That night we were to eat at Rita's house. Since we had never been there, the arrangement was to meet at the post office at 1800. Rita had gone off to the other village on an errand but was supposed to have returned in the late afternoon. At 1800 we were at the post office. At 1900 we shrugged and returned to *Whisper* and made dinner, feeling that perhaps we had misunderstood the hour. At 0200 the next morning I heard a knocking on the hull and peered out sleepily to see a bleary, red-eyed Rita alongside in his canoe. He was very apologetic and also very drunk. I thought I heard him say that his wife had had dinner ready. However, we didn't know where his house was and we didn't want to go there without Rita.

"Another time," I said and went back to sleep.

We found out the next day that it was just as well we didn't go to dinner, for at 2000 the previous evening Rita's wife had given birth to a child! Rita, no doubt feeling the strain of fatherhood, had gone out for a few beers with his friends.

The next evening we went to Rita's house to meet his wife Pare (pronounced Pa-ray), to see the new baby, and to have a glass of wine. Pare was sitting up in bed. She was a tiny, pretty woman from Raevavae in the Tubuai islands south of Tahiti. She had wonderful white teeth, and when she smiled the whole world seemed to glow. She gave us more shell necklaces and Rita presented us with a dried shark's jaw.

A few days later we returned to the house for dinner. Pare was up and rushing around and we had a splendid dinner of hour-old *poisson cru*, baked fish with coconut cream, fried fish, boiled fish, big fish, little fish, skinny fish, drinking nuts, coconut pudding—all delicious and all eaten at breakneck speed. No wonder the Polynesians have to sleep after eating.

When we rowed back to *Whisper* the air was sweet with the smell of tiare Tahiti blossoms. The spell of the South Seas was truly on us and I felt totally rested and at peace. I hadn't a care in the world.

The next night, the evening before we left, we invited Rita and his family to dinner on *Whisper*. At 1800 the whole family appeared alongside in the canoe. Rita helped up his two young boys, a girl of eight, the new baby, and Pare, all smiles as usual, who wore a new pareu and a crown of freshly picked and woven flowers. She had made fragrant head leis (called *heis*) for Margaret and me and she kissed us on each cheek when she placed them on our heads.

The water in the pass was smooth and I noticed only the slightest rocking motion. I thought it was soothing, but it alarmed Pare who was worried that she might get ill. Her daughter copied her mother's actions exactly and neither ate much of the good meal that Margaret handed up to the cockpit on plates from the galley. Rita and I paid no attention, but Pare and her daughter were soon doubled up over the rail, much to the disgust of Rita. Without much ceremony he bundled his family into his canoe.

"Goodbye," we said.

"Not goodbye yet," said Rita. "I take family home and then come back to finish enjoying the evening. Polynesian women on board ships! Bah!"

The distance to Tahiti was 198 miles, and the next morning— Sunday, July 9—we slipped out of Avatoru pass and headed southeast between Tikehau and Rangiroa. At lunchtime on Monday our feet were tapping to the lilting music from Papeete that was coming in clearly over the radio. At 1500 Margaret ducked below and shouted, "Wake up! Wake up! I can see the green mountains of Tahiti ahead."

5 /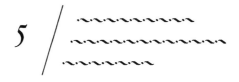

Everybody's Paradise

ONCE IN A FARAWAY PORT SOMEWHERE I WAS APPROACHED by a well-dressed young man about seventeen years old.

"Excuse me," he said cautiously. "But have you been to Tahiti?"

"Yes," I answered. "I have just come from Papeete, where I had a good long visit."

"Did you see the girls dance?" he asked eagerly.

"Why, yes, I did," I answered.

"Did any of them dance nnnnnaked?" he said, glancing over his shoulder to see if anyone was listening. "I mean with bbbbbare breasts and aaaaall?" He blushed when he asked the last question and I had the feeling that although he knew the words he had never pronounced them before.

"Perhaps," I told the young man without answering his question. "I saw lots of lively dancing to spirited drum music. I met a slim Chinese-Tahitian girl with golden skin and lovely black hair that reached to her waist. She wore a trim red-and-white pareu and kept fresh hibiscus flowers in her hair. Her eyes were big and brown and as soft as butterfly wings. She wore fragrant tiare Tahiti blossoms that she had woven into a necklace, and she played the guitar and sang in a low husky voice. . . ."

"Oh, mmmmmy!" said the young man. "And did you go out sailing in outrigger canoes?"

"Oh yes. In the big lagoons under the shadows of the blue mountains. We fished and swam and . . ."

"Could you pick fruit off the trees and eat it free?"

"At an owner's invitation you could have bananas, papayas, oranges, limes, mangoes, coconuts. . . ."

"I wish I could go," said the young man. "I'm going to save hard and maybe someday. . . ."

I don't recall whether my questioner was from Japan, Canada, the United States, New Zealand, or where, because I have heard the same inquiry in many places. But the one thing I do know is that the young man had a typical case of the *romantic dream*, the infectious idiocy that obscures, weakens, and otherwise dilutes any realistic appraisal of Tahiti. *Everybody everywhere* has heard about Tahiti. *Everyone* plans to go.

When we headed for Tahiti in *Whisper* I didn't know what to expect. I had read half a dozen books about the island, thumbed through perhaps fifty magazine pieces over the years, and talked to a few—not very many—people who had actually been there. All the opinions added up to a general impression that the good old days

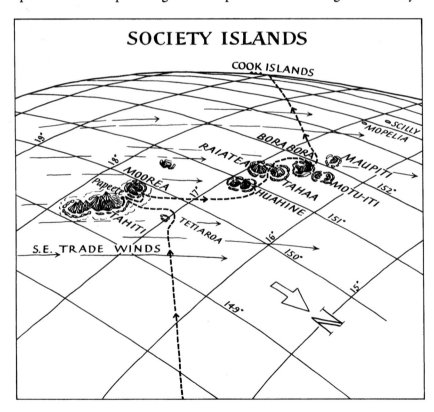

were gone, that most of the flowering beauties had been picked off by the French Navy, that Papeete was crowded and dirty, that prices were out of sight, and that every year the French authorities added a few more sticky rules about visas and length of stay. I knew that jets were now winging in tourists by the hundreds, that new hotels were growing faster than palm trees, and that, in 1968, for example, seventy-two cruise ships put 46,574 excursionists ashore. Mr. Geraud Gilloteaux, the capable director of the tourist bureau, told me that 72 percent of the 28,402 tourists were from North America, stayed one week, and spent $32.25 a day. I knew also that most tourists met only one another and stayed pleasantly isolated in their deluxe hotels and that their impressions of Tahiti were utterly superficial and deceiving.

Yet we had been told that the Bastille Day celebrations were fun, the island itself was high, verdant, and particularly lovely, and that nearby Moorea was a dream. We enjoyed the spirited Tahitian music and we had already met a few Tahitians who were hospitable, mercurial, and endless fun. In Papeete we would see yachts from all over the world, and we knew that if we stayed away from the tourist circuit we might sample a little of the real Tahiti.

It was true, both the good and the bad, the old and the new. The island lay in front of us with its hovering clouds, green mountains, and coconut palms. A noisy bumblebee turned into a jet aircraft that swooped low over the airstrip at Faaa to the southwest. Across the foaming reef we could see the tops of the warehouses, the masts of ships, and the acacia trees along the red-roofed waterfront of Papeete.

It was mandatory for foreign ships to take a French pilot, so at 0600 we were outside the harbor entrance with flags requesting a pilot and *pratique*—the clearance granted to a ship after compliance with port regulations. I felt very correct and proper, but no pilot appeared. Suddenly we heard the deep boom of a ship's horn and we turned to see an enormous white high-sided cruise ship slide past us and disappear into the harbor without stopping for a pilot, waiting her turn, or anything else. As the ship passed us a Chinese messboy emptied a big garbage bucket over the side and we rolled in the swells along with orange peels and grapefruit rinds. "What a way to begin!" I said. Several fishing boats chugged past us on their way out for tuna and a little later a small ferryboat hurried toward Moorea.

Finally at 0700 a fiberglass launch with two outboard motors came churning out of the pass, made a high-speed sweeping turn in front of us, and a man in a purple-flowered shirt—who I had to assume was the pilot—waved impatiently for us to follow him. He led us to a quay where we tied up with fifteen other yachts, and in a few minutes the agriculture, immigration, customs, and quarantine officials had cleared us. The golden rule to easy entry was the French visas we had gotten in California.

After three months of Pacific solitude the noise and bustle of Papeete astonished us. In a way we were eager for a change, but it came too quickly. Cars, large and small trucks, and crowded open buses clattered and snorted along Quai Bir-Hacheim, the waterfront road. Women and children, often two together, one behind the other, hurried past on wheezing motor scooters. One official wanted me to sign a form, so we hopped on his motor scooter and bounced off to an office somewhere. Everyone was well informed and courteous, but the pace was double-quick. Sign this! Do that! Go there! Step up! Fill this out! Fast! Quick! Hurry! Maybe I had been away from civilization too long.

Back at the ship, Margaret was still adjusting our lines to the seawall, for we had dropped a bow anchor and twenty-five fathoms of chain and had backed stern to the quay. It was exciting to see flags from all over and such home ports as Paris, Juneau, Zeebrugge, Mooloolaba, Vancouver, Southampton, Toulon, Plymouth, Basel, Glasgow, and Vlaardingen neatly lettered on the yachts. Some of their crews took a lively interest in our arrival. We looked over the sloops and schooners, the cutters and ketches, squaresail yards, awnings—everything. We met the Belgian yacht *Procax* again, saw our friends the Sykes on *Escapee*, and were tied up next to *Eryx*, Jean de Vogué's handsome eighty-three-foot topsail staysail schooner that we had met in the Marquesas.

In the harbor to the north we looked over to several big cruise ships and toward half a dozen small, work-worn motor vessels. Across the way we noticed what seemed to be a whole fleet of French naval ships with hundreds of uniformed sailors rushing around. To the west were four or five trading schooners, one of which was hoisting a new canvas mainsail. Another schooner was discharging a load of outer islanders who were all laughing and shouting.

Almost the first story we heard was of *Skunda*, a thirty-two-foot schooner from San Francisco owned by Bruce and Suzanne Lamb. A few days earlier the ship had been on course between the Tuamotus and Tahiti when a strong current pushed by the southeast trades had set the ship far to the northwest. At 0330 one morning, while the owner was below ill, the little ship struck the reef on Tetiaroa, a four-mile-long atoll thirty miles north of Tahiti. The schooner was holed but not badly and she hung on the edge of the coral. The owner summoned a tug from Tahiti which pulled the ship off the reef. Unfortunately the high-capacity pumps on the tug failed to work, and the schooner sank in 120 feet of water while the horrified owners watched all their worldly possessions get swallowed by Davy Jones. It was a dreadful incident.

Bruce Lamb reckoned he had been exposed to a two-knot current on his port beam which had set him to leeward about fifty miles in twenty-four hours. Both Eric Hall on *Manuma* and we in *Whisper* had experienced similar currents. At noon on July 10 I figured I was thirty-six miles from the northwest corner of Tahiti. I had taken morning and noon sights, but foolishly I hadn't worked them out, since I thought we would see Tahiti in a few hours. I had expected the atoll of Tetiaroa, the island on which *Skunda* had foundered, to be out of my sight to *starboard*. Imagine my surprise at 1400 when I saw Tetiaroa to *port*. What a current!

Now we were safe in port once more. Above us on the Papeete waterfront trucks kept unloading piles of plywood and lumber. The sound of hammering pounded through the air. Workmen covered light framing with plywood and palm-frond mats, and stalls and temporary buildings began to fill the mall along Quai Bir-Hacheim. As soon as a building was completed it was decorated with crepe paper, cardboard flowers, and palm fronds and filled with cases of Hinano and Manuia beer. Signs advertising this bar and that went up, and gambling games, sideshows, restaurants, cafés, chance boards, dance floors, sidewalk bingo, and all the highlights of a midway fair blossomed on the waterfront. It was as if we were outside the main tent at a circus.

The next day—July 13—people converged on the waterfront and soon filled all the streets. At 1000 a cannon was fired from a French warship and the *fête*—one day early—was on. One man got so carried away—no doubt taken in wine—that he celebrated the start of the two-week Bastille Day holiday by jumping into the water, clothes and all. We heard drumbeats of a parade and turned to see high-stepping dancing teams rush past. On the following day we watched the race of the fruit carriers, men who staggered under poles laden with giant stalks of bananas, long strings of breadfruit, and heavy stems of plantains. We took photographs at a spear-throwing contest where expert Polynesian men hurled javelins at a coconut target thirty feet up on a pole. During the week we saw a speed contest between native women to find the fastest weaver of palm-frond baskets. How their fingers flew! We stood on the shore of the lagoon and admired the skill and strength of both men and women paddlers in the outrigger canoe races. One morning we took turns using the binoculars to pinpoint action in a race between sail-driven outrigger canoes. With the gray-blue mountains of Moorea in the distance, we held our breath as an outrigger with a colossal spritsail from the island of Anaa inched past a gaff-rigged sloop with a huge jib from Raiatea. How quickly the outrigger canoes, with their big sails to hurry them along, glided on the smooth lagoon.

Every night for a week we attended the native dance competitions, which were superb. Expert teams from all over Polynesia competed for cash prizes. Each team had a percussion orchestra and generally about twenty men and twenty women, although one of the best teams was all male. Prizes were awarded for dancing, for the orchestra, and for the costumes.

The men and women wore finely combed grass skirts that were accented with elaborate waistbands decorated with shells and tassels. Everyone sported high headdresses—often with colored feathers—and many had pretty circlets of woven flowers around their necks and wrists. The sharp staccato of drumming started, a spirited *otea* perhaps, and the women's hips gyrated smoothly and quickly. The men took fast steps to the right and left while bowing each way, perhaps acting out the beginning of a song. Forty pairs of bare feet stepped neatly together, and the words the dancers sang blended into a splendid melody. How fast and exciting it all was! How much fun it must have been to do, for the dancers loved to perform. Happiness seemed to flow from every movement.

No matter how complicated the dances were they always included a tamure. But words to describe a tamure! A man faced and stood close to a girl. The drumbeats were quick and strong. Her hips pulsated and her long grass skirt followed in an oscillating, swishing blur. He danced in a bit of a crouch with his bent knees rapidly opening and coming together like scissors. The two performers were close together and soon their bronzed bodies gleamed with sweat. The drumming was loud and the steps were quick, sexy, and wild. The limbs of the dancers flashed faster and faster. The drumming crackled

like spring thunder, and we edged forward to catch a blur of flesh and costume.

Suddenly it was over and we saw the partners smiling and laughing as they crumpled from exhaustion after the dance. How abruptly the Pacific dancing stopped! A troupe would be going full tilt and then bang! Not a sound. Not a movement. You felt that someone had pulled an unseen electric switch.

Some of our greatest fun was going around Tahiti on the public buses, which were open along the sides and back. A ride was a good way to get the feel of the lush and uncrowded countryside and to travel to the beaches. *Le truck*, as one was called, ran out to the various districts from the central market in Papeete, where you pushed from one to another to find a bus that was going to Papara or Taravao or wherever. Almost everything was transported by bus, and the driver or several passengers would always turn to help a woman with three pigs or a small boy with a big tuna. Bicycles, cases of beer, battered foot lockers, pieces of iron pipe, and stalks of bananas were piled loosely on the roof, and the whole topload threatened to roll off with every frequent lurch.

A delightful habit of the Society islanders was their quickness to laugh at anything. One day we were on a bus going to Mataiea when a front tire exploded with a tremendous bang. The wounded bus slumped to the side of the road and the men and women laughed until their eyes brimmed with tears and they almost fell from the side benches. Their laughter ranged from deep earth-rumbling belly laughs to squeaky soprano giggles, with a whole cacophony of in-between chuckles and guffaws. When the Tahitians laughed, every bone and fiber of them laughed. You felt happy just watching them and you had to join in.

We found it easy to meet people on the buses and we got acquainted with several Tahitian and French families who took us for rides, invited us out for meals, and visited us on the ship. But we had lists of stores to buy and it was imperative to repair the forward deck leaks on *Whisper*. Since deck leaks were common and fifteen world-circling yacht captains were nearby, I asked three of them to inspect my problem.

"I think your trouble is from leaking front ports," said Ron Mitchell, owner of the Australian ketch *Calypso*. "I suggest that you put new sealing compound under each port."

"From my study of your leak I think you need a waterproof canvas boot to cover the joint between the mast and the mast step on the coachroof," counseled Dr. Guy Cappeliez, the bearded skipper of the Belgian cutter *Procax*.

Edward Allcard, the merry master of the British ketch *Sea Wanderer*, had other ideas. "Deck leaks are troublesome but the results are worse," he said. "For your peace of mind you should remove all the important stored goods in the area that gets wet and place them in sealed plastic boxes."

Since we were anxious to stop the forward deck leaks that had plagued us all the way from California, we followed all three suggestions.

Practically all the commerce in the Society Islands was in the hands of the Chinese. Instead of stores that specialized in ship's goods, sportswear, tools, lumber, or rubber products, however, the tiny Chinese shops carried a hodgepodge of items that defied classification. A typical store that measured twenty by thirty feet might have anchors, butter, radios, swim suits, bicycle fenders, plastic buckets, ice cream, welding rods, and stationery. You started out in the morning with your list and went from store to store and felt victorious if you captured two items in five.

In one shop I entered, the Chinese owner shook his head as I advanced with my list.

"Why are you shaking your head already?" I asked. "I haven't even told you what I want yet."

"That's O.K.," he said glumly. "I won't have it."

Finally the rush of the people, the noise of the *fête*, the congestion in the harbor, the expense associated with the city—all these things made us yearn for peace and quiet. We put two sailing friends —Tony and Anne Carter, who lived in Papeete—on board *Whisper* and slipped out of the harbor. We headed across to Moorea, a lofty, dark-green island about ten miles northwest of Tahiti, and entered Opunohu Bay. Tareu Pass was easy and we glided southward on the tranquil, perfectly protected bay into the very heart of the island itself. Tall volcanic peaks rose on three sides and the high skyline of the wooded mountains was complete somehow and soothing to the eye. We handed the jib and ghosted along on the dark water with the mainsail scarcely pushing us. There were a few houses but we saw no one. We didn't hear a sound until I pulled the windlass pin and the anchor splashed down in eight fathoms. Margaret swam ashore with a long line that she tied around a coconut palm, and we warped the ship shoreward almost under the branches.

Here again was the romantic dream of the South Seas: the calm blue-black water, the green palm branches shimmering in the warm sunlight, the towering, swordlike mountains, and the trade winds softly brushing the palm fronds together. Fragrance from a flowering tree drifted out from shore and its odor almost became legendary incense.

All of a sudden two Tahitian girls clad in yellow pareus and riding bicycles wavered around a bend in the road along the edge of the bay. What a fine sight they made!

"*Ia ora na*," they called, waving at us and blowing us kisses and almost falling off their bicycles with laughter.

"*Ia ora na* yourself," we shouted back, waving and smiling as the girls disappeared along the shore.

Two generations of small-boat sailors had agreed that Opunohu Bay was the most beautiful anchorage in the world. We concurred

fully and were content to sit and look, to walk around the shores, to swim half a dozen times a day, and to do easy jobs such as varnishing the tiller and scrubbing weed from the waterline. It was good to unwind from the fast life of Papeete. When Tony and Anne Carter left us they wrote in our guest book, "The most restful weekend ever."

From Moorea we headed to the leeward islands of the Society group. Huahine was the first, eighty-five miles to the northwest, a night and a day away. We arrived at the small village of Fare, where the French schooner *Eryx* was already tied up. Her skipper, Jean de Vogué, kindly met us in his dinghy, invited us to dinner, and took a stern warp ashore. It soon began to rain hard while a gray beat-up motor vessel unloaded drums of gasoline and kerosene and took on copra from a large tin-roofed warehouse on the cement wharf. The quayside was filled with scampering children, elders sitting and chatting, and vendors selling drinking nuts, mangoes, and ice cream from hand freezers. Above us stevedores slung thick rope nets around greasy bags of copra. The men and women wore wide-brimmed hats woven from pandanus, and when they walked you heard the soft flip-flop of their sandals.

Late that night we had to shift our anchorage twice because of strong currents charging through Avamoa pass and swirling around the lagoon. The weather worsened. *Eryx* left the dock and steamed up and down inside the reef until dawn. I didn't want to take a chance with coral patches, so we tied up alongside the quay, put out four automobile tires to protect the hull, and laid out an anchor abeam to keep us from bashing into the dock. Even so we bent most of the lifeline stanchions on the starboard side. At first light we cleared out and went to a nearby small bay, suggested by local fishermen. We dropped two heavy anchors on long cables and a light stern anchor to keep us from swinging, and we lay stormbound for three days while a southeast gale—locally called a *maraamu*—whistled overhead.

At 0300 one morning during the height of the storm I heard a car horn frantically beeping. I looked out to see a pair of yellow headlights rapidly flashing on and off at us.

"Halloo . . ." came the windswept voice of the local gendarme. "A . . . tidal . . . wave . . . warning," he shouted. "Take . . . any . . . action . . . you . . . need . . . to . . . take," he said.

I took an aspirin and went back to sleep.

On the third morning the gray motor ship—in spite of warnings of heavy head seas—left for Papeete, her passengers and crew confident of a quick trip. That afternoon the ship limped back to Fare, her passengers gray and pale, her crew ashen and weak, her main cargo hatch damaged, and much of her cargo wet.

When the storm blew out we walked up to the north end of the island to Maeva, an old village partially built on stilts along an inland arm of the lagoon. The village looked a bit battered, but it still had one old-style Polynesian meeting house, a large structure that looked like an enormous upside-down plaited basket. A number of *maraes*—ancient stone platforms once used for religious purposes—were being restored by archaeologists. The area had obviously been inhabited for hundreds, perhaps thousands, of years, and we looked at the remains of extensive stone fish traps.

The next day we left Fare and sailed inside the lagoon to the southwest corner of Huahine, where we tied up at Haapu, the most remote village we had seen. All the houses were of native materials, and several dwellings were on stilts over the water. Transport was still entirely by outrigger canoes, and along the shores we saw many new canoes under construction. Each hull was shaped from a single log that was hollowed out with a curved ax blade.

We were a great attraction, and soon half the adults and all the children seemed to be on board. In a short time the decks were black from the dirty feet of the youngsters who spent hours looking in on us through the ports. The Tahitians were on the ship early in the morning and late at night, with short breaks for meals. In the evening the women would come down to look in. Everything we did seemed fascinating to the people.

We met Tetuanue Nanua, who took us off to see the new church. The village had only 218 residents, and we were puzzled when we saw several other reasonably sound churches standing unused. Generations of competing missionaries had formed groups that favored first one religious sect, then another. Each had built its own church, made its converts, and then faded from prominence. No traveler to the South Pacific can fail to observe the idiocy of such squabbling.

"Is the new church Catholic?"

"No."

"Protestant?"

"No."

"Mormon?" (Very big in the South Pacific.)

"No."

"Seventh-Day Adventist?" (Also very big.)

"No. The new church is Christian."

"Christian?"

"Yes, Christian. We worship God, sing hymns, read the Bible, and conduct services. So many of the white preachers have come and fought with one another and gone that this time we decided to have our own church.

"Do you like our new building?" Tetuanue was proud and his face beamed with satisfaction as he looked up at the high ceiling. "We have worked hard and soon the building will be finished."

The volunteer labor of the untutored Tahitian builders had resulted in a sturdy, crudely constructed church that completely lacked any sort of unified design. A journeyman American carpenter would have cried at the waste. How foolish it was to spend so much energy and money to duplicate existing structures. How much copra was cut to pay to import the cement, the boards for the pews, the glass windows, and the metalwork! How much more useful a new dispensary, a small hospital, or a school might have been. All through the Pacific we were to see the dreary results of futile squabbling among shortsighted missionary groups whose measure of success was not the general good of the people but the number of supposed converts whose devotion was often bought with gifts.

The local Tahitian chief, Nanua Mai, visited us on *Whisper* and asked us to his home for a meal. It turned out to be a colossal affair. We had steaming pig from the earth oven, crisply fried slices of breadfruit, *épinard* with coconut cream, baked reef fish caught that morning, juicy chunks of spicy *poisson cru*, hour-old drinking nuts, and fresh mangoes and oranges. We ate until we were ready to burst.

"Eat more!" urged the chief.

"Full up absolutely!" we chorused.

The chief disappeared in the direction of the cookhouse.

"I hope he's bringing coffee," Margaret whispered. "I'm so stuffed."

In a few minutes the chief returned, smiling broadly and bearing a platter with twelve fried eggs.

"A special treat for our guests," he said triumphantly.

I groaned when the eggs were put in front of me. All the guests stopped to watch. What could I, the visiting captain, do but try? I managed two, and passed the platter to Margaret who somehow ate three more before she gave up.

We didn't eat again for two days.

One night we stopped at the home of Tetuanue to hear

hymn singing, known in the Society Islands as a *himine*. Polynesians are born singers, with a natural ability to harmonize and to use counterpoint. While their children slept on the floor and a pressure kerosene lamp cast flickering shadows over their faces, seven women and six men sang powerfully and well, a chorus that breathed gusto and spirit and took your breath away with its intensity. The woman in charge sang a strident, high-pitched counterpoint that was a bit screeching at times, but it added a depth to vocal music that I hadn't known before. We went back several nights. I will always re-member Haapu as the singing village.

On August 18 we sailed from Huahine, touched briefly at Raiatea, skirted Tahaa, and slipped through Teavanui pass into the big lagoon at Bora Bora. The island was high, with steep, craggy mountains up to 2,386 feet. Bora Bora looked something like Moorea except that the lagoon was larger and the mountainous interior seemed more open and less wooded.

We were just in time to see a big stone fishing party, a kind of super fish drive. Whether the stone fishing was an excuse for a happy social occasion or put on by the need for fish I don't know, but it was certainly a joyous time. About 400 people gathered on the west side of a peninsula that jutted into the south lagoon. The Tahitians began to weave palm fronds into a long bushy net about three feet wide and maybe 1,000 or 1,500 feet long. The net was carried and pulled into the water and positioned in the shape of a large V with its fingers open to the west. The net holders—mostly women—stood every few feet and held the net out as far as they could, the tallest woman out farthest.

The women all wore bright pareus, the men colorful loin cloths, and everybody had crowns of flowers. We stood on the white sand beach above the shining azure of the shallow lagoon and looked at the rainbowed clothing, the bronzed bodies, the shining black hair of the women, and the dark green leaves in the long net.

Meanwhile 100 men in fifty outrigger canoes spaced about 150 feet apart had formed a long line far out across the lagoon. As I looked the fleet began to advance. At a signal from the leader of the fleet, a man standing in the bow of each canoe tossed a stone tied to a short line into the lagoon. He then retrieved the stone and at the next signal threw the stone again, chasing any fish ahead of the canoes. The canoes at the ends of the advancing fleet moved faster to make a curved line that gradually moved toward the open net. The stones

continued to fall like beats of a drum, and the canoes moved both ahead and closer together.

Everybody was shouting and yelling when the line of canoes arrived at the net. The Tahitians began to close the ends of the trap, and most of the boatmen jumped in the water to help the women. Little by little the perimeter of the now unbroken net began to shrink and the forest of legs of the net tenders blocked and scared the fish. An excited ring of people grew closer and we began to see fish jumping and splashing. The net was drawn near the beach—the legs were solid now—and the fish were speared or seized and tossed up on the beach, where they flopped around until a head man made a general distribution. Everyone was laughing and the general glee made your heart sing. The fish were of all kinds: green, yard-long spotted fish with jutting lower jaws, fat red snappers, blue parrot fish, round yellow fish with gray stripes, funny-looking skinny white fish with sad eyes, orange fish shaped like dinner plates—heavens! All kinds and all aimed for the evening dinner pot. The stone fishing was wonderful and we were amazed at the spectacle.

We had a good time in French Polynesia. In spite of all the talk that "paradise was finished," we found the Marquesas, Tuamotus, and Society Islands lovely beyond hope. We admired the people, enjoyed their customs, and had the fun of sharing many experiences. We wish we could have spoken their language, but except for a few words their three tongues were impossible to learn in three months. Marquesan is as distinct from Tahitian as Italian is from Spanish. Maybe next time we could learn more.

Now it was goodbye. The course was 220° M. and the distance to Rarotonga was 540 miles.

6 / Where Are the Cooks?

WE KNEW RIGHT AWAY WE WERE BACK AT SEA, FOR A strong blast of wind hove *Whisper*'s starboard rail down to the water. Bora Bora rapidly fell astern, and in less than two hours I was up on the foredeck reefing the mainsail. Margaret was sick, King Kong, our new Tahitian cat, was sick, and even I—old iron stomach—lost my lunch. The rot had set in.

At dusk we saw the 700-foot mountain on the small island of Maupiti a few miles off to starboard. Fortunately the east-southeast wind was fair over our port beam or a little aft, a reaching wind, but it continued to freshen. At 1815 I put on my safety harness and began to steer by hand because the vane could no longer cope with the seas, which pushed the ship first to the right and then to the left. Our course was good, our speed excellent, and I hesitated to slow the yacht because we were making such good time. However, I soon had my hands full steering, and an hour before midnight I realized that more sail would have to come off.

While I was thinking about the sail changes there was a sudden roar and everything turned white. A big sea had broken over the port side and had filled the cockpit up to the tops of the coamings. The rush of water had swept me onto the side decks and against the life-line stanchions. The next thing I knew I was spitting water like a civic fountain and thinking that an airplane had crashed on top of me. In the cabin the floor was swept by an avalanche of books that

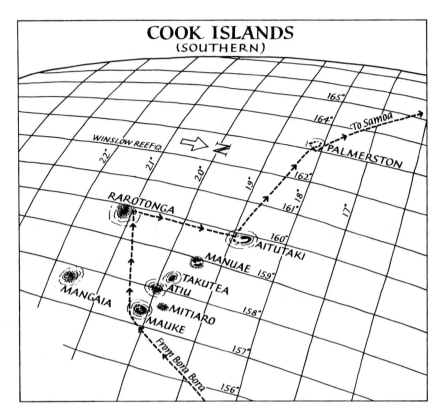

COOK ISLANDS
(SOUTHERN)

was well sprayed with water and tapioca pudding from pans that were flung off the gimballed stove.

I climbed back in the water-filled cockpit and watched motes of phosphorescence swirl round and round as the water slowly drained back into the sea. Some of the water slopped out when the ship rolled, but it still took fifteen minutes for the cockpit to empty. At that moment I lost all interest in large cockpits. I later calculated that up to the tops of the coamings the cockpit had a volume of about sixty-four square feet or a water capacity of two tons, an astonishing weight for a ship that displaced only six tons.

After the wave we took the hint that we were moving too fast. I hauled down the working jib and we hove to until 0700 the next morning, when we bent on the storm jib. The wind was still thirty knots—a moderate gale—from the east-southeast with large seas. After we got under way again we steered carefully and bore off whenever we saw a big swell approaching. Finally at 1430, after a squall, the wind abated somewhat and we managed to get the self-steering working by sheeting the jib flat. When we had hove to during the night I had forgotten to pull in the line and rotator of the Walker log, our distance recorder. The log line had gotten around the rudder, and the rotator continued to turn until the line was in an awful tangle. Margaret made some heroic stabs with a boat hook, triumphantly retrieved the horribly snarled line, and retreated below to untwist the mess.

Obviously we weren't used to being at sea again, for in the afternoon Margaret wrote in the logbook: "I have been having hallucinations of palm trees alongside the ship. Hal keeps hearing cars start up."

A little later the wind increased again, so we pulled down the mainsail completely and continued at hull speed under the storm jib alone.

At noon on August 27, the third day, the sky cleared and we had bright sunlight. The ocean seemed calmer and we hoped the gale force winds were over. We hoisted the reefed mainsail, which lessened our rolling, and celebrated the end of the storm with a substantial hot meal. The improvement was a false alarm and at 2100 the wind increased again. *Whisper* began to race through the water. Two waves thumped over the port side and broke heavily on board before we could hand the mainsail. We continued under the storm jib alone.

Ever since we had left Bora Bora, water had been flying everywhere. There seemed to be as much below as outside. Heavy spray drummed on the coachroof with every roll of the ship, and the water worked under the main hatch and dribbled into the quarter berth and galley. The forepeak deck leaks began to run as usual. Altogether the situation below decks was more suited to tropical orchid growing than to sailing. "Where oh where can I hide the ship's logbook to keep it dry?" I said.

August 28. 0400. Reset steering vane after squalls. Still running under storm jib alone. Wind from the port quarter. Heavy rolling. Bad ventilation with everything shut. Need more Dorade vents. A bit cooler 1200 miles south of the equator and a wool shirt feels good at night. Boy am I tired! What I want more than anything else is sleep.

At 0830, after a series of squalls, the wind decreased. While I was hoisting the reefed mainsail the clouds opened up a bit and I saw both the sun and the moon. Margaret quickly handed up the sextant and wrote down the time while I measured the angles. The observations put us ninety-seven miles from Mauke and 245 miles from Rarotonga.

We had shaped our course to pass slightly south of Mitiaro and Mauke because we had been warned of a strong current near the two small islands.

We were going through the southern limits of the southeast trades and the squally weather continued. At noon the next day we had both the full mainsail up and the working jib set, but later we pulled down one third of the main again. On the evening of August 29, star sights of Betelgeuse, Canopus, Achernar, and Capella put us thirty-one miles from our destination.

We kept a careful lookout because Rarotonga was only a few miles long and would have been easy to have passed in the dark, which would have meant beating back. At 0300 I stood in the companionway looking around while I drank a cup of hot chocolate. Suddenly I saw two lights, a red and a white, off to port. By staring hard under the weak glow of the new moon I was just able to make out the shadowy profile of an island to the southwest. It was wonderful to see navigational lights for mariners after the slim pickings in French Polynesia. My heart was full of thanks.

We immediately came about and put *Whisper* on the starboard tack to work north of the island. As dawn broke across the sea the green bulk of Rarotonga hove into the yellowish sky. From a distance the island appeared as a triangular stone fortress that seemed strong and enduring but somehow terribly alone and isolated. The island had such *clarity* in the early light. It was almost as if you had removed a pair of dirty glasses from in front of your eyes and saw the scene now sharp and clear and brilliant all in a twinkling.

It probably sounds silly, but as I watched Rarotonga grow bigger and its distant pyramid change into a miniature range of mountains and valleys I felt a little tinge of achievement at having found the island. Not that it was hard particularly, but I suppose somewhere there is a bit of Columbus or Captain Cook in all of us, and though today we only play at discovery, the game is still thrilling.

How exciting it is to sail to a new island! Suddenly all those hours —watching the compass, the eyestrain over the charts, the celestial observations, the calculations, the sail changes at night, the wet clothes—suddenly all those things are behind you and mean nothing, for the prize is at your feet.

The island stands before you, green and golden in the early-morning light. The mountains rise boldly, soaring up to rocky summits and descending in wrinkled ridges and swooping escarpments.

On the lowland the ever-waving palms look familiar and you wonder what is growing on the cultivated fields. Closer still a blue wave booms once on the fringing reef and in a magical instant is split into a million fragments of white. A red building, a steep-roofed church, and a flag stiff in the trade wind appear from behind a headland.

You check the chart for rocks and depths and ease in toward the shore. Now you can see houses in the village and a white-fronted store. A fisherman in a canoe outside the reef smiles and waves his arm in greeting as you glide in close to the land.

Now is the moment to go in. Down with the mainsail. Hard around on the tiller. Change the jib sheets. You work the tiller with one foot as you stand on the cockpit seat to judge distances. You run in through the pass, nervously watching the claws of coral on each side. Now down comes the jib, its white folds fluttering to the deck. As you round up into the wind the ship loses way and you fling a line to a pair of arms that materializes from the crowd on the pier head. The yacht swings for a moment and then settles down as her dock lines are made fast.

"How long 'de trip take, capt'n," calls out a friendly voice.

"Four and a half days from Bora Bora," you reply.

"Good time, capt'n."

You have arrived.

Tiny Rarotonga, a mere twenty-five square miles in area, is one of the fairest islands in the Pacific and easily ranks with Tahiti, Moorea, and the Marquesas. The administrative center and largest of New Zealand's Cook Islands, Rarotonga is formed of an oval-shaped cluster of mountains seven miles long and five miles wide that pushes grandly above the sea. The highest peak is Te Manga, 2,110 feet, but there are half a dozen more only a little lower. Below the skyline of wrinkled green, the island slopes off into ridges heavily wooded with banyan, breadfruit, tamanu, chestnut, and candlenut trees. In the higher valleys you can pick tiny orchids and walk beneath enormous tree ferns. Downslope you see thousands of orange trees, thriving fields of tomatoes, and lush swamps of taro whose leaves look like giant dark-green butterfly wings at rest.

The climate is one of the best in the world. During the day the temperature is always between 76 and 84 degrees. At night it ranges between 66 and 74. The island has a small fringing reef but no lagoon to speak of, and the only shelters for ships are at Avarua and Avatiu on the north shore. Both places are mere cracks in the reef, although Avatiu is being continuously improved to give modest protection to vessels up to about 100 feet over-all, the length of the motor ships used for inter-island transport.

Before *Whisper*'s dock lines had stopped swinging at Avatiu, two little cars squeaked to a stop on the jetty. Four young men, who represented the departments of agriculture, health, customs, and immigration, pushed through the crowd of onlookers and jumped on board. All were neatly groomed and immaculately dressed in white shirts, white shorts, and high white stockings. We shook hands and filed below.

"How long do you want to stay?"

"Clearance papers from your last port, please."

"Have you any guns aboard?"

"What do you have in the way of spirits?"

"Your smallpox vaccination certificates expired in California. How did you get through French Polynesia? Come to the hospital for shots, please."

"What fruit have you on board?" (A grapefruit, three or four papayas, two dozen limes, and the fruit basket were whisked away and never seen again.)

The men were good-looking Polynesians—called Maori in New Zealand—who spoke excellent English. They obviously liked to come aboard the ship and were pleased to look around. But they seemed so efficient and formal and unbending that I was somewhat awed by their white-starched presence. (Maybe it was because things were so casual in French Polynesia.) I thought of offering the men a drink, but I wondered whether I would be arrested and carted off to jail if I produced a bottle of California brandy. I thought I had better not. I asked a few questions, promised to go to the hospital, handed over the fruit, and went forward to lower the yellow Q flag. As I watched the men drive off I was breathless from their efficiency, which seemed to belong more to a rifle drill team than to dockside formalities.

The first thing that surprised us when we went ashore was the general feeling of orderliness. Everything appeared to be arranged and planned somehow. The men wore trousers and shirts and the women European-style cotton dresses. No longer did you hear a gentle *ia ora na* but a snappy *good morning*. The people walked quietly along the sides of the neatly paved asphalt roads, and although it was a Wednesday morning I had the feeling that church was just out. The New Zealand government—which did furnish good medical and dental care—was more paternalistic and rule-conscious than the French, who ran things without interfering with the natives so much. Or if you changed the words you might say there was a certain gusto and spirit in the Tahitians that was dampened and ironed flat—or almost flat—in the Cooks. We were to learn that only occasionally would the inner quicksilver of the Cook Islanders show itself.

I went to cross the paved road along the shore and looked first to my left and then to my right as I stepped across, something I had done a million times before. A horn beeped and brakes screeched and I leaped out of the way and turned to see a Land Rover automobile coming toward me on the right-hand side of the road. Yipes! I was back in England, where the traffic runs opposite to the rest of the world.

After I recovered from almost getting run over we walked three fourths of a mile to Avarua, the main village of Rarotonga and the government center of the Cook Islands. Dozens of small Honda motorcycles buzzed past us, usually with two people aboard, and life seemed to be prosperous around the busy stores and trading companies. The government buildings, neatly constructed and painted, with metal roofs, were the featureless, one-story offices you might see anywhere. Tall, pale New Zealanders and stocky, somewhat darker Maori dressed in the shorts and immaculate white stockings that we saw everywhere hurried from office to office with papers and briefcases. Signs read H.M. CUSTOMS, H.M. POLICE, H.M. IMMIGRATION, and so on. I thought the Gothic churches of the London Missionary Society (LMS) might have been appropriate in England, but on a tropical island they were monstrous, ugly, and singularly out of place. I was appalled at the waste of good land for the LMS cemeteries, which were marked by acres of hideous gravestones.

On the Union Steamship Company dock hundreds of cases of orange juice were on their way out to a freighter anchored off the reef. Dozens of jovial stevedores loaded the boxes on a tiny railroad system that took them to the end of the pier, where they were passed from hand to hand to whaleboats and lightered to the ship and the world market beyond.

We knew that three of the Cook Islands had airfields, but we were surprised when we found out there was no regular air transport and no airmail service. We had asked our bank to send us funds, but we discovered there was no bank in the Cook Islands. Our mail was no doubt in Wellington, New Zealand, waiting for the monthly steamship. Without money our stay looked bleak, but the government treasurer, Tom Overhoff, understood our problem and kindly advanced us funds.

We found the government freezer in Avarua a wonderful place to shop. Friendly girls in white were delighted to gossip about our trip and to sell us fresh vegetables, eggs, and delicious frozen meat from New Zealand. The prices were low, the variety excellent, and the quality high. After a sea passage and visits to islands where the diet was mostly fish, taro, coconuts, and tinned meat, we doubly enjoyed the fresh food.

Everyone kept inviting us to go dancing, so the next night we walked along the shore, past the rusting wreck of the 100-ton schooner *Yankee*, to the dance hall, where I paid our admission charge of thirty cents each. The dancing was sensational, and the din from three guitars, a tambourine player who sang, and a determined drummer was incredible. You had to talk by sign language, for all you could hear was music blasting out of a bank of shoulder-high electric amplifiers turned to full volume.

The dance hall was packed. Most of the girls and many of the men wore flower garlands of frangipani called *ei*. Everybody seemed to be there—not only the young and the old, but the very young and the very old. *Everyone* danced *every* dance. The music was mostly modern, and the steps were a helter-skelter combination of the twist, frug, rock and roll, jitterbug, tamure, and any quick step you care to name. To call the dancing spirited hardly describes it at all. When the music started the scene was like a volcanic explosion, and the energy burned up on the dance floor was enough to blow a hole in the sky. Two hundred couples shook, lurched, swayed, quivered, seesawed, wriggled, staggered, zigzagged, and squirmed. I thought 400 firecrackers had exploded.

The dancing was such fun! If you tried to sit out a number and to feebly fan yourself back to normal, a girl would appear and drag you off to the floor. On one turn near the stage I looked up at the orchestra. I almost fainted when I saw that the leader, clad in a chartreuse-and-magenta shirt, with a big flower garland around his neck and a crown of blossoms circling his head, was the staid immigration official who had been on *Whisper* the day before. He had a big smile on his face and he was frantically strumming away on his amplified guitar and hugely enjoying himself.

Part way through the evening a troupe of twenty teenagers put on a special exhibition of traditional dancing. Such a show was called an "item" in the Cooks, and the young performers were led by an older, expert dancer. This night the leader was a woman from Aitutaki who was a superb dancer and who shepherded and prodded her grass-skirted charges through their intricate steps. Afterward the leader did a slow solo number. Her dancing was astonishingly graceful and sensuous. Her face beamed, her hips talked, and her hand movements literally sang. The dancing was earthy, and radiated voluptuousness and life. In no way was the effect prurient or lustful. The dancing was the essence of shining beauty. It is impossible to describe art with words, but I might be able to suggest a measure of her skill when I say that no one applauded when she finished. Everyone in the hall leaped to his feet and cheered spontaneously.

On the way back to *Whisper* I kept humming the new tunes I had heard and the next morning I caught Margaret trying out a few dance steps on the foredeck.

Next to us in the little harbor were two small yachts that we had seen in Papeete. Ed Boden from California was genial and handsome, a forty-year-old civil engineer who had purchased a twenty-five-foot *Vertue*-class cutter named *Kittiwake* in England. He had thrown away the engine, stoutly rerigged the ship as a masthead sloop, and was having a wonderful time sailing leisurely around the world. Though he was by himself he was by no means a loner, for he made dozens of friends wherever he went. The Polynesians were

hopeless at mechanical repairs, something that Ed was particularly good at, and he fixed dozens of motorcycles and outboard engines wherever he went. His small sloop was always a social center, and—though he made big disclaimers—when the pretty girls were around I am sure he liked to see them. Ed was a good sailor and he taught me many tricks of sail handling.

"My ambition is to be the first person to sail around the world and not write a book about it," he said.

Our other neighbor was Eric Hall, who sailed by himself on *Manuma*, a Nicholson 32 fiberglass sloop built in England. Eric was an ingenious fellow, and one day he showed me a rope ladder he had made that he could hoist to his masthead in case he had to go aloft while at sea. Eric was older, a retired naval engineer, who—though always willing to lend a hand or to give advice—kept more to himself and liked to go for long walks. He was taking his ship from England to New Zealand.

The contrast between the two captains was astonishing. There were always several motorcycles or bicycles parked on the dock above Ed Boden's ship, with people coming and going and half a dozen adults and children on board. Someone would be strumming a guitar and Ed would be tinkering with an outboard engine or playing his tape recorder. His ship was loaded with gifts of fruit and fish and we always wondered when he slept. On the other side of us Eric Hall would be reading or cooking a solitary meal. I don't think he was lonely. He preferred a quiet kind of existence. Perhaps we saw the races personified: the gregarious American and the retiring Englishman. Certainly you could choose the sort of life you wished when you were on a small yacht.

While we were in Rarotonga we met all the island characters, or at least the prototypes. We bicycled out to Rutaki and called on Andy Thomson, the legendary South Seas schooner captain who had skippered trading vessels in the Cook and Society islands for forty years without an accident. Andy had retired and was energetically tending an enormous vegetable garden behind his house.

"I'm over eighty now," said Andy with a big smile. "My health is quite good but my wife suffers a bit from arthritis. My only problem is a continuing thirst for alcoholic spirits."

We exchanged visits with Andy several times and he told us yarn after yarn while he consumed glass after glass of whisky. ("The hurricane was a double one and with the lee shore only five miles away I took over the wheel myself . . .")

We shook hands with Father George, a sympathetic, cigar-smoking, old-time Dutch priest who taught us a few phrases of Maori and gave us rides on his powerful motorcycle. He proudly showed us his small church near Titikaveka, where he made us coffee and played opera records on his gramophone. Father George was keen on sailing ships. He kept a large logbook and asked each visiting skipper to fill in a page with details of his ship and trip. You could scarcely read some of the entries without your eyes getting a little misty, for life and death was down in black on white.

The book recounted that in 1966 a Canadian yacht had struck the reef on the northwest side of Rarotonga in the middle of the night. A large number of local men worked four days to free the ship.

"The sight of the *Trendaway* sliding into the boat passage and to the sea along with the roar of over one hundred helpers will live in my memory forever," wrote the captain.

We got acquainted with Walter Hambüchen, an American who spoke bitterly about his homeland. Walter, once an ecologist, edited the island newspaper. "Rarotonga is my home now," he said. "I will never go back to the nervous confusion of the United States."

The local fishing expert, Peter Nelson, came aboard *Whisper* and explained how he used the Japanese long line method to catch tuna. Peter was a quiet, curly-headed New Zealander who described the different islands with soft-spoken precision.

"You see, on Puka Puka the men have plenty of time," said Peter. "When they buy a box of matches they carefully split each matchstick down the middle. That way they get two boxes of matches and pay for only one."

We had dinner with Graeme and Rosemary Wallis, two schoolteachers from New Zealand who were experts on local history and who took us hiking in the mountains. Later they loaned us a Honda motorcycle. We inspected a forty-foot catamaran being built by Brian White, the shipping manager of the Cook Islands Trading Company. We met Maori families and were often invited into their homes when out for walks, especially on the weekends, when we were sometimes given a glass of bush beer, vile stuff made from oranges.

We attended the dedication of a new community hall at Titikaveka and got involved in a Maori feast with chicken, pig, noodles, taro, breadfruit, yams, eggs, rice, orange juice, and various salads and desserts whose Maori names I never managed to sort out. Everyone ate with his fingers, quite an adventure in slippery eating, especially when you tried a dish that was a kind of jello . . . oops—there it goes. The food was laid out on tables, and flies were a problem that was solved by young girls who stood behind you all through the meal and kept long fly whisks moving back and forth.

Officially there was no racial discrimination in the Cook Islands and many white men had Maori wives. I was surprised to discover that few of the men taught their wives to speak English. It seemed a pity, for it cut the wives out of so much of the social life that the men enjoyed. English was taught in school, but in the past—especially on the outer islands—not all the young people attended. Perhaps as schooling is improved the problem will ease. I can't imagine being married to someone and not to speak his principal tongue.

Everyone was kind to us. We had hot showers at the little government hotel, the laundry did our work free, and the head of the woodworking department at H.M. Public Works, Malcom McQuarry, helped us with several repairs to the ship. All throughout the Pacific, people assisted us and freely gave us goods and services. Though we were ordinary people we were on a great adventure, the kind that many men and women dream of and with which they can identify. Perhaps by helping us they participated a little in our journey.

Whisper's deck leak was no better. The next suspect was the forward coachroof portlight. It was poorly made and had always leaked a little. After some deliberation I removed it and fiberglassed the opening with twelve layers of cloth. I backed up the repair with a piece of plywood and laid a piece of teak—a gift from the local coffinmaker —across the inside to match the paneling. Certainly the leak would have to stop soon!

Almost every night during the fifteen days we were in Rarotonga we heard drums and the sharp crack of sticks on wood blocks in the packing shed above the little harbor. Twenty or thirty teenagers would gather to practice traditional dances, and we often watched an older expert lead his pupils through intricate steps and songs again and again as a beautiful bit of island culture was passed on. The young people liked to gang together every night and to work at their steps. We thought it was a good way to grow up.

On September 14 we sailed from Rarotonga. We had reached the southernmost point of our trip and henceforth we would head north and west until we got to Japan. Our first destination was Aitutaki, 140 miles north.

A stranger to the Cooks might consider the islands a unified group like Hawaii or the Azores. The truth, however, is that the Cooks are fifteen tiny bits of land scattered over 750,000 square miles of the

Pacific between French Polynesia on the east and Samoa and Tonga on the west. The Cooks—whose land totals less than 100 square miles—are really two groups of islands 500 to 750 miles apart. Aside from their name and flag they bear little relation to each other. Tops of extinct volcanoes form most of the southern islands, while coral atolls make up the northern group. Transport is by ship and usually slow and infrequent.

Captain James Cook discovered five of the southern islands in the 1770s and the rest of the islands gradually became known. Beginning in 1822 the London Missionary Society (LMS) moved in and quickly converted the natives to Christianity. Soon the islands were controlled by the missionaries, who meant well but imposed unreasonably burdensome moral laws on the easy-living Maori. The rules were based on Calvinism and directed by zealous evangelists who worked from grim, thick-walled churches that looked more like fortresses than places of worship. On Sunday, to take just one example, no work, sport, or relaxation was permitted. No fires were allowed, not even a cooking fire. The entire day and evening were devoted to scripture reading, prayers, sermons, studying gospel messages, and catechizing. The missionaries on each island worked hard to get funds and goods from their converts to extend the church work elsewhere.

During the nineteenth century, France, England, Germany, and the United States were busy claiming islands in the Pacific, but no one paid much attention to the Cooks. It wasn't until 1901 that the islands were placed under British sovereignty. Constitutional government was gradually introduced, and the excesses of the Protestant church were whittled down. We had heard that the Blue Laws—the LMS rules—had been especially strong in Aitutaki. Now the island was on our skyline and we would find out.

The sail from Rarotonga had been delightful. High aloft a few soft smears of cirrus had floated like swirls of whitewash on blue paper. The wind was from ahead, about ten knots, the seas were slight, and with all our sails set we had glided along like a feather on a quiet pond. We arrived at night and hove to until morning.

I had been told to sail back and forth in front of the Arutanga anchorage on the northwest side of Aitutaki. We did so and soon a small government launch came out of a narrow pass that led from the lagoon, which was studded with coral patches. The launch chugged alongside and a short man clad in a white shirt and white shorts stepped on board.

"Welcome to Aitutaki," he said with a smile and a warm handshake.

"My name is John James MacCauley, but everyone calls me Jock. I'm the resident agent and I'll give you a few directions as we go in."

Jock helped us furl the sails and then took a towline from the launch which was guided by a native helmsman who expertly piloted us to the tiny anchorage at the main village of Arutanga. We dropped an anchor and put out two stern lines to trees on shore. *Whisper* was well protected by land on three sides and had three miles of shallow lagoon on the fourth. Unlike Rarotonga, there was no surge. Eight big whaleboats, two power launches, and two other yachts lay nearby. Our friend Ed Boden in the twenty-five-foot *Vertue* sloop *Kittiwake* had sailed ahead of us and was waiting with a pot of coffee.

"Would you like some bananas?" he said as he poured. "I have already fixed eleven outboard motors and I just happen to have five stalks. Also I can let you have twenty giant papayas. Would you like a fish for dinner?"

On the other side of us we looked at *Clarinda*, a straight-stemmed, twenty-nine-foot gaff cutter, surely built before World War I. She was a Plymouth hooker, a converted fishing boat with a long bowsprit, and had been sailed from England by Colin Iles and Martin Mitchell. A third crewman, Peter Harrison, had joined later. Colin planned to settle in New Zealand and take up farming. However, there was a slight delay because the three fellows had made a wonderful discovery in the Cook Islands: girls!

Aitutaki was four miles long and one and a half miles wide, a fertile summit land of volcanic origin that was surrounded by a much larger triangular-shaped lagoon that measured twenty-seven miles in circumference. The highest point on the island was Maungapu, 390 feet, from whose windy summit you could look down on a lagoon of sparkling green, across to palm-topped patches of white coral sand along the barrier reef, and to the purplish ocean beyond. The 2,500 people raised oranges and bananas and made copra, but after Rarotonga the pace of things seemed slow.

Like all the outer islands, Aitutaki suffered from the exodus of its young people, who were attracted by the bright lights and money of Rarotonga and New Zealand. Unfortunately the smartest often went first and tended to leave the less talented behind. We were to see few people between fifteen and forty. With an official policy of discouraging tourism, poor transport, and the flight of its vigorous youth, the future of the outer islands was doubtful.

During our 16 days at Aitutaki we became good friends with the resident agent, Jock, and his wife, Mate (MAH-tēy), a delightful New Zealand Maori woman. We had many meals with local people, watched native dancing, toured the island, and even played tennis. One day Jock and a few friends took us on a picnic and shell hunt to Akaiami, a small motu of white sand and utter peacefulness on the eastern barrier reef. Once the motu had been a stopover point for inter-island seaplanes, but the traces of man were almost gone. Now above the untouched sand the leaves of the palms, tamanu, and hibiscus trees swayed and dipped before the fresh wind of the southeast trades as they always had, and when I walked on the dazzling beach and felt the warm Pacific water wash across my feet I thought how transient and puny man was.

A Maori friend, Dora Harrington, taught me the words of a local folk song. Sometimes we went to the dance hall, where—as in Rarotonga but on a smaller scale—the people managed to burn up a few million calories. We learned to eat *uto*, the fibrous filling of a sprouting coconut which some people compared to ice cream. Somewhere I picked up a bug and spent a few days in my bunk feeling unhappy

until the local native doctor paddled out and gave me a bottle of sulfa tablets which soon cured me.

Because of the LMS Blue Laws, now modified but still not to be ignored, it was improper for a man and woman—young or old—to be seen walking together. In a group, O.K., but two alone was severely frowned on. Affairs of the heart had to be carried on with extreme discretion. You met someone miles out in the bush, each party having arrived from the opposite direction. All the people in a village knew of the meeting but no one saw anything.

The three fellows on the yacht next to us, *Clarinda*, had made friends with girls but unfortunately had carried on too openly. Gossip started that the girls were common. The mothers lost face and became resentful. To regain prestige one mother went to the police and swore out a complaint against one of the *Clarinda* crewmen. The charge was serious and dealt with the rape of a girl under fifteen. After the resident agent initialed the charge a chief judge would have to come from Rarotonga to hear the case.

Jock was an old hand at such problems. He managed to delay initialing the complaint while he ordered the yacht to leave.

"I won't be sorry to see the boys go," he said, shaking his head. "You see, if the woman could have publicly vilified the man in question— 'Pig! Pig! Miserable pig!'—her standing with her peers would have reverted to normal. Now there is trouble for me, the police, the woman, other yachts—it's a mess."

The captain of *Clarinda* promptly hunted up the indignant mother, apologized profusely, and somehow got her to drop the charge. People were disgruntled but everyone was able to breathe again.

While this was going on we had our own problems. During the gentle sail from Rarotonga, Margaret had appeared in tears one morning. "It's the deck leak," she wailed. "Everything is wet again. We've spent so much time for nothing. If the ship leaks under these easy conditions what is it going to do in a really bad storm?"

Jock offered to have one of the local boat experts look for the leak. "However, if that doesn't work, you should memorize a Maori chant to Tangaroa, the god of the sea," he said. "Whenever you see a big wave coming you shout '*Tangaroa i te Tiitii. Tangaroa i te Taataa.*'"

I took pains to learn the chant, but I also decided to remove four feet of toerail on the starboard side, to plug some of the bolt holes, and to see what happened on the run to Samoa. We did several other small jobs, spent a morning filling our water tanks, and gave a little party for our friends.

On Sunday, October 1, the day before we left, the pastors in each of the Aitutaki churches made the following announcement: "The black yacht *Whisper* will leave for Palmerston Island tomorrow morning. The captain has offered to take any mail, citrus fruit, flour, sugar, cabin biscuits, and small packages. No chickens or pigs or lumber."

7 /

The Smallest Island

PALMERSTON WAS 219 MILES WEST OF AITUTAKI, AND with a fair southeasterly wind I reckoned the trip would take two days. However, the weather was unsettled and overcast, and the trade winds were stronger than I had anticipated. By 1700 the second day we had logged 157 miles plus an estimated twenty-four additional miles for the current swept up by the prevailing wind. Because of cloud cover and rain I was unable to get sights, so I hove to on the port tack since I didn't want to pass Palmerston in the dark and have to beat back.

We *had* to find Palmerston, the westernmost island of the southern Cooks, for *Whisper*'s saloon was piled high with mail, flour, sugar, shiny tins of cabin biscuits, burlap sacks stuffed with oranges, unwieldy stalks of bananas, and large and small packages. At 0630 on the third morning I let the backed headsail draw again and we resumed our course of 270° M. Half an hour later, as a rain shower cleared, I was pleased to see a sliver of land ahead. At first I thought the land was a long way off, but the tiny islet on the north side of Palmerston was only four miles away. It *was* tiny.

When I looked ahead and saw the small atoll in the middle of the turbulent ocean it seemed a miracle of existence. How could such an insignificance of land, a mere scrap of nothing, survive when the sea was angry? Before me was a rudimentary piece of the universe, a shadowy outline without real dimensions, a collection of earth fragments like those a small boy would use to build a sand castle on a beach.

Yet—unlike the small boy's handiwork that always washed away—the land had risen from the bottomless deeps of the Pacific, a wheel of life that had somehow endured and grown and had finally flowered in plants and birds and fish and man himself.[10]

In factual terms I could write that Palmerston was an uneven, almost submerged thin oval of brown and reddish coral seven and a half miles long and five and three quarters miles wide on which six lumps of sand, each holding a bouquet of palms, were scattered like white beads on a dark string. Fifty miles from Palmerston the ocean was over 16,000 feet deep; not until you were within nine miles did the tiny atoll begin to climb from the floor of the ocean. There was no central land mass at all. From my perch up the mast I could see directly across the shallow lagoon, past the short whitecaps, to the far reef. Under the gray sky the diamond greens of the shallow lagoon were muted to soft emerald and quiet cobalt.[11]

The island was uninhabited until 1860, when an Englishman named William Marsters settled on the remote atoll. Marsters, born in Birmingham in 1821 and brought up by his grandmother in Leicestershire, went to sea at fourteen as an apprentice and eventually became a mate on a whaling ship. He changed jobs during the gold rush in California and worked at mining for a while, but later went to sea again until he jumped ship at Penrhyn in the northern Cook Islands. Penrhyn was a wild place in 1850, but Marsters got along well and even married the daughter of the chief. He traveled among the Cooks, visited Samoa, and in 1860 sailed to Palmerston with a labor force of islanders to establish a coconut plantation for a Tahitian businessman named Brander, who owned the little atoll.

In addition to one wife from Penrhyn, Marsters married a second woman, who was his first wife's cousin. The labor force on Palmerston had been recruited for one year but no one from Tahiti appeared until 1866, when Brander's son-in-law came with the news that Brander had died. Marsters promptly gave Brander's relative a bill for the labor and for necessary supplies that he had bought from passing whalers and had paid for with gold nuggets he had gotten in California. Brander's relation responded by giving Marsters the island in lieu of payment. The new owner pondered his future and must have wondered what his grandmother in Leicestershire would have said.

The lagoon was filled with fish, there were always coconuts, and the people made copra and collected a few supplies for whaling ships. Marsters acquired another wife, a woman from Manihiki, and eventually had a family by each of his three wives. The virile Marsters had seventeen children in all. The number grew to fifty-four in the second generation and to more than 1,000 in the fifth generation, now spread far over the Cooks and New Zealand.[12]

According to Christian ethics, old white-bearded Marsters' sins were manifold. However, he was a practical man with a good deal of common sense and he ran the island reasonably well. He taught his children to worship God carefully and insisted on a rigorous upbringing of all the young people.

"The boys were frequently made to row to the other side of the lagoon and back—nine miles—before breakfast, and had learned to battle with the elements in boat and canoe, to fish with spear, rod and line, and net, to catch birds, to work with tools, build houses, and a score of other crafts before they were in their teens," wrote Commander Victor Clark, who spent eleven months on the island in recent years.[13]

A test of manhood was to build one's own boat, which had to pass the scrutiny of the other islanders and to stand up to the rigors of the sea.

Many stories have been circulated about inbreeding on Palmerston. According to Commander Clark, such tales are myths. You need only to meet the present-day Marsters to see how healthy and alert they are. Old William did not allow a brother and sister to marry. Half-brothers and sisters could, but only one couple did. The others took Maori wives and husbands from elsewhere in the Cooks. In more recent generations the Marsters have married within the family but no closer than cousins. More often they have chosen mates from distant islands, and new blood has flowed into the family.

In the early days the atoll developed somewhat as Pitcairn Island did, with little contact with the outside world. Old William taught his descendants to speak the English of his native Leicestershire, but over the years the phrases became strange and hard to understand. It wasn't until the present days of radio, the influx of a few outsiders, and occasional travel to the other islands that the accent of the English got back to normal. Many of the young people of each generation have gone to other islands where there has been more opportunity. But in spite of the emigration, a colony of eighty to one hundred has remained, interwoven in a giant family of three main branches with incredibly complex relationships.

A visitor in 1929 who called on the son of old William (who—like his father—had also married several times) discovered that the island magistrate had a very young wife, a daughter a good deal older than the wife, and a granddaughter older than both his wife and daughter.[14]

When England assumed control of the Cook Islands at the end of the nineteenth century, Palmerston was run under a lease from the British government. In 1953 the island was given to the inhabitants, who largely run their own affairs. An acknowledged head of the family keeps order and any disputes are settled by a family council.[15]

If you look at a map you might think that Palmerston would be visited by vessels from Samoa, Tonga, or Fiji, but the reality of island commerce is that an island group tends to be served by its vessels alone which voyage for definite commercial reasons. Palmerston's main cash crop is twenty to thirty tons of copra annually, not very much really, and trading ships call only about twice a year.

I put *Whisper*'s helm down and hauled in the mainsheet as we rounded the north point of the atoll and headed toward the principal islet. Our sails had been sighted, and four boats and a dozen men came out. They were a healthy-looking lot, dark from the sun, with heavily calloused feet. They wore shorts or trousers, a mixed-up collection of tattered sweaters, and well-mended jackets. Most had on hats or caps of some kind. Though we were only 1,100 miles from the equator, the wind was cool under the gray sky. Warm garments were clearly valued possessions.

"Welcome to Palmerston," said Bob, who was first on board and handed us four drinking nuts. He was a tall, handsome, thick-set man in his fifties whom I liked at once. The way he smiled and moved around the decks put me at ease.

The passes into the lagoon were shallow and encumbered with coral, so Bob directed us to an anchorage on a sand patch about 200 feet outside the barrier reef some three fourths of a mile from the village. The trade wind was steady, and it held us away from the reef. We unloaded all the packages and fruit.

"You and Margaret come ashore with me," said Bob. "Joe will stay on the ship until you return. If the wind or current shifts and the ship swings toward the reef, he can slip the anchor and sail away from the island."

I had never left *Whisper* with a stranger before, certainly not in such a hazardous position. But the Marsters had excellent reputations as boatmen and the condition of the boat that Joe had built and come out in indicated a good deal of knowledge. *Whisper* was in the lee of the island, so there was no sea swell, but the twenty-knot trade wind kept a heavy strain on the anchor chain. Before we left I put out a second anchor, also buoyed, and went over the details of the anchor winch and sail handling with Joe.

The small village was on the lagoon side of the westernmost islet and, like most atolls, was composed of sand and gravel and small lumps of coral. The beaches were white and sandy, and the shallow water felt warm when we waded ashore. Young palm trees, perhaps fifty feet high, were everywhere, and their leafy top-hamper rattled noisily in the wind. We walked past a row of small palm-thatch boathouses near the shore to Bob's house, where his family was waiting to greet us. When we shook hands, each person held onto our hands and smiled and said a few words of special greeting that made us feel particularly welcome. Two chairs were put out for us and we had tea and cookies. Bob's wife was a big woman who sat crosslegged on a pandanus mat on the floor, a position she was obviously well used to. Another woman was about to have a baby, and several youngsters frolicked around the room.

Bob's house had a tin roof, but many roofs were made of plaited palm leaves. The floor was concrete and the crossbeams and rafters were shaped from coconut wood. A kerosene pressure lamp was suspended overhead, and a splendid pandanus hat trimmed in red hung on one wall. In a corner stood a sea chest and the inevitable foot-operated sewing machine. Every bit of fresh water on Palmerston was rainwater. There was enough, but I noticed that when Margaret finished washing, her bowl of soapy water was carefully poured on a young lime bush that Bob was trying to grow in the coral.

A little later a stout young girl named Tupou appeared. "Compliments of Mr. Ned Marsters," she said. "Please come to tea."

Ned Marsters, the magistrate, was the grandson of old William, the first settler, and though Ned was hospitable and remarkably courteous, there was no nonsense about him. You soon learned that he was in charge of the island and that was that. Ned must have been in his mid-sixties, a serious, stocky, clean-shaven man with white hair, bushy gray eyebrows, and the healthy bronzed skin of all the Marsters.

"We had better eat now," said Ned as soon as we entered his house and met his family. Ned's place was a sort of island headquarters that included the medical station, a water catchment storage system, and various rooms. "We can talk at the table."

We sat down to a first-class meal of chicken in curry sauce, taro, rice, and a dish called po-ke, a mixture of pumpkin and arrowroot. There were lots of flies around the food, but Tupou stood opposite us and fanned them away with an elaborate fly whisk made of six long bosun-bird tail feathers.

Margaret asked Ned about the weather. "Do you think it will get worse?" she said.

"No, not just yet," said Ned thoughtfully. "Let's see. . . . Today is October fourth. The strong winds don't generally come until January and February, although in 1883 a December storm destroyed all our coconut palms. In January 1914 our houses and crops were wrecked by a hurricane which swept many islands in the South Pacific. In 1923 most of our houses were leveled and the crops destroyed, and at the end of March in 1926 the atoll was completely devastated. Early in 1931 we had much damage by heavy gales, and in February 1935 practically all the coconut palms and ground crops were swept away. Another bad one came in 1942.[16]

"We used to have eight islands on Palmerston, but two of them washed away in the storms."

He spoke with a mixture of pride and resentment in recounting how the people of Palmerston had resurrected themselves with little help from the outside after the major storms of 1926 and 1942. "The incentive for schooners to call is copra," he said. "After the hurricanes had destroyed all the coconut palms we had no copra to sell and hence no schooners came.

"It was a difficult time," said Ned. "I had many young mouths to feed and all we could eat was fish. I fished all day every day and slept little at night worrying about getting enough to eat. The women dug in the center of the island and made several small taro plots. We scarcely had any tools to move coral and earth and had to construct wheelbarrows from wood. No schooners came for a very long time and we had no sugar or flour or matches or coffee. As soon as possible we got a thousand sprouting coconuts from Manihiki and planted them.

"But I don't want to scare you with all this talk of hurricanes. A bad one comes only every dozen years or so. Most of the time the weather is good."

We got on the subject of music and I mentioned how good the people of the South Pacific were at playing ukuleles and guitars.

Ned shook his head. "Both of those instruments are new to these parts," he said. "When I was in Tahiti in 1912, neither was known. But a few years later—in 1917—the ukulele and guitar had reached Rarotonga by way of Tahiti, and in 1925 we got them here. Before that we played the accordion and the mouth organ."

After we had eaten, Ned sent Tupou with us on a tour of the island, which didn't take long because the atoll was only one half mile wide. The houses of the eighty people were neatly arranged and built either of wood or thatch. Each had a separate cookhouse, a washing shelter, a toilet, and often a fenced enclosure for small black pigs. The lanes between the houses were swept clear of leaves, and here and there was a bed of flowers. We admired several fine breadfruit trees, walked along underneath the rustling palms. whose slender brown trunks arched before the wind, and had a look at the taro and arrowroot patches.

We passed the cricket pitch and stopped at the school, where we talked briefly with the teacher and the eighteen pupils and shook hands with each one. In spite of the occasional hurricanes the island seemed reasonably prosperous. We walked beneath a few small banana and papaya trees and noticed many chickens strutting around. In the center of the atoll we were surprised to see a few large tamanu trees, thick-trunked heavyweights that might be compared to the oak trees of the temperate zones. The wood is hard and is used for canoe hulls, boat frames, cabinet work, and wooden bowls.

The occupants of almost every home we passed rushed out to see us, to shake hands enthusiastically (an island passion), and to invite us in for a visit. Palmerston is a low island, without navigation lights, and is hard to spot from the sea, especially at night. In the past a number of ships were wrecked on its reef. Among the houses we saw ships' cabin doors, bits of staircases, paneling, and stoutly built bunks with sets of drawers underneath.

We were tired and returned to Ned's house, where we met Ben Samuel, a lively, wide-awake chap who was the "dresser," the first-aid man. Ben had just come in from the reef with four big blue-green parrot fish. We were invited to spend the night on the island, but I elected to return to *Whisper*. Ben gave us one of his fish for dinner and we looked forward to eating the tasty, thick, boneless meat. Bob took us back to the ship and returned home with Joe.

During the night the wind increased a little, and when Joe came out at 0700 the next morning we winched in the main anchor and chain and hung on a light Danforth anchor and a nylon warp which was easier to cast off in case of trouble. I bent on a smaller jib and tied a deep reef in the main. Joe seemed happy to stay on board and look after *Whisper*, so we went ashore.

We walked around the island, met the radio operator, and had a look at the church—a dark, weather-stained, incredibly decrepit structure that was built of salvaged wood and bits of old ships. The steps to the pulpit were fashioned from a companionway whose shiny brass rail and brass treads had surely rolled across many a seaway.

During the last hurricane the church was blown some distance away, but the men of Palmerston salvaged the remains and patiently rebuilt it, although the building lists to port. Ned showed us a special stormproof house whose timbers were eighteen inches square and sunk deeply into the coral. The massive beams and stout planks were salvaged from a wrecked ship that was hauling bridge timbers from America to Australia.[17]

We looked at photographs of Commander Victor Clark, an English sailor whose yacht *Solace*, in the same position that *Whisper* now occupied, swung onto the reef and was wrecked in 1954. With the help of the islanders in an epic effort, the thirty-four-foot ketch was hauled across the reef to the village, where she was rebuilt to continue her voyage around the world.

At our request dinner that day was curry chicken again plus rice, taro, coconut and arrowroot pudding, small crispy-fried fish, and coffee. As before, Tupou stood opposite us with her fly whisk and chased away the flies. Ned muttered about political troubles and how outsiders were trying to get control away from the people of Palmerston, but I didn't think he had much to worry about.

We heard the bang of a gun and Ben rushed past with an old rifle. "A nice fat bosun bird is flying around," he shouted as he ran toward the beach.

Margaret walked over to visit Joe's wife, and a little later Ben—he had missed getting the bosun bird—and I went fishing on the reef. We put on stout plastic shoes to protect our feet from the sharp coral and waded west from the village to the edge of the fringing reef, where the raging seas thumped and thundered as they crashed on the reddish-brown coral. You couldn't watch without wondering how the reef could withstand the endless cannonading of those tons of furious water. A ship wouldn't last ten minutes on such a reef, I thought to myself. A steel hull was the only hope. I looked nervously to the north where *Whisper* lay anchored a little offshore. She was safe and her position unchanged.

Ben used a heavy three-pronged spear about fifteen feet long with remarkable success. We stood together and peered into the deep pools. I saw nothing. Ben, his eyes glinting with delight, pointed excitedly at a fish, raised his spear, held it for a moment, and flung the javelin. About half the time when he pulled back the spear there was a fish impaled on its tip. He then strung the fish on a length of tough fiber stripped from the central leaf stalk of a palm frond. With so much fishing on Palmerston I thought such expeditions would be old stuff to Ben, but he beamed with delight the whole time we were out. In forty-five minutes Ben had four parrot fish from eighteen to thirty inches long and half a dozen smaller ones.

I happened to glance to the north toward *Whisper* and stood horror-struck when I saw the ship spin around and head away from the island. Ben and I rushed back to the village, wading through the shallows as fast as we could. As we neared the beach, people began to appear from everywhere.

Those who live close to the sea realize that when there is trouble everyone must work together, smoothly and quickly. There is no time for arguments, only time for cooperation and help. Long-practiced plans go into operation and emergency measures take precedence over everything. We had to get to *Whisper*, which was getting smaller and smaller, both to retrieve the ship and to bring back Joe, who without knowledge of celestial navigation would be unable to find the island once it got out of his sight.

The Palmerston boats, twenty feet long, were stoutly built, with closely spaced frames and thick planking. The open boats were very heavy, but when the order went out to put one in the water, the nearest four people—men or women—picked one up at once on a sort of double-yoke arrangement and quickly carried it from its boathouse to the water. Willing hands loaded the rudder, sails, spars, oars, containers of fresh water, line, tarpaulins, and a small outboard engine.

Then I was in the boat with Ben at the tiller and Ned, Tupou, Margaret, and a young boy. We poled through the pass and chased *Whisper*, which was several miles away, drifting slowly, while Joe, without sails, steered across the wind toward the southeast. We made good time in the trim Palmerston boat and soon got alongside the yacht.

"The ship started to swing toward the coral," said Joe when I climbed aboard. "There was barely time to slip the anchor."

With the boat in tow we sailed back to our anchor off the reef. The wind was still over twenty knots and its change from the southeast to the east was probably responsible for the vagrant current that had swung *Whisper* toward the reef. The unsettled weather was worsening.

Clearly it was time to go. By now four other boats had come out from the village. Everyone climbed on board and we tied the boats astern.

"I had hoped to stay a few days so we could have gotten to know you a little," I said. "To leave now simply tears the heart out of me."

"Don't worry," said Ned. "We understand."

We gave the assembled people two pieces of line, a sack of fresh limes, and some requested tubing fittings and valves and bits of hose and clamps. Ned had asked us for Vaseline. Fortunately we had a large can that I was glad to give him. We passed up all our old clothing and what few cigarettes we had. I gave Joe a knife and several hand tools along with some canned and powdered milk for a new baby.

The people began to press letters and packages on me, along with greasy coins and well-creased New Zealand dollar bills for the postage. I took the mail but refused the money. A man I had not seen before gave Margaret a lovely bowl of tamanu wood. A girl handed me a fresh loaf of warm bread. Margaret held up two rare seashells. Suddenly I had a fish, a piece of exotic wood, two coconut bowls, a crown of fragrant flowers. . . .

"We had planned a feast in your honor," said someone. "We're sorry that your hat's not ready. After you admired the hat in Bob's house we wanted to make one for you."

We all shook hands one last time, and the many Marsters climbed into their brightly painted boats and headed toward the lagoon. Margaret sailed slowly ahead with the mainsail while I hauled in the nylon warp. Finally I reached the fathom of one half inch chain at the end and with a mightly heave flipped the anchor on board. As Margaret bore off I winched up the jib and with both the wind and current behind us we were quickly carried away from Palmerston.

I could hardly look back for the tears in my eyes.

An epilogue to our visit to Palmerston came more than a year later. When we were on the island, Ben Samuel, the first-aid man, had an ailing Seagull outboard engine that needed a vital part. The engine meant a lot to his family, and I told Ben that I would try to get the part in Samoa and send it to him.

"But I need it now," he said. "By ship it will be a year or more."

Three or four times a year a plane of the Royal New Zealand Air Force flew from American Samoa to Aitutaki to calibrate the radio direction-finding equipment of the airport. I knew the plane flew over

Palmerston during its flight, and I thought I might be able to arrange an air drop.

When we got to Apia in Western Samoa a friendly mechanic found the part, which I wrapped in a rag and stuffed into a large coffee can together with a dozen ball-point pens the Marsters had asked for. I put a note inside, wrote the destination outside, taped the can shut, and attached a long yellow ribbon streamer. A pilot at Polynesian Airlines kindly agreed to take the can to Pago Pago and leave it for the next New Zealand plane. I had done what I could. Now it was up to others.

More than a year later I received the following letter:

> *Palmerston Island*
> *December 20, 1968*
>
> DEAR HAL:
>
> *Thanks very much for the part of the Seagull that you sent on the calibration aircraft. It was dropped down on the water catchment roof. Now I have confidence in you because I didn't trust you when you told me you were going to send the part on the calibration plane. When the plane circled around the island several times I knew the plane was going to drop something. I remembered what you told me. So thanks for your kindness. I send you greetings from Ned, Bob, and the other people on Palmerston. I passed on your best wishes and love to all the people here.*
>
> *Now I would like to give my greetings to you both for Christmas and the New Year. Also I convey my greetings to your families.*
>
> *Thank you for the ball-point pens that you sent. I have been in Rarotonga for two months and have just returned to Palmerston. So Hal please would you send some of the pictures. I would like to have some to remember you in the future. Also send some old clothing for the families here on Palmerston. If you need any local things please let me know.*
>
> *I conclude my short letter here with Thanks to God for all your best. I wish to hear from you and Margaret.*
>
> *Cordially*
> BEN SAMUEL
> *Dresser, Palmerston*

8 / The Heart of Polynesia

"SOMETHING IS AHEAD," I SAID TO MYSELF ON THE MORN-
ing of October 10. "Tall mountains seem to be mixed up with those
clouds. It must be Samoa."

"*Land ho!*" I shouted.

Margaret came on deck and studied the horizon ahead. "Oh no,"
she said, shaking her head. "I don't agree at all. You're dreaming.
Those are only clouds with bluish tops."

It was hard to pick out land when a cumulus build-up towered in
the distance. I knew we were close to Tutuila, but were those 2,000-
foot mountains ahead or not? How easy it is to wish things in front of
your eyes and to lose arguments with yourself when you want to see
something! We continued to the west-northwest for another four hours
before a dark line on the horizon thickened slowly into green and blue
mountains fronted by bold cliffs with necklaces of white where the
ocean broke on the fringing reef.

Whisper had logged 466 miles between Palmerston and Samoa, a
five-day run with mostly heavy stuff from the southeast, gale-force
winds and seas that had whipped us down to a solitary storm jib. ("All
shipping in Tonga, Fiji, and Samoa is in port because of storm force
easterly winds and heavy, disturbed seas," croaked the radio between
bursts of static.) On October 8 we had made a run of 121 miles with
only 103 square feet of canvas flying. Fortunately the steering vane had
worked to perfection, and we scarcely touched the mechanism except

98

to change the wind-blade adjustment a few degrees one way or the other.

The seas rose up big and irregular and lots of water slammed on board. The forward deck leak was worse than ever, and for several days we mopped up a bucket of sea water from the lee side of the cabin sole every two hours or so. Boarding seas filled the cockpit to overflowing several times, and plenty of water squirted in around the main cabin hatch.

The most insulting deluge came through the Dorade vents, the special coachroof ventilators with water traps that usually stopped everything but air. I was asleep when the top of a wave rolled on board, cunningly filled the ventilator above the head of my berth, and suddenly poured in on me. I was asleep one moment and spouting water and cursing the next. Margaret couldn't keep from laughing, and I had to smile to myself when I realized what had happened.

October 7. 1600. Speeding along under headsail alone. Cloud cover gray and dark but not thick and I can see blue sky in places. Waves

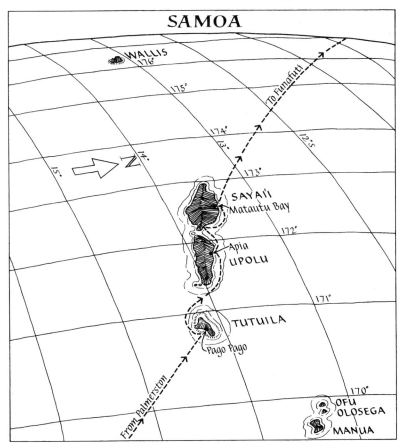

large and the yacht skims forward on big rollers several times a minute. About every 30 minutes or so the top of a wave slops on board with a noise that is a little unnerving. Surprising how chilly it is without the sun. Good to have on oilskins and a stout safety harness when I go on deck. I have been sitting in the cockpit chuckling over a book by Nancy Mitford called The Blessing, *a paperback that is completely soaked through. As I read I tear off the pages and watch them flutter away. . . .*

The wind, the irregular up-and-down motion, and the leaks combined to make the passage damned unpleasant for four days. We had the ship's hatches and ports mostly closed because of all the water flying around, and the ventilation below was poor. The air was hot and stuffy and it was too rough to cook much. But on the morning of the fifth day the wind eased, the sun came out, and no longer were we on a roller-coaster ride. Maybe a little adversity heightens beauty, for after the storm the sky seemed bluer, the sun warmer, and the sea had a quality of magnificent gentleness. I stood in the companionway for hours, filled with delight at the sparkling ocean and the too blue sky. The air was as clear as the rays of a star, and I felt that I could see all the way to eternity. My uncluttered life was indeed sweet, and it seemed—as it always does—that the simplest pleasures were best.

Not only is the sea unspoiled and without artificiality, there is a primeval quality, a *purity* surrounding its environment. Maybe you appreciate the sea because when you are lost upon its vastness your life is not jammed up with the trivia, the meaningless detail, and the foolish stuff of civilization. Somehow a fundamental strength—a mysterious and independent energy—seems to flow from the wild and undisciplined ocean. Perhaps on some level we recognize an affinity with the ultimate powerhouse of nature.

Samoa consists of three large islands plus a handful of smaller ones. The islands are high, bluish-green, and wooded, their rounded summits sticking up from a great submerged range of volcanic mountains that surfaces from the deeps of the Pacific. Tutuila, owned by the United States, is the smallest of the big three islands but has the best natural harbor in the South Pacific. The highest peak on the fifty-four-square-mile island is 2,141-foot Matafao which rises above a 1,200-foot ridge that runs along much of Tutuila's nineteen-mile length. The opening to the great harbor of Pago Pago (pronounced Pango Pango) faces south,

and as we approached we had to watch out for breaking seas that were sometimes kicked up by heavy swells that erupted on off-lying banks of coral a few miles south of the island.

The weather was light and we sailed shoreward, close-reaching with a gentle northeast wind while we glided up and down on big swells. Through the binoculars I picked out radio towers, and soon we were even with the red-and-white entrance marker on Breaker Point. The *Pilot* books warned of Whale Rock in the middle of the fairway, and as I looked ahead off to port there was a tremendous whoosh and rush of white water as a swell broke on the rock. We saw a red bus creeping along the shore and we began to pick out a rusty roof, a slab-sided warehouse, a wisp of smoke. Tall cliffs and mountains rose on three sides of us and it seemed that we had reached the end of the bay and that the charts were wrong. But as we drifted slowly northward the main harbor magically unfolded to our left, and we headed into a quiet bay where we were totally protected from ocean storms. An aerial tramway spanned the harbor overhead and a few small ships were tied up to docks along the south shore. Across the way on the north side I saw dozens of large fishing ships with high prows and sharply curved sides. The yellow sun hung low in the sky and the long shadows of the jutting mountains cast shimmering patterns on the still dark water. Altogether the scene was beautiful and we were thrilled to sail into American Samoa.

My reverie was short-lived.

"Hey, buddy, you can't tie up here," bellowed a hoarse voice when I approached a dock near the main settlement. We continued a little farther and saw a car drive up, a man get out and motion us toward an old pier, where we went alongside. The pier was particularly rickety and the edge toward the water bristled with enormous nails and spikes. We quickly put out tires to protect the hull. Several more cars drove up with Samoans who were customs and health officials, but the immigration and agriculture officers were busy at the airport and weren't able to come for several hours. I wanted to go out and anchor, but we had to stay at the terrible dock until our incoming clearance was finished. *Whisper*'s hull got badly scratched by several fiendishly long spikes that stuck out from the old pier. Finally we were ready to go.

"You can tie to a mooring in the harbor without charge for four days," said one of the officials. "After that you have to pay port dues. For your thirty-five-foot length the charges are twenty-five dollars for the first month, fifty dollars for the second month, and seventy-five dollars for the third."

The charges seemed enormous.

"I'll anchor then," I said. "This is an American ship and I have good ground tackle and—"

"You still have to pay," said the man. "It's no good to anchor because the bottom of the harbor is foul with pieces of old ships and cars and trucks and whatnot dumped in by the Navy. You had better tie to a mooring and think about it."

We did as he suggested and went to bed.

The next morning I was awakened by a squeaking noise and I suddenly realized that I was listening to birds. I climbed on deck and sat in the warm sun and looked at the magnificent harbor which lay under the green bulk of Rainmaker Mountain. A big Australian ship had docked at the main pier, and we heard the shouts of the stevedores as they unloaded cargo. Near us half a dozen other yachts—including several trimarans that I later found out were abandoned—lazily circled their moorings. The motor ship *Dick* of Apia, flying the red-and-blue ensign of Western Samoa, chugged past with a load of waving Samoans and a deck cargo of giant taro. *Dick* was a funny old ship about fifty-five feet long, painted many shades of blue and white and red, with a toilet perched aft above the water on two timbers that stuck over the stern.

Margaret and I went ashore in the dinghy and walked to the post office, where we found a long line of people in front of the windows. We collected a bundle of letters and several parcels and mailed all the letters and packages that we had brought from Palmerston. The little post office was a popular place, for the Samoans not only received and posted letters, but they sat around reading their mail and industriously penning long letters. The women tended to be large, often with broad shoulders ("Good football players," I said), and generally wore bright cotton print dresses. The men were stocky, dressed mostly in shirts and trousers, and often rode bicycles or motor scooters. Outside the post office a Samoan policeman directed traffic with a lot of fancy hand signals that used up so much energy he had to be relieved every few minutes.

Margaret went shopping for fresh food while I hobbled off to the hospital. On Aitutaki I had gotten coral cuts on the Achilles' tendons of both ankles and the wounds had steadfastly refused to heal, probably because they were always wet when sailing. The hospital was a large, impressive-looking, old-fashioned series of buildings with busy departments and plenty of patients.

The doctor sucked his breath in sharply when he pulled the bandages off the backs of my ankles and uncovered horrible festered wounds. He prescribed gentian violet ("never lime juice") and antibiotic ointment. "You must keep your ankles dry," he admonished, an order I dutifully followed for the next three weeks until the coral cuts healed.

When I returned to *Whisper* I had to look twice to find her, for Margaret had all the wet things from the forepeak hanging out in the sun to dry. The ship was festooned with sheets, trousers, cushions, charts, sails, and things I'd forgotten we had. I took drastic action to solve the forward-deck leak and removed five feet of toerail on each side and filled the bolt holes and hull-deck joint with epoxy resin. The appearance of *Whisper* suffered a little, but I was quite ready to trade beauty for dryness.

On the next mooring was the thirty-six-foot Carol ketch *Myonie*, an American yacht registered in Ashland, Wisconsin, of all places. Al and Helen Gehrman were on their way around the world for the second time. Al was a podiatrist, a foot doctor, and from time to time the voyaging would stop while he repaired a few feet to raise further cruising funds. Al was in the midst of a big job. The casing of the reduction gear on his auxiliary engine had broken so he removed the engine, extracted and repaired the broken part, and put the units back —all by himself while on a mooring.

It was possible to rent an automobile, but we found bus rides much cheaper and more fun. As in Tahiti, the buses were the main transport, and everything was hauled in the ancient vehicles, often castoffs from Kansas City or New Orleans. There were long benches down each side of the buses and the sides were windowless and open. The scenery along the south shore of Tutuila was spectacular. We often climbed high above a beach or a bit of dazzling shoreline lagoon as our old bus groaned along the steep and bumpy roads.

We passed many Samoan villages, collections of thatched huts that looked like brown cupcakes amidst the tall trunks of the coconut palms. A Samoan house is called a fale (FAH-lee) and consists of a high, dome-like roof that rests on inner and outer posts of breadfruit wood ranged around in a circle. The supporting posts—set on a raised stone or concrete foundation—entirely replace the usual walls and partitions of a house. The high thatched roof is particularly effective against the heat of the sun, and the absence of any walls means that cooling breezes can blow right through the house. Privacy doesn't seem to be a problem, since everyone can see everyone else. In case of windswept rain a series of woven screens, something like venetian blinds, can be let down from the roof. Pandanus mats are put on the floor for sitting and sleeping, and the fales are usually free from Western-style furniture except for a foot-operated Singer or White sewing machine. Cooking is done in a smaller shelter in back.

The native structures near Pago Pago were quite junky in appearance, with pieces of rusty iron sheeting in place of thatched roofs. But farther away the villages were more unspoiled and prettier, with swept paths and flowers growing around the fales. In the outer districts the men wore wrap-around skirts called lava-lavas and the women dressed in pulatasies, ankle-length skirts with fitted tunics—usually of contrasting colors—that extended down to the thighs.

Each village had an extra-large fale in the center, a sort of meeting-house, and we often saw a group of men sitting around in a circle crosslegged on mats in the traditional Samoan manner while they discussed some problem or other. As they talked they made sennit, coconut fibers that were twisted and rolled into a twinelike cordage that was used to lash things together.

On the way back to the harbor a young boy hailed the bus, indicated that someone in a nearby fale wanted a ride, and said something in Samoan. I was surprised when a number of the passengers got off and walked to the fale. Each reappeared with a case of beer, which he stacked down the main aisle of the bus. Soon there were twelve cases of beer on board. Finally the passenger appeared, an older man with a tailored lava-lava who was carrying a briefcase and seemed to be someone of consequence. We continued along for a few miles to another village, where the scene was repeated, except that the beer was off-loaded. The passengers lent a hand as a matter of course, and the bus waited until the delivery work was completed. I found out later that if you had an errand in a store the bus driver would wait for you if you asked him. Never mind the schedule!

The ultimate in bus assistance came a few days later when we rode westward along the south shore. Evidently a woman was building an addition to her house, for the bus left the main road and stopped at a lumber yard. Everyone got out and helped load long two-by-fours, unwieldy pieces of plywood, and heavy iron pipe—not a little but a lot. The loading took a long time. The springs of the bus were bent way down, and Margaret and I wondered whether we had gotten into a work detail by mistake. Finally the driver indicated that we were ready to go, and everyone got on, climbing around the enormous load down the middle. The bus staggered off, never daring to leave first gear.

In Tahiti we had met several officers from large Korean fishing ships because the men had stopped at all the yachts to ask for foreign postage stamps for their collections. Their calls were clever, since the yachts received mail from many places and usually could give the Koreans a few new stamps. The Koreans also liked to practice speaking English. In Pago Pago the two large tuna canneries—Star Kist and Van Camp— were supplied by big fishing fleets from Japan, Taiwan, and Korea, and we soon met a Korean officer ("Stamps, please, for my collection"), Captain Myung Ki Moon of the Nam Hae fleet ship #270. Captain Moon was a short man, about five feet tall, with a round face, long black hair, a rumpled blue suit, and endless enthusiasm.

"Come to my ship, please, for a little visit," he said with a bow.

The following afternoon we took the bus to the north side of the harbor. At the shipyard next to the canneries we found an amazing scene, one that must have made the old Polynesian gods up above shake their heads. Fifty or sixty motor fishing ships from the Far East lay rafted together in long rows as they underwent repairs and painting. The ships from Japan and Korea were modern steel vessels, but those from Taiwan were wooden with high, amazingly curved sides, the sort of sheer you might expect to find on the emperor's launch in an old Chinese scroll. Without the weight of tons of fish in their holds the Taiwan ships lay at odd angles, their decks canted and the masts leaning way over.

Hundreds of energetic Oriental crewmen swarmed over the ships, hammering, wire-brushing, sawing, riveting, and painting. Japanese welders knelt on the decks, their hoods masklike and their sparking welding rods blue and ghostly. Sweating Formosans threw fishing floats into shore boats while gangs of begrimed Koreans sat balanced on crude rafts on the water while they scraped on the sides of the hulls. Some ships were diseased with rust. Others gleamed in antiseptic white. Laundry fluttered from a dozen decks, and loudspeakers shook with the tremulous vibrato of Cantonese singers from Hong Kong, squeaky flutes from Taipei, and scratchy violins from Pusan. The water was streaked with heavy oil, putrid with fish waste, and stinking from garbage and sewage. A ship out of the water had new bottom paint and was about ready to skid down the ways while the crew madly polished the bronze propeller. In front of us a Chinese carpenter shaped a curved plank with a long chisel and a leather mallet. On the side of the quay a dozen Orientals hurried around measuring out new fishing lines which lay in long, starkly white rows on the oily earth.

We found Captain Moon buttoning his trousers in the wheelhouse.

"Ah, postage-stamp people," he said, waving us in. Captain Moon's 160-ton steel vessel was one of sixty-one identical ships that had been built in Le Havre, powered with Fiat Diesels with German reduction gears, and outfitted with radios from England, fishing tackle from Japan, and hardware from the United States. "A truly international ship," said Captain Moon, chuckling at his little joke.

Ship #270 had been laid up for months waiting for a new engine part from Germany. In the meantime the vessel had been painted inside and out. We saw that half the deck space was filled with fishing floats, buoys, and lines, and that most of the space below was taken up by the large engine and refrigerated hold. The quarters of the officers and crew were tiny, but the men seemed well used to climbing over one another and were cheerful and busy although perhaps weary of the long stay in port. After having seen Polynesians for so long the energetic and fast-moving Koreans seemed nervous and high-strung to us.

Most of the Far East Samoan fleet practiced the long line method of deep sea fishing in which a stout main line about 1,000 feet long is attached to flag buoys and is paid out overboard. From this main horizontal line, five to thirteen branch lines hang vertically downward and are provided with hooks baited with eight-inch frozen fish from Japan.[18]

"This assembly is called a basket," explained Captain Moon. "When we are on the fishing grounds my men put out about 375 such baskets which means that we have some 3,375 hooks strung out on fifty to seventy-five miles of line. We adjust the buoy lines to control the depth of the hooks to meet the bluefin tuna or albacore which generally swim thirty-five to 120 feet below the surface."

The men fished for albacore, yellowfin, big eye, and marlin. The albacore ran ten to forty pounds, the big eye 100 to 400 pounds, and the marlin 140 to 600 pounds. The capacity of the refrigerated ship was seventy-five tons which hopefully had been reached after a trip that was sixty days long and included forty-five days of fishing. The twenty-four crew members worked on a share basis of thirty-five percent of the catch, with the rest going to the Korean government which provided the ship and took care of its expenses.

In 1967, the Star Kist cannery paid $380 for one ton of albacore, $280 for yellowfin, and $180 for big eye. A little arithmetic told us that the contents of the refrigerated hold were exchanged for about $21,000. The crew shared $7,350, or an average of $360 if the catch was good and of high quality. It seems that commercial fishing—no matter where practiced—is a tough life, with long hours of drudgery at low pay. "Of course our life would be better if it weren't for the sharks, which take twenty to twenty-five percent of all the fish we catch," said Captain Moon.

Before we left we had a drink of iced pink punch and were given a few fish hooks and a dried shark's jaw. "Save for me all postage stamps from foreign countries, please," said Captain Moon.

We gave him our promise.

One day a sailing enthusiast named Grant Masland came down to *Whisper*. Grant was a director at the television station and he took us on a tour of the station and of several elementary schools. Since Tutuila was small and the schooling had been widely criticized in the U.S. press, a major island project was the transmission of lessons by television. A master teacher working under ideal conditions in Pago Pago could prepare an arithmetic or language lesson that could be beamed all over the island together with expensive artwork and teaching aids that could never be justified for one teacher alone. It seemed a good scheme until we learned that $6,000,000 had been spent on the station and its equipment (six video tape recorders at $60,000 each), money that could have trained perhaps several hundred Samoan women to be teachers or have established a small teachers' college. In the schools we visited we felt that the television lessons were presented as *a substitute for* a teacher rather than as *a supplement to* a teacher. It seemed to us that the young people spent entirely too much time passively watching television. The pupils were bored, unchallenged, and quite outside active participation in the lessons.

We met Don Farrell, the capable and talented principal at Pavi'e'i, a fine new school in a village on the south coast. Don was in love with his job, thoroughly happy to work with his Samoan pupils and teachers, and he thanked his lucky stars at having such a fortunate opportunity. Don was a good amateur painter, he liked to play the valve trombone in his spare time, and he was keen on gardening which showed up in the borders around the school buildings which were bursting with flowers and decorative shrubs. But Don was not typical. Too many of the Americans I met were interested only in high overseas pay, extra allowances, travel, and U.S.-type housing. They tended to erect exclusive enclaves ("Samoans keep out") where they sat around drinking and complaining about their sacrifices at leaving home. "I am here for only one reason," an American schoolteacher from Oklahoma told me.

"I want the money and when my thirteen months and twelve days are up I will leave here forever."

I have no respect for such people, for in turning away from those around them—in this case the interesting Samoan people—they cheat themselves dreadfully. Certainly they could learn a few words of Samoan, if for no other reason than to impress the people back in the United States!

Although I met some good people in American Samoa I did not enjoy the visit. The Samoans were well aware of the position and money of the Americans, and I often felt tension and hostility in the air. The Americans got stateside wages; the Samoan women at the canneries received 60 cents an hour. Yet the prices in the stores were not significantly different from those in San Francisco. The ramshackle native housing around Pago Pago, the rundown shops, the rickety stores, the polluted bay, and the greedy merchants around the harbor were an absolute disgrace. I failed to see how a jet airstrip and a luxury hotel would help the average Samoan on Tutuila.

We paid our harbor dues, fivefold more than anywhere else on our Pacific trip,[19] and with Grant and Lynne Masland on board for the overnight sail to Apia we slipped seaward under the lofty brow of Rain-maker Mountain.

9 / ~~~~~~~~~~~~~~~~~~
~~~~~~~~~~~~~~~~~~~~
~~~~~~~~~~~~~

Twice Adopted

WHEN I LEFT PAGO PAGO IN AMERICAN SAMOA AND sailed the eighty miles to Apia, the capital of independent Western Samoa, it was like going from a dark closet into a large, well-lighted room. The ghosts from the dark were gone. The room was filled with relaxed, hospitable people. A big bowl of fruit sat in front of me and I found that the coins in my pocket were worth three times as much.

We liked Western Samoa at once. We arrived on a Sunday evening, usually a time when clearance officials are away and return grumbling to charge overtime. But the first official who stepped on board smiled pleasantly.

"Welcome to Western Samoa," he said as he stamped our passports. "How long would you like to stay with us?"

It took only a few minutes to clear and we tied to a large mooring buoy in the harbor. The amazing thing about anchoring in a harbor at night is how different the appearance becomes at first light. Mysterious shapes turn into ordinary buildings; a shadowy hull becomes a whale boat on a mooring; from the sound of the surf you worry that you've anchored almost on the beach, yet in the morning you're half a mile away. Screams in the dark are only shore birds scrapping over a piece of fish. The red winking light that seemed so close is really on top of a radio tower two miles away.

We were on the north coast of Upolu, anchored in the middle of the harbor of Apia, a city of 25,000, about one fifth of the country's people. Western Samoa is made up of two main islands, Upolu and Savai'i (sah-vye-ee), both forty-eight miles long and up to twenty-five miles wide. The islands have mountains from 3,000 to over 6,000 feet, but the high places are usually hidden in clouds, and from the ocean the main view is of swelling hills of green that roll gently upward until they disappear into wispy layers of white.

The last land of any consequence that we had visited was Tahiti. The islands of Upolu and Savai'i were of comparable size but immeasurably more fertile, with large coastal lowlands of deep rich soil. There was plenty of rainfall and a big local population that was both friendly and would work cheaply. It was no wonder that white planters and entrepreneurs had cast covetous eyes on this fair land a century ago, and that Germany, England, and the United States had sent warships to look after the interests of each country's greedy nationals. Indeed the ships might have fought and begun a war if a hurricane hadn't wiped out the competing warships in Apia harbor in 1889. Germany ran Western Samoa until World War I, when New Zealand assumed charge. In 1962, Western Samoa became independent, although she still leans heavily on New Zealand aid and British-trained leadership.[20]

We took the dinghy and rowed ashore. Apia harbor is roughly semi-circular in shape, about one mile across, and open to the north, with the entrance somewhat encumbered by reefs. A new wharf and warehouse have been built on the eastern side. Landward of this is a long, tree-shaded beach on which the local tugs and ferries are dragged up on crude marine ways for repairs and painting. We left the dinghy under a breadfruit tree and headed along the main road, which circled the bay.

An English Austin chugged slowly along and we passed many Samoans walking. The men wore lava-lavas and were generally big and full-fleshed. We passed a hotel, half a dozen small churches, a noisy bus depot, various shops, and the big trading stores of Burns Philp and Morris Hedstrom. Many of the women were dressed in pulatasies, the long Samoan skirts that seemed to impart such a graceful motion to their walk.

Where Main Beach Road intersected Vaea Street we watched a Samoan policeman direct traffic. He was dressed in a gray lava-lava with a Sam Browne belt and stood on a small platform under a large square umbrella. He controlled the pedestrians and vehicles with an amazing display of arm, hand, and elbow motions. His white gloves pointed up, then down, sideways, together, his arms crossed, uncrossed,

spread apart, stood at right angles. He was an artist with his hands, a conductor of movements and motion. No one could describe his gestures, but everyone understood them. The people and cars and trucks followed his directions and flowed smoothly through town with hardly a stop.

The Samoan women sold fruit and vegetables along the main street. The produce was exhibited in palm-thatch baskets behind which the women sat on mats holding aloft black umbrellas to shade them from the hot sun. You could buy such things as cucumbers, pineapples, limes, mangoes, passion fruit, and green beans very cheaply. In American Samoa one or two papayas cost twenty-five cents; in Apia you could buy a whole basket of enormous papayas—a load you could scarcely lift—for the same price.

All the produce was big, well-formed, and beautifully ripe. The people too were healthy and vigorous, with sturdy, muscular bodies, glistening skin, and shiny white teeth. The abundant land gave them an excellent diet—though they often ate too much. It was a local joke that a beefy Samoan could destroy an enemy by merely sitting on him.

The next afternoon we stopped at Aggie Grey's Hotel. In Rarotonga, Captain Andy Thomson had told us to call on Aggie. "I once did her a small favor and at Christmas time she always sends me a bottle of whisky, which helps me get over New Year's Day, a troublesome holiday," Andy had told us.

Many years ago Aggie started a small hotel with beds for twenty-two people. Now she could take 160 in a jumble of modern buildings and gardens next to the Vaisigano River on the east side of Apia. One took it for granted that her rooms were clean, her formally served set meals good, and her people dependable. It was the depth of her welcome, the people you met, the happy way her dining-room girls danced the siva-siva, and the fact that she served an honest drink and managed to straighten out your jumbled currency that made you remember. And a generation did and passed the word, and Aggie became famous.

I found myself face to face with a tall, dignified woman perhaps in her late sixties. Half Samoan, the daughter of an English pharmacist, the widow of a New Zealand businessman, and the mother of five well-educated children, Aggie was unlike anyone I had ever met. She wore a long red mumu with a white flower print that, together with her gray hair and erect carriage, gave her a thoroughly commanding appearance.

She spoke softly and slowly, almost as if she were choosing the best word from a list of many, and I found myself listening intently. She told about her early days, her house in the Bay of Islands in New Zealand, the problems over money and transport, and how she had put up the passengers from the flying boats during the seventeen years they had flown to Apia. We talked for only a little while, but it seemed that I had known her always. From time to time an aide would whisper some problem in Aggie's ear. She would make a decision, utter a few commands in Samoan, and return to the conversation with hardly a break in her delivery. She was a completely gracious woman who radiated poise and character and had the stuff and substance of royalty. I hoped that all queens were like Aggie.

She chuckled when I told her that Andy Thomson said he often dreamed about her and thought she was the most beautiful woman in the world.

"That goddamned old liar hasn't changed a bit," she said. "He always was full of hot air and whisky. I guess that's why I love him so. . . . Now I know you're off the little black yacht and I want you to have dinner with us."

I protested that I hadn't come to cadge meals and that we generally ate on board.

"Young man," said Aggie imperiously, suddenly standing huge and tall above my chair, "you're my guest. One of the girls will tell you when your table is ready."

The following day I went to see Captain Benson, the harbormaster. It was now the end of October, and the South Pacific hurricane season would begin in a few weeks. Samoa was along the northern edge of the danger area, but our planned course was northwest and hopefully would take us rapidly away from the hurricane danger.

"Stay with us here in Apia until March," urged Captain Benson. "If a hurricane comes, we'll take care of you. My boys will haul you up on the beach over in the corner. It's the only way a small ship can survive.

"If you remain here until the southeast trades return in March, you can continue with a fair wind," said the harbormaster. "It's pleasant here in Apia. The people are good, the water in the bay is reasonably clean, and there are no harbor dues."

Benson was right. Apia was pleasant and I thought hard about the invitation to stay. However, if we waited five months our sailing schedule would be completely upset. It was important for us to time our passages to miss the typhoon season in Japan and the winter gales in the Aleutians. Benson's invitation was tempting, but I decided to continue.

For a long time I had considered putting canvas weather cloths around *Whisper*'s cockpit to cut down the amount of spray that flew up on the helmsman. We inquired about a sailmaker and were told to see the local expert, a man named Tapasu who lived in back of Main Beach Road. The principal streets of Apia had European type buildings—the usual stores and shops and offices and schools—along with several notable structures left over from the days of German rule. But once away from the waterfront area you rapidly left most of these buildings behind. You were back among trees and fales, cooking huts, and paths in the woods. In a twinkling you were in *fa'a* Samoa, the Samoa of tradition and antiquity.

Tapasu welcomed us at once and the women spread mats for us to sit crosslegged on. I thought our visit would be only a few minutes, but I didn't know much about Samoa.

Tapasu was an alert, slim man in his late forties who was delighted, simply delighted, to see foreigners and to talk about ships. In his earlier days he had sewn sails, worked on inter-island schooners, and had even survived a shipwreck.

Tapasu's fale was surprisingly large inside, about forty feet across, and with its high airy roof and lack of furniture had lots of room. We met several of Tapasu's married children and said hello to his younger children and grandchildren. Various women were cooking out back, and Tapasu's immense wife, Sivaiala, a skilled seamstress, was busy sewing on her foot-operated machine. We began to get a notion of the Samoans' love of oratory from all the questions. How old were we? When was the ship built? How tall was the mast? Did we have oars or an engine? Where had we gone to school? How much did it rain in San Francisco? What was snow like? And so forth. We sat so long that our crossed legs ached terribly.

The next day Tapasu paddled out to *Whisper* in a handsome green-and-white bonito canoe to measure the ship for the canvas weather cloths. He spent an hour looking over *Whisper*, pronounced her O.K., and told us more about his experiences on schooners. "You had better come to tea at four o'clock," he said as he left. "The women will have something nice and I might cook a steamed pudding myself."

That evening we had steak, pig, green beans, fish, drinking nuts, and taro. The Samoans are very fond of taro, a root crop something like a giant turnip, and were continually munching on the big white tubers. I thought taro tasted like library paste and ate as little as possible.

During dinner I noticed Sivaiala looking critically at my shirt.

"That's poor material and the shirt doesn't fit very well," she said. "Go down to the store tomorrow and pick out a few fathoms of nice cloth and I'll run off some shirts for you."

During the next few days we spent a great deal of time with Tapasu's family. Sivaiala made shirts for me and dresses for Margaret, marveling at M's slim figure and at the small amount of material needed for a dress. "No Samoan in her," said Sivaiala wistfully.

We took half a dozen of the women from Tapasu's family out to *Whisper* for a visit. After the ladies had looked around the ship and played with the cat they sat in the cockpit under the broad awning and sang Samoan songs, clapping and laughing like young children, their voices carrying far over the still water.

I would hate to get in a fight with a Samoan, for they are generally powerful men and in addition are expert rock throwers. For supper one night Tipeni, Tapasu's fourteen-year-old son, was told to kill a certain chicken that was strutting around outside the fale. Tipeni was with me at the time and while he went on talking he picked up two rocks. He casually threw the first rock, which knocked the chicken down. The second rock hit the chicken's head and killed it. When I commented on his prowess at throwing, Tipeni shrugged, picked up another rock, and pointed at a flower on a distant hibiscus bush. A moment later a shower of red petals floated down.

A few nights later when Tapasu, Margaret, and I were out for a walk along the waterfront I happened to mention Captain Benson's invitation to anchor in the harbor until March. "A good idea," said Tapasu. "You can stay with us. We're your family now. You can move right in and live in the fale as long as you want."

At first we were flattered at the invitation, but we soon realized that Samoan hospitality was overpowering. You were expected for every meal and if you were late or missed a meal the family would be quite distressed. There would be a knock on the hull and a sad-faced member of the Tapasu family would hand up a warm fish and some goodies wrapped in a banana leaf. We enjoyed the family and liked them, but we wished to look around the island on our own sometimes.

We got acquainted with an American family from Hawaii, Charlie and Mary Judd and their three children. Charlie was the chief surgeon at the main hospital in Apia. He had given up a flourishing practice in Honolulu and had traded an income of several thousand dollars a week for one of a few hundred dollars a month. Charlie was a gentle man, a tall rangy fellow with glasses, balding gray hair, and a soft voice full of confidence. He had come to Apia for three years and liked his job immensely.

"I have the chance to do a whole range of surgical work," he said, beaming with satisfaction. "Back in the U.S. you are termed a specialist of some kind and usually do a limited type of work. Here I am called on to do everything. The job is difficult and challenging and I love it. And the Samoans are so appreciative of what I do."

One morning we went to the main station for a bus to the eastern part of Upolu. The driver waited until his vehicle was bursting with people, hand-cranked the engine into life, and started off. Soon it began to rain and the Samoans commenced to close the windows, which weren't glass but pieces of old plywood that you pulled up from slots down along the side of your seat. Soon all the shutters were up and the interior of the bus was as dark as the inside of a cave. The tropical rain thundered on the windshield and wooden roof and I wondered how the driver could see.

Inside we were all snug and the talk was animated and lively. We got into conversation with several men but politely declined their invitations, for we were determined to walk around a bit and not to spend the day sitting crosslegged on mats answering questions. The rain stopped, the shutters descended into their slots, and we looked out on a narrow track that cut through the leafy jungle of tall trees and shrubs. To our left the trees fell away toward the sea, and here and there we saw clusters of dark-brown oval-shaped fales and strings of fluttering laundry.

"Let's get off and walk," said Margaret.

The bus groaned away from us and we were alone at a place called Lufilufi. Below the road were half a dozen small fales spaced around a stream that coursed along beneath palms and breadfruit trees. The air was heavy with moisture from the rain, and fragrance from frangipani and tiare Tahiti blossoms. We walked for a while, worked around several hills, and then cut down a path toward the sea. Suddenly we were face to face with a startled Samoan girl.

"My name is Rosita," she volunteered after she recovered from her surprise. "Come—come to my fale and meet my aunt." Since we were a little tired from walking in the heat we followed Rosita and soon met Mrs. Taialii Alafaga, who quickly produced mats for us to sit on. We met her husband and mother and over a cup of tea found Mrs. Alafaga a relaxed woman who, though interested in us and our trip, didn't press us with too many questions.

We were a long way from the tempo of Apia. The little cluster of fales among the dark-green trees on the edge of the quiet sea was enchanting. Rosita took us on a little tour of some nearby caves with fresh-water pools. We watched Mrs. Alafaga grate coconuts for a sauce for a fish that was to be steamed for supper. Rosita wrapped the fish in a banana leaf, placed it parallel to and on top of the central mid-rib of a palm leaf, and then deftly plaited the leaves across the fish to enclose it in its own special basket, which then went on the hot coals.

Mrs. Alafaga discovered that she was the same age as Margaret, and the two women gossiped like old friends. She asked if she could see *Whisper*. The next morning she and Rosita took the bus to Apia and waved their handkerchiefs from the shore to attract our attention so we could gather our visitors in the dinghy. Another day her husband came to see us and we all went back to Lufilufi for the evening.

"You're part of my family now," announced Mrs. Alafaga during supper. "Come and stay with us. Forget the ship for a while."

I smiled acquiescence but my heart sank, for Tapasu had been urging us to quit the yacht and to move in with him. Two families had adopted us! Clearly our social life had become too much. The next day Mrs. Alafaga sent Rosita with a basket of taro and a message inviting us to tea. At the moment Rosita arrived, Tapasu's son was asking us to dinner.

According to the coconut radio a man with a long red beard had been towed into the next island in a dismasted yacht. We had thought of visiting Savai'i briefly, so we left at once in the hope of helping the disabled ship. Margaret sent Mrs. Alafaga a small present and wrote her a letter explaining why we were leaving. We walked up to Tapasu's fale to say goodbye in person. We didn't realize what would happen.

Farewells in Polynesia are bad news. As soon as we said that we were leaving everyone in the Tapasu household started to cry. It was terrible. All the women and children began to moan and weep and the men's faces were as long as yardsticks. Margaret gave Sivaiala a little present to thank her for her expert sewing and she burst into uncontrollable sobs, her big body trembling while she dabbed at her red eyes with a lace handkerchief. We thought we were only casual friends, but according to Tapasu we were important members of his family and would be sorely missed. Finally we left after much handshaking, many embraces, and more weeping. We promised to return, to write, and to exchange packages.

We were so depressed at the farewell that I swore never to do it again but to write a letter and to sail off quietly.

While we were tacking across Apolima Strait to Savai'i we caught a four-foot dorado on our trailing lure. When we arrived at Salelologa after the twenty-five-mile trip a crowd of several hundred Samoans collected to watch us sail in. A little later I hoisted the gold-colored dorado up on the main boom. The people on the dock wanted to buy the fish, but we had planned to have it for dinner. Several women demanded to buy the fish. Since Margaret was in charge of the money, what there was, I turned the problem over to her. The women on the wharf held up coins. Margaret shook her head. More coins. No! Still more coins. No! Finally one of the Samoan women jumped on *Whisper*, seized the fish, gave Margaret a whole handful of small silver coins, hopped back on shore, and triumphantly disappeared into the crowd with her fish while Margaret—in her new role of commercial fisherman—sat down to count her hoard.

Next to us on the dock we saw our old friend John Cotton sitting dejectedly on the deck of *El Viajero*, a crudely built, forty-foot, ferro-cement ketch. John had been engaged to ferry the ship from Villa in the New Hebrides to San Francisco. It was an ambitious trip for a single-hander, especially in an ill-equipped ship that sailed poorly to windward and whose engine would not run. North of Savai'i a spreader in the rigging had carried away. The mast crashed to the deck and John narrowly missed going on a reef. A local ship had towed him to Salelologa, where John had made arrangements for a tug to take him to Apia. We heard later that it took months for John to get the mast repaired. He finally delivered the ship to San Francisco from Apia after a seventy-six-day, nonstop voyage.

We found Savai'i a good deal more primitive than Upolu. The island was steeply mountainous, with recent lava flows, few roads, and even fewer white visitors. The villages were quite unspoiled and many of the men had extensive body tattoos. But it was hard for us to walk around because a crowd tended to gather wherever we appeared. The local police inspector put a guard on the ship at once, for Samoans—especially in remote places—have a different sense of values and tend to help themselves to what they want. In former times—and still today in some places—a Samoan could take the food or personal property of others for his own use.[21]

According to Western notions we would call many Samoans petty thieves, but the traditional Samoan concept is that everything should be shared. This modified communism may be O.K. for Samoans, but it is hard on visitors and I dreaded to leave *Whisper*. We heard a story that when a Samoan wants to grow beans he plants one seed for himself and a second for the thief who will certainly appear in the night at harvest time.

In Apia we had talked with several schoolteachers from New Zealand and they had asked us to call on them at Avao on the north coast of Savai'i. Since the charts were poor we made inquiries about Matautu Bay on which Avao fronted. We were assured that it was well sheltered with a sandy bottom in which our anchors would hold well. Late in the afternoon of November 21 we eased *Whisper*'s sheets and glided into Matautu Bay. The anchorage, however, was open to the north, and where the water shoaled over the white sand, big swells formed that thundered into white spray on the fringing reef farther inshore. The weather was settled and the barometer remained high, so we anchored the ship, tidied up her gear, and prepared to go ashore in the dinghy.

"Look what's coming," said Margaret, looking shoreward. "I hope they're friendly."

A fleet of thirty outrigger canoes had set out through the surf and was rapidly closing in on our little ship. I thought that if we pulled away in the dinghy the fleet might follow us and leave the ship alone. But as I rowed toward the reef the canoes converged on *Whisper*. I felt that my little ship was Captain Cook's *Endeavour* in Matavai Bay in Tahiti in 1769, for while she rolled merrily at anchor the primitive canoes surrounded the ship and the husky, dark-skinned natives swarmed on board. The scene would have made a wonderful photograph, but of course I had no camera.

I turned to look at the swells bursting on the fringing reef and realized we would have to ride a wave across the coral barrier. In the twilight the approach seemed quite hazardous and we would not be able to get back to the ship until morning. I looked back at *Whisper* and saw one of the Samoans dancing up and down the decks with a life ring around his neck. I wondered whether someone had sliced off the mainsheet. I swung the dinghy sharply around.

"Sorry," I said, "but this is one place we're leaving." As soon as we got aboard I began to winch up the anchor while Margaret hoisted the mainsail. As we began to move seaward the canoes gradually left us. Savai'i faded into the dark.

10 / ~~~~~~~~

~~~~~~~~~

~~~~~~

The Back Door to Yesterday

So far on our trip we had voyaged over routes reasonably well known. Now we left the paths of the round-the-world sailors and headed northwest toward the British crown colony of the Ellice and Gilbert islands. It was in these seas a century ago that Yankee brigs and barks from Nantucket and New Bedford had come to search for the elusive whale. A generation ago mighty fleets of Japanese and U.S. warships had fought grievous battles. But now the equatorial ocean highways ahead of us were silent and empty except for an occasional inter-island schooner whose masts we might not spy once in a dozen years.

We had decided on the route but our charts were sketchy, the *Pilot* books vague, and authors had seldom found these seas. I counted sixteen islands in the Gilberts and nine in the Ellice group. But where to stop? It was the travelers' old dilemma: At which stations on the train trip should we get off? There was no conductor to ask and no Baedeker to consult. A good anchorage was equal to a travelers' hotel for us, so we looked for a lagoon where we could safely drop an anchor. The choice became name picking based on passable lagoons. Should we go to Nukufetau or Nanumea? Nukulaelae or Funafuti? We took pot luck and shaped our course toward Funafuti.[22]

The distance was 659 miles, the course 290° M., and the passage took seven days—no, six days, or was it seven? We had crossed 180° W. longitude and lost one day when we passed the International

Date Line. This always confused me and I let Margaret sort out whether Sunday was now Monday. Was Tuesday really Tuesday or was it Wednesday?

The trip to the Ellice Islands was easy, with mostly light following winds and periods of calms and variables. As we neared the equator the sun burned down and obliged us to wear shoes when we walked on the hot decks. The hesitant wind flickered between north-northeast and south-southeast and brought us half a dozen squalls every day, which cooled off the ship and gave us delightful fresh-water showers.

November 23. 0630. A little while ago I watched the light strengthen as the new day rose from the depths of the night. The colors were marvelous to see as they grew from the black that little by little became gray and then blue and pink. But not one shade of color formed before my eyes; there were a dozen, perhaps 50 separate grays and blues and pinks. The ineffable delicacies were far beyond any mere words. The experience of seeing whole civilizations of color was almost beyond human comprehension.

Combined with the colors were the cloud shapes: Trade wind clouds that stretched long and thin; clouds that towered high and reached low; streamers of white scudding east at one level while feather-edged ribbons of gray floated southward higher up. An enormous cumulus blocked the rising sun but soon the dark cloud was rimmed with pink that shimmered into gold before it became the white of day. All around me the colors changed, grew, combined, and disappeared. Dawn was finished. The new day had begun.

The wind picked up from the east and the next day our noon-to-noon run was 133 miles. Before supper I discovered that a jib sheet had slipped over the side and had gotten around something below the waterline. No amount of tugging would free the line, so we hove to. I put on a face mask and dived over the side to recover the line, which had somehow managed to knot itself into a loop and to lasso the rudder. That night at 0210 I looked out to see the exploding crimson of a meteor flash in the sky off to starboard. It was the biggest I had ever seen and, while I watched, the meteor burned out and its curving glow died like a spent firework.

On a certain point of sailing when the wind was not quite behind us and not quite abeam, we couldn't hold the headsail out to windward with a pole (our usual running arrangement) because when the ship rolled on a wave and skidded toward the wind, the breeze would get behind the headsail and backwind it. The drive of the mainsail then soon put the ship way off course. Conversely, if we set the headsail behind the mainsail, the headsail tended to be largely useless because it was shielded from the wind by the mainsail. This also put us off course.

With both arrangements the headsail was forever filling and emptying with bangs that threatened to blow the sail to shreds. The self-steering gear was quite unable to cope with this problem, which we usually solved by altering course a little. One day we tried running under a headsail alone when the wind came from this troublesome direction. The wind vane then steered the ship perfectly, but without the support of the mainsail *Whisper* rolled and rolled—even on a relatively placid ocean.

I was soon aware that Margaret was hoisting the mainsail and changing the course. "I'm tired of all this rolling," she said angrily. "You would think with a calm sea we could manage some comfort. I would rather take a day longer and arrive in one piece. I feel like pepper in a salt shaker."

November 26 was a tiring day, with little wind, two tremendous squalls, and heavy rain showers. At noon the fiddle rail on the stove broke and several dishes launched themselves to destruction. It was very chilly during the second squall and I blessed my oilskins. While I was on deck lashing the handle of the faulty roller reefing gear in place a small gray bird with pointed, sweptback wings suddenly fluttered to the deck. I carried it below and got out the bird books. With a bird in your lap the identification is positive. Length? Let's see—eight inches. White rump? Yes. Notched tail? Yes. Dangling webbed feet? Yes. Nostrils in tube on bill? Yes. The bird was a Leach's storm petrel, a delicate little fellow who stayed with us for several hours before continuing his flitting flight just above the waves over the open ocean.

At 2035 our position was an estimated seventeen miles from Funafuti. We hove to until dawn, when we got under way again with dark clouds frowning across the horizon from west to north, just the direction we were headed. I wondered whether we would be able to see the low atoll, but at 0740 Funafuti showed up ahead. Rain plummeted on deck and it was too gusty to use the vane. The wind worked from dead aft to the starboard beam as a rain squall passed going northward. Goonies, shearwaters, and a bosun bird flew around the ship. We headed for a tower structure of some kind and held our course until we were about half a mile from a point of land where we suddenly noticed a small group of people watching us. One man waved a large red flag. Red flag! Was landing prohibited? Was there a danger of some sort? Had I broken a rule? It later developed that he was just waving it for fun.

We gybed and ran southwest along the island for five miles to Te Puapua pass. Opposite the pass two more squalls bore down on us and erased all visibility more than 200 yards. While Margaret stood out to sea on a compass course I went below to check the engine. However, the little Diesel would only splutter and sneeze. It was the first time I had tried the engine since Samoa, and I found the fuel system choked with dirt and water from contaminated oil. While Margaret dodged squalls and tacked back and forth I spent a sweat-filled hour cursing and smashing my knuckles on the greasy monster. Again and again I took apart the three filters, cleaned them, and tried to get fuel through the lines, which were plugged with sludge.

It was hopeless. The fuel system needed major work. I emerged from the hell-hole covered with sweat and oil and fuming with rage at myself for not having personally strained every drop of oil I had bought in Apia. The cat meowed. Margaret said nothing. I cooled off by pouring buckets of sea water over me to clean up. We headed across the pass by sail. "The devil take his machinery," I muttered blackly.

Funafuti lies 510 miles south of the equator, almost astride the International Date Line, and is about 2,300 miles southwest of the Hawaiian Islands. The atoll measures eleven by fourteen miles and is shaped something like a man's head facing west, his profile outlined with the dot-dash pattern of a broken reef surmounted here and there by palm-topped islets which total about thirty in all. During World War II, Funafuti was a U.S. naval base and I have seen a photograph with twenty capital ships at anchor. The cautious directions in the *U.S. Pilot* had evidently been written for these battleships and heavy cruisers, for we had no trouble at all entering the large lagoon. The *Pilot* glibly spoke of rows of buoys, leading marks, and beacons, but except for a stone marker on Funamanu Island all were gone. World War II was a long time ago.

Inside, the weather improved, and in the calm lagoon we tacked back and forth up to the village of Fongafale where we anchored in the early afternoon while the Ellice Islanders lined the shore.

The village was along the center of the largest islet, a boomerang-shaped thread of coral six miles long which varied in width from a third of a mile to only sixty yards. The atoll land was so narrow! If you faced the green water of the lagoon and then turned around, you could always see the purplish seas of the open ocean gleaming between the palm trunks. During World War II a small airstrip was carved out of the widest place, and two or three times a month a small plane from Suva landed with mail and a few passengers. There were 685 natives and five New Zealanders on Funafuti.

After the flamboyance of the Samoans we found the Ellice people quiet and unobtrusive. Life on the atoll was fairly close to subsistence. The men fished every day and the women were experts at preparing coconuts, chickens, small pigs, bananas, and taro. The houses were open and built of pandanus-thatch roofs set on posts that stuck above foundations of lime or concrete. Sometimes a sheet of rusty iron was tacked on the roof or a few old boards were nailed across the sides. In general the houses were featureless and drab.

The people conversed in Ellice, a Samoan offshoot, but many of them knew some English and a few spoke excellent English from having worked at the phosphate diggings on Ocean Island. When the men fished they sailed in small outrigger canoes with spritsails of an inverted triangular pattern.

Like most places in the Pacific outback, the people were not only short of cash but had little chance to earn it. A new London Missionary Society church (LMS) was under construction at Fongafale, and when the foundation had been poured, a large amount of sand was needed, which was available at the south end of the main island. There were two automobiles and a truck on Funafuti. The local officials offered to rent the truck to the construction workers for one day for $1.50 so the sand could be hauled to the site of the church. The islanders had other ideas. The women plaited baskets of palm thatch, which the men put in their canoes and paddled south to the sandy beach. There the baskets were filled with sand and loaded into the canoes, which were paddled back to near the church site. Moving several tons of sand took many trips and much paddling over a number of days, but the job required no cash at all.

"Why spend money?" said one of the men. "We have plenty of time. Hauling sand by hand costs nothing at all. Besides, it's fun." He chuckled with glee.

Now the church was partially finished, and one day while we were walking around we happened to go past the new structure during a time of great excitement. That morning the roof had been completed, which signaled the start of a feast. As we walked in front of a nearby meetinghouse a woman darted out and put crowns of freshly woven flowers on our heads. We were invited to enter the meetinghouse, and a fine mat was spread for us to sit on. While I looked around I felt something and was astonished to see a woman sprinkling talcum powder on my shoulders. This, we found out later, signified that we could sing and dance, and we saw that all the other people—perhaps a hundred—had talcum powder on their shoulders too.

We ate with our fingers from a mound of island food that was placed in front of us on a banana leaf. A young girl sat before us as we ate and fanned the food to keep the flies away. Then the elders gave short speeches. Since I was a visitor I was called on to talk, and someone translated my English into Ellice. I told how glad I was to be on the island and how fortunate the people were to live on such a beautiful place. I said I was pleased to see so many happy people and to be at the feast. I complimented everyone on the new church and thanked them for their hospitality.

After the speeches the women ate. Then came singing and dancing. The women had powerful, low-pitched voices and were good at harmonizing. They loved to sing and their faces beamed with pleasure as the notes came out. The men sang in short, strident phrases and almost shouted at times. The women dancers dressed in white or patterned sleeveless blouses crisscrossed with bright bands of orange-and-red cloth and paper and wore short, very full grass skirts decorated with more strips of color. Around their necks and heads were garlands of tightly woven flowers, and tied to each arm between the hand and shoulder were four or five circlets of bright flowers made of colored paper.

The dancers didn't perform like Tahitians or Cook Islanders at all. Six of the Ellice women stood in line in front of a group of singers and acted as if they were in a stylized trance. They looked straight ahead or to one side or the other without smiling, purposely grim, sometimes holding their arms rigidly ahead or sideways and moving slowly in a formation of six. Meanwhile the men sat packed around a low wooden platform about six feet square that was covered with a mat on which they drummed with the flats of their hands. At the beginning of a song the drumming was light and intermittent, but at the climax twenty fellows pounded the drum for all they were worth while they sang at the tops of their voices.

It was quite a lunch, and afterward I reflected on how much

pleasure and happiness these people achieved on their tiny, primitive island.

I looked up from the village and noticed that the palm branches had begun to blow in a different direction. The wind had changed from the southeast to the west, which put *Whisper* on a lee shore with a coral reef only 100 feet behind the ship. We returned to the yacht at once.

A problem with calling at atolls and anchoring in lagoons is that if a strong adverse wind comes up, you really have no place to go except to head out to sea. But the new wind or the tidal stream conditions during the storm may make the pass impossible to use. Furthermore, if the pass is intricate you can leave only during daylight when you can see. Sometimes an atoll will have a few small islets or motus that you can work around to gain shelter, but generally your only defense is heavy anchors and stout chain. You have to stand and take it.

In extremes a ship can begin motoring into the wind to relieve some of the pressure on the anchors. Captain Andy Thomson told me that once when the *Tiare Taporo* was threatened by hurricane winds in the Suvarov lagoon in the Cook Islands he had full power on steaming into the storm. "We stood regular watches hoping to go nowhere," said Andy. "On the second day the storm passed over."

Within the eleven-mile sweep of the Funafuti lagoon the west wind soon raised choppy waves. However, the barometer was high and we had no intelligence of a major weather disturbance, so I elected to keep *Whisper* where she was. We let out more chain on our main anchor and I laid out a second anchor on a 200-foot nylon line. Putting out the second anchor in the dinghy was hard work, and as I rowed into the wind and waves my arms felt as if they would fall off. Our little drama went quite unnoticed on shore, but it was important to us and we did everything we could to anchor *Whisper* securely. Margaret sewed strips of canvas around the second anchor line to prevent chafe where the nylon ran over the bow fairlead. I put on a face mask and swam out to the anchor buoys to check that both anchors were properly dug into the coral sand and that the chain and line were not fouled on coral patches. We took down the awning and various lines aloft to reduce windage. The storm increased, and soon the lagoon was a froth of whitecaps, but after twelve hours the wind went back to the east and dropped to nothing.

The New Zealanders worked at the airstrip and both families had been amazed to see *Whisper* sail in. ("Nobody comes here. In fact nobody ever heard of Funafuti. How did you ever find us?") One quiet evening they all came out to the ship for drinks and a look around. ("Bloody amazing how you live on this little thing.")

We ate with both families, took showers, got ice, did our laundry, and were freely invited into their homes. Norman Jones was the works officer at the airstrip and Chris Rogers was the meteorologist. We liked them both, though the men were totally different. I almost wished Somerset Maugham could have met them.

Rogers was a quiet and reserved professional weatherman who was perhaps a little on the stuffy side, although certainly generous and helpful. He was closemouthed and wasted no time at all on social small talk. His pretty wife, Jocelyn, kept their house neat and perfect, and when we ate it was punctually at seven. Each course was served on gleaming, unchipped china with the correct spoons and forks. Jocelyn was clever at making small Christmas gifts for her people back home, and Chris showed us his immense shell collection, which he had catalogued with mathematical exactitude. We heard a lot of words, but I felt there were layers and layers of protective coatings surrounding their isolated lives.

Norman Jones, the affable works officer at the little airstrip, kept no secrets at all and soon told us all his problems, his hopes and fears, his worries and joys. He was only in fair health—pale and sallow in spite of the tropical sun—but he ran his house as an open establishment, dispensing ice to the hotel next door, beer to the Ellice men, and hospitality to all, including Saturday night bingo. He insisted on giving me tools from his home workshop and stores from the family kitchen. Norman and his wife had a Fijian man and an Ellice woman who were newlyweds staying with them and, together with Norman's six-year-old daughter and the house girl and various others, generally had ten or twelve for meals. Their screen door was always banging open or shut, the gossip and jokes never stopped, and the coffee pot percolated from morning till midnight.

We hoped to get a few loaves of bread before we left, but there were too few customers on Funafuti to support a regular baker. However, when I inquired, the assistant executive officer of the island, an Ellice man named Sapoa Nitz, said his wife would be glad to bake for us. Sapoa's wife offered to leave the loaves at the hotel.

The hotel was a funny little place that opened when the island had official visitors or when the plane from Suva was late and had to stay for the night. An Ellice man ran the hotel, but he showed enthusiasm only when it was time to close up. In theory the hotel was open one hour each evening, but in practice you had to make an appointment to buy a bottle of beer, which you were supposed to drink on the premises. Meanwhile, the manager stood around and made it very plain that he wanted to close up. When I asked him whether his closed-door policy didn't work against good receipts for the hotel he smiled impatiently. "Time to close up now," he replied. "Sometimes I don't open for weeks."

Sapoa Nitz's wife appeared with two giant loaves of bread, beautifully shaped and baked to a delicate golden brown. "Splendid," I said, handing her the two shillings. But when she gave me the loaves I almost dropped them, for each loaf seemed to weigh twenty pounds. They had been made with coconut-palm yeast and, instead of being light and airy, the bread was as hard as flint and as heavy as blocks of lead ballast.

We of course said nothing but thanked Mrs. Nitz profusely, and as we rowed out to *Whisper* for the last time Margaret sat in the stern holding the two loaves like golden trophies. We found out later that the bread was totally indigestible, and when we finally jettisoned it over the side, each loaf sank like a cannonball!

11 / ∿∿∿∿∿∿∿ ∿∿∿∿∿∿∿∿ ∿∿∿∿∿

Close to Shipwreck

THE GILBERT ISLANDS ARE ROUGHLY 700 MILES NORTH-west of the Ellice group, and with the rainy season well advanced I wondered how long the trip would take. The fair southeast trades had weakened into unsettled weather from every direction, with a prospect of westerly gales and a remote chance of a hurricane.

On *Whisper* we found light headwinds as we worked toward the equator. The trip was slow and easy and my recollections are of gentle winds across a smooth, silvery, untroubled ocean. How lovely it was! Sometimes we were becalmed for twelve or fifteen hours until a little wind would ripple the enormous, very long and gently lifting swells that moved with a wonderful steadiness. If you closed your eyes you could scarcely feel them. It was only when you watched the horizon that you could gauge the rise and fall of the water. Sometimes I felt that I was on the hump of the earth and that the movement was not the sea but the earth herself, a throbbing pulse that came from the heart of the universe.

Whisper was at her best in these conditions. We had all our sails set, of course, and the ship went along incredibly well. The vane steered perfectly, far better than any helmsman who would have been cooked on deck.

On December 4 we passed Vaitupu, the last of the Ellice Islands. Vaitupu was a densely wooded atoll a mile and a half wide and three miles long, a shimmering ribbon of green stitched to a delicate thread of golden yarn. It seemed a very dream on top of the horizon. People on shore watched us as we crept past and we could see the palms, pandanus, and the oaklike fetau trees behind the long beaches of white sand. It was amazing to think that 900 people lived on the little island. We had barely enough wind for steerage way, and it took most of the day before the atoll dropped out of sight astern.

Closer to the equator we had expected the south equatorial current to give us twenty to thirty-five miles of westing per day. Instead we found that *Whisper* was getting set *east* about twenty miles a day. But it didn't matter. We were in no hurry. We had plenty of food, good books to read, and always a few odd jobs to do—fix a cockpit locker hinge, reeve a new topping lift, or sew a pair of torn trousers.

We still had the forward deck leak to think about. We were definitely close to solving the problem, which was in the hull-deck joint. At Funafuti we had removed three more feet of forward toerail on each side, cleaned the areas underneath, puttied the seams, and laid four-inch strips of special fiberglass cloth over the joint in epoxy resin. Each time we hacked off a piece of the toerail and covered more of the hull-deck joint, we found less water below. The outside appearance of the hull suffered and we lost the security of a toehold when changing sails on the foredeck, but gradually we seemed to be winning the battle.

One night at dusk the sea around *Whisper* exploded with life when a hundred porpoises suddenly surfaced around the ship. They splashed water up and down the decks as they circled around and around, diving, rolling, twisting, and frolicking, their sleek steel-gray bodies half out of the water. The cat, Kong, sat on the edge of the deck and watched wild-eyed, perhaps savoring a bite of fresh fish but afraid of the powerful, seven-foot sea creatures. Sometimes several of the porpoises would pause for a moment and emit a great *paaaahhhh* as they breathed, a sound that terrified Kong and sent him racing below. His curiosity was too great, however, and a moment later he would be back looking intently over the side.

December 7. Becalmed again and we sit quietly on a silent ocean at dawn. . . . It is an amazing experience to be becalmed and one that every sailor should know. . . . The wind gets less and less, the slatting of the sails and gear increases, the ripples on the water disappear, and you realize you are not moving. Down come the sails, one by one, and the ship sits stripped of her canvas. The sea is smooth and quiet. The only movements are from the long swells

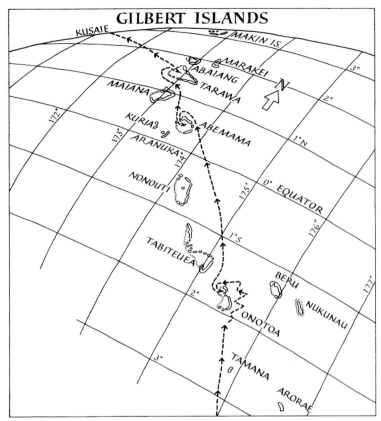

GILBERT ISLANDS

KUSAIE
MAKIN IS.
MARAKEI
ABAIANG
TARAWA
MAIANA
KURIA
ARANUKA
ABEMAMA
NONOUTI
TABITEUEA
BERU
NUKUNAU
ONOTOA
TAMANA
ARORAE
EQUATOR

that appear on one side, gently lift the ship, and run away on the
other. On all directions the distant horizon is perfectly even, an
encircling rim of dark water that seems hard and powerful in
contrast to the airy sky above.

The sky now — at 0540, before the sun—is full of soft blues and
grays. Two squalls are nearby, a small one whose rain slants steeply,
and a bigger squall with straight-down rain. A few clouds float at
perhaps 1,500 feet but they too are becalmed and only move a little
in the still air. Already in the eastern sky the sun has brushed a few
clouds with white and pink and shiny yellow.

With the unsettled weather we knew it was only a question of time
until we had wind. It came gently at 1000 the next day when we
began moving slowly with all sails set. By 1300 the northwest wind
had increased to twenty knots and we put on a smaller jib and
cranked three rolls in the mainsail. Four hours later we were skidding
along at seven knots and I was on the foredeck hanking on a storm jib
and rolling down the mainsail still more while black-edged storm
clouds tumbled in from the west at mast-top height. Large waves began to form and the sea grew rough. But by 0200 the next morning

the westerly gale was suddenly over, the seas were down, and the big sails were going up again.

We inched along day after day through calms and squalls, light airs and small storms, and slowly made miles toward the northwest. When westerly weather blew up, great forks of lightning often splintered the dark clouds. The rain poured down, the wind blew hard, and we sailed fast, happily toward our goal. A few hours later the wind would be gone and *Whisper* would be gently rocking on a windless ocean with the sun scorching down.

Without wind the sun was oppressively strong. Though we were quite brown we smeared ourselves with sunburn cream, gulped salt tablets, and drank lots of water, usually in the form of citron, a lime-and-sugar drink that was sweet, refreshing, and nutritious. We wore our largest straw hats, sunglasses, long-sleeved shirts, and rigged an awning over the cockpit. Though the sun shade was a droopy and ill-conceived affair, it helped cool the ship and us. Margaret fanned herself with a big Samoan fan she had gotten from Mrs. Alafaga in Apia.

When we left Funafuti an Ellice family gave us a large stalk of small green bananas. After a few days at sea the fruit began to ripen and we had unlimited bananas. We had excellent bananas to eat out of the hand and sliced bananas with sugar and tinned cream. We ate banana fritters, fried bananas, crushed bananas, rice pudding with bananas, sliced bananas with rum, banana cream pudding, and bananas with cereal. We finally got to the stage where we couldn't stand their sight. Even the cat, Kong, who would eat anything, growled and stalked away angrily when we put a banana in his bowl.

Much of the passage was into headwinds, and when the sea was rough we had to shut the ports and hatches to prevent water from getting below. But closing the ship stopped most of the through ventilation and it was stifling below. However, the freshwater showers from the frequent squalls were refreshing and there were so many that we couldn't have been cleaner. When the wind was behind us and the mainsail was let out, the rain collected and ran off the sail at the forward end of the main boom and we took showers at the mast. When the wind was from ahead and the boom was pinned in we stood aft under the end of the boom to let the delicious cool water run over us. Kong hated to get wet, but a few times he got shut out by accident during squalls. Then we heard frantic meowing from an animal that looked more like a rat than a cat.

On December 12 we crossed a moon sight with a morning sun line which gave us a noon position of 1° 58′ S. and 176° 10′ E., thirty-five miles east of Onotoa atoll in the southern Gilberts. At 1800 Margaret sighted the island, but it was too late in the day to go closer, so we hove to for the night. We expected to be pushed away from the atoll by the east-setting current, and sure enough at dawn there was no trace of land. It took us until 1030, the tenth day from Funafuti, before we tacked a half mile off the eastern shore.

"The lagoon looks marvelous," Margaret shouted down from the ratlines. "Like Rangiroa in the Tuamotus only more sand and larger beaches. I can see lots of tall palms. Oh for a nice cool drinking nut!"

There was a recommended anchorage, according to the sparse comments in the *U.S. Pilot*, but it seemed wide open to wind and swells from the west. I hoped we could enter the lagoon. We would have to sail to the opposite, northwest corner of the atoll where we could perhaps get local help to guide us. The distance was only eleven miles in a straight line, but it took us to the middle of the afternoon before we tacked north of the island and headed west. The breakers boomed along the fringing reef; however we held our own and with the sails strapped in tightly and water flying everywhere we passed through the disturbed seas that fronted the top of the island. The weather was worsening, with many squalls and some low clouds.

Our 1910 sketch chart showed a stone beacon on a motu called Temuah which we rounded in a hurry with eased sheets. I doused the genoa while Margaret steered toward the anchorage shown on the chart. Suddenly we were in an area of coral sand and coral heads with depths of three to four fathoms. I let the anchor go, but the chain was fouled in the locker from all the motion during the long passage from Samoa. The barrier reef was only fifty feet away.

"Gybe at once and run back out," I shouted at Margaret, who threw the tiller over hard and eased us back into deep water. We got the chain in order and went back and anchored in three fathoms. The wind was fifteen knots from the north-northwest with about two squalls every hour. There was not much wind with the rain, but each squall seemed a river from the sky.

I saw at once that the anchorage was wide open to the west and very rolly in any case. Already we were pulling hard on the chain, which creaked a bit, so I rigged a thirty-foot anchor spring of half-inch nylon line—a sort of giant rubber band to take the minor shocks of the ship jerking against the anchor. Suddenly all was quiet except for the fall of the topping lift, which *rat-tat-tatted* on the mast as we rolled. To keep the line quiet I led it aft and tied it off, a step I was to regret.

Margaret got ready to go ashore, about three quarters of a mile across the lagoon, while I blew up the inflatable dinghy. It was now 1700, with maybe an hour or a little longer before dark. A small rain shower whipped across us and was gone, but I could see an enormous squall coming. In a moment heavy rain bucketed down and the sky became sea, indistinguishable except for the cooler fresh water. The rain erased the reef and the island completely, and I could scarcely see the bow of the ship. Half an hour later the rain still plummeted down; now it was too late to go ashore. A good thing Margaret hadn't been caught when halfway to shore or she couldn't have seen to row without a compass. We would wait till dawn.

The prospects for dinner were good. A silvery-blue four-foot wahoo had taken our trailing feather lure while we had tacked along the island and we had a splendid fish. I cleaned the beautiful creature as the rain tapered off.

"How many steaks do you want?" I called down to Margaret from the cockpit. "How thick? The fish looks great."

"Oh, cut eight steaks about three quarters of an inch thick," she said, holding up a thumb and forefinger an inch and a half apart. "I'm starved and I bet you are too. I'll have the frying pan hot in a minute and we can eat shortly."

My hacksaw made quick work of the request, but there was enough fish for fifty steaks. It was a pity we hadn't someone to give the rest. Without refrigeration there was no choice in the tropics. Meat or fish was eaten at once or tossed over the side.

I went below and dried out a bit. *Whisper* was straining hard at her anchor. I decided to take off the genoa and put on the working jib in case we had to leave. However, once I got on deck I realized that conditions were changing rapidly and I hurried to change the headsail. The wind had veered to the west and we were on a lee shore, a sailor's nightmare. The wind was not too strong, about twelve to fifteen knots, but large swells began to roll into the anchorage. While I knelt on the foredeck and changed the jib, two waves broke across the front of the ship, the second about two feet over my head. As I tied on the jib sheets there was a small bang. The nylon anchor spring line had chafed through and broken. I rushed below.

"There's some nasty stuff rolling in here now," I said to Margaret. "We've got to clear out at once!" The ship rose on another breaking crest and the chain and windlass groaned terribly.

"Do have some of this nice fish," said Margaret. "We'll eat a little and go." I wolfed a little of the wahoo, but I was too nervous to eat.

Ten minutes later the chain was screeching against the windlass gypsy whenever the ship rose on a heavy swell, which surged in about every two minutes. On deck the ship was rolling and pitching so that I had to crawl along the deck to reach the mast. In the dark and confusion I tried to hoist the mainsail without bringing the fall of the topping lift forward from the cockpit. The sail jammed, of course, with the topping lift fouled around the main halyard. Down mainsail.

Clear topping lift. Hoist away. But the sail refused to go up more than a dozen feet.

With the ship plunging and yawing, the top of *Whisper*'s mast was scraping wild arcs in the sky. On one lurch the burgee halyard had whipped around the main halyard and jammed it. By now the motion of the yacht was simply ghastly. As we rolled back and forth, the deck on first one side and then the other slammed into the sea. I knelt at the mast, clawed down the mainsail, got a grip on the burgee halyard, and cut it away. Then I hoisted the sail again.

This time the halyard whipped around the starboard spreader. I pulled the sail down for the third time. Margaret crawled forward and managed to keep tension on the halyard while I cleared it and reeled up the slack on the winch. This time the mainsail climbed the mast smoothly and quickly. At this point it would have been dandy to have fired up the auxiliary engine for a little quick help out of the untenable anchorage. But the fuel system of the engine was still full of sludge. We would have to sail the anchor out.

Margaret ran back to the tiller while I prepared to hoist the jib. All this time waves had been surging into the anchorage, lifting the yacht, and churning past with a hollow sound as they broke behind us and walloped against the barrier reef in back of the ship. The waves were on the point of breaking, but so far only two had actually crested and sent white water across the decks. Nevertheless, the strain on the chain and windlass was enormous, and I expected both to be snatched into the sea.

Suddenly a colossal wall of water was in front of the ship. Though daylight was gone I could see the milky white of the foaming crest as it thundered across the face of the breaking wave. It looked huge and heavy. I was horrified.

"Hang on!" I shouted.

The wave broke clear across as it got to *Whisper* and with a roar lifted the ship up to an angle of perhaps 75 degrees as the water thundered down the decks. I lay flat with my head down, seized a mooring cleat with each hand, and held on with all my strength as the water rushed over me. The windlass in front of me gave a lurch and shriek as suddenly all the remaining chain was ripped out of the gypsy and stripped into the sea. There was a bang and a great jerk from aloft. The ship wallowed in broken water as the wave passed. I spit out a mouthful of warm salt water.

"The chain must be broken," I said aloud. "We must be on the reef." I had visions of fragments of *Whisper* strewn along the reef and mixed up with pieces of bones—*my bones!* "No!" I said. "We are still rolling and must be afloat." I looked up and wondered what had broken aloft. The snap at the end of the 75 degree climb and then again when the ship had plunged were frightful. Something must have broken. The rigging? The mast itself? It was too dark to see anything except that the mainsail was flapping. Rain rattled down from the inky sky. My eyes burned from the salt water.

I clawed at the windlass and found the chain limp. We were in a momentary calm after the great wave had passed. I groped at the chain and found a piece of metal that had been torn from the gypsy. With energy produced by desperation I hauled in the chain at a fearful pace—until my arms throbbed and my breath came in gasps. Finally I came to the shackle that had held the nylon anchor spring. My pliers had been swept away, so I raced back to the cockpit, got a hacksaw, and hurried forward to cut the iron shackle. Again I stripped in chain as fast as I could pull. To my amazement the chain got tight. The anchor still held. Or I hoped it held. The shock of the breaking wave had broken the hold of the windlass on the chain and it had merely run out.

"Haul in the mainsheet! Put the tiller to starboard!" I yelled at Margaret. "Stand by for the jib. Back the jib to starboard and as the ship's head swings to port, haul the jib to leeward."

As I winched up the jib halyard, *Whisper* payed off on the starboard tack and began to move. I cranked the anchor windlass until the slack chain became taut and pulled the head of the ship around to the port tack.

"I'll change the jib sheets," Margaret shouted above the noise of another breaking wave.

We were on the port tack now and moving smartly and the force of the wave—though knee deep down the deck—angled off *Whisper* somewhat. We kept short tacking as I worked in the chain. God, how black it was! I was afraid the anchor would foul a coral head and I might need the hacksaw—if I could find it on the waterswept deck— to cut the cable. But the chain kept coming. I glanced to starboard and saw that we were moving past the little motu at the end of Onotoa. The anchor was free! I winched it on board, gave Margaret a compass course to steer, and collapsed in the cockpit. Once out at sea we hove to on the offshore tack to recover from the evening.

Half an hour later a gale roared in from the west. Our late anchorage must have been a maelstrom of white water and breaking waves, a death trap for ships and sailors. We had saved the ship and probably our lives by clearing out in time. I thought back to the days when we had practiced sailing out an anchor in Drake's Bay north of San Francisco. There we had propped open Eric Hiscock's *Cruising Under Sail* on the coachroof and followed his directions like a cook baking a cake. Eric's instructions and our practice had saved us.

The next day I discovered that the shank of the forty-five-pound CQR anchor—a two-inch I-beam of drop-forged iron—was bent, and a tough, six-ton-test iron shackle at the end of the anchor chain was stretched to almost twice its original dimension, with its pin bent one quarter of an inch. Beryl Smeeton had given me that shackle and I thought of her with a good deal of affection at that moment. During the pitching caused by the great wave, both the top and bottom aerial insulators on the port backstay had shattered, and the outhaul fitting at the end of the main boom had been partially torn off. It was a wonder we still had a mast!

How comforting it was to be on the deep sea again! The motion of *Whisper*, the motion that we knew so well, seemed steady, reassuring, and almost homelike.

Had I learned anything? I hope to tell you. Forget doubtful anchorages when the weather is uncertain. Stay at sea if you would live.

12 / ∿∿∿∿∿∿∿∿∿
∿∿∿∿∿∿∿∿∿∿
∿∿∿∿∿∿∿

The Porpoise Is Dead,
the Whale Is Sunk

TWENTY-FIVE MILES NORTH OF THE EQUATOR WE SIGHTED Abemama in the central Gilberts, and a few hours later we anchored off the village of Binoinano deep inside the quiet lagoon. Because of the calms and headwinds and the anchoring misadventure off Onotoa, the 640 miles from Funafuti had taken us two weeks. We had sailed 1,171 miles.

Now the trip and the bad weather were behind us. We sat above the calm sapphire of the lagoon and doddled with coffee after a good meal. Outside the pass we had caught another big wahoo, and in the late afternoon Margaret and I and the cat munched contentedly on fish steaks while *Whisper* lolled easily at anchor.

I heard the snort of an outboard motor and looked up to see a small boat approaching. In a few minutes the local constable, the island executive officer, and several assistants, all Gilbertese, climbed on board. They welcomed us cordially but were curious to know our business and who we were.

We had crossed the border into Micronesia. The skin of our visitors shone with a deep copper. The Gilbertese were short and lean—there was no Tahitian fat here—and the men moved with a natural vigor and confidence. They had handsome, good-looking faces set off by prominent cheekbones, short straight noses, well-formed shiny teeth, and merry brown eyes. Their black hair was short-cut, straight, and glossy. Altogether the fellows looked quite alike, and I thought of a team of good-humored, small-sized athletes. I liked them at once.

"We ask you to come ashore to sign the visitor's book," said Ioane Kaitabo, the executive officer, in excellent English.

We all climbed into the launch and motored toward the land some three quarters of a mile away. The lagoon soon shoaled to a foot or so and the boatman and his helper jumped over the side to push and pull the launch over the white sand in the shallow places. I had a chance to look around.

Abemama, which means Land of Moonlight, was typical of the sixteen atolls of the Gilberts. The island was shaped roughly like a horseshoe pointing west, with its outside dimensions about nine by thirteen and a half miles. The iron rim of the horseshoe supported a thin wall of green with golden beaches on each side. At most the land measured a half mile wide and ten feet high, with a sandy marginal soil that supported coconut and pandanus palms and an inferior taro called babai. Geologically the atoll was very old, and inside the lagoon much of the coral had disintegrated into dazzling sand, often swirled into motus, shoals, and sandbanks by the force of currents.

It was dark when we touched the shore, but the sand on the village beach flared up from the harsh light of kerosene pressure lamps held by several men. We were suddenly aware of a crowd of perhaps seventy-five to a hundred people watching us. Ioane led the way to the small headquarters office of Abemama—the crowd followed—where he produced and dusted off the visitor's register, a large bound book. I opened it and saw that it had been started in 1946. In more than twenty years only a handful of outsiders had come to the island. I signed my name at the top of page three.

"Are we the first yacht, Ioane?" I asked.

"I think so," he said. "I have never seen one before."

We were taken to Ioane's comfortable native Gilbertese home across the way. The crowd was still with us and we all filed inside the high-ceilinged main room, which was lighted by gently hissing kerosene pressure lamps. Two rickety chairs, hastily fetched from God knows where, appeared, and we were bid to take them. Everyone else sat crosslegged on mats. We were given two freshly husked drinking nuts, and when we finished Ioane began to speak.

"Ships come to Abemama very seldom and the people are excited and interested in you. With your permission we would like to ask you a few questions. I can translate—"

"Where did you come from?" asked a man in back.

"America, the United States," I answered. "My home is in San Francisco." The names got no response at all. "On the other side of the Pacific," I said, trying again and motioning toward the east, "is a big land where I live. We came by way of Tahiti, Samoa, and Funafuti."

Now I mentioned names that got nods and recognition. I would have to answer in terms that these atoll people understood.

"How many days from your land?" asked an old woman who squatted in front of us in a thick grass skirt.

"Nine months, but we stopped at many islands for rest and food."

As Ioane translated into rapid-fire Gilbertese, the frowns of the people dissolved in understanding.

"Why did you come to such an isolated place as Abemama? No one ever comes here."

"To meet you, to see how you live, and to become your friends."

"But what of storms?" asked a voice in back. "How were the waves beyond the horizon? What of the gale-force winds from the north that we call Nei Bairara, the Long-Armed Woman?"

"We had a few storms," I said. "Mostly though we have sailed in the trade winds. Our ship is decked over and when the sea becomes angry we put up small sails and wait until the ocean becomes our friend again."

More and more villagers, especially women, kept crowding into the room. A few people rolled shreds of tobacco inside pandanus leaves to make particularly foul-smelling cigarettes that were passed from person to person, each of whom took a puff or two.

"Do you have plenty of coconuts and fish in your land?"

"My country is too cold for coconuts. However, our land is good for growing cold-weather fruits and vegetables—things we call apples and corn and beans and potatoes. We eat some fish but we raise animals for meat. Your staple is the coconut; our mainstay is bread made from wheat flour."

"How much did the ship cost?"

How could I reply sensibly to a man who in one day would gather and split 300 coconuts whose dried meat might fetch three dollars? "I got the ship by trading the proceeds of all my work for five years," I said, holding up five fingers. "The ship is my most valued possession."

"How was the fishing on your trip? What kinds?"

"The best fish was wahoo, a strong fighter," I said. "But too large. We ate so much that we grew great stomachs. The cat on the ship got a belly so big that he cried for two days. He almost died of pleasure."

While Ioane translated I made motions of a big stomach on me, on Margaret, and on an imaginary cat. Everyone hooted, and when I imitated an overstuffed cat the room rocked with laughter.

The questions went on and on. We were tired but our audience was delighted with the show and we saw eager brown eyes on every side. Someone handed us cups of coconut toddy, a sweet, slightly thick, amber-colored drink.

"You have come a long way," said a man whose hair was thin. "You are only two, one a woman. Were you afraid when you were out there far from land? You found your direction by the white man's method but what did you feel in your heart? Tell us now."

"Old friend, you must know the sea, for you speak wisely. The Pacific is big and powerful and when her temper is high her rage knows no limit. We were late in the year to come here and we almost lost the ship and ourselves at Onotoa because I was foolish. Now we are safe at Abemama. But of the sea . . . I have often been frightened but I don't know fear. If your ship is good, luck is with you, and the sea is on your side, you have a chance. When the Pacific smiles you must hurry. When she screams you must wait. Above all you must acknowledge that the sea is the master in your heaven. You are merely a dot of nothing, an insignificance."

Margaret and I stood up. Suddenly everyone began to applaud. Without realizing it we had put on a performance, an entertainment in remote Abemama. As we left Ioane's house on our way back to the ship the people smiled and nodded to the actors.

The next day we went ashore in the dinghy. It was a long row, the current against us ran swiftly, and my arms soon felt as if they would fall off. Finally the water shoaled enough so that I could wade and pull the dinghy along. Loss of an oar in such a place would have been serious and I was glad we had a small anchor with us.

In the bright morning the atoll was a world of dappled sunlight and shadow, of brown palm trunks reaching toward a green heaven, of long beaches of white diamonds. A crowd of golden-skinned youngsters escorted us to the village along wide pathways of coral gravel and sand that were outlined with small rocks and bordered with fluted hibiscus and milk-white crinum lilies. We began to see the quiet browns of peaked roofs and the tawny sides of native cottages.

A few children scampered in front of the houses and shrieked as

they ran past. We heard the chatter of women as they walked along the roadway and we saw several young men with handsome bronzed bodies pushing bicycles on which were balanced enormous bags of copra. I caught a sniff of delicate frangipani, and the stronger smell of something cooking drifted up to us. My heart soared for a moment as a magic curtain flapped open and I looked at the simple beauty and essence of the South Pacific.

Each home stood by itself on a raised foundation of lime made from burned coral. The corner posts, rafters, joists, and thatch for the roof had been cut from pandanus palms. Coconut-leaf mid-ribs lashed side by side were placed upright to make walls, and thin slats of bent coconut wood covered with lattices woven from white pandanus roots formed the window frames and doors. More coconut mid-ribs became flooring and the whole house was tied together with intricate cross-lashings of coconut-fiber string.

But this bald description suggests in no way the pleasant geometry of the Gilbertese houses in among the palms and the magical neatness and order of the village. The houses were light, airy, and perfectly suited to both the eye and the atoll environment. Even the arrangement of the footpaths was harmonious, and I noticed that they were swept clean of leaves and debris. We saw no rusty iron, no junky old boards, and no litter.

Ioane met us and introduced us to the assistant medical officer, Tomasi Puapua, an Ellice Islander from Vaitupu. There were no cars on the island, but both men had small Honda motorcycles. Margaret climbed behind Tomasi, I got back of Ioane, and we zoomed off to look at the island, most of which had a roadway. However, the land was not continuous, and every mile or so we came to a crude causeway that had been constructed to bridge the swift channels of water that raced between the lagoon and the sea and isolated one part of the atoll from another. We dismounted and trod gingerly across these rickety bridges, which were nothing more than haphazard collections of odd branches from trees pegged together with a few nails—teetery matchsticks that threatened to collapse with a hard step and to plunge us into the swirling waters below.

We drove through small villages, passed fields of wide-leaved babai, saw the skeletons of World War II airplanes, waved to women washing, and interrupted men making copra. Someone asked us for matches. We all searched our pockets.

"No matter," said the man. "I can use uri wood." He called to his son to bring him two pieces of the dry wood. Then he pressed the end of the first piece against the side of the second, and stroked the first rapidly back and forth. In fifteen seconds smoke began to rise; in thirty seconds the smoke thickened and we saw a spark. The man pushed his pandanus cigarette into the young fire and lighted up. Then he turned to us, held up the cigarette victoriously, and smiled a happy toothless grin.

We smiled back and drove on.

At Manoku we stopped at the Catholic station, where we were surprised to meet a French priest, Father Dureihmer, who was astonished to see two white people.

"But there's been no ship," he stammered. "Wh . . . where did you come from?"

We told about our trip and Father Dureihmer stood spellbound. He was a small, energetic, bespectacled man in middle age who had been in the Gilberts most of his working life. In his little school he was training sixteen native priests who would study for three years.

Father Dureihmer invited us all to lunch, but he didn't eat much, for he was starved for conversation rather than food. We discussed De Gaulle, the Common Market, island medicine, World War II, men in space, American politics. . . . "Ah, it's good to talk," he said, relishing the words. "I'm in another world out here."

"I regret that I can only offer you this inferior Australian wine with lunch," he said. "It's vile-tasting but all I have. Can you imagine a Frenchman offering guests such bilge? Or drinking it himself?"

We left after promising to call at the station again. Ioane and Tomasi took us back to the main village and our dinghy.

The next morning we went ashore again, but Ioane was busy with tax court. He came out to see us for a minute.

"We collect one dollar for each parcel of land regardless of size," he said. "Some people pay and some people argue but we still collect, although the rate and scheme are ridiculous."

We had lunch at the hospital with Tomasi. The hospital was a self-care institution in which each patient's family moved in with the sick person to feed and take care of him under the supervision of the doctor. Instead of a central building the hospital complex was a tiny dispensary plus a scattering of several dozen small native houses, one for each patient and his family. Several lepers were in isolation in back.

"On an island such as Abemama the only trained medical people are myself and my nurse," said Tomasi while we ate. "A self-care hospital is the only way to achieve reasonable care for the seriously ill."

I was very impressed by Tomasi. His title was assistant medical officer, but he was the doctor for three islands and he was astonishingly capable. He had been picked as an adolescent and sent to Suva, where he received rigorous schooling and practice for six years. The emphasis was not on *theory* of medicine, although there was some, but on *practice*. Each assistant medical officer, or AMO as he was called, performed dozens of complex operations under the tutelage of the staff of the Fiji School of Medicine.

"We can take care of ninety-five percent of all medical problems on our islands," said Tomasi. "For difficult cases we can radio for assistance to the general hospital in Tarawa. Much of our work is routine childbirth, fractures, or perhaps removing a fishhook from a man's nose. We spend a lot of time discussing diet and passing out vitamin pills, for malnutrition is a problem on atolls. However, when someone comes in with appendicitis we must operate at once or the patient will be dead."

Tomasi was proud of his tiny dispensary and his stocks of medicines and equipment. The United Nations, through UNICEF, had given him a motorcycle, a launch, and an outboard motor to conserve his energies for medicine instead of walking and paddling. An autoclave, scales, a number of expensive medical books, and various medical items also bore the stamp of UNICEF. I made a mental promise to support the organization forevermore.

Before we left Abemama we were invited to Baretoa to see Gilbertese dancing, which we had previewed on Funafuti. We heard the stentorian chanting of the men as they sat around a raised platform and pounded the rhythm with the flats of their hands. We listened to the earnest voices of the women and we watched the brightly dressed dancers who moved with the stiff and inflexible steps that seemed so unreal yet were so typical of these atolls.

That night Ioane and Tomasi came to dinner on the ship and they enjoyed the meal immensely. Both were exceptional men who had the twin blessings of intellect and education. The two men chafed in the backwater of Abemama, but they were wise enough to realize that their place was with their people—to heal them, to guide them, to lead them. When Ioane and Tomasi left *Whisper* late that night to cross the star-swept lagoon my heart felt the wrench of the peripatetic traveler: to make a good friend and then to leave him.

The following morning we were to start early. We had promised to take the royal mail to Tarawa, and a prisoner brought out the mail bags in a canoe and took the signed receipt back. I rowed ashore with a bottle of good French wine I had bought in Apia. I saw Father Dureihmer pushing his bicycle along.

"Father," I said, "we're leaving this morning and I want to say goodbye." As we shook hands I said that I had enjoyed the lunch the other day but that the Australian wine was simply terrible.

His face fell.

"It pains me to think that a Frenchman will have to celebrate Christmas by himself and have only that bilge to drink."

His face fell further.

"But cheer up, Father!" I said. "I've brought you a present of a good bottle of Saint-Julien Médoc that we had on the ship. We want you to have something nice for the holiday." When I whipped the bottle out of its paper sack Father Dureihmer's eyes grew big and responsive.

"You shouldn't have . . ." he began.

"Nonsense," I said as I climbed in the dinghy and began to row away. "It's my pleasure. We hope that you'll remember us with a kind thought."

"A kind thought?" he shouted across the water. "A kind thought indeed! I'm going to pray for you forever!"

Tarawa was an easy overnight sail, and shortly after lunch on December 22 we crossed the pass into its giant lagoon. Gilbertese fishermen after tuna had sighted us and a parade of their swift sailing canoes flashed by on both sides. We were aware of a large population (8,000) at once, for we saw rows of native houses along the shore and crowded ferryboats heading across the lagoon.

But we were prepared in no way for the reception we got when we pulled down the sails and glided against the seawall in the tiny man-made harbor at Betio. Above us stood 200 or 300 Gilbertese men shouting and pointing and laughing and gesturing. The sun blazed down on their handsome brown bodies, brilliant with the cheerful whites and reds and blues of trade-store prints. News of *Whisper* had been radioed from Funafuti and Abemama, but the men couldn't believe that our little ship had crossed the Pacific. Waves of delight rippled across the yelling mob when someone saw an anchor or the compass or a navigation light and pointed it out to his friends. I was overwhelmed at all the fuss; the noise and laughter seemed a little too much.

A bird circling high in the sky might have seen that the reef of Tarawa (pronounced Tare-a-wah, with no accents) looked like a vast triangle bent from a piece of rusty iron rod. The three-sided, milky-blue lagoon measured nineteen miles from north to south, and the main islets of Betio and Bairiki lay on the southern base of the triangle which ran sixteen miles in an east-west direction. Americans first heard of Tarawa during World War II when a stoutly entrenched Japanese force made the beaches of Betio run crimson with the blood of men from the U.S. Marines and Navy. Seventeen percent of a 18,313-man attacking force ended up as casualties to secure an atoll that no one had heard of before or remembered since.[23]

When we went ashore to deliver the mail we heard English spoken with accents of New Zealand, Australia, and Great Britain and saw tall men in white shirts, white shorts, white stockings, and brown laced shoes, for this was the main island of the colony and 200 Europeans lived on the atoll. Not only was Tarawa the center of government administration, but the island was also the principal shipping center for the twenty-five atolls of the Gilbert and Ellice group, headquarters for the trading company, and home of the colony hospital, secondary schools, missionary offices, copra warehouses, machine shops, and a surprisingly busy boatyard. There was a feeling of prosperity and industry in the air.[24]

We began to make friends and in a day had half a dozen dinner invitations. We got acquainted with the head of the trading company, Keith Ussher, a curly-headed New Zealander who moved fast, was capable, aggressive, and generous, but a man who never stopped talking. He and his gentle wife, Evie, were building a small yacht alongside their house and they were good to us during our visit. We were offered the facilities of the boatyard, so we unstepped *Whisper*'s mast, which needed repairs and varnishing, made arrangements to paint the bottom of the ship, and I began to overhaul the fuel system of the engine, which we hoped to get back into operation.

The mast was propped up on sawhorses at the boatyard, and as Margaret and I sanded and varnished each morning we got acquainted with the Gilbertese workmen who often stood and watched every move we made. With supervision the Gilbertese were excellent workmen. For instance, the claim at Betio was that the stevedore gangs, using barges, could unload 400 tons of general cargo per day as against 300 tons per day in a modern quayside port. The men were an enthusiastic lot, perhaps a bit irresponsible and clownish by Western standards, but they had rules of their own, main ones being the concepts of courage and shame.

A Gilbertese man constantly exhibited his courage by his performance in daily tasks. If his courage failed, he was shamed, which was tantamount to death or severe social ostracism. The standards were black and white; there was no middle ground.

The men often took their small, undecked sailing canoes into the ocean where the seas were big and currents strong. A man might sail his canoe for years and have no trouble. But if he capsized or his mast broke or the sail ripped, the owner would have to get back to the atoll by himself. His countrymen might watch—and be beside themselves with laughter—but they would offer no assistance. The victim would accept no help anyway, for if he did he would be totally ashamed and probably kill himself.

When a veteran office worker at Betio was reported missing after going fishing, the Europeans were about to send a launch outside to search for the man.

"No sense going," said one of the local men. "You won't find Kimaere alive, for I saw him drown."

We heard about a Gilbertese who had been out on the reef at low tide. The fishing had been so good that he forgot to watch the time and suddenly found himself cut off by the flooding tide. He couldn't get back to land, for the undertow sucked him seaward as fast as he swam shoreward. He was in a desperate position and covered with blood from cuts when he was slammed against the coral as he went back and forth. A group of islanders on shore guffawed at the fisherman's plight.

A European called to the men, "Why in God's name don't you help the poor fellow? Take him a canoe or throw him a line."

"Oh, sir, we couldn't do that. If the man saw us coming to help him he would drown himself."

Fortunately the man kept his wits and managed to work ashore.

A well-known fisherman from Abaiang was plucked out of the ocean by a colony ship that happened to pass when his canoe was seen upside down and his mast and paddle gone. The man lost all interest in the sea, and after cowering in the hospital for a week he announced that he was going to Tarawa and learn to be an electrician!

Gilbertese children usually obey their parents without exception. However, when a father told an errant daughter who was involved in a complex romantic situation that he was taking her back to their home island, the girl refused to go. Shamed, disgraced, and utterly ruined, the father stuck a knife in his belly.

In other words, a man must be a winner; he must not lose. The victor is courageous—according to the Gilbertese use of the word— but shame destroys him before the eyes of his fellows. I suppose this was the reason the natives were so enthusiastic when we arrived on *Whisper.* We were heroes as long as we stayed ahead of the game. I would hate to be shipwrecked in the Gilberts!

But this was only a single color from the rich rainbow of Gilbertese culture, a people we wanted to know better.

To understand those who are different from you, a person needs patience, knowledge, and respect, three traits possessed in large measure by the late Sir Arthur Grimble. He was a long-time administrator, yarn-spinner, and a prince when it came to a sympathetic ear for the Gilbertese, who less than a century ago were tough warriors who decimated their enemies with swords of fire-hardened palm wood rimmed with sharks' teeth.

Grimble wrote of the poetry, songs, legends, sorcery, magic, and wisdom of these complex people who on their last voyage might be swept into the zone of wildfire (where a man had two shadows) before he sailed over the lip of the world.[25]

The Gilbertese logic was sometimes scathing: "God and Jesus do not belong only to the Protestants and Roman Catholics," said an old man of eighty who was thoroughly fed up with the missionaries, their biased teaching, and constant infighting. "God and Jesus belong to the pagans also. They are not surrounded by a fence up there in Heaven, and we do not have to run into a mission fence to find them here on earth. They are everywhere . . . we can take them for our own friends if we want them."[26]

The Gilbertese could celebrate the end of a long dispute between two villages with a rollicking poem:

Behold! the back-and-forth, the dartings, the stabbings of my
 words are done!
For the talk is ended, the judgement judged
And there he goes now sailing over the horizon.
The porpoise is dead, the whale is sunk,
The thundercloud is fled from the sky,
The storm is over: a small, cool wind blows between the villages.
A cool wind-o-o-o! O-o-a![27]

On Boxing Day, the day after Christmas, Margaret and I went to a grand party on the *Teraka*, the colony training ship that was anchored in the lagoon. Most of the Europeans were on board and we were served by ninety enthusiastic cadets who were learning to become stewards, engineers, and seamen. The training scheme was clever and I was filled with admiration for the British.

Commercial shipping lines in the Pacific and Far East are in constant need of good seamen. The Gilbertese made excellent crewmen, but there had been no way of training the men and the shipping companies didn't take native apprentices. Someone in the colony suggested buying an old steel coasting vessel from Germany that was for sale at a reasonable price. Qualified training officers were expensive to hire and there were no funds in the slim colony budget, but the scheme looked so promising that the United Nations offered to pay the salary of the captain. Several major shipping companies from Germany and Great Britain furnished the other principal officers, since their lines hoped to hire the trained cadets. It was a wonderful idea and the thinking behind it could well be copied by others.

Margaret and I completed the mast work, and one afternoon we asked for the crane and six men. Sixty (!) showed up, all shouting and joking, and amidst pandemonium we stepped the mast, under the supervision of Sam Murdock, the capable foreman at the boatyard. A few days later we put *Whisper* on the hard white sand and at low tide painted most of the bottom and scrubbed what we couldn't reach to paint. The engine now worked, and one by one we crossed jobs off the list. Some of the deck leak was still with us, so we removed the rest of the toerail between the mast and the stem and laid fiberglass over the hull-deck joint. Finally it was dry below.

One day I happened to glance up and I saw something that appeared like an enormous kite up so high that it was among the low trade wind clouds. It *was* a kite and we noticed others. We discovered that kite flying had been a favorite Gilbertese pastime for as long as memory. The kites were huge—often twelve to fifteen feet long—and we measured one that was twenty-five feet overall. The construction was of thin sticks lashed together and covered with light cloth or plastic. The ball of string was often the size of a volley ball. We couldn't get over the size of the kites!

Large whaleboats were used throughout the colony to haul copra from shore to ship. Such service was severe, for the boats often had to go through the surf and sometimes capsized, and there were always eight or ten bashed-up whaleboats awaiting repair at the boatyard. Often the boats would sink, and as they went down the copra bugs and cockroaches would scramble higher and higher. Whenever a whaleboat foundered near us the horrible insects would begin to swim toward *Whisper*. I had always thought that cockroaches would drown, but I can assure you that the two- and three-inch brutes can swim well. We seized oars and fought them off, repelling the odious invaders with vicious smashing blows against the hull and water.

We sailed across the Tarawa lagoon in the astonishing Gilbertese outrigger canoes, perhaps the fastest in the world and one of the miracles of the islands. So-called modern concepts such as asymmetrical hulls, low wetted area, light weight, and large sail area were old stuff to the Gilbertese. Our lagoon canoe was thirty-five feet long and entirely built of small boards lashed edge to edge with coconut string. There was no metal in the entire canoe. To change direction you didn't tack or wear the ship but you physically shifted the entire triangular sail from one end to the other and carried the steering oar to the opposite end while always keeping the outrigger to windward. This was not as awkward as it sounds, for the reaching winds were steady and the courses often ran for miles.

When the mainsheet was pulled in we flashed across the turquoise lagoon at eighteen knots. Two men danced in and out on the balancing outrigger, one man steered, and the captain handled the mainsheet and ran things. The idea was to attain a balance between the wind and the sail so that the outrigger would be just clear of the water. With no drag from the float and the enormous sail full of wind, our knife-edge canoe hurled across the lagoon fast enough to bring tears to my eyes. When a puff of wind came, the acceleration was unbelievable. What excitement!

The other miracle of the Gilbertese was the maneaba. This was

the great meetinghouse of each village, and somewhere among each collection of native houses you would see a lofty peak and a huge mat of thatch pushing almost as high as the palms. The maneaba was not only an attraction for the eye; it was the social hub, the assembly hall, the dance emporium, and the news center of the village. Each clan in a village specialized in one part of the construction. According to Sir Arthur Grimble:

> One manufactured thatch pieces for the roof, another lashed them into place; there was a clan to gather the timbers, a clan to dress them, a clan to lay them in place; and so on for the capping of the ridge pole, the trimming of the eaves, the setting up of the corner-stones, the shingling of the floor, the plaiting of the coconut-leaf screens to cover the shingle and hang below the eaves. The ridge soared sixty feet high, overtopping the coconut palms; the deep eaves fell to less than a man's height from the ground. Within, a man could step fifty full paces clear from end to end, and thirty from side to side. The boles of palm trees made columned aisles down the middle and sides and the place held the cool gloom of a

cathedral that whispered with the voices of sea and wind caught up as in a vast sounding box.[28]

On New Year's Day we heard shouting and clapping from the great maneaba at Betio, and we walked up to watch half a dozen groups take turns singing and dancing. The performance had some of the aura of a revival meeting, with a thousand or more people involved, and the leaders, who stood in back of the puppetlike, brightly dressed dancers out in front, whipped up the shouting and singing to a frenzy. Another day we saw youngsters from the island of Tabiteuea practice crab and ghost dances. A leaf skirt around the wriggling hips of a three-year-old was quite a sight.

On the day before we left we gave a small party for the friends we had made on Tarawa. Forty-five people signed our guest book. The next morning we discovered that *Whisper* was hard aground.

"No problem," said Sam Murdock. "I'll call out the fire brigade."

Fifty men appeared, waded into the water, and put their shoulders against *Whisper*'s hull. "Hip hip hip *haaaaaaw*," shouted the leader, and the ship began to move. The men got laughing so hard they had to stop, but at the signal of their leader they soon boosted the yacht into deeper water.

As we sailed away from Tarawa I thought of the richness of the Gilbert and Ellice islands and the wise and unmeddling government. A child's good night poem kept singing in my brain:

> Mr. Star, thou, the little one,
> Wink once, wink twice.
> Thee I have chosen: thou art sleepy!
> Thou sleepest, Mr. Star, thou, the little one,
> In a little cloud.
> O-o-o-a-a-a! Sleep![29]

13

A Large Outrigger
Has Been Sighted

AT FIVE O'CLOCK IN THE AFTERNOON ON JANUARY 16, we had logged 332 miles on a course west and a little north from Tarawa. It was the third day out and we ran easily before light easterly winds and a favorable current, halfway to Kusaie, the easternmost of the Caroline Islands.

With 8,662 miles behind us since San Francisco we knew our sailing routine well. When a fair wind blew we put the mainsail out flat before the wind, with one line to hold the boom firmly forward and a second line on a tackle to pull the boom and sail down so the belly of the sail wouldn't chafe on the rigging. Opposite to the mainsail and a little forward, the genoa was held out with a long white pole whose inner end was clipped to the mast and whose outer end was controlled by three lines. The thrust of the wind pushed evenly on the balanced sails—one out to port and one out to starboard—and we sped along hour after hour while the wind vane easily steered the ship.

I looked up at the neat triangles of sails enclosed by the strong rigging and varnished spars and marveled that man could harness the wind in such splendid fashion. Like the steam locomotive, the windmill, and the stagecoach, sailing was hopelessly outdated, a kind of archaeological oddity; yet it was a wonderful, free kind of life where money and possessions counted for little. You lived at a level where a simple act like identifying a curious bird became profound and surrounded with wonder. You would see a coconut be-whiskered with barnacles and grass and speculate where its parent tree grew. A fish would jump out of the water and you had time to think about the complex world of sea creatures below you. At night there were the stars! I never saw the world above until I went to sea.

January 19. The stars are so brilliant and beautiful that it is worth taking extra naps during the day so that you can sit up at night to watch them. (Those of the equator and northern hemisphere are much more splendid than the paltry few of the south.) Orion's complex is the best with its leading lights of Sirius, Betelgeuse, and and Procyon. Early in the morning (here at 5° N.) the Big Dipper comes up and with it (on the sweep of the arm) Arcturus and Spica. Capella is then a glowing guidepost of blue in the western sky. Surely the splendor of these night skies is the best thing I have ever seen. And it's all free.

Margaret and I played games with the stars. On a good viewing night we would try to impress each other by rattling off a dozen stars— and then point out a new one.

"Look! There's Schedar," Margaret would say, gloating with su-periority after some secret homework with the star charts.

"Oh? Where's that?"

"*Everybody* knows Schedar. It's at the bottom and right of the W of Cassiopeia. See, over there . . ."

As we neared Kusaie (Koos-eye) we had lots of squalls. Most lasted only fifteen or twenty minutes but they persisted, and when we were below we always listened for the sudden calm and severe silence that presaged these minor wind and rain storms. Then one of us would go topsides and douse a sail until the disturbance passed. We were slowly working north but still in the unsettled southern fringes of the north-east trades, a wind pattern that got increasingly vague as we sailed toward the Far East. ·

At 0715 on the sixth day from Tarawa, Margaret looked up from feeding the cat to see the high silhouette of Kusaie scratched across the horizon. We were in the American Trust Territory, on the outermost fringes of the Carolines, a scattering of 963 small islands that was sprinkled from Kusaie (163° E.) all the way west to the Palau Islands (130° E.), a distance of 2,000 miles. In addition the Trust Territory also includes the Marshalls and all of the Marianas Islands except Guam. In total the territory takes in three million square miles of the Pacific and encompasses 2,137 mostly tiny islands whose land area adds up to 687 square miles on which live some 94,000 people who speak nine different languages.[30]

The islands belonged first to Spain, then to Germany, and finally to Japan. After World War II the area became a United Nations strategic trusteeship with the United States as the administering authority. Or to put it more simply, the United States promised to look after the islands in exchange for rights to build military bases. But the islands are far-flung, conditions abysmal, transport nonexistent, and the United States—with little colonial experience—has had only slight concern over its distant possession. Few Americans have ever heard of the Trust Territory and care less.[31]

We knew all these things and wondered what we would find. On our chart we saw that Kusaie was roughly a circle about nine miles in diameter, and looking ahead we watched verdant, green-clad mountains slowly take form and substance.

By late afternoon we were off Lele on the eastern shore, and I was surprised to see two boats come out to escort us into the harbor. As we glided through the pass we saw perhaps 100 people lined up along the village shore on the north watching us. We glanced at the people, but our attention was drawn to the village. And what a village!

It was worse than Pago Pago in American Samoa. I saw an eye-smashing horror of huts, warehouses, boat shelters, and houses, mostly roofed with torn scraps of rusty iron sheeting. Everything was built up from beat-up scrap boards and junk lumber roughly nailed or propped into place without any sort of plan or guideline. Some of the decrepit, unpainted structures were built around old concrete foundations and walls of Japanese style from an earlier era. Several shiny motorcycles bounced along the dusty waterfront, which was bordered with thickets of weeds. Piles of broken wooden boxes and debris littered the foreshore. I thought back to the neat villages of the Gilbert Islands and groaned.

"I don't understand Americans," said Margaret. "It's truly incredible how junky the waterfronts of these U.S. islands are. It almost seems there has been a carefully worked-out plan to make the villages as ugly as possible.

"We've visited French and British islands and I've seen photographs of these places during the German and Japanese times," she said. "Each administration except the American manages to have neat villages, reasonable roads, and some order. The money is here for new motorcycles and outboard engines. Plenty of energy is present, for I can hear hammers pounding away. Can't the American authorities furnish a little enlightened control? Must the slums of America be exported?"

Shortly after we anchored, five officials came out to see us. We met Leo Delarosa, the acting district administrator, who jumped on board and showed us a message from one of the elders of Lele.

A LARGE OUTRIGGER HAS BEEN SIGHTED. TWO SAILS AND COMING VERY FAST. ALL THE PEOPLE OF THE VILLAGE ARE WATCHING. YOU HAD BET-TER COME.

Leo asked whether we had "authorized permission" to visit the Carolines.

"Authority? Permission?" I said, dumbfounded. "I am an American citizen. This is a U.S.-documented vessel. President Kennedy said over and over that it was official policy to encourage visits and tourism."

"I will radio the U.S. Navy strategic command on Saipan to see about authority for you to visit here," said Leo, surprised at my outspokenness.

You have to get away from America to realize that no officialdom on earth is worse or more cumbersome than that of the United States. Any action on an administrative level is years behind policy statements. Second-echelon officials hide behind phrases such as "Headquarters says . . ." or "According to present regulations . . ."

The next morning we went ashore to look at Kusaie, which has the reputation of being the garden isle of the western Pacific. The soil was extremely fertile, the growth lush and heavy, and we were soon eating delicious oranges, brimming with juice. We met two men almost at once—Paul Ehrlich of the Peace Corps and Frank Grossmann, an American teacher from Idaho, who took us on a tour of Lele. We visited some old stone ruins that were said to date from 1500 and were supposedly once the residence of the kings of Kusaie. A series of stone walls built up from columns of black basalt laid horizontally on top of one another rose from the floor of the forest. Each stone column was five- or six-sided, ten or twelve inches in diameter, eight or ten feet long, and resembled the trunk of a small tree. The stone walls looked like the sides of a log cabin, except that the walls were longer and higher and overgrown with giant banyan trees and heavy vines and creepers. The ruins covered perhaps a half square mile, at least the parts we saw, but were hard to envisage as a dwelling place because of the jungle growth and the roofless, tumbled-down condition.

Leo drove up in his Datsun truck and took us for a bouncing ride along a road that finally petered out five or six miles north. Along the perimeter of the high tropical island we saw a thick confusion of brown palm trunks soaring to a green overhead, and we looked at the big-leafed breadfruit trees, a few hardwoods, and the cream and crimson of flowering hibiscus. We listened to the twittering of small birds—something we hadn't heard for a long time—and walked along the edge of mangrove swamps, which, according to Leo, were found only in a condition of both fresh and salt water. We inspected nipa palms—short, nutless trees—whose tough leaves were used for roof thatch. The road was truly terrible and got no maintenance at all.

Back in Lele, Leo's wife had us all to a big lunch, which included mangrove crabs, giant fellows with enormous pinchers whose red legs had big chunks of rich and succulent meat.

We found Frank Grossmann great fun. Though not quite up to the appearance of a Hollywood leading man, Frank was a number-one character actor who was well traveled, urbane, and kept us forever chuckling.

"I was on one of the islands during an outbreak of disease," said Frank later in the day, "and I was instructed to brief the local chief about an emergency air drop of vaccine.

"O.K., Chief," said Frank, with many motions of his hands. "Listen carefully. Tomorrow—next sun—a great silver bird will come over the island past the tall mountain—over there. The medicine will—

" 'You mean the DC-6?' said the chief. 'Let's see. Medicine is Code Yellow. I will alert my men to watch for the airdrop of the paratyphoid bacillus in the primary target area. . . .'

"But seriously," said Frank, "you must forgive me for my small jokes. It's the only way to keep your sanity in this place."

We visited the small hospital in Lele, the sole medical facility for Kusaie, and were shocked at the peeling paint, the sagging doors, the rusted screens, and the insects buzzing around inside the decrepit building which had plenty of patients but hardly any medical equipment. I opened my mouth to speak but Frank held up his hand.

"I know what you're thinking," he said. "And I agree. It's a grim community joke that when an operation is over, not only are the doctor's tools counted, but so are the bits of plaster that fell from the ceiling.

"Every Congressional committee that comes here is horror-struck just as you are," said Frank. "The Trust Territory hired a special team to make an expensive study which pointed out that the whole village of

Lele was situated in the wrong area and should be relocated across the bay on higher ground where the drainage is better. Then when the new village is built a proper hospital can be constructed. It's a grand scheme but only a ridiculous notion, for the five million dollars it will cost is never going to come from the paltry budget."

"Such grandiose schemes are hopeless," said Margaret. "Americans mean well but are too idealistic. It's not necessary to rebuild the entire world like a suburb of Philadelphia. People resent too much intrusion anyway. Do you think the natives of Lele are going to want to leave their ancestral home?

"What is needed is not five million dollars in the vague future," said Margaret, "but five thousand dollars this month to paint and patch the existing hospital. In fact I could make a good start with five hundred dollars and a couple of local workmen."

Later Frank showed us the school where he taught that had been constructed after long planning and fought-over funds. The new building had tiny windows because the stateside architect had specified artificial illumination. Unfortunately there was no electricity. The small windows allowed no ventilation.

"Everybody knows that windows should be floor to ceiling when you're on the equator," said Frank. "Too bad the architect never got out of Washington, D.C. In addition the rest rooms and the general plumbing are unusable because there is no way to get water down the mountain. It's regrettable the architect didn't put a water-catchment system on the roof, which is the usual, simplest, and cheapest arrangement in the tropics."

Back in Lele we saw some excellent local handicrafts made from native fibers. I bought a hat and Margaret got several shopping baskets. Strips of material dyed purple had been cleverly worked into the weaving. "Probably root dyes discovered by the people of Kusaie in ancient times," I said.

"Nothing like that at all," answered Leo Delarosa, who happened to be walking past. "The purple coloring is from A.B. Dick mimeograph ink!"

We stopped at Kusaie only a few days. It was a pretty island whose lofty greenness reminded us of the Marquesas. When we went hiking with Frank Grossmann he took us through great gardens of jungle where we saw guavas, mangoes, papayas, and giant stalks of bananas. (Little did we know it would be the last good fruit until we got to Japan.) It was hard to realize that in 1874, Kusaie was the place where

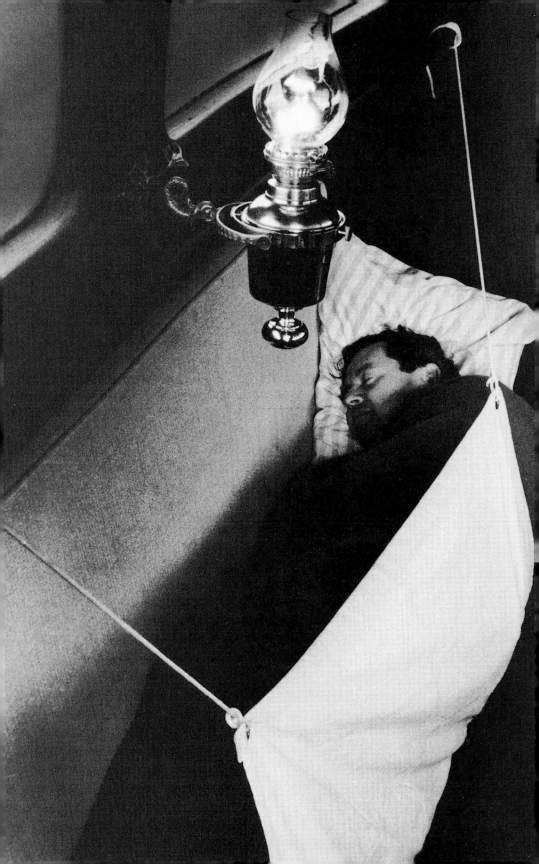

Captain Bully Hayes had reached the zenith of his career as a forger, ship stealer, swindler, confidence man, child raper, kidnapper, black-birder, murderer, thief, and general nuisance to the human race.[32] Kusaie too, on the other end of the human scale, is where present-day native Protestant pastors, trained by zealots from Boston, still exhort their people to "confess" in public.

From the top of the hill above Lele, Frank pointed out the traces of Japanese days—the alcohol plant, the fish factory, the shipping docks, and the dim outlines of fields where rice and sugar cane once flourished. We had seen Japanese features in some of the Kusaie people, had heard Japanese spoken, and had bought Japanese foodstuffs in the trading stores.

"I sometimes think these places might be better off under the Japanese," mused Frank. "Of course the Japanese colonized the Carolines for their own benefit. We Americans have a lot of plans . . . if we only had better people out here."

The trip from Kusaie to Ponape was an easy 320 miles with northeast winds of fifteen to twenty knots behind us. On the second day we passed Pingelap atoll just as the swift night of the equator fell on us. We were exactly on course, but it was good to have the low island behind us before dark. When the daylight was gone I stood on deck and hunted in vain for the atoll which was astern and to starboard only a mile or two. In the moonless, overcast night I could see nothing, though I have good eyes and looked carefully. No wonder atolls are dangerous at night!

When the wind was fair we were often able to open all the hatches and ports, which allowed lots of fresh air below. Kong, our cat, liked to jump from the floor of the toilet compartment up through the open ports to the deck. He would wait until the middle of a roll and then jump. Sometimes he did this a dozen times in an afternoon and then would scamper up and down the decks looking for flying fish.

One morning about 0700 I was dozing on the port settee and I vaguely heard the cat jump on deck. A little later when I got up to check our course and to look around, I suddenly had the feeling that Kong was gone. I called Margaret and we raced to search the ship. We were running hard at six knots with a small jib flying and when Margaret and I stood on deck and looked back at the heavy swells that reached endlessly toward the rising sun we knew it was hopeless to go back. I had no idea when Kong had gone over the side. His little head would have been impossible to find in the seas that were running. I think he would have gone right down.

We were sick about losing Kong, absolutely disconsolate. People get attached to pets more than they realize and even as I write these lines twenty months later I feel regret and sadness.

January 24. 0900. Of all the islands we have approached, the landfall here has been the most frustrating. Yesterday we ran our distance and were confident of our course but saw nothing except misty clouds to the west. Finally after a lot of hard looking I made out part of a mountain. We piled on all sail and hastened to the west for hours until we could distinguish a bit of the north and south extremities of Ponape. We carried on until dark, feeling that the island was on rollers and that as we approached Ponape it was automatically pulled away from us another ten miles. We finally gave up and hove to at sunset.

This morning at first light, we again made all sail westward. But the men had pulled the island away from us on the rollers again. No sign of land. Finally we saw a bit of mountain through the mist. (Our eyes ache from all the searching.) We carried on but it took us two hours before the bearings on the north and south points were the same as yesterday afternoon. Now an hour later we can begin to see the separate peaks, knobs, and ridges through the heavy veil of mist. No doubt there is a stream of hard-running current from the west. We expect the island to be pulled back on rollers any minute as we hurry toward the phantom.

We knew the main settlement of Ponape was at Kolonia on the north coast. However, we wished to visit the ruins of Nan Matal, so we sailed into the big bay of Matalanim on the east coast, glided around the protecting hook of south-facing Pantieinu Point, and anchored in four and a half fathoms. The waters of the bay were opaque with particles of soil carried down by the Retao River above us, and the dark water reflected a tumbling waterfall, mountains mantled in heavy green, and afternoon cumulus clouds billowing above the highlands. Three rickety native houses on stilts stood near us on shore, and two miles to the south the buildings of Father Costigan's big Catholic school loomed up from clearings in the velvety growth. *Whisper* swung with a cat's paw of wind and I looked at a thick mangrove swamp 150 yards away. Bird calls fluted across the quiet water.

The next day several outrigger canoes came alongside. We saw at once that the people were darker than those we had met before, and their standards of dress were poor. The long, lean canoes were hollowed from logs that sat low in the water and needed constant bailing. The owners paddled, set rude sails before the wind, or used outboard motors. Any women on board invariably carried big black umbrellas.

We soon found that the ambition of every young Ponapean man was to install a large Johnson or Evinrude motor in his outrigger canoe and to flash around the waterways at high speed with a great rooster-tail of water splashing up behind. The larger the motor, the more ecstatic was the smile of the owner. Last year ten horsepower. This year twenty-five. Next year fifty!

We rowed across Matalanim Bay to Nan Matal, the site of an ancient stone city that is spread across perhaps 100 low islets near the southern entrance of the bay. Long known as the forgotten Venice of the Pacific, Nan Matal has the appearance of a series of feudal fortifications. The stout, dark-colored walls are built up from stone logs of columnar basalt ten or twelve inches in diameter and eight to ten feet long, stacked in log cabin fashion like the ruins we had seen on Kusaie.

We rowed along the mangrove-choked canals and tied the dinghy up at the front of a giant ruin whose black walls jutted thirty feet above us. We walked up broad steps through a large entrance and, once inside, we found the stone ruins cool and strangely quiet. Some of the low chambers had roof beams of stone logs. We speculated on the people who might have constructed this ancient city with its straight canals and precise walls which presumably once supported colossal peaked roofs of wood and thatch or else harbored hundreds of small individual dwellings. Except for the water, Nan Matal reminded us of the Inca city of Machu Picchu high in the mountains of Peru. Certainly these departed races had a good knowledge of civil engineering and stone work. U.S. scientists have recently dated charcoal fragments that were 700 years old, showing that native fires burned in Nan Matal in the thirteenth century, but how the ancients transported stones that weigh many tons remains a mystery, a puzzle for future archaeologists.[33]

Before we left we met an old man with wide vertical bands of blue tattooing on his legs who was collecting breadfruit and carrying them to his canoe. We returned to *Whisper* by way of another canal route—passing tumbled-down ruins everywhere—and glided down waterways with heavy steaming jungle on each side. It was good to break into the open and to feel the cool northeast trade wind again.

The next day we sailed along the east coast and around the north barrier reef to Kolonia, the principal settlement of Ponape and the head of the eastern district of the Caroline Islands. In my mind's eye I had hoped for a neat little town nestled beneath the dark-green mountains that rose behind the Tawenjokola River, but we saw the usual junky American waterfront, an ugly amalgam of rust, dust, and debris. Wags have sometimes called the Trust Territory the Rust Territory, which is not far from the mark. So much World War II debris still litters Micronesia that scrap metal is the territory's second most valuable export a quarter of a century after the war.

When I landed I was handed a copy of the harbor regulations, but I soon discovered that the river near the settlement hadn't been dredged since Japanese days and was silted with mud so that we went aground at low tide. I leafed through the regulations and found that I would have to pay harbor dues of $5 a day even though I anchored out and had access to no facilities. Once ashore, however, I explained that I was a small pleasure vessel and after some trouble managed to get the harbor dues waived.

In Western Samoa and Kusaie we had met members of the U.S. Peace Corps and now we got acquainted with many more. For the most part these were young people who had come to a foreign place for several years to work with the local residents on a grassroots level. They instructed island women about balanced diets and nutrition, helped with better village sanitation, taught elementary school, worked on roads and water reservoirs, and cheerfully labored in a dozen disciplines. There were a few misfits and some wheel-spinning because of inexperience, but the men and women of the Peace Corps had the twin advantages of youth and energy, and best of all they lived at the level of the local people. The Peace Corps volunteers generally stayed in native villages, often wore local dress, and tried hard to speak the language of the land. Their goals seemed realistic and practical.

But it was quite a transition for Martha Bridges, aged twenty-two, from Grand Island, Nebraska, who suddenly found herself distributing anti-filariasis pills in a remote village in the Kiti district of Ponape instead of attending classes at the University of Chicago.

"I liked the Micronesians very much," said Martha when I spoke to her in Kolonia, "and as I learned to speak Ponapean better they accepted me more and more. I had a little house of my own and my life was secure and interesting except for one thing: I could get no privacy. Every hour of the day and night the villagers were with me or looking at me. In the evening I would be in my house reading or cooking or combing my hair and there would always be a few locals peering in the window. I liked the people but their constant presence began to bug me."

Martha knew the Micronesians were intensely superstitious, so one night at dusk she wrapped herself in a white sheet and lighted a tall candle, which she placed on a saucer in the middle of her one-room hut. Then she knelt in front of the candle and began to wave her arms and wail a high-pitched chant.

"*Whish!* The Peeping Toms were gone," said Martha, "and have never come back—even at noon!"

We met Jim Zeiger, the plant pathologist at the agriculture station. Jim gave us a grand tour of the impressive plantings and trees—begun by the Japanese—and we saw such exotics as the mangosteen, star apple, cherimoya, Malabar chestnut, ixora, soursop, tiarre gardenia, and Surinam cherry. Jim showed us pepper vines which grew on neat rows of fern posts and explained about the processing and marketing of this new Micronesian crop. Jim's most important project was research on breadfruit disease.

"The breadfruit is a major staple of tens of thousands in the South Pacific," he said, pointing to brownish spots on infected fruit. "We are working to inject a plot of sterile breadfruit seedlings with different viruses to learn about the course of the blight and possible ways we can attack its cause."

A number of American teachers came to see us on *Whisper* and we got to know many men and women—often married—who had come from the United States to teach school for two years. Invariably someone would appear who was keen on sailing or travel and who would ask a hundred questions about our trip and the yacht. Without doubt the social acceptance we got in many places depended largely on the fact that Margaret and I were doing something that represented a dream to many people. The romantic delight of sailing at leisure from one island to another is enormously appealing, and during our Pacific trip hundreds of people told us that they too had similar plans—uh—someday.

A parallel consideration of such a trip pivoted upon the needle point of fear. Many people told us they would like to make a similar journey but they were obviously afraid of the sea. When I tried to explain how small-ship sailors worked to minimize the hazards of the sea by careful planning, I got only stares, hesitations, and vague answers.

Or to say it another way: Most people like the known, the positive, and the certain. Our friends on land distrusted what we said about the dangers of the sea. When I said that storms were infrequent and we tried to be where the gales weren't, my listeners didn't believe me. When I suggested a coastwise trip for a starter, I saw heads slowly shake. Their minds were made up in advance. Twice I invited keen schoolteachers to come with us to Guam to try out an ocean trip; neither the man nor the woman accepted. Yet the fascination with our trip continued.

We had some splendid evenings with the American teachers who worked in Kolonia, but we began to discover that the different groups from the United States squabbled fiercely among themselves. The educators—themselves split in factions—hated the plant people, who reciprocated with gusto. The head of the cooperatives was quitting, he said, because his plans were constantly frustrated by headquarters and those who controlled his finances. Public Works wanted more money and less work, and the transport people claimed their shipping schedules were reduced to shambles by the demands of the Peace Corps. Even after twenty-five years, a dozen studies, and untold expenditures, a proper airfield hadn't been constructed on Ponape (the Japanese had two fighter strips during World War II), and the only official transport was via tiny amphibian planes that used the lagoon. A good administrator could have dealt with these problems, but unfortunately the number-one man on the island had a drinking problem and was often absent from his office.

The situation was humorous in a way and Ponape would have been a good place for a novelist. But it was a pity, an absolute shame, that so much energy was wasted in petty bickering—foolishness that dissipated the time of expensive people whose talents should have been used for the good of the Micronesians. "Misfits are the plague of the administration," wrote Willard Price after a long visit.[34]

This is a book about a sailing adventure, not a political work, but if I can be allowed one comment it is this: The U.S. will never have any success running the lives of foreign people until it establishes a *career* colonial service based on the British model. The service should be staffed with outstanding, carefully chosen people—*employed for their entire working lives*—who wish to deal fairly and firmly with foreigners under U.S. control.

The question at the moment is not intent, for our intentions are pure. The question is not money, for we spend far more than anyone else. The question is not motivation, for we want to do well. The question is *experience*. We are bungling amateurs.

"Few of the Trust Territory positions are even under our civil service," writes James Ramsey Ullman. "There is, on the one hand, neither the machinery for preparing a man for a career in the islands, nor, on the other, the rewards to make it attractive once he has undertaken it."[35]

The use of the words "wards" and "colonial service" may sound presumptuous today, but the need for these concepts exists. The Pacific people I saw weren't a bit concerned over the blue-sky slogans of nationalism, colonialism, and self-determination. These people were worried about getting something to eat.

You can't rule stone-age people with computers and pie-in-the-sky planning studies. The Micronesians need leadership. They have to be told what to do. Money is important but *leadership* is the critical thing. The Gilbert Islands were run for only a fraction of the money spent in the Carolines. Yet we saw busy, happy people who lived in neat villages in the Gilberts. In the Eastern Carolines we saw confusion, indolence, and apathy in an environment of abysmal living conditions. The young people don't need to study the humanities and social studies (whatever that means) but to learn to read, to write, and to perform simple arithmetic. What Kusaie and Ponape lacked was craftsmen of all kinds—carpenters, welders, cement workers, seamen, offshore fishermen, plumbers—men with practical skills. This shortcoming was quite unrecognized by U.S. officialdom, and met so far as I saw by only a single Catholic priest, Father Hugh Costigan, a twenty-year Ponapean veteran, who ran a useful industrial trade school designed to help the actual *needs* of his island.[36]

As we got ready to leave Ponape we thought of Adriano Selhar, who had come aboard *Whisper* in Matalanim Bay and had told us about the astonishing yam culture on the island.

"Growing yams is very important on Ponape," said Adriano. "They are raised for food but more important they are cultivated for prestige."

We found out that over one hundred varieties of yams are grown, some long and skinny, and others short and round. The individual tubers grow up to six feet long, six to eight inches in diameter, and weigh 200 to 250 pounds. Sometimes six men are required to carry a single yam! The Ponapeans often grow the yams deep in the forest in hidden places where each farmer works with secret techniques, special fertilizers, skills handed down from father to son, and varieties of yams that date from pre-Spanish days.[37]

"The cult of the yam is complicated," said Adriano, smiling broadly. "If you grow a yam bigger than anyone else and give it to the chief at the annual festival, you become famous and the chief awards you a special title. To present the biggest yam is a wonderful honor, which not only reflects a man's ability, generosity, and initiative, but shows his love and respect for his elders. I would give anything to be able to grow a two hundred-pound yam. Just think of it!

"Who knows?" said Adriano, pausing in glorious thought, "maybe I will be lucky with the plants I have in the forest."

Where Are You, Magellan?

As we slipped northward through a pass in Nankapen-param Reef, a full-throated northeast wind ballooned out *Whisper*'s sails. The overcast dawn of February 6 was an hour old, but in the dim light the dark mountains of Ponape were already fading behind us in the mist.

The great game in small-ship cruising is to arrange your passages so that you go from one place to another without intermediate islands in the way. Or if that is impossible, to plan things so you will see the intervening obstacles during daylight hours. In more civilized parts of the world, powerful flashing beacons and various signals help the mariner. But in the trackless voids of the nether regions you are on your own. God forbid any surprise atolls in the middle of a moonless night!

The complex of the Caroline Islands bulked to our west. We aimed to leave these reefs and atolls to the south by holding a course of 296° T., which gave us a straight run for Guam, 900 miles away. We were in the northeast trades and had plenty of fair wind across our starboard quarter. The wind was squally, however, and for the first few days we seemed to be forever pulling the sails down and running them back up.

On the second day we logged 156 miles noon to noon, our best ever for twenty-four hours, but the motion was too wild as we whished ahead on big rollers, so we carried on with less sail. Even so our average remained 137 miles per day, good daily runs for a sailing ship twenty-five feet on the waterline, especially when we generally flew a double-reefed mainsail and a storm jib. The wind varied from twelve to thirty knots.

With *Whisper* guided unfailingly by the self-steering vane we had to be careful not to fall overboard. A sailing yacht is designed to come into the wind and stop if no one is at the helm. If you were steering by hand and fell over the side you could probably swim to the stopped ship. But with the vane in control of the helm, the yacht would merrily continue on course while you—alas—watched forlornly from the water. For this reason we had double lifelines around the ship, and when the sea was rough we wore safety harnesses so that we could clip ourselves dog-leash fashion to the ship somewhere. Alone up on the foredeck at night with the other person asleep you had to be especially careful—one hand always firmly on the ship or your legs jammed against something.

Margaret and I wore police whistles around our necks so that we could summon each other in case one of us fell over the side, got fouled in a line, or otherwise desperately needed help. Fortunately we never used the whistles.

We spent a lot of time studying the next charts and reading the *Pilot* books for the islands ahead. Of course if you took the *Pilot* books seriously you would never leave your home harbor. No writing on earth is more filled with gloom and black warnings than the sailing directions of the various governments. We read of "uncharted rocks, numerous and fang-like," "hostile tidal streams that seethed with sudden over-falls," "poisonous shell fish," "severe magnetic anomalies," and about "vicious undersea volcanic activity."

Margaret and I often held contests to see who could come up with the most melancholy passages and we would soon be hooting with laughter.

"Listen to this one," I said. " 'The anchorage is obstructed with a loaded ammunition ship below the surface.' And here's happy news: 'The life-saving station has been shut down.' "

"Try these," said Margaret. " 'Unlighted concrete fish traps obstruct the channel.' Or 'Mariners are warned that oyster farmers have some-times fired on small ships thought to be poaching.' "

Guam is the southernmost of the sixteen Marianas Islands which extend northward for 420 miles and include such well-known places as

Tinian and Saipan. Our plan was to work north along the chain and to cross 280 miles to the next group north, which was the Nanpo Shoto, some two dozen small volcanic islets which extended north another 640 miles to the Japanese coast. I spent days studying the charts, reading the *U.S.* and *British Pilots*, and examining weather maps.

As I read the *Pilots* I followed the descriptions with the appropriate charts. This was slow work with Japanese place names because the names were sometimes different. Was the mountain called Hagashi Yama the same as Mihara Yama? Was I right in assuming the Kyodoga Hana was a spelling variant of Koiwadoga Hana? Was the village of Yaene the same as Kanado? Was the 215-foot cape named Funatsuke Bana that I saw on the chart the same 215-foot place that the *Pilot* called Funetsukega Hana?

I began to have serious doubts about my scheme to work northward along the two island groups. The strong Kuroshio current—the Japanese current—set toward the northeast at thirty to forty miles per day, and the prevailing winds above 25° N. blew from the north and northwest. I feared that we might find ourselves beating against the wind on the port tack trying to make westing as we headed north while being set eastward by the Kuroshio current. The prospect was dismal. After much deliberation I decided to strike out boldly for southern Japan directly from Guam. According to my studies, a gale or two was likely, but we would have plenty of room in the Philippine Sea, with Okinawa and Chichishima as refuge places on the extreme limits of our route.

"The distance between Guam and the southern tip of Kyushu is 1,310 miles," I said to Margaret. "We should stay in the northeast trades for 64 percent of this distance or some 840 miles. That leaves 470 miles —call it 500—of more uncertain winds. Typhoons are unlikely in February. We can cope with gales, though not pleasantly. With luck we can make the 1,310 miles in ten days."

I had made my decision. So much for the homework.

We were somewhere over Nero Deep, a submarine trench whose bottom lay 31,680 feet beneath us, an inverted Everest of the Pacific. The weather continued to be overcast and the moonless nights were black. The illusion of speed was remarkable with the ship running hard. When the wind blew strongly and the seas stayed moderate, we seemed to hurl along in the darkness. At such a time it always appeared to me that we were running downhill—maybe into the other world of the Gilbert Islanders. It is strange how the notion persists. But the feeling of sailing down and down recurs and I have experienced it many times at night.

An hour before dawn on the seventh day I saw a brightly lighted Japanese fishing vessel lying quietly on the sea. That morning was gray, but at 1135 we saw the sun for a moment and a questionable position line put us twenty-seven miles from Guam. I was worried about passing the island and having to beat back, but two hours later we sighted Guam some twelve miles to starboard. How beautiful it was! We immediately put *Whisper* hard on the wind and began to beat toward the island, which, with its cloud cap, looked like a fairy-tale illustration.

February 12. 1340. I am quite pleased to see how well we are going to windward with the storm jib and three rolls in the main. The wind force is 24 knots with fairly large but quite regular seas. There is water over the foredeck but only occasional spray in the cockpit. This landfall has been something like Rarotonga. Twice now I have not allowed enough leeway for the trade wind drift.

Guam is a big American military base and the approach by sea is controlled by the U.S. Navy. We were required to radio twenty-four hours or more ahead for permission to enter Apra harbor, a gigantic military installation on the west coast. Since we had no transmitter, I had asked the radio people on Ponape to contact Guam, which they did. However, when we arrived at Apra at night, no one had heard of us. We were not allowed to enter the commercial harbor but were sent to a remote quarantine anchorage on Cabras Island, a place known locally as Outer Siberia. We were soon cleared, but we discovered that we were miles from stores, shops, supplies, main roads, and transport. I wanted to apply in person for permission to tie up at the docks in the inner harbor, but the gate at the main Navy area meant a ten-mile walk.

We were told to sail to the small-boat harbor at Agana, the main city of Guam. After bashing to windward for most of a day we followed the leading marks through the tiny windswept pass and bang! We were on the coral! We managed to get turned around and off, and fled out to sea, feeling particularly bitter at a Navy that would send a small ship to a harbor that required local knowledge. Wet, tired, and discouraged, we returned to Apra. Again I tried to go to the commercial docks—where a Navy band was serenading a cruise liner—but we were sent to Outer Siberia. What was particularly frustrating was that I couldn't even get to anyone to plead my case. We had no choice but to stay among the area of broken-down docks, moored barges, and new construction.

We saw a parade of big U.S. Navy ships, nuclear submarines,

immense drydocks, and tall, giraffelike cranes, presided over by swarms of dungaree-clad sailors and civilians in hard hats. Overhead a steady procession of B-52 bombers departed and returned from missions in Vietnam. The bombers were painted a dull black and, with their long droopy wings, looked immensely forbidding. Not far from us an ammunition ship was unloading bombs, and trucks stacked with the ghastly missiles rumbled past *Whisper*.

Now on the third day at Guam we were particularly anxious to get ashore and to Agana, where we hoped to find several months of mail. Margaret managed to ride into the city with a friendly construction worker and brought back packages, film, books, charts, a few urgent parts for the ship, and letters from our friends.

We looked on our chart and saw that Guam was about twenty-nine miles long and four to eight miles wide, with a spine of 1,000-foot mountains paralleling its major dimension. Once heavily wooded, the vegetation is now sparse and the general color of the island is light brown. Our attention was drawn to the automobiles, which were everywhere. The island's 230-mile road system was choked with 28,000 motorized vehicles. The biggest problem was to get across the main street in Agana at quitting time when the Navy workers headed for home. After a year in the South Pacific the traffic seemed unbelievable.

"I discovered that the two-car family is out of style," said Margaret. "Modern families have three!"

Technically Guam is a U.S. territory run by an appointed governor and a legislature of twenty-one members, but in practice the island is operated by the military establishment (for example, since most telephone calls are military-oriented, the Navy furnishes free phone service for everyone). The local people number 55,000, with another 38,500 connected with the armed forces.

Guam might easily be called an aircraft carrier with trees, although its used-car lots looked suspiciously like those of Los Angeles and New York.

We found that food prices were higher than the sky. Food cost more on Guam than in San Francisco, and a 25 percent cost-of-living bonus was added to wages. What we could not understand was why certain Japanese and American foodstuffs cost more in Guam than in the Caroline Islands, where the transport charges were infinitely greater. Margaret was amazed that bananas cost fifty cents a pound in the markets.

"The bananas are *grown* here," she said with incredulity. "In California I buy bananas from Costa Rica that cost only ten cents a pound."

With *Whisper* tied up in Outer Siberia it was a miracle that we made any friends, but several schoolteachers happened to drive past and kindly invited us to their homes for meals. One day when we were out walking, a man named Marshall Bridge picked us up in a very battered car. "I thought you were in the Peace Corps with your camera bags," said Marshall. "No matter. I recruit people for the educational program out here and if either of you can teach and are fluent with Japanese and can pass a security check I can offer you a job with a vast salary."

A little later we met Bill Moody, a foreman at one of the Navy shops, who helped us with a repair of *Whisper*'s tiller fittings. Two people loaned us automobiles, which made shopping easier and gave us a chance to look at the island.

We sailed to the southwestern coast of Guam to visit Umatac Bay. This was something we had dreamed of when we had first outlined the Pacific trip, for it was in Umatac Bay in 1521 that Magellan had anchored his three ships after his long Pacific crossing.

At dawn [writes a historian] *they coasted along until the watchers crowding the rail sighted a break in the cliffs and saw a little bay between the shoulders of the highlands. They could make out a number of canoes drawn up on its sandy beach while back from the shore a row of thatched houses on stilts was visible.*[38]

Now 447 years later we sailed *Whisper* along the same coast. The wind whipped down from Jumullong Manglo mountain as we skirted the fringing reef. We tacked in toward the little bay and thought of Magellan and his men, sick, scurvy-ridden, and dying, after crossing the strange Pacific from South America. We wondered at their emotions.

The bay was small, only 350 yards wide, and I was surprised that Magellan's weakened men could have worked their unhandy ships inside. Like Magellan we saw the village, now with a church, built along each side of a narrow road. And we saw the Chamorros—the natives of Guam—who were generally small people, a mixture of Micronesian, Filipino, and Spanish stock. We heard the staccato Chamorro language, a Micronesian tongue with Spanish and Tagalog words.

That night we thought how fortunate we were in our little ship. Four centuries ago Magellan had no food, no charts, little medicine, and his navigation was pitiful. On *Whisper* we had a variety of excellent health-giving foods, first-class charts, ample medicine, and we could navigate with ease. The design of our little ship was good and she was made of materials beyond Magellan's dreams. Yet he was the first Western man to cross the world's largest ocean and to demonstrate its existence to an unbelieving world.

That night we drank a toast to Magellan.

We left for Japan on February 24 and learned right away that the Philippine Sea in winter has a mind of its own. An hour out we put one reef in the main, followed a little later by a second reef. Before midnight we pulled down the number two working jib and replaced it with the storm jib. We were headed a little west of north, bashing into big seas churned up by twenty-five to thirty knots of wind from the northeast. Our lives had suddenly become wet and noisy. Japan seemed a long way off.

Margaret was ill and out of it all in her bunk and I didn't feel too well myself. About every third wave thumped on board and bombarded the coachroof and cockpit with sea water that sluiced everywhere. The sea conditions were different from those we had experienced before, and water ran all over the ship, especially around the main hatch, which leaked alarmingly. We had long known a few drips, but now we had first a trickle, and then a stream which soon flooded out the quarter berth, the chart table, and sloshed over the tools stowed beneath. I tried to lash a piece of canvas around the hatch, but without proper fastenings the canvas came adrift.

When we sailed against the wind we pounded into the waves, and big ones would almost stop the ship. *Whisper*, angled closely into the seas, climbed the swells as they passed and crunched into the troughs that followed. You felt the ship rise on a wave, hesitate, and then fall with a great thud into the pit between the last wave and the next. Below in your bunk hanging on, you wondered how the ship could take such knocks. Certainly her stout hull would break in two.

In heavy windward going, the self-steering vane was not too good because the head seas shoved the bow sideways. Adjusted to go more against the seas, the vane steered well until we got into a calmer patch when the vane headed *Whisper* into the wind and tacked the ship. With no one to release the jib sheet, the ship wound up hove to, riding easily on the seas but going nowhere.

"This will never do," I said. "We've got a long way to go." At midnight I began to steer by hand and we got along much better. I was able to stay on course until a big sea approached, when I headed off a little to take the wave on its side. This way we kept the ship moving and lessened the terrible banging.

We were still in the tropics and the sea water was warm. During the night I wore oilskins without boots. After a while there was as much water inside the oilskins as outside, but I was warm and comfortable and cheerfully steered hour after hour. In the dark you could see the big seas coming by the flash of their crests. The water churned and tumbled as it approached and I sometimes thought there were a thousand crested dragons charging the ship, their spines erect and mighty as they converged on our little world. The dragons hissed as they approached and sighed as they swept past, leaving a tingling smell of iodine that freshened the cool air of the black night.

In the first eighteen hours from Guam we logged eighty-two miles. At noon on the second day the gray sky darkened in the north and the wind increased to a steady thirty-seven knots, almost on our nose. We hove to on the starboard tack and I retired to my bunk with a handful of crackers and a book. Margaret was listening to the short-wave broadcasts on the radio.

"It's marvelous to tune in to the political broadcasts of each nation," she said. "The reports of Radio Moscow, Radio Peiping, Radio Australia, and the Voice of America are so different that you think each announcer must be reporting separate events. What pretenders people are! How they bend the truth to fit their own purposes!"

Margaret had her sea legs at last, and we soon had a hot meal, which we ate from bowls while we wedged ourselves against the cabin bulkheads. At first light on the third morning I looked out on a lead-colored sea striped with foam-crested rollers that marched in unflinching rows from the north-northeast. The wind was a little less, and the Ventimeter read twenty-four to thirty-two knots. I was fed up with being hove to because we weren't getting anywhere, so I began to steer again. Close-reaching on the starboard tack, we made good time, but water flew everywhere. Before noon a sea bounded up over the coachroof, filled the port Dorade ventilator, and poured in below. About half the time there was a foot of water in the cockpit. However, *Whisper* scooted along, and by 2300 the log read ninety-seven miles, an average of six knots, a figure I doubted. A little before midnight the wind became very gusty. We hove to on the port tack.

At 0700 on the fourth day Margaret cautiously slid the hatch back, looked outside, and measured the wind. "Oh joy," she said. "There's an easterly wind of only twenty-four knots."

We got under way at once. During the morning the cloud cover dispersed a little and celestial observations put us 235 miles northwest of Guam. The weather stubbornly stayed foul and in the afternoon the wind backed to the northeast and increased to thirty-five knots with gusts that put the sides of our lee coachroof in the water. We hove to again and I pulled down the third reef in the mainsail. Later I doused the storm jib.

February 28. 1230. We have been steering since dawn and have made 33 miles northward but during the last two hours the seas have gotten bigger. One broke on board and washed Margaret to the opposite side of the cockpit. While I was steering I got caught by a large wave which swept me and a sail bag on to the lee deck, filled the cockpit, and snapped the boat hook in two. Margaret and I have both been wearing safety harnesses plus an additional bight of line tied around us and made fast to a cleat. After a second wave put me across the lee deck I hove the yacht to.

The sky has a low roof of slate-colored clouds with patches of sun here and there which make me think the gale will soon be over. However, the waves are a bit frightening now, and the largest I have seen. In the last 24 hours we logged 31 miles.

When the third wave broke on board Margaret saw the kettle fly upward from the sink and cross to the outboard part of the chart table without spilling a drop. A remarkable act of levitation!

The next day the gale went on. The seas were easier—perhaps more regular—and we banged along and did 135 miles. The yacht was a shambles inside. We had rolled heavily from a big wave and everything flew off the shelves above the chart table. A pair of pliers smashed the stove pressure gauge to bits and spread glass all over the galley floor. While I was asleep the books catapaulted off the shelves above the port settee, flew across the cabin, and landed on top of me.

"Help! I'm drowning in books," I shouted, suddenly awake, with dozens of books piled on top of my head.

February 29. 1900. Incredible how you see glimpses of life beneath the surface. Yesterday at the height of the big waves I spotted a whale 25–30 feet long. A little later when the sea was quite wild I saw something off to starboard which after a few minutes proved to be a dozen porpoises leaping and frolicking. How rich with life the sea must be beneath the surface.

2100. Wind up to 40 knots from the east. I tried steering for an hour and filled the cockpit again. Hove to on the starboard tack now. With the current, fore-reaching, and leeway, we are probably making 2 or 2½ knots straight for Japan.

Whisper was so hard pressed that on the next morning—the seventh day of gales—we put up the number three storm jib (fifty square feet) and continued to thump along. At midnight warm rain began to fall. A frontal system was passing over and the wind was definitely less. I was grimy, salt-covered, and weary beyond belief. I sat in the cockpit with the warm rain running over me and watched a ship ten miles off to port.

"Hooray!" I said. "There are other people in the world after all."

The next day we reveled in fine weather and sun. The wind and seas both decreased, and we ran up bigger sails and cautiously opened the hatches and ports. The lifelines were festooned with clothes drying out, and while I picked up below and replaced a few lengths of running rigging, Margaret cooked several hearty meals. Our spirits, now immensely restored, climbed higher when our noon position showed that we had only 680 miles to go.

I had begun to think that in the Philippine Sea the prevailing winter winds always blew from the northeast at forty knots. For a week the sailing had been rigorous, with the ship shut up like an agitated oyster and the sails of laughable size—so full of wind I expected them to blow into a million threads.

At times one perhaps has doubts about sailing in a small ship, but the storm always passes and with it the uncertainty. Like the smile of a pretty girl after an argument, the blue sky, the warm sun, and the easy seas soon restore one's faith in the enterprise.

By March 3 we were at 22° N., and a shirt and a pair of trousers felt good. At night we spread blankets on the bunks, and sea boots began to appear from their long storage. We even fired up the cabin heating stove to dry out the ship below. No one complained about the heat.

I started the engine to charge the batteries. The little Diesel was running nicely when suddenly there was a horrendous bang, followed by a crash, and then silence. I opened the engine-room compartment and was surprised to find the engine gone. The flimsy, built-up wooden mounts had fallen to pieces and the unsupported engine had dropped into the bilge. Once again we were a true sailing ship.

We began to see an occasional smudge of smoke on the horizon, and we kept careful watch for ships, particularly at night. One morning I sailed near an old moss-covered floating tree that was almost twice as long as the yacht. From time to time we had dolphins around us, and once we ran alongside a big turtle. Under the clear skies the sea was no longer blue but dark-colored, for we had worked into the mainstream of the Kuroshio current—the black tide—that swept northeastward from the Philippines to Japan and beyond.

At noon on March 8—1,221 miles from Guam—we were smoothly broad-reaching in front of a twenty-knot southwest wind when I noticed a swell from the northwest. Rain splattered on deck and the wind began to veer and blow harder. I knew something big was coming. Our little vessel was strong, but she was only a tiny ship and we had to drive her sparingly. We yanked down the mainsail, set the storm trysail, and put up the number three storm jib, our two smallest and stoutest sails.

Two hours later we were hove to in a gale with a steady forty-six knots of wind from the northwest. The swells from two directions tumbled against one another, and the sea was as nervous as a caldron of boiling water. *Whisper* lurched into a complex of roads and pathways that capered and bucked like scenery waving in an earthquake. The lanes and ditches not only formed and disappeared in a twinkling, but of a sudden rose and heaved down as the ship tried to go ahead. When she hobbled east she was knocked south, and when she was shoved north she was jerked west. Cross seas banged and slapped on all sides.

I stood in the hatchway and looked out on a leaden scene of bitter gray sparked now and then with a stray shaft of sunlight. The wind had real weight in it and I could scarcely turn to windward because needles of spray hurled against my face and blew my eyes full of water.

The ship rose on a swell, and all at once I looked out on several miles of snorting ocean. Here and there wave tops exploded into block-long cascades of foam, etched white against the dark sea. In the distance immense combers broke and toppled, and when the light was right you could see green water furiously tumbling down.

Then the ship slid into a trough and our world shrunk to a single wave mountaining up behind us. As the sea climbed higher and higher I wondered whether the ship would lift as the swell swept forward. Somehow the ship always rose, and as the water roared ahead, the wave whished under the hull with a bubbling sound.

Storms in the ocean sometimes give the crew a good drubbing. But though you get weary, your senses become immensely heightened. You grow alert to every movement, every shudder, and every vibration of the sea. You hear better, see farther, and somehow touch toward the nerve of the shrieking wind and ocean. You take great breaths of super-clean air, and your nose and tongue pick up the sharpness of the iodine and the faint aroma of sea creatures. You learn the sense of the sea itself.

I stood in the hatchway for hours watching it all, sometimes shouting for pure joy as the big waves scoured past. "You haven't got me yet," I yelled like a blubbering fool, with my words twisted by the wind. "You may be big, but I've still got my wits and my ship."

The grandest experience of my life was to look upon the sea in storm and later at the sea in calm. It's a thing everyone should experience. Reading about it won't do, and photographs are a poor substitute. You need to gaze upon the brooding soul of the tempest itself, and on another day to ponder an ocean of utter tranquility.

During heavy weather we always saw storm petrels, small soft-gray birds that fluttered a few inches above the wave tops seeking bits of food on the surface. The storm petrels often flitted behind the yacht to look over the water churned up by the passage of the ship. The birds would dance above the wave tops a few feet from you and almost touch the water with their tiny webbed feet. In the lee of the waves the wind must have been less, for the gales didn't seem to bother the birds. I often wondered why they weren't swallowed up by the toppling crests, but the petrels somehow rose just enough to stay above the water. No matter how close they were the birds never took any notice of us. Their job was to get food, it appeared, and the task seemed to take their entire attention.

I grew very attached to these slender-winged little fellows—called Mother Carey's chickens by sailors—who came next to us again and again and never showed the slightest fright. Sometimes when I was on the foredeck changing sails and rising up and down on the plunging deck I would look out and see these dainty little birds fluttering—there is no other word—a few feet away, only inches above the water.

By noon on the fifteenth day the gale was gone and we were under way again. The next day we saw a ship, a glass float, and a waterlogged Japanese basket. The following night Margaret called me at 2200 and nodded toward a Japanese coasting vessel about a quarter of a mile astern.

"This fellow has circled us twice," she said. "I haven't made any

motions nor changed course. Evidently the honorable captain has never seen anything like us."

At 0345 on the seventeenth day Margaret picked up a lighthouse signal on Tanegashima, a small island south of Kyushu. We skirted its east coast and in thick weather headed across the Osumi Kaikyo, the broad strait leading to Kyushu.

I was asleep on my berth when I heard a familiar voice. "Oh do come up," called Margaret. "I see Japan."

The visibility was poor—driving rain, low clouds, and light squalls —but we caught glimpses of a high, rock-bound coast. The scenery was wild. Steep mountains disappeared into clouds, and along a black and white and gray coast gigantic rocks were dashed and buffeted by the wind and sea. Hiroshige would have liked our landfall.

We kept plenty of sail up for power since there were strong tidal streams and our engine was only ballast. When we rounded the entrance to Kagoshima Bay we got becalmed behind a current-swept rocky headland and had a few worrying moments when I wished for a big sculling oar. But we finally got wind and began to work up to the city of Kagoshima, the port of entry at the head of Kagoshima Bay, forty miles to the north.

In the middle of the next afternoon, with the magnificent volcano on Sakurashima erupting mightily to starboard and a ferryboat hooting for right of way off to port, we glided into Kagoshima. While the port officials blinked at us with astonishment we clumsily climbed on the docks with our lines and bowed deeply. We had reached the Far East.

15

A Sail in Japan

FIVE MINUTES AFTER WE HAD TIED UP *Whisper* IN KAGO-
shima a crowd of a hundred Japanese looked down on us from the
big commercial pier. A sailing yacht like ours was unknown, and under
the shadow of hulking freighters and enormous, double-decked ferryboats the people gazed with fascination and curiosity at *Whisper*'s tiny
hull, her diminutive mast and sails, our little anchors, and the toy self-
steering vane. The children pointed at our U.S. flag, the Japanese courtesy flag, and at the yellow quarantine flag that flapped idly.

We weren't quite sure what was going to happen, so we busied
ourselves with furling the sails and tidying up the lines.

"Good afternoon, Captain."

I looked up to see three uniformed Japanese officials lowering themselves on deck. They were nattily dressed in dark blue, with crisp white
shirts, carefully pressed trousers, and elegant officers' hats. Two carried
briefcases.

I ushered them below and had just begun to get out the ship's
papers and the clearance from Guam when I felt more people step on
deck.

"Immigration, please."

Four more men filed below, and as I looked still others appeared on
deck. Some of the men were young and smooth-faced with plain uniforms, while several of the gray-haired officials had lots of gold braid
on the visors of their hats.

"Customs inspection, hello." More Japanese officials stumbled on

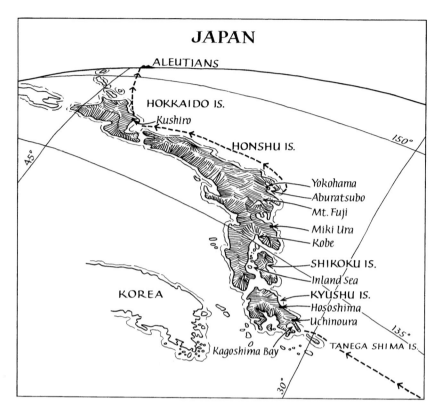

JAPAN

ALEUTIANS

HOKKAIDO IS.

Kushiro

HONSHU IS.

Yokohama
Aburatsubo
Mt. Fuji
Miki Ura
Kobe

SHIKOKU IS.
Inland Sea
KYUSHU IS.
Hososhima
Uchinoura

KOREA

Kagoshima Bay

TANEGA SHIMA IS.

45°

150°

135°

30°

board. Someone asked for passports, but there were so many men in the saloon that I couldn't get forward. Margaret had half a dozen in the cockpit, more were along the side decks, and I heard heavy footsteps on the foredeck.

"Health and agriculture officers, please." A new face smiled in the hatchway.

It was all too funny and I began to chuckle. I guffawed. I giggled. I laughed. I roared. I wept. It was hilarious. I made motions of a little ship, pointed at all the people, and began to count on my fingers. Everybody began to laugh with me and the ship trembled with the gusto of a good joke. The contagion spread to the crowd on the dock, and the laughter rose like a great wave of happiness.

What had happened was that the word had spread that a strange little sailing ship, a yacht with a woman on board, had suddenly come in from across the sea. All the officials wanted to have a look. It was a vast entertainment, an amusement on a dull winter workday. Everybody who could came—apprentices, clerks, inspectors, supervisors— and we were suddenly overrun. Twenty-eight uniformed officers had climbed on board and each claimed to have serious business.

We soon satisfied the agriculture and health men, and the immigration authorities stamped our passports. The customs people, however, concerned with smuggling, searched the ship from the chain locker to the after lazarette. But instead of opium they found rusty cans, in place of gold bars they uncovered wet blankets, and the guns they sought turned out to be dirty laundry.

We wanted a change of scene, so we tied the ship securely, snapped the padlock on the hatch, and left the yacht to the crowd that still watched.

Kagoshima was a bustling seaport of 300,000, and, like so many Japanese cities we were to see, it had a quality of rawness, a feeling of not being quite finished. Many of the streets were torn up and dusty, building projects stabbed the sky with steel and concrete, and the sidewalks were invariably incomplete. The first thing we wanted was a hot meal. We had brought a few yen from Guam and were eager to do business, but first we had to find a restaurant.

We were far from the tourist routes and, once away from the port officials, heard only Japanese. We couldn't read a single letter, much less a word or sentence. We couldn't decipher a street sign, a bus designation, and we could only gaze upon a sign which said 危険建物破壊中 (Danger! Building Demolition!) with idle curiosity.

However, a friend we had made in Guam, Ria Bridge, had loaned us a special English-Japanese dictionary prepared by Oreste Vaccari which had the Japanese words in both Japanese characters and spelled phonetically in Roman letters. This meant we could look up the word for restaurant (*ryoriya*), for example, which we could read and pronounce. If that didn't work, we could show someone on the street the word written in Japanese characters (料理屋). Without the little dictionary our life would have been hard indeed.

Westerners were unusual in the streets of Kagoshima, and people stopped to stare at us. Once downtown, and very hungry by now, we entered a little eating place which had *noren*, half-curtains with large Japanese characters written on them, hanging across the entrance. As soon as we entered, the waitresses began to giggle. One timidly approached and bowed.

"*Hai* [yes]?" she said.

I pointed to the dish being eaten by the person next to us and gestured that we wanted the same. The waitress made the motions of small, medium, and large. I chose medium. She withdrew, immensely relieved, and soon brought bowls of Chinese *soba*, delicious thick noodles in a steaming broth. We each paid 70 yen (19 cents).

As we walked around the city we were delighted with the Japanese food markets, which had dozens of varieties of oranges, all arranged in geometrically precise rows. The early strawberries were individually wrapped, and each early melon lay resplendent in a separate gift box with a window. Enormous bottles of dark-brown *shoyu* sauce alternated with giant bottles of *sake* of half a hundred varieties. We saw stacks of scrubbed carrots, fat cucumbers, giant white radishes called *daikon*, and cabbages with heavy green leaves.

The fish counters gleamed with a circus of colors and shapes—the pink flesh of salmon, the silvery-blue sides of salted mackerel, and big solid chunks of dark-red tuna. The fish sellers stacked up heavy slabs of dried bonito and arranged trays of crayfish whose feelers waved above the edges. Some fish were long and eel-like, others round and thick, and still others flat and spined. There were neat mounds of tiny shrimp, pungent shreds of squid, and purplish sections of octopus.

It was good to have wholesome fresh food again, and we soon had a variety on board, which kept quite well since we were almost 2,000 miles north of the equator. We found the winter nights cold in Japan and we usually fired up the cabin heater.

The harbor authorities moved us next to the ships of the Maritime Safety Agency, the Kaijohowancho, the Japanese equivalent of the U.S. Coast Guard, whose sailors and officers tied us alongside one of their patrol vessels and helped us with the crowds. We were glad to see people and to talk with them, but the men and women and the uniformed students never stopped coming. Night and day we heard them loudly reading our name and home port, *Wheez-pear*, Sahn Frahn-sees-ko. Fortunately for us the Maritime Safety Agency acted as a buffer and a question-answering service about the strange black sailboat. One man who was particularly helpful was a slight-figured chap named Kenrow Iwamoto, a junior officer.

Wherever we went in Japan we tied up to these friendly ships which flew a dark-blue flag with a single eight-pointed gray star on a gold shield. The crews helped us with repairs and shopping and we became good friends with many of the men, who loved to practice their rudimentary English. Most of the Japanese sailors seemed extremely cautious and at the slightest sign of wind or rain came rushing over with the latest weather maps, urged us to double our lines, and pleaded with us not to go sailing—even when the wind was fair and moderate. Their idea of a good day to go to the next port was a flat calm. How they thought we had ever gotten across the Pacific by sailing on windless days I will never know.

As a visiting captain I was invited to many *sake* parties, which were held at the drop of a noodle. The duty hours of the Maritime Safety Agency men often dragged and a few cups of *sake* helped brighten the gray hours. Then a few more cups and soon a full-blown celebration was under way.

Sometimes at 0200 the main hatch of *Whisper* would suddenly bang open and a seaman would shout: "Very important, Captain, this ship go my ship."

I would sleepily step on deck and climb to the next ship to find half the crew drunk and singing and pounding their fists on the table in the cabin. The captain was generally way ahead in the drinking and in the consumption of little cans of smoked oysters, some of which had dribbled across his uniform. I was hailed as a hero and heard a lot of bubbling Japanese amidst red eyes and empty *sake* jugs. A new bottle would be opened, heated, and I would be given a stiff glass together with handshakes and vows of United States–Japanese friendship forever.

Since I was four hours late for the party and couldn't understand a word, I was a little out of it and could only smile and feign unmitigated happiness until I could slip away and go back to bed.

The next afternoon the honorable captain, now alert and in a fresh uniform (you should have seen him last night), would nod curtly at me. I wondered whether he remembered the night before and all those pledges of international good will.

We found the docks filled with life and vitality. Most of the ships were Japanese, but we saw freighters from the Philippines and Australia, and trading ships from Taiwan and Indonesia. We watched green-helmeted crane operators hoist bright-red farm machinery into cargo holds. Stevedores lugged sacks of fertilizer and pushed carts piled high with crates of brooms and straw baskets overflowing with cabbages wrapped in plastic. Men with bulging shoulders wrestled steel rods into long piles on the dock while frantic train brakemen waved striped signal flags, which brought strings of dwarf railroad cars that were pushed by nervous, soot-belching locomotives. Funny little three-wheeled trucks backed into impossible corners to pick up giant bottles carefully cushioned with straw and tied with straw rope. Sometimes the dock workers paused to drink from miniature plastic teapots or to slurp down a fast bowl of noodles. Then back to work quickly, for other ships waited and hooted with impatience.

When we first got to Kagoshima we had a visitor, Sukefumi ("Fumi") Kabayama, a university student whose home was in a nearby village. Fumi was very keen on sailing and a member of the Nippon Ocean Racing Club, a national sailing organization, and he wrote a number of letters of introduction to various members along our route. Fumi was on vacation from his Kyoto school and came to *Whisper* each day to help us on the yacht. He was a good worker and, unlike most of the dreamer types, didn't have to be watched and constantly supervised. Fumi had a twenty-five-foot sloop which he kept on a lake near his school.

We became quite fond of Fumi, who not only worked hard but insisted on bringing us presents. He appeared at 0900 each morning after a one-hour bus ride from his village, smiling brightly and carrying a blue sailbag with his work clothes.

"I am like Santa Claus," he would say, sitting down and opening his blue bag. He would extract a bag of oranges, a cake, or a box of sweets.

Fumi had studied English for many years, but his conversation was terrible. However, we spoke with him every day and after a week we began to notice remarkable improvements in his English.

Kagoshima was a key transport center for the many small islands south, and ferryboats arrived and departed at every hour. No people are more sentimental than the Japanese, and fierce tears appeared at farewells. The departing passengers bought rolls of colored paper tape and held one end while their relatives on shore grasped the other. As the ship left—the loudspeakers blaring "Auld Lang Syne"—the people on each end of the paper tapes held tightly as the streamers unrolled and stretched farther and farther. Amidst more tears and frantic waving, the colored tapes finally broke as the ship got up speed. Then the music changed to a spirited march, and the people on shore dried their tears and went home.

I had been working on the engine of the yacht and had managed to get the mounts partially rebuilt. A local machinist made several critical parts, and with his help and some hoisting with the main halyard we got the engine up in place and working, though the repair was incomplete.

After a day of struggling with the ailing engine, and well infected with spots of grease and splotches of fiberglass resin, I was only too ready for the curing grace of the *o-furo*, the Japanese hot bath. Margaret and I took our towels and clean clothes and walked to a nondescript building with a tall iron smokestack. Men (男) entered on one side and women (女) on the other.

I paid 25 yen (7 cents) and stepped into a small room where I undressed and put my clothes in a straw basket. With my towel and soap in hand, I slid back the glass door to the main bathing room and heard gasps of astonishent as a dozen or so Japanese men turned to see a *gaijin*, a foreigner, enter their hot bath. However, I had learned to merely nod hello, and I picked up a plastic bowl, sat down on the tiled floor in front of hot- and cold-water taps, and began to wash myself.

The drill in a Japanese *o-furo* is to wash and rinse completely before you lower yourself into the steaming main bath, which is *very* hot. (You must show no emotion as you descend.) As you soak in the hot water for perhaps five or ten minutes you find that the heat relaxes all your tense muscles. Though a bit enervating, the Japanese bath is totally refreshing and sensible and something the Western world should adopt.

"I paid twenty-five yen plus an extra five yen because I washed my hair," Margaret told me later. "The women and children couldn't believe what they were seeing. The children, especially, had never seen blue eyes, and they put their little faces so close to mine that our noses almost touched.

"And such washing," said Margaret. "The women scrubbed every square inch of themselves so hard I thought their skin would come off. We all helped one another with our long hair and then had a good soak.

"I always wondered how the women survived the winter weather wearing only light kimonos," said Margaret. "You should see the layers and layers of woolens they put on underneath."

Stories and photographs about us and *Whisper* appeared in the newspapers and on television, and we continued to have many visitors, several of whom invited us to their homes for dinner. One night we took the streetcar to the house of Manabu ("Mab") Fukudome, another college student. We left our shoes at his door and put on slippers before we stepped onto the woven tatami mats with which all Japanese homes are floored.

Mab's widowed mother and sister welcomed us with bows and smiles, thick cushions to sit on, beer to sip, and little Japanese cakes to eat. The family was worried that we might have missed some vitamins on our trip, so we had an enormous salad of delicious mixed vegetables. Japanese women concern themselves particularly with the appearance of food, and the ingredients of the salad were chosen both for taste and arranged for prettiness.

We then moved to a room next to the kitchen and sat crosslegged around a small table with a thick blanket tacked around the edges and an electric heater underneath. The rooms were chilly, and we all put our feet and legs beneath the table and drew the blanket around for warmth. Mrs. Fukudome began to cook sukiyaki in an electric frying pan on the table. The two women had dishes of beef sliced thin as onion skin and plates of carefully washed cabbage, carrots, mushrooms, bamboo shoots, bean cake, and various ingredients. When the food was cooked we helped ourselves with chopsticks, dipping each mouthful into a beaten egg before we ate it.

We hadn't sat crosslegged since Samoa, and my legs began to tingle with stiffness. However, I feared to straighten them out because I didn't want to upset the little table and to electrocute myself on the rickety electric-plug arrangement which had wires radiating octopus-like to the frying pan, electric rice cooker, room lights, phonograph, heater, and television set, all of which were going.

American Westerns were big on Japanese television, and the sound dubbing was astonishing. I heard gun-toting desperados from West Texas suddenly spout a mouthful of rapid-fire Japanese. Mab asked me whether I had a gun and my cowboy suit on the yacht.

"I have my horse too," I said, and we all roared with laughter. I motioned toward the TV cowboys and thumbed through my diction-ary. "*Otogi-banashi mattaku desu* [fairy tale absolutely]," I said, which put our hosts into such hysterics that they almost upset the table.

The evening was good fun for everyone. We got along surprisingly well with Mab's modest English, our scraps of Japanese, and lots of gestures. The next day the family visited us on *Whisper*.

On our last night in Kagoshima our friend from the Maritime Safety Agency, Kenrow Iwamoto, whom we had seen every day for several weeks, gave us a sukiyaki party aboard *Whisper*. Kenrow and Fumi, our voluntary crewman, got our permission, rushed off to shop, and returned a few minutes later with a big box of vegetables and groceries. We fired up a one-burner Tilley cooking stove in the main cabin, and Kenrow and Fumi took turns putting in the thinly sliced beef and the precisely cut vegetables. The meal was wonderful—hot, tasty, fine-smelling, and novel to eat—a supper to linger over while we chatted and told jokes.

"This is the second sukiyaki feast in two days," I groaned. "I will get big like a sumo wrestler," I said, indicating a big belly. "*O-sumo.*"

Kenrow had brought us a going-away present of green tea. "I will be very lonely when you go," he said wistfully. "It is good to have you in Kagoshima."

I was quite touched by his statement. Earlier in the week I had been ill. Kenrow had looked in and had been genuinely distressed to see me flaked out in a forward berth. "Do you need a doctor?" he had asked. "I can call one right away."

He went over our itinerary and approved or disapproved our various stops. "Be careful of the headland of Sata Misaki," he counseled. "Hard currents there. Go far outside before you turn."

Kenrow was twenty-six and had been with the Maritime Safety Agency for eight years. He had two children, and his wife was a tea-ceremony instructor and a pupil of flower arranging. He was thrilled by our trip and liked to come aboard *Whisper* (with his two dictionaries) for a hot rum punch and a chance to practice his English.

Kenrow was a junior officer. His rank badge had two stars and two horizontal bars and he was qualified to command ships up to 1,500 tons. "But I want to get better certificates and to go to the Maritime Safety Agency University," he said.

I will long remember his slight figure in his trim blue uniform. I hope I can see him another time.

Again and again as we made friends with the ordinary people of Japan we were convinced that ghastly wars would be impossible if countries exchanged more visits on a person-to-person level.

We sailed from Kagoshima on a sunny April morning with Fumi on board for a few days. As we left, Sakurashima erupted mightily and spewed bits of rock that floated and covered the water with a froth of pumice that extended for miles and looked alarmingly like land. We touched briefly at Yamagawa and Odomari in the Kagoshima area and headed north along the east coast of Kyushu. We had the choice of continuing north via the Inland Sea or of going on the Pacific side of Shikoku and Honshu. We elected the Inland Sea because we had heard vaguely of its scenic attractions.

Sailing in Japan was a new experience. Close in, the hills and mountains were distinctive, but once a few miles offshore the land disappeared in a gray haze that seemed part fog, part industrial pollution, and part the nature of the country itself. We had to steer careful compass courses and to note our distance run. We were better off at night, for the Japanese had excellent aids to navigation, and the light signals were frequent and powerful.

Of course when we were close to shore during daylight we kept track of our position by reference to land features, using Japanese charts and the usual books of sailing directions. But the pilotage was a muddle in gray.

Our *Pilot* books identified places by solitary mountains. I saw mountains everywhere. The *Pilot* books described prominent points of land. I saw dozens of spurs of high land. The books spoke of small islands and conspicuous trees. We saw scores of islets and I often wondered whether the energetic Japanese woodsmen had spared that conspicuous tree so often mentioned but so seldom seen. Indeed with enough patience you could fit a given landscape—especially when it was half submerged in gray—into almost any description.

What we did find were small and large coasting vessels whose captains skirted in closely to shore with knowledge learned from lifetimes of working along the Japanese islands. Whenever we saw ships appear out of the murk we knew we were near the shore and on the shortest course between the two nearest towns. As we worked north we saw more and more Japanese fishermen in the big offshore tuna fishery in the warm Kuroshio current. The fishermen had ships of every sort, usually high-prowed wooden vessels twenty to forty-five feet long with thumping Diesel engines and decks cluttered with nets, poles, floats, gaffs, barrels, rows of night lights, laundry, fish boxes, and sometimes a small riding sail at the stern.

All fishing stopped when we came near. The crew would line the decks, pointing and smiling at us, and eagerly discuss the ship and flags and sails. "Yacht-o, yacht-o," the men would exclaim.

The Japanese seamen were always helpful. When I was unsure of a headland I only had to point and to shout "Hetsuka Ura?" for example, and I would get eager nods or aggressive head-shaking. When I gestured toward several villages and called out the names, the Japanese sailors would smile and nod. If I indicated a detour around a danger with my hand they assented eagerly. If I questioned the depth of the water in a nearby harbor I got immediate motions to indicate how many men high the water was deep. If I shook my fist at an approaching squall the fellows on the other ship knew exactly what I meant. In short we were all from the sea, and though from different cultures, we understood and helped each other, for one never knew who would need help tomorrow.

Fumi knew the Kitamura family in Uchinoura and had written them, so we sailed into Ariake Wan and slipped behind the quiet breakwater next to a few fishing boats. Uchinoura was an old-style Japanese village surrounded on the land side by rows of orange trees whose dark foliage climbed the surrounding hills. Time had darkened the wooden sides of the small houses, and the gray tile roofs curved gracefully above the narrow lanes. We put out a bower anchor from the ship and tied up stern first to the concrete quay, a method we were to become expert at before we left Japan.

The whole Kitamura family—father, mother, daughter, four sons, and grandmother—was along the shore when we docked and we were whisked away for a bath and meal. It was comfortable in the Kitamura house and we felt well settled and at ease at once.

In Japan the rooms are sized according to the number of soft straw mats, tatami (each measures about three by six feet), that make up the floor, a single mat being the smallest area in which one person can sit, work, rest, and sleep. You have six mat rooms, eight mat rooms, and so on. The entire house is conceived in multiples of this fundamental modular unit, and every dimension—the width of the sliding doors, the height of the room, the size of the veranda—is worked out in terms of the basic tatami.[39]

We sat in the parlor of the Kitamura house, a ten-tatami room walled in by sliding panels (*fusuma*) and translucent screens (*shoji*) that opened to the formal garden a few feet away. One wall had a small Shinto shrine with a purple cover raised above it. A photograph of grandfather, the late patriarch, hung above the shrine. An old Japanese scroll (of sailing ships, to honor us) decorated another wall. An *okoto*, a thirteen-string harp, lay at the foot of the scroll, and we admired a Japanese doll in a glass case. The ceiling was high and the upper parts of the walls were finished in hand-sawed cedar embellished with long wood carvings. The main furniture was a low table with surrounding cushions on which we knelt and later were told to sit.

We ate meals of many courses, each exquisitely prepared and served on dozens of small dishes that were carried from the kitchen by mother and sister. There was no clutter of wires and no sound of television. Only the peacefulness of the traditional room and garden and the quietness of the sea and countryside.

The next morning we ate in the same room, but the environment of breakfast was quite different. The shoji screens had been opened, and with the garden beyond, the feeling was that the room was part of the garden. The flowering cherry and plum seemed to flow right inside the house. The ordered rocks and sea shells and green shrubs all worked together with the cedar walls and roof tiles. The feeling was a satisfied one of neatness, order, and tranquility. Just over the garden wall we saw the varnished mast of *Whisper* with the Japanese courtesy flag leisurely flapping in the morning sun.

The people of Uchinoura all wore kimonos and bowed deeply, their knees and hands and foreheads touching the floor when they greeted you or departed. We were startled at such bowing, but the people—of all ages—kowtowed from habit without a thought. We were the first foreigners that the Kitamura family had ever entertained and the first that the grandmother had ever seen. We stayed for several days and visited the nearby family farm, where on ten acres of rich Kyushu land some 1,500 orange trees each bore about 200 kilos of sweet-tasting fruit every year. True to the Japanese custom of gift-giving, Margaret was given a beautiful kimono. Grandmother presented us with a set of "married couples tea cups" of special pottery. The next night we countered (after much hunting in the yacht) with a fancy Swiss handkerchief for the grandmother, a piece of costume jewelry for the sister, and a Samoan fan for the mother.

We of course invited the Kitamura family to *Whisper* for a meal,

but the tide was low and the women had trouble getting down to the ship with their long kimonos until we found a ladder.

"I feel as if I am deep in the heart of old Japan," I told Mr. Kitamura through Fumi, who translated. "The values in your life are much the same as mine. You respect beauty and tranquility as I do."

Mr. Kitamura nodded gravely and looked thoughtful behind his thick glasses. I thought I saw the beginning of a tear. All of a sudden there was a deafening explosion. I jumped up.

"O.K.! O.K.!" said Mr. Kitamura. "Only Japanese rocket firing at nearby rocket base of Tokyo University."

Obviously the twentieth century had come to Uchinoura. I wondered if the rocket man bowed before he pushed the button.

Fumi left us and returned to college. We sailed north into the Bungo Suido, the strait between Kyushu and Shikoku, and stopped at several places before we entered the Inland Sea. This great finger of the Pacific, encumbered with islands and peninsulas, is about thirty miles wide and 230 miles long in an east-northeasterly direction. We had had many warnings about strong currents, but with the appropriate tidal tables we had no difficulty. What we did find was heavy shipping traffic and that new terror of terrors, the hydrofoil, a ship that looks like a giant mosquito and skims on top of the water at forty knots with a siren and a red light to clear the way.

The buoyage and navigational light system was excellent. However, instead of clear skies and fresh winds combined with exciting scenery we often found a murky atmosphere and calms, and generally we didn't see the picturesque volcanic islands with their splendidly formed pines until we were close to land. At Saganoseki we left behind a colossal smokestack hundreds of feet high that spewed reddish dust from blast furnaces into a somber sky.

Margaret and I stood watch and watch as we sailed from buoy to buoy and island to island, steering careful compass courses. We heard the sound of big and little ships and felt the vibrations of their engines. Sometimes we saw ghostly silhouettes appear and disappear, but generally the sounds receded without us seeing anything. We came upon frail little fishing boats, floats that marked submerged fishing gear, plastic debris, and derelict fifty-five-gallon oil drums that were easy to confuse with buoys.

When the tidal stream ran against us we anchored. At Obatake Seto the current roared by at eleven knots in the 850-foot channel, and when we started out with a fair stream we rushed by a signal tower with the ship making fifteen knots over the ground. We covered five miles in twenty minutes, the fastest *Whisper* has ever traveled. I was at the helm and Margaret was in front of me. I asked her to move. There was a misunderstanding because of the noise of the water, and during a brief argument the chart flew over the side and somehow got into a counter-eddy of the violent current.

"Look!" shouted Margaret above the roar. We watched unbelieving as the chart was swept out of sight in a twinkling.

April 15. 1100. Much heavy industry along the Honshu coast off to port. Sounds of riveting from new oil storage tanks carry across the water. Jet fighters overhead (one formation of three close-flying, dark-colored, bat-wing planes). Many ships loading at a refinery. The whole area smells as if it's ready to blow up. Small wooden ships jammed with barrels, big and little oilers, and super tankers. A moment ago I looked at the super tanker Gloric from Monrovia through the glasses and I suddenly realized that the pier I thought she was against was the forestructure of the Gloric herself!

We anchored near several ferries at the shrine of Miyajima on the island of Itsukushima. We took the dinghy ashore to see this famous attraction, which was thronged by hundreds of Japanese, who are certainly the world's most energetic tourists, carrying their maps and cameras and lunch baskets. Some of the Japanese wore kimonos, some sported Western clothes, and a few young people had on jeans and leather jackets. However, we all stopped to exchange our shoes for the straw sandals of pilgrims before we stepped onto the wide camphorwood walks of the Shinto shrine which led to various places of worship, rows of stone lanterns, ancient buildings with religious relics, two remarkable pagodas, and to a near view of the *torii* gate itself.

The great red *torii* of Miyajima, perhaps the most impressive of the 100,000 *torii* in Japan, is built of six enormous camphorwood trunks and is so located on the edge of the sea that the tide alternately covers and uncovers its impressive base.

"The universal presence of the *torii* in Japan is, I think, comparable to the sound of church bells in the West," writes Japanese scholar Fosco Maraini. "The popular belief is that to pass under a *torii* is a first stage in purification."[40]

April 18. Hiroshima. On Tuesday we had dinner at the apartment-office of Dr. Keiichi Tanaka, a sailing enthusiast and a busy throat specialist. The dinner was pleasant and the talk was all about yachts

*and cruising. Dr. Tanaka, however, made it sound as if he was about
to go off on a big sailing trip which I think is doubtful because
of his enormous one-man practice and his level of living.*

*Dr. Tanaka hired Watanabe, one of Japan's leading naval
architects, to design a new 33-foot sloop for him. Tanaka employed
Okazaki, a small shipyard on Shodoshima, to build the yacht. But
in order to afford all this, something not common in Japan, Tanaka
works very hard and has a practice so big that he cannot find
time to enjoy his ship and certainly not to go away on a long or
even a short cruise.*

*His life is a paradox, as are the lives of many Americans, sort
of quivering ulcers, who in order to afford something they want
very much, must work so long and hard that they have neither the
time nor the energy left to enjoy their hard-won gains. Perhaps
their salvation would be to reduce the height of their goals a
trifle. . . . Maybe a 30-foot yacht instead of 33 feet. And must it be
double-planked with expensive teak on the outside? Better a modest
trip to paradise than no trip at all.*

In Hiroshima we tied up to a Maritime Safety Agency ship. One
morning Margaret was on the dock washing clothes in a bucket with a
hose and a box of detergent when a sailor happened by. He watched

Margaret closely for a moment and hurried away to return a little later with a friend. The two sailors stood next to Margaret and vigorously discussed her box of detergent. Finally the second man spoke.

"Wrong box," he said. "Only for vegetables. Please wait."

The two men disappeared and soon came back with a box of detergent with different Japanese writing on it which they gave to Margaret. "Please use now," said the second sailor. "Other for vegetables only. No power for clothes."

We discovered later that the Japanese have at least three detergents. One for vegetables, one for dishes, and one for clothes, all used in cold water.

We continued east through the Inland Sea and found more heavy shipping traffic. We saw old rust-streaked sailing hulls that had been repowered with lumbering engines, high-sided trading vessels, sleek low-slung steel oilers, big fishing boats on their way to the Pacific, cargo vessels from Europe, and small undecked dories without paint that were patiently sculled by a fisherman's wife while he fiddled with his lines and hooks.

Often the motor vessels would come near to have a look at us. A ship stacked with lumber and bamboo would slip alongside, the door of the pilot house would slide open, the helmsman would step on deck, and we would exchange waves and smiles. But we had to be careful when ships approached because sometimes they ran on automatic pilot with no helmsman visible. Three times during our stay in Japan, vessels came close to us on collision courses and I saw no one in the pilot house.

The little islands were exquisite—steep and rocky with delicately branched pines and always with a tiny Shinto shrine, a few statues to Buddha, and perhaps a small *torii* arch. We marveled at the patience and resourcefulness of the hard-working Japanese farmers who grew such splendid crops in the rocky soil. If the weather or the season was too cold for strawberries, for example, a little bamboo frame and plastic cover was fitted over each plant, which was tended with what seemed almost like adoration.

The islands were timeless and blemished only by the national curse of Japan: plastic. On every beach and road, in every river and harbor, in every estuary and pond—everywhere—we saw plastic junk. Plastic toys, plastic buckets, plastic bags, plastic everything littered the shores and roads and lanes in wearying windrows which will never disappear.

Whisper's hull was foul with marine growth, for we had not taken the ship out of the water since California. Dr. Tanaka had suggested that we go to the shipyard where his new yacht was under construction. The yard was on the island of Shodoshima, in the eastern part of the Inland Sea, and on a rainy April afternoon we sailed in silently to the little settlement of Kotozuka on the north coast. Mist-shrouded green hills rose up in back of a sandy beach on which were scattered the ramshackle buildings of the boatyard and the few houses of the hamlet.

The shipyard was a small place that specialized in yachts and sailing dinghies and was run by a smiling Mr. Okazaki and his four sons. The yard employed forty men, mostly locals who had been trained as apprentices and who worked cheaply and well. We hauled *Whisper* out on a rickety marine railway that seemed certain to collapse. Indeed the power windlass used to pull the ship from the water looked as if it had been designed and built by Archimedes. The Japanese knew their job, however, and we were soon high on the beach. While the carpenters did a few jobs inside I repaired the rudder, which we had damaged on the coral at Guam, and I replaced all the shut-off valves below the waterline.

"Good morning" in Japanese is *ohayo gozaimasu*, but in these remote Shikoku islands the dialect eliminated the first word and used only the final sibilant of the second. "Good morning" sounded like a plain "ssssss." We presumed the morning smile and hiss was a pleasantry, so we smiled and hissed back.

The Japanese carpenters used tools I had never seen before. Most of their work was by hand and their saws cut when you pulled (instead of when you pushed as in America or England). Each man had five or six small pull saws made of thin, high quality steel that cut quickly and precisely. Every carpenter had a dozen planes and chisels and seemed a fanatic at sharpening them, for we often saw a man bent over a set of abrasive stones flushed with water while a steel blade was rapidly scraped back and forth.

To make a long line for a saw cut or other measurement a worker employed a kind of ink pot with a roller and a string, something like a miniature spinning wheel. In use the carpenter stretched the string between two points raised slightly above a plank. He plucked the ink-stained string and presto! A sharp black line—perfectly straight—appeared on the plank between the points.

Women do hard physical work in Japan. Often you would see them slaving on road construction gangs or cutting trees in a forest. In the shipyard two little women with their hair wrapped in white towels

worked as janitors. For some reason they were terrified of me, and whenever I appeared they would seize a basket of shavings and rush down to the beach to burn them.

Every day we looked at Dr. Tanaka's new wooden ship. Plastic and steel and aluminum may be good for yachts but for romance and feeling nothing equals wood. I don't know whether it is the fragrance of the flying wood chips or the delight of watching the skilled joiners and shipwrights expertly fit the planks together. Maybe we all know wood better (everyone has whittled) and feel an acquaintance with teak and oak and fir and spruce.

The island newspaper reporter did a story on us, and every day the newspaper was delivered to the ship with great seriousness, as if the paper were a document of huge importance. No one seemed to realize that we couldn't read a word.

One morning the number-one Okazaki son, Yoshihira, rushed down from the office. "Shipping Bureau telephone. You must go mainland Shikoku quick. Big trouble if no go."

I sighed and began to change my clothes. We had been plagued by the Shipping Bureau all through Kyushu. The problem was that certain large specified ports in Japan are open to foreign shipping. All other ports are closed and can be entered only with special permission, which is tedious to get.

By their nature yachts prefer the smaller and more isolated ports rather than Tokyo, Nagoya, Sasebo, and so forth. Japanese vessels are not subject to this rule, of course, and practically no Japanese has ever heard of the Shipping Bureau. The first problem was to find the agency (whose existence was usually denied). The second was to explain what I wished to do, which usually took several hours of earnest talking (through a translator) to unbelieving civil servants. In the end I found the best answer was to say that I had put in at so and so for emergency repairs, a white lie perhaps but a reasonable defense against regulations drafted in 1912, long before tourism.

We liked the Okazaki shipyard whose men did excellent work and even cast and machined their own metal fittings. The language was a problem, however, and sometimes Yoshihira and I had to work hard with our dictionaries, which fortunately for scholars have lots of terms that deal with love and poetry but have few words for practical sailors. We hoped to end the floods of water into the accommodation of the yacht with a box to contain the main sliding hatch, which had leaked so badly. In addition an expert carpenter fitted splash boards from the new hatch box to the sides of the cabin to direct water that fell on the coachroof to the decks instead of at the hatch and cockpit.

With two coats of anti-fouling paint on *Whisper* and number-two Okazaki son on the windlass, the ship was lowered into the water. We paid our bill, exchanged bows with the whole staff, and headed east toward Kobe. At Nishinomiya we met Professor Kensaku Nomoto, an expert single-handed sailor who kindly marked our charts for the rest of Japan.

We had been in the Far East for two and a half months and the summer typhoon season was approaching. It was time to get north. At the end of May we sailed toward the Tomogasima Suido, the channel between the Inland Sea and the Pacific.

We were with a vast flotilla of big ships going in and out from Kobe and Osaka. Swarms of fishing boats crisscrossed around us, independently pursuing their business of straining the sea with nets or trying to outsmart the fish with baited hooks.

May 28. 1300. 60 ships in sight. Mostly coasters and fishing vessels. One giant passenger ship, a tug pulling six barges, a large ferry, small cargo ships, and various tankers. I can feel the vibrations of fishing boat engines as I write. Incredible amounts of smoke and fumes stream skyward from the Wakayama steel mill and refinery complex to the east.

A little later Margaret called me on deck. "Look ahead," she said. "I see what looks like a breakwater with city buildings at the far end. I've plotted bearings of it but the chart shows open water."

We watched with interest. Half an hour later the breakwater and buildings turned into a vast white super tanker being maneuvered by tugs.

By nightfall we were in the Pacific and surrounded by red and green and white ship lights on all sides. We marveled that there were no collisions, but each helmsman watched carefully and sorted out the lights as they approached. Many of the Japanese fishing boats used bright floodlights to attract their prey. A row of the little ships blazed like a downtown street at carnival time. As we passed the individual boats we saw that each captain carried a green light over a white light to indicate that his trawl was down. The wind had been fitful, so we started our little Diesel to help us through the traffic. However, the vibration of the engine was severe and we shut it off. The engine mounts needed to be rebuilt entirely.

By dawn we were around the southernmost point of Honshu. The shipping traffic from the Inland Sea had fanned out and we were almost alone. We headed northeast along the east coast of the great Kii peninsula and by early afternoon glided into the steep and wooded shores of Kata Wan, where we followed a fish boat flying an enormous flag into a protected anchorage. We tied up stern to at the village of Miki.

The people of this remote village had never seen anything like us or our ship, and they were as delighted as children with a new toy. We tied the ship near the familiar iron chimney of the *o-furo*, but Miki was small and had the hot bath only three days a week. It wasn't long before we were invited to someone's home, where we scrubbed and soaked and then shared a meal of raw fish, octopus, tomatoes, and beer.

Soon after we sailed in, four beamy net-tending boats appeared. Each of the unpainted tenders was about forty feet long, weighed many tons, and was entirely handled by two men with sculling oars. All the crewmen wore large round straw hats with white towels wrapped around the brims. *Whisper* was in the docking space of the net tenders, but with a little pushing and shoving there was room enough for all.

The men put up awnings over the four boats and kindled a wood fire on the deck of one. They soon had tea and rice and raw fish before them. It was a wonderful scene. The chattering men in their straw hats. The cooking under the awning. Hawks circling overhead watching for bits of food. Ribald comments from one ship to another. The putt-putt of a passing boat. The sounds of children raking leaves and scraps of paper from the quay. The old man on shore recollecting his fishing days. . . .

I adjusted several tires for bumpers between the ships by slipping a clove hitch on one of the lines holding a tire. One man didn't know that knot. He distrusted it and insisted on adding two half hitches to each of my clove hitches. This amused his fellow fishermen as much as Margaret and I, and we all smiled. Then someone gave us fish for our dinner and another man passed a hose with fresh water to us.

Of the seventeen ports we visited in Japan we liked the village of Miki and its neighbor Kuki more than any others. Everything was new and novel and exciting.

We watched the busy fish market and learned that when a fish boat came in with a big flag flying it meant a huge catch. We looked over the shoulders of Japanese shipwrights while they hammered away on new wooden fishing ships. We took long walks in the lovely countryside. One morning the returning crew of a night fishing boat hailed us on board and we shared their breakfast of beer, raw squid, and *sake*, a powerful diet at 0700.

Even mailing letters was fun. Japanese stamps are beautiful and I hoped to put a variety of stamps of small denominations on each letter to my friends in America. But how to explain this? In Miki I opened the stamp tray of the postmistress and helped myself to stamps (while the whole staff watched with big eyes). When I had my letters checkered with a variety of bright colors I totaled up and pushed my yen across the counter. Suddenly one of the clerks understood that someone in America collected stamps. Smiles all around and chuckles of delight.

The day before we left, a Maritime Safety Agency Patrol launch came to check the strange foreign ship. Communication was difficult, but I dutifully filled out the papers which had questions in English and Japanese. The captain of the launch asked me to fill out a second set and then a third. I felt a bit harassed and I suppose my impatience showed.

Satisfied at last, the captain took the papers, bowed, and rushed to his launch. The crewmen started the engines, threw off the lines, and the ship started away. Suddenly it came back and the lines were tied up again. I watched as the captain jumped ashore and headed in my direction.

"Oh no," I thought. "Not more forms!" But the captain merely handed me a slip of paper on which he had laboriously printed in unfamiliar block letters: BON VOYAGE.

The trip to central Honshu took three days. Tokyo Bay was unsuitable for yachts, so we sailed to Aburatsubo in Sagami Wan, the next bay west. Aburatsubo was one of the main yachting centers in Japan and over 100 sailboats lay on moorings. Most were twenty-five feet in length because of the 40 percent tax on larger yachts. We tied alongside our friends Jens and Keiko Jensen, who lived on their thirty-two-foot gaff ketch *Tortuga*.

To get *Whisper* ready for the North Pacific I had three big jobs and many small ones. I took six of my eight sails to a Yokohama sailmaker to have a third row of stitching zigzagged along every seam. I had been using a jury-rigged port backstay since the anchoring misadventure in the Gilbert Islands, so I ordered a new backstay plus two new upper shrouds and one lower shroud, all of which had broken strands of wire. Jens Jensen and I removed *Whisper*'s engine with the main halyard and got a local shipwright to strengthen the mounts by adding immense specially welded angle irons which were through-bolted to the hull.

While I was busy with the ship, Margaret and Keiko Jensen bought many cases of stores and patiently tracked down the charts and *Pilot* books for the North Pacific.

These jobs often took us to Tokyo and Yokohama where we learned that patience and time are the requisites for Japanese shopping. Taxicabs are cheap in Japan, but the problem is the address, since houses and businesses are numbered according to when they were built. To go to a company you have a Japanese friend telephone ahead for instructions. Your friend then writes out the directions in Japanese, which you hand to the cab driver.

"O.K., O.K.," the cab driver would smile, his gold teeth glinting. He would pin the directions to the windshield with rubber suction cups, which left him only a narrow slit for forward vision. The driver would then pull on his white gloves, gun the engine, and we would lurch away ready for combat with traffic.

Japanese drivers pass on hills, around curves, and think nothing of swerving around big trucks and buses. Once a Japanese driver pulls out he never retreats. "Full speed now!" is his cry as he floors the accelerator. The only saving grace is that everyone drives alike and expects cars from all directions. When I would think a head-on collision was imminent, everyone would honk and squeeze aside just enough so that all would get through. "O.K., O.K. Plenty room," my driver would say, turning from his narrow slit to face me while he practiced his ten words of English.

A critical part of the directions was the telephone number of your target so that when your driver got lost he could telephone for additional help. ("Follow the double streetcar tracks until you come to the blue noodle factory. . . .")

The other terror of shopping is that the Japanese hate to say no ("Yes, I would not like another cup of coffee"). Often after you had arrived at a business house which had assured you by telephone that it had the tubing or wire or chart or whatever, you would be told (after a cup of tea and much time-wasting talk) that last year the Primus franchise was sold to a company on the other side of Tokyo. Or "Yes, we will have the parts in a few days as soon as the next shipment arrives from Sweden."

But the Japanese were kind and meant well. Sometimes a clerk would accompany me for hours while we went from store to store. When we finally got the part, the clerks would laugh with pleasure, a delight so genuine that you had to smile with them.

The day before we left for Hokkaido another cruising yacht came to Aburatsubo and we met Paul Hurst and his Filipino crewman Abraham Magpator. Paul had sailed from the Philippines in his sleek white-hulled Alden ketch *Staghound*.

When we headed north to Hokkaido we sailed offshore far enough to get outside of coastal shipping. The first night, however, we had plenty of company.

June 29. 2150. Seventy-seven fishing boats in sight, each with five powerful floodlights directed at the water. When we pass one of the ships we can feel the Diesel chugging away, hear the screeching

Japanese radio, and see the busy hands of the fishermen as they pluck the silvery fish from the lines as they are hauled in.

The passage north was slow. The 671 miles to Kushiro took eight days, generally with gray weather and fitful winds. At the start we were helped by the north-flowing Kuroshio current, whose temperature we measured every day and found to be 73 or 74 degrees. But by the time we had reached 41° N. we had left the warm current behind and were in the cold Oyashio current. The water temperature fell to 55 degrees, and under foggy skies and unused to the cold, I found myself wearing long underwear, two pairs of woolen socks, a heavy shirt and trousers, sweater, neck scarf, oilskins, sea boots, a winter coat, and two pairs of gloves. In July!

Along the southeast coast of Hokkaido we saw that the fishing boats were big and strong. The bulwarks, ground tackle, engines, and gear in general indicated severe conditions, and the way the men worked showed they were tough and rugged in these northern waters. None of the tissue-paper boats and frail crews of the Inland Sea in these waters.

We found Kushiro a raw, unfinished sort of place, a center for fishing, shipping, and paper- and plywood-making. Gray and colorless, the foggy bit of Hokkaido that we saw must be a frigid terror in winter. In every office and home was a giant stove. The windows were double, and when the stove fuel was wood I saw cord after cord of it piled high against the side of a house. The sidewalks of Kushiro always seemed to be under construction on both sides of the street at once, and with the taxicabs and trucks roaring along the narrow streets, walking was an exercise in survival. But the people were cheerful and friendly and the women seemed better dressed than anywhere else in Japan.

The Japanese fishermen are masters of the sea. In American Samoa we had watched their ships come in from the Pacific almost sinking under the weight of gleaming tuna, shiny blue wahoo, and whopping big-eye and yellowfin. In the Japanese ports we had looked at ships laden with bottom fish of every kind and with almost every edible crustacean known to man. The Japanese netted millions of tiny fish that were chopped into meal or made into paste.

A Japanese fishing vessel bound for the South Pacific had tied alongside us in Guam because of engine trouble. What was the first thing the men did? They all started fishing. "To see what fish are in this distant ocean." In a little village in Kyushu I had watched a shrimp specialist spend two hours baiting 100 tiny hand-made traps and then lower them to the bottom of the harbor in a *selected* place in a *selected* pattern at a *selected* time. Now in Kushiro a fisherman gave me four *ka-re*, delicious flatfish caught in gill nets set at forty meters. "Higher depth no good," said the fisherman. "Lower no good. Must be forty meters exact."

Fishing is a national passion in Japan. The people excel because they practice. They specialize. A father teaches his son and the skills go down the line of generations. "When I seek the tuna I become a tuna and I think like a tuna," an old man told me. The Japanese are not too hidebound to change, however, and they are often the first to adopt new machinery or an advanced technique.

A popular game in Hokkaido is indoor fishing. You buy a ticket and enter a room mostly taken up with a tank about thirty feet long, twelve feet wide, and four feet deep. The tank is filled with water dyed an opaque blue to keep the fishermen from too much success. You fish for goldfish (which you can keep) with a sliver of bamboo for a rod, a thread for a line, and a hook you can hardly see.

The tough fishermen of Hokkaido loved this game and on their days off would spend hours hunched over the opaque water staring at a red-and-white bobber the size of a pea while their buddies shouted encouragement and made jokes. Yet when the bobber went down, the fish came out. I like to think I am clever, but when I tried it I caught nothing.

On the day of our departure we secured our clearance for the Aleutian Islands and walked to the regional weather building. No one spoke any English and we were sent from office to office. Finally we got to a large room with dozens of small desks around the walls. At each desk sat a clerk with weather maps and one or two telephones. As the reports came in the charts were marked and sent to the chief forecaster, who sat surrounded by telephones at a huge desk in the center of the room. The desk was cluttered with weather charts, reports, clip boards jammed with statistics, and an ashtray full of cigarette butts.

The forecaster was a small, nervous, tired-looking fellow with deep lines in his face. Barometric pressure seemed to ooze from his skin. He had obviously worked up through the ranks and was responsible for storm warnings for thousands, perhaps millions of people. He was treated with vast respect and obeisance by his underlings, who approached him in a semi-bow as one might a king.

I explained that I was about to sail to the Aleutian Islands in a ship eleven meters long and—

He held up his hand. "You have come at the right time," he answered in excellent English. "My new forecast is ready now." He explained how weather information came to his office from ships all across the North Pacific.

Suddenly the telephone rang. The forecaster listened. Another phone rang. The inscrutable face of our friend collapsed into a horror of uncertainty. He slumped forward with his face in his hands.

"No use," he said. "All changed now. But for you going northeast, O.K. Winds ten knots from the west."

As we bowed, more telephones rang. We fled before we heard something bad. We hurried to the ship, cast off the lines, and left Japan.

16 / ~~~~~~

Are the Aleutians Cold?

WITH A SPRIG OF PINK CHERRY BLOSSOM LASHED TO THE headstay and a friendly hoot from an escorting Japanese customs launch, we left Kushiro and headed east across the North Pacific. The date was July 11. We wondered what was ahead.

The start was our poorest ever. We sailed out into four days of calms and fog off the southeast coast of Hokkaido. On the first day we did four miles—our all-time low. The following three days we had runs of fifty-six, twenty-five, and forty-seven miles, not much better. We heard the dim hum of fishing boats from time to time, but in the cottony mist around us their sound seemed to carry for miles and we didn't worry until the thump of their engines was quite loud.

Our last contact with Japan was one morning when six mackerel ships discovered us waiting for wind on the fog-shrouded sea and motored near us. I motioned that we would like a few fish. One ship maneuvered alongside on the calm water and a crewman passed us a tub with seven salted mackerel. We threw packs of American cigarettes across and soon the whole crew—in long underwear shirts and with towels tied around their foreheads—had lighted up and was smiling. We had a good look at one another, exchanged bows, and the ships moved off to continue fishing.

It was a small incident but one of the things that makes travel so worthwhile.

When we were becalmed it was important to pull in the rotator and its fifty-foot line which drove our distance-recording Walker's Log. Otherwise the rotator would sink and pull the line down, which would foul the rudder or the propeller. I had issued stern orders to *always* pull in the log line when becalmed or hove to. But when we lost our wind gradually, it was easy to forget. On my watch the log line got wrapped around the propeller. I took down the jib to stop the ship, stripped off my clothes, put on a face mask, jumped into the sea, and freed the line. I was only in the water half a minute or so, but the Oyashio was cold and I was soon gasping. Afterward I dried off and put on my warm clothes but I shivered for a long time and was a little sick.

A dark-brown seal appeared on the still water and followed the ship. He went faster than we sailed and was soon swimming in circles around *Whisper*, mocking our progress. Margaret translated a French magazine article and I spent an afternoon with a novel by Joyce Carey.

We saw a number of headfish, sometimes called ocean sunfish, gigantic relatives of puffers or porcupine fish, that swam just below the surface with a ragged black dorsal fin that knifed through the water like the fin of a shark. Only the fin flopped lazily from side to side. The headfish were strange creatures, perhaps from the age of dinosaurs, and seemed only the remnant head of a larger fish. Yet the heads—up to ten feet long—had fins and eyes and mouths and gills and swam around us curiously. We read in our fish book that their leathery skin was two inches thick and they weighed up to 2,000 pounds. The book added that headfish were not good to eat, but the fish were safe from me in any case, for the last thing I wanted aboard was a one-ton sea monster! The headfish showed no fear of us. We watched the great gray creatures with awe and wondered what else we would see if the ocean remained calm.

During the third night we got a light northeast wind, which increased with rain during the morning of July 14. By noon we had enough breeze to change to the number two working jib and to tie one reef in the main. The wind backed to the north, and at last we began to make good our course toward the northeast. We had been worried about being too close to the Japanese coast in case of an onshore gale, but with a run of 131 miles on July 15 we had a good offing. Laysun albatrosses, parasitic jaegers, and both Leach's petrels and fork-tailed petrels flew around the ship.

We had thought of visiting the Russian islands. However, we had neglected to ask permission at the Russian embassy in Tokyo. In addition, the Japanese Maritime Safety Agency officers in Kushiro strongly

advised us not to go to the Kuriles or to the Kamchatka peninsula. In spite of the warnings and lack of visas we were tempted when we saw several of the Kuriles dimly off to port. Our main reason for not stopping was the lack of time. The summer sailing season in the North Pacific was short and we had far to go.

On July 16 we passed a small Russian trawler and on the radio we heard Russian stations from Petropavlovsk and the Siberian mainland. The music was heavy and syncopated (often with soapy tenors) and the announcers were always women.

When we had planned our Pacific voyage we had three basic weather problems. The first was to avoid the South Pacific hurricane season. The second was to get away from Japan before the typhoons started in the late summer. The third was to miss extensive gales in the North Pacific.

We had worked past the first two problems and now we faced the third—to cross the North Pacific at the most favorable time.

The monthly *Pilot* charts indicated the average gale frequency for each five degree square of latitude and longitude, and we had spent a long time studying the little blue squares and their inset numbers. In

January—according to the charts—we would find gales up to 14 percent of the time. In February one square read 17 percent. April looked better, with only one reading of 10. June was mostly 1 and 2 with a maximum of 3. In the westernmost Aleutians the gale frequency rose to 5 percent in July and 7 percent in August, while most of the northern Pacific had 0, 1, 2, or 3. In September three squares had 8, and the percentages of gales increased sharply during the rest of the year.

Clearly we would have the most storm-free passage in midsummer. An easy July–August passage was tempered, however, by heavy summer fog, which ran from 30 to 40 percent south and west of the Aleutians to 10 percent in the Gulf of Alaska. In the vicinity of the Aleutians the sea temperature was about 45 degrees, and whenever a warm wind blew from the south, fog formed at once. Ice was not a problem.

We had already run into plenty of fog. It blocked the horizon and reduced visibility to a few hundred feet. Yet though it was thick it was not high, and often we could see blue sky if we looked overhead. Sometimes the fog rose as a body and we could see the horizon but no sky.

For celestial observations we needed both the sun (or another heavenly body) and the horizon at the same moment. The fog was a constant problem, however, except during the nights, which were sometimes clear. But when the sun rose it heated the air, which formed convection fog on the cold water. All in all we found that star sights at dawn were often our best chance for celestial observations.

We had unlimited sea room now and were north of the steamer lanes. The ocean was surprisingly calm, the barometer remained high (as much as 1022 millibars), and we made good daily runs. The winds were generally light, with a southerly component, and we carried a lot of sail area. We wore plenty of warm clothes and at night we often used the cabin heating stove. We were pleased with our progress although I wondered about a fog-bound landfall. We still had our wits about us, though, and lots of confidence.

Even if we arrived in thick fog there would be plenty of signs of land. We knew that the bird population was enormous in the Aleutians and that many birds flew out to sea to fish in the morning and returned to their nests in the afternoon. We would see kelp and seaweed on the ocean and could listen for the booming of waves on the rocks and the swish of the sea on the beaches. Large populations of seals and sea lions and sea otters lived in the Aleutians, and we would see them and hear their snorting and barking. The *Pilot* books spoke of strong tidal streams between the Pacific and Bering Sea, but we had read of various fog-bound ships that had been safely swept from one ocean to another by the currents, which sometimes ran swiftest in the deepest channels between the islands. We had no reason to doubt our excellent compass and we could sense a shoaling bottom by the difference in the feel of the swells. We had a good depth sounder to tell us the fine measurements when close to land, and we would certainly sail slowly if we approached in fog. The Aleutian land masses would tend to upset the sea winds and at some stage we ought to have a fog-clearing wind. And if we watched for the sun and horizon carefully there would be a few chances to fix our position.

In any case we had asked for adventure. Our undertaking was bold and exciting and I was anxious to press on.

As far as we knew we were the fifth yacht to sail from Japan to the American continent via the Aleutian islands. Five British naval officers pioneered the route in 1933 in *Tai-Mo-Shan*, a fifty-four-foot ketch that displaced twenty-four tons. The second was *Tzu Hang*, a forty-six-foot ketch (twenty-two Thames tons) owned by Miles and Beryl Smeeton, who with two others for crew sailed via the Aleutians in 1965. *Stormvogel* (seventy-three feet and forty-two tons) with six aboard made the trip in 1966. The American yacht *Awahnee* (fifty-three feet and twenty-four tons), owned by Bob and Nancy Griffith, together with three crewmen, crossed in 1967. *Whisper* was number five. She measured thirty-five feet and weighed six tons. But though she was the smallest, we like to think that she was the proudest.

On July 21 I got a good round of observations. "We're three hundred and eighty miles from Attu, the westernmost of the Aleutians," I said. "But Petropavlovsk on the Kamchatka peninsula is only three hundred and twenty miles away."

"I knew it! I knew it! *Whisper* wants to go to the Russian ports," cried Margaret, who secretly wanted to go too. "All these southerly winds and north-setting currents are trying to tell us something."

The next day remarkable clouds formed overhead. From the northeast to the southwest great horizontal bars of dark gray reached across the sky in colossal wavelike rollers as far as we could see. It was almost as if a gray-haired sea were upside down. The water temperature was 49 degrees now, and the weather had turned crisp. We were almost to 50° N. latitude and in the eastern sky the summer night began to turn pink and pale blue at 0200.

On July 23 the light southerly winds increased to gale force. We changed to a small jib and triple-reefed the mainsail. The sails were still too large, and solid water exploded on board, so we handed the main altogether. The seas got up, of course, but they had started over a calm ocean and were even and regular. The wind vane steered the ship perfectly and we stayed right on course with the jib pulling us at hull speed.

I stood in the companionway for hours with the hood of my winter coat around my head while I watched the gray seas push up from astern and rush forward, hissing as they passed the ship. *Whisper* rolled from side to side as she hurried along, while the vane, the ever-steady steering device, kept our heading true. I say "device" but surely the steering vane has a heart and soul, for how else could she hold the ship so firmly in her cord-bound grasp, safely steering the yacht in gale and calm, by moonlight and sunlight, day after day, mile after mile?

Three black-footed albatrosses flew round and round the ship, sometimes dropping behind the swell of a wave. Yet they never wet a wing. "Surely they are God's answer to perpetual motion," I said, as the thin seven-foot wings dipped and wheeled with scarcely a flap. We had last seen the dark profile of the squat brown bodies and the dusky, saberlike wings off the California coast. The birds seemed like old acquaintances.

By 0300 the next day the gale was over, more sails began to go up, and we slatted and rolled on a windless North Pacific. One might expect a gradually diminishing wind after a gale, but it seems that when a big wind is over, the curtain bangs down and there is little or nothing until the next scene opens some hours later.

July 24. 0700. Wind light. Hoisted genoa. Log line around rudder again. Spent two hours getting it free. Lashed small spinnaker pole and boathook together. No luck. Cursed log line finally freed by dropping a dinghy anchor over the side to pull the line down from the rudder. Stone-age sailing.

Yesterday the fog cleared a bit. I was asleep when Margaret saw a ray of sun. "Sun! Sun!" she shouted. I rushed on deck with a sextant and took a series of observations. After dinner I shot star sights of Deneb, Altair, Arcturus, and Polaris which gave us a good fix. Fierce headache from the eyestrain connected with the star sights and their arithmetic.

On the fifteenth day from Japan I climbed on deck at 0415, swathed in layers of clothes. The midnight fog had dispersed and the cold air was as clear as the lens of a telescope. The eastern sky glowed reddish in the dawn and I saw two islands to the northeast, more than forty miles away. We identified the long island with snowy mountains as

Attu, the westernmost of the Aleutians. It lay off to port. Agattu, dead ahead and smaller, was overlaid with a mushroom of thick fog.

If you were to put the point of a giant compass on the North Pole and swing an arc between the southernmost tip of the Alaskan mainland and the middle of the Kamchatka peninsula near the end of Russian Siberia, your curving line would follow the sweep of the Aleutian Islands. These fifty islands—depending on how many fragments you count—extend through 24½ degrees of longitude or 885 miles at 53 degrees N. latitude.

The Aleutians were discovered in 1741 by Vitus Bering, and the severe and cruel occupation by Russian freebooters that followed soon erased most of the native Aleuts together with practically all the fur seals and sea otters. The United States acquired the islands as part of the Alaska purchase in 1867. Dutch Harbor on Amaknak Island became an important transshipping center after the discovery of gold in 1898

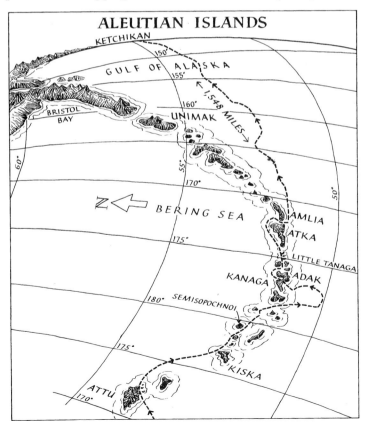

turned Nome into a boom town. In June 1942 the Japanese bombed Dutch Harbor and occupied Attu and Kiska as a diversionary action for events farther south in the Pacific. The United States launched a counterattack from bases that were established on Adak and Amchitka. In 1943, after bitter fighting, U.S. forces took Attu, and the Japanese withdrew from Kiska with the message, "It's all yours, Yank."[41]

Most of the American GIs who spent time in the Aleutians during World War II cursed the weather and isolation. A number of myths have grown from the experiences of the soldiers, and most people shudder at the mere mention of the name. The Aleutians are a land of ice and snow (false). The scenery is depressing and monotonous (false). The islands are a military outpost where poor Army recruits

resolutely march back and forth (false). Only Eskimos live there (false).

Margaret and I looked across twenty miles of sparkling Pacific to the bold skyline of Attu, topped by the flashing teeth of snowy mountains. The supporting land mass was a stony arctic blue, a heavy and powerful indigo, rather than the easy cobalt of the tropics. Even in the sun the ocean air had a chill to it and our gloves and wool caps felt good.

Birds flew everywhere now, especially large glaucous gulls with frosty white wingtips and pink feet, fork-tailed petrels, and murres. As we neared the southeast coast we saw thousands of tufted puffins. They had stocky black bodies a little over a foot long, bright orange-red bills, and tufts of white hanging down the backs of their heads as if it were time for the whole flock to go to the barbershop.

The puffins were truly the comedians of the sea. As we sailed along, the ship startled the young birds resting on the water and they attempted to take off. The puffins flopped and splashed and made a colossal commotion trying to get airborne. Some made it and then flapped madly a few inches above the water, their little wings drumming the crisp air. We stood on the foredeck and laughed as we watched. The puffins' ultimate defense was to dive just as the ship went over them. They would reappear far astern, shaking their clownlike heads as if to say, "You so and so."

Attu is thirty-five miles long and fifteen miles wide and uninhabited except for a thirty-two-man U.S. Coast Guard Loran station. The wind was light as we approached Massacre Bay, the best anchorage. Fog began to appear in the west. We took continuing bearings of principal points—all with unnerving names—and as we tacked past Murder Point under the shadow of Terrible Mountain at the western entrance, white mist swirled around us.

Margaret steered a careful compass course while I stood on the foredeck and we worked near several enormous tumbled-down World War II docks. The fog lifted a bit and we saw a U.S. flag above the main Coast Guard building. Through the glasses I watched a man disappear. In a moment the front door opened and a dozen men ran out. They jumped into a truck and speeded toward the rickety pier we were approaching. We handed the jib, dropped an anchor, veered fathoms and fathoms of chain, and as the ship swung we passed lines to the men on the pier.

"Where—where did you come from?" asked Lieutenant Martin

Hoppe, the commanding officer, as we furled the mainsail. "You suddenly appeared out of the fog. It was like a dream. We couldn't believe it. No one *ever* comes here. You are the first ship since the yearly supply vessel. Most of our food and goods come by air—uh, when the fog lifts," he said, motioning at the clammy mist.

"We left northern Japan fifteen days ago," I said. "We . . ."

"Come up to the building," chorused the men, "and tell us about it."

Our five-day stay on Attu was like a wonderful vacation. We were invited to take our meals with the men, who seemed always to be having steak. Margaret was the only woman on the island and she was treated royally. The area around the bay had been a military base for both Japanese and U.S. troops during World War II and there were hundreds of disintegrating buildings and Quonset huts and tons and tons of abandoned war goods. But over the first hill these rusting relics were largely gone. We visited inland lakes and plunging cascades and marveled at the steep, ice-carved Aleutian slopes that were so incredibly green, a solid and powerful green that seemed to represent a whole year's growth compressed into the short weeks of the northern summer. There was no tall growth, but we walked through waist-high wild flowers everywhere. Patches of fog alternated with the sun, which was warm and delightful. In the streams we caught Dolly Varden trout and along the shore of the bay we saw tens of thousands of silver salmon. Every cast brought in a big fish.

Reeves Aleutian Airlines had a monopoly on the least wanted air route in the world, and a DC-6 flew in mail, food, new men, gossip, and a stewardess (!). In theory the plane came every three or four days, but fog often canceled the flights week after week. When the plane finally arrived it was like Christmas.

There was a legend that dogs were needed on Attu (false), and whenever anyone wanted to get rid of a dog from Anchorage westward, he was put on the plane and sent to the last stop. The dogs were fed choice scraps from the kitchen and were soon sleek and fat. When we walked, the pack always came along, and a romp in the hills was good fun for all.

The morale at the Loran station was excellent. Most of the men were young recruits who treated their twelve-month tours on Attu as an adventure in the north and a lark. They were full of life and in their spare time were radio hams, beachcombers, photographers, fishermen, stamp collectors, and so forth. All were kind to us and curious about our trip, which we told about at length.

On July 31, with all thirty-two Coast Guard men waving goodbye, the dogs barking, and a gift of vegetables and frozen salmon in the galley, we headed east. Two small false killer whales crossed in front of us as we left Massacre Bay and sailed north around the island into the Bering Sea.

We wanted to visit an uninhabited island in the Aleutians but sheltered anchorages were rare. We finally decided to stop at Semisopochnoi in the Rat group, attracted by the jaw-breaking Russian name, which meant "seven extinct volcanoes." Although I was a bit wary, the three-day sail was a delight and we stayed on the northern, Bering Sea side of the Aleutians where the *U.S. Coast Pilot* said we would find better weather and less fog. We stood watch and watch, followed the compass carefully, and took celestial observations when we could. Fog was part of the scene, but it occurred in patches and often streamed above an island in high caps of white vapor. Or the fog billowed leeward in long horizontal teardrops with the bright sun behind. The differential in both temperature and wind velocity around the small islands made the fog a local condition and often it formed and disappeared before our eyes. As the sun heated a land mass it too influenced the fog.

The panorama of the islands to our south was a fluttering screen of changing weather. We used the hand-bearing compass together with vertical sextant angles to establish our position, and one by one we checked off the islands as we passed some ten to twenty miles to the north. At one time we had eleven small islands in sight. There was un-limited sea room to the north, west, and east, and if a prolonged north-erly gale arose we could run between the islands to the south.

We anchored in a bay on the eastern side of Semisopochnoi, well protected on three sides but open to the east. We buoyed the anchor, tied a reef in the mainsail, and as night fell we hanked on a storm jib. The next morning the barometer was high and the weather settled, so we went ashore.

No trees grow in the Aleutians, but the beaches were piled with thousands of logs and pieces of driftwood carried by the ocean cur-rents. We found glass floats from Japan and remnants of fish boxes with Russian markings. As we walked along the beach we heard a barking noise and turned to see a blue fox romping over the big logs. The fox looked and sounded like a small dog except for his magnificent bushy tail. He was as curious about us as we were of him, and we inspected each other for several minutes before he bounded off. Almost at once we saw a fox kit among the rocks and wood debris. Margaret picked up the little fellow and we marveled at his fluffy brown fur and endearing manner.

We kept an eye on *Whisper* and the weather and walked up on a ridge behind the beach, where we found a small, stoutly constructed building surrounded by waist-high grasses. The weather-worn structure was an Aleut fox trapper's cabin and probably dated from the late 1930s. It had been heated by a wood stove and we saw a pile of wood and a hand saw as if the trapper had just stepped outside. In back was a grave marked with a tall, weathered Russian Orthodox cross engraved with beautifully chiseled Cyrillic letters. You couldn't help but wonder who had lived in the cabin, what his story was, and who lay buried out in back.

The island measured ten miles across and we wanted to go to a small lake in the middle, but we found what looked like an easy walk to be a boggy swamp masked by tall grasses. It was both hard going and you needed hip boots. On the better drained shoreside ridges, however, we discovered the same wildflowers that we had seen on Attu—big bushes of blue lupine, clumps of golden paintbrush and purple irises, and sunny showers of yellow asters and daisies.

I found the land forms of the islands exciting. The slopes of high, snowy peaks plunged into ice-hollowed ridges of intense green. Reddish volcanic domes rose above lettuce-colored valleys. Sometimes you could look up precipitous avalanche slopes that climbed hundreds of feet above sea-dashed cliffs. With the trees entirely gone there was no softening of contours, and the general feeling was of new landscapes that had just emerged from the heart of the earth. It was only when you went over the land on foot at close hand that the birds and animals and plants and fish and streams and beaches eased the harsh impression you got from a distance. The changing light and cloud forms made the scene new every hour. Seals and sea lions and sea otters swam in the bays, and we watched colossal flights of birds so thick they were like smoke before a wind.

August 2. 1530. Away from Semisopochnoi with a light northerly wind and a warm sun. Three Japanese fishing trawlers nearby. Correct time and date unknown since we are astride the International Date Line. I am totally confused. Margaret has moved the clocks ahead two hours and decided that yesterday's date will remain today's. Just so tomorrow doesn't become yesterday!

At 2000 I was asleep and Margaret was reading. We were twenty-one miles east of Semisopochnoi, almost halfway to Gareloi Island. Suddenly I heard Margaret's voice.

"On deck! On deck!" she shouted.

I jumped up to see an enormous U.S. Coast Guard vessel almost alongside. Many of the crew lined her decks to look at the strange little sailboat in the Aleutians.

"Do you need any assistance?" boomed a voice from the bridge through a loud-hailer.

Margaret passed me the Aldis signaling lamp and I replied in Morse that we were quite O.K. As I flashed "thank you" the big white ship with its cheery red-and-blue bow stripe moved off. I later wrote to the master of the *Taney* and thanked him for his kindness and offer of help. That November we had a cordial letter of reply from Captain R. F. Young. The *Taney* was a 327-foot cutter built in 1937 and driven by steam turbines, which explained why Margaret had been caught unaware by the almost silent vessel when she slipped alongside.

It was still quite light at midnight and we had Gareloi Island in sight. The south-setting current had pushed us back into the Pacific and the northerly wind increased, so we handed the genoa and put up the small working jib. At 0200 we tied a reef in the main and paid

close attention to our course, for the Delarof Islands, a series of small islets and rocks, lay only seven miles to leeward and we were uncertain of our southern drift. By 0500 the tidal stream had begun to set toward the Bering Sea and the opposing, increasing wind kicked up severe, irregular seas over the mountainous bottom, which varied in depth from twenty-one to over 500 fathoms, according to our charts. It was light now and we took bearings of the southern points on Tanaga Island to check our position. The wind increased and the clouds lowered.

At 0900 we had three reefs in the main and the storm jib up. It was crucial to keep sailing eastward to pass the dangers to the south, but the force of the wind had the starboard deck entirely under water. The push of the seas from the north shoved us bodily to the south almost wave by wave. However, by 1030 I stopped steering because I judged that we had sufficient sea room so that the storm couldn't drive us among the rocks and shoals of the Delarof Islands. We then pulled down the storm jib and mainsail and hoisted the storm trysail. How easy it is to write what was such a struggle! Under the trysail, *Whisper* lay relatively quiet. No longer were we bashing across the seas but riding with them.

"The wind registers a steady forty-six knots on the Ventimeter," I noted, "and it takes a real hero to look to windward, because the spray feels like hot gravel."

August 3. 2215. The gale has stirred up a tempest above this shallow sea bottom and our cockleshell rolls and pitches like a tea leaf in a boiling pot. We lie huddled under a pile of blankets in the lee berth. I am astonished at the nastiness of the seas in the supposed lee of Tanaga.

During the afternoon Margaret went forward to secure a loose anchor. She came back choking from swallowing sea water and was very red in the face from wind-hurled spray. She has lots of pluck. Deck leaks fierce. Maddening to be stopped like this when our goal of Adak is so close.

The gale lasted twenty-four hours and afterward we found that under the storm trysail we had jogged along on a course of about 50 degrees to the north wind at a rate of one and a quarter knots while we made leeway of half a knot. In twenty-four hours we blew offshore some twelve miles and made roughly thirty miles of easting.

As usual, the gale ended as quickly as it began. We soon had more sail up, headed northward, and managed a sun sight through thin clouds. The barometer began to drop again as we picked up Kanaga Island. We hunted along the southeast coast for a protected bay mentioned in the *Pilot*, but the land was deeply indented and the rocks and kelp extended far offshore. I was hesitant about getting too close to shore in the rough water and foggy cliffs. We bore away for Adak Strait and by 2000 on August 4 we had two anchors down in the inner-most finger of Three Arm Bay on the uninhabited west shore of Adak. For the next two days we lay in this calm anchorage while gales whistled outside and fog howled down the mountains above us. It blew so hard I thought the wind would whisk away the green of the grass. Finally on the third day we sailed around the northern part of Adak to Sweeper Cove in Kuluk Bay, where the U.S. Navy had an airstrip and 5,000 sailors and civilians.

Contrary to our experiences with the Coast Guard, we found the people at the Navy base generally colorless. Adak was as starkly beautiful as the other Aleutians, but most of the Navy people and civilians we met seldom looked farther than the rim of a glass during their off-duty hours. They seemed to regard their northern duty as a jail sentence and spent a lot of time watching abysmal reruns of old television programs. There was an incredible number of automobiles for a place with scarcely any road system.

We called on the base commander, Captain Hubert Glenzer, who in turn visited us. Glenzer was also the local game warden and keen on sea otter management and Aleutian geology. We met Jim and Muriel Welte, two civilian workers who were old hands at world travel and who spent their spare hours hiking, identifying flowers, taking photographs, and studying correspondence courses. We also met Ken Van Horen, an officer who worked as a commercial halibut fisherman on the side and loved it. But these people, we felt, were out of the ordinary. It was the old story of well-adjusted people leading useful and productive lives while the complainers were bored and frustrated. The main business of the base was supposed to be military surveillance of the northern waters, but from what we saw, it seemed mostly a memorandum-passing game between dreary bureaucrats.

We sailed for Atka by way of Little Tanaga Island. We were in the Andreanof group now, in the middle of the Aleutian chain, and fog was often around us. We found it best to sail only by daylight and to go from point to point with our compass and elapsed mileage to guide us when the swirling mists descended.

However, on many days there was no fog and the air was so clear that we felt we could see all the way to the North Pole. On such a day we sailed past Great Sitkin and marveled at its 5,740-foot peak and nearby volcano which pushed a steady stream of smoke and ash into a sky of silk-ribbon blue. We could see the sun glinting on the snout of a glacier high on the main peak and a black rim of ash around the huge caldera lower down.

On foggy days our world was different, a constricted arena only a hundred yards wide. You stood at the front of the ship and peered into a thick shroud of gray. The fog was cold and wet and I felt thankful for the layers of wool and the oilskins and the thick gloves. My nose dripped like a leaky faucet.

I couldn't afford to daydream. The land was near and my eyes were all that stood between success and disaster. The only things I saw were fog and water, both featureless and unchanging. All at once three murres flew in front of the ship, their narrow wings beating in a whir. Then the silent hand of fog again. A few broken pieces of olive-green kelp appeared in the water and looked like enormous, water-soaked

noodles. The swells were smoother now. Certainly we were across the strait that separated Tagalak Island from Atka and were in the easier water behind Cape Kigun.

"A sea otter to port," called Margaret from her position at the helm. We saw a gray-whiskered otter leisurely paddle away on his back while he watched us closely.

"Depth," I called.

"Thirty-one fathoms," shouted Margaret after glancing at the dial of the echo sounder.

The fog was thicker now. I could see only seventy-five or a hundred feet. We continued to sail fast, too fast.

"Ease all sheets," I called. "Let the sails luff."

We passed more kelp and I watched for protruding rocks. Suddenly I saw something whiter than the gray of fog. The white was water breaking at the base of a rock or a cliff.

"Change course to 060 degrees," I shouted.

"060" came the response as the ship swung to port.

Now I could see cliffs and the shore of an island, certainly north-western Atka. The fog cleared higher up and mountains rose above the mist. I dashed aft for the hand-bearing compass, took bearings of every-thing in sight, and began to match the angles with the chart.

More murres flew past, along with puffins and guillemots. We saw otters paddling around and big patches of kelp appeared to starboard. I had calculated that we should be abeam of Bechevin Bay at 1803. But our speed across Atka Pass may have exceeded four knots. At 1753, ten minutes earlier, I saw the land close to starboard begin to fall away.

"Stand by to gybe," I called, hurrying aft to haul in the mainsheet. Margaret shoved the tiller to windward and we changed course to 170 degrees. As we headed almost south we passed high cliffs that I hoped led to Bechevin Bay. I looked for the gray bluffs of White Point men-tioned in the *Pilot*—and there they were. We followed the cliffs toward land, and the fog was suddenly less. The echo sounder read twenty-five fathoms, twenty, fifteen, ten, eight, five, and I let go the anchor and lots of chain. We were safe in a protected bay. Now let the fog and wind come.

We found the isolated Aleutian anchorages wild and exciting, a part of America that no one knows. Your footsteps pushed into untrod-den sand and in a few minutes you might discover a Japanese broom, a piece of Russian fish net, a coil of old rope, and the skeleton of a whale. The shore birds and foxes and sea otters scarcely noticed you, and where a stream entered a bay you walked over boulders and sandbars. Often the river bottom became the way across the land. The cliffs and hills above the beaches loomed enormous in the changing fog and the growth was thick and almost impenetrable, a green jungle of grasses up to your waist. It sometimes took half an hour to struggle up a small hill, and we soon learned to wear our oilskins when we went for a walk. The land was harsh but it had a fascination. The longer I stayed the more I liked it.

We headed for the Aleut village at Nazan Bay on the east coast of Atka. As we sailed past Korovin Volcano on the north point of the is-land, a great blast of wind—a williwaw—came hurtling down the black mountain. A moment before we had had all sail up and barely made two knots. Now the port deck disappeared under water.

"On deck," I shouted. Margaret hurried topsides from below. "Pull down the genoa." I kept the ship on course while Margaret clawed down armfuls of madly flapping Dacron. We were only a mile from land and the water was quite smooth in spite of surface whitecaps. But great torrents of icy wind thundered down on us. The port deck re-mained a boiling river.

"Never mind a small jib," I yelled, tossing the roller reefing handle at Margaret. "Reef the main."

Margaret quickly cranked the reefing gear and the mainsail got smaller and smaller. The wind shrieked louder, and with no jib and the mainsail area reduced by half we whished across the calm water mile after mile while we held our breath and marveled at the strength of the wind and the speed of the ship. Finally near Cape Shaw it began to get dark. It was too late to enter Nazan Bay, so we headed offshore until we got out of the big wind and hove to until morning.

At first light we sailed into the bay, slipped between two islets, and while rain brushed our faces and clouds swirled above the mast top, we rounded a low bluff. As I looked ahead a handful of gray houses and white and red buildings swept into view, a remarkable contrast to the firm green of the undulating hills.

We anchored in front of the village. Two Aleut teenagers in a pulling boat soon came out and told us to take the ship to the shelter of a small nearby island. We moved at once. A squally wind gusted at forty knots, so we veered all our chain for the main anchor and laid out a second anchor on a 200-foot warp.

Atka Village had eighteen families and a hundred residents. The Aleuts are short, dark, and muscular. Most have round faces, large eyes of a remarkable brown, and vague traces of Asiatic features. The men and children dressed in ordinary Western working clothes, often with boots and jackets and baseball caps from Sears, Roebuck. The women wore cotton dresses or slacks. Except for their stature the people might have been from a farming community in Iowa when viewed from a short distance. We soon learned that the Aleuts had little in common with the Eskimos who lived farther north and whose culture was materially different.

"Would you like to come in for a warm-up?"

The greeting came from Sally Snigaroff, a teenager who dashed up to us and led up the steep hill to her home. We were welcomed into the weatherbeaten frame house by Sally's mother, Clara Snigaroff, a stern-looking, thickset woman with a pleasant smile who held a big coffee pot into which she was rapidly spooning fresh coffee.

We talked with Mrs. Snigaroff about our trip and passed on news from Adak. We met her other daughter, Frances, and a son. Both the girls and the young man were about to leave for schooling on the mainland. The girls had a battery-driven phonograph going full blast with country and western songs and couldn't wait to show us their photograph album. Their father was away working on a commercial fishing boat.

Mrs. Snigaroff didn't quite understand where we had been on *Whisper*, but when we told her we planned to sail to the mainland she got very upset.

"The mainland from *here* in that little boat!" she cried. "That ocean is terrible. I'll worry a lot until you write me that you're safe." Mrs. Snigaroff jotted down her address and made us promise to send a letter.

Most of the houses we visited had little furniture. The principal item was a large coal or oil stove, generally the center of family life. Rows and rows of woolen stockings hung on nails or from string clotheslines above the stove. In a nearby sink sat the evening meal—a couple of salmon or a piece of caribou meat. Kerosene lamps furnished light.

We looked at the new red schoolhouse, a two-room affair up through the eighth grade that was modern, large, well designed, and impressively equipped. It was to replace a decrepit old building. The villagers hoped to have the new school ready for the fall semester. The almost completed quarters for a teacher from the mainland were commodious. A new generating plant chugged nearby, and half a dozen Aleut workmen scurried around with tools and equipment.

As we walked through the windswept village we often saw a face in a window watching us, a face that flashed out of sight when it saw

that we had noticed it. We visited different families and began to realize that the Aleuts were painfully shy. They were self-conscious about being Aleuts and greatly feared shame and ridicule. It was a pity, for when the Russians first traveled to the islands more than 200 years ago the fifty-odd islands had an Aleut population of perhaps 25,000. But the unbelievable cruelty brought by the Russians, together with those familiar footprints of the devil—smallpox, tuberculosis, typhus, syphilis, and influenza—destroyed these people who had had a remarkable and highly developed primitive culture related to their seaside existence. Agattu Island, our landfall in the Aleutians, for example, had had thirty-five native Aleut villages when the Russians first came. Now there were no villages and no people at all.[42]

The faces that we saw were the remnants of the Aleuts whose strain has been weakened by successive waves of hunters, fishermen, and soldiers. According to the 1960 census only 2,099 Aleutian Islanders have 25 percent or more Aleut ancestry. Even today their health is generally poor, and, because of inbreeding, dullness is a problem. With their old skills largely gone and a strong desire to copy mainland life, the villagers probably couldn't make it without government assistance, too much of which goes for drink, canned goods, and worthless U.S. junk.[43]

However, in spite of these dismal facts we saw lots of life and plenty of children in Atka Village. The green hills were wonderful for running and the kids charged up and down the slopes laughing and tumbling, their cheeks red and their yells shrill. The men brought in enormous halibut and heavy pieces of caribou. The teenagers appeared with salmon and trout, and everywhere we saw racks for drying reddish strips of smoked salmon. The people were clever with their hands, and Nadesta Golley, a bright-eyed young woman with beautiful long hair, let me see a small basket she was weaving from fine grasses.

Her father, Sergius Golley, showed us the Russian Orthodox church with its two green balloon-shaped domes on top of a neat, white wooden structure. The inside was white too, with carefully painted blue diamonds and squares around the altar area. Sergius, who was seventy-four and one of the village leaders, read a few lines from the big Russian Bible. During services the interior was lighted by a large brass candelabra that held two dozen candles. There were no seats or pews. Everyone stood for the infrequent services when a priest came from Unalaska.

The Aleuts speak a language akin to Eskimo. The sound was unique to me and totally indescribable. The word for "hello," for example, is *du-lù-maqx*. "Thank you" is *kaxgasikuq*. "Come again" is *akaqdali-daq*.

The people were astonished at our interest and delighted to teach us a few words, though they roared at our fumbling pronunciations.

Shortly before we left Atka three teenagers came out to *Whisper* for a visit and brought us a piece of halibut. Edward Nevzoroff, Ronald Snigaroff, and Frank Snigaroff sat around eating cookies and examining a chart of their island. Frank was a smart lad and about to leave for an Indian school in Oklahoma, where he hoped to learn to be an automobile mechanic.

"Will you come back?" I asked. "Do people come back?"

"No," answered Frank. "They don't come back 'cause there's nothin' to do here. They just keep goin' . . . nothin' to do here but hunt, fish, and camp."

The Aleuts often went camping during the summer. They fished and hunted and gathered edible seaweed, shore plants, and shellfish— perhaps as they had in the old days. There was lots of driftwood for fires and in good weather the climate was mild. Margaret and I went to several of these camps, where we were given shells and a few late flowers.

"What do you see here on Atka?" I asked Clara Snigaroff at her family camp one day. "The life is hard and there's no future. You say you've forgotten much of the Aleut lore, and the old customs are dying."

"I know," she said. "But this is my land and I love it. This year the wildflowers came early and they were so lovely. We had fresh bouquets every day for a month."

Clara's eyes lighted up as she spoke, and she touched a tall stalk of grass with affection.

"The young ones go," she said, "but I want to stay. My heart would break if I left."

17 / 〜〜〜〜〜〜〜〜〜〜〜〜〜〜〜〜〜〜〜〜〜〜〜〜〜

Gales, Totems, and Eagles

WITH HALF A DOZEN SLEEK KILLER WHALES DIVING AND spouting around the ship, we sailed from Atka and headed south across Amlia Pass. The winds blew lightly from the east and we glided along the uncharted south shore of Amlia Island, whose mountainous skyline looked like a fairy's dream in the hazy sunlight of the golden afternoon. I had laid out a course across the Gulf of Alaska, and as we headed roughly eastward from the center of the Aleutians we began to leave the islands as they curved northeastward.

The pleasant weather didn't last.

August 20. 2110. Three hard days. Weather black and nasty and a southwest wind up to 40 knots. Enormous seas, large enough so that the vane is powerless and humans are powerless too. We started out with the genoa and full mainsail. Then one reef and the #2 working jib. Next two reefs in the main together with the storm jib. This was followed by the storm jib alone, and then bare poles. The last, bare poles, does not work for Whisper. *Too much windage aft and the ship gets pushed around and drifts sideways with the rudder useless. In any case we lay a-hull for seven hours today.*

With no sails the motion was horrible. I fixed a torn batten pocket on the mainsail and repaired a broken part on the steering vane. Finally at 1400 today I got the trysail up after a struggle but afterwards I was so tired I could only sit in the cockpit and steer weakly.

Margaret hoisted the tiny #3 storm jib which got the ship going again and later we hooked up the vane. Now we are making three or four knots with somewhat better motion since the seas are more regular. (Actually the ride is still pretty wild but compared to what it was, the ship seems positively comfortable!) Wind southwest at 32 knots. The ship is a shambles below, a jumble of oilskins, bedding, books, cooking pots, charts, and you-name-it.

When we ran into these severe seas I got violently ill, the sickest I have been on the whole trip. This coupled with two sleepless nights and the grim motion along with many sail changes took all my strength. Never have I been so feeble. Tonight I finally ate a hot meal, had a two-hour nap, and feel much better.

By midnight the following night the gale had blown out and we were becalmed on a windless, lumpy sea.

We were headed for Ketchikan in southeast Alaska by way of Dixon Entrance, the twenty-five-mile strait between Alaska and Canada that opens into an island-studded archipelago that runs northwest above Vancouver Island for 560 miles. The center of Dixon Entrance was at 54° 28′ N., so our course was 84° T., a little north of east. The distance from Amlia Pass in the Aleutians to the seaward side of Dixon Entrance on the mainland was 1,548 miles. We hoped to make the crossing in two weeks.

After a day of light westerly winds the breeze backed to the southwest and stiffened into a gale again. We stripped *Whisper* down to storm canvas and whished to the east with nasty-looking seas curling up astern. We found the gales in the Gulf of Alaska to be of short duration and rapidly moving. The pointer of the barometer marched up and down with alarming jumps as the storms tracked their way across this northern corner of the Pacific. The wind veered when the eastward-moving depressions went north of the ship and backed when they passed south of us.

The second gale lasted the eighth and ninth days of the passage and then eased off with the wind out of the west. Though both gales had been from the southwest, we found that we had been set far to the south and at one time I thought of squaring away for San Francisco. However, we continued pushing north and east. By noon on the tenth day we had made 750 miles and had about 800 to go.

One dark night we were changing a headsail with the spreader lights on when a small gray bird suddenly fluttered to the deck at our feet. I picked him up and stroked his soft, high-domed head. He seemed quite content to rest, so when we finished with the sail we carried the bird

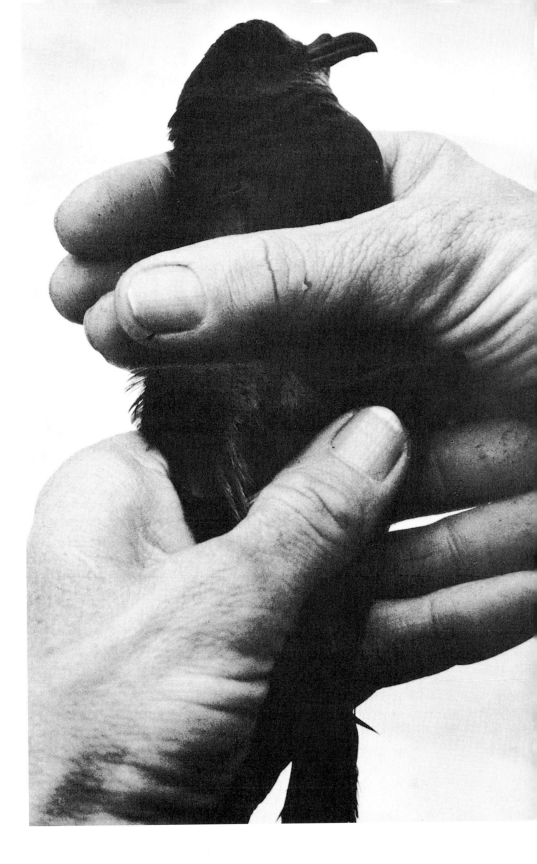

below for a good look. He was entirely dark gray except for a patch of white near the end of the top of his tail. His long, jointed legs and black webbed feet were not made for land use at all, and when he walked he had to help himself along with a wing for a crutch. His bill was slender and hooked and had nostrils on top in a tube. His eyes were two dots of bright black.

Margaret had the bird books. "How long are his wings?" she asked.

I opened one wing and measured it. "Five and a half inches," I said. "The tip is pointed and swept back," I added, feeling that at last I couldn't miss an identification.

"Is his tail notched?"

"A deep V-notch."

"A Leach's storm petrel," said Margaret. "Sailors know them as Mother Carey's chickens."

Margaret put the bird in a cardboard box, but he didn't like it and spent the night under the saloon table. The next morning we photographed him and he peeped a little while we held him. Margaret then tossed him into the air and he raced off, diving and skittering a few feet above the wave tops.

I felt I knew a storm petrel well after our interview, and I often saw several of the little soft-gray fellows flitting over the sea, especially when the weather was stormy and the seas were disturbed. I might be kneeling on the foredeck, encased in oilskins, with my safety harness clipped to a piece of rigging, and be stuffing a sail into a bag, when I would hear a quiet squeak. There in front of me would be two storm petrels dancing and diving like joyous butterflies just above the wave tops. Whenever I saw the birds I felt I was no longer alone. I had company, lively company, and we shared our ocean world together.

Margaret did wonders with meals and I never regretted the lack of refrigeration. We went the extreme from munching a few dry crackers during gales to elaborate dinners when the weather was reasonable. One memorable night Margaret handed me a warm plate with crispy pieces of golden fried chicken, sauteed Maine potatoes, and well-buttered Japanese corn—all from cans. Dessert was New Zealand peaches and cream (two more cans) plus almond cookies followed by many cups of lapsang souchong tea. But usually the meals were simpler. Our two-burner kerosene Primus stove worked well, although sometimes the motion of the ship made the stove swing so violently in its gimbals that we had to lash it down. Then we missed the stove sorely, for its top was always level and the only place where a hot cup or pot could be left unguarded for a few minutes.

August 27. 0145. The night is black and a two-foot-wide stream of phosphorescence glows behind us as we hurry along and leave a luminous path. The log line is a glowing bluish thread afire on the dark sea. The air is dry and the deck does not run with condensation which is unusual. At sunset last night the sky was layered with clouds. . . .

The barometer had begun a dance downward and the wind backed from the west to the south to the east, indicating that the center of a depression was moving south of us. In twelve hours the barometer fell from 1013 millibars to 1001, and we went through the usual sail drill and wound up hove to under the storm trysail as the wind increased to a steady forty-five knots from the northeast. By late afternoon the barometer had plunged to 993 mb., the drone in the rigging had become a remarkable hum, and the storm trysail was clearly too much for the ship, which lay with the starboard deckhouse ports entirely under water. Spray and scud grayed out the windward ports and the ship below was plunged into aquarium darkness. (I thought of Vito Dumas and the canvas he carried over his deckhouse.) The bend in the mast from the strain of the trysail was scary. How I wished for running backstays and a lower headstay to brace the mast!

If a big ship had passed us 100 feet away I think we would have been invisible, half submerged in the hiss of spray and sea.

I could have handed the trysail, but I hoped to keep a little canvas up to preserve life down below. After some thought we took down the trysail and hoisted the mainsail which flapped madly in the strong wind. I then quickly rolled the boom fourteen turns with the roller reefing gear, lashed the handle in place, and hauled in the mainsheet. With only the top twelve feet of the mainsail showing—half the trysail area—we lay reasonably well about six or seven points off the wind.

The seas that streamed toward the southwest were large and surprisingly even, for the wind seemed to have blown away much of the crests. The horizon was gone and the ocean and clouds had melted into a single element, a substance that was new to us. If you darted a glance to windward you saw only gray-white patches and streaks of dense foam in the moment before your eyes were stung with salt. As the hours went by we became aware of a tempest that was chilling in its intensity and fundamental in its violence. We learned that the heart of the storm gave the sea a rolling, thundering motion, and our tiny ship staggered as she heeled to the shocks that snapped through the water.

Just before dark Margaret pumped the bilge and captured the end of a spinnaker pole topping lift that had escaped. I prepared some tools

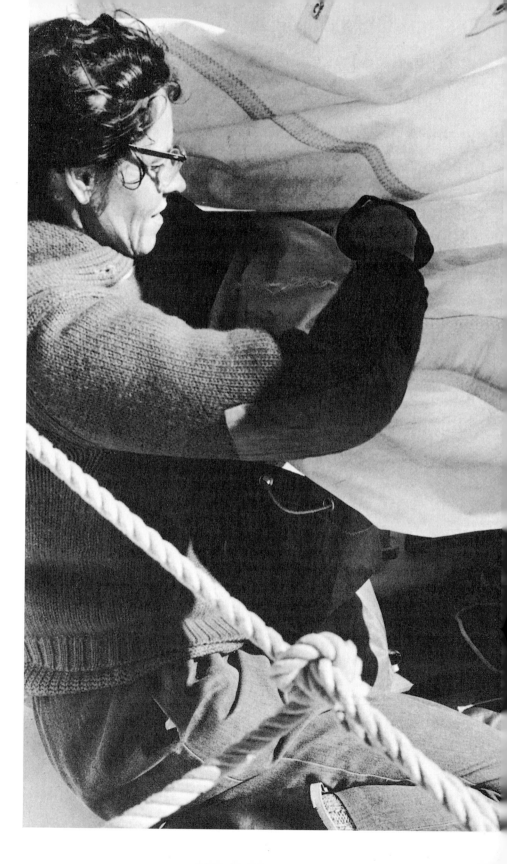

and pieces of stout plywood in case one of the cabin ports got broken. We had done what we could and retired to the lee berth, where we napped, read a little, and played nonsense word games. I fell asleep trying to think of a river that began with Q.

On the morning of the twelfth day of the passage I awoke to hear the wind much less, but I missed the sound of the steering vane, which made a slight clatter from time to time.

"The vane's gone," I said to Margaret when I looked out. "From now on we'll have to steer by hand." The gale had snapped the one inch stainless steel shaft and we lost the wind blade that had steered us so faithfully for 16,530 miles. I had a spare blade, but I never thought the shaft would break.

As the wind went down and the barometer climbed we got under way again, missing the help of the vane. We took turns steering, four hours on and four hours off.

The sea was vile after the great storm. Without the drive of the wind, the water tumbled and fell every which way. Cross-seas smacked against one another, and instead of a regular, oscillating, predictable motion, the feeling on board the ship was like going up in an elevator during an earthquake. A steady rising motion was interrupted by a sudden sideways push. Then the bottom dropped out and the ship plunged into a pit where the sea no longer was. The ocean was a huge rock quarry, and the ship kept falling into abandoned holes.

We had become so accustomed to the help of the steering vane that guiding the ship by hand soon became a bore. It was a cold, wet business in spite of thick clothes. Since we were still 580 miles offshore, I put blocks on the lifelines outboard of the tiller on each side and led steering lines from the tiller below deck. We then remounted the compass on the forward side of the bulkhead aft of the port settee and zing! We had a warm, inside steering position. True, our movements were backward and the helmsman sat facing aft, but you soon got used to the reversed steering.

We pushed to the northeast and gradually got closer to the Alaskan coast, changing a sail now and then and heaving to when the wind freshened from ahead. On the fourteenth day we had a fair westerly wind, so we took down the mainsail and poled out a jib on both the port and starboard sides. We led the sheets to the tiller and got the ship to steer herself for forty-one hours. The icy rain squalls stopped, the weather warmed up, and we opened the hatches for a great airing and drying out. Jaegers and black-footed albatrosses circled the ship, and with clear skies and reasonable seas we determined the ship's position each morning and afternoon. On the seventeenth day our radio picked up a fine Mozart piano concerto from CBC, Vancouver.

September 3. 1145. Because of a wind change, Margaret called me to gybe the running sails. We finished and while I steered for a moment she went aft to free the log line which had gotten around the self-steering gear. She then accidentally put her left hand into the mechanism of the powerful vane gear, which, routinely swinging, crushed her hand and particularly her third finger. Suddenly I saw 1½" of bone, alarming in its whiteness, and blood everywhere, the red violent against the hard yellow of Margaret's oilskins. We managed to piece together the flaps of bloody skin across the wound by using sterile butterfly bandages. Then we bound up all the fingers. I gave the patient a codeine pill, cleaned the blood out of the cockpit, and took a slug of brandy for my shot nerves. Margaret took it all very calmly.

We were within twenty-five miles of land, and during the afternoon a fishing trawler appeared south of us. Toward evening, fog thickened around the ship, so we hove to for the night, each of us keeping a look-

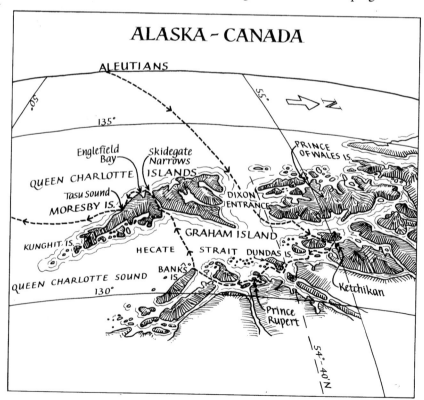

out in turn. The next morning we continued eastward, and as the sun rose the fog dispersed. At 0718 a longitude sight put us seven miles west of tiny Langara Island, at the north end of Queen Charlotte Island, and I suspected we were over Learmonth Bank, because the sea had a different feel to it and we saw fish and birds and large tangles of floating kelp.

"I see a blue swell of land off the starboard bow," Margaret announced at eight o'clock. "At first I thought it was more clouds, but what I see is stationary and solid."

Our longitude was no problem. We knew we were at the west coast of America, but we wanted to be very sure of our north-south position in case an onshore storm came up. At 0942 the position line from a second sun sight angled through Dixon Entrance, and as a wonderful landscape of bluish clouds lifted, a complex of land forms unfolded around us.

I thought back to the scenery of Japan, which, though adequate and sometimes splendid, was often shrouded in grays. Japan's landscapes had seemed as diminutive as her people, lovely but on a modest scale. The Aleutians were isolated volcanic remnants, carpeted lushly in green for the few months of summer, but essentially austere and harsh. However, the landscapes of southeast Alaska and northwest British Columbia now on all sides of us were totally big and powerful. Islands and capes and high mountains and promontories climbed above the ship on every side. We saw row upon row of hills and spurs and ridges, all on a grand scale and all forested with tens of thousands of tall and untouched conifers. We glided along calm expanses of water cut on three sides by a giant country that seemed to climb to the sky. The air was clear and we felt we could see until the limit of vision dimmed our fancy.

The earthy smell of the land was good, and the fragrance from the trees almost brought tears to our eyes. We sailed past Dall Island, headed north up Clarence Strait, and anchored in the first good bay on Prince Charles Island. Gardner Bay was completely protected from the sea, and after our crossing from Atka we slept the sleep of the dead for a day and a night to recover from the exertion of the long sail. During the nineteen-day passage we had changed headsails and reefed and unreefed the mainsail sixty-one times. We had been becalmed on three occasions for a total of twenty-three hours. We hove to five times for a total of fifty-three hours.

The principal town of southeast Alaska is Ketchikan, a haphazard collection of gimcrack houses that clings precariously to the steep southwest slope of Revillagegedo Island a few miles north of the Canadian border. The entire town of 8,000 looks as if it is ready to slide down the slope of Deer Mountain into the still waters of a tree-lined strait named Tongass Narrows. Ketchikan is about seventy miles from the Pacific and is a free-spending frontier town that lives on logging and fishing and summertime tourism. The people make vast wages, but they pay colossal prices for everything, so they are about even in spite of the flamboyant economy.

It was a busy place. Most of the transport was by air, and as we approached, our ears droned with the distant hum of jets and the nearby snort of float-equipped lightplanes, waddling amphibians, and spidery helicopters. We tied up next to the Coast Guard cutter *Cape Romain*, whose crew helped us find a doctor who took charge of Margaret's injured hand.

On the first night we thought we would eat in Ketchikan.

"Excuse me," I said to a fisherman. "Can you suggest a restaurant?"

"Well, stranger, there's no place real good, but you can try the Elks Club."

We weren't members, but the man kindly introduced us at the club, where we were led to a table and given menus engraved on thin planks.

"Why don't you have the special?" suggested the waitress, pouring water. "It's only eight-fifty each and you get—"

Seventeen dollars! We swallowed our pride and walked out. During much of our trip we had spent $50 a month for everything.

The next morning Margaret tried to buy short lengths of wool to darn our stockings.

"Oh, we don't have anything like that up here," said the woman in the store. "If people get a hole in their stockings they throw them away."

We got acquainted with the men of the Coast Guard on the *Cape Romain*, who were keen to see the yacht ("Imagine coming from the Aleutians in this!"). Chief Bosun's Mate Dick Benson helped me repair the wind vane. Quartermaster George Porter fixed us up with charts, and the skipper, Jake Jacoby, gave us a tour of Ketchikan. George Porter was a great moose hunter and every November he shot a huge animal that furnished meat throughout the year for his family. Mrs. Porter gave us a big piece of the frozen meat and we had moose roast,

moose steaks, mooseburgers, mooseballs and spaghetti, moose hash, and finally moose soup!

The area was the center of salmon fishing, and every summer hundreds of big purse seiners—worth up to $120,000 each—chugged north to Ketchikan from the state of Washington. The salmon ran thick and heavy and the fishermen made lots of money, often $3,500 for ten weeks' work. The fish boats were stout and husky, with a whopping Diesel, and generally carried a crew of eleven who worked on a share basis. Many of the purse seiners flew a broom at the starboard mast spreader to indicate that the ship had taken 100,000 salmon worth ten to twenty-five cents per pound at the cannery. We got to know some of the fishermen, ate on various purse seiners, and soon realized that most of the money the fishermen earned wound up in the pockets of the owners of the saloons and bars which lined the short, roisterous streets of Ketchikan.

A typical fisherman was Al Orton, the cook on the *Mary Elizabeth B*. Al was an amusing, chatty fellow in his fifties, very bright and friendly, and only slightly sad that he no longer worked as a lawyer.

He had run a collection agency, among other things, and over several glasses of wine he told us about the business.

"An American values his car more than his wife, children, or house," said Al. "If you threaten to repossess his automobile he will sign anything, especially if you rouse him at 0500 and confront him with a document and a sheriff."

Al's stories never stopped: "One day we were out seining and I was on my way back to the galley from the food storage box on deck. I planned to make corned-beef hash for lunch, and in addition to the meat I carried a large green bell pepper, a tall bunch of crisp celery, and several onions.

"The skipper stopped me," said Al.

" 'Say,' he said, 'I don't care for green peppers. Leave them out of the noon meal, will you?'

"O.K.," said Al, and he tossed the green pepper over the side.

"One of the crewmen spoke up. 'I'm not much on celery,' he said. 'The strings get in my teeth. Don't put celery in the corned beef.'

The cook nodded and threw the celery into the water.

" 'Oh, I can't eat onions,' said another man. 'They make my breath bad. No onions, please.'

"All right," said Al, and he heaved the onions into the sea. "The hell with you guys," he roared. "I won't eat corned-beef hash without green peppers, without celery, and without onions." He threw the meat over the side. "You can all go hungry until supper."

Our new friends urged us to look at the totem poles which were unique to southeast Alaska and western British Columbia. We went to parks at nearby Saxon and at Mud Bight, where we saw dozens of these remarkable carvings, some of which were sixty feet high. The poles were sculptured with ravens, bears, fish, owls, frogs, humans, and so forth, cleverly carved around the outside of each log. The totems had been collected from deserted villages and restored by the U.S. Forest Service with the help of Tlingit and Haida Indian carvers, who repaired and painted and in many cases entirely made anew the tall cedar logs whose strange forms sparkled with bright blues and reds and yellows. Each pole illustrated a legend, and the topmost figure symbolized the clan that owned the totem. The interpretation of the poles and legends was complex, but even with no knowledge of the individual myths we found the totems amazing to inspect. We heard that modern Indian craftsmen often carved with chain saws and used cans of spray paint, which seemed a bit disappointing but inevitable, I suppose.[44]

A few days later we sailed southward from Ketchikan and anchored at Village Island, almost on the Alaskan–Canadian border. A century ago this tiny islet was home for a tribe of Tongass Ravens who drew their canoes up on the sandy beaches, perhaps with freshly killed deer from the mainland and salmon ready for smoking. Today, however, the Indians were gone and their canoes and dwellings had vanished. Yet their totem poles remained, now largely rotten, with many taken away, and the rest grown over with scrub and trees.

The carvings we saw in their original environment on Village Island had a wonderful primitive quality about them. We looked at images that had a feeling of agelessness, of simplicity, of depth, of power, properties the modern totem poles lacked. The figures reminded us of the carvings we had seen in the Marquesas Islands and in photographs of statuary on Easter Island. Without paint, splitting apart, rotten, and vandalized, the remnant totem poles were superior in every way to the recent work we saw near Ketchikan—in spite of the chain saws and the cans of spray paint.

Sailing in the archipelago along the northern west coast was a new experience. We anchored every night and traded the sextant and *Nautical Almanac* for a hand-bearing compass and binoculars. We sailed from point to point and rejoiced in the superb charts, first-class navigational aids, and protected waters. The air was clear and the scenery grand. I would trade all the scenery in Japan for one bay in Alaska.

Logging was big business along the coast, and as we crossed into Canadian waters we often passed tugs that were pulling enormous rafts of logs toward pulp and lumber mills. A few of the logs escaped and were very dangerous, so we sailed only during the day when we were able to keep a lookout for these deadly battering rams, many of which were half again as long as the yacht.

September 19. 0830. This morning we got under way before dawn because wind commenced to blow into our anchorage near Dundas Island and we were poorly anchored in rocks. When I came on deck in the black night the stars were as crisp as new snow on a zero morning and I was glad I had pulled on long underwear and had my heavy coat tightly around me. The fragrance from the fir, spruce, and cedar forests was enchanting in the cold air. Margaret put up the main and jib while I shortened the chain. She then steered and handled the sheets while I broke out the anchor and we began to make short tacks toward the Green Island light.

There was no point in two of us being on deck, so when our position relative to the north wind improved, I sent Margaret back to bed. The wind was 15 knots or so with a short chop, and I was busy with the tiller, adjusting sheets, and making sure that I was away from Whitesand Islet, a place bordered with rocks.

Red-streaked fingers of dawn filtered over the dark-blue mountains that ringed the scene above the black water. Scattered clouds and fog banks lay balanced above the sea in the distance, and far away the bases of the taller mountains were hidden, making their blue-black summits appear like islands in the sky. The water had a surprising tumble, yet when I looked below I saw Margaret sound asleep with only her nose and unfurrowed forehead showing from beneath a pile of blue blankets. How peaceful she looked.

I thought of the kindness of the men of the Coast Guard in Attu and Ketchikan. Surely if I had military service to do again I would choose the Coast Guard. Not only is it a small organization with superb esprit de corps but its work is worthwhile. You help someone instead of trying to destroy him.

We headed into Prince Rupert by way of Venn Passage, a narrow backdoor channel. I had worked out the bearings and headings beforehand, and I sat on the mast spreaders with a chart and a hand-bearing compass directing Margaret. The day had become warm and sunny, the wind light, and as we glided through the riverlike passage with grasses and shrubs and trees around us, Indians from the village of Metlakatla came from their houses to watch us.

Prince Rupert, the western terminus of the Canadian National Railway and home of a large cold-storage plant for fish, had a population of 12,000 and a splendid position on a bluff on the south side of a fine protected bay, large enough for all the ships of Canada. But Prince Rupert seemed a town that time had forgotten. The buildings dated from the 1920s and I felt that nothing much had happened since in spite of the hopes of stockbrokers and the promises of politicians for a new gateway to the Orient.

We discovered that the fuel barges of the big oil companies had laundry machines, dryers, a kitchen, hot coffee on tap, and first-class showers, toilets, and washbasins for both men and women. All were free if you bought fuel, so we filled our tanks, although I felt foolish buying only four gallons of Diesel oil and nine gallons of kerosene.

The Prince Rupert chart agents had poor stocks of Canadian charts and we were obliged to ask various fishing-boat captains whether we could buy any extra numbers they had. We got several charts from Sergeant Lorne Musclow, the skipper of the blue-hulled *Nanaimo*, a Royal Canadian Mounted Police patrol ship.

"Do you jig?" asked Lorne.

"Beg your pardon?"

"Do you jig?"

"Fox trot a little."

"No, no," laughed Lorne. "Do you fish for cod and snapper with a jigging lure?"

"You'd better tell me about jigging," I said.

"You use a heavy Norwegian lure about six inches long," said Lorne. "It's shiny with treble hooks and you stop over a good ten or twelve fathom patch and lower the lure to the bottom and then heave hard on it three or four times. If there are any fish around they will strike at once. If nothing happens you move on. You need spend only two or three minutes in a place to catch dinner in a hurry."

We bought a jigging lure at once, which we used with signal success thereafter, blessing Lorne each time we bit into fresh red snapper or ling cod.

The day before we left Prince Rupert we were astonished to see the Australian yacht *Calypso*, which we had tied next to in Tahiti more than a year earlier. Florence and Ron Mitchell and their son Ronald had sailed their thirty-foot Tahiti ketch to Hawaii and then to Sitka, Alaska.

"We worked up the coast to sixty degrees north and saw glorious scenery—especially in Glacier Bay," said Florence. "We caught halibut and salmon and crabs, gathered clams and abalone, and picked five kinds of wild berries. We made friends everywhere, and they almost sank the ship with kindness and gifts of meat from moose and elk and deer and caribou.

"When we sailed into Juneau, the governor personally welcomed us," said Florence. "No amount of money could have bought a happier or more exciting summer, yet we hardly spent anything at all, except a smile, a handshake, a helping hand once in a while, and the simple story of our trip."

Our friends in *Calypso* headed south while we sailed west to the Queen Charlotte Islands. It was now the end of September and time for southeast gales. We had heard many stories of fish boat disasters in Hecate Strait, the fifty-mile channel between the mainland and the Queen Charlotte Islands. Hecate Strait was shallow, the tides ran strongly, and a southeast gale against an opposing tide over the shoals could raise a maelstrom that was death for small vessels. The fishermen knew this well and never crossed the strait unless the weather was clear.

We stopped at Larsen Harbor at the north end of Banks Island, where we lay with half a dozen small gill net fishing boats that had been stormbound for five days. It had blown so hard the day before that the fish boat we rafted with had had one of its wheelhouse windows blown out. However, the weather improved and the next day we all left, the gill netters traveling together in case one had an engine failure.

The fifty-five-mile crossing was easy, although the sun had an evil-looking ring around it. We passed many patches of tangled kelp on the surface, while above us we watched dozens of geese and large, long-necked birds, white below and black above, that we later identified as western grebes. The wind was light and we didn't sight the dim outline of land until 1730. At that time the depth of the water was only thirteen fathoms and the sea sounded like a river, gurgling and chuckling in the shoal depths. We were headed for a small place named Queen Charlotte City, but the entrance was obscured by an enormous sandbar whose pass was many miles to the north.

The night was black and it began to rain hard and to blow from the southeast. We felt our way through the pass into the shelter of the bar, but the buoys and lights were different from our chart and *Pilot*. Where we sounded four fathoms we should have had twenty. An hour before midnight we anchored, hoisted a powerful light in the rigging, and turned in, to wait until morning, when we sorted out things and continued another fourteen miles to Queen Charlotte City.

A bird flying high among the clouds could tell you that the Queen Charlotte Islands look like a long, skinny triangle with its base at the north and its pointed tip curving toward the southeast. The triangle measures fifty-five miles across at the top, and the north-south dimension is 150 miles. Halfway down the triangle a threadlike east-west channel named Skidegate Narrows divides the mountainous land mass neatly in two, leaving Graham Island to the north and Moresby Island to the south. Near the southern extremity the east-west Houston Steward channel slices off the tip of Moresby Island, named Kunghit Island, making three main islands in all plus a handful of islets on the east side of Moresby.

The latitude of this ocean outpost of Canada is about the same as central Labrador or the northern tip of Holland. The Charlottes are somewhat similar to larger Vancouver Island, except that these islands are farther north and west and more offshore, a wild and unsettled place with only 3,000 people—including 800 Haida Indians—on the almost 4,000 square miles. Even today the islands have not been thoroughly explored, and each map-maker has a different story. Many sailing charts have blank spaces entirely without soundings and details.

The Charlottes have excellent natural harbors, abundant timber, good offshore fishing, and extensive deposits of hard and soft coal, copper, iron, and gold-bearing quartz. Some men reap the profits of this rich land and throw them away. Others husband what they make and become prosperous. But all the people are self-reliant pioneers, for the land is harsh and not used to the ways of twentieth century man.

We sailed into the little settlement of Queen Charlotte City near the eastern entrance to Skidegate Narrows. The day was wet and cold, with hard rain from the southeast. Purse seiners, salmon trollers, and gill netters packed the small harbor and we rafted up alongside. I thought the fishing boats were in the harbor because of the weather.

"Oh no," said Bronson Bussey, the talkative captain of a nearby fish-buying boat. "We're only allowed to fish three days a week. The season is set by the fisheries' people, who count the salmon in each river and arrange the boundaries and seasons accordingly. Their idea is to allow enough salmon to get up the rivers to spawn for fishing in the days ahead. But the officials are always thinking up new regulations and it's rules, rules, rules."

Bussey had 50,000 pounds of salmon on his fish-buying boat and could afford the time to complain.

No matter where you are the fishermen always grumble. In every port in the world you can find a collection of old salts in a coffee shop or on a dock somewhere bitching and complaining and growling. But like the farmers who always plan to get away and never go, the fishermen never stop casting their nets and hooks. In the Charlottes the herring are fished out, the sardines are gone, and nobody wants sharks' livers anymore. You can still find salmon and halibut, but the Greenland turbot have wrecked the halibut market and the fisheries' people are ruining salmon fishing with all their rules. Or so go the stories. The fish prices are low, food costs more now, the boats are poor, the fuel is bad, the weather forecasts are wrong, the sliced bread is too thin. . . .

"My brother made sixteen thousand dollars on halibut and ten thousand dollars on herring in one year," said Bill Greene, who we talked with on his gill netter *Heather*. "However, at income tax time he had to borrow money."

It was the same story we had heard in Alaska. Big money but broke. "He made thirty-five hundred dollars in two weeks, but. . . ." The biggest catch and end product was usually booze. Whether this is the nature of fishermen, a recourse when the fish don't appear, something to combat the cold, nasty, wet, hard work, or because of the loneliness and uncertainty of the job, I don't know, but show me ten bags of groceries for fish boats and I'll wager you can find eight bottles. I don't mean to be a prude, for I enjoy a hot rum on a blustery day. But the amount of uncontrolled hard drinking on the northwest coast was astounding, and a direct blow to the area's vitality.

On their days off the fishermen worked as loggers, sat around playing cards, flew to Prince Rupert in chartered float planes, or went deer hunting. We saw as many as eight deer on fish boats that had come in from remote inlets. A big deer was a heavy load for a man, especially up the steep tidal ramps that rose and fell up to twenty-seven feet. I never understood why the deer had to be unloaded at low tide.

The national bird of the Queen Charlottes was the crow. These big black fellows were all over the fish boats, cawing and hopping about, picking at fish scraps, at untended grocery bags, and at drying venison. I watched a crow drop a clam on the dock trying to knock the shells apart. The crow picked up the clam, flew into the air, and dropped the shellfish on the concrete. Again and again. What a noise a choir of crows could make!

One day Margaret went to a nearby Haida Indian village. She started to walk but was given a ride by a local resident who introduced her to Rufus Moody, a Haida argillite carver. Argillite is a rare, block-like slate that takes a high black polish. The stone was hard work to get. Rufus and his wife took a ninety-minute boat ride and then climbed eight miles up a mountain to reach the deposits, which then had to be quarried and loaded on packboards.

Rufus used a variety of tiny chisels to carve small totems that were five to eighteen inches high and cost from $50 to $180. The totems were embellished with noble-looking eagles and ravens and the usual traditional figures. Mrs. Moody gave the finished carvings an ebonylike luster by buffing the rock with black shoe polish.

A few days later we were anchored in a nearby cove when we heard an outboard engine stop and a skiff glide alongside. Someone knocked on the hull.

"Is anybody at home?" said a tall, flat-faced man who spoke with a strong German accent. "I own the laundry. You left me a note that one of the machines was out of order. I want to refund your forty cents."

"Never mind about that," I said. "Come out of the rain and have a cup of coffee."

We met Werner Funk and his ten-year-old son. Werner had emigrated from the Rhine Valley in 1952, built a home and got married six years later, and now had three sons and a daughter. Werner modestly admitted to driving a Caterpillar bulldozer and cutting logging roads, but we later found out he was the best logger in the area and had just paid $40,000 for the principal business property in Queen Charlotte City.

"It's good country here," said Werner. "Clean and beautiful. We don't see many yachts because the Charlottes are too remote from the big cities. Most boat owners don't go far anyway."

We told Werner about our trip and asked him to sign our guest register. "Our plan is to go through Skidegate Narrows to the west side of Moresby and to visit a couple of the big bays before we head south. But I wasn't able to get a chart of the channel and the *Pilot* is full of warnings," I said.

"The easiest for you is to follow someone through," replied Werner. "I could take you myself, but I think a ship is better. You need local knowledge because at low water, parts of the channel dry out. In fact, at low water we can get a bulldozer down in the channel to work on it."

We arranged to follow a fisheries' patrol vessel, the big *Sooke Post*, through Skidegate Narrows, and at first light on a day when the tidal stream was exactly right, the ship picked us up at the eastern entrance.

"Follow us closely and turn as we do," shouted Ken Harley, the skipper. "We draw nine feet, so you won't get into trouble unless you cut corners."

It was impossible to sail in the narrows. We fired up our little Diesel to the maximum and closely hugged the stern of the *Sooke Post*. I thought it was a miracle there was a navigable channel between the two great islands, for precipitous mountains shot up immediately on both sides.

The *Sooke Post* made abrupt stops at blazes on trees and at other special markers, turned sharply one way or the other, and hugged certain sides of the channel so closely that when we followed, our mast and rigging ripped off bits of tree branches.

Winding through the heart of the mountains was exciting and an adventure I never dreamed of. We passed sets of range markers and I could see Ken Harley's head snapping back and forth as he maneuvered his ship to keep the markers in line. At one place the shrubs on each bank of the channel almost touched. I thought it was the end.

"It's a mistake," I said to Margaret. "We'll both be stuck forever. Future archaeologists will wonder how two ships got entombed way up in the mountains."

The channel widened from time to time and the silent water reflected gorgeous vistas of cedar and spruce. We were at sea level, of course, but we felt as if we were up hundreds of feet. Hawks spiraled overhead and deer looked up impatiently as our little procession split the mountains.

"Look!" shouted Margaret, pointing at the *Sooke Post*. "The captain's crazy this time. He's going right for the bushes."

We watched with apprehension and incredulity until a thread of water appeared. The *Sooke Post* shouldered aside more shrubs and continued westward. In two hours it was all over. I was wringing wet from the excitement but dancing inside from such a thrilling morning.

We tied up briefly with the *Sooke Post* to thank the crew for their help. Ken Harley was a tall, beefy man who wore a white skipper's cap, a neat black tie, and a khaki uniform complete with campaign badges. He was a long-time, practical sailor and when he marked his favorite anchorages on our charts his pencil moved with the confidence of a man who had every inlet and cove and ship disaster fingerprinted on his mind.

"This chart's all wrong," said Ken, jabbing with his pencil. "The bay really goes like this. Look out for a rock here and a shoal patch there. You can tie up near this waterfall and take fresh water easily." When he finished I felt my charts were a hundredfold more valuable.

We continued down a wide inlet toward the Pacific, and as we began to feel the swells of the ocean, the *Sooke Post* left us, easily running at twice our speed while her crewmen waved goodbye. We sailed offshore a few miles and turned southeast. The English sailor Peter Pye, in *Moonraker*, stopped along the west coast of the Charlottes in 1954, and it was from his fine book *The Sea Is for Sailing* that we got the notion to visit the area.

And what a coastline! Craggy mountains climbed directly from the sea to the clouds. Wide waterfalls tumbled into the ocean. Yellow cliffs and black forests fought for space above a nervous Pacific. It was a land as rugged as Magellan's Tierra del Fuego, a splendid paradise in settled weather but an awesome hell in an onshore storm.

With a fair wind in our sails we headed southeast to Englefield Bay. We followed Ken Harley's advice and slipped around Saunder Island to Kaisun Harbor ("The way in looks impossible but keep going"), where we anchored in front of an abandoned Haida village.

Ashore we found the beaches stacked with immense logs that had been washed up in storms along with all sorts of flotsam. The village had long been gone and the only things left were a few rotting totems, a burial box in a tree, a few posts and pits, and wide patches of grass. Streamlets of water had been led to the village, and as we walked among the bear and deer tracks we wished the white man had never brought his smallpox so we could have heard the laughter of the vanished Indian children and seen the long log canoes drawn up on the shelving beach. It was lovely among the tall cedar trees with the bright sun and the blue sky, but we felt that the spirits of the Indians were looking over our shoulders.

The next day a southeast gale blew up and we took refuge in Security Inlet, a finger of the sea that reached four miles into the mountains. While the gale howled for five days we hiked around the shores, fished, wrote letters, read, and—as we had been instructed— helped ourselves to the crab pot of the *Sooke Post*. While I did a few maintenance jobs, Margaret took the big Dungeness crabs and experimented with *soufflé à la crabe*, *crabe à la Newburg*, and *crabe gratine*, succulent delights that she had learned when she lived in Paris. I was always awed at the miraculous meals Margaret prepared on her tiny two-burner kerosene stove.

On October 6 we left Englefield Bay and headed south, but we found that the southeast storms had set up such a strong northwest-running current that we made only ten miles in four hours, even though we sailed hard. We weren't getting anywhere, so late in the afternoon I turned back so we could make shelter before dark.

We now had a strong fair wind and soon neared the intricate entrance to Kaisun Harbor.

"Look behind us," shouted Margaret above the noise of the breakers on the rocks.

I glanced aft and saw a small white fish boat, quite near, alternately appear and disappear in the swells. I couldn't believe my eyes. First I thought the ship was running for shelter as we were, and after we turned a blind corner and she didn't appear in a few minutes we went back out to see where the fish boat was, for I thought she might be in difficulty.

Then I saw her turn out toward the main part of Englefield Bay. No doubt her skipper had seen our sail, a strange sight along the isolated coast, and had followed us to see that we got in safely. Bless his heart! How humble and thankful I felt.

The following day we tried again and found the current less and the wind more favorable. Our destination was Tasu Sound, a large inland arm of the sea twenty-five miles down the coast. The entrance to Tasu, according to the *Pilot*, was especially hard to see when approaching from the north, so we watched the cliffs and mountains carefully as we headed southeast.

When we got near Tasu we worked in to about one mile offshore. There was a good lump in the sea from the northwest-running current, the swells left over from the southeast gales, and new cross-swells raised by the twenty to twenty-five knots of wind from the south-southwest. I didn't want to get to leeward of what we thought was the entrance, so we stayed hard on the wind until we got well to windward of our target.

"O.K., helmsman," I called. "Go for that notch in the castle wall."

We rushed through the mixed-up swells and jumpy waves shoreward of the 100-fathom mark. *Whisper* pitched and rolled, and as we slammed into the short waves, spray rattled in every direction. We sailed fast in the gray and unsettled weather, for we had plenty of sail up so we would have the power to beat out in case we had picked the wrong headland. Margaret worked the tiller like an oar as the ship bounced and turned. I scrambled a little way up the ratlines and was satisfied that Tasu Sound was in front of us, for I could dimly make out a placid inland lake beyond a narrow slit in the mountains.

I glanced behind us and saw an enormous blue-black cloud rearing up astern. It looked like a biblical painting of the end of the world. Fortunately it passed rapidly to seaward of us.

"Pay attention to your compass heading," I called to Margaret. "Here comes a strong squall." We steered by the compass for a minute, and when the sharp rain passed we could see the navigational light on Davidson Point, which confirmed our position.

The wind was now dead aft and the head of the ship yawed from side to side in the turbulent water. The mainsail gybed with a crash and threatened to gybe again. A bell rang in my head and I remembered a lesson I had learned from Ed Boden in the South Pacific. When you are running hard with the wind directly aft and it's impossible to change course, pull the mainsheet in tightly and ease the headsail sheet. You retain control of the ship and have the mainsail up and ready for use in case of need.

We could see the waves hammering into the rocky headland beneath the light signal. On Tasu Head, to starboard, there was an enormous offshore rock, a low rounded dome on which the seas rose up and shattered like glass. As we neared the narrowing channel the edges of the dark sea turned into light green over the rocks along the edges.

Trees suddenly loomed above us and we hurried past the outermost part of the headland. The channel was only three cables wide and the wind hurled down on us from the mountains as squalls ran to the east. Margaret and I had to shout to talk because the waves thundered on the rocks.

As soon as we had passed through the channel into the sound we pulled down the mainsail. The water was smooth and calm inside the bay, but squalls flung their wind and rain on us and the yacht staggered under their force. However, we were safe, and half an hour later we rounded Horn and Gowing islands. We had been told about an iron mining settlement at Tasu, so we sailed in and tied up at a small dock at the little company town.

While I made fast to the float in the dying daylight a slim man in an oilskin jacket appeared out of the rain.

"Hello," he said. "My name is Peter Mylechreest. There's just time. Follow me."

Mystified, we did as we were told. Peter hurried us up the ramp and along a gravel street to a squarish building. When we went inside we realized it was a dining hall.

"Steak tonight," said Peter. "Be my guest."

Peter was the doctor for the company town whose 400 residents lived in a cheerful, new, well-planned community supplied by daily float plane flights from the east. Heavy stores were barged in from Vancouver. The town was adjacent to a deposit of thirty-three million metric tons of rich copper and iron ore which had been readied for mining by an investment of $41 million in the town, complex mining machinery, and docks. All the ore went to Mitsubishi in Japan on such ships as the *Japan Maple*, a colossal vessel that carried 55,000 tons of ore on each trip.

"This must all seem startling to you," said Peter, who took us on a tour of the big open-pit mine the next day. "I could hardly believe it when I first came."

We became good friends with Peter, who was an M.D. by profession but a wildlife biologist in his spare time. He was a studious, well-groomed bachelor from the Lake District in the county of Westmoreland in England and he passionately loved travel in the wild places of the north. One of his favorites was Foula in the Shetland Islands. He had studied trout problems in Great Bear Lake in the arctic north of Canada and had voyaged on mission ships to remote Indian villages. When Peter spoke of these places his eyes grew wide and bright and he became the

restless slave of adventure. If we had been starting out on *Whisper* I would have taken him with us at once.

Tasu was a Haida Indian word that meant "Lake of Plenty." It was a wonderful inland bay that reached into the mountains for five miles with four irregular three-mile arms that stretched sideways parallel to the coast. Except for the iron mine, which was dwarfed to insignificance, the whole area was untouched and virginal. Tall mountains wreathed with fragrant conifers sloped swiftly downward on all sides. The crystal waters of a dozen substantial streams tumbled into the smooth sound, which was home for enormous runs of salmon, along with halibut, cod, snapper, and crabs. Bear, deer, elk, and many wild creatures roamed the shores, which were tough to penetrate because of the thick rain forests of spruce, cedar, and hemlock. It seemed to me that Tasu must have resembled the San Francisco Bay of 200 years ago: largely unspoiled, the waters and shores filled with natural life, and an aura of peace and quiet over the whole place. The land before the rape by man.

One day while Peter was guiding us to a new part of the sound we slipped around a corner and saw an odd little yellow vessel at anchor. As we got closer we saw that it was a decked-over steel lifeboat with a big cabin. A smokestack puffed lustily into the chill air, and a large Canadian maple-leaf ensign strained at the flagstaff. We were waved alongside *Hiram* by a couple who appeared on deck in red shirts.

"Have you seen the eagles this morning?" called the silver-haired skipper. "More than a dozen since breakfast. Look! Here comes another."

For the first time in my life I saw a bald eagle. He was right off a silver dollar, a great black bird with a white head and white tail feathers. His flat wings stretched some seven feet, and as he passed overhead we could hear a swish as his wings dipped and raised.

We got acquainted with the owners of *Hiram*, Neil and Betty Carey, two Americans who had emigrated to the Queen Charlotte Islands. "Something I should have done years ago," said Neil, a big tough-looking ex-Navy officer with the physique of a wrestler and the soul of a violinist. The Careys owned small houses on both the east coast and on isolated southwest Moresby Island. They didn't have much money and did a great deal of beachcombing along the wild western coast, a pastime that got them both a fine collection of souvenirs of the sea and an enviable knowledge of the coastline.

Betty was a famous canoe expert who had made solo paddle trips from Seattle to Alaska in a fourteen-foot dugout canoe. She taught us much about Haida Indian village sites. "Of course you won't find an anchorage for a deep keel near a village," she said. "The Haidas looked for smooth, sloping beaches up which they could pull their canoes to safety."

When we met Neil he was working for the Canadian Fisheries Board, and for a month or two little *Hiram* putted about the west coast inlets, checking fishermen, setting fishing boundaries, and counting salmon. I went with Neil on several counting trips. With a loaded carbine to scare off the bears that were everywhere, munching on salmon, Neil led a blistering pace along the streams that were bordered by almost impenetrable rain forests. I thought I was pretty nimble in slipping through woods, but Neil put me to shame. He shinnied across moss-covered logs, ducked under leaning alders, scrambled over upturned roots, skirted boggy patches, and eased down muddy ravines at a pace I couldn't believe, all the while telling me about salmon.

"The sockeye come in June or July," said Neil. "The pinks or humpbacks arrive in August. The chums or dog salmon appear in the autumn along with the cohoes or silvers."

By means of a well-practiced sampling technique, Neil was able to estimate the number of salmon in a run.

Sometimes we looked into a deep pool and saw fifty or seventy cohoe salmon, each three feet long, each a silvery pink-bellied beauty. We saw a few about to deposit eggs and milt. The female circled over a crude scraping in the sand in a shallow place and deposited her eggs, which were fertilized by the male hovering a few inches away, culminating the life cycle of these remarkable and vigorous fish.

One night before we left Tasu we anchored far out in a remote bay, miles from anyone. There was a light rain, the clouds were low, and away from the yellow glow of our kerosene cabin lamps the night was black as death. We had been hiking in the woods and had turned in early.

Suddenly in the middle of the night I heard a strange scratching noise. I was awake at once. I pulled on a coat, slid back the hatch, and peered out. We were still well anchored, no driftwood was against the hull, and the dinghy was tied aft with two lines. The noise had stopped. I was satisfied and went back to bed.

A few minutes later I heard the scratching noise again. Now it

was louder, an eerie scraping sound. I climbed on deck with a flashlight and swept the powerful light around. Nothing forward. Nothing to the sides. Nothing aft. My heart stopped when the light hit the dinghy, for I saw a man in a rubber wet suit, a scuba outfit, climbing out of the water! My hands clenched the flashlight like a vise. My hair must have stood straight up.

Then I looked again. No! It was not a man. It was a big seal that had decided to take a fresh-water bath in the half-swamped dinghy. At midnight the big gray creature had crawled into our tender to splash around. What a fright!

We sailed from the Queen Charlotte Islands on October 10, bound for San Francisco, 900 miles to the south. It was a fine, clear day when we left, and as the great dark mountains around Tasu receded into the mist behind us I realized that the long Pacific trip was almost over. The Queen Charlotte Islands were the last of the new and unknown places. There had been so many during the nineteen-month trip: Eiao, Moorea, Aitutaki, Palmerston—seventy places in all. The memories made me a bit weak. Already there was a fair volume of correspondence from new friends.

It was good to get to sea again, and as *Whisper* heaved on the breathing ocean I felt a real kinship with the mighty Pacific. But as always the relationship was a cautious friendship, for though the old woman was capable of love she could be cantankerous and difficult.

The season of the equinoctial gales was advanced, so we headed offshore to get an offing of several hundred miles and to stay clear of the shipping lanes. We hoped for an eight- or nine-day passage, but the northwest winds that we had heard so much about seldom materialized. We found mostly calms, fog, and winds from the south.

On the fourth day the wind increased to thirty knots from the southeast, so we hove to for eight hours. At 2300 the wind suddenly died and was replaced a few hours later by an icy thirty knot blast from the northwest.

October 14. 1045. 200 miles west of Tatoosh Island on the latitude of the United States–Canadian border.
   Last night in the dim hours we fought the mainsail down, handed

the jib, and discovered that we were humming right along under bare poles. I knew I could never get the vane to steer with no headsail, so Margaret dug out the 50 sq. ft. storm jib since I was determined not to waste a fair wind. I hanked on the sail, crawled back to the mast, and began to hoist the little sail when I happened to look aft.

A tremendous wave was bearing down on Whisper. *Suddenly the ship looked so tiny and the whole enterprise seemed so insignificant. "She'll never rise to this wave," I mumbled aloud as a puff of wind snatched the words from my lips. I watched, half-holding my breath. The mighty wave rolled forward, the stern lifted, and the yacht rose well, although the foaming crest boomed on board, roared into the cockpit, and bowled along the side decks.*

Margaret, with two safety lines around her, was in the cockpit steering. She suddenly found herself up to her armpits in a bathtub of water only 20° above the freezing point. I saw her spluttering and blowing. She calmly began to take off her clothes and to wring them out.

"It's your turn to steer," she said gamely. "I've had my bath for today."

Later we put up the trysail and continued to make good time. But the following day we were becalmed on an utterly smooth ocean. On the seventh day we hove to for twenty hours in a southeast gale and on the eighth and ninth days we were becalmed for fifteen hours.

And so it went. No wind. Then too much from the wrong direction. Our daily runs were erratic and poor—57, 101, 48, 26—but like chopping at a tree with a dull ax, you keep at it and eventually the target tumbles. Occasionally we saw the lights of ships at night. We constantly watched the big dusky black-footed albatrosses that circled around and around on their thin droopy wings, day and night, in calm and in storm. Sometimes porpoises frolicked around the ship, exuberantly diving, rolling, twisting, jumping, and splashing. Then in an instant they would be gone.

One night near the latitude of the Oregon–California border we were slowly beating into a fifteen-knot southeast wind during a rainstorm when I looked out and saw a light behind us. I immediately pulled on my oilskins and went on deck. I expected a freighter to pass, but as the rain swept the sea the light stayed about the same. After half an hour I realized I was traveling only a little slower than the lights, which were gradually nearing *Whisper.* Closer now I saw the three vertical masthead lights of a big tug pulling something. The rain increased, but I felt safe since the lights of the tug were heading toward my starboard quarter and would safely pass to the west. Then I glanced at my port quarter and suddenly saw a *second* tug. The two tugs were on a bridle hooked to a towline that pulled something which was almost invisible but which loomed huge and awesome in the black night. *I was gradually being overtaken and surrounded by the two tugs, one pulling up on each quarter.* When the rain cleared for a moment I saw the bow waves of the tugs only a few hundred yards away.

I wasted no time but tacked to the east at once and bore off a little to get away from the leviathan that was after me. A few moments later the high sides of an enormous vessel under tow glided past. The unlighted monster would have erased *Whisper* as easily as a man could have stepped on a snail.

At the height of all this the string holding up my oilskin pants came undone. I grabbed at my trousers but only managed to undo my belt. My trousers tumbled about my ankles, which left my bare bottom out in the downpour while I worked the tiller and the headsail sheets.

When it was all over I didn't know whether to laugh or to cry.

On the thirteenth day we were near Cape Mendocino in heavy fog but slowly getting south. The cottony fog formed each morning for three days. It was thick at the surface but not high, and often we could see a sun that resembled an opalescent pearl on a cushion of dull satin.

We began to work inshore and saw more steamer traffic, but fortunately no more vessels under tow. On October 25 our position was 38° 21′ N. and 123° 30′ W., close to Point Reyes. Under vagrant westerly zephyrs, a bright sun, and a cloudless sky we crept south and east. Before noon on the sixteenth day we sighted the Farallon Islands, and a few hours later the sturdy towers and the delicately swooping cables of the Golden Gate Bridge hove into view.

How exciting it was to be within a few miles of our outbound track! At 1400 we passed underneath the bridge. The trip was in our pocket. Margaret produced a bottle of Japanese whisky and we each lifted a glass in celebration of the 18,538-mile voyage.

I toasted the Pacific. I toasted the ship. I toasted the mate.

I loved all three.

A Few Notes on Whisper

I BELIEVE A SAILING YACHT SHOULD BE ABLE TO FUNCTION without an engine. If you are becalmed at sea you simply wait, perhaps a shocking thought to jet-age travelers these days. However, a well-designed ship can do wonders in light airs. Some of my most pleasant memories are of ghosting along and dreaming and feeling very close to the sea and its creatures, something you miss entirely if you turn on a noisy engine.

I do feel that a small Diesel (with emergency hand-cranking) is a useful installation. It can drive a powerful mechanical bilge pump and is a good charging plant to supply power for a few electric lamps. Sometimes an engine is helpful in docking, although I much prefer the excitement of entering and leaving ports under sail. Where an engine is of particular help is when you are becalmed and caught in a strong tidal stream when it is too deep to anchor (I think of the Tuamotus). However, in 1,000 days of sailing this may happen only once. You may be becalmed just outside a port with dirty weather coming up. Or you may wish to go through a canal. These are legitimate uses, it seems to me, for a small engine if the weight, size, and fuel requirements don't overwhelm the vessel and use up its best space. My fifteen-horsepower, two-cylinder Volvo-Penta weighs about 425 pounds and consumes one quart of fuel an hour.

I have experimented with a long sculling oar and find that I can scull and maneuver Whisper (displacement six tons) at one knot in calm water. For a month during the Pacific trip we had no engine and managed to get along reasonably well.

The engines in cruising yachts get larger each year (along with electrical complexities) and a whole new school of cruising, a group that misses much of the spirit of the sea, it seems to me, is growing up. Instead of being sailors, these captains have to be journeymen mechanics and financiers to keep ahead of the repairs and the bills. Everything is engine, engine, engine, more and more fuel tanks, long distance radios, pressure hot water, washing machines, radar, Loran, and so on, *ad nauseam.*

I think you can make an interesting distinction between (1) a pure sailing ship, (2) a sailing vessel with a small auxiliary engine, and (3) a motor vessel with auxiliary sails that are used when the wind is favorable, a *sail-assisted vessel.* I believe that most accidents happen to category number three because many owners of so-called "full-power auxiliaries" are not sailors and don't know how to maneuver and control their ships under sail. These yacht owners often have no concept of storm management, how to sail an anchor out, how to heave to, and so on. Instead of knowledge they rely on engines that may work or may not.

I would humbly suggest that $100 be spent by each of these people to attend a dinghy sailing school. The skills learned and brought to the larger vessel will add immeasurable pleasure, safety, peace of mind, and perhaps commence to build pride in seamanship.

A principal consideration in a seagoing sailing ship is of course the integrity of the hull and deck structures. Without a sound hull and sturdy hatches, ports, cockpit, coachroof, and decks that are impervious to pounding seas, the ship will fill with water and its heavy lead keel will sink the vessel.

Whisper's hull—constructed from many layers of fiberglass mat, cloth, and roving saturated with polyester resin—is magnificent. It has never leaked a drop, and after 25,000 sea miles seems as good today (August 1971) as when it was launched five and a half years ago. However, as has been made evident in the account, I had trouble with the hull-deck joint, which was simply a bond of a number of layers of fiberglass mat placed on the inside where the hull and deck moldings met. For ordinary weekend sailing this would probably be enough, I suppose, but at sea where the stresses are sometimes awesome, the joint was inadequate.

When we returned from the Pacific trip Margaret and I removed the toerail, plugged 140 bolt holes, and radiused the outside of the joint. We then covered it on the outside with seven layers of ten ounce fiberglass cloth of gradually increasing widths set in polyester resin so that the joint would be massively strong and watertight both inside and out. In place of the low toerail we installed a $1'' \times 4''$ teak bulwark (35 feet on each side) bolted one inch above the deck on special stanchion bases spaced six feet apart. (While we're on the subject of leaks I wonder why there must be over 250 holes in the deck of a modern yacht, all of which are potential drips or worse? With a little thought you can eliminate half of them.)

In case you think I overstate my case I will say that when we crossed the Philippine Sea and bashed into head seas day after day we opened up thirty inches of the hull-deck joint at the stem, the point where the hull strength should have been prodigious. The pound-pound-pound of head seas soon uncovers any structural flaws. (The reason many cruising skippers are keen on all-steel yachts is massive strength, no leaks, and freedom from fastening worries.)

All parts of a vessel that go to sea should be painstakingly engineered, and should draw on experience at sea. You need something besides a shell of plastic for a fiberglass yacht. Naval architects who spend their careers working in warm offices have little appreciation of the power of breaking waves (oh, that the sea would get the same consideration as rating rules!). Deck structures, it seems to me, should be low and unencumbered, with generous bracing and reinforcement tied well down into the hull. Portlights should be small and strong. Better to lose a bit of headroom than to compromise with strength. (The importance of headroom is highly overrated anyway.)

Lest this sound like a diatribe against John Brandlmayr, the designer of *Whisper*, let me say that the ship sailed well and never gave me the slightest worry regarding performance. Her motion was wild many times and we had to shorten sail as soon as the wind increased, but she was a whiz in light airs and our elapsed passage times were reasonable.

Whisper's rudder is hollow and built of fiberglass shells. Some of the compartments are open to the sea and filled with water, an engineering feature I don't understand. But though I had doubts, the rudder and fittings proved adequate. When we put the ship on a coral reef at Guam the bottom of the rudder merely got crushed. If the rudder had been steel, the impact with the coral would have torn off the entire assembly. Better to have crushed a few square inches than to have lost the whole thing. I suppose the rudder of a cruising yacht should be set a few inches above the keel so the keel takes any grounding strains rather than the rudder.

This is not the place to discuss the pros and cons of various rigs, but I can say that when you cross oceans in a sloop, your shoulder development is assured, for you will make many sail changes. I would definitely fit running backstays to help support the upper part of the mast. Though *Whisper*'s mast has a reasonably large cross-section, the upper portion moves around alarmingly in a seaway. Of course if you fit backstays you might as well fit an inner headstay on which you can fly a staysail. You then have a sort of cutter rig. If you sew a set of reefing points on the staysail you have four choices of headsails without physically manhandling sails, not a small consideration. You can fly a jib and staysail, jib alone, staysail alone, or a reefed staysail alone.

I don't understand sailors who readily accept the chore of cranking enormous sheet winches yet who complain about setting running backstays—which take only a moment.

I would definitely not fit twin headstays again, for I had much trouble with (1) chafe of the headsail against the unused stay and (2) with the unused stay working open the jib hanks of the sail set on the other stay. I would make all the mast fittings of Monel, silicon bronze, or galvanized iron—in that order—rather than stainless steel, for I broke four mast tangs during the trip. The stainless steel appeared to work-harden and become brittle. Never weld stainless steel mast hardware.

It is useful to carry some sort of a swaging tool to help with repairs to running and standing rigging, both for yourself and for other small ships you will meet.

Whisper's original sails came from Rolly Tasker of Hong Kong and served us well. Our later sails were made in Seattle by Franz Schattauer whose skill and personal attention resulted in much better setting canvas. In consultation with Franz we now have stout, triple-stitched sails with hand-sewn bolt ropes and ample reinforcements. The sails are very strong, but quite light. Franz used eight-ounce Dacron for the mainsail and six-ounce for the genoa. The full cut main has three short fiberglass battens, each enclosed in envelopes of Dacron built up to three thicknesses to control chafe. For offshore cruising you need sails of the highest quality; skimp elsewhere if you must, but not when buying sails.

On future trips I will definitely take a spare mainsail (rather than the useless and expensive RDF set in which I invested) for when you get down to basics it is sailpower that drives the vessel. I prefer slab or tied reefs (three rows) to roller reefing because (1) the sail sets much better, (2) the strains on a roller reefed sail that is rolled slightly unevenly are severe, (3) you get away from dependence on a possible faulty roller reefing gear such as we had, (4) you can have a lighter boom with better sheeting arrangements, and (5) it's cheaper. Tying reefs is of course slower than using a roller reefing mechanism.

On *Whisper* we cook and heat and light with kerosene, which I think is the perfect fuel for small ships. Kerosene—or light clear Diesel fuel or stove oil which seem to be the same as kerosene and half the price—works to perfection in Primus stoves and appliances. The fuel is cheap, safe, dependable, hot, and in all ways satisfactory. (Kerosene is smelly only if you have leaky appliances.) My second choice is a Diesel stove, which is excellent in the high latitudes but a furnace in the tropics. Bottled gas is dangerous, expensive, hard to get in many ports, and the fittings on the containers are always different. Alcohol is excellent but costly and sometimes impossible to get. (I recall a yacht that bought alcohol from the pharmacy in Papeete at prescription prices.) Solid fuel is dirty, bulky to store, and often expensive and difficult to find. On a long trip you use a good deal of fuel, no matter what sort. We carry twenty gallons of kerosene on *Whisper*.

Your tastes become simple when you cruise in a small ship. It's amazing how little you really need to exist pleasantly and comfortably. The more gadgetry the more problems. Possessions as such mean little on extended trips.

Although we generally use electric lights for reading—especially in the tropics—we planned our equipment so that we can get along with no electricity at all. We had no refrigeration, not because I don't appreciate the advantages of ice but because I refuse to put up with the complex machinery and the noise of a charging plant. I recall a big all-electric yacht whose main generator was out of order and whose auxiliary generator had a broken part. The existence of the people plummeted to utter squalor since their electric toilets wouldn't work, they were unable to cook, their frozen food spoiled, they couldn't raise their anchors. . . . We finally loaned them some candles and a pressure kerosene lamp.

I carry lots of spare parts. In many cases I carry spares for the spares. My theory of spare parts is to fit the spare so you know it will replace the original. Then to tuck the original away for a rainy day.

For example I installed the spare water pumps for the galley before I left on the trip. I stored the originals, *which I then knew would fit in all ways*.

The Hasler wind vane gear was completely successful and made most of the trip a pleasure instead of a steering marathon. We lost the wind blade in heavy weather in the Gulf of Alaska, but the fault was mine, for I should have removed the blade in such weather. The vane gear steered perfectly downwind when I generally ran with the mainsail eased forward (with a guy to prevent gybing and a vang to hold the boom down to minimize sail chafe on the lee spreader). To balance the drive of the mainsail we carried a headsail boomed out on the windward side with a spinnaker pole. It is good to carry poles of different lengths to boom out a variety of sails, particularly storm sails. The use of a mainsail and a poled-out headsail does a lot to minimize rolling. We used twin headsails a few times but experienced a good deal of rolling since twins are essentially squaresails and fail to give much lateral support.

With a steering vane you must be careful not to fall over the side. In bad weather and at night we always wear safety harnesses, which we clip to a lifeline or a piece of rigging. We hang police whistles on cords around our necks for emergency signaling. We also have a long bamboo overboard pole with a flame-colored flag on top, two life rings, and a floating overboard light with a high-intensity flashing light.

Recently I have learned about small pocket-sized waterproof mini-flares, which certainly will go along on our next trip. With such a flare in your pocket you would be able to pinpoint your position to someone on a returning yacht.

I carry two radio receivers, principally to obtain time signals. We have no transmitter, for I feel that if we get into difficulty we should get ourselves out. I feel strongly about calling for help, for U.S. small-boat people have abused the privilege so abysmally that I am horrified at the whole concept. My situation would have to be very desperate before I would ask for assistance. There is the matter of *pride in doing it yourself*, a value not often thought of these days, but something I believe is important.

I can see one use for a transmitter and that would be to ask for medical advice in case of a mechanical injury or a major illness. Our battery power is modest, however, and I have none.

In general we had good weather during the Pacific trip. You plan carefully to take advantage of fair winds, summer temperatures, and seasons free from gales. The literature of sailing has entirely too much storm talk. Like the newspaper and its daily tabulation of murders, one's ideas may get distorted. The newspapers never mention how many men peacefully come home from the office, kiss their wives, and spend an evening with their stamp collections. That wouldn't be news, even though it is the truth. Likewise the sea, though sometimes stormy and downright nasty, is often smooth and easy.

Without question the most important piece of mechanical gear on the ship is the anchor windlass, in our case a Simpson-Lawrence 500 two-speed lever action device which enables Margaret or me to handle the anchors with ease and to assist in warping the ship when in harbor. We carry four anchors—two forty-five-pound CQRs, a forty-two-pound fisherman, and a thirty-pound Danforth. We generally use one of the CQR anchors, which we have arranged to be self-stowing over a stem roller. Most modern yachtsmen use CQR anchors because they hold well and don't bend, a problem with the Danforth design. The fisherman, of course, is the old standby, and though it automatically gets fouled when the ship swings on a tidal change, the anchor holds well on a short length of cable and is often good in rocky holding ground.

We generally anchor with all chain and carry thirty-five fathoms of ⅜″. We had little trouble with dragging anchors. The only difficulty in seventy places, strange to say, was over gleaming coral sand in Rangiroa atoll in the Tuamotus, where the white sand appeared to have a hard crust. We spent a perplexing hour with all three types before we got one to dig in. In the tropics I often put on a face mask and swam out to inspect the anchor after we had put the ground tackle down. I learned a good deal about anchors and anchoring. Sometimes you think you are well anchored and the chain is wrapped around and around the anchor. It is a good policy to buoy the anchor, although it is one thing more to do when you are busy sailing into a new place.

We carry seventy-eight gallons of fresh water in two tanks, plus eight or ten gallons of water in plastic jugs. This is ample, in fact more than twice what we have ever used on a passage. Two quarts of fresh water per person per day is sufficient. The best way to replenish water in the tropics is with a water-catching awning. Not only is it simple and quick but the water is clean and easier to get than rowing jugs ashore and walking long distances to catchment tanks where the water may be of doubtful purity.

Cruising yachts should have two dinghies. If you lose one you have a spare. (A small tender can fit inside a larger, or you can have an inflatable for a second.) If you are anchored out and someone is ashore with the dinghy, anyone on board is immobile unless you have a second tender. A good sailing dinghy is useful, for the distances you must row in foreign places are sometimes considerable. Also you can often take pleasant trips to far corners of a large lagoon in a sailing dinghy. Carry spare oars and rowlocks. I do not have an outboard because I refuse to have gasoline on board.

We carry no guns, which are illegal in most parts of the world anyway. Your best ally, if you are worried about protection, is a smile, a handshake, a small joke about the weather, and perhaps an offer of a cup of coffee or an inch of whisky. Guns are made for killing, not friendship.

Rather than to worry about what to *do* about people, our problem was often what to do *for* people when they had done us great kindnesses. In the future I plan to carry a number of cheap stainless-steel knives, large fishhooks, and inexpensive rope to give friends who are especially good to us. Again and again we were asked for used clothing. A Polaroid photograph of everyone is a fun gift, and a picture of the ship and crew is appreciated. People like to go for short sails. Always carry a guitar in the South Pacific.

You must take the advice of natives with caution with respect to the suitability of a place regarding depth. Most people of the South Pacific use outrigger canoes, which draw only a few inches. The natives generally have no concept of the underwater shape of ships with keels and will enthusiastically wave you in to a place with only a few inches of water. It's a good idea to put a dinghy over the side and to make a few soundings yourself if the water is unclear.

What does it cost to take such a trip? I consider that a small yacht in good condition is worth the same as a modest house. In 1966, *Whisper* cost approximately $20,000, to which I added another 25 percent— $5,000—for the steering vane, charts, navigation equipment, stores, spares, dinghies, warps, medical supplies, and so on and on. Cruising equipment is astonishingly extensive. You need *everything*, for you have to be self-sufficient in both items for living and for keeping the ship going. A vessel at sea is a miniature, self-contained world. It takes months and months to get ready.

Actual cruising costs are something else. The very nature of a long trip takes you to places where it is often impossible to spend any money at all. You find instead that you barter a pair of old trousers for two fish and half a dozen drinking nuts. Where the money goes is when you reach a large port and eat out in restaurants, something we seldom did. If you have modest resources the best scheme, we believe, is to buy first-class foodstuffs and to prepare them yourself. Even in San Francisco today Margaret and I can both eat a good meal on *Whisper* for $1 or so. If we eat out it is hard to spend less than $4 for the two of us.

I believe that in 1971 two people can cruise in a small ship for from $100 to $200 a month if the ship is well prepared beforehand, has no complex machinery or electrical gadgetry to maintain, and if you watch your expenses in every way. This means avoiding places with high port charges and in general being frugal. Often you can stock up when you find food bargains. The fun you have is of course in no way related to what you spend. We have seen the crews of yachts in the $100-a-month class have much better times than those who spent ten times more. You don't have to deny yourself sightseeing, for most places have cheap public transportation. We carried take-apart bicycles which we stored in the forepeak.

Cargo and passenger ships travel mostly between large ports where there are generally excellent aids to navigation and pilots you can hire to help you enter and dock. The smaller places, however, often have no aids to navigation and you must find your way in alone. The volumes of pilot instructions that cover practically the whole earth tend to reflect this situation. The big ports are well described, but the remote places generally have only skimpy and outdated notes. The disparity is increasing, for large ports are growing bigger while small places are falling into disuse, except for local traffic.

The only literate strangers to many small ports are the crews of cruising yachts. I feel it is important for small-ship captains to write in changes and corrections to the *Pilots*. It takes only a moment and one sentence to say that "such and such a beacon no longer exists," that "harbor X has a mean ground swell and it is better to anchor out than to lie alongside the dock," or that "you need to hire a watchman if you leave the ship." The correctness of sailing directions can be maintained only if everyone concerned helps. Who knows? Maybe your son will profit from a change you have written in.

There are many aspects of seamanship involved when you cross an ocean in a small ship. One lifetime seems hardly long enough to learn all you should. I have a theory that preparation for passage-making is worse than the actual sailing. I am always nervous and unsettled before sailing and calm and untroubled once we get under way. The contemplation of danger is sometimes far worse than the actual hazard itself. Small ships seldom get in trouble at sea. It's around land where difficulties begin. If things look nasty when you draw close to a strange coast, heave to and wait awhile. What is one more day? You have to throw away the calendar when you go cruising.

You must do all you can to stay rested and to keep reserves of energy tucked away, for a tired captain can easily make a stupid move.

I have talked enough. If you have the urge to go you will in spite of what I say. If your heart isn't in the sea you will never leave the safety of the land, a pity perhaps, but not many people have the fire of adventure in their bones. But if you want to go don't wait until everything is perfect or you'll never get away. Most adventuring is done on a shoestring. Perhaps that's part of the fun. ("If you have all the money you need, you lose the adventure," says my friend Bobby Uriburu.)

The very nature of exploration, pioneering, and adventure is quest and curiosity, not safety and security. Only a few berths from where *Whisper* is now tied up is another yacht whose owner watched us arrive fresh from the shipyard. He saw us set out on the Pacific trip, return, edit a film, write a book, give lectures, and now he sits and watches the parade of visitors from the Pacific climb onto *Whisper*. Yet he still talks of his trip and how he is going. If you have the urge by all means set a date and go!

Notes

1. J. C. Beaglehole, *The Exploration of the Pacific*, Stanford University Press, 1966, pp. 65–68. Also see *Pacific Islands*, published during World War II by the Naval Intelligence Division of the British government (B.R. 519B Geographical Handbook Series). The five volumes are a superb source for Pacific information. The Marquesas are covered in detail in Vol. II, pp. 260–99, and in Vol. I, pp. 246–47.

2. J. C. Beaglehole, *The Journals of Captain James Cook*, Cambridge, Hakluyt Society, 1961, Vol II, pp. 372–73.

3. Charles A. Borden, *South Sea Islands*, Philadelphia, Macrae Smith, 1961, p. 116.

4. Robert C. Suggs, *The Hidden Worlds of Polynesia*, New York, Mentor Books, New American Library, 1962, p. 59. A highly readable book about recent archaeological work in the Marquesas. Chapter Two has a good summary of the troubled history.

5. Willowdean C. Handy, *Forever the Land of Men*, New York, Dodd, Mead, 1965, p. 167.

6. Population figures in French Polynesia are sketchy and incomplete. See Handy, *op. cit.*, pp. 223–26. Also *Pacific Island Year Book*, Sydney, Pacific Publications, 1963, p. 151. Useful but often highly inaccurate.

7. Many small-ship sailors have called at the Marquesas and written accounts, including Stevenson (1888), London (1908), Muhlhauser (1921), Seligman (1937), Le Toumelin (1951), Crealock (1952), Van de Wiele (1952), Hiscock (1953), and Pye (1953).

8. Bengt Danielsson, *Forgotten Islands of the South Seas*, London, Allen & Unwin, 1957, p. 165. Danielsson, as Alain Gerbault did a generation earlier, demonstrates that with proper motivation—as in sports—the 'lazy islanders' have astounding energy, vitality, and endurance.

9. Bengt Danielsson, *The Happy Island*, London, Allen & Unwin, 1952, pp. 155–75.

10. For the ultimate description of Palmerston, viewed from the air, see James Ramsey Ullman, *Where the Bong Tree Grows*, Cleveland, World Publishing Co., 1963, pp. 227–28. Charts of Palmerston are difficult to get. H.O. 1980 has been discontinued. The best I have been able to find is in a little booklet, *Maps of the Cook Islands*, by the Survey Department, Rarotonga, printed by the Government of the Cook Islands (undated).

11. Data for the ocean floor around Palmerston can be found in Helen Raitt, *Exploring the Deep Pacific, the Story of the Capricorn Expedition*, Denver, Sage Books, 1964, Chapter Fourteen.

12. Commander Victor Clark, *On the Wind of a Dream*, London, Hutchinson, 1960, pp. 134–97. By far the most authoritative account of Palmerston. Clark, whose yacht was wrecked and rebuilt on the island, had an excellent chance to study the place for eleven months. His lucid account debunks the stories of inbreeding.

13. *Ibid.*, pp. 136–37.

14. W. A. Robinson, *Deep Water and Shoal*, London, Rupert Hart-Davis, 1957, pp. 115–17. Also see Ralph Stock, "The Dream Ship," *National Geographic*, January 1921, pp. 49–50.

15. *Pacific Islands Year Book, op. cit.*, p. 144.

16. *Pacific Islands, op. cit.*, Vol. II, pp. 561–62.

17. Another visitor to Palmerston was Irving Johnson, *Westward Bound in the Schooner Yankee*, New York, W. W. Norton, 1936, pp. 124–26. A view of a churchman is by Bernard Thorogood, *Not Quite Paradise*, London, London Missionary Society, 1960, pp. 66–71.

18. Jan-Olof Traung, editor, *Fishing Boats of the World: 2*, London, Fishing News (Books) Ltd., 1960, pp. 73–74.

19. The high harbor dues are typical of American shortsightedness. With a little encouragement and the most modest of facilities the magnificent harbor of Pago Pago could become the center of yachting and sailing in the South Pacific. In Papeete, long the mecca of yachts, the little ships from all over the world are made welcome and form a colorful part of the waterfront. Contrary to what some Americans think, yachtsmen are not bums and do spend reasonable amounts of money locally.

20. *Pacific Islands, op. cit.*, Vol. II, pp. 591–607. For a modern

account of the 1889 confusion, see Edwin P. Hoyt, *The Typhoon That Stopped a War*, New York, McKay, 1968.

21. John O'Grady, *No Kava for Johnny*, Sydney, Ure Smith, 1966. A delightful novel of modern Samoa that deftly reviews the conflict between old and new customs.

22. For an invaluable guide to mariners, see Captain E. V. Ward, *Sailing Directions*, Tarawa, Gilbert and Ellice Islands Colony, 1967. Price $1 (Australian). This detailed and up-to-date seventy-four-page handbook is far superior to *Admiralty* and *U.S. Pilots*.

23. Samuel Eliot Morison, *History of United States Naval Operations in World War II, Aleutians, Gilberts, and Marshalls*, Boston, Little, Brown, 1951, Vol. VII, p. 185.

24. For general information, a reading list, and statistics of this well-governed atoll colony, see *Gilbert & Ellice Islands Biennial Report, 1964–65*, London, Her Majesty's Stationery Office, 1967.

25. Sir Arthur Grimble, *Return to the Islands*, New York, William Morrow, 1957, pp. 50–51.

26. Sir Arthur Grimble, *We Chose the Islands*, New York, William Morrow, 1952, p. 174. The classic of the Gilberts, a bit exaggerated occasionally but the writing is often breathtaking and always penetrating and conscientious. Grimble should be required reading for all Americans in overseas government. For an early account of Abemama, see Robert Louis Stevenson, *In the South Seas*, New York, Charles Scribner's Sons, 1923, pp. 329–409.

27. *Ibid.*, p. 276.

28. *Ibid.*, pp. 78–79.

29. Sir Arthur Grimble, "War Finds Its Way to Gilbert Islands," *National Geographic*, January 1943, p. 85.

30. *Sailing Directions for the Pacific Islands*, Washington, U.S. Government Printing Office, H.O. Pub. No. 82, Vol. I, pp. 6–9. A handy source of miscellaneous information is *Trust Territory of the Pacific Islands*, Washington, U.S. Government Printing Office, 21st annual report, July 1, 1967 to June 30, 1968.

31. The Trust Territory is fertile ground for crusading reporters who have found plenty to write about. See Willard Price, *America's Paradise Lost*, New York, John Day, 1966; E. J. Kahn, Jr., *A Reporter in Micronesia*, New York, Norton, 1966; and Don Oberdorfer, "America's Neglected Colonial Paradise," *Saturday Evening Post*, February 29, 1964. An older and more idealistic sketch is by Robert Trumbull, *Paradise in Trust*, New York, William Sloane, 1959. For a broader background, see J. C. Furnas, *Anatomy of Paradise*, New York, William Sloane, 1947.

32. James A. Michener and A. Grove Day, *Rascals in Paradise*, London, Secker & Warburg, 1957, pp. 223–58.

33. David S. Boyer, "Micronesia: the Americanization of Eden," *National Geographic*, May 1967, p. 735.

34. Price, *op. cit.*, p. 170.

35. Ullman, *op. cit.*, p. 81. Mort Colodny, the district cooperative officer in Ponape, has made excellent suggestions for economic improvements in an eighteen-page paper *Economic Development in Micronesia* (unpublished, a copy is in the possession of the author of this book).

36. For an account of this remarkable priest, see Kahn, *op. cit.*, pp. 268–74.

37. A good synopsis of this unbelievable crop is by John Wesley Coulter, *The Pacific Dependencies of the United States*, New York, Macmillan, 1957, pp. 268–70.

38. Charles Parr, *Ferdinand Magellan, Circumnavigator*, New York, Thomas Crowell, 1964, p. 333.

39. Fosco Maraini, *Meeting with Japan*, London, Hutchinson, 1959, p. 337. This superb book is so good that one sentence can hardly sum up the depth, wisdom, information, and *feeling* of Japan. An excellent translation and first-rate photographs. A basic book is by Ruth Benedict, *The Chrysanthemum and the Sword; Patterns of Japanese Culture*, Boston, Houghton Mifflin, 1946. Helpful also is Laurens Van der Post, *A Portrait of Japan*, New York, William Morrow, 1968.

40. Maraini, *op. cit.*, p. 133.

41. For war reminiscences, see Murray Morgan, *Bridge to Russia*, New York, E. P. Dutton, 1947. A formal account of World War II military affairs is in Morison, *op. cit.*

42. *U.S. Coast Pilot 9, Pacific and Arctic Coasts*, Washington, U.S. Government Printing Office, 1964, p. 237. For a general historical sketch, see Harold McCracken, *Hunters of the Stormy Sea*, New York, Doubleday, 1957. A specialized work is by Waldemar Jochelson, *History, Ethnology, and Anthropology of the Aleut*, The Netherlands, Anthropological Publications, 1966.

43. Ted Bank II, *Birthplace of the Winds*, New York, Thomas Crowell, 1956, pp. 64–115.

44. Viola E. Garfield and Linn A. Forest, *The Wolf and the Raven*, Seattle, University of Washington Press, 1948.

Two Against

Cape Horn

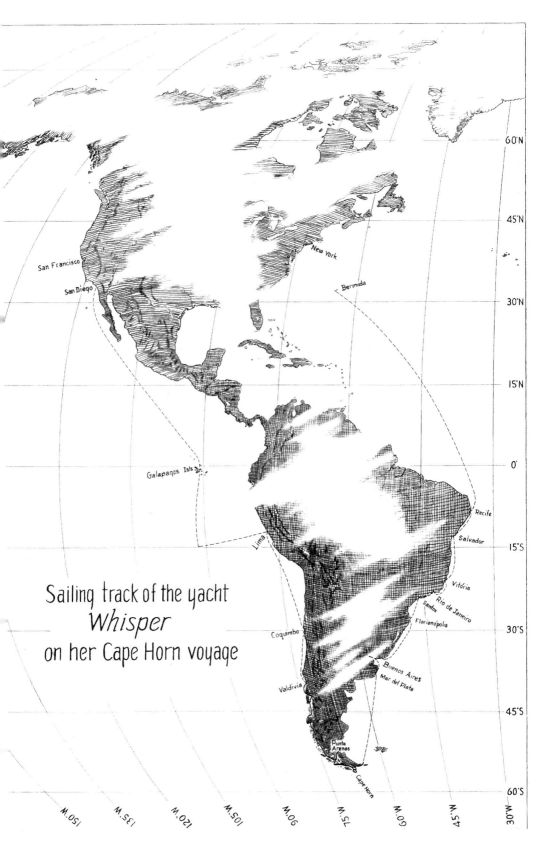

Sailing track of the yacht
Whisper
on her Cape Horn voyage

HAL ROTH

*Two Against
Cape Horn*

Maps by Sam F. Manning

PRECEDING PHOTOGRAPHS

The mountain world of the Chilean channels: an aerial view of Estero Reloncaví.

Looking north–northeastward from Caleta Voilier across the Northwest Arm of Canal Beagle on a winter afternoon toward the snowy peaks of Tierra del Fuego. Whisper *(home port: San Francisco) is both firmly anchored and has lines ashore to strong points.*

In the Chilean channels.

Cape Horn from the southwest.

Headed south near Cape Horn. This view looks back across the stern of Whisper *and northward toward the Wollaston Islands which are about twenty-five miles north of Cape Horn island. Vessels normally don't fly flags at sea (the flags wear out too quickly), but this was the special day when we sailed around the famous cape.*

*T*o all of my dear friends in Chile, and in particular to those who helped us after our misfortune:

Eduardo Allen	Guillermo and Marina
Horacio Balmelli	Herrera
Isvaldo Benivente	Roberto Kelly
Salvador Camelio	Jorge and Carmen Merino
Fernando Camus	Luis Ocampo
Hector Chavez	Jorge Piñeiro
Juan Espinosa	Peter Samsing
Orlando Figuerola	Osvaldo Schwarzenberg
Raul Ganga	Oluf Torres
Rafael Gonzales	The crew of the *Castor*
Edwin and Jane Leslie	The crew of the *Fuentealba*
The crew of the PTF *Quidora*	The crew of the *Águila*

Contents

vessel — a shipyard — everybody rows — collecting
shellfish — church at Achao

Maps

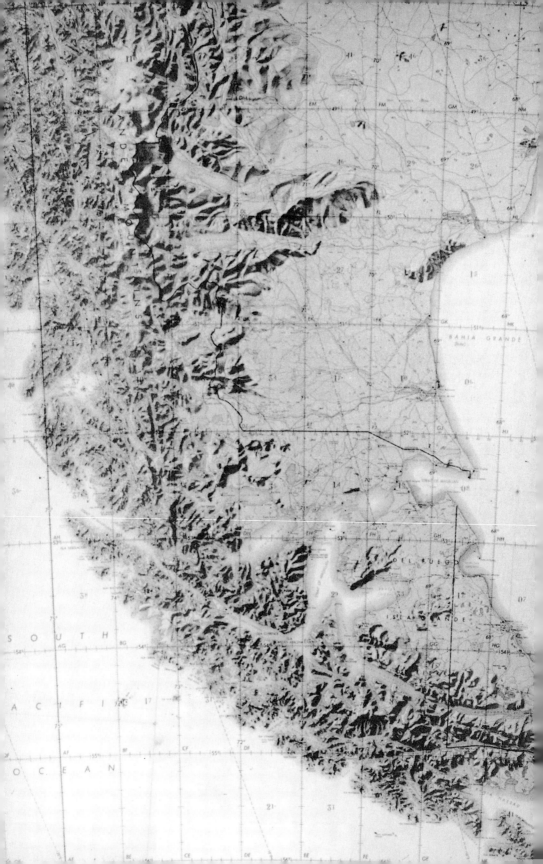

*T*HE SEA is a mistress oft wanton and cruele,
Upon her bosom no man plays the fule;
And if he would her power conquest,
He must of himself give his true best.

—ANONYMOUS

ONE

Where Do Ideas Come From?

SOME fifteen years ago I read a book by W. A. Robinson entitled *To the Great Southern Sea,* an account of a voyage from Tahiti to the west coast of South America. Robinson had hoped to visit the thousand miles of fjords and waterways in the Chilean channels north of Cape Horn, so after crossing the eastern Pacific he sailed his big sixty-six-foot brigantine into the twenty-mile-wide channel of Boca del Guafo at 44° S, at the southern end of Chiloé Island. The weather was thick and the tidal streams were formidable. Robinson lacked suitable charts and tidal tables but he thought he could easily sail his powerful fifty-ton vessel into the sheltered waters behind the Chilean islands facing the Pacific. A strong tidal stream pouring westward out of Golfo Corcovado showed him how contrary the Chilean seas can be.[1]

"A sudden boiling millrace stopped us in our tracks," he wrote. At the same moment, black clouds swept in from the west. Robinson turned his ship to the northwest and fled out to sea.

The next day he tried to enter the channels at Canal Chacao, 120 miles to the north. Again the yacht was flung seaward by water roaring westward from the inland water-ways. With the barometer plummeting and squalls driving down from thickening cloud banks in the west, Robinson gave up his attempt to enter the channels in his own vessel and sailed north into easier waters. Later he visited the southern region on a local steamer.

Robinson's descriptions ("the glint of sun on snow-peaks"), his delight with the country ("I was insidiously attracted"), and his feelings of excitement ("a glimpse of a new frontier") all combined to give me a severe case of Cape Horn fever—a contagion with which I was soon plainly infected. My forehead was hot. My tongue was dry. I was covered with spots.

In my mind's eye I could clearly see a shiny hull and the white sails of a small vessel gliding quietly along the dark waters of a narrow channel. Above the shore rose the strong green of thick forests. Higher up, the trees became brown-streaked granite spurs and cliffs as the mountains climbed to thickening patches of snow and ice. Higher still, at the top of the image, lay a splendid jumble of shadowy glaciers, jagged summits, and swirling masses of clouds, all of whose forms were softened by the blue of distance.

My dream was marvelous but it was only fantasy. I would have to learn more facts.

I began to collect books about Cape Horn. I soon found out that although there were a good many recollective sailing accounts by men who had gone around Cape Horn in square-rigged ships (say from Australia to England), there was little about Cape Horn itself and the lands and waterways to the north. I discovered that Pigafetta's famous account of the discovery of the Strait of Magellan ran to only a disappointing 778 words and that most historical accounts about Magellan finding his great waterway are utter fantasy simply because no detailed records exist.[2]

My tiny collection of Cape Horn books grew slowly, two or three volumes a year. The collection happened to be mentioned in the author's blurb on the book jacket of *Pathway*

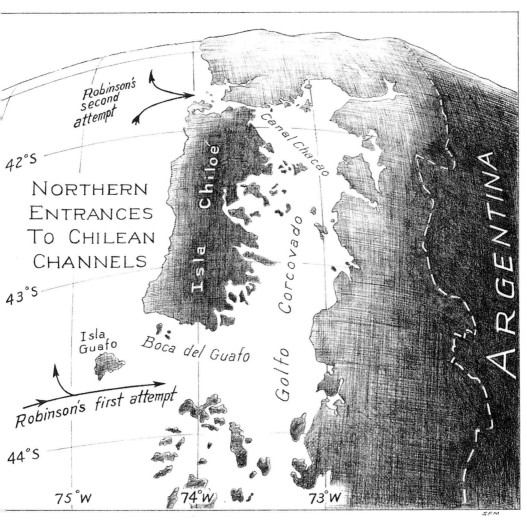

NORTHERN
ENTRANCES
TO CHILEAN
CHANNELS

To Cape Horn
1,000 miles

in the Sky, a book I had written on mountaineering. Though the description clearly stated that I was merely collecting books on Cape Horn it was too late. The pregnancy had begun.

The book reviewers described me as a Cape Horn sailor, which was completely untrue. I had never been to South America. I had never gone near the Southern Ocean.

My friends were no better.

"When are you going to Cape Horn?" they chorused.

"Cape Horn? I'm only collecting books," I said.

"Ha! Don't kid us," they said. "When are you leaving?"

But year after year the Cape Horn notion persisted. It pulsed through my head like the penetrating clang of a church bell. Just as mountaineers dream of climbing in the Himalayas, sailors muse about Cape Horn. Some small ship sailors are horrified at the thought of going around Cape Horn in a tiny vessel. Others are fascinated by the idea. For them that cape of capes is a kind of altar, a Mecca, a place where a man is blooded, a symbol of adversity and achievement, of hardship and conquest.

The sailors of old complained and boasted about Cape Horn in the same breath, cursing the experience but loving it every minute because—like going off to war—it was the greatest adventure of their lives. A journey around Cape Horn was a trip to the ultimate classroom of the sea; the graduate was a deepwater sailor. No more needed to be said.

In the past, Cape Horn and the Strait of Magellan were the decisive marks between the world's two greatest oceans, and for four hundred years there was a mixed-up squabble for rights and sovereignty by Spain, Holland, France, England, and Germany—all of whom schemed and plotted, and who dispatched their best officers and ships to control this strategic southland.

In time, however, world trade became more important than sovereignty. Starting with the 1849 gold rush in California and continuing until World War I, manufacturing and international commerce expanded hugely. By the last two decades of the nineteenth century there were more than 10,000 deepwater sailing ships—5,000 British, 2,000 Norwegian, 1,200 French, 1,200 Swedish, and 1,000 German—almost ten million tons in 1895. Most of the ships were three- and four-masted vessels that carried a few passengers and cargoes such as case oil, coal, guano, manufactured goods, nitrates, rice, wheat, wood, or wool past the southern tips of Africa or America on their way to foreign terminals. These ships employed thousands of sailors, and it is from their records and writings and stories that the legend of Cape Horn arose.

The first steamship crossed the Atlantic in 1819, an idle curiosity with both paddle wheels and sails. By 1875, however, the compound engine and screw propeller were in full use and there were fifteen steamship companies engaged in transatlantic commerce alone. Steamships kept to precise schedules and sailed directly from port to port, made quick turn-arounds, and completed four ocean voyages a year while sailing vessels could do only one. The opening of the Suez Canal in 1869 suddenly halved the mileage between the Far East and Europe, and steam traffic through the new canal soon took the place of the sailing routes around the Cape of Good Hope. Nevertheless, the big Cape Horners which went from 3,500 to as much as 8,000 tons (27,000 square feet of sail up to 60,000 square feet) continued to operate profitably on long routes.

A large sailing commerce continued between Europe and Australia, and between Europe and the west coast of North and South America until the Panama Canal opened in 1914. This second transoceanic canal was the final fall of the axe for long-distance commercial sail, except for a marginal Finnish effort that hung on for another quarter of a century. In 1938 a dozen three- and four-masted barques loaded with Australian wheat paraded past Cape Horn on their way to Ireland. It was the end. By the time World War II began in the following year the perilous Cape Horn route was finished, a scrap of history at once remote and forgotten. Today only an infrequent giant oil tanker or a diesel-powered cargo ship rumbles past the black rock of the south. The albatrosses and the pintado petrels have the Southern Ocean almost entirely to themselves.[3]

Cape Horn remains a distant symbol of a vanished age when men drove their ships by harnessing the wind in folds of canvas. A relic of the past. Yet the lonely rock was a meaningful signpost to me. I wanted to sail around it. I wanted to try the Strait of Magellan. I wanted to see the waterways of Chile. My wife—Margaret—and I hoped to compare the Chilean channels with the fjords of Norway and the inside passages of Alaska. We had both read about the ragged Indians of the south and we wondered whether we would see any Alacalufes or Yaghans. A friend had told us that we would be able to sail in company with a splendid fleet of small sailing workboats on the east coast of Chiloé Island. We had heard tales about giant shellfish.

"Will we be able to sail close to the glaciers in Canal Beagle?" we asked one another.

"Will it be possible to see the great mass of Mount Sarmiento itself?" we wondered.

I had read so much about Cape Horn and the Strait of Magellan (Cabo Froward, Isla Tamar, Cabo Pilar) that I had to see these places for myself. I had heard (or imagined or fancied) that no sailor was a real sailor until he had tried the currents and winds down there. This was probably a lot of romantic balderdash but nonetheless it was a small factor.

We decided to go.

Margaret and I had already gone to many places in our thirty-five-foot yacht *Whisper*. She was designed as a stock racing-cruising sloop by the late John Brandlmayr and built by Spencer Boats, Ltd., of Vancouver, Canada. Her hull and deck were made of fiberglass. She had a lead keel, a spruce mast, and a small two-cylinder diesel auxiliary. We supplemented her normal rigging with an inner forestay and running backstays to strengthen the mast for additional security. Besides the usual sails, we carried a small staysail on the inner forestay and could easily run up a storm trysail which we kept permanently mounted at the bottom of its own track on the mast. These two small sails were handy when the wind was strong.

Over the years we had made dozens of improvements to *Whisper*, generally to strengthen her and to simplify the gear and to make the vessel more suitable for short-handed ocean cruising and living aboard. We had a windlass, four anchors, and lots of stout chain and lines. A self-steering device guided the yacht at sea and a powerful diesel stove warmed the cabin below. We had shelves of books, plenty of stores, and a radio to bring us music and time signals. *Whisper*'s cabin was comfortable, airy, and pleasant. Her only bad point was that she was burdened with perhaps four thousand pounds of cruising gear which put her low in the water. We fought a constant battle to take weight off the vessel.

(Overleaf) The interior of Whisper *as seen in a wide-angle photograph looking forward. In the foreground to port is the chart table. To starboard is the galley with hand pumps for fresh and salt water. The saloon has a table to starboard, and settee berths to port and starboard. Forward is the head compartment. Beyond that is the forepeak with two berths. Light at night comes from three kerosene lamps plus various twelve-volt reading lights as required. There are stout handrails at shoulder level on each side to grab when moving from one place to another. The cabin sole is teak as is the interior joinery. A six-foot bookshelf is above the port settee plus a three-foot athwartships shelf for large books on the forward bulkhead. Two additional six-foot bookshelves run fore-and-aft above the forepeak berths. At sea each person sleeps on a saloon berth or in the single quarter berth out of the photograph to port and aft. (The forepeak berths are suitable only for use in harbor.) Various bits of gear (barometer, fire extinguisher, spice rack) are dotted around the cabin, as are a few souvenirs from our travels. Four china dishes, two coffee mugs, and a crock of butter rest on the galley sink so we must be in a smooth and quiet anchorage.*

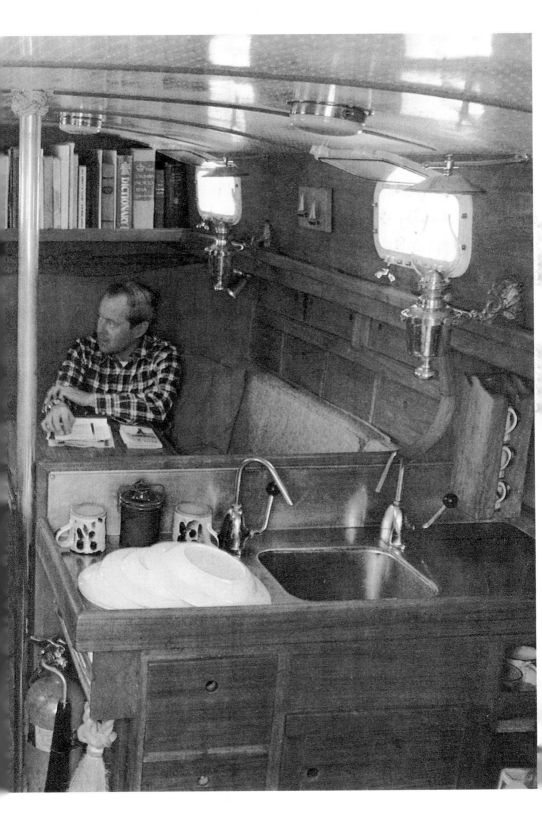

Whisper's specifications were:

overall length	*35 feet*
waterline length	*28 feet*
beam	*9 feet 6 inches*
draft	*5 feet 11 inches*
sail area	*527 square feet*
displacement (empty)	*12,000 pounds*
displacement (laden)	*16,000 pounds*

Our maximum speed through the water was 7.4 knots (or 178 nautical miles in twenty-four hours). Except for rare bursts, however, we never sailed at that speed in the ocean because normal sea conditions made the motion too uncomfortable. On a long passage we considered 100 to 135 miles per day as good runs. Some twenty-four-hour periods

were a great deal less, but we could generally count on 90 to 110 miles even in slow going.

Now *Whisper* was in California. We wanted to go to Cape Horn. We studied the charts, various volumes of sailing directions, and an enormous blue book entitled *Ocean Passages for the World*. At first we thought of sailing south to Panama, east to Trinidad, and then south along the coast of Brazil. However the contrary trade winds and powerful opposing currents looked too strong. We gave up the Caribbean plan and began to check the routes in the Pacific, the ocean that *Whisper* knew so well.

When you use the wind for power to travel on the world's oceans you soon learn that the long way between two points may be the easier, because fair or reaching winds (with following or beam seas) are kinder to the crew and mean less broken gear from bashing to windward. In addition, fair or reaching winds translate into faster sailing, so a long detour for favorable slants of wind is often the most prudent course. We could have sailed *Whisper* from California to Cape Horn via Tahiti (8,533 miles) which would have meant lengthy passages in the northeast and southeast trade winds and finally a voyage eastward in the westerlies of the Southern Ocean.

I liked sailing with the wind in the trades but I didn't want to make a long passage in the Southern Ocean in *Whisper*. I knew from the books of Smeeton and Moitessier and Knox-Johnston, and from my friends aboard the small yachts *Carronade* and *Manuma*, that the open wilderness of the Southern Ocean was not a good place for yachts—or even medium-sized ships for that matter. The odds are not on your side because the longer you sail in the Southern Ocean the greater are the chances that you will get into really heavy weather, that is, sustained storm force or hurricane winds. The winds, however, are not the problem. In a flat sea with plenty of room, a properly designed and handled yacht can survive almost any force of wind. The difficulty is the wind-driven seas which when heaped up and irregular with cross seas can humble almost any vessel, large or small. The last thing I wanted was to get turned over and dismasted by a monster breaking wave which had grown and run unchecked before the strong westerly winds of the Southern Ocean for perhaps thousands of miles.

I knew from oceanographic studies that one wave in three hundred thousand waves was four times the height of the average. The English sailors of old never heard of oceanography but they knew all about *graybeards,* the name the sailors gave to giant waves. The Chileans called them *tigres.* The French sailors knew them as *les vagues énormes.* Regardless of their nationality, however, all sailors shook their heads at the mere mention of these dragons of the sea.

It was true that we would sail in the Southern Ocean from time to time during the trip to Cape Horn, but the more I minimized my exposure to this tempestuous place the better. Margaret and I had seen plenty of gales in the Gulf of Alaska, the Bering Sea, the Philippine Sea, and elsewhere on other voyages; nevertheless in the Cape Horn region the gale frequency was 26 percent in June and 15 percent in December. This meant that in the southern winter we would experience winds of thirty-four knots or more, one day in four. During the southern summer (starting in December) we might well find similar winds one day in seven. Of course these figures were averages; the weather could be much worse or infinitely better.

Quite aside from the clinical graphs of wind and weather, we had heard unnerving tales about the strength and power of the squalls—the sudden windstorms—which in the vicinity of the mountains of southern Chile were called *williwaws.*

In the end we rejected the route via Tahiti because of the long and uncertain passage in the Southern Ocean, and additionally because we didn't like the prospect of a fifty-day voyage from Tahiti. Twenty or thirty days at sea were acceptable but longer nonstop runs were not.

"I want to stop after a few weeks and see something," said Margaret. I could hardly ignore her urgings, for Mar-

garet was a champion traveler who had gone from Bombay
to England via the Suez Canal five times before she was
eight years old and had never unpacked her suitcase since.

"If we harden in the sheets a bit we can go south via
the Galápagos Islands and Peru," she said, pushing back her
glasses and thrusting a forceful finger on a map of South
America. "Then if we go south along the west coast we'll
miss most of that stupid Southern Ocean."

From California to southern Chile was a hard business.
We sailed to the Galápagos Islands (west of Ecuador), a

*Once away from the immediate environment of land, we often
saw pintado petrels, small sooty-brown birds that flitted about
behind us, gliding, wheeling, skimming low over the water, and
turning every which way to show off their white checkered
mantles. These common petrels often follow ships for days and are
also known as cape pigeons.*

passage of 2,947 miles in twenty-nine days, mostly to windward against the northeast trades which blew mostly from the east. We continued to Peru but the sailing was more difficult because the force of the contrary southeast trade wind was augmented with the north-flowing Humboldt Current. It took twenty-one and a half days and 1,956 miles to make Callao, the seaport of Lima.

We carried on southward in light and variable winds toward Coquimbo, Chile, which we reached after 1,610 miles and seventeen days. From Coquimbo south to Valdivia (929 miles and twelve sailing days) we entered our fourth weather system and found southwest winds that were sometimes fresh enough to oblige us to anchor behind a sheltering headland (or Isla Mocha in one case).

As usual, a trip at sea was a powerful lesson in geography. I had always assumed that the west coast of South America was roughly south of the west coast of the United States. I was astonished at how far *east* we had traveled. The longitude of our departure point in California was 117° W. Far to the south, we learned that Valdivia, Chile, was at 73° W, about the same longitude as New York. We had been obliged to make 2,640 miles of easting as we went south. We had had to slug it out to windward much of the time because we had discovered a lot of easterly wind in the trades. In spite of all my scheming we had experienced a good deal of uncomfortable sailing. We were quite ready for a change of wind.

To begin our Cape Horn adventure we had come 7,604 miles which had required eighty-one days of sailing, a showing of only ninety-four miles a day. To demonstrate the absurdity of toy sailboats, an ordinary jet aircraft could have made the same trip in twelve hours and at a cost of only two meals instead of almost two thousand hours of sailing and two hundred fifty meals! Nevertheless we now had our floating home less than two hundred miles from the northern entrance of the Chilean channels—an isolated and little-known archipelago almost at one end of the earth. On

The trip from California to the northern entrance
of the Chilean channels.

Ports	Mileage	Days	Months	Winds	Course	Notes
San Diego, Calif. (33° N), to Isla San Cristóbal, Galápagos (1° S)	2,947	29	December January	E 18–24	SSE	Much east in NE trades
Galápagos to Callao, Peru (12° S)	1,956	21½	March April	SE 18–24	SSW & ENE	Against SE trades and Humboldt Current (near coast); two long tacks
Callao to Coquimbo, Chile (30° S)	1,610	17	October November	S 8–14	WSW & ESE	Light winds and much tacking; against Humboldt Current
Coquimbo to Valdivia (40° S)	929	12	December	SW 20–35	SSE & WNW	Obliged to shelter at times
Valdivia to Canal Chacao (42° S)	162	1½	January	W 20–25	S	Good beam winds

7,604 miles in 81 days, or an average of 94 miles per day

board our little yacht we had everything we needed for a pleasant existence—our beds, favorite books, a writing table, and a few treasured possessions. The wind was free, food was simple and cheap, and we had a whole new world to explore.

T W O

A Change of Wind

A LITTLE before noon on December 31, Margaret and I sailed from the dock at Valdivia and glided down the eight miles of river that separated the city from the Pacific. The trip to, and now from Valdivia, a place of 91,000 people, was great fun, for along the river we had fresh beam winds blowing warm and fragrant from the bordering farmlands. We sailed rapidly and easily in perfectly smooth water, even passing a Chilean tug hauling two barges laden with cargo. Everybody waved and smiled while all concerned kept a nervous eye on the wind and on *Whisper's* slowly increasing distance from the towline between the tug and the barges.

At the mouth of the river we slipped beyond the seaport of Corral and headed out into the Pacific whose familiar swells we soon felt. At five o'clock in the afternoon, the bearing of Punta Galera, the first headland southwest of Corral,

Here, nearing land, we steered carefully. The sea was rough and I wore my safety harness to keep me attached to the ship. The instrument with the white dial is a taffrail log which registers mileage. A life ring and a spare anchor hang on the stern pulpit. The strange-looking apparatus with the blue cloth at the upper left is a self-steering device which is excellent for use at sea where the wind is steady, but a good deal less helpful around mountains and cliffs and inland waterways where the wind is gusty and fickle.

43

bore 080° and we changed course to 185°, sailing almost south, with 115 miles to go to the Canal Chacao entrance of the channels. For the first time in thousands of miles we had a fresh westerly breeze and we drove through the approaching night with eased sheets. *Whisper* surged along splendidly without the miserable pounding that we had known so much since California. I felt free somehow—as if chains had been taken off my ankles.

The problem in sailing along a coast with an onshore wind is that if the wind blows up into a gale you have a dangerous shore on your lee side—a seaman's worst horror. On some coasts there are harbors or headlands or islands where you can find shelter, but on this part of the Chilean coast there were no real refuges. The only hope of a sailing vessel when hard on a lee shore is to claw off under reduced sail and to get far enough from land to be out of danger— say twenty-five to fifty miles or more. It is unusual, however, for winds to blow exactly at right angles to a shoreline which gives you a chance to work offshore easier by choosing the more favorable tack.

We had the hazard of the lee shore well in mind and I had chosen a course to take us twenty miles offshore. Fortunately, the barometer was high and steady and it was the season of best weather. In the early evening the wind increased to twenty knots, but instead of changing to a smaller headsail we let the yacht romp onward with the genoa because we had an appointment with a tidal stream.

We were quite aware that we had to pass through the entrance of Canal Chacao during slack water or with a favorable east-setting tidal stream. Our friend Captain Roberto Kelly of the Chilean navy had given us careful instructions when he had visited us further north.

"You must attempt Canal Chacao only when the conditions are favorable," he said. "Otherwise I think it will be impossible for a small yacht. The problem is that an enormous volume of water flows back and forth between Golfo de Ancud and the Pacific. Canal Chacao is narrow and the streams run hard. In addition, when the ebb, the west-going stream, meets the prevailing westerly swell, the result is an appalling sea—even for our large naval ships. When coming in you must arrange your program to be at the western entrance when the tidal stream is beginning to flood, that is, going eastward with you."

We followed Captain Kelly's advice and had worked out the proper hours. Now we were on schedule. *Whisper* made good time throughout the night. A few squalls passed over, one of which dumped a load of tiny hailstones on deck and obliged us to hand the headsail for a time. While the genoa was down I swapped it for the working jib. Margaret hoisted the smaller headsail at 0715, while I changed course to aim for the land to the eastward. Unfortunately, the morning sky was partially overcast; in any case, an early-morning sextant sight would have been useless for precise latitude, our chief concern. I tried my radio direction finder on the signal presumably sent out by the Punta Corona light station. The transmitted characteristics I received were the Morse letters OC instead of the letters CONA listed in the Chilean book of radio aids, which was only two weeks old. This meant I could place no reliance on the signal. As usual, when a bearing would have been handy, the RDF set was useless. Fortunately, however, I had no reason to doubt our dead reckoning plot based on the compass and the elapsed mileage indicator.

As the sun rose in front of us a little to the north, we steered southeast and ran before a twelve-knot westerly wind with maximum sail set again. Shearwaters and small black-browed albatrosses skimmed the water around us. At 1035 we saw a distant headland on the starboard bow. I knew the ocean depths were less because the westerly swell was increasing as it felt the floor of the sea. We busied ourselves trying to identify the land. The instructions in both the Admiralty and Chilean *Pilots*, our ever-useful volumes of sailing directions, warned of dangers to the north of the entrance, so we headed a little south to favor the southern

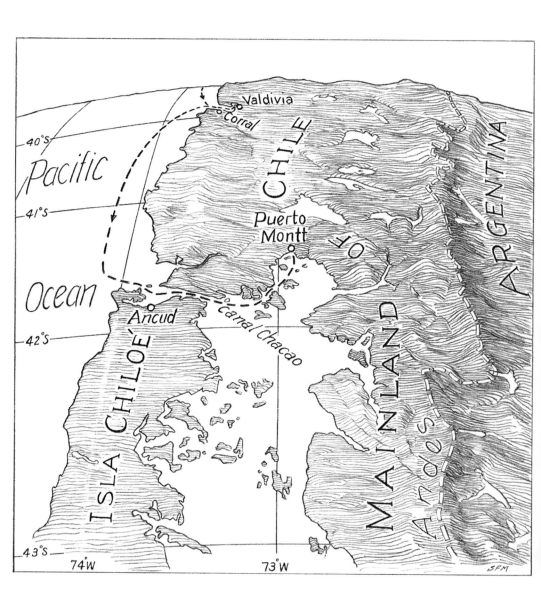

approaches. The key to the channel was the white tower of the Punta Corona light station, which we hoped to see shortly.

The ocean swells soon became enormous; there was no doubt about being in shoaler water. Sixty miles to the west the Pacific was 13,000 feet deep and extended in an unbroken sweep for thousands of miles—to Australia and beyond. The ground swell that we now felt was resonant, alive, and awesome. The yacht was bouncing all over the place in seas that were brittle and threatening to crumble; we had scarcely enough wind to keep the sails full.

All of a sudden I became aware of a thundering noise. Somewhere ahead the seas were exploding. As I peered nervously eastward from the top of a crest I could see mist and white water two or three miles in front of us. The great swells of the Southern Ocean were breaking on rocks.

The land appeared to be continuous to the right, so we eased off to port and gradually left the white water to starboard. The swells increased in steepness, and when we were down in the troughs we were quite becalmed and could see nothing except towering walls of gray water on all sides. Then up again for a look at the excitement toward the land. Margaret muttered something about taking a photograph but I had lost all interest in cameras. I wanted to get the hell out of there. My nerve ends were tied in knots and my stomach muscles were a mess.

I will never forget the force of those breaking swells. It was not a crashing waves-on-the-rocks-along-the-beach sort of action. It was a low-pitched boom, a vibration in the sea, a cataclysmic violence that I could easily feel from two miles away and which made the entire yacht tremble. The effect was a pulsing, a quivering, a wholesale shaking of the ocean, as if I were experiencing an earthquake or standing next to a warehouse of exploding dynamite. I was conscious of an enormous release of energy as thousands of tons of water were brutally halted at the edge of the continent. The angry water tried to continue onward and hurled itself into a froth of whitened fury. The forces in the Southern Ocean were truly astonishing.

Each transmitted shock of exploding water was enough to give any sailor palpitations of the heart. I had a momentary horror of being caught by one of those breaking monsters which would crush a large or small vessel like an elephant stepping on a peanut. I could almost feel a rippling of new grey hairs on the top of my head.

While I was edging away from the breaking shoal, Margaret was busy with the hand-bearing compass and the chart. She worked out that we had started to enter a small bay named Bahía Guapacho at the southern entrance to Canal Chacao. The breaking shoal was Rodal Guapacho. We took bearings of two small islets to the northeast which were in the right places, but we were unable to see the Punta Corona light tower which should have been in front of us. It wasn't until we passed into smoother water and went further east that we were able to pick out the hard-to-see tower, which needed a coat of paint and was quite inconspicuous—at least on the bearing we were on. For some unknown reason the light was on a point of land in back of Punta Guapacho, the obvious headland for the light.

In another hour we were behind the double projecting fingers of Punta Guapacho and Punta Corona. Here the water was calm, the tidal action insignificant, and we sailed slowly into a small cove named Puerto Inglés in Bahía de Ancud, well protected from the ravages of the Southern Ocean. When I let the anchor go, the sound of the chain rattling out echoed across the hills. A church overlooked us half a mile to the southwest. Green fields and patches of dark forests climbed to the uplands of Peninsula Lacui, the northwesternmost part of Chiloé Island. I could hardly believe the sight. We had arrived in the channels.

The little settlement of Ancud was five miles away to the southeast and I silently saluted the memory of the Norwegian singlehander Al Hansen, who had sailed through these waters from Buenos Aires via Cape Horn in 1934.

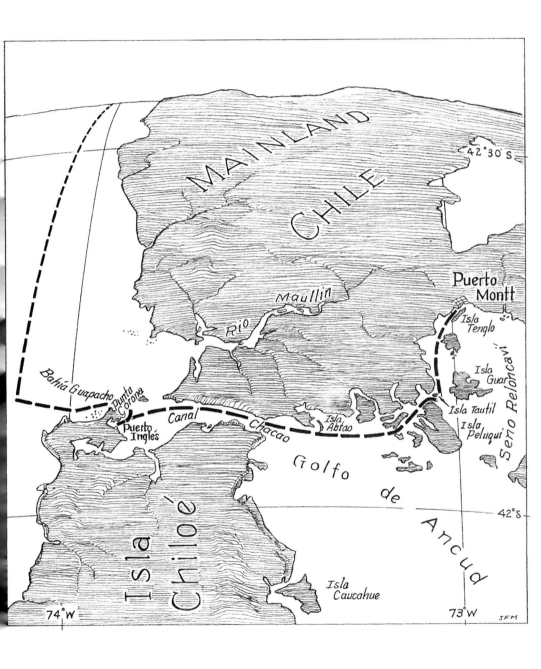

Hansen was the first small-boat sailor to make the classic big ship passage from 50° S in the Atlantic to 50° S in the Pacific against the strong current and winds from the west.

He sailed an eleven-ton gaff-rigged pilot cutter named *Mary Jane* that was thirty-six feet long, with a beam of twelve and a half feet and a draft of six feet, designed and built by Colin Archer in Narvik, Norway, in 1904. The former lifesaving vessel of the Norwegian coast patrol was a double-ender, painted gray with light bulwarks and a dark rubbing strake. She had a pleasant sheer and was constructed of wooden planks fastened with hardwood pegs called trenails. Unlike most gaff rigs she was sailed without running backstays. The mast, however, was a colossal solid spar whose diameter at its base was half the width of a man's shoulders. *Mary Jane* had a reefing bowsprit that projected forward of the stem more than eleven feet; the vessel carried three tons of iron and stones for ballast. The area of her three flax sails totaled about nine hundred square feet. To balance the cutter for self-steering, Hansen adjusted the tiller with wooden pegs that could be pushed into a series of holes across the aft cockpit coaming. The yacht had no engine.

The Norwegian sailor was a good-looking, muscular man in his middle thirties with enormous hands and a shock of dark blond hair that tumbled across his forehead. He always sailed with a dog and a cat that he carried as mascots. He was especially proud of his library of a hundred books and of a large photograph of a bathing beauty contest that had been autographed by Miss France, Miss Germany, Miss Russia, Miss Rumania, Miss Hungary, and Miss Tunisia.

Hansen had been a sailor all his life and had worked as a pilot in the merchant marine. He had logged twenty-two thousand miles in *Mary Jane* when he set out for Cape Horn from Buenos Aires in February 1934. He was keen to get around the tip of South America and to Chile before April when the season of strong gales began. The long passage to

Ancud took him almost sixteen weeks, by the end of which *Mary Jane's* sails were so ragged and patched and blown out that they were worthless. Hansen asked for new sails to be sent from Argentina.

In June 1934, almost at the opposite end of the world from his home in Forvik, Norway, he left for the port of Corral to the north. His vessel was wrecked in a violent storm along the coast and Hansen lost his life. No one knows the details except that some burned fragments of wood fastened with trenails were found. Now almost half a century later I thought of the death of this enthusiastic sailor—surrounded by his pets and books and his autographed pin-up picture—with regret. Hansen certainly belongs to the history of long distance ocean sailing in small vessels.[4]

Nothing can compare with the accomplishments of these solo sailors who—when the going is tough—have no choice but to carry on. The singlehanded ocean mariner is most assuredly the champion of all sportsmen and needs to be the master of a dozen disciplines, most of all himself. As a famous seaman once put it: "When they are tired there is no one to take their watch, when they are anxious there is no one to relieve them of their anxiety, when they think they are sick there is no one to laugh them out of it, when they are fearful there is no one to lend them courage, when they are undetermined there is no one to harden their resolve, and when they are cold there is no one to hand them a warm drink."[5]

The next morning we figured out compass courses and the bearings of different headlands and beacons to bypass the various shallow banks and rocks during the twenty-mile transit of Canal Chacao. We were so cautious that we laid out a course suitable for a squadron of battleships. The east-going tidal stream began at 1327; we left a little after 1200 to be at the right place at the best time.

What did we find? A light following wind, a clear sky, a

hot sun, and calm water. Our transit of the channel was so easy that I was a bit deflated after all the horror stories. We even took off our oilskins.

Now at last we were in the great archipelago of southern Chile, an inland sea of bays, inlets, waterways, fjords, gulfs, estuaries, and coves. Every sort of term was applicable because in a thousand miles of drowned mountain range the water assumed all possible forms. As we sailed east we began to see small islands which made position finding simplicity itself. We merely took compass bearings of three prominent land features in different directions and drew the bearings on the chart. The three lines crossed and made a point—or more usually a tiny triangle called a seaman's cocked hat. We were in the middle of the cocked hat.

The yacht Whisper *followed the Chilean channels and water-ways in the shadows of the Andes for 2,438 miles.*

While Margaret was steering I had been taking photographs, only to find when changing film that the camera had had no film in it. First I was mad at myself but soon I was laughing at my idiocy. We worked through a scattering of islands to the northeast on our way to Puerto Montt. The afternoon buildup of cumulus clouds brought rain showers, and the islands were first dark and then light as shafts of sunlight flickered through the moving clouds.

The countryside was hilly and dark green. Thick forests of low trees and bushes reached down to the water. Here and there stood solitary houses or small settlements with cleared fields outlined by wooden fences. The clapboard houses, generally unpainted, rose up tall and narrow with peaked roofs broken by smoking chimneys. We could see horses and cows, laundry on lines, and youngsters watching us. The country was like Norway except that the climate was softer and the slopes were easier.

The beaches on both sides of us were broad, of gravel or small stones, and were well marked with high water lines, for the considerable tidal action had scoured the shelving slopes into broad ribbons of seaside highways. Sheep and cattle patrolled these thoroughfares, chewing unknown fodder. We passed a church, and watched a black-hulled sailing vessel in the distance.

When the favorable tidal stream was about to turn we anchored in fifty feet of depth at Isla Tautil, not far from the first church that I had ever seen covered in brilliant pink paint. In the morning we continued northward, now in Seno Reloncaví, an inland gulf about twenty miles in diameter. To the east the sky was gorgeous, with several layers of marbled clouds—high cirrus, a pebbly layer at middle altitude, and ballooning cumulus at lower height. Bluish, snow-topped mountains seemed to rise directly from the eastern shore.

Ever alert for local knowledge, we followed a small passenger launch chugging along with people and a great mound of sacks of potatoes. From time to time the vessel, the *Chauquear* of Calbuco, would stop and a rowboat would shoot out from shore with a passenger and another sack of potatoes.

The harbor of Puerto Montt is formed by the protecting mass of Isla Tenglo, a skinny islet about three miles long, separated from the mainland by Canal Tenglo. As we neared the canal we passed several small shipyards, one of which was building a two-masted sailing ship whose image looked as if it should have been on a commemorative stamp or in a history book. We followed the canal to the main harbor which had very high docks along which lay an assortment of small cargo and naval ships. The tidal range was a problem so we threw our lines to the Chilean naval tender *Colo-Colo* whose crew lined the rail above us. We looked up at a row of black-topped heads with bright and curious eyes.

The interrogation that we had come to know so well in South America began. The questions, particularly the first, were always the same:

"When are you leaving?"

"Who knows? In a week or so."

"What was your last port?"

"Valdivia, with all the pretty girls."

"Where are you going?"

"Cabo de Hornos."

"How many on board?"

"Two."

"How much did the yacht cost?"

"The same as a small house."

"Do you like Chile?"

"Oh yes. Especially the beautiful mountains. And the Chilean red wines are very good."

"May we look at the yacht?"

"With pleasure. Tomorrow."

With a smile and a lot of handshaking we shouldered our way past the questioners and climbed up on the wharf to take our clearance papers to the officials.

THREE

A Rustle of Fabric

*I*LIKE to play a game with myself in which I carefully describe a place that I have never seen. I work it all out—the physical setting, sizes of things, people, what they do, colors, sounds, smells—everything. Then when I arrive at my unseen target I see how close I was. Sometimes my speculations are quite good, but with Puerto Montt I was a long way from an accurate description.

In truth this city of 80,000 was at the extreme north of the Chilean channels, nestled in the green foothills of the province of Llanquihue (lan-KEY-way) of which it was the capital. To the east and northeast a dozen high Andean mountains stabbed the sky with towering spurs of stone that were eternally frosted with white. Osorno was especially notable. It rose in a precise cone to 8,728 feet and loomed so close and huge above the sea that it somehow seemed artificial, almost as if a public relations firm had arranged for its presence. After each rain the surrounding peaks were dusted with a new layer of snow whose brilliance was often so silvery in the afternoon light that your eyes were hardly able to stand the glare.

The city had distilleries, flour mills, breweries, tanneries, wood product industries, and was a center for timber exports and sheep raising. People on holiday liked the nearby recreational lakes. In addition Puerto Montt was the southern terminus of the Chilean railroad system and—with few exceptions—the area marked the end of the national roads. To the south lay a wilderness of high mountains and thick forests, of isolated islands and intricate channels, of heavy rainfall and stormy winds. Isla Chiloé, to the immediate southwest, had a sizable population, but the numbers of people fell off abruptly further south. The only feasible transport in all this southern region was by water, and the shipping followed the natural waterways—called *canales* in Chile—which paralleled the north–south spine of the Andes for hundreds of miles. A half dozen small coasting ships handled cargo and passengers for the towns of Chiloé, for the hamlets of the mainland along the west slope of the Andes, and for the Chonos archipelago further south. Other ships brought limestone from Isla Madre de Dios south of Golfo Trinidad at 50° S. Some ships were on their way to

These oxen pull a cart laden with potatoes and farm produce through the streets of Puerto Montt. The stalls in the back sell baskets plaited by Chilote women.

Skimming along northeastward on a fair flood tide with a reaching wind from the southeast, this Chilote gaff sloop slips along in the shadow of Isla Tenglo near Puerto Montt.

and from the city of Punta Arenas on the Strait of Magellan. The Chilean navy had various patrol, work, and supply vessels. Finally, large cruise ships—generally painted a gleaming white with bright flags flying from every halyard and crammed with snapshooting tourists—occasionally stopped for a day.

With all these activities, a pleasant environment, and a reasonable climate, Puerto Montt was a lively little city. There were, however, other attractions.

As soon as we had entered Chile we were asked whether we ate food from the sea. "Do you eat shellfish?" was a question that we heard again and again. The Spanish word for shellfish is *mariscos*, and in Chile the word fairly rang through the air. In general the many varieties of *mariscos* were cheap and plentiful. Even the poorest man included shellfish in his diet.

Further north we had eaten scallops or *ostiones*, which were baked with butter and cheese and were so good that you immediately ordered more. We soon learned that the Chilean people ate *locos*, a kind of small abalone, as a first course with almost every meal. *Locos* were generally eaten cold with mayonnaise or a special sauce, were nourishing and quite filling, and had a smoky taste of the sea. *Choritos, cholgas,* and *choros* were mussels of different sizes which were eaten raw with lemon, fried, curried, or could be made into a hearty and aromatic soup. Clams were *almejas*, whose meat was fried or used for a thick and steaming chowder. *Langostinos* and *camarones* were small shrimp that were eaten uncooked with a spicy hot sauce or fried or concocted into a rich and filling broth. The orange parts from the insides of *erizos* or sea urchins were eaten raw with chopped onion and were considered to be the ultimate energy food for sexual power and longevity (always served by waiters with lots of sly and knowing winks). The *picoroco* was the giant barnacle, a five-inch stonelike crustacean—heavy as lead—that seemed to be of no use to man except maybe to be broken up in a rock crusher and used as paving gravel. Yet the center of the *picoroco* had a tasty white morsel of seafood—perhaps a cross between heart of palm and a chewy oyster—which you extracted and popped into your mouth. In addition there were *piures, machas, jaivas,* and so on and on, all sorts and shapes and colors of shellfish that were new to us.

These many creatures of the sea plus a dozen varieties of freshly caught ocean fish were sold at the market of Angelmó, which was on Canal Tenglo about a half mile from where *Whisper* was tied up. Angelmó was a functional place, strictly unfancy, and its stalls did a colossal business. Margaret and I often walked there to buy something to take back to the yacht for lunch or supper. The market was fascinating in the morning when the stalls were opening and the men were bringing in fresh seafood. Two husky fellows would hurry past, staggering under the weight of a pole from which hung a dozen great blue and silver mackerel, still glistening with sea water. A shout from behind would clear people to the sides as a wheelbarrow load of fresh

The food staple and delight of the Chileans in the south are shellfish. Here we see palm-sized mussels which are a main foodstuff and occur naturally by the millions.

clams was rushed along the walkway and dumped with a clatter of shells at a stallkeeper's feet. Perspiring men carried heavy boxes of *congrio colorado*, Chile's tastiest fish, to the counters where the big congers were fileted and exhibited and snapped up by housewives who couldn't wait to get the fish into their string shopping bags. Sure-footed boys brought in boxes of prickly sea urchins, beautifully packed in neat rows like hen's eggs. The boxes were handled as carefully as new babies in order not to break the delicate shells until a professional opener deftly cracked the sea urchins and extracted the orange meat just before selling it.

The smells of the market were sharp and pungent and pricked at my nose like the offerings of a spice market. Never had my nostrils been assaulted by such aromas. Something undefinable told me at once of the wholesome power in these seafoods. I was repelled and attracted at the same moment.

The sellers in the stalls were a confident and cocky lot of fat, merry, and ribald entrepreneurs who would crack open a shellfish, give you a taste, and then double up with laughter watching your face as you sampled something you had never tasted before.

The seafood market at Angelmó, however, was only half its business. The tiny bay was a gently sloping drying harbor that was safe in all weather. We were amazed to discover that over three hundred small commercial sailing vessels from the extensive waters around Chiloé, the Cordillera, and the surrounding islands came to trade.

The little ships were all single-masted cargo carriers from twenty-eight to forty-five feet long that were sailed in protected waters in sight of land. The black-tarred hulls had a beam of some 50 percent of the overall length, sharply flaring topsides, long keels, and almost flat bottoms which enabled them to be easily run aground and to lie at shallow angles when the tide was out.

Most were identical in design, with transom sterns and outboard rudders, and were rigged as gaff sloops with small jibs tacked to the ends of short bowsprits. The wooden hulls were carvel planked with *ciprés* which was copper fastened. Round beach stones made up the ballast. The anchor warps were braided from a tough local vine called *peta;* the parrel hoops around the mast to hold the hand-sewn canvas sails were formed of circlets of a native vine called *quilineja*.

The workboats had no engines, no lights, no compasses— nothing complicated to get out of order. The idea was to move cargo and people at low cost. Sails, oars, and the skills of the sailors were quite enough. I had the feeling that this commerce had gone on for ages and would continue long after automobiles, airplanes, and atomic bombs were forgotten. Indeed except for an occasional piece of synthetic line there was nothing of the twentieth century on these vessels at all.

The little Chilote ships came laden with colossal loads of firewood, bags of potatoes, sacks of wheat, and heavy boxes of shellfish. With high flush decks and the entire inside of the hull given to stowage, the carrying capacity of the small ships was unbelievable. In addition, the decks were often piled high with lumber, scrap boards, empty demijohns for wine, and three or four miserable sheep. The island women sometimes wove great stacks of shopping baskets to sell at the market and neat piles of them were sandwiched into odd corners on the deck. The upshot of all the bulky deck cargo was that the poor helmsman often had to stand tall and erect and to peer around things in order to see where he was going.

Besides the cargo were the owner, a sailor or two, plus various wives, girl friends, children, relatives with enormous suitcases, and sailing acquaintances. Cooking took place on deck over a large, three-legged black iron pan in which a wood fire was kindled. An iron grill over the fire held a kettle and a cooking pot.

A trip to Puerto Montt was not only for business but provided a social and shopping excursion as well. When a *lancha Chilote a vela* came in you could hear the excited chatter of the people on the boat carrying over the water. The children would be laughing and jumping about and all

Here are eight of the fleet of three hundred sailing vessels that take care of commerce around Isla Chiloé, the Cordillera, and Puerto Montt. With their

black-tarred wooden hulls, single masts, and highly peaked gaff mainsails, the little ships are distinctive and unique.

on board were anxious to get landed and see their friends who were waving from the shore.

The sailors of these cargo vessels worked the strong tides masterfully, sometimes anchoring during foul tides. If the weather was bad the captain sought shelter in any one of a dozen handy coves or he nipped around to the lee of a nearby island. If this wasn't possible, he simply ran his boat ashore. With smooth water, an ebb tide, and a weather shore, the ship—like that of Ulysses—was soon high and dry and safe. The lack of a compass wasn't serious because the sailing routes were well known and the helmsman usually had a few familiar islands or mountains in sight.

In a calm a couple of long oars appeared and the people took turns rowing or sculling. When a boat came into the shallow waters of Angelmó she was poled near the shore until she was aground close to her neighbors. A rusty anchor was tossed into the mud. Usually twelve or fifteen gaff sloops were in the harbor at one time. They stayed two or three days, did their business, and then slipped out quietly at the beginning of high water.

These small cargo vessels were unloaded by the owners and helpers who threw the goods into two-wheeled horse-drawn freight carts that were backed alongside the hulls. Often four or five carts worked at a single ship, the horses

A trip to market is a wonderful family outing. Here a man and his wife and their seven children glide southwestward along Canal Tenglo toward home after a visit to market to drop off island produce and pick up a few necessities. Junior steers while father pauses at an oar. Mother, in the bow, fondles a young child. This vessel is a double-ender—less common—and has been fastened with iron nails, now bleeding and streaking the topsides with rust. The sails are enough to make a yachtsman weep, but seem adequate for this family workboat.

(Overleaf) At low water in the drying harbor of Angelmó, eleven sailing sloops rest on one side of their hulls and prepare to unload cargo from their home ports.

wading in belly-deep water while being jockeyed into position by expert draymen who snapped their whips and shouted friendly curses at their plodding charges. The cargo was handed or tossed into the carts which went back and forth to shore like water beetles.

Horse carts easily work around the grounded sailing fleet, taking firewood, potatoes, and sheep, and returning with sacks of flour and sugar. The entire interior of the vessels is for cargo so the crews live on deck, cooking over little wooden fires that are set in three-legged iron braziers. Arrival time is a great chance to see friends and exchange information and gossip, so the crew do a lot of socializing.

We listened to the squeak of the carts' wheels, the splashing of the horses, and the banging of the sticks of firewood against the sides of the carts. We heard the squawking of swallowtail gulls on the alert for food and the yells of the men from one boat to another. We smelled horses and sea-weed and freshly sawn lumber. We inhaled aromas of dried fish and potatoes and onions as grunting men carried loads past us.

All these sounds and smells mixed with the movements of the people and animals and birds and water. These impressions merged further with the colors and forms of the masts and sails and hulls of the grounded fleet. We heard the babble of fish buyers, the lament of sellers, the screaming of children, and the gossip of women. A grand scene had exploded before us; it was a true opera of life, complete with comedians, martyrs, self-proclaimed tycoons, city slickers, country rubes, heroes, and fools. We never got tired of watching.

When Margaret and I walked back to *Whisper* we heard the clip-clop of horses' hooves on the bricks of the waterfront streets. Sometimes we saw oxen in front of wagons of farm produce. At the docks the gondola railroad cars filled with limestone were pulled by small locomotives freshly painted black and neatly trimmed with red. Their whistles screamed through the air, and the coal smoke rose from their stacks in widening swaths of black that looked glossy and hard against the satin white of the distant mountains.

Puerto Montt was a good place to stock up on food for the trip to Cape Horn. We had no idea what we would find on Chiloé Island or further south. Experience had taught us that when we saw something we needed we should buy it at once because we probably would not find it again. We already had many food stores on board. Margaret topped up her supplies of flour, sugar, cooking oil, potatoes, and onions, plus the usual fresh food. We had bought plenty of canned goods in Peru.

Whisper was in good order except that the compass was suspect. We had had the instrument adjusted by a professional in California and it worked perfectly as far as northern Chile, where we began to get too far offshore on some of our coastal hops. I took azimuths of the sun and discovered that we had a significant error. Since we were now tied up to a naval ship with a professional navigator on board I asked the lieutenant to help us.

There were half a dozen precisely placed buoys and towers in the harbor area so the navigator went out with us and constructed a deviation curve for the compass. While I was turning one of the adjustable magnets at the bottom of the compass, however, the whole built-in adjustment system fell to pieces, another casualty of red brass and salt water. Upon looking into the system I found that one of the adjustment magnets was loose and rolling around. No wonder we had had problems! I made a twenty-eight–dollar telephone call to the makers, E. S. Ritchie of Pembroke, Massachusetts, who airmailed new parts. Unfortunately, they—like other packages in southern Chile—never arrived. I finally junked the entire correction system and swung the compass without the correctors. I learned to verify the new deviation chart by checking the compass whenever I got between two points of land that were accurately charted.

The crews of the various commercial cargo ships heading south were forever trying out their lifeboats in Canal Tenglo. The boats were sturdy and well built, with flotation tanks and water breakers. The trials were serious business and the coxwains tolerated no fooling around. The orange-painted boats not only had small diesel engines and sailing rigs, but they had great bundles of long oars. I was astonished at how well the men used the oars. All these preparations of lifeboats and emergency equipment were a bit upsetting. When I mentioned where *Whisper* was bound, the eyeballs of our listeners invariably turned toward heaven and the people crossed themselves.

All vessels traveling through the Chilean channels were required to have a pilot. We had asked for an exemption because we would be traveling by day only and had a full set of charts—ninety or so—plus four volumes of detailed sailing directions. We told the authorities where we were going and gave them an approximate schedule. We were requested to report at several places on the way and to stay in the main channels ("No exploring, please").

We asked the local naval commander, Osvaldo Schwarzenberg, and Luis Macias, the captain of the Chilean naval tender *Lautaro*, for their advice about several alternate routes and about anchorages in general. One afternoon we spread out an armload of charts which the two officers were kind enough to mark with cautions, favorite anchorages, good watering places, and friends' names.

"You will find three places with very dirty weather," said Comandante Schwarzenberg. "Golfo de Penas, Isla Tamar, and Cabo Froward. I suggest that you have a good rest before you try those areas. Also you should rub your favorite rabbit's foot and get what help you can from up there," he said, looking upward while making the usual gestures toward heaven.

Puerto Montt had a tiny yacht club with a few power launches and sailing dinghies. The sole cruising yacht was a small ketch with red sails named *Odin* that was owned by Guillermo and Marina Herrera. Willi and Mari, as they were called, became good friends and we often ate at their home on the hill above the city. The Herreras were good prospects for the sailing life because they kept their little house as neat as a ship, with everything tidy and perfectly in place. Willi and Mari took us for drives to see the lakes north of Puerto Montt. They suggested that we move *Whisper* from the congested environment of the docks to an anchorage at the yacht club about two miles southwest on Canal Tenglo.

We found the anchorage quiet and pleasant and near a local bus line so we could ride into Puerto Montt. In South America most people don't have automobiles so the bus transport is highly developed. There are lots of small buses, they run frequently, and go everywhere for trifling fares. The buses—bouncing along and often smoking frightfully—move quickly because the drivers make it a point of honor to race from stop to stop at full throttle.

We didn't like the Puerto Montt museum, but we saw a wonderful private museum dedicated to early life on Chiloé Island. The owner and curator was an author and woodcarver named Narciso Garcia, who had assembled a superb collection of historical artifacts. Most museums are dullsville, but Garcia's collections were grouped to give surprising insights into the island life of a century ago. Garcia gave us a good tour and even with the language problem had us laughing or astonished in turn. The Chilote people of generations past had curious ways. On wash day, for example, a woman put her dirty clothes into a large wooden tub on the ground. She added soap and water and then climbed into the tub and trod on the wash with her bare feet to agitate and clean the clothes. In one room we saw tools and plumbing parts and farm implements—even complex threaded parts—that were constructed almost entirely from wood. Garcia's wife was hard at work on a definitive Chilote dictionary. Certainly the worthwhile work of this energetic couple should qualify them for assistance from the Chilean government.

One morning I watched an enormous Mercedes bus try to turn a corner into a narrow street in downtown Puerto Montt. The driver saw that it was hopeless so he stopped and backed and filled and backed and filled. Behind him was a horse pulling a milk delivery cart. The horse and cart were small; the bus was very much larger. I watched the pleasant sight of the bus being stuck while the horse nimbly slipped around and went on about his business.

The following night when we were on *Whisper* I saw a mouse in the forepeak. The creature had probably gotten on board when we were at the commercial docks. The mouse was playing among some newspapers—perhaps building a nest. I got out a trap, cocked the spring, and baited the trigger with cheese. Later I happened to mention the mouse to Willi Herrera who was on board at the time.

"We have a mouse on board," I said.

Willi shook his head. "Oh no," he replied. "You are mistaken. Mice never come to yachts. I am positive of that. Besides I—"

At that instant there was a sharp snap from the forepeak. I rushed forward and returned holding the trap from which the mouse dangled. Willi was dumfounded.

It was pleasant in Canal Tenglo. We had never been anchored in an area with a tidal range of nineteen to twenty-six feet. At low water we were down in a canyon; at high water we were level with the trees on the shore. The sailing lives of the black-hulled Chilote boats were regulated by the tides. On every flood tide we saw a sail or two or three coming northward. On the ebb a few boats dropped down from Angelmó and headed southward and home.

The windward ability of the local sailing vessels was poor, but with a fair breeze and a favorable tidal stream they raced along at eight or nine knots over the ground. In calms an oar or two appeared. If a Chilote vessel seemed to be making much progress to windward you could be sure that an oar was working on the side of the vessel away from you.

The helmsman of a local sailing sloop generally bent his course a little when he spied the hull and mast of *Whisper*. The passing vessel would come close alongside so the crew could look us over. The people on board always seemed to be having a good time, almost as if they could hardly believe their good fortune at having a free ride on the wind and water. The nautical traffic went on in rain or sun, during the day and at night.

From my journal:

January 30, 2200   The air is warm and sultry and the stars are lovely and clear. Margaret and I were sitting talking in the cockpit earlier tonight when we heard a rustle of fabric. We looked up and there was a lancha Chilote a vela *only a few feet away with her big gaff mainsail silhouetted against the dark sky that was brightened a little by a new moon. There were no lights on board and the black hull glided slowly along, the helmsman's cigarette a dot of red in the black.*

The sailing vessel skimmed along slowly when suddenly the main halyards were let go and the canvas flapped to the deck in loose folds, the blocks squeaking as the halyards flew up. Someone tossed over an anchor and as the vessel swung away from the moonlighted sky, she disappeared in the night.

Puerto
Montt

Isla
Guar

Isla
Puluqui

Isla
Abtao

Isla
Tabon

Isla
Queullin

Seno Reloncaví

Estero

Cordillera

Reloncaví

42°S

Golfo

de

Ancud

Isla
Caucahue

Isla
Llancahue

Estero Quintupeu

Buta
Chaques

Isla
Mechuque

Estero
Cahuelmó

Isla
Tac

Estero Renihue

42°30'S

Isla
Caquache

73°W

72°30'W

SFM

78

FOUR

The Fjord in the Mountains

*W*E SAILED southward from Puerto Montt on a sleepy January morning bound for a place deep in the heart of the Andes. A sail in the mountains was something new to us and I fretted about the probable lack of wind. As we glided along in *Whisper* I marveled at the bluish scenery. Everything was part of a rainbow of blues—the mountains, the forests, the sky, the water, even a series of warm and gentle rain showers that looked like blue teardrops as they moved with the wind. In pouring rain we could only see to the end of the yacht. Ten minutes later the rain would drift away and the massive bulk of the *Cordillera de los Andes* was suddenly revealed with super clarity: a broad ribbon of cliffs and headlands and steep forests that climbed away to dazzling flashes of snow on distant summits.

Our destination was a place called Cahuelmó, about fifty-five miles to the south-southeast. By the late afternoon

(Overleaf) One day while anchored in Cahuelmó we had a visitor from another fjord who sailed over in his eight-foot dinghy, which used a slim branch for a mast, a couple of willow cuttings for a boom and sprit, a scrap of cotton cloth for a sail, and an oar for a rudder.

We became friends with Don Pedro, here seen with two of his sons on a calm day in this elegant fjord.

we had crossed Seno Reloncaví and part of Golfo de Ancud, two large inland gulfs. All day long we saw black-hulled gaff sloops piled high with sacks of potatoes and wheat going northward. Sometimes we had six or seven sails in sight at one time. We were in another century, in another world, with never the sound of an airplane or an automobile and only rarely the slow thump-thump of a fishboat engine or an inter-island ferry.

A friend named Jorge Piñeiro had suggested that we visit Cahuelmó. "It's an idyllic place and has wonderful natural hot springs," he said. "A half-hour soak will take ten years' wear and tear from your bones." Jorge clapped his hands together with pleasure as he spoke. "It makes me feel younger just to think about those marvelous soaks and all

that mountain grandeur. You'll be entirely by yourselves because the only resident is a man named Don Pedro who is a friend to all visitors as long as they don't steal his cattle."

"The Chilean *Pilot* says that winds of the fourth quarter —westerlies—blow in this estero with great violence," I said.

"Nonsense," said Jorge, who had been a Chilean naval officer and was now the master of *El Trauco*, a large Chilean yacht. "I have personally visited the fjord many times and have always seen it calm and peaceful during our summer trips. You *must* go."

When Margaret and I sailed in to Cahuelmó we saw that it was about one mile wide and three miles long, with a narrow entrance, forested walls that rose steeply from the water, and a cascading waterfall some 230 feet high that plunged noisily into the northeast corner of the bay. Most of the fjord was about 130 feet deep so we followed the local advice and dropped an anchor near the waterfall and ran a stern line ashore.

We were soon entranced by the utter tranquility of the place. We met Don Pedro and his four children. He was a cheery, quiet man who was raising his children single-handed because his wife had been drowned in a boating accident. Unfortunately, she—like many people close to the sea—could not swim. Don Pedro had formerly lived in Ancud but his home was destroyed in the earthquake of 1960. He had moved to Cahuelmó, built a house, and in addition to a few scratch crops and some chickens he ran a few cattle. He eked out his income by selling shellfish and smoked fish. He took his wares to Calbuco in the usual Chilote sailing sloop because there were no roads within fifty miles. The children went to school in the next inlet north, but it was too far to sail or row each day so the youngsters boarded with friends until the weekends when Don Pedro brought them home.

Cahuelmó seemed such a remote place for this man and his children. We gave them our old clothes and they brought us fish and beef. More important, Don Pedro rowed over for a little visit each day. It was fun to blow gently on the spark of our new friendship. I would pour a glass of wine and hand it to Don Pedro who would drink it down and hand back the glass with a shy smile.

At Don Pedro's suggestion we piled into the dinghy and rowed up to the steaming thermal springs which were so hot that you could scarcely touch the water. The local people, however, had led several cold rivulets of water to the hot springs, and by partially damming up the hot with a handful of moss and letting in some cold you could adjust the temperature. In addition the locals had hollowed out several bathtub-sized depressions in the soft volcanic rock. It was marvelous to have a hot soak under the warm summer sky with trees and ferns and wildflowers around you. If you turned your head a little you could see mountains topped with snow.

Sometimes in Cahuelmó we saw a pulling boat twenty or twenty-five feet long come in for a load of shellfish. The two-man crew worked in a strange fashion. One man put on a headpiece breathing apparatus and plunged over the side

with a collecting bag. The diver's partner on board cranked a large handwheel connected to a small compressor that pumped air to the diver via a long hose. The men took turns diving and pumping. It seemed eerie, somehow, for a man to be below the surface of the sea with air pumped to him by his buddy above in the real world. There wasn't a sound connected with this lonely fishing. The only sign of the man below was the unending motion of the fisherman above slowly cranking the big iron wheel. It was spooky.

Cahuelmó was a good place to do a few small jobs on *Whisper*, to write some letters, and to study the next batch of charts that led toward Cape Horn.

Early one morning I suddenly awoke and felt the yacht pitching and rolling. I looked out and was horrified. The calm fjord was whipped by a westerly wind, the wind that supposedly never blew in the summer. We were trapped at the east end of the fjord near the shore and had to leave immediately. I cursed myself for ignoring the warning in the *Pilot* and for not having cleared out the evening before when the barometer had begun to drop and low clouds had blocked out the stars. Fortunately we had hanked on a small jib and had reefed the mainsail. I jumped into the dinghy and pulled myself along the stern line toward the cliff where the line was tied to a tree. As soon as I was afloat in the dinghy I realized why we weren't feeling well. *Whisper* was rolling all over the place in a wicked chop caused by the wind against the strong ebb that was pouring out of the fjord. The short waves slopped into the dinghy which was soon half full of water. I got as close as I could to the end of the warp and reached up with a knife, cut the line, held to the end, and signaled Margaret who quickly pulled the dinghy and me back to the yacht. We hoisted the dinghy on board and lashed it down.

Now we had the problem of beating out of the fjord against a headwind that was increasing by the minute. We ran up the mainsail and backed a small jib to get moving. I bent over the anchor windlass while Margaret tacked back and forth. The difficulty was that the strong wind wasn't steady but thundered down on us in irregular squalls from slightly different directions. The sails flapped frightfully when the wind headed us. After some effort I got up the chain and anchor and we began to beat toward the entrance.

If the wind had been a constant thirty or forty knots we could have thrashed our way out. But the wind was first twenty knots and then forty or fifty knots as the squalls shrieked down from the mountain heights. The wind heeled us over until the sides of the coachroof were in the water. Then all of a sudden the punch of the wind would be gone and we would be sailing along quietly. In the distance, however, I could hear another squall coming. With all the violent movement the engine wasn't much help because the propeller was out of the water half the time. (Over the years we have found that in really hard going the engine is relatively useless.)

The clouds began to lower and the wind increased in force until it threatened to blow me off the foredeck. The gusts buffeted me as if someone were punching my shoulder. I realized that it was hopeless to try to get out of the fjord because the squalls were rocketing down from the entrance every couple of minutes. The fjord itself had no shelter except at the upper end which was encumbered with unknown sand banks and shoals that dried out at low water, certainly not a place to explore with such winds behind us.

The only hope was to anchor out in the middle of the fjord. The holding ground was excellent white sand, but the depth was 130 feet which meant that we needed some 650 feet of cable. I dragged an anchor and two long warps to the foredeck, tied the lines together with a carrick bend, and began to fake down the lines. But as fast as I got a pile of line in order, a squall heeled the yacht and half the line skidded over the side. There was nothing to do but to start over. Again and again the line got tangled. There was some unintelligible shouting from the cockpit and gesturing about rocks but I waved Margaret onto the other tack. I went on sorting out the foredeck knitting like a seamstress gone wild.

The wind force escalated and the squalls whipped the water to a white froth. I had never seen such violence from wind and water in a restricted place. All land disappeared, the ship vanished, sight itself was blocked, and my eyes felt only the piercing sting of hail from the squalls. It probably sounds stupid, but the violence of the weather was beautiful in a way. I know that sometimes one's senses seem suspended, and an eternity of impressions flashes before the camera of the mind. For a second I seemed to look into the heart of the storm and to feel a strange kinship with the winds that were trying to destroy my little world.

Down at my feet the line tangles were hopeless because the deck was a teeter-totter that fell first one way and then the other. I looked around and saw that by some clever sailing in the lulls, Margaret had been able to get within a mile of the fjord entrance so we had a little sea room behind us. I motioned to Margaret to ease the mainsheet and then to come forward and hand the jib. Meanwhile I let out a forty-five-pound CQR anchor and all 210 feet of chain. The scope was less than two to one, but I figured the drag of the anchor would slow us down and hold the vessel somewhat until we got the line sorted out. With the yacht no longer heeling so violently, and with four sets of fingers frantically untying the tangles, we quickly sorted out the warp and let go a twenty-pound Danforth anchor and eased out 560 feet of line—a very long string. Both anchors held. We dropped the madly flapping mainsail and took careful bearings of landmarks. Even in the squalls we didn't drag. We were safe.

Around the perimeter of the fjord a dozen new waterfalls poured down from the heavy rain. During a clearing in the storm Margaret suddenly noticed a group of small figures huddled together on shore. Don Pedro and his children had watched our whole little drama.

We measured the wind when it eased a little. During the shrieking gusts, the indicator on the Swedish Ventimeter immediately shot to the top of the scale which meant sixty-three knots. Two days later this turbulent wind still blew and it wasn't until the third day that the noisy storm passed over and we were able to leave the fjord. The experience at Cahuelmó was a bit sobering. We were still twelve hundred miles from Cape Horn and already we had been severely flattened. Now when we sailed, one part of my brain would be tuned in to the nearest protected anchorage. No more open fjords for us.

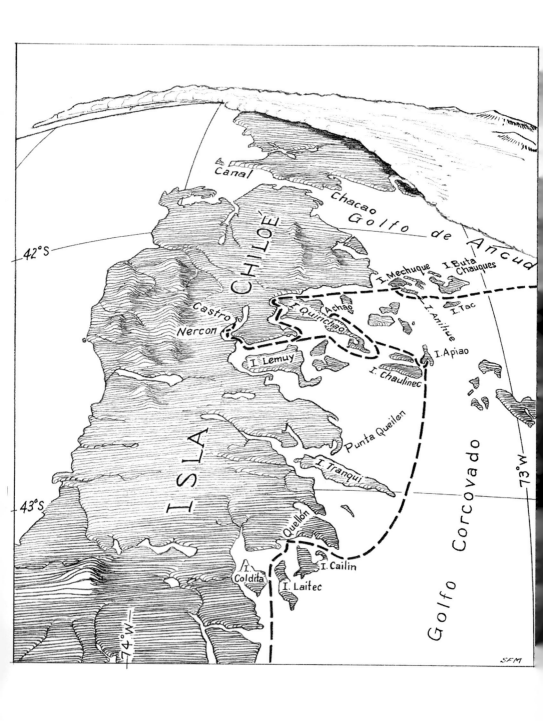

FIVE

Black Hulls and Shellfish

W E SAILED toward Isla Chiloé which lay fat and green on the western horizon. The date was February 13 and a sixteen-knot wind blew warm and steady from the southwest. Margaret was in a good mood and she sat in a corner of the cockpit while she chuckled over a book by James Thurber. We worked up to a small island named Buta Chauques and skimmed along the southeastern shore past a band of kelp that floated parallel to the land. Above us rose the brown cross of a small church on the cliffs of the rocky island. Two hours later—with the setting of the sun—we rounded Isla Añihué close to starboard and slipped into the quiet water south of Isla Mechuque. Under the mainsail alone we slowly sailed near a small village. We noticed a group of people watching us. No one took his eyes off *Whisper.*

We anchored off the village in the place suggested by the Chilean *Pilot,* but three pulling boats came out at once and told us that we were in the way of night traffic. We were conducted to the *puerto* around the corner where we were surrounded by land on all sides. By the time we had anchored for the second time we seemed to be major news.

A half dozen boats were now tied up alongside. One man wanted to sell us chickens ("only 2,000 escudos. Very plump"). While I was declining the offer of the chicken salesman I saw out of the corner of my eye that a fishing boat as big as *Whisper* was coming alongside. And a second! One tied up forward and the other began to maneuver toward us. It was too much. I untied the first fishing boat, pushed it away, and asked the crew to come the next day. I turned to see two *carabineros*, with boots and smart uniforms, climbing on board from a pulling boat. Two girls who had come with the policemen also wanted to inspect the yacht, as did the rest of the welcoming committee. By the time night fell and everyone had left we had shown *Whisper* to forty visitors. Chicken feathers were all over the cockpit.

Mechuque (meh-CHU-key) was a small hamlet of some seventy or eighty gray and unpainted clapboard houses with peaked roofs that were built around several low hills near the shore. We had been invited to the house of Fermin Grandón the chief *carabinero*, so we called on him to present our papers. Fermin invited us in for a breakfast of fried clams. The *carabineros* were the national policemen of Chile and had a reputation for fairness and uncorruptibility. (Unlike elsewhere in South America we heard that if you offered a bribe to a Chilean *carabinero* you were liable to go to jail.) Instead of being a national secret police, however, with all the undertones of that phrase, the *carabineros* that we encountered were more like friendly patrolmen on a neighborhood beat. We often saw these men in remote places where they kept law and order and always appeared neat and well groomed.

We met Fermin's two children and had a look around his house, which seemed somewhat overfurnished and cluttered with souvenirs. His wife was busy cooking in the kitchen. Fermin had a wind-up phonograph and was keen to play stirring *carabinero* marching songs, which seemed a bit much at 0830.

We went for a walk to see the village with Fermin's sister and another girl. The church was closed because there was no priest just then. We saw several small stores which had the usual canned goods, dried beans, sugar, rice, cooking utensils, and a few rolls of cloth. The island had too much rainfall for wheat and barley so the various cereal crops were often cut while green and taken into the kitchens of the homes and placed near the warm cooking hearths to ripen. Most of the men worked as woodcutters or fishermen and the village reflected these modest endeavors. We saw a few fishing boats up on the beaches, and one man was building a new cabin on an old hull. All the drinking water in Mechuque was fetched by hand from several wells and the people lighted their homes with kerosene lamps. There was daily mail service from Chiloé. The people had a simple life, but it seemed wholesome and pleasant.

We visited Fermin's house before we left and once again plates of delicious seafood appeared, accompanied by stirring *carabinero* marching songs on the phonograph. Fermin was delighted with our visit and presented us with a bottle of hard cider. He was a dear fellow but he was obviously miscast as a policeman. He should have been the leader of a brass band.

When we sailed from Mechuque, three old men stood on the beach and watched us, absorbing every move that Margaret and I made with the anchor and lines and sails. The three old men stood entranced. I felt a little self-conscious as if I were doing something wrong, so when we began to pull away I turned and waved good-bye. No one moved. The three old men stood perfectly still, filming us with their eyes. I went back to my steering and the chart. Before we changed course at the end of the island I turned and looked back. The old men were still watching. No one had moved. *Whisper* must have represented a dream, an escape, a change, a curiosity, a novelty, a transitory link with the universe beyond. Never have I seen three men look with such penetrating intensity.

We sailed westward to Canal Dalcahue where we an-

chored off the eastern shore of Isla Chiloé. This big island
measured about a hundred miles from north to south and
was thirty miles from east to west. In the early nineteenth
century when Chile rebelled against the Spanish crown,
the Spanish governors fled to Chiloé and in despair offered
the island to England. George Canning, England's foreign
secretary, turned down the suggestion, and in 1826 the last
of the Spanish royalists was driven from the island which
was Spain's final foothold in Chile.[6]

At the end of the eighteenth century Chiloé had three formal religious districts and fifteen Franciscan missionaries.
Perhaps it was from these ambitious men of God two centuries ago that Chiloé derived its tradition of churches. Margaret and I saw churches everywhere—on prominent peninsulas, on high hills, in villages, along waterways, even on
tiny islets. The churches were small, but astonishingly numerous. The Chilean sailing charts of this region were dotted
with Maltese crosses.[7]

Everywhere were churches. Ahead, behind, to the right, to the left . . .

To find our position we only had to take the compass bearings of three churches on three different islands or headlands and then draw the lines on the chart. On foggy days we tried to follow the lead of the local sailors who kept track of land by listening for the barking of dogs.

Chiloé had a population of 111,000 that was clustered on the sheltered north and east sides of the island. There were two cities, Ancud in the north, and Castro in the east. Castro, with a population of 22,000, was located up a protected inlet far from the sea. I had read that the city had been settled by a Spanish explorer in 1567. I had also read that Castro had been looted, burned, and had suffered various earthquakes, fires, and floods during its four centuries. I expected a venerable walled city with an ancient church, old colonial buildings, and men on horseback.

The first sight of Castro revealed a skyline with the twin spires of a graceful church. The skyline also revealed the large A-frame of a new tourist hotel. Instead of men on horseback I saw men in Volkswagens. Instead of the mellowing stone of large colonial buildings we saw hundreds of small modern structures, warehouses with tin roofs, a bus depot, the towers of a radio station, and a crowded open market along the waterfront.

We had come in on the flood tide with a half a dozen black-hulled Chilote sailing sloops that were laden with people and produce. These local vessels sailed directly to the beach near the market to dry out. We anchored in a depth of thirty-three feet and lay near the route of motor launches that went back and forth between Castro and a swimming beach several miles across the channel. Each of the big fifty-foot wooden launches took fifty or sixty people and was pushed by a single twenty-horsepower Swedish Archimedes outboard motor, a low-rpm powerhouse that we often saw in Peru and Chile. It was a remarkable demonstration of the useful application of power.

My sea boots had begun to disintegrate so I rowed ashore to hunt for patches. Shopping is slow business in remote corners of the world but it gives you a chance to meet the people. The key is patience. I walked down the sleepy main streets, and after half a dozen false leads I found a likely looking hardware store. Inside I interrupted a card game to ask the clerk—the chief player—whether he had patches for rubber boots. After the clerk finished his hand he put down his cards, disappeared into a back room, and brought out a small patch made in Germany.

"Perfect," I said. "Have you a larger one?"

The clerk went to the back of the store again and after a few minutes returned with a bigger patch. "Give me six large and six small," I said.

The clerk was astonished. "Your boots must have many holes."

"Like a sieve," I replied, holding the fingers of each hand at right angles to the other to get across the meaning. "What about cement?" The clerk stopped for a minute to take a few sips of tea, disappeared into the back, and after some time returned with a tiny tube of cement.

"More," I said. "Bring me a dozen." By this time the card game had been forgotten. All the players had collected at the counter where they took a keen interest in my leaky boots and the patches. I had to explain who I was and where I had come from. Distant place names were meaningless so I said that I had sailed from Valparaiso, which resulted in a lot of worried looks.

Finally the clerk returned from the back room for the fourth time and triumphantly displayed twelve tiny tubes of cement. "Do you own a shoe repair shop?" he said. We all had a good laugh. My purchases were carefully wrapped and tied, and after some lengthy calculations the bill was worked out.

"Enough for many years," said the clerk as he presented me with my package. "No more wet feet." With smiles on every side I paid my bill (500 escudos), shook hands with the clerk and all the card players, and left.

Margaret and I shopped for food at the outdoor market along the Castro waterfront. We bought big purple onions and fresh string beans only a few hours from the vine. We loaded our canvas shopping bags with crunchy apples, luscious green cucumbers, heavy bunches of fat carrots, and eggs that were still warm. It was hard to stave off the women selling dried fish (very smelly) and those who

(Overleaf) We watched the little sailing vessels come in along the waterfront of Castro. We saw the men unload bulky sacks of potatoes and chupones, *heavy boxes of shellfish, and the omnipresent sheep or two. Life for these people revolved around the barter system, but they always retained a sense of dignity, independence, and cheerfulness.*

hawked lottery tickets ("Today is your day"), but we readily bought *chupones* which were the fruit of a thorny upland plant and looked something like artichokes. Each *chupone* had several dozen protruding seed stalks. You pulled out a single stalk, crushed the white inner end with your teeth, and sucked on it for a delicious pineapple flavor. When the taste was exhausted you plucked out another stalk, and so on. Children loved *chupones* and people all over town were chewing the stalks. When Charles Darwin visited Castro in 1835 he also noted that the locals were sucking seed stems from *chupones*, "a pleasant sweet pulp, here much esteemed." [8]

There was a great deal of sampling and checking in the market. A man would ask for an apple, take a bite, shake his head, and go on to the next seller. A woman would take a few cereal grains and earnestly inspect and taste them before deciding. A fish was never bought until the gills were looked at to see if the fish was really fresh.

All of the produce was sold by an old Spanish dry measure called an *almud* which is equivalent to a peck or a little less. Each seller had a neatly made box—roughly eight inches on a side—that had been handed down from mother to daughter for generations. You bought an *almud* of plums or half an *almud* of peas.

Local boats often came to market with some of the women on board clutching lovely bouquets of flowers. I am a sucker for ladies with flowers, so we always had a fresh bunch on the saloon table while we were in Chiloé.

Many of the women in the market wore thick hand-woven woolen skirts with a fringe at the bottom. The patterns were large squares of orange or dark green or brown with contrasting lines at the edges. Margaret liked the heavy wool and bought a one-kilo ball to knit a sweater. Meanwhile I negotiated for a fresh mackerel for dinner.

We discovered that an ordinary glass bottle was a treasure that was carefully saved for refilling or to turn in for a full bottle. There was no chance of purchasing wine, mineral

water, ginger ale, or cooking oil unless you had bottles to surrender. To get around the container shortage the house-wives of Chile practiced constant bottle larceny. Margaret managed to collect a dozen bottles only after the most involved purchases.

"Six bottles of ginger ale please."

"Do you have the bottles?"

"No. Sell me the bottles. I will pay extra."

"Completely out of the question, *señora*."

"Where can I get bottles?"

"At the distributor's warehouse."

"Where is that?"

"I can tell you the address, but I must inform you that the company only sells wholesale and will not sell to you."

"Sell me three bottles. I will . . . ah . . . bring them back tomorrow."

"Ha!"

While we were in the south we found that shopping for ordinary items used by the people who lived in the region was easy and direct. We could buy local food, simple clothes, basic hardware, kerosene, soap, and aspirin without too much trouble. Getting unusual items or services was much harder. Nonregional foods, flashlight batteries, complex hardware, typing paper, radio repairs, and visits to a dentist were often hopeless.

To mail a package of exposed camera film to the U.S. was an all-day job.

"What's in the package?"

"Tourist films."

"You will need a stamp from Customs."

This meant a trip across town. The Customs man was about to go fishing and looked at my package with suspicion. "But it's going *out* of the country, not in," I pleaded. He stamped it.

Back at the post office the clerk didn't like my package.

"You must have a hole in it for inspection in Santiago."

"But I already have a Customs stamp."

"You must have the hole."

The postage charge for a kilo was 5,000 escudos or eight dollars. The only stamps, however, were in fifty-escudo denominations. Where can you put a hundred stamps on a small package? After some trial and error I stapled a piece of paper to the package and glued the stamps in place. I registered the parcel of course, but *certificado* was run by a bewildered woman who had obviously never handled an overseas package before. After thirty minutes at her window (with an impatient, lengthening line behind me) I was ready to swear off photography forever.

By now we had been around Puerto Montt, the cordillera, and Chiloé Island long enough to soak up a few impressions. The Chilote people were part Indian and part Spanish, with sparkling brown eyes, tanned faces, and coarse jet-black hair. The men were short and wiry; the women tended to be short and dumpy (the slim, stylishly dressed *señoritas* of Chile lived elsewhere). The Chilote men often wore tams or knitted caps and heavy sweaters of thick wool. They were almost all confirmed chain-smokers and great talkers who delighted in standing around discussing the weather, the qualities of old girl friends, or the next trip to Calbuco or Chonchi. Meanwhile the women worked industriously—selling at the market, cultivating in the fields, carding wool, and looking after the numerous children (once I saw a young lady nursing a child while she sorted mussels in a sailing vessel). It was common to see men talking and smoking in a boat while the women rowed. The men were clearly in charge, but I suspect that on an operational level the Chilote society was run by women.

The style of life was rustic and pleasantly primitive. The people were open and sincere and you couldn't help but hold out your hand to them because they were so trusting and direct. Our Spanish was terrible, but the Chilotes made an effort to follow our blundering efforts and somehow we were understood (gestures and diagrams on paper helped).

(Left) The hull sections of these load-carrying Chilote workboats have sharply flaring topsides. The main driving power comes from the large canvas mainsail. Note the brailing line from the leech of the sail to the gaff boom. This line leads down the mast to a convenient position so the sail area can be reduced quickly in case of a squall.

(Above) These vessels have gaff sloop rigs with crude fittings and gear, but the sailplan works well in these waters. The main boom is supported by fixed topping lifts which chafe the sail badly when the mainsheet is eased. In most parts of the world, gaff rigs have adjustable topping lifts which can be eased to reduce chafe. When I suggested this scheme, my idea was met with horror. "My grandfather used fixed topping lifts and what he did is good enough for me. Besides, a little sail sewing gives the women something to do."

How the Chilotes liked little jokes! I was keen to go for a sail on a local sloop so one day I went off in the *San Pedro* from Huequi to the next port. Margaret followed in *Whisper*. The *piloto*, Bernardo Peredes, and the *propietario*, Marcelino Nuñez, doubled up with laughter and amazement when they saw Margaret hoisting *Whisper's* sails, trimming them expertly, and beginning to overtake the *San Pedro*. I made a motion to Bernardo and Marcelino that Margaret might beat their sloop (we were running downwind). First the two men looked worried, but when they realized that I was joking with them, their laughter and good spirits knew no bounds.

We learned that the Chilotes have a rich and varied folklore of traditional beliefs, superstitions, and legends that rival the ancient Greeks and Romans. *El Millalobo* is the king of the sea. *La Huenchur* is a mysterious medicine woman. *La Pincoya* is the golden-haired daughter of the seashore and beaches who controls the shellfish. Dozens of

(Left) The piloto, *Bernardo Peredes. (Right) The* propietario, *Marcelino Nuñez.*

While I sailed on the San Pedro *and watched Bernardo Peredes steer, Margaret sailed alongside. Here she is forward adjusting a line while* Whisper *looks after herself.*

intricate stories and characters tell about everything from the creation of the land to man's sicknesses and death. To explain the birth of a child, for example, the legend of *El Trauco* introduces a sort of demon spirit of love in the form of an ugly dwarf with hypnotic charm who goes around seducing young unmarried women who want to run away but can't . . .[9]

(Overleaf) The fishermen's village of Nercon was built on wooden piles along the shores of these lovely hills that climbed westward from the sea a little south of Castro. On the water people traveled by boat; on the land they walked or used donkeys.

At Nercon we saw this ship's carpenter planking up Chilote workboats.

We sailed to nearby Nercon, where there was a small shipyard, and walked among a collection of old fishing boats, a new launch under construction in a shed, and a twenty-six-foot double-ended sailing vessel being built outside. The work was rough and crude. Half a dozen frames were cracked and one of the planks was split, but the whole job from the order to launching was to take only fifteen days. The planks were fastened with copper nails which were bent over where they emerged from the frames. The men eyeballed most of the planking and worked quickly. The yard crew also sewed the sails. Previously the men had built a sailing workboat that was fifty-nine feet long and the year before had constructed a thirty-foot sailing yacht named *La Pincoya*.

As we traveled south we passed fishing villages whose dwellings were built on high pilings along the edge of the water. One morning we dipped our flag to a big government health vessel which traveled from island to island with a medical staff on board.

All transport moved by water and a man's boat was as important to him as an automobile is to an American. Often we had half a dozen sails in sight when we traveled. In calms, oars appeared. Until I went to Chile I never realized how effective oars could be. We saw people rowing everywhere. It was common to have several oarsmen, each pulling on an oar ten to thirteen feet long. When the wind dropped, we watched heavily-laden sailing craft moving steadily and smoothly with a couple of oars. Once I was in a heavy *lancha* sixteen feet long (with a dozen people and their baggage) that was pushed by oars and which made reasonable progress. The blades of the oars were narrow and the rowers generally pulled with a short jerky motion, not a long smooth sweep.

The blessing of southern Chile was the abundance of shellfish. No one ever went hungry. On a minus tide the people scurried along the wide shorelines as the water receded with gurgling and sucking sounds. The trees and banks seemed high above us as we floated on a lowered ocean.

The water was low—down twenty-six feet—and a whole new world of sloping shoreline lay exposed. The women were humped over, bent down after clams and other goodies, their finds dropped in baskets carried in their left hands. Men dug

with wooden rakes among the seaweed or with old shovels in the mud. Loudly yelling boys competed with one another to get something choice. Old men carried string bags and scratched with hoes. Dogs sniffed and barked and ran along the exposed shores. A thin man in high boots industriously raked up a special sort of seaweed and shoveled it into baskets which he dumped into his rowboat. Young children clutched toy containers and mimicked their elders.

Everything was hurry! hurry! because the extreme low water lasted less than an hour. Once the crops were covered, the chance was gone. You could easily tell the sex of the picker by his track. The women seemed more patient and their nimble fingers quickly turned over rocks while their bodies scarcely seemed to move. The men all used tools, dug violently, and left disturbed mounds behind them.

Other people worked in the shallows from small boats and employed long poles with wire nets on the end. A man in yellow oilskins reached as low as his tall pole could go and groped blindly for special small shells. A little way down the beach a cow munched uneasily on yellowish seaweed that had been exposed by the low water. Across the channel on a point of land in the distance I could see other human figures bent over plucking a harvest of shells.

I listened to the sounds of the digging: the rasping, scratching, scraping, the clunking of rocks, the squeal of

This church at Achao was said to be the oldest on Chiloé. We heard a date of 1832 mentioned, not far from the time of Darwin, Fitz Roy, and the Beagle. The architectural style is curious and includes arches, two types of windows, three kinds of shingles, and a square-sided tower surmounted by an eight-sided cupola. Obviously the structure is very old and has gone through many restorations, including the recent concrete piers for the columns that support the arches. Looking at the church made me feel that a carpenter from England or the northeastern U.S. must have had a hand in the design at some stage. Inside, the church was surprisingly large with an open plan, but the interior seemed damp, dark, and drafty.

shovels on stones, the slurping of a pole being withdrawn. I watched while the shellfish people furrowed and inspected, probed and fingered, and dug and sifted in the mud and sand along the edge of the vast inland Chilean sea. Now, however, the water began to rise. Suddenly the work was finished. The men and women stood up and stretched their stiff backs. The tools were wiped off; baskets were measured and combined. The women disappeared in the direction of their homes. The cattle climbed to the fields. The children ran elsewhere to play. The men sat on the high shoreline to talk and smoke.

We called at Achao to see a century-old church, and at Isla Apiao because I was intrigued by a U-shaped island whose interior was accessible to our draft at high water. In the sheltered inlet of Apiao we found a shipyard on a hill, a large oyster-farming operation, and we saw a marvelous woodcarving by a Chilote artist. We could have spent a month, a year, or a lifetime sailing around Chiloé which seemed endlessly intriguing. Many of the anchorages were beautiful. We had a date with Cape Horn, however, so we took advantage of fair northerly winds, sailed southward, and soon began to leave the neat checkerboards of cultivated fields behind us. The settlements became fewer and the familiar brown churches grew less common. No longer did someone immediately row out to see us and crash alongside when we anchored. I had often been cross at all the interruptions by the Chilotes. Sometimes I had complained bitterly to Margaret about the lack of peace and quiet. When we were no longer bothered, however, I confess that I missed the knocks on the hull and the questions from the alert and curious Chilotes. I suppose I was like the man who fussed about the noisy violin practice of his daughter but who missed the music when she was gone.

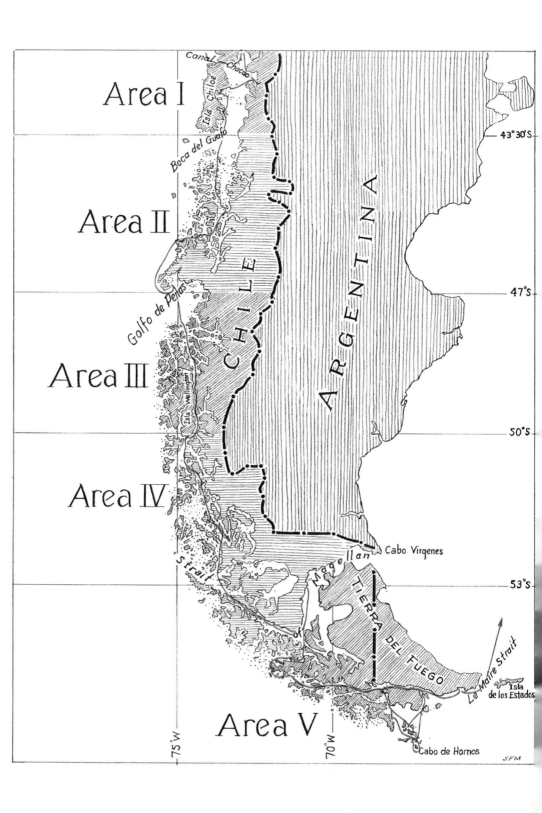

SIX

Who Was Anna Pink?

FOR PLANNING purposes I found it convenient to divide the Chilean trip into five parts. We had just sailed south from Isla Chiloé (Area I) and now were crossing the Boca del Guafo into the Chonos archipelago (Area II) which extended to about 47° S. Area III ran from Golfo de Penas to the fiftieth parallel of latitude at the south end of Isla Wellington. Area IV reached from 50° S to the Strait of Magellan and the city of Punta Arenas. Area V included the big island of Tierra del Fuego and Cape Horn.

Measured in a straight north–south direction, the distance lay between 42° and 56° S, which was fourteen degrees of latitude or 840 nautical miles. Our route was by no means direct, however, and when I totaled up all the bends, twists, backtracks, detours, false starts, and roundabout tracks of the whole trip, we found that we had logged 2,438 miles between Puerto Inglés in Canal Chacao and the west end of Isla de los Estados in Le Maire Strait.

Just now, however, we were entering Area II, the Chonos archipelago. We sailed across the Boca del Guafo in twenty-five-knot, gray, northwesterly weather. Astern, Isla Chiloé fell from sight. Four hours later we saw the first views of las Islas Guaitecas ahead to starboard. The islands rose up low and wooded at the base to somewhat barren and rounded heights of 1,200 feet. With this landfall we began a series of daylight runs from one isolated anchorage to another. Dense woods replaced the farming communities further north and the few fishermen that we saw were poorly dressed. The fishing sloops of the Chonos were small and crude, with high-peaked gaff mainsails of dark-brown fabric. Soon even those were behind us.

Margaret and I had four thick volumes of sailing directions or *Pilots* from the Chilean navy plus ninety-six nautical charts. In addition we had two volumes of British Admiralty *Pilots* and a few English charts to supplement the Chilean plans. We found the Chilean charts excellent and up-to-date. A small point was that land heights were sometimes poorly shown. I recall sailing alongside great cliffs in one place and looking at the chart which showed only blank white spaces —as if we were sailing on the Argentine pampas. The Chilean navy wanted mariners to stick to the main tracks so soundings were purposely omitted from side channels.

We liked the charts. The *Pilots* were also good and written in simple, direct Spanish so that even a couple of foreigners could work out the directions. The Chilean physical aids to navigation were poor, however, and some navigational lights were out or inoperative. Most beacons, markers, and monuments desperately needed repairs and painting. My guess was that the lights and maintenance had been neglected because of Chile's abysmal financial plight and because all transiting large vessels took Chilean pilots who had intimate knowledge of the waterways.

We found it regrettable that many of the beacons that marked channels and various critical places were not maintained. These monuments were all mentioned in the *Pilots* and drawn on the charts and obviously had been erected at great cost and effort by the navy in the past. In spite of this problem, however, the *Pilot* books and charts were quite adequate for daylight traverses of the channels.

Day after day we sailed southward along the various waterways—Perez Norte, Perez Sur, and Moraleda. We generally logged thirty to fifty miles on each run and found lots of good anchorages. It was early March and the prevailing winds blew from the north. With fair winds the

sailing was easy and pleasant. We seldom saw settlements or people.

One afternoon I had a nasty scare. A big rusty steel-hulled fishing boat steamed close to us. For a moment it reminded me of the vessel that had come alongside us off the Peruvian coast four months earlier and had demanded whiskey and cigarettes. When I demurred, the scowling Peruvian captain had threatened to ram the yacht and had sheered off only when I got out the Winchester thirty-thirty rifle and fired two shots into the air. But now as I looked across a bit nervously I saw only smiling faces on a Chilean navy workboat. We quickly ran up our U.S. flag and dipped it and watched a Chilean crewman hurry to lower and raise his trim red and white flag with a white star on a blue canton.

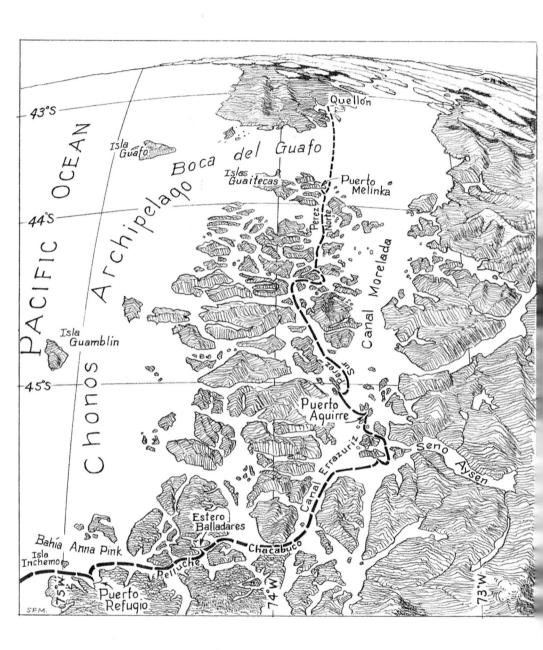

We stopped at a little village named Puerto Aguirre, near the entrance to Seno Aysén. The settlement was way out in the wilds and was a ragged little place that existed on fishing, and shellfish collecting and canning. Large or small, however, these remote hamlets always had two *carabineros*, a generating plant for electricity, radio communications, a proper schoolhouse, and an alert group of fishermen. When we changed course to sail up near the settlement, the wind came from ahead so we began to tack back and forth. All at once we noticed a group of people on shore watching our approach. As we sailed abeam of the men standing on the beach next to their open boats we began to get the unmistakable hand motions that indicated we should anchor. We sailed a little further, dropped the jib, anchored, and fell back to the suggested spot. Soon a dozen of the locals were on board to check us over.

Late that afternoon when everyone had gone, a leaky old rowboat pulled alongside. A pretty young woman sat in the sternsheets and held a baby on her lap. A rather disreputable-looking, unshaven man was rowing.

"Do you want to make a lot of money?" asked the woman.

"Why not?" I answered without risking anything.

"You must give me things to sell."

"What do you want?"

"Good clothing."

I made a motion to take off my trousers.

"Oh, no," she said with a marvelous laugh. "I mean **extra** clothing. New things."

While this conversation was going on I noticed that water was creeping up inside the rowboat. The woman moved her feet upward on the curved sides of the boat to stay ahead of the water. I motioned to the couple to climb on board *Whisper*. The woman shook her head. I offered a bucket to the man and made motions of bailing. He was clearly not interested.

"Do you have any French perfume?" asked the woman.

"French perfume?" I almost dropped the bucket. "What would you do with French perfume?"

"Sell it! There are many opportunities here." She gave me a sly glance and made vague motions toward the shore. I looked where she indicated but all I could see was a great pile of purple mussel shells and a dozen old whaleboats.

"Er . . . how much do you want?" I said.

"Bring me many large bottles of French perfume. I can sell them all. You will get much money—and perhaps more." She smiled up at me mischievously. "I must go now," she said. I swallowed nervously. Who was this charmer?

By this time the rowboat was one-quarter full of water. The woman continued to work her feet up along the sides of the hull to stay ahead of the water. Her child eyed the water fearfully and clutched at her mother's neck. The man at the oars had boots on and sat dumbly waiting until the woman nodded and he began to row.

I watched the boat go to the shore. The people climbed out, pulled the boat up on the beach, and trudged up the muddy track without looking back. What could this woman possibly do with French perfume? Sell it to the crews of passing vessels? But how many ships stopped in Puerto Aguirre in a year? How could I find the woman again? Would I want to? If the woman made money smuggling, she certainly didn't spend much on her water transport. Her boy friend didn't look any too prosperous either. In any case she was certainly an appealing smuggler, and if she had worn a few drops of the French perfume she could have unfrozen the cold heart of any passing captain.

That night the wind blew at thirty knots from the north but the holding ground was good and we were well anchored with plenty of chain out. Once when I got up to check our position I noticed that our kerosene anchor light had blown out. While I was relighting it I saw that a small coasting ship had anchored behind us. Maybe with a cargo of French perfume.

The next morning we watched the village while we got ready to leave. Wind-blown smoke raced downwind from

As we traveled south, the local vessels got smaller and cruder.

each house and the branches of the scrub trees rattled in the gusts. The fishermen worked at their boats drawn up on the beach and unloaded mackerel and sea bass. An old woman in a ragged brown sweater struggled to carry heavy firewood to her house. Children played nearby (no one offered to help the old woman). Higher up on the beach a new boat was under construction but there had been delays and its partial planking was gray with time. A man staggered along with a sack of flour and disappeared up the track into the woods. In the distance young girls skipped rope and their laughter rang across the water. Two women stood talking on the porch of a house while another woman shook out a blanket from an opposite upstairs window. Several boys took turns shinnying up the mast of a boat and then sliding down with shouts. Meanwhile the old woman in the ragged brown sweater struggled by herself with the firewood.

We sailed south along Canal Errazuriz and east by way of Canales Chacabuco and Pulluche. One night we stopped at Estero Balladares and anchored near a freshwater stream that ran into the protected bay. The water was smooth and quiet except for some commotion caused by a dozen ducks that beat the water frantically with their wings. At first I thought the birds were driving small fish before them into the shallows but later I found out that we had been introduced to loggerheads or steamer ducks which, unable to fly, beat the water to a froth in their frenzy to run away from danger. We got to know these strange birds well and often saw them madly flapping away when we entered isolated anchorages. According to my friend Bill Tilman, who had sailed these southern waters in his Bristol Channel pilot cutter *Mischief*, you had to be mighty hungry to relish a steamer duck.

Whether steamer duck should be called food is "a point verging perilously on the moot" [he wrote]. Our duck had been hung for three days, boiled twice, cooked in a pressure cooker, and served curried, yet still it had about it a pungent flavour of steamer duck —that is, of fish oil. Many years have passed since the Rev. Dr. Folliot justly observed that "the science of fish sauce is by no means brought to perfection—a fine field of discovery still lies open in that line"; yet in Patagonia the field has been neglected, as yet no sauce has been discovered that will disguise the fishiness of steamer duck.[10]

We had a good rest at Balladares and since we had a sparkling mountain stream next to us we filled the water tanks and did the laundry. Passing ships sometimes stopped for water at Balladares and a dozen signs with the name of a vessel and the date were nailed to a tree next to the stream.

We followed Canal Pulluche a little south and then west into Bahía Anna Pink where we began to feel the familiar swells of the Pacific. With dramatic high cliffs to the south on our left we edged along past four small islands and slipped into an anchorage.

Puerto Refugio lay on the edge of the Pacific and was surrounded by cliffs and mountains except for the entrance on the northwest side which was protected by half a dozen islets. While rain thundered down and low clouds swirled around the headlands we anchored off a beach on the southern side in sixty-five feet. When I had first seen the term *puerto* on a Chilean chart I thought that perhaps docks or ship facilities existed, but in truth *puerto* was merely a protected or partially protected place to anchor. The last three anchorages had been quite deserted and there didn't seem to be a soul within a hundred miles.

Puerto Refugio and Bahía Anna Pink dated from Commodore George Anson's voyage of 1741 against the Spanish. Anson's English fleet consisted of six fighting ships and two supply vessels, a 200-ton pink named *Industry* with twelve crew, and a 400-ton pink named *Anna* with fourteen crew (the term *pink* referred to a small three-masted bark with an especially narrow stern). The men of the expedition suffered terribly from scurvy during the long trip from England to the Pacific via Cape Horn.

(Overleaf) From our anchorage at Puerto Aguirre we looked at this scene of small houses, whaleboats, fishermen, and wood-gatherers.

While off the coast of Chile at about 46° S, the *Anna*, separated from the rest of the fleet, got involved with a westerly gale and was driven eastward toward the land. The captain—Master Gerrard—attempted to anchor near Isla Inchemo but squalls drove him toward the mainland and it seemed that the *Anna* would be wrecked for sure. At the last minute, however, the crew spied an opening in the cliffs ahead and steered into a well-protected bay. The ailing men lived in the refuge for two months and cured their scurvy by adding shellfish and wild vegetables to their diet before sailing onward. The anchorage was named Puerto Refugio and the larger area was called after the pink *Anna*, which in lubberly fashion has been corrupted to Bahía Anna Pink.[11]

Thirty miles to the south lay Rescue Point which was named by Fitz Roy aboard the *Beagle* on December 28, 1834:

While we were furling sails, some men were seen on a point of land near the ship, making signals to us in a very earnest manner. Being dressed as sailors, it was natural for us to conclude that they were some boat's crew left there to collect sealskins. A boat was sent to them, and directly she touched the land they rushed into her, without saying a word, as men would if pursued by a dreaded enemy; and not till they were afloat would they compose themselves enough to tell their story. They were North American sailors, who had deserted from the *Frances Henrietta* (a whaler of New Bedford), in October 1833. When off Cape Tres Montes, but out of sight of land, and in the middle of the night, these six men lowered a boat and left their ship, intending to coast along until they should arrive at Chiloé. Their first landing was effected on the 18th, but owing to negligence the boat was so badly stove that they could not repair her, and all their hopes of effecting a coasting voyage were thus crushed in the very outset.

Here in Estero Balladares, with unlimited fresh water from a mountain stream running into the anchorage, Margaret does some laundry.

(Overleaf) Looking across Bahía Anna Pink we see dark cliffs and hills that ring Puerto Refugio. It was here in 1741 that the pink Anna found refuge.

Finding it impossible to penetrate into the country, on account of its ruggedness, and thick forests, which, though only trifling in height, were almost impervious, they began a pilgrimage along-shore; but it was soon evident, to their dismay, that there were so many arms of the sea to pass round, and it was so difficult to walk, or rather climb, along the rocky shores, that they must abandon that idea also, and remain stationary. To this decision they were perhaps more inclined after the death of one of their number: who, in trying to cross a chasm between two cliffs, failed in his leap, fell, and was dashed to pieces. Their permanent abode was then taken up at the point which shelters Port San Estevan, now called Rescue Point; where they passed a year in anxious hope. Of course the few provisions which their boat had carried ashore were soon exhausted, and for thirteen months they had lived only upon seals' flesh, shell-fish, and wild celery; yet those five men, when received on board the *Beagle*, were in better condition, as to healthy fleshiness, colour, and actual health, than any five individuals belonging to our ship.[12]

From Bahía Anna Pink it was necessary to sail in the ocean for about one hundred forty miles because of a gap in the inland waterways. Part of this mileage was across the Golfo de Penas which had an evil reputation for storms, poor visibility, and unpredictable shore-setting currents. A weather forecast would have been helpful, but we had found it impossible to get such information in southern Chile. What broadcasts there were merely referred to conditions at the moment.

We waited until we had fair weather and a high and steady barometer and sailed from Puerto Refugio on a sunny clear morning with a fourteen-knot westerly wind blowing. We headed south and a little west to get an offing and by midnight we had logged sixty-three miles and were making good progress. At 0200 Margaret saw the flash of the Cape Raper light. I thought of the three watchkeepers at the remote lighthouse and the description written by Roz Davenport when the forty-six-foot Australian cutter *Waltzing Matilda* had visited the station in 1951:

The light was lit by paraffin. It had to be turned by hand, each man taking a watch through the night. It was beautifully kept, every single part polished and sparkling like a modern kitchen. I climbed inside the light itself while one of the men turned the handle—I felt like a white mouse in a cage, running on a toy wheel. Two hundred feet below, the Pacific crashed against the cliffs. Even at that height the noise of the wind and the seas was deafening and we could feel the building swaying with the force of the wind.[13]

At 0300 we changed from the genoa to a working jib when a series of light squalls dumped cold rain on us. At dawn I worked out a sextant sight from Venus to verify our position at the northern entrance to the Golfo de Penas. By 0800 we had double-reefed the mainsail and were running east-southeast with a thirty-five-knot wind on *Whisper*'s port quarter. The dark bulk of Peninsula Tres Montes was ahead to our left with Cabo Tres Montes somewhere in gray clouds in front of us. Because the wind was increasing I decided not to run for Canal Messier, which was fifty miles to the southeast across the Golfo de Penas on one of the worst lee shores in the world, but to sail instead to Puerto Barroso behind the shelter of Peninsula Tres Montes. It looked like an easy twenty miles. As we got close to the land, however, the fair wind that I had counted on gradually turned against us because it somehow worked behind the peninsula and mountains and headlands and now came charging toward us. Furious squalls began to dart out from the land, and the yacht heeled drunkenly as the wind hit the sails. By noon the wind was Force 8 from the north. Because of the weather shore there were no waves to speak of, but the sea was all white. Spray flew everywhere. Not only was the wind contrary, but we were obviously bucking some current or tidal stream—maybe both—and our progress was pathetic. It took us eleven hours to make good the last twenty miles to Puerto Barroso, no doubt our slowest twenty miles ever. When we finally anchored, we stripped off our soaking wet clothes and threw them on the cabin sole. Our faces were white from caked salt.

"I'm fed up," said Margaret. "How can you sail with such a sneaky wind? This Cape Horn route is paved with problems."

SEVEN

Condors and Shipwrecks

SLEET clattered on the deck and squalls whooshed over the bay every few minutes as we lay in Puerto Barroso waiting for an improvement in the weather before continuing south. The surprising thing about the place was that a squall would pass, the sun would come out, and the bay would be calm and quiet for a few minutes. But if I went on deck to do a small job, I would look up to find the sun suddenly gone and another squall roaring down on *Whisper*.

Quick! Grab the tools and get below.

The wind continued to blow hard from the north, switching abruptly to the south on the second day when the center of the weather system passed us moving eastward. Margaret and I watched streamers of storm-driven clouds run swiftly before the wind. Yet through breaks in the moving clouds we could see higher clouds that seemed almost stationary. The strong winds appeared to be below an altitude of a thousand or so feet.

The early nineteenth-century British survey ships had

In Puerto Charrua we sailed past this waterfall that was 432 feet high.

stopped near our anchorage in 1828 while charting these waters for the first time. Margaret and I had the distinct feeling that few people had been here since. We looked at untrodden sandy beaches and thick tangled forests of deep green that thinned out as the trees climbed the slopes.

On the third morning the sun shone brightly in the March sky and the needle on the barometer moved steadily to the right. While I recovered our anchors a condor circled overhead. The giant vulture had black plumage with white wing patches and a white neck ruff. Its flat lead-colored head was featherless and the neck had a wattle of loose skin. As the bird wheeled above the mast I could distinctly see light between the curved and separate dark feathers at the tips of the nine-foot wings and hear a rush of air with each flap. The bird was remarkable to see and made me think of dinosaurs and pterodactyls.

"Some bird," said Margaret. "Let's hope its appearance is a good omen."

We still had to cross the Golfo de Penas so we got out the chart and books to examine the fifty-mile gulf again. Normally the crossing of a small gulf was a trifling matter. Volume II of the Chilean *Pilot* suggested otherwise:

The gulf is particularly notable for the continuous and violent storms that sweep through the area, and for the large seas caused by the gales. A strong current from the west runs between Cabo Tres Montes and the entrance to Canal Messier. Great vigilance for navigation is advised during thick weather and in periods of poor visibility.

We started out with light winds which gradually freshened from the north. A few hours later we were running hard under shortened sail toward a frightful lee shore. We watched the fading summits of Tres Montes behind us and took bearings to check our east–west set, but low clouds and rain made it hard to see. We kept the mountains in sight for fifteen miles and then had only thirty-five miles to go, which should have been an easy dead-reckoning run. The problem, however, was how much to allow for the east-

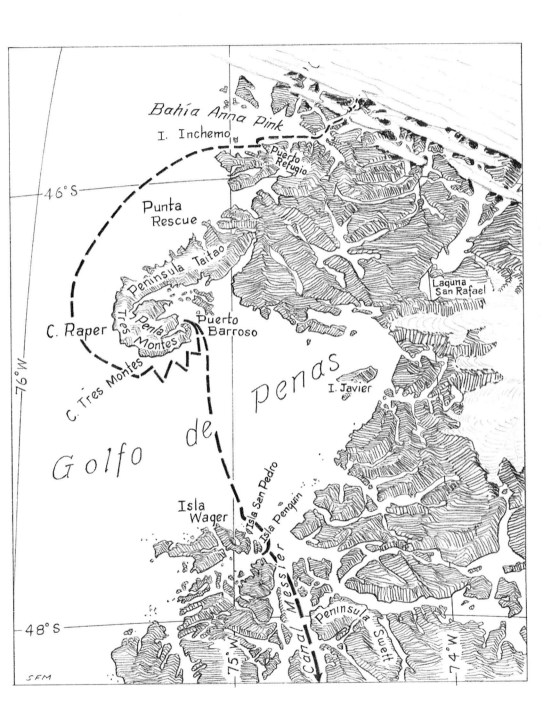

setting current. I figured fifteen degrees, but as the wind and seas increased, the steering was hard and our course was not exact.

I went below to tune our radio direction finder to the powerful San Pedro lighthouse radio beacon at the northern end of Canal Messier. I was quite astonished to find that San Pedro transmitted on 500 KC (Servicio QTG). My Brookes & Gatehouse RDF set stopped at 475 KC. In addition the station transmitted only on request which meant that with no transmitter on *Whisper* and an RDF set unable to receive the San Pedro signal there was no chance of radio assistance. Once again the RDF set was useless.

Because our east–west position was uncertain as we neared the southern shore of the Golfo de Penas I kept up enough sail to be able to push back into the thirty-knot wind if it became necessary to head northward into the gulf. Margaret steered while I stood forward with an arm around the mast and looked carefully ahead and to each side as I had done so many times before.

Sometimes a patch of dark cloud resembled a mountain-top. At other times I thought a breaking swell was a rock, but the only things I saw for sure were storm petrels and small black-browed albatrosses. Rain fell heavily. No wonder the trees and shrubs grew so thickly at this latitude. I said a silent prayer for all mariners running toward lee shores.

Suddenly I saw land ahead. We immediately turned eastward, hardened in the sheets, and began to see waves dashing against rocks and islets close to our right. We headed up a little to work offshore a bit and went along while I tried to fit an ill-defined shoreline into the sopping chart I held in my hand. All at once we saw the big steel towers of the San Pedro lighthouse. Marvelous! Now we knew exactly where we were. Margaret turned south-southeast and we left the land—Isla Wager—and the light station to starboard. An hour later we were seven miles south in Canal Messier, running nicely in smooth water, and about to round Isla Penguin into a good anchorage.

Isla Wager, the island we had just passed, got its name in

1741 when the twenty-eight-gun three-masted British ship *Wager* piled up on the north shore. Part of the same fleet that included the pink *Anna*, the *Wager* was one of Anson's ships bound against the Spanish. The beamy, bluff-bowed oak vessel had left England the year before, painted a proud yellow with a bold blue stripe around her upper works. Her cheering crew of a hundred sixty had hoped to become rich from plunder. But nine months later the ship was scarcely workable because of scandalous shipyard preparation, damage from heavy weather, and bad management. The officers and crew were miserable and only half alive because of scurvy. Thirty men were already dead; another hundred ten were to perish on Isla Wager and elsewhere; only twenty men got back to England.[14]

The next day the strong north wind continued. It was fair for us, however, and we were in sheltered waters so we hurried southward along Canal Messier. The north–south waterway was about three miles wide with small side branches here and there. The sailing was glorious. We had excellent charts, no navigational worries, and with only a headsail up we were able to surf along when a squall overtook us. High cliffs and mountains rose on both sides of this great natural canal. From time to time ravines filled with dark-green foliage ran back from the sides. Waterfalls poured down from unseen lakes and streams that had been charged to overflowing by the rain. Sometimes the storm clouds lowered to a few hundred feet and made a sort of wall between the sides of the channel. Masses of gray mist swirled and thickened and billowed while the rain and wind poured down.

A Swedish cargo ship passed us headed northward. I was glad that *Whisper* wasn't plowing into the seas and wind and wind-induced current that the big vessel seemed to take so easily.

When Margaret and I had sailed in Alaska we had learned that it is necessary to allow supplies and time for storm-bound days in port when you travel in such regions. No small vessel should try to make her way against great winds and seas unless such progress is very important, because such sailing is slow, uncomfortable, and hard on the yacht and the crew. The weather in many high latitude regions changes regularly, however, and if you wait a day or two or three you may get following winds and seas where before everything was against you. Often it is worthwhile to wait because you can make more mileage in one good day with fair weather than in three bad days with contrary winds.

We anchored in Caleta Connor after passing the Swedish cargo ship. That night the northerly storm blew itself out and gave us a week of light weather.

The next day while Margaret was steering she spotted another freighter. "There's a ship ahead," she called below. "Come up and hoist the flags so we can dip the ensign when we pass."

I ran up the Chilean courtesy flag and the U.S. flag. Something was wrong. Although the big ship was headed toward us our closing speed was slow; in fact the other vessel appeared to be dead in the water. It was only when we got close that we realized the ship was an abandoned wreck sitting on top of Bajo Cotopaxi, a mid-channel shoal. When we finally sailed past the blue, rust-streaked hulk we saw that she was the *Capitán Leonides*, an unfortunate Greek freighter.

Our route continued through Angostura Inglesa (English Narrows) about which the *Pilots* had pages of warnings and advice. We passed through at slack water with scarcely enough wind to fill the sails and wondered what all the fuss was about. In the northern part of the narrows lay Islote Clio, a tiny islet with a prominent white statue of the Virgin which had been erected by a well-wisher to give protection to passing mariners. At several places we saw the remains of Indian dwellings marked by enormous piles of purplish shells of clams and mussels. Granite domes and cliffs climbed high above the water, and snowfields glittered in the distance. When the weather was sunny it was a friendly and hospitable region and I was glad that we had come.

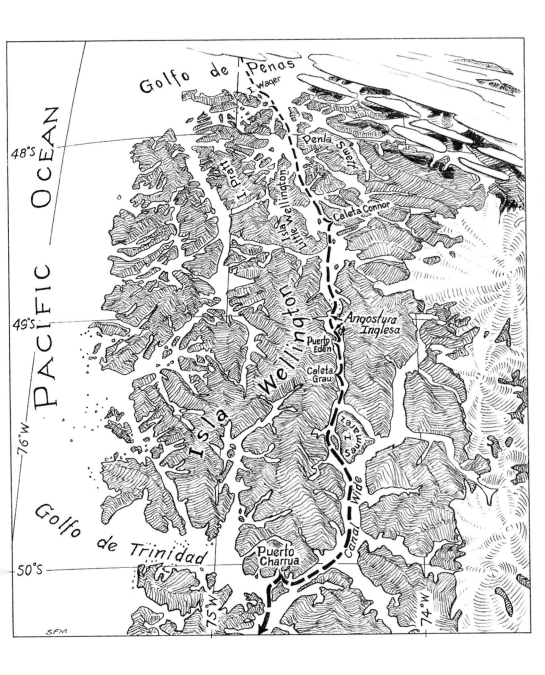

This vessel, the Capitán Leonides, *was a wreck jammed on top of a rock named Bajo Cotopaxi.*

We sailed into the little Indian settlement of Puerto Edén to have our clearance papers endorsed. We saw the usual uniformed *carabineros*, two good-natured souls who here took turns being the official welcomer, mayor, recorder, judge, dispenser of social welfare, crisis avoider, harbormaster, closer of the saloon, jailer, patient listener to one's woes, and in general a Father Superior. Like Indian settlements in most countries the two hundred or so Indians lived in a hodgepodge of tumble-down houses, but the village also had a dock, a school, and a post and telegraph office.

The next morning an Alacalufe rowed over to ask for used clothing. The man was one of twenty-three remaining pure-blooded Alacalufes, according to a *carabinero*. Our Indian visitor spoke softly but cleverly: "If you don't have any old clothes, new ones will do as well," he said. "I like blues and smart stripes." The man had a marvelous face, tanned and craggy, with large features and a mop of black hair.

Whether it was a face of resignation, suffering, cunning, or simply boredom I could not decide. We also got acquainted with an Alacalufe woodchopper who was incredibly skilled at shaping square timbers from *ciprés* logs with an ax.

A coasting ship anchored near us to unload a few supplies. I asked the radio operator whether he could unlock the secret of Chilean weather forecasts. He smiled, waved me inside his tiny wireless shack, flicked several switches, and suddenly—between bursts of nervous static—he was speaking to a confederate somewhere down the line.

"Hey, Luís, how is the weather?"

"The weather is very good today."

"Is it raining where you are? Look out the window and see."

At each port we stopped at in Chile we added an endorsement to our clearance which was soon almost six feet long.

"Just a minute. . . . Yes, it's raining hard."
"How's the wind?"
"Just a minute. . . . Yes, plenty of wind."
"What direction?"
"Just a minute. . . . Southwest, forty knots."
"The weather is very bad today."
"*Si*, the weather is very bad today."

Alacalufe Indian, Puerto Edén.

Our next destination was the Strait of Magellan, which took us seven more days of sailing. Each night our anchorage was increasingly dramatic as we voyaged closer to the heart of the high Andes. We crossed the fiftieth parallel of south latitude.

As we approached Canal Wide and skirted the high mass

of Isla Saumarez in a light rain I noticed a wisp of smoke ahead. Far out in the wilderness we came upon an Indian house where a man was splitting firewood. The figure looked up as we hove into view with our sails pulling hard. The chopping stopped in mid-stroke and the man turned to watch us, spellbound, as if we were an apparition of some sort. He didn't respond to my wave or shout but conintued to look at us as if we were a strange bird or a novel fish. Another man moved into the scene, also watching us. The two figures kept their attention on *Whisper* until we passed out of sight. A hundred, two hundred years ago, their forefathers might also have stared transfixed at earlier voyagers.

In Puerto Charrua we anchored near a 434-foot waterfall that roared into the water near us. I got in terrible trouble that night when I opened a portlight to let in a little air. I forgot that Margaret's bread was rising and that bread is temperamental stuff. The chilled loaves suddenly collapsed like punctured tires when the yeast stopped making CO_2. Margaret lost her temper. "No more bread ever," she cried. "I'm through. You'll have to make your own."

The next day we followed Canal Concepción and slipped into Puerto Molyneux where we anchored near two wrecks. The larger one was the *Ponderosa* of Monrovia, which was beached and in fair condition. Its cargo of rotting wheat smelled ghastly. The anchorage was a hundred feet deep so we put out five hundred feet of chain and nylon.

On March 22 we sailed through a wonderful mountainous narrows called Angostura Guia whose glacier-carved granite cliffs and canyons and ravines and domes reminded me of 10,000-foot mountain passes in California's Sierra Nevada. It seemed unbelievable to be sailing at sea level with such scenery around us. The northerly winds still held as we entered Canal Sarmiento and hurried south.

We stopped at Puerto Bueno which the Spanish explorer Pedro Sarmiento de Gamboa discovered and named in December 1579, some four hundred years ago. It seemed unreal to think of a sixteenth-century ship with a crew of fifty-four officers and men anchoring and mooring, taking on wood and water, collecting shellfish, drawing the seine, and climbing the local mountains to make the first crude charts of the region. As we looked around our comfortable yacht with her dry and rot-free fiberglass hull, Dacron sails, durable cordage, useful auxiliary engine, electric lights, winches, wire rigging, excellent charts, and healthy foodstuffs, we tried to imagine what sailing in these channels must have been like in 1579. Any sort of rational comparison was beyond us.

It is a mark of my ignorance that until I began to read the personal narratives of the early Spanish who explored the south and west coasts of South America I thought them all dolts who were almost always outwitted by the clever English. Such thinking is completely untrue and perhaps comes from my defective and oversimplified textbooks at school. Sarmiento, Cordova, Ladrillero, Hojea, and many others were talented and resourceful, as their accounts plainly show.[15]

We began to see large glaciers when we turned into Estrecho Collingwood. As we headed southeast the ice fields and glacier snouts on the northwest slopes of the mountains stood out bluish and enormous. The barometer was dropping again.

It was a bit upsetting to see the wrecks of so many large ships. We passed two more in Canal Smyth about twenty miles north of the Strait of Magellan. One big steel ship was on her starboard side with her propeller and rudder in the air. We read about two other wrecks near Boston Island and a third directly on our route. "If big ships get turned upside down, what chance do we have?" I said to Margaret.

We hove to at the Islotes Fairway lighthouse near the western entrance of the Strait of Magellan. I hoisted the flag signal uu ("I am bound for . . .") and then pa (Punta Arenas). We could see two uniformed lightkeepers watching us, one with binoculars and the second with a black volume, presumably the code book.

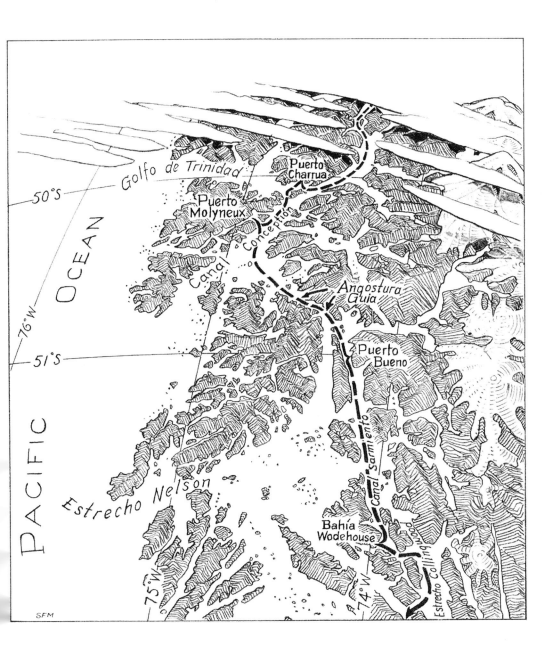

As we crossed into the Strait of Magellan and headed toward Isla Tamar the wind veered from the north to the west and began to blow hard. In the middle of the strait the waterway opened out and the scenery was awesome. I was keen to take a photograph of Cabo Pilar, the famous landmark at the southern side of the western entrance, but as I groped for a camera the historic cape disappeared in swirling mists of darkening rain and wind. Everything around us was gray—gray water, gray cliffs, gray mountains, and gray clouds. I could hardly believe that we had reached such a long-dreamed-of goal. It was wildly exciting, yet a bit unnerving.

Fifty miles to the northwest lay the Evangelistas lighthouse whose keepers put up with the worst weather anywhere. The lantern is 230 feet above sea level, yet during bad weather spray is flung on the glass. Taking supplies and a change of keepers to the light is a hard job for the Chilean navy. Once a relief ship waited for forty days to transfer men and desperately needed food. The ship stayed in the protection of islets southwest of Isla Pacheco about ten miles from the light while hoping for a respite from the westerly gales.

In the channels we navigated by constant reference to landmarks. Our main tools were the binoculars, the hand-bearing compass, and the charts.

(Overleaf) As we sailed south into Estrecho Collingwood we began to see bluish glaciers on the northwest slopes of the mountains bordering the Strait of Magellan.

Today these islets are called Grupo Cuarenta Dias (Forty Days Group).

I thought of the small ship sailors who had been here before and had gone westward from this place. It took Joshua Slocum (1896) seven attempts before he made a successful offing into the Pacific from the Strait of Magellan. Louis Bernicot (1937) made it on his first try. I shuddered to think of heading out into those Pacific graybeards.[16]

We spent an uneasy night behind Isla Tamar in Caleta Rachas (Squall Bay). The yacht did a ballet sequence all night and in the morning the two anchor cables were wound round and round each other. We cleared out promptly and were soon running eastward under a small working jib. We found the seas surprisingly large, caused by the gale pushing against the tidal stream from the east. The wind increased and we were soon surfing along. I knew that we were overpowered, but the sailing was so exhilarating and our progress so good that I hesitated to shorten sail.

From the log:

March 27, 1500 East of Cooper Key light. Whisper broached to under the poled-out working jib. M. was steering and a wave shoved the stern to starboard. The sail got backed against the spinnaker pole. The wind pummeled down in furious gusts. (I was on the port side forward taking photographs.) M. got jammed against the starboard cockpit coaming by the tiller which was unmovable. We should have cut the jib sheet, but there was a lot of water flying around and some confusion. The eight-ounce sail blew out in a zillion pieces and we resumed course, making about three knots under bare pole. We consigned the remnants of the sail to the deep, a noble burial for an old friend.

The anchorages were getting more chancy and the sailing was getting harder by the minute. No wonder we had seen so many big shipwrecks. Maybe the condor that had circled around us earlier was trying to tell us something. What lay ahead?

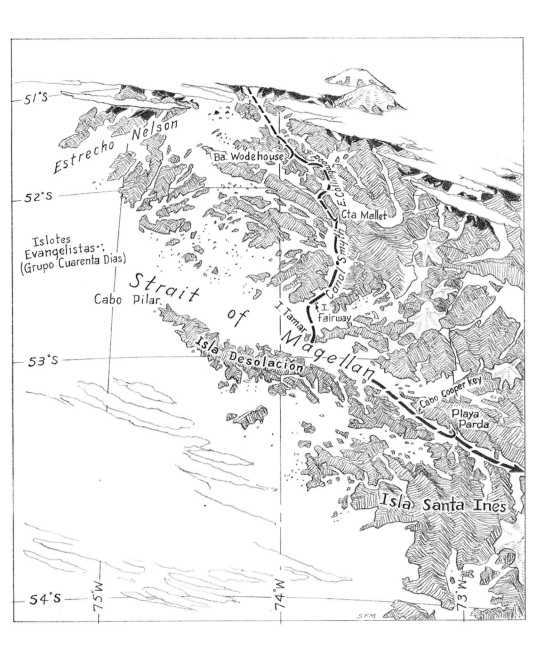

EIGHT

Strong Winds

S AILING in Cape Horn waters is like walking on a
tightrope. As long as each of your steps is surefooted and
in the right direction, all is perfection. In my view, small-
boat handling in the vicinity of the great Chilean mountains and glaciers is the most exciting sport in the world.
Trouble lurks on all sides, however, and it takes only one
slip to plunge into disaster.

The big problem is the wind, which can blow with violence that is hard for a distant reader to believe.

Cape Horn gales blow primarily from the west. As the
depressions move eastward in the Southern Ocean at say
60° S, the wind to the northward blows first from the northwest, veers to the west, and finally blows hardest from the
southwest. For more than one hundred twenty-five years,
ship reports have verified that winds of at least Force 8
(34–40 knots) blow 23 percent of the time in the Cape
Horn area. This means that you will find winds of thirty-
seven knots and upward one day in four.

*(Overleaf) Looking south across Bahía Playa Parda toward the
Strait of Magellan which here runs east and west (to the left and
right). There is a strong west wind blowing and you can see the
wind-blown water streaming eastward in the distance. Whisper
rocks from side to side as squalls strike the yacht. In the distance
is Isla Desolación.*

This is only part of the problem. Around mountains, the uneven heating and irregular topography introduce a turbulence factor of some 40 percent more and cause violent gustiness. Force 13 and 14 winds (72–89 knots) are no strangers to the Chilean channels, and Force 15 (90–99 knots) is more than casually known. A portion of the blame can be directed to the williwaw or Cape Horn squall:

The williwaw [according to the British *Pilot*], unlike most of the squalls which occur in tropical and temperate regions, depends largely, if not entirely, on the existence of strong winds or gales at sea at a height of several thousands of feet over the land. These strong winds generally prevail over an area of several thousand square miles. As they strike the rugged mountains of the archipelagos, they set up eddies of varying size and intensity. . . . During the strongest williwaws, which occur most often westward of Cabo Froward and near the main coastline adjoining the stormiest region at sea, the wind almost certainly exceeds 100 knots.[17]

For the fellow snug at home, such figures are mere numbers. Coming face to face with winds of these magnitudes in a small vessel, however, is an awesome test of man and boat.

Obviously no yacht or fishing boat or naval vessel or cargo ship goes sailing in hurricane winds by choice. You anchor in a sheltered place if possible and wait for better weather. In the channels there are many suitable bays, but ordinary anchoring techniques are quite useless when the wind begins to blow hard. In southern Chile all vessels— unless they are large enough to keep up steam and have crew to stand anchor watches—take lines ashore; otherwise they use radar and travel day and night.

Unfortunately, in the beginning you doubt the necessity of tying ashore. *My* anchors are better. *My* anchoring techniques are good enough. *My* judgement is adequate. Lines ashore? Mooring to trees? Humbug!

It is only after some months in the region, a careful reading of mariners' accounts, and discussions with other captains that you begin to get an idea of the scope of Cape Horn anchoring problems.

The strong winds blow from the west so you seek a bay or inlet that will protect you from westerly seas. Ideally, an anchorage should be on the east side of a long low finger of land that runs north and south or perhaps is a horseshoe open to the east. Low land to the west is preferred because the wind turbulence and resultant williwaws are less. Usually, however, a sheltered bay in the channels has mountains or steep hills on three sides. What you must do then is to try to predict where the westerly winds will funnel down, and to head the vessel in that direction. This means anchoring in front of a canyon or draw or low place in the hills that leads roughly westward. You sail up to such a place and creep as close to the shore as possible.

Sometimes a deep anchorage will allow you to go within a few feet of the shore; the water is often clear and you can watch the bottom come up. In addition the charts sometimes have detailed plans. Then you launch the dinghy and take lines to the land—generally two lines secured to separate strong points. If there are substantial trees or logs, you can tie to them. Otherwise you carry anchors ashore and dig them into the beach or earth, or jam the flukes in cracks in the rock if you're near a stony shore. The westerly winds will hold you off and it is easy to veer a little line and to drop a stern anchor to keep the yacht from swinging. Obviously anchor- and line-handling techniques are important as is a good rowing dinghy.

If all this sounds complicated, it is; but such a scheme is the only way of survival when the hurricane winds begin to blow. And exactly half the time the winds start at night which means that you are quite helpless in the pitch black because you can't see anything. Even during the day the visibility is often poor because of windblown spray. With a couple of lines to the shore and a little thought about protecting the rope from chafe, however, your vessel can withstand any strength of wind. The noise may be wearisome and the heeling from the gusts may upset your nerves a little, but you and your vessel will be safe.

I don't want to give the impression that the westerly gales are unremitting and that the sailing in the south is an endless nightmare of anchoring and storm sail handling. Sometimes the weather is beautiful with sunny skies and light winds for a week or two. Birds sing around the yacht. Seals play in the water. Laundry is on the line. All the portlights and hatches are open. The camera is out. A paint pot appears. You take delightful walks in the woods.

But one day the barometer begins to plunge. It is time to think about shelter and security. The sun vanishes. Heavy clouds race in from the west. The sky drops to mast-top level. The temperature falls. Rain and sleet begin to beat on the deck. The world becomes constricted and sullen and gray. Look out!

In the Strait of Magellan we were blown out of two anchorages in spite of substantial anchors, lots of scope, and good holding ground because I hadn't caught on to the idea of tying ashore at night or during violent storms, a concept I was to learn little by little. On March 30 we had anchored in Puerto Gallant, the inner part of Fortescue Bay.

My journal noted:

I happened to look out and noticed that we were very close to Wigwam Island, the islet that divides Fortescue from Gallant. The island had a lot of bushes of the most marvelous shades of light green. I was fascinated by the colors and how the bushes were moving in the wind. Wait a minute! The bushes weren't moving. It was the yacht! Yikes! We were dragging merrily down the bay. I had the sense to pull on my oilskins before I went on deck and it was fortunate that I did because I was out in hurricane force winds for the next three hours.

We picked up the anchor and put it down four more times, each effort in a different part of the bay. But on every attempt the CQR dragged home hopelessly fouled with sea-weed and kelp. We dropped a 33-pound Danforth only to have it also come to the ship with a huge tangle of kelp. By now it was almost dark so we hurried outside into Fortescue

Bay where the water was deeper. I dropped the CQR and we held on all night, a rolly and miserable time. I had strained my back and the yacht was a mess from the sea-weed and lines and anchors. Fortunately there was a small navigational light at Fortescue which gave us a handy point to take anchor bearings at hourly intervals.

I wasn't alone in my trouble at Puerto Gallant. In January 1768, more than two hundred years earlier, Louis de Bougainville had written: "A dreadful hurricane came suddenly from S.S.W. and blew with such fury as to astonish the oldest seamen. Both our ships had their anchors come home, and were obliged to let go their sheet-anchor, lower the lower yards, and hand the top-masts: our mizen was carried away in the brails." [18]

The next day we rounded Cabo Froward, an impressive, heavy-browed mountain that climbed to 1,178 feet immediately above us. This point marked the southernmost extremity of the mainland of South America. To the south lay Tierra del Fuego and a scattering of small islands, one of which was Cape Horn. Here the Strait of Magellan turned northward.

It was exciting to sail in such famous waters. Thoughts of Magellan and his chronicler Pigafetta flashed through my mind. It was past this place that Francis Drake sailed in August 1578 with his fleet of five vessels. Drake soon learned about the williwaws: "Two or three of these winds would com togeather & meet . . . in one body whose forces . . . did so violently fall into the sea whirleing, or as the Spanyard sayth with a Tornado, that they would peirse into the verry bowells of the sea & make it swell upwards on every syde."

(Overleaf) The southern tip of the continental mass of South America is Cabo Froward, here seen rising above the Strait of Magellan. For many years an enormous iron cross stood at the top of Cabo Froward, but the monument was blown away in a fierce storm. A second, reinforced cross was raised, this time to stand forever. Unfortunately, the wind was stronger than the iron, and the second cross blew down.

Drake made the 334 nautical miles of the Strait of Magellan in only sixteen days (Magellan took thirty-seven). He then went on to terrorize and ransack the Spanish towns and shipping on the west coast of South America and eventually sailed west-about to England with the *Golden Hind* almost sinking from the weight of silver and gold booty.[19]

The Spanish viceroy of Peru sent Sarmiento to the Strait of Magellan to fortify the place against future incursions by the infamous Francisco Draquez, as he was called. Sarmiento thoroughly inspected the strait and then sailed to Spain where he recommended to Phillip II that the strait be fortified and colonized. A great fleet of twenty-five ships and some thirty-five hundred soldiers, clerks, and colonists (including women) left Spain in September 1581. From the beginning the fleet had grievous problems. Many of the vessels were rotten and foundered in severe weather, and by the time the ships had crossed to Brazil the ragtag squadron was sorely depleted by desertions, drownings, disease, and continuing thievery. Some of the leaders went elsewhere, the fleet started, turned back, and restarted. Sarmiento finally reached the Strait of Magellan with only five ships, thirty months after leaving Spain.

In February 1584 Sarmiento landed three hundred people near the eastern entrance and founded a settlement called Nombre de Jesus. One of his vessels was wrecked while unloading stores. Three other ships deserted and fled. Sarmiento took a hundred soldiers and traveled overland and set up a second village Rey Don Felipe, at Puerto Hambre, a few miles north of Cabo Froward. But bad management, marauding Indians, and squabbling doomed both settlements from the start.

This alert creature is a guanaco, closely related to the llama, alpaca, and vicuña. The extinct Indians of the Ona tribe on the eastern end of Tierra del Fuego hunted and lived almost exclusively on this animal. Note the open, flat, rolling land toward the eastern side of the Strait of Magellan, an abrupt change from the mountains further west.

Sarmiento sailed off in the *Maria*, the last ship, to get supplies in Brazil. He loaded new stores and tried to get back, but gales drove him away. He finally decided to return to Spain to organize a genuine relief expedition. On the way, however, he was captured first by the English and then by the French and held prisoner for three years. It was the end of 1589 before he got back to Spain where no one had any interest in the poor colonists at the other end of the world.

When Thomas Cavendish sailed to the strait in 1587, on a voyage in which he tried to emulate Drake, he found only a handful of starving Spaniards. Sarmiento's great scheme had failed miserably. The whole story of Sarmiento reads like a fanciful romance and could be the vehicle for an opera if the actual happenings weren't so tragic.[20]

As we looked at Cabo Froward and the dark waters of the strait, I could almost see the *Beagle* battling westward on her first survey voyage in 1827. I reflected on Theodore Roosevelt's great white fleet of U.S. battleships that had steamed westward from this point in 1908. The Chilean cruiser *Chacabuco* proudly led the sixteen enormous coal-burning capital ships at ten knots as they kept an interval of four hundred yards between ships while hoists of brightly colored code flags fluttered from the signal yards.[21]

I thought of 1914 and the Battle of Coronel and how the doomed British fleet had steamed past this spot on its way to meet the Germans. And finally I remembered the plucky yachtsmen—Willy de Roos of Belgium and Tom Zydler of Poland—who together with their crews had sailed past this place only a few months before us. I said a quiet prayer for all these adventurous men, their countries, and their varied reasons for coming.[22]

That afternoon we anchored in Bahía Bougainville, a snug cove about one cable wide, "completely sheltered from all winds," according to the *Pilot*. In an impressive calm we anchored in forty-two feet—in good holding ground of mud and shells—and with two hundred ten feet of chain out we were unable to drag the yacht toward the mouth of the bay even by jerking the yacht with the full reverse power of the engine. We turned in early and hoped for a good rest, but in the dim hours of the night the wind started to howl. I routinely got up to shine a flashlight at the trees, only to have my hair stand on end when I saw that we had been blown out of the bay—chain and all—and had almost dragged up on a small island to the east.

Sleep was finished. We put up storm sails, recovered our anchor, and sailed forty-three miles northward to Punta Arenas. The wind was forty knots from the west-southwest and the strait was a mass of white water, but we sailed about a half mile off the weather shore where in only eighteen-inch waves we made good time, although we heeled plenty in the squalls.

This business of getting blown out of anchorages was no rarity. Joshua Slocum's *Spray* was repeatedly flung out of anchorages while sailing in the Strait of Magellan area. In March 1896, Slocum wrote: "While I was wondering why no trees grew on the slope abreast of the anchorage, half-minded to lay by the sail-making and land with my gun for some game and to inspect a white boulder on the beach, near the brook, a williwaw came down with such terrific force as to carry the *Spray*, with two anchors down, like a feather out of the cove and away into deep water. No wonder trees did not grow on the side of that hill! Great Boreas! a tree would need to be all roots to hold on against such a furious wind." [23]

The British *Pilot* mentioned tree damage with alarming regularity: ". . . squalls are probably frequent, and must blow with great violence, for there are trees torn up by the roots." [24]

The mountainous geography of the Andes changed abruptly as we moved northward toward the eastern entrance of the Strait of Magellan. The land became low and flat and drier. Trees vanished. The few hills were golden with dried grass and you could see long distances across the land. We

The port of Punta Arenas is a poor place for large and small ships because the Strait of Magellan is eighteen miles wide at this point and there is no protection from the sea. The vessels shown here are on the lee side of the dock while a westerly wind holds them off. A wind shift, however, means that all the vessels must move to the other side of the pier.

began to notice a few ranches and buildings.

Punta Arenas is the principal Chilean city of the south, and is on the western side of the Strait of Magellan at a point where it is eighteen miles wide. The city has a population of 65,000 and, in addition to being the navy headquarters for the region, handles a good deal of wool and mutton. There is a shipyard, airport, some light manufacturing, and the city is a shipping center for oil, gas, and coal, besides handling coastal traffic. Unfortunately there is no proper port,

only a long dock that extends southward. In westerly winds everyone ties to the eastern side of the dock or anchors out. A good deal of the beach area is littered with wrecks of big and little vessels, and accounts of drownings from people going ashore from ships anchored in the open roadstead are dotted all through travelers' accounts.[25]

While we were there a violent local storm called a *panteonero* (a cemetery wind) blew up and brought Force 13 winds (72–80 knots). During the big wind I retreated below and read about early flying in the area:

The French pioneer airman Saint-Exupéry wrote some vivid descriptions of the effects of the cyclones and whirlwinds in southern Argentina, "the country of flying stones," as he called it, because large stones were literally flung into the air and hurled about by the howling wind. On one occasion, after landing his plane with much difficulty he had to fight for hours against the diabolical strength of the hurricane, which was rolling cattle over and whipping roofs off houses. He asked for assistance from local troops, and with hundreds of men lying on the plane's fuselage and others clinging to the undercarriage, holding the plane down, he was able at last to run it into the hangar.

Again, when Saint-Exupéry was pioneering the air-route down South America to the Magellan Straits, for the French postal authorities, strong winds over Patagonia forced him to land when 200 miles from Punta Arenas. He took off again the following day, being airborne in a matter of yards—literally plucked from the ground by the headwind. But an hour later he could still see the landing strip he had taken off from; and after six hours' flying against the wind he had covered no more than 160 miles, although the plane had a 400-h.p. engine.[26]

I looked out from inside *Whisper* and saw that the Strait of Magellan was a mass of foam. The fear among the massed small boats on the lee side of the dock was that the big German cargo cranes would topple over and fall on the vessels. The navy officers all had the visor straps of their hats down under their chins to keep their hats from blowing away. People moved on the dock like cats, mostly on all fours, and went from handhold to handhold. But two days later the storm was suddenly over, and life on the dock was back to normal. Small boys bicycled up and down while stevedores moved crates of onions.

Some years ago Margaret and I made a long trip in the Pacific during which we produced a 16-mm documentary film. We lectured with the film in order to raise funds to continue our travels. Now we were attempting to make a new film about our Cape Horn trip. But the trouble with film work on a small yacht is that when the action is best you are quite busy dealing with various problems and have no time to shoot film. In the Chilean channels there was so much to do that a forty-eight-hour day wouldn't have been long enough. So I hired an American photographer to join us for the sail from Punta Arenas to Cape Horn. The idea was for him to shoot a lot of action footage to make the documentary more exciting, and to cover angles and situations that were impossible for Margaret and me to film.

We put on additional stores in Punta Arenas and met Admiral Eduardo Allen who was the head of the navy in the south. On April 17 we welcomed the photographer and his wife, who we will call Adam and Eve. We set off at once and retraced our route south along the Strait of Magellan,

One day we had a visit from Admiral Eduardo Allen who was the commander of the Chilean naval forces in the south.

and then sailed south and west along Magdalena and Cockburn Channels to the western end of Tierra del Fuego.

Again we were surrounded by high mountains, but now at 55° S the low trees—what there were—leaned severely to the east, wedge-shaped as if trimmed by giant shears. The rock was grayer and more fractured and rounder than further north, evidence of increased glaciation. Most of the place names had been given by Fitz Roy and the crew of the *Beagle*. We passed Islas Stewart, Londonderry, Hamond, and Whittlebury, for instance.

A few days later we sailed into the northwest arm of Beagle Channel where, in a distance of twelve miles, five large glaciers descended from the north side of the mile-wide channel directly into the water at sea level. It was a fine experience to glide slowly along in front of glacial snouts of fissured blue ice that extended upward for hundreds of feet. I say "hundreds" but the ice seemed miles high. Streams of icy water ran down the fronts and there were eerie grumbling and grinding noises as the ice inched forward. We fished out fragments of ice floating in the channel and had great sport fixing cool drinks. It was all so beautiful that we spent two days taking photographs and walking on shore.

Now we were within striking distance of Cape Horn and I was determined to make a fast run for our goal. We were technically bound from Punta Arenas to the Chilean naval base at Puerto Williams. Permission for Cape Horn had been on a "yes you can," "no you can't" basis, and I was worried that we might be denied permission at the last minute on some technicality or other. We had learned that South America was full of technicalities.

On April 28 the four of us aboard *Whisper* pushed hard and made it to the north end of Canal Murray, only seventy miles from Isla Hornos. It was now the end of April and the hours of daylight were short because we were well into the southern autumn. The next morning I got everyone up in the dark and we were underway by 0815. We hurried south-

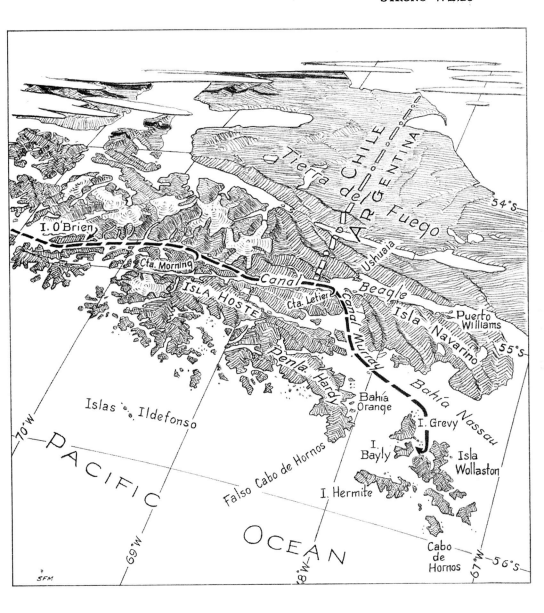

(Overleaf) The western end of Isla Tierra del Fuego seemed a world of gray stone and primordial beginnings. Whisper's sails made a dot of white on a landscape so vast you could scarcely fathom the immensity of this wilderness world.

ward through Canal Murray, dipped our flag to the Chilean lookouts, and sailed southeast.

The day was gray and overcast and the clouds to windward looked ragged and full of squalls so at 0910 Margaret and I tied a reef in the mainsail and put up a smaller headsail. Meanwhile Eve steered and Adam took photographs. At 1025 we were running well before a freshening northerly wind as we sailed away from the snowy mountains of Isla Navarino and out into the open waters of Bahía Nassau. Ahead, rising from the horizon, we saw the dark forms of Islas Wollaston and Hermite, an archipelago with eight good-sized islands, on the southernmost of which was Cabo de Hornos. I could hardly believe the sight. Was this Cape Horn at the foot of the American continent? The fabled and awesome sailing hurdle of centuries? The air was clear, and on Isla Hermite, twenty-five miles away, I could plainly see the tops of a row of bare mountains which stuck up like the teeth on a saw blade.

Margaret wanted to go to the Hardy Peninsula and anchor in Bahía Orange, which was closer and supposedly a good anchorage. I overruled her, however, and chose to head for the Wollaston Islands, a little further to the southeast, and only twenty-four miles north-northeast of Isla Hornos. The *Pilot* books suggested three places in the northern part of the Wollaston Islands: the first was Surgidero Otter, an anchorage for large vessels in ninety-two feet but open to the north. The second was Surgidero Romanche in fifty-three to one hundred five feet, fairly well sheltered, but not recommended because of violent squalls from the mountains on Isla Bayly during westerly gales. The third was Surgidero Seagull, described as being well sheltered and suitable for small vessels of reduced draft. Since the soundings were moderate—which promised less work recovering the ground tackle—and the anchorage was surrounded by islands, I selected Surgidero Seagull. From this anchorage we would be in an excellent position to sail around Isla Hornos during good weather. In addition the approach to Cabo de Hornos from the east would mean that we would be sailing in sheltered waters and should have an easier trip. Also there were more protected harbors on the east sides of the islands.

Our progress was good, but I was concerned about the barometer which had dropped from 997 millibars at breakfast time to 984 by mid-afternoon. We were now sailing fast under the running rig before northerly winds of twenty to twenty-five knots. During a routine gybe while running, I winched in the sheet of the headsail whose clew was held outboard with a spinnaker pole (as I had done a thousand times before). Suddenly the pole collapsed where it pressed against a forward lower shroud. We quickly replaced the broken pole with a spare and resolved to treat aluminum poles more gently in the future. Certainly the thin metal poles should not be subjected to bending strains.

By 1500 we had logged forty miles and were rapidly approaching the Wollaston Islands which consisted of four irregular islands, mostly volcanic, that measured about twenty-five miles from northwest to southeast. From a distance the islands looked brown and bare. Mount Hyde, the highest point, rose to 2,211 feet.

At 1700, Eve reported that the barometer had plunged to 979 millibars, an ominous nine o'clock position, and I knew we were in for a blast from the west. Adam and I dragged a second anchor to the foredeck.

The approach to Seagull anchorage was from the south. I was surprised when we entered because instead of a snug cove we had come to a low basin a mile and a half in diameter. Above us to the west rose the smooth slopes of Isla Bayly. It was obvious that winds would roar down from the island and race out across the anchorage. Even worse was a mass of kelp in the mostly twenty-six-foot depths of the bay. The kelp was as thick as water lilies in a pond.

We had worked out anchor bearings from the chart and *Pilot* so we hurried to the recommended place and dropped the anchor. We began to drag in the twenty-knot northerly wind so I winched up the anchor and found some gray mud on it, along with a ball of matted kelp which I cut away. I let go the anchor a second time. Again it dragged. This time it came up with no mud at all—only a huge sphere of kelp. I hacked away the weed and dropped the anchor a third time. Then a fourth. The autumnal night was descending rapidly.

In lowering clouds and darkness, Margaret took bearings of two mountains. We seemed to be holding, but I had misgivings about what might happen with the low barometer so I let out all the chain on the first anchor and put out a second anchor on a long nylon line.

The north wind began to veer toward the west. I could hear the williwaws begin to race down the mountain on Isla Bayly. A few minutes later we were enveloped in seventy-knot winds. Initially the sound was like screaming sirens. But as the wind increased and gradually swung to the southwest, the roar changed to the low-pitched whine of giant turbine wheels. The noise was a bus engine running at full throttle inside my head.

I peered out of the hatch. Sheets of spray slammed into my face. All landmarks had disappeared. The only thing I could see was the white tracery of excited water flying over the yacht. I thought of moving to a deeper anchorage. I thought of another anchor. I thought I'd never heard such wind . . .

Suddenly we felt *Whisper's* keel grate on the bottom. The yacht fell hard on her starboard side and crunched into rocks. Water came in at once.

We were shipwrecked on uninhabited islands only a few miles from Cape Horn.

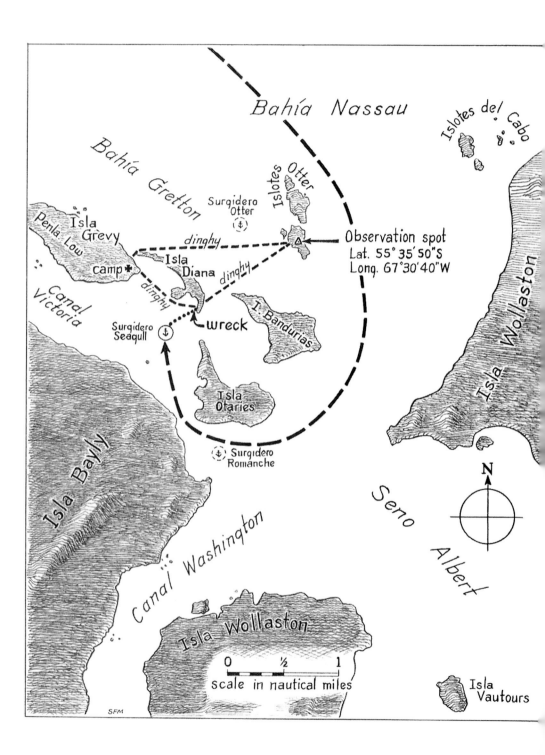

Bahía Nassau

Islotes del Cabo

Bahía Gretton

Islotes Otter

Surgidero
Otter

Isla
Grevy

Penla Low

dinghy

Observation spot
Lat. 55°35'50"S
Long. 67°30'40"W

camp

Isla
Diana

dinghy

Isla Wollaston

dinghy

Canal
Victoria

I. Bandurias

wreck

Surgidero
Seagull

Isla
Otaries

Surgidero
Romanche

Isla Bayly

N

Seno

Isla Wollaston

Albert

Canal Washington

Isla Wollaston

0   ½   1

scale in nautical miles

Isla
Vautours

SFM

NINE

Shipwreck

*T*HE FIRST feeling the shipwreck gave me was one of incredulity. "It can't happen to me," I muttered as I bit my lip. "Wrecks only happen to other people, because *my* preparations and *my* seamanship are too perfect." Yet poor *Whisper* lay wounded on a rocky beach on an uninhabited islet twenty-four miles north-northwest of Cape Horn. At high tide the yacht was one-third full of water, and the pounding of the hull against the cannonball-sized rocks was no myth.

Each incoming wave picked up the vessel a little and dropped her as the water receded, slamming the yacht down on the beach. The hull creaked and groaned and shivered. It was awful. I thought of all the places Margaret and I and *Whisper* had been together—French Polynesia, Rarotonga, Samoa, Kusaie, Japan, the Aleutian Islands, Alaska, the Queen Charlotte Islands, the Galápagos, Peru. . . . We had had a few dangerous moments but *Whisper* had always come through. But now, stupid fool, I had let her down. The mighty captain had allowed his vessel to drag ashore in a heavy westerly gale. The whole thing was monstrous and inconceivable.

(Overleaf) Shipwrecked in the Wollaston Islands near Cape Horn.

Shipwrecked! Obviously the anchors had gotten fouled and were useless. Could I lay out another anchor on a long warp? I looked out into the inky night. Bursts of frigid spray slapped me in the face like shotgun pellets as the waves broke on the stony beach where *Whisper* lay thumping. At that moment another barrage of williwaws exploded down the mountains of Isla Bayly. The moan of the wind quickly increased to a baritone wail. There was no possibility of launching a dinghy and putting out an anchor until the wind eased.

According to the angle-of-heel indicator we lay at fifty degrees to starboard. The visibility was terrible but by waving a flashlight around I could dimly see that we were on the edge of an islet with smooth water only a few yards to leeward. Maybe we would blow or bump our way across. But as soon as I thought of this I knew we would never move to the quiet water beyond the islet because the yacht was so firmly aground. Indeed, the starboard deck almost touched the beach which was composed of smooth, roundish stones eight inches or so in diameter. There were hundreds, no thousands of these stones that clattered together when a wave rolled in, and again a moment later when the water ran out. It was hard to look around because of the flying water and the steep angle of heel of the yacht. It took a good deal of hanging on to keep from falling over the side.

If only I could row an anchor out to windward while the tide was still flooding. . . . I wondered how many shipwrecked mariners had muttered those words?

To keep from getting increasingly soaked with cold water as the waves broke over the yacht I went back inside and slammed shut the hatch. Below, I found water rising inside the hull. We had no doubt been holed or stove in on the starboard side where the yacht was pounding. The date was April 29; the time was 1930. We still had two and a half hours to high water. I made a quick calculation with the tidal tables and worked out that the water would rise less than two feet, not enough to swamp or submerge the vessel.

It was impossible to walk around inside *Whisper* because of the angle of heel. We climbed from handhold to handhold. All the loose gear tended to fall toward the low side which was soon a couple of feet deep in the water. I thought of the women chatting quietly about dinner half an hour earlier. Now we had to shout to talk above the noise of the wind, the waves, and the pounding of the hull. Everything had happened so quickly that I was only vaguely aware that a new chapter in my life had begun. I knew that hard times lay ahead.

There were four of us on board. My wife Margaret, dear Margaret, was as steady as a pillar of stone and completely dependable when the going was hard. Eve—the photographer's wife—had sailed with us for a few days in California at an earlier time. She seemed sensible, calm and thoughtful, full of ideas, and she was always willing to pitch in and help. I had no idea how she would react in a crisis.

I knew less about Adam, her husband. He was a big, well-built man with a huge beard and a deep bass voice. A talented film maker, he was smart, his mind was logical, and he spoke well. In the last few days I had learned that he knew little about sailing and was hesitant about helping with the yacht and various chores unless I directed him step by step. Although he wanted to learn about long distance sailing he considered any sort of detail work—making eye splices and whipping the ends of a halyard, for instance—as "women's work" and "boring" and simply refused to do it which I thought odd. How Adam would act when the going got tough was anybody's guess. I hoped for the best.

We were in a nasty situation. Yet it was far from hopeless. Fortunately the yacht was being battered by relatively small waves because the opposite shore of Seagull anchorage was only a mile and a half away. With limited fetch the waves had little time to build up. The accident had occurred about three and a half hours after low water and what waves there were had shoved us well up on the beach. This meant that we would be high and dry at low water. It would be easier to work on the yacht but harder to get the vessel down to the water to refloat her. Patching the hull and hauling the yacht into the water were not my concerns just then because the refloating would need calmer conditions.

Our biggest problem was exposure and cold. The diesel stove was submerged in salt water; the cabin was soon to be one-third full of 39°F water. All of us, however, were warmly dressed in woolens, oilskins, boots, hats, and gloves. Most of the bedding was dry. The yacht was cold but she gave us protection from the wind.

"We'll stay here until morning," I announced. "Let's turn in and get some rest."

Adam and Eve crowded into the quarter berth which was on the high side of the yacht. Margaret and I managed to nap on the port saloon berth which had a large canvas lee cloth. I fired up the one-burner Taylor kerosene cabin heater which happened to be on the port side. I climbed into the angled saloon berth, intermeshed my oilskinned limbs with Margaret's, and managed to doze a little. The heating stove flue didn't work too well because of the high wind. I wondered whether I should get up and shut off the stove. "Is it better to die of asphyxiation and be warm, or to be cold and alive?" The stove hissed away and I fell asleep pondering the question.

I awoke from time to time because my position was so cramped. In the night the tide fell and the water drained from inside the vessel. The pounding of the hull on the beach stopped. The silence was wonderful. I climbed outside. Though the wind was still strong, the spray was gone. I took a flashlight and dropped to the beach. I wanted to see where we were and I was curious about the land, but the low clouds made the night very dark and my seaboots slipped on the mossy rocks. The walking was treacherous. I went back to the yacht to wait for daylight. The others were still asleep.

At first light I dropped to the beach again and walked around the yacht. Except for a chunk torn from the bottom of her rudder, Whisper seemed in good condition. The entire port side was perfect and looked as if the vessel had just come from a shipyard. The damage, however, was underneath the starboard side on which she lay. I was amazed to discover that the second anchor we had dropped the night before was up on the beach higher than *Whisper*. In fact the anchor had been blown or carried by the water across the end of the islet to the extremity of the nylon cable which was stretched tightly downwind. Think of the power of a storm to do that!

We were on Isla Diana, a scimitar-shaped islet about one mile long and a quarter of a mile wide on the west side of Seagull anchorage. The islet was only about ten or twelve feet above the sea. There were no trees, only large clumps of tall, coarse-leaved tussock grass. Across from us to the west and south rose the brown and withered mountains and hills of the main Wollaston Islands. Patchy snow lay near the heights.

It was impossible to prepare anything to eat on board so we took a Primus stove and some food to the lee side of the islet. The wind kept blowing out the Primus so we got the yacht's dinghy and dragged it around the islet for a windbreak. Margaret cooked hot cereal and made coffee. I took a couple of pictures of *Whisper*.

After eating, Adam and I walked along the slippery beach stones to the opposite end of the islet to have a look at our general situation. While we were picking our way across the rocks, Adam suddenly stopped and turned toward me.

"What are our chances, Hal?" he blurted out. "I mean, do you think we'll ever get out of this?"

I had been so busy thinking about the wreck that I hadn't paid much attention to Adam. Now, when I looked closely at him, my heart sank. He was shaking in his boots. His eyes had become slits and he was almost crying. Instead of looking at me when he spoke, Adam looked at the ground. During World War II and the Korean War, I had seen what fear could do to a man. The stranding of the vessel was bad enough. To be obliged to deal with a terrified photographer who had an acute case of the browns was trouble indeed.

"The yacht is finished," he said. "We don't even have a radio. How much food is there? I want an inventory of the food right away. We must count the cans."

"Relax," I said. "Margaret and I have done a lot of mountaineering. We know how to live out in the wilds. The yacht is extremely well provisioned and we have enough food for at least two months. If necessary we can supplement the food with shellfish. We may have to find some fresh water."

"Water?" said Adam nervously. "How much is there? How many days will it last? How much can we have each day? Let's sound the tanks right away."

I tried to reassure him. "I think we can get the yacht off," I said. "At least we're going to try hard. When the wind drops we're going to run out a couple of anchors, move a lot of stones, and see if we can turn the bow toward the water. At high tide we may be able to slip a couple of driftwood timbers under the starboard side. Then at the next low tide when the hull is empty of water we'll try to bolt a plywood patch on the hull. We may have to work in the water a little. I have a thick rubber wet suit . . ."

"Work in the water?"

I saw that Adam was horrified. It was clear that he wanted nothing more to do with the yacht. His idea of heaven just then would have been for the clouds to open and a helicopter to land and whisk him to the Cabo de Hornos Hotel in Punta Arenas, 188 miles to the northwest.

Back on the yacht Eve and Margaret had taken more food ashore and we all had a hot lunch on the beach. Then, while I worked inside to expose the hull damage, I asked Adam to take the dinghy and row out an anchor. The wind had dropped and the job was easy. I told him exactly what I wanted, but when I looked out later I saw that he had put the anchor out to the south, not the west. A fifteen-minute job had taken two hours and instead of securing the anchor warp to the port bow cleat to help pull the yacht toward deep water, Adam had put the warp on the starboard stern cleat which meant that he was tying the yacht to the land. Maybe on purpose. Poor Adam was wandering about in a daze.

We had thousands of feet of new 16-mm film and two cameras on board. "How about taking some footage of the wreck and what we're doing?" said Margaret to Adam during the afternoon. "After all, a photographer doesn't have this opportunity every day."

"You're entirely right," said Adam in his deep bass voice. "We must start on a systematic shooting schedule and chronicle every aspect of this experience. We need a lot of good sequences."

Adam talked eloquently but he took no photographs—then or in the days to follow. Later he climbed into the yacht where I was working. He was looking for something and began to pick up things from the high dry side and let them fall into the water on the low side of the saloon or the galley. He took a large plastic jar with all my taps and dies and drills from a tool drawer that I had open. His eyes were searching for something else so he simply dropped these irreplaceable tools into the salt water. I gasped. I could hardly believe what I had seen. At first I was angry, but as I moved closer to shout at him I saw that Adam's eyes were glazed and that he was breathing heavily. He was sick with fear and not in control of himself. Instead of anger I began to feel sorry for him.

I took Margaret aside and spoke to her privately. "Adam is pretty upset," I said. "He's in a bad way. We're going to have to set up a camp on shore and forget about *Whisper*."

Margaret had been watching Adam on her own and she agreed with me.

I gathered everyone together and spoke in strong terms for Adam's benefit. "Tomorrow morning, if the wind is down, Margaret and I will take the fiberglass dinghy and row across the hundred yards or so to Isla Grevy, the next island, to see about setting up a camp in the grove of trees that Adam and I spotted this morning on our walk. I know from reading that Indians and seal hunters have lived in the Wollastons, and I believe we'll find water and shelter. We can make a tent with the sails from *Whisper*. Tonight we'll stay on the yacht, but by moving a few things we can be more comfortable. It's possible that we may see a patrol vessel or a fishing boat. In addition, I think there's another Chilean navy lookout station south of us. I don't know whether it's on Isla Hermite, Herschel, or Deceit, but we may find something. So everybody cheer up. Let's all have a whisky and then some dinner."

The next morning Margaret and I rowed across to Peninsula Low on Isla Grevy. We found a good-sized rivulet of fresh water, and in walking through the trees we discovered the remains of an old campsite. A conical tent of some kind had once been arranged over a framework of poles. The tent was long gone but the framework was good enough for us to throw a sail over for shelter. The camp was about thirty or forty feet above the water; a walk of one hundred fifty feet to the north took us to the eastern edge of the peninsula where we had an excellent view north and northeast into Bahía Nassau and of Isla Navarino in the distance beyond. Lots of wild celery grew near the camp. Margaret saw mussels that uncovered at low tide.

During the next few days we rowed several dozen loads of sails, bedding, bunk cushions, tools, line, water jugs, dishes, and pots and pans to the camp, which gradually became quite deluxe. We lashed three sails around the existing tent framework to make a serviceable tepee which we floored with sail bags and the sun awning. Then came cushions and mattresses followed by blankets and sleeping bags. We had two kerosene stoves and a pressure kerosene lantern. There were several hundred cans of food plus larger containers of flour, rice, sugar, noodles, and spaghetti. We dug a shallow ditch around the tent to drain off water and gradually improved the tent with props and lines until it was quite weatherproof. I am sure the sailmaker would have been amazed to have seen what we had done with his handiwork.

Eve worked especially hard collecting mussels which she steamed, fried, curried, or made into delicious soup. She hauled water from the rivulet and gathered wild celery. At first her husband wanted a big nightly campfire until we convinced him that wet wood would make a smoky fire besides being a lot of trouble to get going and keep up. Adam liked the camp but he still acted nervously. He slept at least ten hours a night and spent hours writing furiously in a notebook. We repeatedly asked him to use the movie cameras, but nothing happened.

It is not my purpose to mock Adam and to make sarcastic

Our good-rowing Davidson dinghy was invaluable in exploration and for moving supplies and food.

comments on his behavior, but simply to observe that when fear grips a man it changes him and he becomes wretched and useless. Adam was the biggest person in the party and he should have been the strongest. Fear bled his strength away and he became the weakest.

We tried to assign Adam little jobs. Not much seemed to interest him, however, until Margaret got the idea of giving him the rifle and making him the camp hunter. Adam was a good shot and disappeared for hours on hunting expeditions. He brought back big kelp geese which Eve cooked in the pressure cooker. The meat was dark brown, something like turkey, and it tasted delicious. The trouble was that the thirty-thirty rifle was much too powerful for birds. The big slugs tended to destroy the creatures instead of merely killing them as a shotgun would have. Nevertheless, we were glad for the additional food, even if it was in small pieces.

Working to set up the camp and running it was a full-time job and a half. Collecting naturally occurring food may sound romantic but it takes an unbelievable amount of time and patient effort unless you are a local native and have learned to do it from childhood on. We saw lots of clam shells along certain beaches but we had no rake, which I thought of making from a deck brush and a row of copper nails.

The weather was surprisingly mild. A few days were stormy, but in general the wind and cold were minimal. Maybe we were getting used to Cape Horn living. Of course once on land we tended to ignore sea conditions.

We spent many hours rowing back and forth to the wreck and carrying things across the slippery rocks. The round trip was about two miles or so, but part of the way was through kelp whose long, heavy stalks and leaves would get wrapped around the oars. The person rowing would have to stop, unship the fouled oar, slide it out of the kelp

Unloading supplies on Isla Grevy with the Wollaston mountains in the distance. The moss-covered rocks along the shore made the walking treacherous.

(or cut the leaves away), and then re-ship the oar and begin again. It was always easier to go around kelp patches even if it meant a long detour.

One morning when Margaret and I started out for the wreck I got the idea of rowing along the outside—the north-west side—of Isla Diana to avoid the heavy kelp. The wind was calm and I thought we might see something new along the beach. We started out well but the kelp was thicker

The emergency camp on Isla Grevy was based on this tent made from sails wrapped around poles set up tepee fashion. We were reasonably protected from strong winds in this grove of small trees. We found fresh water, wild celery, and mussels nearby.

than I had foreseen and the rowing quickly became impossible. Every two or three strokes I had to unship the oars to clear them. All of a sudden, gusts of wind from the southwest began to blow at us and to push the dinghy away from shore. I re-doubled my rowing efforts but I only got the oars fouled twice as fast. At first our position was merely annoying, but it quickly grew alarming. Here we were in a tiny dinghy only eight feet long getting blown away from land! I threw out an anchor at once, but it didn't hold in the slippery kelp. I had read somewhere about Indian women mooring canoes by tying to bunches of kelp, so I knelt in the bow of the dinghy, grabbed three or four thick kelp branches, and passed a line around them. The line slipped from the slimy stalks. I tried a second time. The line slipped again.

All this while the wind was increasing—say, to thirty knots. Not a great deal, but in a small dinghy even a little is a lot. We were gradually losing ground and getting blown to sea. I looked shoreward to see if there was any chance of help. Adam and Eve stood watching us, not knowing what to do. I tried to wave to them to send us a float or the inflatable dinghy on a long line, but the notion didn't occur to them in spite of my earnest gestures. I remember so well thinking of two expert sailing friends in San Francisco and wishing that one of them had been on the beach to help us.

Margaret and I were rapidly getting blown away from shore. What to do? I glanced behind us. Fortunately there was another islet about a mile to leeward. Whether we would be able to make our way there, however, and to land in one piece were questions that I couldn't answer or even think about. Already we were skimming along downwind in swells higher than the dinghy's freeboard. I found that by keeping the stern exactly parallel to the swells, we went along in fairly good fashion. I steered by using the oars as drags, digging one in a little to turn the vessel slightly. It was a delicate business and my heart was in my mouth because if we had gotten broadside to the waves we would have capsized at once, and certainly would have perished in the frigid water. Margaret sat perfectly still in the sternsheets and gave me directions as we steered across the swells toward the islet.

The sea got lumpier and we raced downwind. I was afraid that we would be swamped any second. Finally, as we got near the islet, and close to the rocks and small breaking waves on the lee shore, Margaret spied a little sheltered place past a tiny bit of land. We avoided several rocks, managed to steer past a stone ledge, touched bottom, jumped out, and quickly ran the dinghy high up on the shore. I almost wilted from nervous excitement. If there hadn't been an islet to leeward we would have been blown out to sea east of Cape Horn.

During my life I have been lucky to sidestep death many times, but this was the most providential. As I guided the dinghy by selectively dragging the oars, I remember thinking of a book by John Muir in which he described the first ascent of Mount Ritter in California's Sierra Nevada in 1871. Muir had been climbing for hours and he finally got into a situation in which he could neither go up nor come down. He clung high on the side of the mountain with his arms outstretched while noisy ravens chattered nearby. "Not yet, not yet," he cried. "I'm not carrion yet."

"Not yet, not yet," I mumbled to myself. "We're still alive, even though we passed through the shadow . . ."

Margaret and I walked around and around the little islet—its name was Islote Otter, we later found out—for the next eight hours to keep warm. We ate some mussels from tidal pools and collected tiny red berries from bushes. At dusk the wind dropped and we were able to launch the dinghy and row back to the grounded yacht for a load of gear. We then returned to the camp on Peninsula Low and stumbled into the tent in the dark. Adam and Eve had put out the camp light and had gone to bed. Eve got up to fix us something to eat.

"We thought you had bedded down for the night," she said.

"Bedded down?" said Margaret. "Bedded down in what?

If we had bedded down on the islet we'd have died of exposure."

Seagull anchorage was discovered in April 1839 by the 110-ton New York pilot schooner *Seagull* which was part of the U.S. Navy exploring expedition led by Charles Wilkes. Unfortunately, a few days later the *Seagull* left Bahía Orange on a routine voyage and got into a furious gale. The *Seagull* (two officers and fifteen men) was never seen again. In November 1855, W. Parker Snow, the energetic captain of the eighty-eight-ton missionary schooner *Allen Gardiner*, anchored in Bahía Gretton and took a ship's boat into Seagull anchorage. Snow noticed a deserted wigwam and he walked ashore at the precise site of *Whisper's* emergency camp on Peninsula Low. During the same week, Snow and the *Allen Gardiner* went through a five-day hurricane plus squalls that almost tore his schooner apart. He lay with two big anchors out, one on 540 feet of chain.

During the night of the third day of its prevalence, I was on deck when a furious squall of hail and wind, similar to a tornado, burst upon us with a force like the blow of an enormous sledge hammer. The little ship trembled again; you could hear every part of her move under that tremendous blast, and I might easily fancy her a living thing shuddering with the apprehension of the wrath and power of those terrible elements she was calmly striving to resist. On that wild coast, near that dark and frowning land, during that inky night relieved occasionally by fitful gleams of a strange and peculiar light, with the large hail pelting upon one like showers of bullets, I could not but feel deeply anxious.[27]

Louis-Ferdinand Martial, in charge of the 1882–83 French scientific mission, visited Seagull anchorage to chart the region and discovered that Victoria channel ran between Isla Bayly and land to the north. Martial named the separate land Isla Grevy, "in honor of the first magistrate of the Republic." In 1923 the artist-adventurer Rockwell Kent sailed to the area in a small chartered boat from Ushuaia.[28]

All four of these visitors—Wilkes, Snow, Martial, and Kent—found Indians living and working on the islands. A little seal hunting, fishing, and shellfish and crab gathering supported the people in subsistence fashion. The account by Rockwell Kent is charming. Kent even contrived to baptize the half-breed offspring of an Argentine ex-prison inspector and a Yaghan woman.

We in the *Whisper* party thought it a pity that the lives of the Indians had been so tampered with by the missionaries and white settlers. The Indians were all dead—gone forever. We would have liked to have seen them and to have learned from them how to live off the land.

Adam and Eve and Margaret and I began to make reconnaissance hikes to the west and north of the island. Two of us went out on each clear day to see if we could find any people or structures or shipwrecks or a campsite closer to Peninsula Hardy or Isla Navarino.

The land was severe, but it had redeeming qualities. Isla Grevy was mostly open and rocky, with handsome light-brown coloring. Parts of the island were boggy and you had to watch your footing to keep from stepping into little pockets of sphagnum moss. Our routes climbed through flats of matted brush and dwarf wind-blasted trees. In protected canyons and draws along the shores we walked through luxurient thickets of evergreen beeches twenty-five to forty feet high. These small forested areas always had water, tall grasses, wild celery, and thick topsoil. In every one we visited we saw traces of Indian campsites.

We found no animals. The only land birds were a brown mockingbird type about ten inches long with white horizontal lines above and below the eyes. Along the shores we scared up lots of steamer ducks which would rush off, madly flapping away, and leave wakes of foam behind. I was never sure who was startled more—the steamer ducks or I. We saw many kelp geese about the size of small turkeys. The females were a hard-to-see mottled brown. The males stood out in white dress with specks of black. If you saw a male you could be sure that a female was nearby, but it took hard looking to spot her. We noticed a few brown ducks, some seagulls, and black cormorants with white breasts.

Along much of the shoreline of Grevy were large rounded boulders covered with slippery moss. Half in and out of the water, the big rocks guarded the shore like tank traps and made walking extremely hazardous. The combination of the boulders and masses of nearby offshore kelp made any small-boat work unthinkable.

From heights on the island we looked out across at Peninsula Hardy, eight miles to the west. With a sky of blue, the water was blue too, and the sunny Pacific seemed lovely. Below us, at our feet, lay Bahía Beaufort which was wide open to the southwest swell; even from a distance the water had a feeling of power and purpose. From the north end of Grevy we could see across the thirteen miles of Bahía Nassau toward the snowy slopes of Isla Navarino which shimmered in the blue haze of distance.

By now a week had passed. I removed a heavy twelve-volt storage battery from the wreck and took my English Aldis signaling lamp to the lookout point past the camp. The powerful light was visible for fifteen miles—perhaps more —so we signaled from time to time toward Isla Navarino which we knew had some ranches on it. Eve got the idea of spreading a sail on nearby dark trees in case a plane flew over. I began to work on a sailing rig for the dinghy.

On the ninth morning Margaret and I started rowing to the yacht when we saw Adam and Eve run through camp. Adam had my Olin flare gun and began to shoot red and white flares, all of which fizzled out after rising only a foot or two. We hurried to the lookout point and saw a Chilean torpedo vessel about three miles to the northeast.

I grabbed the Aldis lamp and called up the Chilean vessel. She stopped at once and I signaled our identity and condition. Margaret had the binoculars and reported that a rubber boat was being launched. Adam was whooping with joy.

"I'm glad to see the Chileans too," said Eve, "but I'm a

little sad that our camping experience is over. I would have liked to have explored a little more."

Twenty minutes later an officer and three Chilean sailors waded ashore. I ran up to the man in charge and apologized

Another view of the emergency camp looking southwest across Seagull anchorage to Isla Bayly. The growth of shrubs and grasses is surprisingly lush in the southern autumn. We see jugs of water, the U.S. flag, and a few camp chores in progress. We found many signs of earlier camping, presumably by Indians.

for his wet legs and feet.

"Oh it's nothing," he said, his face all aglow. "These patrols are a bore. Rescuing someone is the most exciting thing that's happened to us in years."

TEN

Salvage

THE 118-FOOT Chilean navy torpedo boat *Quidora*
picked up the four of us from the emergency camp in the
Wollaston Islands and whisked us around the east end of
Navarino Island to the Chilean naval base at Puerto Williams.
As Captain Raul Ganga completed the sixty-mile trip and
eased his vessel into the dock that fronted on Beagle Canal,
it seemed that half the people on the base had come down to
see us. Everyone treated us with great courtesy, almost as
if the shipwrecked mariners had been snatched from the jaws
of death. The most disappointed man was a medical aide
from the hospital who had expected us to be suffering from
hunger, malnutrition, and grave injuries. We thanked him
for his concern but assured him that we were all in good
condition and well fed. "Plenty of good Chilean shellfish
down there," said Margaret.

The commander at Puerto Williams, Fernando Camus,
was a tall, handsome man with fair coloring who looked
more like a Dutch naval officer than the head of a military
base near Cape Horn. Camus spoke flawless English, and—

*Seagull anchorage and Isla Diana in the Wollaston group
twenty-four miles north-northwest of Cape Horn. A chalupa with
fifteen men is being rowed from the* Castor *to the wrecked yacht
on shore.*

like the captain of the torpedo boat—was full of charm and confidence. We met briefly with newspaper reporters and television cameramen and then were taken to a small guest house. This was all very nice, but I was terrified at what might be happening to poor *Whisper* languishing on the beach of Isla Diana. News of the rescue was out on the radio and I feared that every fisherman and freebooter within a hundred miles would be converging on the wreck to strip her.

"The yacht represents all my assets," I said to Commander Camus. "I'm worried sick."

"You forget," he replied, lifting an authoritative right forefinger. "You forget that the navy exercises absolute control of this area. No one is going to bother the yacht. If the weather cooperates we're going to help you."

An hour later I was introduced to Lieutenant Horacio Balmelli who was the captain of the *Castor*, an eighty-two-foot workboat that was used for various supply and general utility jobs. Messages had been going back and forth to Admiral Allen in Punta Arenas and a plan developed to send the *Castor* to refloat *Whisper*, or at least to salvage her gear. Everyone was taking a personal interest in the refloating. It was a good sign and immensely reassuring.

Balmelli and I spent several hours discussing refloating schemes and salvage materials. He wanted to take along scuba divers, but I told him our need was for timbers, plywood, wedges, picks, shovels, sledgehammers, a few fifty-five-gallon oil drums, a pump, and a lot of bolts. "The yacht is high and dry on the beach at low water," I said. "If we can expose the damaged side we may be able to bolt or screw a patch over the damage."

Balmelli shook his head. "Machine screws and sheets of plywood are very difficult to get in this remote place. You might as well ask for gold bars or watermelons. Let me think about it, however, and I'll look around the warehouses."

On May 9, two days later, we were back at Seagull anchorage. The *Castor* had been joined by the *Fuentealba*, a slightly larger workboat. We had a great pile of salvage materials plus the twenty-five men of the two crews.

By now I had gotten to know Horacio Balmelli—the commander of our little two-ship expedition—a bit better. A graduate of the naval academy in Valparaiso, he was a quiet Chilean who had been stationed at Puerto Williams for four years. He and his family loved the peacefulness of the south and the opportunity to take long walks together in the absolute wilderness. Sometimes when he was fishing along a stream he would look up and see half a dozen fleet-footed guanacos watching him. Although Balmelli was a professional mariner, his mind had the steplike logic of an engineer, and he seemed happiest making plans for some project or other, complete with major objectives, alternatives, and contingencies. His ambition was to start a U.S.-type coast guard in Chile, and he was keen to study search and rescue techniques in America. Balmelli joked with me about the story of the last two men on earth. One was Argentine; the other was Chilean. Their food was gone and they had only a few hours left.

"What were they talking about?" went the line. "Girls? Money? Sports cars?"

"Heavens no," said Horacio. "They were arguing about the border between Chile and Argentina."

Balmelli was sympathetic to my plight with *Whisper* and he was optimistic from the beginning. "We're going to get her off," he kept repeating. "We're going to get her off." It almost became a litany and soon was taken up by everyone on the *Castor*. "We have another secret weapon," said Balmelli. "My bosun, Oluf Torres, is a Chilote and a clever fellow if there ever was one."

The two workboats anchored about a third of a mile from the wreck. Each vessel carried a six-meter tender called a *chalupa* that was rowed back and forth to Isla Diana with men and supplies.

My idea to recover the yacht was to dig under the starboard side, to slip timbers under the hull, and to through-

bolt or screw plywood patches on the inside and outside to make a firm sandwich repair. Then, after some pick and shovel work to smooth the beach, I hoped to turn the bow toward the water by laying out two anchors and taking a strain on the warps at high water. At this time I could check the hull for watertight integrity. Finally, after more beach smoothing at low water, I would skid the vessel in at high tide.

Balmelli's scheme was to erect a steel A-frame (borrowed from the navy base) over the yacht and to lift her slightly with a set of compound tackles in order to expose the damaged side enough to patch it. He then planned to lay the yacht on a special cradle for small vessels (also borrowed from the base) and then to drag *Whisper* into the water.

While Balmelli and I discussed the merits and disadvantages of our plans, Torres slipped ashore with a few men and took charge. Starting at the stern he put a small hydraulic jack under a strong point on the hull and lifted it two inches or so. He then tapped in a timber and a wedge to hold what he had gained with the jack. Torres then moved a few feet forward and lifted the hull again and inserted another small timber and a wedge. He worked little by little and gradually the hull began to straighten up. Initially the yacht lay at fifty degrees, then forty, and then thirty, and finally at eighteen degrees, securely held by timbers and wedges and several empty fifty-five-gallon oil drums. The work of Torres and his men was impressive. Balmelli and I abandoned our plans and bowed to a superior performance.

I got inside the hull and cleared out several dozen large stones, a couple of hundred pounds of gravel, and a mass of slippery kelp. I took a wrecking bar and a light sledgehammer and ripped out the entire galley, the dinette, the starboard seats, stowage lockers, and shelves. By the time I got down to the hull itself the area had been raised above the beach and enough light came through the rupture so that I could see the extent of the damage. The fiberglass hull had

Torres in charge. Note the small hydraulic jack near the transom of the yacht. The beach is composed of fine and coarse stones up to about eight inches in diameter. The Castor *and* Fuentealba *are anchored in the distance.*

an evil-looking U-shaped tear that measured forty-seven inches long in a horizontal direction. At the forward end the tear turned vertically upward for eight inches. At the after end the tear rose twenty-six inches. In general the hull was a hell of a mess. Nevertheless we saw that if the rupture could be bridged by structural material and padded to make it watertight the vessel would be seaworthy.

In viewing the damage objectively, it was remarkable that the wreckage wasn't worse. The hull had pounded on rocks at each high tide for eleven days. A wooden hull would have been kindling. A steel or aluminum hull might only have been dented.

The weather turned nasty. A cold wind blew from the west. The men wore heavy clothing; some had on woolen face masks. One of the *chalupas* had gotten broadside to the surf while landing and had turned over. Several of the men had gotten soaked. But everyone's morale remained high. As is the custom in these regions a bottle of *aguardiente* was passed around. We all took a gulp of the fiery brandy which was good for a little instant heat and perhaps a momentary mental lift because the work on the beach was truly a grubby job. At high water the sea lapped around the keel and it was impossible to work in the frigid, swirling water. With the hull raised, however, the interior was safe from flooding.

I realized that my behavior was paramount to the success of the mission. I made it my business to be on top of all the action. I got acquainted with the men and learned some of their names. I pulled on the leading oar of *Castor's chalupa*. I jumped ashore in the surf before the others. I passed out tools. I discussed problems with the officer in charge of the *Fuentealba*. I worked inside the hull. I carried hot food ashore. I spoke with Torres. I schemed with Balmelli. I pitched in entirely, not only to work but to lead the work. Again and again I asked: "What can I do to help?" I don't quite know where I found the energy for all this but it came from some hidden resource. I realized that this opportunity was my only chance to get the yacht off the beach and I wanted to spread my enthusiasm to everyone. Also I had no idea how long the navy would support the salvage operation. It could be stopped at any moment. We had to work quickly!

The only sour note in our efforts was Adam, the photographer. Margaret and Eve had had to stay behind at Puerto Williams because there was no place on the workboats for women. Adam asked to be taken along. "I'll photograph everything and I want to break down the camp and help bring our things to Puerto Williams," he said. In a moment of weakness I agreed. But as I feared, Adam did neither

Timbers and wedges were used to hold the yacht as she was lifted by the five-ton hydraulic jack. (Below) I soon learned to appreciate the usefulness of scrap timbers, wedges, and old oil drums. Whisper's hull at 40°.

of his announced jobs. Instead he stood around looking nervous or was asleep ten or eleven hours out of twenty-four. Unlike everyone else, he did no work of any kind and conveniently missed taking down the camp (which I and four Chilean sailors did). The Chileans recognized that Adam was disturbed and acting oddly. "Why doesn't he do something?" I was asked again and again. "The mental stress has been too much," I replied weakly.

Lieutenant Balmelli had managed to bring along a large sheet of half-inch plywood from a packing box. The plywood was soggy and not the best quality, but it was strong and could be bent slightly in two directions—just what we needed. I passed a hand saw to Torres who cut an L-shaped patch that overlapped the hull damage by two inches or so. Meanwhile I ripped out some insulating carpet from the interior. The idea was to pad the plywood with carpet to help smooth the rough places and to serve as a kind of packing. At first I had planned to bolt the patch in place with half-inch or five-eighths diameter machine screws, but these were not available. After thinking about the problem I realized that quarter-inch stainless-steel machine screws were adequately strong and that I could increase the bearing area on each side of the patch with large washers. A sailing friend in California, Lou Goaziou, had given me a good supply of such fastenings and I blessed his generosity.

A sharp quarter-inch drill bit in an eggbeater hand drill easily cut through a piece of half-inch backup plywood, the hull, the carpet, and the plywood patch itself. Torres pushed in a bolt from the outside, and eager fingers put a washer and a nut on the inside. Then a second hole and a second bolt. We faced the complication of bending the patch slightly in two directions—over the vertical curvature of the hull and around the fore and aft curvature as well. This required some levering with timbers. The patch, pulled down bolt by bolt, slowly closed over the hull wound. A dozen hours and two tides later the patch was securely held by an encircling ring of forty-eight bolts. Someone then

Torres marks the damaged area and decides on the size of the plywood patch. (Below) The patch partially bolted in place. Note the padding of carpet between the hull and the plywood.

caulked the edges of the patch with cotton. Torres smeared thick plastic paint over the entire repair. The color even matched the hull.

In Chile and Argentina, vessels under fifty feet are often taken from the water on an *anguilera* or cradle. This is made in two parts, a port half and a starboard half, each contoured to fit the bottom of the hull. While the vessel is in the water, the halves are floated into position on each side and securely chained together. A cable from a powerful windlass is led to one end of the cradle and the whole works is dragged longways up a shipyard ramp. The cradles are generally made in twenty-five-, thirty-five-, and forty-five-foot lengths. The curve of the cradles need not fit a hull exactly because the contours can be padded with sacks of

The patch has been completed and has been caulked and painted. Torres is checking the tightness of the forty-eight bolts that hold the patch to the hull.

straw or bundles of rags.

We had brought along the starboard half of a thirty-five-foot cradle and now dragged it in place alongside the patched hull. Torres did a little work with his hydraulic jack and drove in a few wedges and timbers and soon the yacht rested on the cradle ready for the water. We spent a few hours moving stones and smoothing the path to the sea while four men in a *chalupa* brought a hawser in from *Castor's* windlass. At high water, Balmelli signaled *Castor*. The engineer turned on the windlass. The cable tightened but the yacht didn't move an inch. Again Balmelli waved his signal flags. The windlass strained and strained but nothing happened. Everyone was glum. I felt like death.

Suddenly we saw some movement on *Fuentealba* which was lashed alongside *Castor*. The lieutenant in charge had the hawser belayed on *Castor*. He then fired up the main engines on both work vessels and put them in forward—full speed ahead! *Whisper* lurched, skidded sideways a few feet, and then plunged smoothly into the water. She was afloat!

During the salvage we had used most of the Dacron and nylon lines that had been on board *Whisper*. After the yacht was in the water we gathered all the tools and timbers and line on the beach and rowed them back to *Castor*. Unfortunately a large box with most of the lines and warps was dropped overboard. The coils of irreplaceable line sank into the depths, a bitter loss that was to trouble us for months.

Eighteen hours later the yacht was in Puerto Williams after a fast tow by *Castor*. Margaret and Eve met us on the dock. *Whisper's* interior was a sopping shambles of broken wood, soaked clothing, wet charts, squishy sails, ruined books, and rusting tools. Yet everything was aboard and we were thankfully afloat.

Some unseen keel damage caused the yacht to leak badly. I had to pump three hundred strokes an hour. And—as many mariners have learned to their sorrow—leaks don't stop at sunset. The next day Margaret and I and Torres used *Castor's* cargo boom to unstep *Whisper's* mast. We said good-

Whisper *rests on a cradle or* anguilera *as a hawser is led from the* Castor *to the wooden framework. (Below) The yacht slides into the water as the two lashed-together workboats gun their engines and pull ahead to assist Castor's deck winch.*

bye to Adam and Eve who climbed into a DC-3 and flew homeward. Two days later the Chilean naval vessel *Aguila* docked to unload supplies for Puerto Williams. On her return trip north she was to take the yacht to the shipyard in Punta Arenas. There was no shipping cradle for *Whisper* and no materials to make one, so a masterful Chilean bosun simply picked up the vessel in a cargo net and deposited the yacht gently on her side on a bed of old tires laid on deck. An impossible operation you say? I agree completely, but it was done—at night and in a swirling blizzard.

I was near collapse from the mental strain and all the pumping. A steward led me to a cabin as the *Aguila*'s deck lines were cast off. "We get the funniest cargo sometimes," he said. "A *yacht* is on board. Now what would a little sailboat be doing down here?"

Arrival at Puerto Williams on Isla Navarino after a tow from the Wollastons by Castor.

ELEVEN

A Giant Repair

OUR RESCUE from an uninhabited island near Cape Horn returned us to civilization, but we faced a monstrous problem. Quite simply, it was to repair a gaping big hole in *Whisper's* hull, to fix the keel, and to renew the rudder in a city that was eight thousand miles away from the boatyard where the yacht was built. In addition, every bit of gear on board was soaked with sea water, much was streaked with mud and rust, and some was missing altogether.

The yacht was unloaded from the navy ship and taken out of the water at the Asmar shipyard in Punta Arenas on the Strait of Magellan. Several hundred men worked at the shipyard, which was a military–civil service operation that dealt chiefly with Chilean naval vessels, a few local fishing boats, and did some commercial work. While we were there, the *Monsunen*, for example, a steel coasting vessel from the Falkland Islands, came in for repairs and painting.

The men in the yard were cordial and certainly curious about *Whisper*, but in truth they were terrified of her—perhaps as heavy truck mechanics might be nervous about working on a Ferrari or Porshe sports car. Fortunately I knew the

Whisper *goes into the water after her ride from Puerto Williams to Punta Arenas aboard the* Águila.

yacht inside and out and was well acquainted with fiberglass repairs. I planned to be on hand every minute and to supervise all the work.

Our first project was to take the bedding, books, bosun supplies, charts, clothes, cooking stoves, cushions, dishes, foodstuffs, hardware, lines, medical supplies, navigational equipment, papers, pots and pans, the rifle and revolver, sails, spare parts, toilet articles, tools, my ukelele, and a hundred other bits of gear to a small apartment the navy had loaned us. Everything needed to be washed and cleaned and dried out. To move all these wet belongings required three trips of a fair-sized truck and emphasized once again the quantity of living and sailing equipment necessary for distant voyages. For shipyard stowage we got two enormous wooden boxes into which we put the anchors and warps, bilge pumps, chain, compasses, the depth sounder, engine parts, fire extinguishers, and so on. In addition, we loaded the boxes with all the broken galley and saloon woodwork that I had ripped out in the Wollaston Islands and had piled in the forepeak. It seemed incredible how much stuff we took from the yacht. We needed three days to get the inside cleared out.

The cabin sole and starboard side were still deep in mud. I borrowed a hose and pump from the fire department, put on my boots and oilskins, and signaled a man to turn on the water. I had to laugh at myself. When we had set out for Cape Horn I had never thought that I would ever be standing inside the cabin with a fire hose washing out mud, gravel, and kelp. I have learned, however, that surprise is the nature of world voyaging. Every day is different. You never know what is coming.

Half an hour later I had all the mud and pebbles washed to a central spot. We reversed the pump, sucked out the water, and suddenly the interior of the ship was clean. *Whisper* seemed naked and exposed, but at least we had begun.

The Asmar shipyard was the only repair facility in the south. The Chilean navy ran the yard and had generously offered to repair the yacht free of charge. "We have a tradition of helping people down here," said our friend Admiral Eduardo Allen who was in charge of the navy in southern Chile. "Within the limits of the yard capabilities we want to put your *Whisper* back into seagoing condition."

The shipyard men had taken the yacht from the water on May 20. So far one week had passed. I had been given three weeks to get the entire job done and the vessel back in the water. Already the newspaper reporters were demanding a launching date. The difficult hull repair, unfortunately, hadn't even been started. Re-equipping the yacht seemed a

The hull damage to Whisper's *starboard side was suddenly exposed after the patch put on in the Wollaston Islands was removed. The damage was serious, but after pounding at each high tide for eleven days it was surprising that the problems weren't worse. The resiliency and strength of the fiberglass hull were remarkable.*

distant nightmare. No one at the yard seemed to be in the slightest hurry.

Winter was a month away. The days were getting short. The weather at 53° 10′ south latitude was cold. In order to repair the fiberglass hull we would either have to erect a heated tent around the hull or put the yacht inside a heated building because at freezing temperatures the polyester resin would never harden.

Due to the language problem and my unfamiliarity with the shipyard, a man named Juan Espinosa was appointed to "coordinate all efforts." Espinosa was a pleasant, middle-echelon civil service worker—always courteous and nicely dressed—who spoke some English. I used to think that he looked old until one day I found out that he was exactly my age, which was a real shocker. Espinosa was sincere, dedicated, and well acquainted with the various department heads, but even he sometimes shook his head when confronted by the quagmire of civil service politics. "We all have to be patient," he said to me one morning when I was upset that something hadn't been done as promised. "Don't worry," he said. "We are all working for you."

I discussed the concept of time with Espinosa. If an American or Englishman or German said 0900 he meant 0900. But to a Chilean or Peruvian 0900 meant 0930, 0945, maybe 1000, or, God forbid! even 1100.

"Suppose a navy ship was attacking the enemy," I said. "I suppose the torpedoes wouldn't be ready until tomorrow."

Espinosa smiled and laughed: "Oh that's quite different. It is just the normal custom to be a little relaxed about close timing."

With winter approaching, the best plan was to move the yacht inside the torpedo building, a large, heated, all-weather structure. "It is very secret," said Espinosa in a whisper. "The building is full of classified war materials. No one is allowed inside. You can see the sign and the guard yourself."

"What sort of torpedoes are inside?" I asked. "American?

French? English? German?"

"English torpedoes," said Espinosa. "But don't say I said so."

"English? Well then pass the word," I told him. "Margaret was a petty officer in the British Royal Navy during World War II. Certainly if . . ."

"I will tell them," said Espinosa, hurrying off.

Whether Margaret's background had any effect I don't know, but that afternoon the yacht and her cradle were dragged along a trail of greased timbers into the torpedo building. *Whisper's* mast, boom, spinnaker poles, two dinghies, and the two large wooden storage boxes followed, all piled up against some decrepit English torpedoes that were covered with thick grease. At last we could start to work.

I knew that it is difficult to make major fiberglass hull repairs because it is hard to duplicate the original curves. Strands of fiberglass saturated with wet polyester resin have about the same rigidity as wet noodles. A form or mold is necessary—either on the inside or outside—to hold the wet fiberglass until the resin sets up and the material begins to display its amazing strength and form-holding ability.

Whisper's starboard side midships was a mess. Her port side, however, was in perfect condition. But a mold taken from the good side would have been a mirror image of what we needed. I had two willing carpenters, Luis Ocampo and Hector Chavez, who cut nine vertical hardwood frames spaced ten and a half inches apart on the port side exactly opposite the damaged starboard side. We then reversed each frame by turning it 180 degrees about its vertical axis. We tacked each frame in place on the starboard side by using spacers between the frames and several long battens to hold the whole assembly together. Now we had a pattern for the starboard side. Ocampo and Chavez then took down the form and tacked sheets of thin pressed board on the inside. This was covered with wax so the new fiberglass wouldn't stick to the mold.

The next step was to cut away the hull damage, a large

The first step was to cut nine vertical frames to match the hull contours on the undamaged port *side. Each frame was then revolved 180 degrees on its vertical axis and put on the* starboard *side where it was held in place by spacers and battens as we see here.*

(Opposite) The framed structure was then taken down and its inside contours were covered with thin pressed board to make a mold. Notice the torpedoes in the background.

section of smashed fiberglass about seventy inches long and thirty-five inches high. The edges of the opening were carefully ground so that a long taper was left to ensure adequate area for a good bond between the existing hull and the new material. We then fastened the mold to the hull with a few bolts and were ready to put on the fiberglass.

While Ocampo and Chavez were working on the mold, I had removed the structural bulkhead between the saloon and the galley on the starboard side. This bulkhead was in the way of the repair and needed some fixing of its own.

All the work at the shipyard was on metal or wooden

The damaged hull section was cut away and the edges of the opening were carefully tapered to ensure ample area for a good bond. The saloon-galley starboard bulkhead has been removed. (Below) Layers of mat and roving were laid up from the inside with ample overlaps over the existing part of the hull.

hulls. No fiberglass vessel had ever been at Asmar before. It was fortunate that Ocampo and Chavez occasionally repaired fiberglass life raft containers and their mounts, and understood how to work with resin and glass. I had some fiberglass mat and roving material and a few gallons of resin on board. We managed to get more. Ocampo dragged in several cylinders of bottled gas and fired up a big blowtorch-type heater underneath the hull to raise the temperature. One morning we had a mad fiberglassing scene as layers of mat and roving were alternately laid in place and saturated with polyester resin. To strengthen the patch we glassed in three longitudinal stringers which overlapped both the old and new work. A few days later we installed the repaired starboard bulkhead and glassed it in place.

While all this was going on we had streams of visitors even though the torpedo building was supposedly secret and restricted. Every day most of the shipyard workers managed to detour past the yacht to see what we were doing. We got to know the secretaries from the shipyard office. We saw tourists, visiting brass, merchant seamen, fishing boat crews, and of course the officers from the navy headquarters in town. The newspapers wrote frequent progress reports. The television cameramen were forever shooting film. Some of the visitors thought that the patch would fall off; many were in agreement that the yacht would never leave the torpedo building. A few thought the yacht might float. But no one dared to think of going around Cabo de Hornos *in that!*

While the hull, keel, and rudder repairs were underway, Margaret worked hard taking loads of clothes and bedding to the laundry. She had hundreds of books and papers spread around the apartment drying; clotheslines were strung everywhere for special projects. She cleaned every piece of galley gear and removed thick rust from most of my tools and many of the spare parts. There were no replacements to be bought, so, like the Chileans who saved everything, we learned to make do with what we had. Margaret spent hours cleaning rust from engine oil filters, for example,

After the resin had set up we removed the mold. Here with a powerful light inside the hull you can see the outline of the longitudinal stringers (overlapping the old and new work) that we added for strength. The general appearance is a mess, but the hull is as strong or stronger than when the yacht was built originally. Only grinding and filling and cosmetic painting remain to be done. When completed there was no trace of the patch and it was impossible to tell where the yacht had been damaged. Later on, for fun, we told people that it had been the other side of the hull— the port side—that had been damaged, at which point one of our visitors generally said "I can see it," which was baloney because the port side had never been damaged at all. The object at the lower left in the photograph is not a machine gun but a space heater fueled by bottled gas.

and wire-brushing corroded Primus burners for the kerosene stoves. She dunked rusty cans of food in fresh water, dried them, and then wiped each can with oil.

We desperately needed line to replace the lost halyards and sheets, and we wanted new injectors for the diesel engine. These things were not easily available so we sent off to the U.S. and Sweden. Regrettably, the parcels never arrived.

When we left Punta Arenas we had to be self-sufficient for three months. This required a considerable stockpiling of food which was costly in inflation-ridden Chile. Margaret went from store to store with her lists and shopping baskets. To buy flashlight batteries and woolen gloves required visits to a dozen shops. The stores had an astonishing amount of German goods. It seemed that a couple of German super-salesmen must have passed through Punta Arenas. We saw German bread-slicing machines, tools, towels, barometers, packages of dried soup, sleeping bags, detergent, radios, bedsheets, even cuckoo clocks—dozens of things and all from Germany.

Our Punta Arenas sojourn wasn't all drudgery. Sometimes new acquaintances invited us to their homes for meals. We got wonderful letters of encouragement from friends in the U.S. and Canada. Margaret managed to fit in a few lessons of Spanish, which she enjoyed immensely. Often at noon we walked to a small shop in the center of town where we bought freshly-made *empanadas*, a delicious Chilean speciality of spicy beef or chicken, olives, raisins, onions, and a slice of hard-boiled egg, all baked together in a crispy pastry envelope.

Every morning I got up in the dark and stumbled through the sleeping city at 0630 on my way to the shipyard. Fortunately I had my hiking boots on board so I had good footwear to walk along the dirt roads and across the frozen puddles. Sunrise in June wasn't until 0915; sunset came about 1645, so I got used to walking home in the dark.

As soon as the hull was closed up I began to assemble the galley and saloon. There was no new wood available so I used the wreckage I had torn out earlier. It is amazing how you can glue smashed wood back together. Epoxy glue, splints, and a couple of screws can do wonders. I had no time or materials for a fancy job. I needed to get *Whisper* operational quickly.

Even so, it was impossible to have the yacht ready by the yard deadline. On June 13 Espinosa told me that *Whisper* was to go into the water on the following Wednesday. "Impossible," I said. "She is in no way ready for sea. It will take several days just to step the mast and rig her. The interior is still a shambles." The next morning I asked the navy for two more weeks which was granted. I was requested to leave the torpedo building, however, so over the weekend Margaret and I did some fast cosmetic work on the patch and hull and quickly slapped on topside and bottom paint. On June 18 the yard men moved the ship from the torpedo building and took her to the launching ramp. Heavy snow was falling so we hurried to install the diesel stove and to fire it up for warmth.

I put the repaired alternator, starter-generator, and injectors on the diesel engine. Margaret glued insulating carpet on the inside of the hull repair. I collected the two storage batteries, put them on board, and began to hook up the new wiring on the starboard side. Espinosa and I made a trip to the machine shop to collect the welded spinnaker pole and the straightened lifeline stanchions. Two bronze stanchion bases had been crushed almost flat, but a clever welder had managed to reconstruct them.

One day at noon Margaret appeared with all the upholstered cushions, which had been specially cleaned and dried by the Modelo Laundry. We got the saloon table mounted. A repairman delivered my two typewriters in good working order even though they had been submerged in salt water for two weeks—a real miracle. One afternoon I mounted the galley sink, hooked up its drain pump, and installed the fresh and salt water taps. We borrowed a truck to move all the dried and cleaned gear from the apartment.

Although the exchange rate was 720–780 escudos to the dollar, we spent money at an alarming rate. Starter-generator bearings cost 8,500 escudos; injectors were 26,000 each; one set of foul-weather gear was 35,000. The laundry bills totaled 66,000. Three new Chilean *Pilot* volumes were 26,400 escudos. The charges for a 250-foot nylon warp totaled 40,000. Every time we went to the food shops for stores we spent half a dozen crisp green 5,000-escudo notes. The inflation rate was 1 percent a day and in a store it was a race to buy goods with marked prices before the clerks could change the figures.

When we stepped the mast the usual yard gang of twenty men showed up. Three or four would have been ample but the Asmar shipyard worked by the platoon system and there was no changing it. I bolted on the boom gallows, hooked the main boom to the mast, and hoisted a Chilean courtesy flag that had been presented to us by Rafael Gonzales, the captain of the *Orompello*, in a particularly pleasant little ceremony. *Whisper* was beginning to look seaworthy.

Our sails were still covered with thick mud from the camp in the Wollaston Islands. For a month we had tried to find a large, clean, paved area with running water so we could scrub the sails and inspect the stitching. Finally our friend Peter Samsing introduced us to a colonel in charge of a nearby army barracks who offered us the use of a big shower room. Unfortunately, on the day we arrived with the sails the officer was away and had forgotten to tell his sergeant about us.

Can you imagine two foreigners speaking pidgin Spanish arriving at a heavily guarded armory in a snowstorm and trying to get over that they wanted to wash sails? The confusion was total. But we kept at our story. Finally a corporal recognized us from the newspaper stories. Suddenly there were torrents of laughter and smiles all around on the former stern and worried faces.

Whisper's launching was simple because we were already on a cradle. We slipped into the water and chugged out to an enormous mooring buoy and tied to it with three lines. Right away I knew I was going to miss the bleating of all the transistor radios. The frustrations during the seven weeks in the shipyard had sometimes seemed more than a human could bear. Like civil service operations in the U.S. and England, Asmar appeared to be ready to capsize from the weight of its top-heavy brass, its paperwork, and endless talk. Yet I don't want to complain because I was an invited guest. I will always be grateful for everything that was done for Margaret and me. If there be any complaint maybe it is that Americans are too hard driving, too impatient, and too demanding of deadlines and promises. Maybe we should be more relaxed and loose and try to emulate the charm of the Chileans. But then how can a launching dead-line—or any other—be met?

I felt so alone at times. No one had any idea of the enormousness of the job we had done on our tiny yacht. We had crammed three months' work into seven weeks. The re-sults weren't perfect and lots of work still remained, but by God we were afloat and operational. We had managed to sidestep shortages, to outmaneuver red tape, and somehow to keep pressing on. Margaret had been wonderful—always optimistic, encouraging, and full of resolve. Of course the whole repair job was my fault in the first place because I had let the ship drag ashore in a storm. . . . How tired and weary I was. I felt like a knife blade that had been ground down to the handle on an abrasive wheel.

Suddenly I heard an engine roaring alongside. I looked out to see a large steel launch bearing down on *Whisper*. Espinosa and the Asmar chiefs plus reporters and photog-raphers and their various women friends were coming to see us. Crash! We frantically put out fenders and tried to push the bow of the launch sideways to get the invasion force alongside and stopped, but the driver gunned his engine in reverse, backed off smoothly, and prepared to attack again. Crash! The inexpert helmsman smashed his battering ram into our bow. Crash! Now our stern. Crash! And crash again! Couldn't one of the officers aboard the launch tell the driver to come alongside parallel and at slow speed?

I tried to wave off the launch. Everybody smiled and waved back. The television cameramen were shooting film. I feared that our fragile eggshell would be sunk on the spot if the launch persisted in striking us. We were helpless. The steel projectile circled for a try from a new direction, came alongside, and we threw them bow and stern lines. Everybody scrambled on *Whisper* for a thorough look. The women clucked at the galley and the reporters asked the usual questions. Espinosa proudly lectured the Asmar chiefs about what had been done. We were filmed from all directions. We shook hands with everyone, received their blessings, and finally the launch was gone.

"I think it's time to get the clearance and to head south," I said to Margaret. "One more onslaught like that and we'll have to swim ashore. Certainly Cape Horn will be easier."

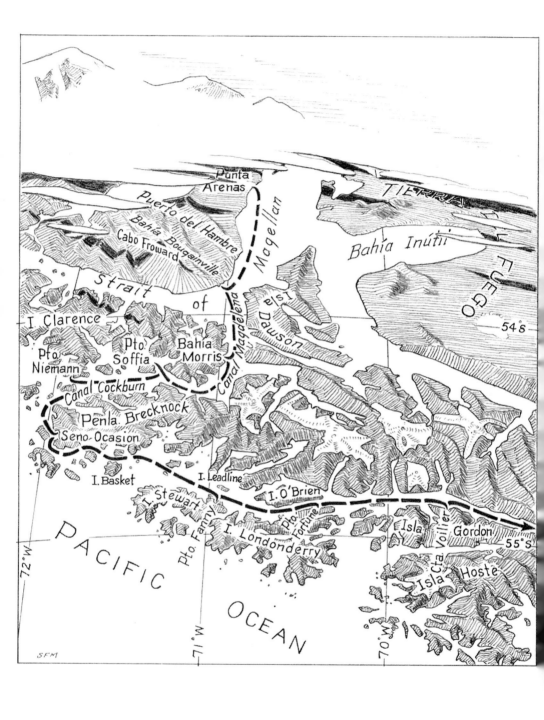

TWELVE

South Again

*W*HEN WE SAILED from Punta Arenas on July 14 for the second attempt at Cape Horn the yacht was barely seaworthy. Margaret and I were exhausted from the seven-week ordeal in the shipyard. We needed a quiet place to rest for a few days and time to complete dozens of small jobs on *Whisper*. We had anchored in Bahía Bougainville twice before, so we immediately sailed forty-three miles south along the Strait of Magellan to the west side of the strait near Cabo Froward. As before, we found the little bay quiet and isolated and pretty with its dense thicket of surrounding beech trees that climbed steeply upward from the rocky shores.

Captain Louis de Bougainville discovered the tiny bay that carries his name in 1765 when he was collecting wood for the Falkland Islands (which were then controlled by the French and called the Malouines). He returned two years later with the frigate *la Boudeuse* and the store ship *l'Étoile* on his way to Tahiti. Bougainville had learned to moor his ships if possible, and he ordered each of his vessels to drop two anchors and to run hawsers ashore to the trees.[29]

Since we had already been blown out of the bay three and a half months earlier and had later suffered our terrible accident, we dropped two stern anchors as soon as we arrived. Then we rowed ashore two strong bow lines which we tied to stout beech trees. During the next two nights the west wind blew hard. When I looked out at the windy black void into which I couldn't see as far as my fingertips, I felt a bit apprehensive. How good it was to have lines ashore to windward in those southern anchorages!

While waiting for an improvement in weather before sailing south along the Strait of Magellan we tied up to this old four-masted iron-hulled barque in Punta Arenas. The dim outline of Tierra del Fuego is across the water to the left.

I mentioned earlier that the yacht was barely seaworthy. Her hull, ground tackle, engine, sails, and interior were all right. The problem was the rig and the crew. We had stepped the mast but the yacht had been launched before I got the rigging adjusted and the turnbuckles secured. I wanted time to rig the spinnaker poles, to install a repaired staysail halyard block, to fix the spreader lights, and to complete many small jobs. The yacht desperately needed to be scrubbed and cleaned. Margaret and I hoped to have a couple of days of rest.

During the salvage at Seagull anchorage we had lost a large box of lines and now were very short of halyards, sheets, and warps. I had tried to have 600-foot spools of half-inch Dacron and five-eighths-inch nylon sent from the U.S., but the shipment never arrived. The only line available locally was three-quarter-inch yellow polypropylene (which was too large for *Whisper's* blocks), and some rather inferior quarter-inch manila (which was much too small and weak). After wondering what to do I got the idea of cutting our few remaining Dacron sheets and halyards in two and lengthening each half by splicing on a long tail of quarter-inch manila to make up for the missing Dacron. We then did the initial hauling on the quarter-inch manila to take up the slack of a sheet or the easy part of hoisting a sail. By the time we got to a heavy strain on the line we were past the manila and the splice and down to the strong half-inch Dacron.

While we were in Punta Arenas I had asked the captain of a cargo ship for a nylon anchor warp. The captain had no nylon but he generously gave me 325 feet of inch and five-eighths diameter manila line. It was heavy and intractable stuff but it served us well. At first the manila was stiff and covered with grease and dirt. After a month of use in clean salt water, however, the line became supple and bleached and reminded me of the braided hair of a Swedish girl.

We sailed south into Canal Magdalena and west along Canal Cockburn. It was now midwinter and there had been

(Overleaf) Monte Sarmiento from Canal Beagle. This prominent peak, named after the early Spanish explorer, is seldom visible because the prevailing westerly winds tend to build up dense clouds around the mountain. Only in easterly weather—not too common—does the double summit appear and then only briefly, giving rise to picnic weather and sunny skies.

a dramatic increase in snow since our first trip. It was easy to tell the times of high and low water because of the snow line at the water's edge. Though the weather was cold, the sailing was magical and we traveled in a fairy world. The mountains of Tierra del Fuego to the south rose up white and gigantic above the dark water. Sometimes the wind blew streamers of snow from the high ridges and peaks. These snow banners blew to leeward for hundreds of feet and made incredible ribbons of white that waved like giant hoists of celestial flags. The winter sun shone low from the northern sky and pinned its reddish rays on snow scenes that flickered before my eyes like the unreal images of a dream.

Margaret and I wore layers of woolens for warmth, and waterproof oilskins for protection from the wind and spray. We kept our heads and ears warm with woolen caps. I put on two pairs of thick hand-knitted woolen stockings inside my seaboots and wore woolen gloves inside large rubber gloves. We alternated short watches of an hour or two.

Each night we moored carefully. Sometimes we stayed over for a day, and gradually got both rested and well into the list of jobs on the yacht. We installed the stanchions and lifelines, repaired the broken cockpit spray dodger, and made new flapper valves for a bilge pump from scraps of a rubber inner tube. The carburetor for the diesel stove never functioned properly after its dunking in salt water, so I finally scrapped the valve and fitted a simple drip feed device, which fortunately worked well. I finished making a spare tiller because the emergency tiller had gotten broken in the accident. The galley sink drain needed a gasket. I braced a weak settee front with two battens and a dozen screws. We spent one day scrubbing the decks and cockpit floor trying to remove an accumulation of mud, soot, grease, rust, resin, and paint from the shipyard.

Near the western end of Canal Cockburn we sailed into Puerto Niemann, an extremely remote and seldom-visited anchorage at the southern end of Isla Clarence. The land was low and partially bare with windswept trees that leaned to the east. As we approached the area I took bearings of various points but none of the land forms shown on Admiralty chart 554 made any sense. I scratched my head and looked again. Margaret, who is good at coastal pilotage, came on deck and was puzzled too. I soon realized that the chart reflected utter fantasy and showed "Duntze islands and channel" where in fact none existed at all. The Admiralty *Pilot* was vague and unspecific. We immediately got out Chilean chart 1201 which was quite accurate and reassuring. Margaret read aloud from the Chilean *Pilot* V which had proper descriptions.

As we jibed and sailed into Puerto Niemann—who was Niemann?—I had the distinct feeling that no one had ever been in the anchorage before. There was no sign of man and I had the eerie premonition that if we had a mishap ashore our anchored vessel might not be discovered for a dozen years. I half expected to see pirates or pixies, Spanish galleons, or green men from Mars. For the real loner this was the ultimate place. Never had I sensed such isolation and remoteness.

The anchorage was well sheltered with good holding ground, but we got into a mess. I elected to anchor near the western shore because of the usual westerly winds. We dropped a stern anchor and headed toward land until the line was taut. I then took the dinghy and started to row a bow line ashore. While rowing the line to the beach, however, a squall funneled down from the land and began to blow me, my warp, and the yacht away from the shore. I rowed harder, furiously, and was only a few feet from shore, but it was no use. Normally this would have made little difference because I would merely have been blown back to the yacht which was anchored. At Niemann, however, the holding ground for the anchor was steeply shelving and in a minute or two the dinghy and I, the warp, the yacht, and her stern anchor —now hanging straight down in deep water—were all blowing merrily downwind.

I shouted at Margaret to give a little forward boost with

During the eight months of our stay in the Chilean channels we filled our water tanks again and again by pouring water into jugs and then ferrying them to the yacht via the dinghy.

the engine, but *Whisper* was drifting astern faster than Margaret realized and the slack from the stern anchor line got into the propeller.

Pandemonium! We had no engine. It was getting dark, and strong squalls of sleet hurled down from the western shore. I rowed back to the yacht in record time and pulled up the stern anchor. We then made sail and beat back very close to the western shore where we anchored. I got two lines ashore and carried out a second anchor. Safe at last!

The lesson I learned was always to carry a line ashore to a windward shore *before* dropping an anchor on a steeply

shelving bottom.

The next morning we tried various schemes to free the line from the propeller. Nothing worked. I put on my wet suit very reluctantly, a bit afraid of the cold water because we had seen chunks of ice in Canal Cockburn. Once in the water, however, I unwound the warp from the propeller in a minute or two and scrambled back on board. The fear of the icy water was far worse than the water itself. I was ashamed of myself for being so slow to go in. Actually I felt wonderful afterward.

To the north-northwest of us at the southern end of Isla

Santa Inés was Seno Dresden, a long, skinny, west-facing fjord that had been a hiding place of the German light cruiser *Dresden,* a survivor of the 1914 naval battles of Coronel and the Falkland Islands. When World War I began, the German China squadron under Admiral Maximilian Graf von Spee steamed eastward to South America. Initially, von Spee had two powerful heavy cruisers which were later joined by three light cruisers.

To oppose this German thrust into the southeastern Pacific, England lined up an armed cruiser, two light cruisers, an auxiliary cruiser, and a decrepit old battleship, the *Canopus,* which could only steam at twelve knots, half the speed of the other vessels.

The Battle of Coronel took place off the central Chilean coast on November 1, 1914, with both fleets steaming southward into a heavy sea and a strong southerly wind. The Germans outmaneuvered and outgunned the British and sank both the flagship *Good Hope* (with Rear Admiral Sir Christopher Cradock) and the *Monmouth.* On December 9, five weeks later, von Spee attacked the Falkland Islands, which he planned to seize and turn into a German base. But the British had reinforced Port Stanley with two large battle cruisers which had been sent at full speed from England and which had arrived only twenty-one hours before von Spee appeared. With Admiral Sir Frederick Sturdee in command, the two big British ships (with twelve-inch guns) plus four light cruisers came out fighting and after a spirited battle sank four of the German men-of-war. Those killed included Admiral von Spee and his two sons. The only ship to escape was the *Dresden,* which fled to the southern Chilean channels where she played a cat-and-mouse game with British cruisers. In March 1915 the *Dresden* steamed to Isla Juan Fernandez where she was sunk by the British cruiser *Kent.*

Reading about these naval actions more than sixty years later, it is hard to realize the problems of fuel and communications. Few ships had wireless sets in 1914, radio direction finding was unknown, there was no aerial reconnaissance, and the big naval vessels used dozens of tons of coal each day and had to be met by fleets of colliers that had been arranged for ahead of time. But the men were tough. Their patriotism was strong and direct even if the motives of the war were clouded. The worst part of the two battles was that some two thousand sailors in the flower of their manhood were killed to little purpose except for the vanity of two countries.[30]

We sailed around the western end of Tierra del Fuego where the gray land met the Pacific. We looked at a brittle world of half-drowned mountain summits, a battleground where the restless water collided with the tops of the Andes which here were near the sea. Most of the land was bare and climbed from the water in massive curves and billows of glaciated stone not long removed from an ice age that had ground the sharp summits into soft surves. A few scrawny trees clung together in heroic clumps whose tops were shorn by the westerly gales. The great swell of the Southern Ocean crashed on a miscellany of rocks and ledges and islets with stunning force, flinging the shattered water high into the air. Captain Robert Fitz Roy, the first man to chart this area, named the region the Milky Way because of its resemblance to the night sky. "The chart of it, with all its stars to mark the rocks, looks like a map of the heavens rather than part of the earth," he wrote aboard IIMS *Beagle* on January 27, 1830.[31]

It was wildly exciting to sail in such a place. But the needle of our barometer was skipping downward in large nervous jumps. We hurried into well-sheltered Seno Ocasión on Peninsula Brecknock as the wind began to rise.

While stormbound I wrote in my journal:

July 20th The view outside is a study of grays and dark greens; of giant granite domes fringed at the bottom with small trees; of noisy waterfalls and cascades trumbling from high overhead; of mist and blowing rain and then periods

of quiet; of curious small birds that dart on deck and peer in at the portlights and companionway; of perfectly smooth water that is clear and dark and cold; of black and white cormorants nesting above us who glide and swoop and flutter when returning home and then sit like waxen sentinels for hours, scarcely moving. The air is crisp and hard and almost tingles with purity. Ashore not a sign of man. No footprint or rubbish heap. No hut or tottering fence or rotting boat. I finger a bush with berries; a vine with small red flowers; a dwarf tree as high as my hand. I take a squishy step across a tiny meadow of sphagnum moss. From the top of a rise we look at a series of small lakes, each dropping into a lower until the last topples into the sea and is gone. Overhead the clouds run swiftly eastward, pushed by the vigorous wind from the west.

Captain Fitz Roy gave names to locations as they were mapped. Places were named after men on the expedition, for famous people, because the place suggested a name, or due to some incident during the survey. As we sailed eastward in *Whisper*, now south of Tierra del Fuego, we passed Seno Courtenay, Paso Adventure, Cabo Fletcher, and Islas Catherine, O'Brien, and Gilbert, all good British names.

The patience and tenacity of Fitz Roy and his men during the tedious survey work in the square-rigged *Beagle* and in open whaleboats was astounding, and the accurate charts are remarkable monuments to the skill and determination of these English sailors. Poor Fitz Roy had one problem after another. One hundred and fifty years ago the Cape Horn region had a population of perhaps five thousand highly independent and clever Indians. While anchored at Isla London, for example, Fitz Roy sent a whaleboat and seven men to an island fifteen miles away. During a stormy night Indians stole the whaleboat. The men from the *Beagle* managed to contrive a sort of basket boat by weaving small branches together and covering the basket with canvas and mud. Three men somehow rowed the basket boat back to the *Beagle* and gave the alarm.

Fitz Roy immediately set out with another whaleboat to recover the stolen boat. At a nearby Fuegian camp the men from the *Beagle* discovered the missing whaleboat's mast. Encouraged, the party pressed on and two days later found the whaleboat's leadline in a camp some twenty miles to the east. A friendly Indian took the party to a nearby cove where the men of the *Beagle* recovered more boat gear. Fitz Roy was convinced that the cove was the home of the thieves. The Indians led the Englishmen on a long and frustrating wild goose chase for nineteen days. Fitz Roy retaliated by taking Indian hostages and their children, but the crafty Indians slipped away and left Fitz Roy to look after the children. In the end, the *Beagle*'s carpenter had to build a new whaleboat.

Now in *Whisper* we sailed along Whaleboat Sound (Canal Ballenero) and passed Isla Basket (named for the basket boat), Isla Leadline, Cabo Longchase, Isla Hide, Thieves Sound (Seno Ladrones), Bahía Escape, and Thieves Cove (Caleta Ladrones). We almost felt the presence of Fitz Roy and his trusty crew. Where was that damned whaleboat anyway?

FOURTEEN

Final Triumph

*A*LTHOUGH the westerly gales sometimes blew fiendishly hard near Cape Horn there were plenty of sailing days when the wind eased to ten or fifteen knots. The light winds generally came with a morning cloud level of three hundred to five hundred feet that cleared as the day progressed. *Whisper* was south of the big island of Tierra del Fuego and we headed eastward and made good time in pleasant conditions, often under full sail. As we glided along in smooth water in the lee of small islands, the world around us seemed still and quiet. Our existence was a mote of nautical dust amidst a galaxy of snowfields and mountains and waterways.

The date was July 22, the middle of winter. It seemed a bad time to be heading for Cape Horn. True, the hours of daylight were short, but it was well documented that the winter weather was better. The most severe gales blow in the southern summer, from December through March.

The advantage of long [summer] days is certainly very great, [wrote Captain Phillip Parker King in an early Cape Horn *Pilot*] but from my experience of the winds and weather . . . I preferred the winter passage, and in our subsequent experience of it, found no reason to alter my opinion. Easterly and northerly winds prevail in the winter off the cape, whilst southerly and westerly winds are constant during the summer months; and not only are the winds more favorable in the winter, but they are moderate in comparison to the fury of the summer gales.[32]

Since leaving Punta Arenas we hadn't seen a single person. Not a ship nor a fishing boat nor a distant man on horseback. All the Alacalufe, Ona, and Yaghan Indians that had amused and intrigued and plagued the early explorers and travelers were gone. No longer would a lone Joshua Slocum sprinkle carpet tacks on the deck of his yacht *Spray* to discourage unwanted visitors at night. The Indians had all vanished—except for a few—pathetic victims of disease, alcohol, a cruelly expanding white man's frontier, and a shattered culture. The handsome and skillful Onas who had lived by hunting the guanaco with bow and arrow had been decimated by tuberculosis and finally wiped out by measles. Margaret and I had seen a handful of Alacalufes in Puerto Edén further north, but they lived mostly on government handouts. We met one Yaghan in Puerto Williams. In reality, however, the Indians of Tierra del Fuego were extinct.

In the old days, the hardy, almost naked Alacalufes and Yaghans had lived in small dugouts or bark canoes and had traveled as nomads from place to place eating shellfish, a few wild plants, seal meat, and occasional blubber from a stranded whale. Each canoe always had a fire in the center, built over a thick bed of clay which served as both firebrick and ballast. Ashore the Indians lived in crude wigwams. Some writers called these people savages because they appeared to live scarcely better than animals. From Magellan in 1520 to Barclay in 1920, travelers' accounts are filled with stories of the canoe Indians who were filthy and greasy by European standards, but who somehow appeared to thrive in a very tough natural environment.

The Indians were seen on all the main islands and pas-

A Fuegian Indian at Puerto Williams on Isla Navarino. This aged survivor lived a simple and pleasant life and eked out his income by making model Yaghan canoes of the old style and selling them to occasional visitors.

sages and even on the most remote offshore islets. When James Weddell of the sealer *Jane of Leigh* anchored in remote St. Martin's cove on Isla Hermite in 1823 he was astonished to see Yaghans coming out to his brig. Soon the Indians were on board entertaining the sailors. Weddell was impressed by the Indians' ability to mimic the Englishmen:

A sailor had given a Fuegian a tin pot full of coffee which he drank, and was using all his art to steal the pot. The sailor, however, recollecting after a while that the pot had not been returned, applied for it, but whatever words he made use of were always repeated in imitation by the Fuegian. At length, he became enraged at hearing his requests reiterated, and placing himself in a threatening attitude, in an angry tone, he said, "You copper-coloured rascal, where is my tin pot?" The Fuegian, assuming the same attitude, with his eyes fixed on the sailor, called out "You copper-coloured rascal, where is my tin pot?" The imitation was so perfect, that every one laughed, except the sailor, who proceeded to search him, and under his arm he found the article missing.[33]

W. H. B. Webster explained how the Fuegians fished without metal or bone hooks: "They fasten a small limpet in its shell to the end of a line, which the fish readily swallows as bait. The greatest care is then taken by them not to displace the limpet from his stomach in drawing the fish gradually to the surface of the water; and when there, the woman watches a favourable moment, and with great dexterity, while she retains the fish by the line with one hand, seizes hold of it with the other and quickly lifts it into the canoe."[34]

Captain Charles Wilkes wrote from the Wollaston Islands in 1839:

We were here visited by a canoe with six natives, two old women, two young men, and two children. The two women were paddling, and the fire was burning in the usual place. They approached the vessel singing their rude song "Hey meh leh," and continued it until they came alongside. The expression of the younger ones was extremely prepossessing, evincing much intelligence and good humor. They ate ham and bread voraciously, distending their large mouths and showing a strong and beautiful set of teeth. A few strips of red flannel distributed among them produced great pleasure; they tied it around their heads as a sort of turban. Knowing they were fond of music, I had the fife played, the only instrument we could muster. They seemed much struck with the sound. The tune of "Yankee Doodle" they did not understand; but when "Bonnets of Blue" was played, they were all in motion keeping time to it. . . . I have seldom seen so happy a group. They were extremely lively and cheerful, and anything but miserable, if we could have avoided contrasting their condition with our own. The colour of the young men was a pale, and of the old a dark copper colour. Their heads were covered with ashes, but their exterior left a pleasing impression. Contentment was pictured in their countenances and actions, and produced a moral effect that will long be remembered.[35]

When Charles Darwin sailed on the *Beagle* he unwittingly made an observation that was to weigh heavily on the Indians' future. "In another harbour not far distant," he wrote, "a woman who was suckling a recently-born child, came alongside the vessel and remained there out of mere curiosity, whilst the sleet fell and thawed on her naked bosom, and on the skin of her naked baby." [36]

The indirect result of Darwin's remark was that tons of blankets and clothes were sent to the Indians. None of the writers or sailors or missionaries or anyone else realized that the Indians' oily skin quickly shed water. ("Indian's body all over like white man's face," noted Barclay too late.) No one considered that the Indians might be acutely susceptible to pulmonary diseases. Great efforts were made to Christianize the Indians and to get them to dress, live, and work like white men. It was all folly. When the Yaghans and Alacalufes and Onas wore damp clothes, the natives got chills that quickly turned to influenza, pneumonia, and consumption. Coupled with the problems of clothing was cultural interference. Once the Europeans began to tamper with the life styles of the Indians and to put them into settlements where they were obliged to learn such pointless idiocy as carpentry and sewing and Bible lessons, their reasons for living stopped.

Little Peter Duncan, once named Multgliunjer, may have learned about Jesus, but if Peter died of tuberculosis at age eleven, what was the use of the lessons if it deprived the child of his life? [37]

Lucas Bridges, who knew the Indians better than any other white man and spoke their language perfectly, visited a large group of Onas who were kept at a Silesian Christian mission on Dawson Island in 1900. Bridges's friend Hektliohlh had escaped from Ushuaia and had been captured once again by settlers and handed over to the Silesians.

"He looked with yearning towards the distant mountains of his native land," wrote Bridges. " 'Shouwe t-maten ya,' said Hektliohlh. ('Longing is killing me.')

"He did not survive very long," said Bridges. "Liberty is dear to white men; to untamed wanderers of the wilds it is an absolute necessity." [38]

It is easy to romanticize about the Indians who in fact became troublesome and thieving when white men began to spend time in the south. Even the most hardboiled sheep rancher, however, had to admit that the Indians' story was tragic and wretched.

We stopped at Puerto Fanny on Isla Stewart, Puerto Fortuna on Isla Londonderry, and at Caleta Voilier on Isla Gordon. Now *Whisper* was once again in Canal Beagle and we sailed past the six large glaciers that flowed down from the north side of the northwest arm of Beagle and discharged directly into the water. The winter snow lay deep on the mountains and we brushed against ice fragments in the channel. In one anchorage Margaret collected three buckets of mussels—of which there were thousands. Some of the mussels measured eight inches long. We kept them in water in the cockpit. At night the buckets froze solid and stayed frozen all day so the mussels were well refrigerated. We ate this batch of shellfish on and off for the next two weeks.

~~~~~~

Peruvian Mussel Soup

36 mussels
2 cups water
1 celery stalk with leaves (or dried celery)
2 tablespoons olive oil
1 medium onion, chopped or grated (or dried)
2 cloves garlic, crushed
1 teaspoon chili powder
1 tablespoon cornstarch
1 tablespoon chopped parsley (or dried parsley)
  Juice of ½ lemon
1 egg, beaten
1½ cups evaporated milk
  Salt and pepper to taste
  Fried croutons optional

.   .   .

Wash and scrub mussels. Place in large saucepan over high heat with water and celery until the mussels open. Remove mussels. Strain liquid through several thicknesses of cheesecloth. Extract mussels from shells.

Heat oil in saucepan and fry onion, garlic, and chili powder. Add mussel liquid and bring to a boil; add cornstarch mixed with 2 tablespoons water. Bring to a boil and simmer 8 to 10 minutes. Take pot from fire, add mussels, parsley, and lemon juice. Mix egg and milk and gradually add to soup. Stir thoroughly and heat but do not boil. Season to taste. Serve with fried croutons. Enough for 3–4 people or 2 hungry sailors.

~~~~~~

One thing a shipwreck impresses on you indelibly is the need for instant action. On July 26 we were asleep at Caleta Sonia during a light snowfall. Suddenly the motion of the vessel was different. I was wide awake. The wind had changed to the east and we were straining at our cable on a lee shore.

We never dressed quicker in our life. In two or three minutes Margaret and I were on deck looking over the situation and ready to move or to put out another anchor. We were bumping slightly on a shallow near a small islet a few hundred feet east of the Yamana lighthouse. We had one hundred thirty feet of chain out, but with the change in wind we had swung into only six feet of depth. I winched in thirty-five feet of chain a little at a time as we lifted on passing swells. We eased into deeper water and headed more into the wind and rode easier. We stood anchor watches until daybreak when we moved to an adjoining bay with better protection. Here I hoped to anchor in twelve or fifteen feet, but even though I watched the plow anchor drop on clean sand the anchor failed to bite in. It took four tries before I was satisfied. Again and again in the channels we found that shallow anchoring was a fraud. We finally got well set in a depth of forty feet with two hundred feet of chain out while we waited for the east wind to change.

When the wind relented we sailed eastward along Canal Beagle. Margaret had washed out some red thermal underwear and had hung it on the lifelines to dry. The underwear froze hard enough to stand up by itself, so we propped it up in a corner of the cockpit to keep the helmsman company. East of Caleta Sonia we passed five black and white killer whales heading westward. One had an extremely tall dorsal fin. On earlier trips we had seen these wide-ranging mammals in the Galápagos Islands and on the west coast of Vancouver Island. The small whales never paid any attention to us.

Two days later we glided into the Chilean navy base at Puerto Williams where we tied up near the *Castor*, the navy workboat that had helped to pull *Whisper* from the beach when she was wrecked. It was marvelous to see Lieutenant Horacio Balmelli and Bosun Oluf Torres and the rest of the crew again and to show them our newly repaired vessel which certainly looked happier than the patched hulk they had hauled off the beach in the Wollaston Islands.

One morning when I was carrying a box of groceries to the yacht a navy truck stopped. "Hop in," said the friendly

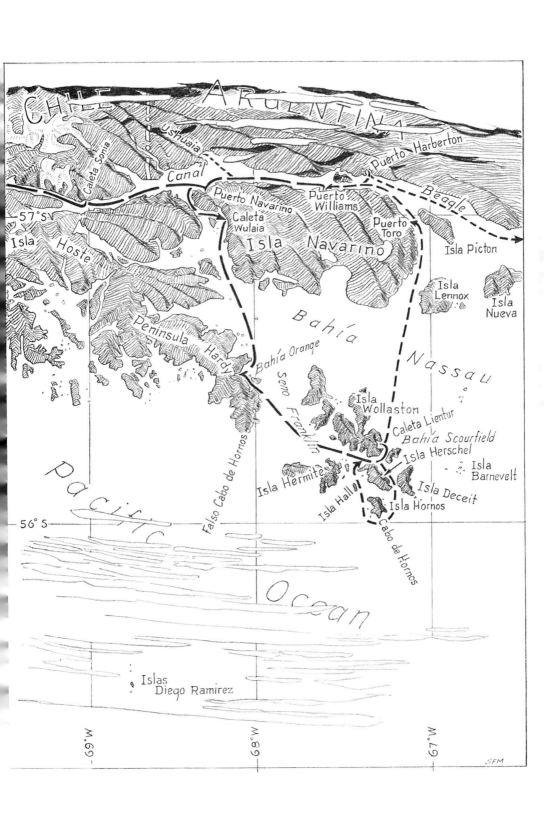

driver. "I'm going down to the dock." I got in and we roared off. The driver had a radio going full blast, he was eating a cheese sandwich, and he was talking nonstop. Unfortunately he was so occupied that he failed to watch a turn in the road and the truck bounced off the track, tore down a row of small trees, and lurched into a ditch. The driver was astonished but he continued to eat his cheese sandwich while the radio blared away. We crawled out of the truck whose starboard wheels were spinning in the air. People came running from all directions and soon had the truck back on the

We arrived at the Chilean naval base of Puerto Williams on Isla Navarino on a beautiful sunny afternoon after a good sail along Canal Beagle. That night, however, a blizzard blew up and in the morning Puerto Williams had a heavy frosting of snow.

road. I had banged one knee hard against the dashboard, but I recovered my box of groceries and limped off down the road, swearing to stay away from dangerous automobiles and trucks which obviously were much more lethal than the risks of Cape Horn.

In the evening Margaret and I walked up to the officers' club where we saw some of our friends. "I feel very humiliated because of my blunder that caused the wreck," I said to a group of Chilean officers.

"Relax," said one of the men. "It was bad luck. Down here we all need divine help to stay out of trouble. Why everyone in this room has been wrecked in the channels at one time or another."

Another man interrupted. "That's wrong," he said with a sympathetic smile. "I've been shipwrecked twice."

We had coffee, much pleasant talk about a dozen subjects, and were given valuable information about anchorages near Cape Horn. The evening was marvelous, but as we walked along the frosty track on the way back to the yacht, I couldn't help comparing my afternoon truck ride with the pleasurable evening, and to speculate on the Chilean character. I thought of the contrast between my frustrations during the repairs at the Asmar shipyard in Punta Arenas in the daytime working hours, and of the many delightful social occasions with the hospitable Chileans during the evenings. The Chileans were certainly not methodical planners nor a punctual, mechanically inclined race, but a people who somehow muddled along in the business world with a different sense of values. I had learned about their carefully prepared, beautifully served meals, their readiness to please, and their cordial manners. If I needed an engineer or a business analyst I would hire a German or a Swiss. But if I wanted a person with the ultimate in charm, a captivating manner, and the height of refinement, I would pick a Chilean. Who else would be an hour late for an important luncheon engagement because he stopped to select and arrange a bouquet of flowers for the hostess?

Just as I was writing this and was worried that I might insult my Chilean friends who had been so helpful and generous there was a great bang on deck. I looked out to see a big chunk of meat on the side deck.

"I just thought you would like half a lamb," said Lieutenant Balmelli. "We have plenty more if you need it."

From Puerto Williams we sailed south through Canal Murray. The mountain scenery rose up on all sides and looked doubly dramatic in the long winter dawn and dusk when the pale, low-angled rays from the sun cast pink and purple light on the snow and clouds and granite crests. A big condor flew overhead, its wingtip feathers flexing and opening with each slow beat. We anchored at Caleta Wulaia at the west end of the Isla Navarino. Ashore we saw a two-story yellow building with a red tin roof and windows trimmed in green with a black iron balcony on the north side. Presumably we were at a sheep ranch because of the outbuildings and fences and facilities for handling animals. But not a person nor a sign of anyone. What a difference from April 1830 when Mr. Murray from the *Beagle* discovered this channel and the broad east–west canal to the north that would be named after his ship.

Murray saw upward of a hundred canoes in one day, each containing from two to six people. The Fuegians had many guanaco skins, and some of the bones of the animals had been made into spearheads. The Indians appeared to be tractable and less disposed to quarreling than those further west, noted Murray. Wherever the whaleboat from the *Beagle* went she was followed by a train of the canoes, each full of people, and each with a fire smoking in the middle of the frail canoe.[39]

By 1859, it is sad to say, relations between the white men and Indians had deteriorated to such a point that the Yaghans murdered eight men of a missionary party whose vessel, the *Allen Gardiner,* had been anchored right where *Whisper* now swung so easily in the sunlight.

"Did you hear a knock?" I said to Margaret.

"A knock?" she replied.

(Overleaf) In rough water south of Isla Navarino.

263

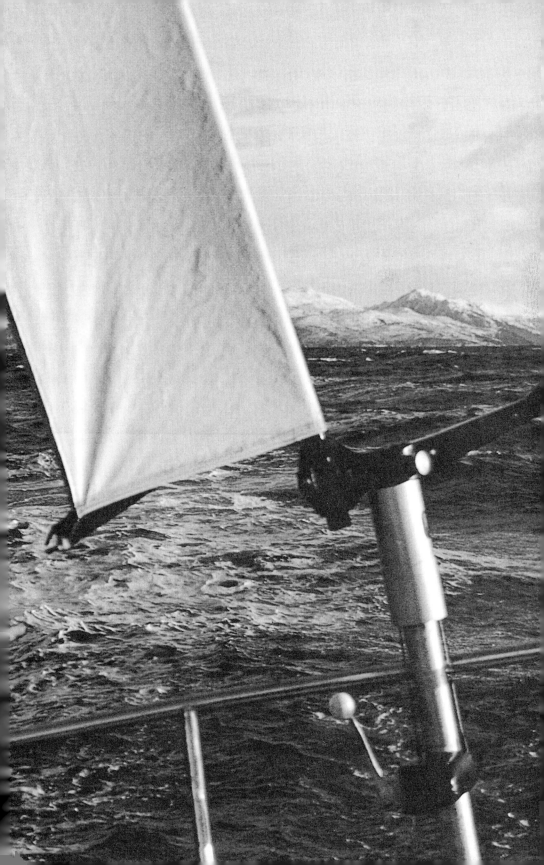

"Yes. A knock from the ghosts of those missionaries," I said.[40]

We were only sixty miles from Cape Horn. The next stop was Caleta Misión in Bahía Orange on Peninsula Hardy. The Chilean navy had asked us to check in at various lookout stations in the southern waters. There were always two men, a radioman and a gunner, who were sent out for several months to keep an eye on an area and to radio in weather information. We had shown our clearances to the lookouts in Canal Murray and now we headed for Caleta Misión. We arrived late in the day during a heavy snowstorm, anchored, and rowed ashore to meet Juan Cordova and Luis Sespedes, two astonished young naval ratings who had seen no one else for several months. They had little to do except to cook for each other and to exercise the dogs. The gunner oiled his weapons and the radioman tapped out daily reports by morse code on a 1940 U.S. radio set. The two sailors told us that at the beginning of July the wind had blown from the west at

These two smiling Chilean navy ratings maintained the lookout station at Bahía Orange.

140 kilometers per hour (70 knots or 85 mph) *for seven days without stopping.* Both men were so pleased to see us—or anyone—that they would hardly let us leave, but we wanted to get to a recommended anchorage west of Isla Yellow before dark. Before we left we walked up to see a bronze plaque that commemorated the 1882–83 French scientific expedition under the command of Louis Martial. The light was already fading in the thickly falling snow when we rowed away from the little dock at Caleta Misión while the men waved good-bye.

On August 6 I sluiced down the decks with buckets of seawater to wash away the snow while Margaret winched up the mainsail. Once underway we headed southeast toward the complex of Islas Wollaston, Hermite, Herschel, and Hornos that lay strong on the horizon. The sky was blue, a yellowish sun was rising off the port bow, and we had a fair northwest wind of fifteen knots. We eased the mainsail, poled out a jib, and hurried toward our goal, once again feeling the swell of the Southern Ocean. Behind us the snowy mountains above Bahía Schapenham on Peninsula Hardy glinted so brightly in the flat light that my eyes could hardly stand the glare.

Though many outlying parts of the world were discovered by the English, Spanish, and Portuguese, it was the resourceful and practical Dutch who first saw the islands before us. In 1616 the 360-ton Dutch ship *Unitie* under the command of Willem Schouten slipped between the easternmost point of Tierra del Fuego and a mountainous island to the east. The Dutch named the strait Le Maire for one of the expedition's leaders; the island was called Staten Island after the States General, the governing body of Holland. On January 29, 1616, while sailing southwest, the *Unitie* passed a high snow-covered islet which ended in a point that was named De Cap Hoorn, after Schouten's home city of Hoorn, Holland. De Cap Hoorn, corrupted to Cape Horn (or Cabo de Hornos in Spanish), soon became famous because it was the troublesome dividing point between voyages in the Atlantic

The snowy peaks above Bahía Schapenham shone golden in
the morning sun as we headed south and east with one reef tied in
the mainsail.

In Bahía Orange we washed the snow off Whisper's decks with
buckets of sea water.

and the Pacific. Cape Horn often meant dreadful weather, discomfort, cold, and sickness, and marked the low point of long and arduous voyages.[41]

Now more than three hundred fifty years later, we sped to the southeast with a freshening wind that backed to the north as we neared the islands. By noon we were in Seno Franklin and approaching Isla Herschel with the mountains of Isla Hermite to starboard. The wind increased to thirty-five knots in Canal Franklin, and with the mainsail down we reached along at a great clip while we checked off point after point on the chart. As we passed the east end of Hermite and several small islets we suddenly had a clear line of vision to the south.

We could see Isla Hall—a rocky summit that rose impressively from the ocean—and *Isla Hornos itself.* Heavens! Here was Cape Horn at last. The famous cape on the south face was in plain sight even from our viewpoint to the north-northwest. If it hadn't been so late in the day we could have sailed around the island.

A few minutes later our view of Cape Horn was cut off by Isla Herschel. Ahead we saw a Chilean motor torpedo boat to which we dipped our national flag and received a similar signal in return. An hour later we exchanged Aldis lamp signals with the Chilean lookout station at the northeast corner of Herschel. I had worked out a simplistic message in Spanish which I dot-dashed to the radio operator. The rapid-fire blinking light that came back quite overwhelmed my modest mastery of Morse, especially in Spanish abbreviations, so I signaled OK to whatever had been sent and we hurried to Caleta Lientur on the northwest side of Bahía Scourfield, another seven miles. Two dozen small seals followed us into the anchorage and played around *Whisper,* leaping out of the water again and again. As we sailed into the bay a squadron of steamer ducks flapped off toward the far shore, their wings and feet making a great commotion as they fled before us.

The weather was going to hell. The darkening sky looked

nasty. Low clouds with ragged bottoms rapidly blew toward us and the wind began to gust strongly. We were soon well set in Caleta Lientur, but the poor yacht heeled first to the right and then to the left as terrific squalls poured down from the mountains of Isla Wollaston. During the night I heard a sail flapping and I rushed on deck to discover that the force of the squalls had somehow blown all the sail ties to the end of the main boom and had allowed the mainsail to escape. Though we were close to a weather shore the violence of the williwaws was enough to fling spray over the entire yacht.

Our salvation during those months in the south was our Dickinson diesel stove which kept the interior of the yacht warm and dry and pleasant. This well-made metal stove measured eighteen by twenty by twenty-two inches and weighed 119 pounds. Its silent pot burner used about one gallon of kerosene or diesel oil every twenty-four hours fed from a gravity tank. Margaret was able to bake four loaves of bread at a time in the oven and usually kept two kettles of water on the back of the stove for hot drinks and for washing.

The westerly gale lasted two and a half days. My journal for August 7 read:

1900 Suddenly the wind is gone. Everything is calm and we hear only the tinkling of water along the hull. It is quiet for a minute, two minutes. Then a low moaning starts in the distance. The noise increases rapidly and climbs higher in pitch as the squall comes closer. I peer out with a flashlight. All is black and the only thing I can see are horizontal streaks of snow. The wind shrieks and a spiraling blast lashes the vessel which shakes like a bundle of rags in the jaws of a playful dog.

I time the wind. Now it is calm (19:11). I hear the wind coming (19:13). Now more quickly (19:13:15). The wind is on us and we heel to 20, 30, 40 degrees (19:14). A line beats against the mast. Water splashes from a kettle on the hot stove and I hear a hiss of steam. I grab the wind indicator, push back the hatch, and rush outside to measure the wind. The red disc flies to the top of the scale. 63 knots. The cold is terrible. I slam the hatch, shake the snow from my hair, and run to the stove. The wind flails at the yacht. All at once the hurricane blast is gone. Again we hear only the tinkling of water along the hull.

It was the sound of the wind that got to me after a while. The continual moaning. The crescendos. The hollow roar. The scream when it was on us. But these words are meaningless because they merely describe the edge of the wind. No one can talk about the squalls of Cape Horn. You must experience their color and shape and size and intensity yourself.

On the morning of August 9 the storm was over. At 0730 we looked out into the clear winter sky and saw Venus, Orion, and the Southern Cross shining brightly in the dawn. We got underway at once. Two hours later we were between Isla Herschel and Isla Deceit, sailing southbound with a single-reefed mainsail and a working jib that pulled us along nicely in a twenty-knot easterly breeze. We passed around an islet off the eastern tip of Herschel. Isla Hornos lay about four miles in front of us to the southwest.

The bleak island was five miles long and two miles wide, with its major dimension on a northwest–southeast line. The land was well elevated above the water and looked somewhat flat and saddle-shaped with a low hill at the northwest end. As we sailed along the east side of the island we saw clumps of beech trees and patches of shrubs. My friend Eugene Anthony, who visited the island in 1974 with the Chilean navy, told me that there were many traces of Indian camping places, no doubt the same type that Margaret and I had found when we camped in the Wollaston Islands twenty-four miles to the north.

I had read about two marginal anchorages on the east side; we had planned to stop and to go ashore for a firsthand look at this fantastic place. Through the binoculars, however, I saw breaking swells all along the eastern side. With the

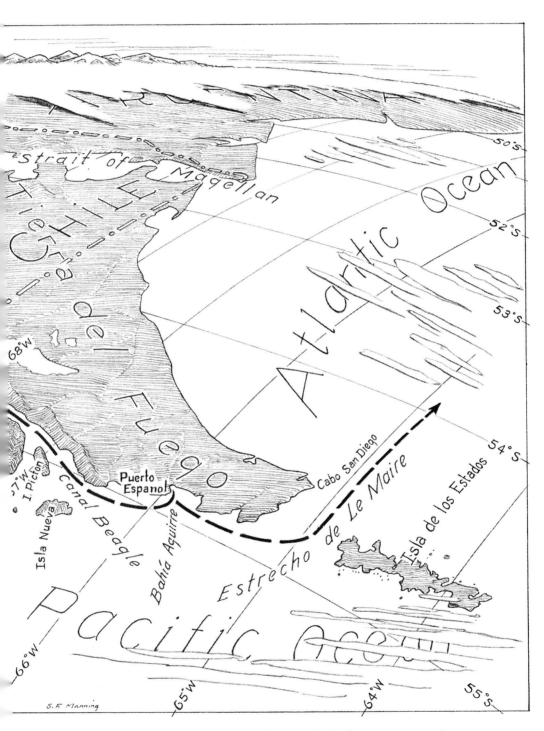

(Overleaf) View south across Isla Herschel. The snowy summit
of Cape Horn rises just above Herschel.

wind from the eastern quadrant the anchorages were impossible.

As we sailed briskly along, all eyes turned to starboard as the south face of the island opened up. We watched Isla Hornos climb to its highest point—1,331 feet—and we looked at the triangular, pointed cliff that tumbled into the Southern Ocean amidst a jagged horror of black rocks and snow and upset water.

I gasped as I looked. Could this be it at last? Cape Horn? I let out a Texas yell. "Yippee! We made her!" I shook my hands over my head, smiled at Margaret, and did a little dance down the port side deck.

"Quick! Write it in the log before you fall over the side," shouted Margaret.

No lightning and thunder clapped down from Zeus. No meteors fell out of the sky. Yet it was a milestone for us to sail our toy boat to Cape Horn via the intricate Chilean waterways with their savage winds. By the time we got to the east coast of the United States we would have sailed twenty thousand miles from California. On the voyage we had had plenty of sail drill, anchoring, the wreck, the salvage, the repair, and the Cape Horn winter run. An intriguing experience. I grew serious and thought of all our friends in the U.S., Peru, and Chile who had helped us. And the wonderful assistance from the navy of Chile when we had been blown ashore. I turned and looked at Margaret— the world's keenest traveler—with affection.

We swung around Isla Hornos toward Isla Hall and as we did a frigid north wind headed us. I thought of the Chilean joke about sailing: "Yes, the wind always blows from the bow." We made our way back to Caleta Lientur, and by stages to Navarino Island where we cleared for Argentina. We sailed to Ushuaia and tied up next to Vasko Arregui's fishboat *Cruz del Sur* and were introduced to the *centolla* or spider king crab, the world's most delicious food. We stopped at Harberton and Puerto Español on the Argentine coast of Tierra del Fuego.

When the barometer was high and steady we sailed for the Strait of Le Maire, the great meeting point of the Atlantic and Pacific, where tidal overfalls have capsized large ships. We arranged to be at the strait exactly at slack water as recommended. Yet the seas were awful, simply horrendous, and we had the added zest of a southwest gale that erupted from nowhere and soon enclosed us in a swirling blizzard. Sailing blind and committed to the strait because

Margaret and her friend, Vasko Arregui, with a spider king crab.

(Overleaf) Cape Horn from the southwest.

of the gale, we rushed through Le Maire at four knots under bare pole with no sails up at all. The seas were enough to make the strong weep, and we had to steer like dinghy sailors to keep from broaching. We knew the wind was strong because the tops of the seas were blown off in streaks of white spume.

But the strait was short and soon we were in the South Atlantic with a weather shore and unlimited sea room. No more would we be obliged to anchor under those mountains and to feel the blasts of the hurricane squalls. No longer would we have ninety-minute anchor drills every morning and evening. I was sick to death of our snail-like progress during the seven or eight hours of winter daylight. I was weary of the intricate pilotage. Now it was all behind us. As we edged our way to the northeast from Isla de los Estados it was grand to feel the regular swells of the South Atlantic.

Once away from land we began to see the familiar brown and white checkered mantles of pintado petrels and the never-ending circling and swooping of black-browed and wandering albatrosses.

We looked at a wandering albatross with disbelief. This great white clown of fluff and feathers that peered down on us across his yellowish bill had a wingspan of fourteen feet. Fourteen feet? Any bird that size was an invention of the mind. A humorous fantasy. But the whole Cape Horn region was a land of wonders and exaggeration, a myth of hyperbole and high coloring. I was Baron Munchausen. I was Aesop. I was Alice in Wonderland. I had dreamed the whole trip.

Whether indeed it was a vapor of the mind or something more factual, the flinty reality of Cape Horn and the channels of Chile was behind us. We had accomplished our goals: a transit of the waterways, a sail in the Strait of Magellan, and a close look at the Tierra del Fuego and Cape Horn. In ninety-seven anchorages and 2,438 miles of sailing between Canal Chacao and Isla de los Estados we had seen another marvelous slice of the wild places on our wonderful planet.

(Overleaf) Headed northward in the Strait of Le Maire between Tierra del Fuego and Isla de los Estados. A southwest storm is behind us and the wind is strong enough so that we are going along at four knots under bare pole without any sail up at all. This strait is the meeting ground for vast quantities of water from the Pacific and Atlantic and is a most hazardous place. We arrived exactly at slack water but found simply horrendous seas. Fortunately it took only a few hours to sail through Le Maire Strait and out into the comparative safety of the South Atlantic.

Notes

1. William Albert Robinson, *To the Great Southern Sea* (London: Peter Davies, 1957).
2. Antonio Pigafetta, *The Voyage of Magellan,* trans. Paula Spurlin Paige (Englewood Cliffs, N.J.: Prentice-Hall, 1969), pp. 19–23.
3. Yves Le Scal, *The Great Days of the Cape Horners* (New York: The New American Library, 1967). This excellent and intriguing book was first published in France under the title *La grand épopée des Cap-Horniers* and is based on the papers of Captain Henri Briend who both commanded Cape Horn ships and gathered reminiscences from twenty-nine Cape Horn masters. The book is particularly valuable because of the overview of world shipping and the role of sail and steam from 1849 to 1914. Also see Raymond A. Rydell, *Cape Horn to the Pacific* (Berkeley: University of California Press, 1952), a general summary with remarkable references.
4. This brief sketch of Al Hansen is based on an interview and photographs in *La Prensa* (Buenos Aires) dated February 18, 1934. Also from recollections of Bobby Uriburu given to the author on January 12, 1969, and a letter dated April 29, 1975. In addition, I have a letter from Germán Frers Sr. dated April 19, 1977, a photograph given to me by Manolo Campos, and a letter from Mr. S. Lyngaas of the Norwegian Government Directorate for Seamen in Oslo dated February 9, 1977. A good summary is by D. H. Clarke, *An Evolution of Single-handers* (London: Stanford Maritime, 1975), p. 121. The three famous Argentine sailors—Bobby Uriburu, Germán Frers Sr., and Vito Dumas—all got acquainted with Hansen

when he stopped in Buenos Aires. It was from this meeting that Dumas conceived the idea for his great voyage of 1942–43. There is a marvelous 1934 photograph of Hansen and Dumas together in Dumas's book *Los Cuarenta Bramadores* (Buenos Aires: Editorial Atlantida S.A., 1944), p. 12. According to a 1934 story in the *South Pacific Mail,* the American wife of Mr. Hansen, Mrs. Mary Jane Hansen, was living close to Boston, Massachusetts.

5. Miles Smeeton, *Because the Horn Is There* (Sidney, British Columbia, Canada: Gray's Publishing, 1971), pp. 86–87.

6. John Brooks, ed., *The 1975 South American Handbook* (Bath England: Trade & Travel), p. 345; *Columbia Encyclopedia,* 3rd ed., pp. 333 & 401.

7. Francisco A. Encina, *Historia de Chile* (Santiago: Editorial Nascimento, 1952), 5:61.

8. Charles Darwin, *The Voyage of the Beagle,* edited by Leonard Engel (New York: Doubleday, 1962), p. 52.

9. Bernardo Quintana Mansilla, *Chiloé Mitológico,* Propiedad Intelectual (Chile), no. 39985, June 21, 1972.

10. H. W. Tilman, *Mischief in Patagonia* (Cambridge: University Press, 1957), p. 102; also see Rae Natalie Prosser de Goodall, *Tierra del Fuego* (Buenos Aires: Foundation of the Banco Francés del Rio de la Plata, 1970), p. 22.

11. Leo Heaps, *Log of the Centurian* (New York: Macmillan, 1973), pp. 25, 116. This book is based on the recent discovery of the Saumarez logbooks and gives new information on Anson's voyage. On page 117 is a crude map drawn by someone on board the *Anna* which sketches Bahía Anna Pink together with four tiny drawings of the vessel which shows the *Anna* rigged as a bark. It is obvious that the first island the *Anna* tried to anchor behind was Isla Inchemo, not in the Inchin group as has been written elsewhere. The best-known account of Anson's voyage was written by his chaplain, Richard Walter, *A Voyage Around the World* (London: J. M. Dent, 1911), pp. 130–138. A few details differ from the Heaps book.

12. Charles Darwin, *Voyage,* pp. 284–285 (quoted by the editor, Leonard Engel, from Fitz Roy).

13. Philip Davenport, *The Voyage of 'Waltzing Matilda'* (London: Hutchinson, 1953), p. 85.

14. Walter, *A Voyage,* This 1911 edition has a marvelous twelve-page introduction by John Masefield who ably sketches the ships and men of Anson's era. Also see John Bulkeley and

John Cummins, *A Voyage to the South Seas* (New York: McBride, 1927); Richard Hough, *The Blind Horn's Hate* (New York: Norton, 1971); S. W. C. Pack, *The Wager Mutiny* (London: Alvin Redman, 1964), the best and most balanced account of a complex story. The crew list and totals of survivors at different times varies from account to account and perhaps never will be known accurately.

15. Samuel Eliot Morison, *The European Discovery of America, The Southern Voyages* A.D. *1492–1616* (New York: Oxford, 1974), the outstanding one-volume digest of all the early voyages. Also see Admiral Don A. De Cordova, *A Voyage of Discovery to the Strait of Magellan . . .* (London: Richard Phillips, 1789?).

16. Joshua Slocum, *Sailing Alone Around the World* (Westvaco Corporation, 1969), p. 125. Slocum's writing about the Strait of Magellan and Cockburn Channel is so accurate that his book can be used as a *Pilot*. Every bit of his voyage can be retraced. Louis Bernicot, *The Voyage of Anahita* (London: Rupert Hart-Davis, 1953), p. 76. A simple sparse book, but one of my favorites. I have always been amazed at how Captain Bernicot contrived to cut and sew new sails inside his small cabin while underway on the ocean.

17. *South America Pilot* (London: Hydrographic Department, Admiralty, 1956), 2:25.

18. Louis de Bougainville, *A Voyage Round the World*, Bibliotheca Australiana #12 (New York: Da Capo Press, 1967), p. 188, a recent reprint of the 1772 English edition.

19. Morison, *European Discovery*, p. 647; Felix Riesenberg *Cape Horn* (New York: Dodd, Mead, 1939), p. 59. Captain Riesenberg is chatty and informative but not as thorough or accurate as Morison. Riesenberg's conjecture about Drake's vanished island is fascinating. Well worth reading for general information.

20. Morison, *European Discovery*, pp. 690–717; Hough, *Blind Horn's Hate*, p. 108; Riesenberg, *Cape Horn*, pp. 96–104; W. S. Barclay, *The Land of Magellan* (London: Methuen, 1926), p. 63.

21. Morison, *European Discovery*, p. 401.

22. Willy de Roos, a Dutchman living in Belgium, sailed *Williwaw*, a 42-foot steel ketch. Sometimes de Roos sailed alone but usually with crew. Tom Zydler, a Pole who now lives in the United States, was the captain of the *Konstanty Maciejewicz*, a 45-foot wooden yawl which had five aboard, includ-

ing a woman psychiatrist. Both passed through the Strait of Magellan in 1973.

23. Slocum, *Sailing Alone,* p. 106.
24. *South America Pilot,* 2:164.
25. R. W. Coppinger, *Cruise of the Alert* (London: Swan Sonnenschein, 1899), p. 37.
26. Yves Le Scal, *Great Days,* pp. 31–32.
27. Charles Wilkes, *Narrative of the United States Exploring Expedition . . .* (Philadelphia: Lea and Blanchard, 1845), p. 145; W. Parker Snow, *A Two Years' Cruise off Tierra del Fuego . . .* (2 vols.; London: Longman, Brown, Green, Longmans, & Roberts, 1857), 2:57–64.
28. L.-F. Martial, *Mission Scientifique du Cap Horn,* (Paris: Gauthier-Villars, 1888), 1:234; Rockwell Kent, *Voyaging Southward from the Strait of Magellan* (New York: G. P. Putnam, 1924), p. 163.
29. Bougainville, *Round the World,* p. 159.
30. Lloyd Hirst, *Coronel and After* (London: Peter Davies, 1934); Riesenberg, *Cape Horn,* pp. 376–382; *Columbia Encyclopedia,* 3rd ed., p. 2016; Oliver Warner, *Great Sea Battles* (New York: Macmillan, 1963), p. 253.
31. *Narrative of the Surveying Voyages of His Majesty's Ships Adventure and Beagle . . .* (4 vols.; London: Henry Colburn, 1839), 1:388–392. These three volumes (plus one of notes and tables) are the best source of channel life in the nineteenth century. Excellent, absorbing stuff. Regrettably, the volumes are rare items.
32. Phillip Parker King, *Sailing Directions for the Coasts of Eastern and Western Patagonia* (London: Hydrographic Office, Admiralty, 1832), p. 140; Martial, *Mission,* p. 244. This French officer, who spent two years at Bahía Orange, also urges westbound travel in the winter because the winds are more favorable, the weather is less bad, and there are fewer chances of damage to the ships. Patrick Van God, *Trismus* (Paris: B. Arthaud, 1974), p. 105. The text of this present-day yachtsman, recently reported lost, includes the comments of Captain Pedro Margalot concerning weather in the south.
33. James Weddell, *A Voyage Towards the South Pole* (London: Longman, Hurst, Rees, Orme, Brown, and Green, 1825), p. 154; for a hair-raising account of a sailor's experiences with southern Indians, see Benjamin Franklin Bourne, *The Captive in Patagonia* (Boston: Gould and Lincoln, 1853).
34. W. H. B. Webster, *Narrative of a Voyage to the Southern*

Atlantic Ocean (London: Richard Bentley, 1834), 1:182.

35. Wilkes, *Narrative*, p. 142.

36. Darwin, *Voyage*, p. 213.

37. Kent, *Voyaging Southward*, p. 158; Eric Shipton, *Tierra del Fuego: The Fatal Lodestone* (London: Charles Knight, 1973), p. 105; Barclay, *Land of Magellan*, p. 130.

38. E. Lucas Bridges, *Uttermost Part of the Earth* (London: Hodder and Stoughton, 1948), p. 267; Armando Braun Menendez, *Chroniques Australes* (Paris: Gallimard, 1961), pp. 163–260; John W. Marsh and W. H. Stirling, *The Story of Commander Allen Gardiner* (London: James Nisbet, 1874). In my opinion the full story of the Indians of Tierra del Fuego still remains to be written. The accounts I have seen are entirely too kind to the missionaries. W. Parker Snow, the first captain of the *Allen Gardiner*, has been quite ignored, as has the aspect of land taken from the natives and used for sheep ranching. Reduced to one sentence, the poor Indians were simply in the way of the white man's expanding frontier and could not cope either physically or mentally.

39. *Narrative of the Surveying Voyages of His Majesty's Ships Adventure and Beagle*, 1:429.

40. Bridges, *Uttermost Part*, pp. 43–45.

41. Morison, *European Discovery*, chap. 31; Hendrik Willem van Loon, *The Golden Book of the Dutch Navigators* (New York: Century Co., 1916), pp. 279–300.

HAL ROTH

~

The Longest Race

Drawings and maps by Heather O'Connor.

Grateful acknowledgment is made to the following: John Farquharson Ltd. for permission to reprint excerpts from *A World of My Own* by Robin Knox-Johnston (published by William Morrow & Co., 1970); Nautical Publishing Company for permission to reprint excerpts from *Capsize* by Commander W. D. King (1969) and from *Trimaran Solo* by Nigel Tetley (1970).

Excerpts from *The Strange Last Voyage of Donald Crowhurst* by Nicholas Tomalin and Ron Hall are reprinted with permission of Stein and Day Publishers. Copyright © 1970 by Times Newspapers Ltd.; and excerpts from *Journey to Ardmore* by John Ridgway are reprinted by permission of A. D. Peters & Co. Ltd. (published by Hodder & Stoughton Ltd., 1971); and excerpts from *The Long Way* by Bernard Moitessier are reprinted by permission of Granada Publishing Ltd.

Suhaili

To Nigel Tetley,
one of the nine sailors
in this astonishing race.
He had a stout heart,
an indomitable spirit,
and incredibly bad luck.

Contents

Illustrations

England
Ireland
Plymouth

ATLANTIC OCEAN

Azores

Madeira
Canaries

Lisbon

0°

Sargasso Sea

Cape Verde

St. Peter and
St. Paul Rocks

Recife

. Ascension

. St. Helena

Rio de Janeiro

.: Trindade

Buenos Aires

Tristan da Cunha .

Cape Town
Cape of Good Hope

Agulha Cu

Rio Salado

Falklands

SOUTHERN OCEAN

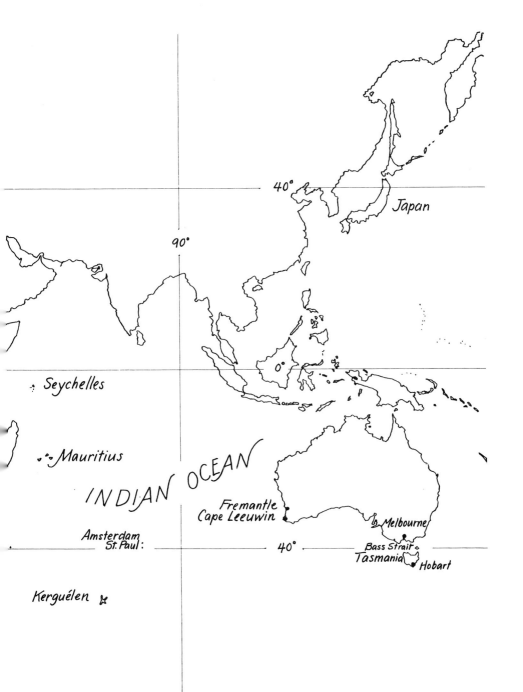

40°

90°

Japan

0°

Seychelles

Mauritius

INDIAN OCEAN

Fremantle
Cape Leeuwin

Melbourne

Amsterdam
St. Paul:

40°

Bass Strait
Tasmania

Hobart

Kerguélen

ix

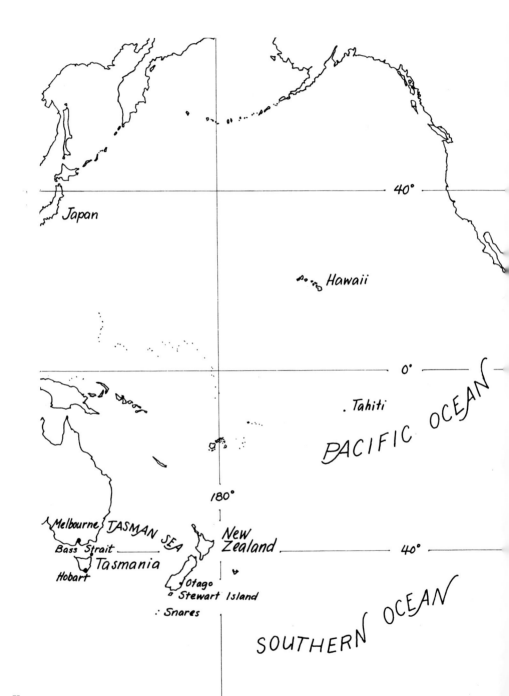

Japan

40°

Hawaii

0°

. Tahiti

PACIFIC OCEAN

180°

Melbourne TASMAN SEA New Zealand 40°
Bass Strait
Tasmania
Hobart
Otago
Stewart Island
Snares

SOUTHERN OCEAN

x

England
Ireland
Plymouth
Lisbon
Azores
ATLANTIC OCEAN
Madeira
Canaries
Sargasso Sea
Cape Verde
Galápagos
St. Peter and St. Paul Rocks
Recife
Ascension
St. Helena
Rio de Janeiro
Trindade
90°
0°
Buenos Aires
Tristan da Cunha
Cape Town
Rio Salado
Falklands
Cape Horn

xi

The Nine Contestants

IN ORDER OF STARTING

John Ridgway • 29, married, one child, English, former paratroop officer and transatlantic rower, in *English Rose IV*, a 30-foot Westerly fiberglass sloop. Started June 1, 1968. Withdrew July 21 (51 days).

Chay Blyth • 28, married, one child, English, former soldier and transatlantic rower, in *Dytiscus III*, a 30-foot Kingfisher fiberglass sloop. Started June 8, 1968. Officially disqualified September 14 (98 days). Really disqualified himself August 15 (68 days).

Robin Knox-Johnston • 29, divorced, one child, English, merchant marine captain, in *Suhaili*, a 32-foot double-ended wooden ketch. Started June 14, 1968. Finished April 22 (313 days).

Bernard Moitessier • 43, married, French, veteran small-boat sailor, in *Joshua*, a 39½-foot steel ketch. Started August 21, 1968. Withdrew for personal reasons March 18 (209 days).

Loïck Fougeron • 42, married, French, in *Captain Browne*, a 30-foot steel cutter. Started August 21, 1968. Withdrew November 27 because of storm damage (98 days).

Bill King • 58, married, two children, English, retired submarine commander, in *Galway Blazer II*, a 42-foot cold-molded wooden schooner. Started August 24, 1968. Withdrew November 19 because of storm damage (87 days).

Nigel Tetley • 44, married, two children, English, navy lieutenant-commander, in *Victress*, a 40-foot Victress trimaran. Started September 16, 1968. Sank May 21 (246 days).

Donald Crowhurst • 36, married, four children, English, electronics engineer, in *Teignmouth Electron*, a 40-foot Victress trimaran. Started October 31, 1968. Empty yacht found at sea July 10 (253 days).

Alex Carozzo • 36, bachelor, Italian, merchant marine officer, in *Gancia Americano*, a 68-foot hard-chine plywood ketch. Started October 31, 1968. Withdrew November 25 because of severe medical problems (26 days).

Beaufort Wind Scale

Beaufort Number	Wind Description	Mean Wind Speed Equivalent (knots)	Deep-Sea Description	Mean Wave Height (meters)
0	Calm	<1	Sea like a mirror.	—
1	Light air	1–3	Ripples with the appearance of scales are formed, but without foam crests.	0–0.1
2	Light breeze	4–6	Small wavelets, still short, but more pronounced; crests have a glassy appearance and do not break.	0–0.2
3	Gentle breeze	7–10	Large wavelets; crests begin to break; foam of glassy appearance; perhaps scattered white horses.	0–0.6
4	Moderate breeze	11–16	Small waves becoming longer; fairly frequent white horses.	1
5	Fresh breeze	17–21	Moderate waves, taking a more pronounced long form; many white horses are formed. Chance of some spray.	2
6	Strong breeze	22–27	Large waves begin to form; the white foam crests are more extensive everywhere. Some spray.	3
7	Near gale	28–33	Sea heaps up, and white foam from breaking waves begins to be blown in streaks along the direction of the wind.	4

Beaufort Number	Wind Description	Mean Wind Speed Equivalent (knots)	Deep-Sea Description	Mean Wave Height (meters)
8	Gale	34–40	Moderately high waves of greater length; edges of crests begin to break into spindrift; foam is blown in well-marked streaks along the direction of the wind.	5.5
9	Strong gale	41–47	High waves; dense streaks of foam along the direction of the wind; crests of waves begin to topple, tumble, and roll over; spray may affect visibility.	7
10	Storm	48–55	Very high waves with long overhanging crests; the resulting foam, in great patches, is blown in dense, white streaks along the direction of the wind; on the whole, the surface of the sea takes a white appearance; the tumbling of the sea becomes heavy and shocklike; visibility affected.	9
11	Violent storm	56–63	Exceptionally high waves. Small and medium-sized ships might be lost to view for a time behind the waves; the sea is completely covered with long, white patches of foam lying along the direction of the wind; everywhere the edges of the wave crests are blown into froth; visibility affected.	11.5
12	Hurricane	64+	The air is filled with foam and spray; sea completely white with driving spray; visibility very seriously affected.	14

This is a true story.
It is not fiction.

1~

Without Stopping

In 1966–67, an English sailor named Francis Chichester sailed around the world in a 53-foot ketch named *Gipsy Moth IV*. The voyage took nine months and included a seven-week stopover in Australia. Chichester had wanted to retrace the routes of the clipper ships and hopefully to beat their sailing times. The sixty-five-year-old sailor failed to achieve the goal he had set for himself by a small margin, but he completed a first-rate voyage.

Chichester was a master at publicity and personal ballyhoo and financed his various sailing efforts with partial sponsorship from newspapers, magazines, commercial firms, and trade associations. He wrote books, endorsed equipment, cooperated with film ventures, and even made radio broadcasts while under way. Unlike many solo sailors, who tend to be quiet and withdrawn individuals, Chichester appeared to enjoy the X-ray of publicity and acclaim, and his battling-the-sea routine sold lots of books.

His writing is filled with overblown passages about fighting the elements, troubles with bad designs, and inferior equipment. He tells about arguments with naval architects, slipshod boatbuilding, fickle weather, and uncooperative waves and winds. If you read parallel accounts written by other sailors in the same races, you wonder if Chichester and the other contestants were in the same race or even on the same ocean. Nevertheless, this crotchety old mariner was the stuff that heroes are made of, and sure enough, it wasn't long before Queen Elizabeth knighted him in an impressive ceremony.

Chichester's vessel *Gipsy Moth IV* was put on permanent display on a concrete pedestal in Greenwich and became a kind of national shrine for English schoolchildren.

All this success and publicity rankled other sailors who wondered if

Chichester's voyage could be bettered, perhaps with less notoriety. After all, reasoned some, people go to sea to get away from the noise of publicity. Yacht club purists said that Chichester was crass and money-crude.

"Baloney," retorted Chichester. "I needed the lolly. How else do you think I paid the bills?"

During Chichester's great trip, Bill King, a former commander of English submarines and also an expert small-boat sailor, had been thinking about an even more venturesome voyage. "Chichester had returned safely to England that summer, and I wondered what adventure remained untried," he wrote. "It struck me that I could set out to sail alone around the world *without* stopping to refit in Australia. . . . It would be one step further in human effort and endurance. An absolutely new experience."

King ordered a new vessel to be built in a hurry, supposedly in secret. He planned to pay for the whole thing himself. It wasn't long, however, until he heard rumors that the great French sailor Bernard Moitessier, who owned the yacht *Joshua*, was also thinking about a world-circling trip without stopping. An English merchant marine officer named Robin Knox-Johnston was trying to raise funds to build a 53-foot steel two-master. Captain John Ridgway was said to be intrigued with the idea.

Finally, in March 1968, *The Sunday Times* of London pulled all these separate efforts together by announcing a nonstop, round-the-world race for single-handed yachts. The prizes were to be a Golden Globe for the first man to finish and £5,000 for the fastest time. The rules did not allow outside physical assistance, and no food, water, fuel, or equipment could be taken on board after starting.

The challenge was to sail the 30,000-mile course without stopping. If the goal were met and the record established, then the contest could never be repeated in the same form. It was the old story: the leader, the groundbreaker, the first to climb the mountain, the first to push aside the impossible. This sailing race would truly be the contest of contests.

As the sponsor of the race, *The Sunday Times* tried to be realistic. The paper repeatedly warned potential entrants about the risks and dangers:

> It must be emphasized that *The Sunday Times* has no desire to encourage suicide attempts. To have a hope of success, yachtsmen must have seamanship of the highest order and a yacht and equipment of high quality, The judges will be ready to comment on the advisability of making an attempt.

The psychological problems raised by seven or eight months alone at sea are largely unknown. Sir Francis Chichester was troubled by hallucinations after only four months. The necessary combination of sea experience and physical stamina would appear to favour men in their forties . . . but younger or older contestants might well have other factors in their favour.

"There was no need to be officially entered, and the rules were simple," noted the Frenchman Moitessier. "All you had to do was to leave from any English port between June 1 and October 31, 1968, then return to it after rounding the three capes of Good Hope, Leeuwin, and the Horn.

"The idea came to *The Sunday Times* after they heard that Bill King and *Joshua* were preparing for the long way," said Moitessier. "My old pal Loïck Fougeron was also readying for the trip. . . . After *The Sunday Times* announcement we decided to sail our boats to Plymouth, hoping to be able to carry off one or even both of the prizes, the good Lord willing."

Already there were five entrants: Bill King, who lived on a farm in Ireland; Robin Knox-Johnston from England; John Ridgway from Scotland; and Bernard Moitessier and Loïck Fougeron from France. Soon there would be four more: Donald Crowhurst and Nigel Tetley from England, Chay Blyth from Scotland, and Alex Carozzo from Venice.

The nine challengers were about to attempt something never before tried by man. Not only did each man hope to sail a small yacht completely around the world without putting into port, but the entrants planned to *race* one another during their nonstop solo efforts. In the Southern Ocean the men would have to battle icebergs, freezing cold, and awesome storms. In the tropics the nine contestants would fight calms and the scorching sun.

There would be no stops in port, no splendid dinners with starched tablecloths and glistening silver, no luxurious rests in comfortable hotels while boasting to newspaper reporters. This race was tough, the ultimate, the Everest of sailing. The contest meant 30,000 miles of risky navigation across the most fearsome oceans known to man. The trip would take nine months of continuous sailing, a gritty test of endurance and determination.

There would be moments of splendid tranquillity, times of anguish and despair, and hours when a man might cry out for companionship and help. Of course if the going grew too difficult, he could always put into port somewhere. But then he would lose his entry in the great race and have to admit defeat. The humiliation of failure was not pleasant once you made the commitment to go—especially if all or part of your entry was paid for with other people's money.

Each of the nine would be responsible for keeping a good course, watching out for big ships, intricate celestial navigation, storm management—everything. If one of the solo sailors became sick he would have to dose himself or die. If he sailed into trouble he would have to work his way out of his predicament or perish. If he fell overboard, his life was gone for there would be no shipmate to return to pick him up. If he broke a leg or got his head bashed in from a swinging boom there would be no one to bind up his wounds or take him to a hospital. If he ran short of equipment or a piece of gear failed or wore out he would have to improvise something. If he got bored he would have to devise amusements.

Each captain would have to cook himself wholesome and nourishing meals or else risk weakness, scurvy, and death. Each man would have to pace himself so he wouldn't burn up his energy faster than it could be replaced by food and sleep. He would have to deal with problems as they came up and laugh at himself once in a while and try to keep a sense of balance and good cheer. Otherwise he might go mad.

He would be without the companionship and tenderness of women; there would be no loving embrace; no gentle hand to wipe his brow or to pass him a warm drink on a stormy night; no sympathetic listener to defer to his leadership; no one to admire and encourage him.

To enter the race at all was a daunting prospect, and the more a person thought about this fool competition, the worse it became.

To finance the race raised another whole set of problems. A good example was Bill King's new yacht *Galway Blazer II*. King hired an English naval architect named Angus Primrose to design a sleek, super-light vessel 42 feet long that displaced only $4\frac{1}{2}$ tons. She had no engine and was driven by a Chinese lugsail rig set on two masts arranged without stays or shrouds. *Galway Blazer II* was beautifully built of laminated wood by Souter's, a famous shipyard in Cowes in the south of England. Wilfred Souter and his men constructed the hull and deck of four layers of mahogany. The first layer of thin strips was placed over a carefully built form of the hull. Each succeeding layer of wood was crisscrossed and glued to the preceding layer. This resulted in a laminated hull of great strength and lightness.

Initially the vessel was to have cost £7,000. But during the six months of her construction the costs jumped to £10,000. Fortunately the increase was met by the *Daily Express* newspaper, which offered King £3,000 if he would "speak to no other paper" during the race. After the launching and during trials and outfitting, the costs escalated further. King had to find another £7,000, which obliged him to throw in "the final savings for my old age," to collect £200 for television and film rights, and to get an advance for a book "which might never get written." In addition, King leased the grazing rights on his farm, sold all his cattle and sheep, and put his car on the market. All this effort was just to get to the starting line. Was any competition worth so many pledges and sacrifices? What had he gotten himself into?

The whole thing was madness.

2~

The Early Starters

THE FIRST MAN TO SAIL IN THE GREAT RACE WAS JOHN Ridgway, who had already had the incredible adventure of rowing across the Atlantic Ocean with Chay Blyth during the summer of 1966. Army Captain Ridgway and Sergeant Blyth had spent ninety-two days in an open boat while they rowed from Cape Cod to Ireland. Now on June 1st, 1968, the day the round-the-world competition began, Ridgway sailed from the Aran Islands on the west coast of Ireland in a 30-foot-sloop named *English Rose IV*.

The twin-bilge-keel Westerly 30 fiberglass yacht had been specially prepared by the builders. Ridgway wanted simplicity, so the engine and all through-hull openings had been eliminated. The ship carpenters had installed heavy teak dropboards in place of the usual weak door to the cabin. Instead of vulnerable windows, the men at the yard bolted small circular metal portlights in place. Ridgway elected a hand-cranked Clifford and Snell Lifeline radio, and at a stroke got rid of charging engines, fuel stowage, storage batteries, and an expensive long-distance radio. The Horlicks Company packed 1,100 pounds of special rations—enough for 400 days—in 400 separate packages. A pilot friend brought eighty charts and eight books of pilotage instructions. Ridgway's helpers loaded sixteen sails on board.

The £4,250 cost of Ridgway's basic vessel was met by trading endorsements and advertising rights (in case the voyage was successful) for pledges of fiberglass material, resin, spars, winches, rigging wire, paint, and so forth that had gone into his vessel. Ridgway raised a further £4,000 for fittings and additional equipment by signing newspaper and book contracts and soliciting other sponsors.

"I was not willing to embark on a voyage untried by anyone before, with the added mental strain of financial worry," said the twenty-nine-year-old Ridgway. "If the worst came to the worst, then there must be no question of . . . [my wife] having to face creditors."

Ridgway considered himself to be a hard-boiled adventurer. To him the race was an experiment in physical survival and human toughness. The voyage was simply a military project. One made a program, delegated authority for the preparations, and carried out the plan like an exercise in an army field manual. The actual sailing, according to this stern disciplinarian, was a secondary problem.

JOHN RIDGWAY

In spite of a flintlike approach that von Clausewitz would have appreciated, Ridgway was apprehensive about crossing the Indian Ocean during the winter months. Although he really didn't know much about this region, he regarded the Indian Ocean as a greater hazard than Cape Horn itself.

Surprisingly, this tough soldier believed in occasional prayer.

Captain Ridgway decided to leave from the Aran Islands on the west coast of Ireland because his Atlantic rowing trip had ended there and he had many friends on the three small islands. Ridgway wanted a quiet start, but he failed to reckon with the officiousness and zeal of British journalists.

On the morning of June 1st, there were two rival television launches filled with competing reporters, photographers, and sound engineers. Each group wanted to outdo the other, and they recklessly jostled for position.

As *English Rose IV* got under way, one launch nudged the yacht on her stern pulpit and narrowly missed the self-steering gear.

"I was furious," said Ridgway. "All my pent-up self-control evaporated, and I screamed abuse at them. At the press conference I had taken great pains to point out the need for care while we were at sea. I knew this to be one of the most hazardous phases of the entire voyage."

Ridgway's outburst was in vain because a little later the other television launch slammed into his yacht, striking her midships on the starboard side. The heavy green trawler rolled her 25-ton hull against the stressed monocoque hull of the yacht.

"There was a horrible crunch," Ridgway wrote later. "Everything and everybody shuddered. . . . I looked down at the splintered strip of wood that masked the bolts joining the deck to the hull. I felt that awful sickness; defeat filled my mind. The bloody despair of trying to do anything with anyone—all that mattered to them were their blasted pictures."

The stubborn Englishman took a deep breath and prayed that the collision damage was only superficial. Ridgway sailed out into the Atlantic and headed south. He had 30,000 miles to go. If the damage was serious he could always put into a port along the south coast of England for repairs and start out again. For two days the wind was light and fitful. Finally a west wind blew up and *Rosie,* as Ridgway called his little vessel, hurried southward, apparently in good order. Soon *English Rose IV* was south of the approaches to the English Channel.

One evening with a blood-red sunset [wrote Ridgway], 240 miles west of the French coast at the northern end of the Bay of Biscay, I was lying back on my bunk. . . . The clock on the bulkhead over the chart table said 2200 hours. I rolled out to check the log and the main steering compass. Far out on the port side, a catamaran seemed to be coming our way. A quarter of an hour passed and there was no mistaking his intentions. The number 12 on her side meant she was in the Atlantic race, which had started from Plymouth on the day I left Aran. My competitors' sheet told me number 12 was the *San Giorgio,* a giant fifty-three-foot catamaran, sailed by Alex Carozzo, "the Italian master navigator" as the *Observer* newspaper had called him. Our meeting was quite a coincidence.

As he closed with *Rosie*, a black-bearded figure at the wheel raised a megaphone to his lips.

"Hello there, can you give me a position?" I smiled to myself. It was the supreme accolade for one who passed O level Navigation at the fourth attempt.

"I'll try. I'm not in your race, you know. I'm sailing south—round the world."

"What is your name?"

"Captain Ridgway."

"Oh, I have read about you. I hope to be joining the race when I

spread
1 line
short

return from America." He wheeled the big multi-hull around *Rosie* with typical Italian verve and élan. I dreaded a collision.

From the position at three-thirty that afternoon, I quickly calculated our present position and called it out to him over my own powerful Tannoy hailer. He wrote busily on a scrap of paper.

"Thank you, goodbye, and good luck." He swung away to starboard, and headed for the crimson sunset. I returned to my bunk. . . .

"Hello there." Ten minutes had passed; he was back again, sweeping his acrobatic circles around us.

"I lost the paper! Can you give me another position check?"

It was like some kind of pantomime, two madmen screaming at each other in the gathering dusk, way out on the ocean. We could have been the only two men left alive in the world, for we both spoke with sufficient gallantry, savouring the moment.

I gave him the position again, and this time I stayed in the cockpit and watched him go over the horizon, feeling a strong bond with this man I had never met.

ON JUNE 8TH, Chay Blyth, the second contestant in the race, sailed from England in a small red yacht. Blyth, Ridgway's partner in the Atlantic rowing effort, left from the Hamble River near Southampton in a borrowed 30-foot sloop named *Dytiscus III*. The vessel was a shoal-draft Kingfisher with twin bilge keels, a class of family cruising yachts that was barely suitable for the English Channel and an abysmal choice for the Southern Ocean and Cape Horn.

Not only was Blyth's vessel marginal, but the captain had practically no sailing experience. Of the nine men who competed in the race, Blyth was near the bottom of the list in sea miles. Yet the twenty-eight-year-old paratrooper, the youngest man in the race, had proved himself a tough nut in the rowing marathon in the Atlantic. Prior to leaving on the round-the-world race, Blyth surrounded himself with expert advisors who gave him crash courses in celestial navigation and in handling a small vessel.

On the morning when Blyth sailed, however, he had so little confidence in his sailing ability that he enlisted friends to help him raise and set his sails. His friends then got on board their own vessels and—like bodyguards—escorted *Dytiscus III*, one in front and one behind. Blyth was to watch the sailor on the yacht ahead of him and copy every move his friend made. The yacht in back was to head off boats that came close because Blyth had no idea how to avoid them. Once through the busy waters of the Solent area and out to sea, there would be less traffic, and presumably Blyth would be able to deal with the sailing. At least the eyes of the press would be away from him. In retrospect this little ruse seems incredible, yet it was carried out and Blyth slipped away on June 8th.

Prior to leaving in his £5,000 vessel, mechanics riveted twin metal tracks to the mast to take one end of the poles he carried to boom out twin headsails. Both the fore and aft deck hatches were sealed. The chain locker was filled with foam to make a watertight bulkhead and to add buoyancy. The engine was replaced with a 30-gallon water tank. Experts installed a large radio, and Blyth learned to operate and repair a small Honda gasoline generator. Meanwhile Blyth's helpers loaded hundreds of food packets, charts, sails, foul-weather gear, books, music tapes, and a motion picture camera on board.

On June 13th Blyth entered the Bay of Biscay off the west coast of France. By now the captain had learned that his vessel's directional stability was poor—her bow often yawed from side to side. Yet Blyth pushed on.

> Sunday, June 16, brought me my swordfish—a splendid fellow who came quite close, leaping out of the water, [wrote the Scots exparatrooper]. I dashed for my camera but I was not quick enough. It was also the day when I worked out a sight which indicated that I had sailed out of my first set of books and charts; and the day for my weekly shave and all-over wash. . . . It is really marvelous, the feeling of sluicing the salt from your beard and then of banishing the beard itself. Suddenly, you are clean again. You feel you can take whatever the next seven days have in mind for you.

Right from the beginning, Blyth's advisors had doubts about the running ability of his chunky, shoal-draft yacht, and during a mild gale on July 1st, Blyth began to agree with his friends. "The waves curled around it, lifting the stern, and *Dytiscus* simply turned sideways on. . . . These were conditions with which the self-steering gear had never been intended to cope. So I lowered the sails again, and once I had lowered them there was nothing more I could do except pray. So I prayed. And between times I turned to one of my sailing manuals to see what advice it contained for me.

"It was like being in hell with instructions. I was lonely and frightened. And I realized that this was but a foretaste of what was going to come once I reached the Roaring Forties in my strong but totally un-suitable boat."

In spite of doubts about himself and his yacht, he pressed on, and by July 18th, his forty-second day at sea, Blyth was south of the equator. He had grown increasingly familiar with his vessel, and he continued to improve his sailing skills.

ROBIN KNOX-JOHNSTON, the third man to depart, was a professional mer-chant marine officer who was especially keen for an Englishman to be the first person to sail around the world nonstop. He was terribly worried that a Frenchman might achieve this distinction. After an earlier ocean race in the Atlantic, which a Frenchman had won, a French magazine had boasted: "Frenchman supreme on the Anglo-Saxon ocean." The in-ference was that English seamen were inferior to French sailors. "This had made my blood boil at the time," said Knox-Johnston.

Robin was born in Putney—a part of London—in 1939, one of five children of northern Irish stock. In addition to his schooling, when he was eight he took up boxing, which he continued until he was seventeen. In training he generally did poorly, but in matches he nearly always won. He was good at individual sports—boxing, running, and swim-ming—but poor at team games.

Knox-Johnston joined the merchant navy as an apprentice when he was eighteen. During three years of sailing between London and East Africa, he achieved a reputation for being both hardworking and stub-born. He passed his second mate's examination in 1960 and joined a ship running between India and the Persian Gulf. He eventually got his first mate's certificate, and by twenty-five he had his master's papers.

Later he commanded a coasting vessel in South Africa. Married for a short time and then divorced, Knox-Johnston had a young daughter named Sara. The twenty-nine-year-old seaman hoped to compete in the round-the-world race in a new 53-foot steel vessel designed by Colin Mudie.

Like the other contestants, however, Knox-Johnston was stuck for money. He wrote to fifty business firms and asked for help and sponsor-ship. No one offered any funds, so he decided to enter the race in Suhaili, a sturdy, somewhat rotund ketch that he already owned. The word "suhaili" is the name given to the southeast wind in the Persian Gulf by Arab seamen.

Knox-Johnston had Suhaili built in Bombay in 1963–64. He and a crew of two had sailed her to South Africa, and then to England in a nonstop, seventy-four-day passage from Cape Town. The ketch was

CHAY BLYTH

built of teak and measured a little over 32 feet long (plus bowsprit) with a beam just an inch over 11 feet. Though she was serviceable and a good sea boat, she wasn't fancy at all.

Rough or not, however, the captain needed money, so he enlisted the help of a hardworking literary agent. Prior to Knox-Johnston's sailing, his representative lined up partial sponsorship from English and American book publishers, the *Sunday Mirror* newspaper, and *True* magazine in the United States,

When *Suhaili* left the port of Falmouth on June 14th, she floated suspiciously low in the water, so low that a stranger might have thought she was sinking. The reason, of course, was that a few days earlier Knox-Johnston and his friends had loaded an entire truckload of food into the small white ketch, enough food for one man for 330 days. Into *Suhaili* went some 2,500 cans and jars and packages, each averaging almost a pound in weight. Knox-Johnston took 216 cans of corned beef, 72 cans of runner beans, and 24 tins of apricots. He put on 72 cans of orange juice, 28 pounds of nuts, 350 pounds of potatoes, and 250 pounds of onions. Somewhere in the boat were 24 dozen eggs, 56 pounds of rice, 112 pounds of sugar, 216 cans of condensed milk, and 14 pounds of hot curry powder. The captain included 1,000 vitamin tablets, 24 tubes of toothpaste, 3,000 cigarettes, and a case each of Grant's Scotch whiskey and Martell brandy.

Like the other contestants, Knox-Johnston filled up the forepeak of his yacht with a mass of spare sails, extra line, rigging wire, and tools. He had nine 5-gallon drums of kerosene and diesel oil, 86 gallons of fresh water, an emergency life raft, a battery charger, and spare gasoline. He took along an armload of nautical charts and seventy-five big books for navigation and recreational reading. He had clothes, bedding, oil-skins, a large radio set, a spare tiller, a rifle and ammunition, 20 sail-maker's needles, 2 cameras, fishing equipment, 24 tea towels, and a massive first-aid kit. The list of gear went on and on and resolved itself into two problems: *where to put everything* and *how to find anything*. It's astonishing how much food a man consumes in a year and how many things he must have in order to keep a sailing vessel going across an ocean.

THREE OF THE NINE contestants had now left England. Ridgway was two weeks ahead of Knox-Johnston with Chay Blyth somewhere in be-tween. When *The Sunday Times* had made the rules for the race it had set the starting dates between June 1st and October 31st because it was thought prudent not to arrive in the Southern Ocean until the southern winter was over. Indeed some people thought that Ridgway, Blyth, and Knox-Johnston had left too early and would get into unnecessarily heavy weather in the south. Yet little by little the first three men were gnawing at the 30,000-mile carrot at the rate of roughly 75 to 100 miles a day.

In the meantime, *Galway Blazer II*, Bill King's new yacht, was rap-idly nearing completion. Moitessier and Fougeron, the two French en-trants, were in Plymouth putting on supplies.

ANOTHER CONTESTANT WAS Donald Crowhurst, a thirty-six-year-old elec-tronics engineer, an ex-flying officer in the Royal Air Force, a former army lieutenant, and a onetime village politician. Crowhurst was ex-tremely bright, but his character was streaked with behavior that was un-even, moody, and at times cheeky and overpowering. He had a wife and four small children and operated a struggling electronics business in a small village located in a rural part of southeast England.

After a vigorous but unsuccessful attempt to borrow Francis Chich-ester's *Gipsy Moth IV* for the race, Crowhurst decided to build a 40-foot Victress trimaran designed by an American named Arthur Piver, who was at that time the leading proponent of multihulled craft. Unfortunately, Piver had recently been lost off the coast of California in one of his small trimarans, which may have capsized, broken apart, or been run down by a large ship.

A trimaran is an unballasted vessel with three slim hulls linked together by crossarms. The great beam gives the multihull considerable stability, and without ballast the total weight or displacement is minimal. On its pencil-like hulls the vessel can skim across smooth water at great speed and needs only small sails to drive the yacht. Unfortunately, in disturbed water and gusty winds it's possible for a trimaran to flip over.

A capsize is an unusual occurrence, but when a trimaran is upside down, the vessel is more stable than when upright because of the weight and drag of the mast and sails hanging down in the water. Though various schemes have been proposed, there still is no reliable way for a man on board a capsized trimaran to right his vessel.

The performance of a trimaran against the wind in rough seas is not much better than a normal monohull. Yet with a following or beam wind a trimaran is capable of speeds at least twice that of a conventional ballasted monohull. The choice becomes a trade-off between the thrill and achievement of high-speed performance versus the risk and danger of capsize.

Crowhurst had elected a trimaran. Like the other contestants he had no money and had to go around pleading for funds—trying to convince reluctant people to pledge assistance in return for publicity.

"My estimates indicate that the boat would only cost about £6,000 so that with yacht mortgage facilities the outlay is very modest in comparison with the returns, which do not merely accrue to this company but include film rights, communication and story rights, and advertising revenue," said Crowhurst, who sounded a little like a movie producer.

Not only did Crowhurst envision fame and riches from the publicity, but he claimed to have invented a whole new series of electronic devices to make his trimaran—and all multihulls—safer. One gadget monitored the yacht's performance while the captain was asleep: anything unusual would be signaled to the crew by warning lights and alarms. If the vessel was overpressed by increasing wind, another invention eased the sails automatically by letting out the controlling lines or sheets. In case his trimaran capsized, Crowhurst had a rubber buoyancy bag at the top of the mast that he claimed would inflate and right his vessel.

Like con artists who have been operating since the time of the Egyptian pharaohs, Crowhurst brazenly claimed to have all this equipment developed, tested, and "now operating successfully." He said he was applying for patents. In truth, these inventions existed only in Crowhurst's mind and had not been built or tried out at all.

In spite of statements that he had "been to sea in small boats over a period spanning almost thirty years," Crowhurst actually had little sailing experience and had never made an ocean passage in a small sailing vessel. He was like many small-boat fanciers who allow themselves to be carried away by the romance of the idea and attempt to let whim and fancy replace experience and actual sea miles.

Reading an exciting sea story transforms these sea dreamers into intrepid captains and born-again Walter Mittys. This fancifulness is well-known to naval architects and yacht builders. Nevertheless, Crowhurst was clever and convincing in his arguments and created a plausible case for his entry. Even the usually conservative yachting magazines accepted his statements and said that his inventions were sensible.

The man who had invested in Crowhurst's electronics business finally agreed to sponsor a new trimaran. But the race was about to start, and the construction of Crowhurst's new trimaran hadn't even begun. Armed with financing, however, Crowhurst arranged with two boatyards to build the yacht in a hurry. One firm, Cox Marine, was to construct the hulls. A second company, L. J. Eastwood, was to assemble the trimaran and complete the interior and rig.

"I must say that at this point I was most impressed," said John Eastwood, one of the owners of the second boatbuilding firm. "Donald seemed to know precisely what he wanted. He had a good technical background and an imaginative mind."

The hulls were built and delivered to Eastwoods on time, and two dozen workmen rushed to complete the vessel. Crowhurst's continuing inventions and changes, however, interfered with the work and caused one delay after another. For example, the normal mast and rigging and sails could not be used because of the masthead buoyancy bag arrangement, so a special rig had to be designed, ordered, and custom-made. Crowhurst wanted an oversize rudder and different interior shelving. There was a dispute about the fiberglass sheathing that the builder wanted to eliminate in favor of paint. Besides the design changes, there were problems because of material shortages, all of which were aggravated because of the rush job. Soon the yardmen were put on a seventy-hour work week; later a night shift was arranged with workmen coming from nearby boatyards. Bothersome shortages plagued the hurried building. For example, one item was soft rubber on which to bed down the tops of the watertight hatches in the two floats of the trimaran. Only hard rubber was available, and it was unsatisfactory because it was too stiff and unyielding. The hatch bedding problem was only one item on a long list.

Building a yacht in a hurry, it seemed, was the same as trying to teach manners to a child overnight; it just wasn't possible without terrible penalties and unending difficulties.

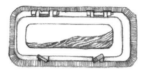

3

Sharks and Giant Yachts

WHILE DONALD CROWHURST WAS IMMERSED IN THE HELLISH business of trying to build a complicated new yacht in a few months, the first three competitors hurried southward, getting farther and farther from England. By July 1st, John Ridgway and Chay Blyth, the first two starters, had crossed the equator and passed into the South Atlantic. Robin Knox-Johnston, the third man to leave, had sailed only 1,200 miles in sixteen days, but he was largely across the horse latitudes or variables, the light-weather area between the trade wind and the westerlies, and he looked forward to better daily runs.

> I had settled in by this time [wrote Knox-Johnston], and was working to a daily routine which I had developed on my previous voyage but which, obviously, had to be adapted to lone sailing. I tried to get to sleep at 10 p.m. if the sailing conditions allowed, and apart from a check at 2 a.m. (more frequently in the shipping lanes or bad weather) I slept through until 6 a.m. when I got up and made my rounds of the deck, setting what adjustments seemed necessary to the rudder, the Admiral [the self-steering] and sails. Breakfast followed, usually fried eggs and something else, followed by a mug of coffee and the first cigarette of the day. If it was fine enough I always sat on deck for this. Nothing can compare with the freshness of the early morning at sea.

During good weather in warm waters, Knox-Johnston often went for a swim. Around noon he would pay out one of the sheets for a trailing safety line and jump overboard. He dived ahead of the boat from the bowsprit and swam as hard as he could until the stern came up to him. Then he would grab the safety line and haul himself on board. Next he scrubbed himself with saltwater soap before jumping in for a rinse. This routine kept him clean and fit. Robin was careful not to miss the safety line. . . .

ROBIN KNOX-JOHNSTON

During his third week at sea, Knox-Johnston began to be alarmed by a persistent leak. Even in easy going he had to pump twice a day—more if the sea was rough. If the yacht leaked in the settled waters of the tropical Atlantic, what would she do in the stormy waters of the Southern Ocean?

> Two days past the Cape Verde Islands [he wrote] we ran into a
> calm patch and I reduced sail. Donning a mask and snorkel, I dived
> overside and went straight to the spot level with the mainmast about a
> foot above the keel where we had had trouble on the previous voyage.
> The trouble was there all right and a large gap was showing along the
> seam for about eight feet. I swam under the keel and checked the
> other side. It was the same, and as *Suhaili* pitched and rolled easily in
> the water I could see the gap opening and closing slightly. I swam to
> the surface, hauled myself on board, lit a cigarette and started to think
> the problem over. What really worried me was the thought that maybe
> all the floors, the brackets that join the frames to the keel, were work-
> ing loose and that this was just the beginning of real trouble. It would
> be suicidal to carry on with the voyage if this were the case, but at the
> same time it was very difficult to see if the danger was serious, as the
> floors were for the most part hidden by the water tanks which were

built into the boat. Those I could see I checked and they seemed firm enough, so I convinced myself that they were all basically strong, and the trouble was just a continuation of the old problem and could be put right by caulking. If I was wrong in this, I just had to hope that not all the floors would go at once and I would be able to manage to make a port before *Suhaili* broke up. . . .

Having decided that caulking was the answer, I had to think of some way of doing it five feet below water. Normally dry twisted raw cotton is hammered into the seam, stopped with filling compound and painted over, but I could not do that. I decided to try and do the job with cotton anyway and hope that the fact that it would be wet would not make too much difference. We had had to do the same thing when in the middle of the Arabian Sea. It had not been easy, but at least I had had two other people helping me and keeping a lookout for sharks. This time I would have to do the job on my own and hope that I would notice any sharks whilst they were still circling.

I got out the cotton and twisted up some pieces in 18-inch lengths, a convenient length to handle although ideally I should have done the whole job with one piece. Next I put a long length of line on a hammer and lowered it overside near where I had to work. Finally I dressed myself in a blue shirt and jeans to hide the whiteness of my body, something that sharks, great scavengers, always associate with refuse, and strapped my knife to my leg. I put the cotton on deck where I could reach it from the water and taking my largest screwdriver as the most convenient caulking instrument, I went overside.

The job was impossible from the start. In the first place I would run out of breath before I had hammered enough cotton in place to hold it whilst I surfaced, and each time I came up for air I lost all the work done. Secondly the cotton was just not going in properly, and even when I changed the screwdriver for a proper caulking iron I made no progress. After half an hour of fruitless effort I climbed back on board and tried to think of some other way of doing the job.

A while later I was busily engaged in sewing the cotton on to a strip of canvas 1½ inches wide. When the whole strip, about seven feet of it, was completed I gave it a coating of Stockholm Tar and then forced copper tacks through the canvas about six inches apart. I went into the water again and placed the cotton in the seam so that the canvas was on the outside; I then started knocking the tacks into the hull to hold the whole thing in place. The finished job did not look too bad but it was a bit ragged at the edges and I thought that it might be ripped off when *Suhaili* got moving again so I decided to tack a copper strip over the canvas to tidy it up. . . .

So far, although I had kept glancing nervously about me whilst I was in the water, I had seen no fish at all. But whilst I was having a coffee break, having prepared the copper strip and made holes for the tacks so that I would have an easier job under water, I suddenly noticed a lean grey shape moving sinuously past the boat. The sharks had found us at last. I watched this one for ten minutes hoping it would go away as I did not want to have to kill it. I was not being kind to the shark; if I killed it, there would be quite a bit of blood in the water and the death convulsions would be picked up by any other sharks near at hand who would immediately rush in, and I would not be able to get the job finished. After ten minutes, though, during which the shark kept circling the boat and showing no signs of leaving, I got out my rifle and, throwing some sheets of lavatory paper into the water, waited for the shark to come and investigate. On its first run round, the shark passed about three feet below the paper, then he turned and, rising slowly, came in again. I aimed the rifle at the shape and with finger on the trigger, followed it as it came in. Three feet short of the paper the top of the head broke surface and I squeezed the trigger. There was an explosion in the water as the shark's body threshed around but within half a minute the threshing ceased and the lifeless body began slowly to plane down until it disappeared into the blue. For the next half hour I watched carefully to see if any other sharks would appear, but apart from two pilot fish, which, having followed their previous protector down until they realized he would never feed them again, now decided to join, a larger and apparently stronger master, *Suhaili* and I had the sea to ourselves. I went overside and in an hour and a half had the copper tacked over the canvas on the port side. A light wind getting up forced me to leave the starboard side until we were next becalmed. But in any case I was quite chilled from four hours immersion, and also a little tense from constantly glancing around expecting to see a shark coming in behind me, and I was quite glad to give the job a rest for a while.

Two days later, when becalmed again, I went overside and repeated the job on the starboard side without incident. The leaking into the boat almost stopped completely.

This modest account of an ingenious repair while at sea and all alone demonstrates the toughness and resourcefulness of the single-handed sailor at his best. Knox-Johnston's caulking repair would properly have been a shipyard job when the vessel was out of the water. His first solution was not satisfactory. Yet he kept at it until he had the problem solved even though he was obliged to stop in the middle of the job to kill a shark. In all it was a remarkable example of courage and fortitude.

NOT ONLY WAS Donald Crowhurst trying to complete a new trimaran for the race, but the Italian entrant, Alex Carozzo, was hard at work building an enormous 66-foot ketch (as yet unnamed). This vessel was almost twice as long as the average length of the other eight entries, and no one knew whether one man could handle such a giant craft. The thirty-six-year-old Italian captain had no doubts at all, however, and appeared to have unlimited confidence in himself.

ALEX CAROZZO

Carozzo was a slim, bearded Italian from Venice who was known as the Chichester of Italy. He was a bit pushy, but a likable chap, and when you saw him from a distance you immediately thought of a character out of Shakespeare, particularly with his willowy figure and the dark, tight-fitting clothes that he often wore. A bachelor, he was a merchant marine officer who during a later trip to the Far East built a 33-foot hard-chine sloop in the hold of his cargo ship. He then sailed the *Golden Lion*, as he called his new sailboat, from Japan to San Francisco by himself in eighty-two days during an especially chilly winter. (I got acquainted with Alex in 1966 when he spent a few weeks in Sausalito, California, after his Pacific trip. He had a meal or two with my wife and me aboard our yacht. He was short of cash, trying to sell his boat, and I often saw his forlorn figure around town.)

When the round-the-word race had started, Carozzo was sailing an enormous catamaran named *San Giorgio* in another race across the Atlantic and (as we saw in Chapter Two) actually met John Ridgway sailing in the Bay of Biscay. Carozzo did not complete the Atlantic race but returned to England, where he commenced the construction of a single-hulled vessel for the round-the-world competition. The new project wasn't even begun until August 20th, but the Medina Yacht Company claimed that its expert workers could build the new yacht in a hurry and launch her well before the deadline. Fifteen men were soon toiling around the clock on three shifts to complete the new Italian yacht in record time. The local yacht watchers were dubious, but the black-bearded Carozzo, chain-smoking throughout and nervously tapping his feet, radiated confidence.

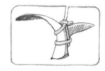

4~

The Middle Starters

Back in southwest England, a fair wind blew from the north. Light patchy fog lay over Plymouth Sound. The date was August 22nd, and the two French entrants headed out to sea. Both men were trim and fit, had their yachts in good order, and looked forward to the race.

The first was Bernard Moitessier, who was forty-three years old when the race began. Bernard was born in Saigon, Indochina in 1925, the eldest of five children. His parents had emigrated from Paris during the French Colonial period, and young Bernard grew up in a sleepy tropical environment of rice paddies and reed-covered plains. As a child he learned to speak French and Vietnamese perfectly. His mother was an artist; his father ran an importing and merchandising company. Bernard's father tried to interest his oldest son in business, but Bernard hated it and took after his mother.

He learned about sailing little by little and built (and wrecked) two crude yachts, one on Diego Garcia Atoll in the Indian Ocean, and a second on St. Vincent in the Caribbean. In the years surrounding the two mishaps, however, Moitessier sailed thousands of miles across the Indian and Atlantic oceans and gradually learned about the sea. He was an expert swimmer and worked for a time as a spearfisher on the island of Mauritius in the southwest part of the Indian Ocean. In 1953, he was attacked by a large shark. Badly bitten on one foot, he was lucky to get to shore and the hospital before he bled to death.

Moitessier named his third yacht *Joshua*, after the pioneering American single-hander Joshua Slocum. The vessel—designed by Jean Knocker of Rue, France—was a $39\frac{1}{2}$-foot steel double-ender (plus a 6-foot, 10-inch bowsprit) with a lofty two-masted ketch rig. The yacht had normal wheel steering in the cockpit, but Moitessier arranged a second position so *Joshua* could be steered from inside the cabin, where the captain could keep watch from beneath a closed bubble hatch reinforced with steel.

The ingenious Moitessier had built his three yachts largely with his own hands, generally scrounging materials and doing things on the cheap because he had little money. For years he lived as a sea gypsy, eking out a minimal material existence but reaping a richly satisfying life in spiritual terms. He was a gentle soul, full of impractical ideas, but likable and charming.

In 1965 Moitessier and his wife, Françoise, had sailed from Tahiti to the Mediterranean via Cape Horn, a phenomenal nonstop voyage of 14,216 miles that took 126 days at sea. At that time the voyage was by far the longest nonstop passage ever completed by a small vessel, and it earned Moitessier publicity, awards, and a growing reputation along with the proceeds from a book he wrote about the trip titled *Cape Horn: The Logical Route.*

Now, at the start of the 1968 round-the-world race, the wiry Moitessier slipped away from Plymouth in his beloved, red-hulled *Joshua* and moved smoothly and steadily toward the open Atlantic. He was rested and confident and hoped that he could gradually overtake the leaders. During his previous Cape Horn trip Moitessier had averaged 113 miles a day; since then he had made various improvements in *Joshua*. In addition he felt that his skills were sharper.

Moitessier claimed that he was not making the trip for money. "Money is all right as long as you have enough for a cup of tea," he told a reporter. "I don't care for it any more than that. The people who are thinking about money and being the fastest around the world will not win. It is the people who care about their skins. I shall bring back my skin, apart from a few bumps on the head."

The second French entrant, Loïck Fougeron, sailed a 30-foot cutter named *Captain Browne*, which had been designed by a Belgian named Louis Van de Wiele. His vessel was originally called *Hierro*, but Fougeron had renamed it *Captain Browne* in honor of an old bearded English sailor who once roamed the Casablanca waterfront and whose pictures now graced the yacht's cabin. Fougeron had bought the four-year-old yacht in Belgium in January and had sailed her to England on a roundabout trip via Casablanca and Toulon. He had arrived in Plymouth in the early summer and immediately began work to prepare her for the race.

Captain Browne was a gaff cutter with a sturdy steel hull, a long low coachroof with five small circular portlights along each side, a tiny cockpit, fairly high freeboard, and a stout transom-hung rudder. The boat sported a short, thick pole mast with ratlines across the shrouds so a man could climb aloft to check ahead.

Fougeron, who was forty-two years old, was a handsome, quiet Breton, born by the sea. He had lived in Casablanca for twenty years, where he had managed a motorcycle engineering company. On an earlier voyage he had crossed the Atlantic in a converted lifeboat. He had no solo sailing experience, but he was confident that he would be able to look after himself and *Captain Browne*. The French captain was meticulous in his preparations and even put aboard spare valves for his pressure cooker. He planned a basic diet of rice and carried 40 gallons of fresh water in his tank plus another 40 gallons of Evian mineral water in small cans.

During the months of the voyage, Fougeron's wife stayed in Morocco. She did not like the sea but tolerated her husband's passion for a sailor's life. Before he left Plymouth, Fougeron cut down his dinner service to one plate and one cup and—apologizing profusely—offered visitors a gulp of gin straight from the bottle. He was very superstitious and went to great lengths to placate the old gods and traditions. For example, when he was at sea he never mentioned rabbits, which was a sure sign of bad luck.

In order to have a little company during his long voyage, Fougeron decided to take a spirited kitten from Morocco.

"When it was time to get underway, my little sister brought me an adorable half-wild kitten called Roulis," said Fougeron. "On seeing my surprise and annoyance, she assured me that the kitten would keep me company, that he was well behaved, ate like a bird, drank still less, and was sweet as a lamb. The kitten hastened to confirm all this by bestowing on me a scratch of which I am still able to find the scar."

ON AUGUST 24TH, two days after Moitessier and Fougeron had left Plymouth, Commander Bill King, the sixth entrant and, at fifty-eight, the oldest man in the race, sailed into the Atlantic on *Galway Blazer II*. Though Moitessier and King were both well-seasoned sailors, their backgrounds could not have been more different. King had begun his sea career at the Royal Naval College when he was fourteen. Three years later—in 1927—he went to sea in a British battleship. At twenty-one he was posted to a submarine in Hong Kong and traveled all over the Far East. Back in England he became second-in-command of HMS *Narwhal*. At the beginning of World War II, King served as a submarine commander and led an incredibly active life for the next six years. He patrolled the Dutch coast, torpedoed eight ships off Norway, blew up a tanker by shellfire, dueled with German submarines, and fought in the Mediterranean. In between times he played polo, skied, delighted in tennis and foxhunting, and hobnobbed with the titled and famous.

After the war, King got married, had two children, and became an expert at ocean racing aboard fast yachts. When *Galway Blazer II* was finally launched on May 24th, it was King's sixteen-year-old daughter—holding a bouquet in one hand and a champagne bottle in the other—who did the christening while an audience of dignitaries clapped its approval. The fitting out of the new yacht, the sea trials, the various changes and improvements, and the supplying took nine weeks more. It wasn't until August 24th that King finally sailed from Plymouth into the Atlantic.

Now six yachts were away on the race: Ridgway, Blyth, Knox-Johnston, Fougeron, Moitessier, and King. The trimaran of Donald Crowhurst and the giant ketch of Alex Carozzo were still in the building yards. Nigel Tetley was preparing to depart. But just about the time that Fougeron, Moitessier, and King were leaving England, news came from Captain John Ridgway, the first starter.

RIDGWAY, IN *English Rose IV*—his *Rosie*—had crossed the Bay of Biscay. Then he slipped past the Spanish and Portuguese coasts and headed for Madeira, a small island 475 miles west of Casablanca on the northwest coast of Africa. *Rosie* had found mostly northeast winds, so Ridgway dropped his mainsail and hoisted twin running sails, one to port and one to starboard forward of the mast, each held out with a pole. The self-steering vane guided the yacht nicely, and she made 100 miles a day with scarcely any effort. It was all too easy.

At night Ridgway put up a kerosene lamp to warn shipping, and every few hours the captain rolled out to check the compass and log reading. As he sped along under twin headsails, with much of the mast loading on the backstays, Ridgway wondered what would happen when the wind came from ahead and the sailing pressure was changed to the side rigging. Then much of the sailing load would be concentrated on the shrouds, their turnbuckles, the shroud plates that were bolted to the side decks, and the side decks themselves.

It had been midships on the starboard side where the trawler had rolled heavily against *Rosie* on the day she had left Ireland. Now when the wind blew hard and his vessel touched 7 knots, ominous creaks came from this area. When Ridgway reduced sail, the noise stopped. During an inspection of the mast and shroud plates, the captain discovered hairline cracks in the gelcoat around the lower shroud plate on the *port* side of *Rosie*, on the opposite side of the yacht from the collision. What did these cracks mean? In addition, the captain saw that the foot of the mast, stepped on deck, appeared to have shifted in its mounting shoe.

Ridgway, who was a persistent worrier, grew increasingly morose. "The collision had upset me more seriously than I cared to admit," he said. "The loneliness tied my stomach in knots. I found myself far too tense after a day in the cabin." He tried to send radio signals, but his set refused to work. Something had gone wrong inside. He would have to get along without radio transmissions.

Each day got a little warmer, the sea turned a deep blue, and Ridgway ate the last of the avocado pears from England. He generally had lunch—sardines, crackers, and cheese—in the cockpit. Dinner was often a favorite curry. At Madeira he met a reporter from his sponsoring newspaper who came out in a local fishing boat. Ridgway passed across his diaries, films, and tapes, had a brief talk, and pushed on southward.

Rosie continued running before the northeast trade wind that sometimes freshened and necessitated smaller sails. The little sloop had fabulous luck with fair winds and at times covered 140 miles in twenty-four hours. Every day Ridgway oiled the self-steering gear and rubbed candle wax on the lines and sails at points of wear.

On the morning when he passed the Cape Verde Islands the wind picked up. The yacht rolled to one side and broached, and the twin headsails were backwinded. This completely stopped the 30-foot vessel. The rising wind ripped one sail right off the headstay and all the bronze hanks were torn open. Ridgway fought the sails to the deck.

"I crept below and burst into tears," he wrote. "For some reason I could not shake off the emotional strain of loneliness. I noticed that I had cried at some point on each of twenty-seven consecutive days. Something must surely be wrong—I was just unable to relax."

A few days later *Rosie* slatted on the quiet waters of the doldrums, the region of oily calms between the northeast and southeast trade wind zones. The boat doddered along at 50 or 60 miles a day. Sometimes Ridgway sniffed the cod-liver oil smell of plankton, which often signaled whales. "Soon we were up with them, shiny jet black with vertical foreheads dropping straight down to their mouths. . . . Like small submarines they would surface and dive; passing right under the yacht they assumed a beautiful brown color, but they would never surface closer than twenty-five yards."

Early on the morning of July 8th—Ridgway's thirtieth birthday—he

ENGLISH ROSE IV

headed more to the west. *Rosie* was through the doldrums and close-hauled on the port tack, heading a little west of south, into the 20-knot southeast trade wind. The next destination was Tristan da Cunha, 2,250 miles to the south. Now the lazy days and easy living were over. *Rosie* slammed into head seas and bucked and pitched. From time to time the wind freshened and Ridgway reduced his sails accordingly. "As a wave moved along the hull, we would be left floating on air, and then the bows would fall like a lead balloon, plunging into the trough with a bow-shaking crack," he wrote. Ridgway hoped that Rosie's designer had made the yacht strong enough.

Sometimes squalls brought more wind and rain. If there was not too much spray flying about, Ridgway caught rainwater by hanging a bucket at the forward end of the main boom. He lifted the after end of the boom with the topping lift to form a belly in the mainsail, where the rain collected. At first the water was a little salty, but it soon washed everything clean and could then be bucketed into the tank and containers.

Ridgway kept inspecting the shrouds and fittings on Rosie's port side because these were the parts that supported the mast as the yacht bounced along on the port tack.

"We were about 600 miles south of the equator and some 600 miles east of Brazil," he wrote. "This was no time to lose the mast, for we had no engine. With a small no. 2 jib and a heavily-reefed mainsail we were making nearly four knots. The seas were long and high, with the white crests sparkling in the sun. Every so often *Rosie* would stumble, taking a sea awkwardly, then she would shudder to a halt, decks streaming. [Suddenly] I was horrified to see the deck bulging around the damaged shroud plate while the cracks opened and closed, bubbling spray."

The army captain from Scotland quickly dropped both sails and lashed the single lower shroud to a strong point on deck. He then undid the two bolts holding the shroud plate to the deck and replaced it with a new plate, adding a 6-by-15-inch piece of $\frac{3}{4}$-inch plywood for a backing piece underneath the deck before he tightened the bolts. Then he reconnected the lower shroud and sailed on. Everything seemed to be OK.

"Next morning I noticed that the plywood had taken on a curve and was creaking ominously," wrote Ridgway. "I checked the situation from every angle. There were at least 700 miles of trade winds ahead and it was the southern hemisphere's equivalent of January. I thought for several hours on the predicament. One thing was sure, if the deck plate went, then the mast would definitely go with it. The only way to avoid the strain on the plate was to turn and run downwind to some South American port."*

"The strain would then be transferred to the twin backstays. If I did this, it would mean the end of the voyage, the end of the chance of a lifetime.

"To go on meant the Roaring Forties in winter; no one in his right mind would go there in a damaged boat."

The captain tried to puzzle out what had happened. He concluded that when the trawler had struck *Rosie* on the starboard side, the impact had caused the mast to whip and strain the deck around the lower shroud plate on the port side.

Ridgway, raging with frustration and disappointment, turned downwind and sailed to Recife, Brazil, which he reached on July 21st, fifty-one days after he left England. "It would be easy to say I would have

---

*This type of flimsy construction is totally unsuitable for an oceangoing yacht. The normal arrangement is for a long, substantial metal chainplate to be bolted to the hull with six or eight stout bolts, or for a large transverse plywood knee to be massively glassed to the hull and deck underneath and then to bolt a chainplate to the knee. A single lower shroud fastened to a U-bolt pulling on a small area of thin deck is exactly what *Rosie* was designed for: Sunday afternoon sailing around a town harbor. More experienced sailors—Moitessier, Knox-Johnston, or Tetley—might have beefed up the deck with a large strongback or have fashioned a pair of chainplates out of something on board, bolted them to the hull, and pressed on. Ridgway had no background for this sort of repair.

won the race but for the damage . . . but I don't think I would have made it anyway," he wrote later in an honest admission.

The first man to leave the race was out. Eight were left.

ON JULY 23RD, Chay Blyth was 480 miles south of the equator and far out in the South Atlantic, almost midway between Africa and Brazil. *Dytiscus III* was banging along close-hauled into the southeast trade wind, much like *Rosie* had been a few weeks earlier. *Dytiscus III* was headed west of south, about 60 or 70 degrees off the wind, which generally blew between 20 and 25 knots. Blyth logged 95 to 120 miles a day while his Kingfisher, heeled to 20 or 30 degrees, zipped along in big seas.

"Jiggling like a tambourine on overtime," wrote the captain.

Blyth ran his life on positive, up-tempo lines and spent a lot of time thinking about his wife and infant daughter. Four days earlier he had celebrated his daughter's first birthday with an onboard party: a special breakfast of grapefruit juice, scrambled eggs, coffee, and biscuits, along with a birthday cleanup and a shave. During the day he opened a parcel that his wife had packed and found a little cake (with one candle) and a few special treats of candy and pâté, a pocket solitaire game, and a book of crossword puzzles. Blyth listened to a tape that his wife had made before he left. The tape had music, the sound of his daughter squealing, the doorbell ringing, and the dog barking. It was just like home.

So far in the race, Blyth's major concern was that his 30-foot twin-

DYSTICUS III

bilge-keel sloop was entirely wrong for ocean sailing. On the rough Atlantic the light shallow-draft Kingfisher tended to yaw and bob around instead of tracking straight and true like a heavier, deep-draft vessel. Nevertheless, *Dytiscus III* was going along quite well.

Blyth's immediate curse was a series of small, never-ending leaks typical of mass-production boats. The ventilators leaked, a forward pump leaked, the coachroof leaked, the shroud plates leaked, and there was a puzzling mystery leak in the forward anchor compartment. Blyth rushed around with a tube of synthetic rubber compound trying to squeeze in caulking here and there. The yacht had no proper bilge drainage so the captain had to mop up the water with a cloth.

All this was small stuff. When *Dytiscus III* was about 750 miles west of Ascension Island, however, Blyth discovered that salt water had gotten into his 30-gallon gasoline supply through the air pipe to the starboard bilge keel tank. It was another example of bad design and poor boatbuilding.

Blyth considered the discovery a disaster. "The petrol was a sickly white," said Blyth. "The Honda electrical generator would not run on the contaminated fuel, which meant no power for the navigation lights or the radio."*

"Try as I might, I could not bring myself to fancy the prospect of crashing through the night with no lights," said Blyth. "But it was the radio business that really bothered me. My wife would neither know where I was nor how I was, and if I decided to stick it out it would be another eight months at least before she would know that I was alive."

Blyth went through a lot of self-doubts and arguments with himself as he continued south. "Morally, had I the right to let my wife wait eight months, with people constantly asking if she had heard anything, just to satisfy my ego?"

Blyth considered putting into South Africa to replenish his gasoline and then to continue. He would be disqualified, but what did he care? He added up his problems: broken doors, leaks, torn sails, no mileage log, and salt water in the petrol. He finally decided to sail to Tristan da Cunha, an obscure Atlantic island at 37 degrees south latitude, about 1,440 miles west of Cape Town, where he hoped to send a letter to his wife.

Dytiscus III ran out of the southeast wind on August 1st. The weather was cooler so Blyth put on warm clothing. On some days he made only 60 miles in light southwest breezes. When fresher winds finally came they were too strong, and the 30-footer broached before a gale. Then

---

*It never occurred to Blyth to filter out the water by straining the gasoline.

came fog and calms, followed by another gale with rain and lightning. ("At sea and at night, it terrifies me," he wrote.) The weather turned steadily colder so the captain added a pullover and thick stockings to his outfit.

Blyth arrived at Tristan da Cunha on August 15th. His vessel was in reasonable order. He was not short of food, and he was rested and alert.

Yet his actions were enough to make a seaman wince.

"Sent up first flare," he wrote. "It's a big decision to make because a flare means a ship in distress. I am not in distress, but I have got to make somebody see me somehow."

A ship from South Africa, the *Gillian Gaggins*, was anchored near the island pumping gasoline ashore. After asking the ship's engineer to repair his generator, Blyth moved aboard the large vessel. He accepted food and lodging and a load of new gasoline. These actions disqualified Blyth, of course, and though he eventually sailed to East London in South Africa, he is no longer part of our story.

Now two men were out of the race: one because of an unfortunate mishap; the second because he broke the rules of the competition.

Seven men were left.

NIGEL TETLEY WAS the next man to sail in the round-the-world competition and is the only entrant we haven't met. Lieutenant-Commander Tetley, like King, was a career officer in the Royal Navy. He was born in Pretoria, South Africa, and had been close to the sea ever since he was a boy, when he learned to row on a Scottish loch.

Tetley joined the navy in 1942 directly from Marlborough College and served all over the world, finally working up to the command of a frigate in 1957. Forty-four years old and happily married to a geography teacher in Plymouth, Tetley had two teenage sons from an earlier marriage.

This handsome, pleasant man had owned and sailed a whole series of dinghies and yachts. During the winter of 1962–63 he had his Victress trimaran built, and he gradually modified and strengthened the big three-hulled craft on trips to Holland, Denmark, and Sweden. The multihull was the same design that Crowhurst was building except that Tetley's vessel had been properly completed and was nicely outfitted. In addition Tetley had added a center keel to improve steering and windward performance. The ketch-rigged yacht had a total beam of 22 feet and carried 900 square feet of sails on her two masts. *Victress* sported a large, high coachroof surmounted at the rear by a boxy cabin that allowed inside steering.

In 1966, Tetley and a friend sailed *Victress* in the grueling 2,000-mile round-Britain race. Tetley and his wife Eve lived aboard *Victress* year-round, keeping warm in cold weather with a stove fueled by anthracite coal. Like Knox-Johnston, Tetley had tried hard to find a sponsor. He sent off letters to dozens of tea, tobacco, and drink firms.

> Dear Sir [wrote Tetley]
> You may have seen a leader in *The Sunday Times* some weeks ago announcing a Round The World Sailing Race for yachts leaving the United Kingdom by October 31st, 1968.
>
> Being very keen to compete and a serving Naval Officer also, I have taken the initial step of applying to the Admiralty for unpaid leave from early September to cover the period up to my normal retirement date, age 45 in February, in order to take part.
>
> Although my present yacht, a 40-foot trimaran, would be capable of making the voyage, a yacht built specially for singlehanded sailing would be much better, and I am writing in hope that your firm may be prepared to sponsor all or part of the building cost in return for advertising rights.
>
> The yacht I have in mind is a 50-foot trimaran, to a design by Derek Kelsall and myself, which could be built in his boatyard at Sandwich for an estimated £10,000 fully fitted. This is a realistic figure for a light weight, yet extra strong, trimaran of sound design and first-class materials.
>
> My sailing experience covers thirty years, and includes the Round Britain Race in which I achieved fifth place in my family trimaran *Victress*.
>
> In view of the short times now remaining to build and equip a new boat, I would greatly appreciate an early answer. . . .

As Knox-Johnston had discovered, a sponsor was a hard fish to find. "The replies . . . all wished me luck, but regretted that no special funds could be allocated for the project," wrote Tetley. "What they really meant, was that the whole thing was much too risky a proposition."

Tetley realized that if he wanted to enter the race he would have to sail the family yacht, just as Knox-Johnston had done. "But how would she stand up to the wild Southern Ocean?" he wondered. No multihull had ever been through the 14,000 miles of the Roaring Forties before. Could the *Victress* do it? He would find out.

> The days of speculation and indecision were over [wrote Tetley]. I notified *The Sunday Times* of my entry. Some financial help would

still be needed if *Victress* was to get all the equipment she needed. How I disliked the thought of publicity. If only one could complete the voyage without anyone knowing until it was all over: to be remembered as a seaman, not a conquering hero. As every sailor knows, the sea can never be conquered, merely held at bay. But sponsorship would only come through accepting publicity. If one took money, one should give a fair return. . . .

During the week, Michael Moynihan came down to interview me for *The Sunday Times*. He was racking his brains for a likely sponsor and when I demonstrated *Victress*'s stereo system, he immediately hit on the idea of a record company. I was delighted at the prospect. That weekend *The Sunday Times* printed an article under the title "Around the World in 80 Symphonies." It showed a picture of Eve and me seated in the cabin, drinking beer and laughing our heads off. Bob Salmon, the photographer, was very good at making us laugh.

Unknown to us at the time, Richard Baldwyn, a director of Music for Pleasure, was returning by air from the south of France and, as the aeroplane was about to land, had just read the piece in the paper. Suddenly the captain announced there was some doubt whether the wheels would go down. While their fate hung in the balance, he made a silent vow that if the plane landed safely, he would help with the venture. The next morning, Terry Bartram of Music for Pleasure telephoned me at Naval Headquarters at Plymouth. Could he come down? Tomorrow? Certainly! This sounded like real efficiency. In the afternoon a telegram arrived from a rival company. Publicity was showing results: the sponsors were biting.

Tetley had worked out an arrangement for downwind self-steering using twin headsails held out on long poles led from the foredeck. He immediately hired an expert machinist to build a mechanical self-steering unit as well. Tetley strengthened the masthead fitting on the mainmast and installed additional rigging. Meanwhile Eve studied books on diet and food and began to load stores aboard *Victress*. In addition to helping pay some of the bills, the Music for Pleasure people made sure that Tetley had plenty of music for the yacht's sound system. No matter what happened, there would be music for every mood: stirring marches for the morning, chamber music at noon, string quartets in the afternoon, symphonies for the evening, plus a variety of singers, Scots balladeers, flute concertos—a little of everything.

Just before Tetley's departure on September 16th, a report came in from *Suhaili*, the leader in the race. No longer did Robin Knox-Johnston have time to play chess by radio or while away the hours singing songs from Gilbert and Sullivan. He had been in a frightful storm off the Cape of Good Hope and there had been some damage. The merchant navy captain had made repairs, however, and was continuing eastward into the Indian Ocean.

"Robin's radioed report appeared in *The Sunday Mirror*. He said that throughout his service in the Merchant Navy he had never seen such seas," quoted Tetley. "Even allowing for press embellishment, the experience sounded hair-raising and I wondered what madness I had let myself in for."

Nigel Tetley's departure was a little more emotional than he had planned.

> As *Victress* headed for Plymouth Sound the knot of small craft fell back on either side. I was in luck, a fair wind blew from the north, wafting the trimaran down harbour like some stately queen attended by her courtiers. It felt strange to find her the centre of attention, though in the splendour of her new paint I knew she deserved it. I had one of Music for Pleasure's brass band records playing over the wheelhouse speaker, and I must have been unconsciously beating out the time, for I could see Eve, in a small boat near by, copying me. Just then, the music changed to a slow soulful passage, my eyes blurred and the sobs came; I could not look at the club launch for several minutes. What had I to feel sorry about? It was Eve whom I had condemned to long months of loneliness and waiting. And there she was, standing up bravely in the bows of the open boat. "Come back soon!" she called as the launch, unable to keep up, turned away. Mustering all the confidence I could, I cried, "I will!"

As Tetley cleared England he began to hurry south in the Atlantic in hot pursuit of the four men ahead of him. According to his studies of the pilot charts, the winds during the months he had selected for his voyage were more favorable for running and reaching, which would mean high speeds for the spidery, three-hulled trimaran. Tetley was far behind the leaders; he was confident, however, that he would win the race.

5 ~

Different Captains

I<small>T WAS ALREADY THE MIDDLE OF SEPTEMBER.</small>
Donald Crowhurst and Alex Carozzo were still struggling to get out of the boatyards and away on their mission before the October 31st deadline. Meanwhile the sailors already at sea were sailing as hard as they could.

Of all the competitors in the race, the Frenchman, Bernard Moitessier, was the great romantic. In temperament, he was a violinist who drew his bow hard across a tuneful ocean. Moitessier listened to the flute calls of the wind, the bassoon notes of the waves, and the rhythmic snare drumming of water slapping along the sides of the hull. To him, the ocean and the sailing life made up a wonderful symphony filled with dreams and delight.

> All *Joshua* and I wanted was to be left alone with ourselves [wrote Moitessier]. Any other thing did not exist, had never existed. You do not ask a tame seagull why it needs to disappear from time to time toward the open sea. It goes, that's all, and it is as simple as a ray of sunshine, as normal as the blue of the sky. . . .
>
> The wake stretches on and on, white and dense with life by day, luminous by night, like long tresses of dreams and stars. Water runs along the hull and rumbles or sings or rustles, depending on the wind, depending on the sky, depending on whether the sun was setting red or grey. For many days it has been red, and the wind hums in the rigging, makes a halyard tap against the mast at times, passes over the sails like a caress and goes on its way to the west, toward Madeira, as *Joshua* rushes to the south in the trade wind. . . .
>
> Wind, sea, boat, and sails, a compact, diffuse whole, without be-

ginning or end, a part and all of the universe . . . my own universe,
truly mine.

I watch the sun set and inhale the breath of the open sea. I feel my
being blossoming and my joy soars so high that nothing can disturb it.
The other questions, the ones that used to bother me at times, do not
weigh anything before the immensity of a wake so close to the sky
and filled with the wind of the sea.

All the contestants except Moitessier and Fougeron, the two Frenchmen, carried radios to keep in touch with the rest of the world. Most
people in a ten-month race would want news from home once in a while.
In addition, the contestants might wish to send messages to their families or sponsors. Certainly the men in the race would want to know how
they were doing in relation to one another. This would mean occasional
transmissions. Moitessier and Fougeron, aboard *Joshua* and *Captain
Browne*, refused to take radios.

"The big cumbersome contraptions were not welcome," said Moitessier. "Our peace of mind, and thereby our safety, was more important,
so we preferred not to accept them." Moitessier was a virtuoso with a
slingshot, however, and had agreed to shoot an occasional message and
a few rolls of exposed film to big ships when they passed close to him.
"A good slingshot is worth all the transmitters in the world!" he said.
"And it is so much better to shift for yourself, with the two hands God
gave you and a pair of elastic bands."

In spite of his fierce independence, however, Moitessier sometimes
relented when he thought of his wife.

> September 1. We meet a ship early in the morning. I get out my
> mirror, and she answers with an Aldis lamp. She has understood and
> will radio my position to Lloyds. Françoise will know that all's well;
> I'm happy—right off, my day is made.
>
> Feeling great, I go below to finish my mug of coffee; glancing out
> the hatch, what do I see . . . the ship coming back! She has made a big
> circle (I can see her wake on the calm water) and is bearing down on
> me from astern. Wow! I get pretty rattled . . . She comes by about fif-
> teen yards off, towering like a wall far above my masts. The ship is
> enormous; she must be well over 300 feet long. When the bridge
> draws abreast, an officer shouts through a megaphone, "We will report
> you to Lloyds. Do you need anything?"
>
> I wave "No" with my hand, my throat is so tight. The monster

takes forever to go by; I pull the helm all the way over to get clear, afraid she would wobble in her course and sweep both my masts away. But the captain of the *Selma Dan* has a good eye and knows what he is doing. I have cold sweats just the same, and my legs feel like rubber. At this range I could pelt the bridge with my slingshot, but there was no time to prepare a message. And I dare not try to get them to understand by signaling: they are so nice they would turn around and come back. I have had enough thrills for one day, and I know someone who is not about to take on any more ships with his mirror for a while.

Little by little the Frenchman—with the advantage of his long experience—gained on those ahead.

The average speed climbs day after day, on a sea full of sun [wrote Moitessier]. I am glad to see that *Joshua* sails definitely faster than before. This improvement is largely because she is much lighter. Also, the longitudinal weight distribution is far better; she is less loaded down with useless gear, and I was able to completely clear out the forward and aft compartments. In the old days, we had two dismantled dinghies in the forepeak, one dead and the other useless, not to mention an incredible pile of junk collected over the years. When in Plymouth, I unloaded the engine, anchor winch, dinghy, all unnecessary charts, a suitcase full of books and *Sailing Directions* that did not cover my route, four anchors, 55 pounds of spare zinc anodes, 900 pounds of chain, most of the ¾″ diameter line, and all the paint (275 pounds!) after splashing a last coat on deck and topsides. . . . Naturally, I did not completely disinherit myself, in spite of cutting to the bone. Though I kept a strict minimum of charts, they covered all possible landfalls around Good Hope, Australia, Tasmania, the northern and southern islands of New Zealand, the Horn waters with parts of the Patagonia channels, and even a few atolls in the Pacific. . . .

Continued fair weather, but very little wind. The speed is still impressive, as *Joshua* can carry more than 1,560 sq. ft. of canvas. I rigged a 54 sq. ft. storm jib as a bonnet under the main boom, in addition to the genoa bonnet, and a lightweight 75 sq. ft. storm jib as a second staysail. The sea is calm; my rig picks up the slightest breeze. I watch the boat slipping along at nearly 7 knots on a smooth sea in the setting sun. What peace! Two weeks already, and a daily average of 143 miles since Plymouth. . . .

The wake stretches on and on. The Canaries are now astern, the

Cape Verde islands on the right, Africa to the left. Flying fish hunted by the dorados glide in big schools in front of the boat. At times a beautiful rainbow plays with the foam of the bow wave. I film it, securely wedged on the bowsprit pulpit.

The doldrums are fairly close now. It is a zone of calms and light variable winds, with rain and squalls, caused by the meeting of the two trade wind belts near the equator. At the latitude of the Cape Verde Islands, the doldrums stretch approximately between the 15th and the 5th parallel north, or about 600 miles.

For the big square-rigged vessels of old, the doldrums meant long, exhausting days handling the heavy yards in the damp heat under a leaden sky, taking advantage of the least shift in the wind, continually coming about. For our small yachts, the doldrums are annoying but nothing more, since coming about is easy; the zone should normally be crossed fairly quickly. Just the same, a sailor will always take on the doldrums with an uneasy conscience. I wonder where my friends will cross? I have not quite settled on a course to the left or right of the Cape Verde Islands.

Joshua has been dragging along for days that feel like weeks. When the breeze drops completely, I have to sheet everything flat and drop the 650 sq. ft. genoa-bonnet combination which would chafe too much, slatting against the staysail stay as the boat rolls. Every time the inconsistent breeze picks up, the genoa has to be raised again and the sheets trimmed to the inch to catch the faintest puff, to sail south at all cost. . . .

On a trip this long, every drop of fresh water is a gift from the heavens. I left Plymouth with enough water to reach New Zealand, though, and will have a dozen opportunities to top up my tank between here and Tasmania. Just the same, I collected 15 gallons yesterday and today, with a bucket rigged under the mainmast gooseneck.

WHILE MOITESSIER WAS patiently sailing through the fitful winds of the doldrums on *Joshua*, another yacht was close behind. It was Bill King aboard *Galway Blazer II*. Both King and Moitessier were consummate small-boat sailors. Both had distinctive yachts, and both had left Plymouth within twenty-four hours of each other. Each of the two men was thin, wiry, intense, and full of nervous energy, yet the two sailors were galaxies apart in temperament, habits, background, and equipment.

The vessel of each man reflected his personality: Moitessier's yacht was strong, well-equipped, powerful, and entirely adequate. Fully stored for the trip she displaced about 12 tons. Yet she was rough, without electricity, crude in fittings and finish, with a studied emphasis on practicality rather than fanciness. Like an earlier famous voyaging yacht named *Tzu Hang*, *Joshua's* hull was painted bright red. She had the feel of distant oceans about her and looked comfortable on the water, as if she belonged there, a true workboat of the sea.

King's vessel was also strong and well equipped, yet she was more graceful than powerful in appearance. Her 4½-ton displacement was less than half the weight of *Joshua*. *Galway Blazer II* had the latest electronic instruments, a life raft, a long-distance radio, and the finest self-steering gear. Her interior furniture was nicely designed and built. There was a large comfortable chair with a seat belt, and King's bed was a swinging cot that pivoted along its fore-and-aft axis and could be locked at any angle of heel. *Galway Blazer II* had a glass-smooth finish and impeccable paint and varnish that befitted a proper yacht. She was elegant, yet somehow the gray-and-white vessel had an aura of daintiness, more a perfection of detail than of a solid, unified small vessel.

It was the ballerina versus the stevedore.

Even the rigs of the two yachts were different. Moitessier had a well-tried lofty ketch rig with conventional solid wooden masts that were massively stayed in place with a forest of wires. Each of the heavy wire shrouds and stays was oversize and strongly fastened to the steel deck. The rig was thoroughly conventional, and every aspect of its handling had been practiced and perfected by seamen for generations. With its multiplicity of halyards, sheets, pendants, outhauls, shrouds, stays, preventers, guys, stropped blocks, and other rigging, *Joshua* looked a little like a tea clipper coming from China in an old nautical painting.

King, meanwhile, was sailing southward with an entirely different rig. *Galway Blazer II* had two large-diameter hollow spruce masts on each of which was fitted a fan-shaped Chinese lugsail—a roughly rectangular sail supported by six full-length horizontal battens whose after ends held the controlling sheets that were led to the cockpit area. The forward part of each sail lay along its mast, which was freestanding, without support wires of any kind. Without stays and shrouds, the sails could be eased right ahead for downwind sailing.

The performance of the lugsail rig was outstanding across the wind and with the wind. Against the wind, the performance was mediocre; in the doldrums and light airs, the sailing ability was poor because of the limited sail area. King could have carried large staysails of light cloth to have dealt with this problem, but it was a complication and might have subjected the masts to unfair loads in squalls.

GALWAY BLAZER II

Yet *Galway Blazer II*'s sail arrangement had the significant advantage that it could be easily shortened from the safety of an inside position. Even better, there was no sail changing at all. The yacht had two circular control hatches protected by spray hoods. All King had to do to adjust the sails was to poke his head out and to haul on or ease a few lines. The arrangement must have reminded King of his days as a submarine commander because controlling the yacht from the deck hatch was a little like running a submarine from a conning tower.

While *Galway Blazer II*'s rig had great handling abilities for ordinary sailing, such unstayed mast arrangements had never been tested in the severe weather of the Southern Ocean. King had prepared for the worst by fitting an emergency bipod mast arrangement, which was kept on deck.

Once at sea, King showed that he was no idler and was soon averaging 150 miles a day. On August 26th, near the coast of Spain, *Galway Blazer II* logged 188 miles in twenty-four hours with a fair northeast wind. Unfortunately, King had problems with the Chinese rig, whose 14-foot fiberglass battens began to break. He was obliged to sail under the foresail alone while he handed the mainsail, extracted the broken battens, and put in spare stiffeners made of hickory. Little by little King made adjustments to the Chinese rig, which he found both exasperating and marvelous in turn. The unconventional sail plan wasn't nearly as close-winded as her competitors, but King's yacht moved superbly at an angle of 65 degrees off the wind.

As befitted an old salt, King gradually succumbed to the spell of the

BILL KING

sea. "I fell into the wonderful basic routine of living as a sea creature with nothing between me and the sky and the depths, with only the sun and stars to guide me," he said in a glowing moment.

King was a slender, spare man with a deeply tanned face and a halo of silver hair. He looked more like a college professor or a clergyman than a world-circling sailor. He was a vegetarian who ate sparingly. No cases of preserved meat or whiskey or brandy went with him. Years before he had made a sailing trip across the Atlantic and had lived on soaked raisins, almond nut paste for protein, whole-wheat biscuits, and cress grown in jars for vitamin C.

"Never had I felt better than after twenty-three days of this carefully balanced diet," he said, "and I was sure it would suffice me for a year if necessary. Flying fish always add themselves to the menu in tropical waters. I would take no medicines and only one large tin of instant coffee to use as a stimulant when I must not sleep."

Throughout the northeast trades, King often logged 160 miles a day. But when he left the welcome fair wind and entered the doldrums, his Chinese rig was slow and underpowered. In the poky and unsteady winds, he could make only 40 miles a day. King gradually slatted his way south toward the wind belt of the southeast trade wind, which began 300 miles north of the equator at his longitude. But it wasn't until September 27th that King again found a good sailing wind.

"Today as the sun got up we came into the true trade winds," he wrote. "Their chief herald was the lovely sky; long French-bread, roly-poly, floccular clouds, replacing solemn menacing piled-up blackness, and a nice steady wind enabling me to set course for the next point."

Sometimes King wondered about himself.

> After the morning chores, I tried to rationalize my various anxieties [King wrote]. Up to now they have been entirely connected with the feeling that I could never get my boat ready this summer. Now, of course, I am beset by other bogies. Why have I undertaken this venture? To sort of teach myself a lesson? I do not experience either a fear of death or dejection at the prospect of spending eight or nine months alone; but I do have a choking fear of failing to be able to cope with the possible situations which may arise. Things will be going wrong from now on, things I did not think of in time, and which now must be put right by myself.

King said that he undertook this long voyage to purge himself of a portion of his past. He wanted to be healed of the terrible mental scars inflicted by the war during the six years that he had spent as a submarine commander—an experience that most of his fellow submariners did not survive. During World War II he had lived half his life submerged. The worst months were the patrols up and down the Norwegian coast during the summer of 1940, when the long days and short nights meant that King's submarine had to keep submerged eighteen hours out of twenty-four. "At the end of those eighteen-hour dives, the air became so deficient in oxygen that our breath came in heavy gasps," he wrote.

Fortunately life on board *Galway Blazer II* wasn't all grimness and introspection. King often looked out of the yacht and away from his black memories and was thrilled by the beauty around him.

> Last night the fresh trade wind slackened [King wrote], and instead of spurting and scooting off the wave crests, we sailed serenely on under a star-spread sky. I sat riveted by the beauty of it for hours; the mast wheeling against the veil of the Milky Way, the apex of our universe. How tiny we seem when one becomes aware of the immensity of the firmament. How much more aware one is in a little boat on a wide sea under a jeweled darkness.

King had the bad luck to accidentally burn his hands with acid while servicing the yacht's batteries. Later he fell and bruised his ribs on the cockpit coaming. These mishaps reminded King how slight the margin of error was in personal accidents for an adventurer on an extended trip. An injured sailor would not be able to guide his ship across an ocean.

> This evening I learnt that Bernard Moitessier has worked out a big lead [King wrote]. This, of course, must be a great disappointment to me and destroy my peace of mind. I built this boat specifically to pioneer this trip, not for ocean racing. When it transpired that a race was on, there was nothing else to do but to join it, but now I have to realize I have little chance of winning it. Already I face the same sort of emotional situation that must have faced Scott when Amundsen reached the South Pole first, or the earlier Everest Expedition which did not quite make it, after superhuman efforts. This sort of thing is a test and discipline of one's character which must be faced, but I did not set out to test my character. I just wanted to achieve a terrific new experience and forget six ugly years spent fighting *under* the sea.
>
> I cannot *drive Galway Blazer* against faster boats. I will plod on around the world, reveling in my boat's special poetic beauty, in her strength and power. I will put disappointment from me—but I wish now I had no radio contact. Much as I like Mike [King's newspaper radio correspondent], family, and value news, I would rather be alone and immersed in the job.

6~
The Late Starters

On SEPTEMBER 21ST, THE FIRST DAY OF SPRING IN THE southern Hemisphere, five of the nine entrants in the race were sailing southward in the Atlantic. The leader, Robin Knox-Johnston, had already turned east and was south of the Cape of Good Hope, at the southern tip of Africa. Moitessier was nearing tiny Ilha da Trindade at 20 degrees south latitude, some 600 miles east of the Brazilian coast. Ilha da Trindade and Ilhas Martin Vaz are two small islands in the South Atlantic. The islands are owned by Brazil and have Portuguese names. Trindade is often confused with the island of Trinidad in the Caribbean. To further complicate the terminology, at one time Ilha da Trindade was called Trinidade and is so indicated on old charts. In this book, I will use modern names and spellings as far as possible.

Loïck Fougeron and Bill King were both still slatting their way through the frustrating dead-air region between the northeast and southeast trade wind zones near the equator. Nigel Tetley had just left England in his speedy bluc trimaran, *Victress*.

John Ridgway and Chay Blyth were both out of the race, one because of damage and the second because he was disqualified for breaking the rules.

The last two men—numbers eight and nine—had not left England. The Italian, Alex Carozzo, was madly working on his enormous 66-foot ketch. In just two days, on September 23rd, Donald Crowhurst was to launch his Victress trimaran, which had been named *Teignmouth Electron*.

The name "Teignmouth" (pronounced TIN-muth) had come from Rodney Hallworth, Crowhurst's publicity agent, who was also the public relations man for the town of Teignmouth, a summer resort of 13,000 people located in Devonshire on the southwest coast of England. Crowhurst's home was nearby, and Hallworth proposed that if the yacht were named Teignmouth and if Crowhurst started his voyage from there and agreed to mention the place as often as he could, Hallworth would start a £1,500 fund-raising campaign. Crowhurst's company was Electron Utilisation, so Hallworth and Crowhurst decided on the name *Teignmouth Electron*.

In truth the naming of Crowhurst's new vessel was not very important because it was doubtful whether she would get away before the October 31st deadline. The original launching date of August 31st had come and gone, as had the "final" date of September 12th. In spite of Eastwoods' efforts of a seventy-hour workweek plus a night shift, the yacht simply wasn't ready. Crowhurst wrote Eastwoods a stern letter.

"The entire project is now in jeopardy," he said in part, and set September 23rd as the absolute last date for getting into the water.

Eastwoods countered with a bill for £900 for Crowhurst's continuing alterations and demanded that all other arrears be settled as well. Another volcano erupted over the fiberglass deck sheathing called for in the design. Eastwoods said there was no time. Crowhurst fumed. He argued that the fiberglass was necessary and was part of the contract. Eastwoods rejoined that painting was good enough because the deck thickness had been doubled at Crowhurst's insistence. The yard tried to telephone Crowhurst about the matter, but he was away. The painting had already begun, and if he wanted to launch on September 23rd. . . .

According to Nicholas Tomalin and Ron Hall, Crowhurst's biographers, it was a time of acute crisis.

> That night, with Donald Crowhurst in an angry, unhappy mood, was the only time during the entire venture when Clare [his wife] pleaded with him to refuse delivery of the boat and give up the project [wrote his biographers]. Somewhat to her surprise, he seriously considered her arguments. "I suppose you're right," he said, "but the whole thing has become too important for me. I've got to go through with it, even if I have to build the boat myself on the way round." Later Clare felt she had put her case too strongly because after this Donald became more secretive about the further difficulties that arose. And there were many more of those.

When *Teignmouth Electron* was finally launched on September 23rd, it was Clare Crowhurst who made the christening remarks and swung the traditional bottle of champagne against the bow. Unfortunately, the bottle didn't break. The builder had to step in behind her and help finish the christening and try to laugh off the bad luck omen.

The builder's yard was in Norfolk in the east of England facing the North Sea. Crowhurst and the crew were to sail the sleek new Victress trimaran to Teignmouth on England's southwest coast facing the English Channel, a distance of 325 miles. By the time the yacht was rigged and various squabbles with the yard had been settled, however, it was already September 30th. Crowhurst and his two crewmen hurriedly sailed into the North Sea and shaped a course south for the Strait of Dover.

Crowhurst soon became violently seasick in the ocean swell but gamely steered as *Teignmouth Electron* streaked south with a fair wind. The three men on board calculated that they would be in Teignmouth in three days. Unfortunately, the wind changed, the contrary tidal streams were strong, and the Victress trimaran—an abysmal performer to windward—scarcely made any progress at all. Crowhurst began to tack back and forth across the English Channel and even used the trimaran's outboard motor at times. Nevertheless, after seventy-two hours of steady sailing and a great deal of back-and-forth work, the vessel had made scant progress toward Teignmouth. Indeed, she was just a little west of Boulogne, France, scarcely 40 percent of her goal.

Crowhurst was puzzled and angry and began experimenting with small and large sails, hoping to find combinations that were more effective. Peter Beard, one of the two crew members, asked Crowhurst whether this sort of sailing performance was really adequate for ocean passages—especially the difficult work of coping with big seas and strong winds.

In an astonishing reply, Crowhurst told Beard that the question was academic because during the round-the-world race the winds would always be behind him and fair.

Beard asked what would happen when the winds were against *Teignmouth Electron;* what would the captain do?

> "Well, one could always shuttle around in the South Atlantic for a few months," said Crowhurst. "There are places out of the shipping lanes where no one would ever spot a boat like this." Then he took Beard's logbook to show him how it could be done. He drew Africa, and South America. He placed two small triangles between them to represent the Falkland Islands and Tristan da Cunha. With his pencil he lightly traced a lozenge-shaped course, round and round, between the two. It would be simple, he said, no one would ever find out.

Crowhurst laughed: it was obviously a joke. The diagram is still in
Peter Beard's logbook.

It took four days to reach Newhaven on the Sussex coast halfway to
Teignmouth. Crowhurst's crew had allowed only three days for the entire trip and had other commitments, so Donald telephoned the builder
and asked for a replacement crew. Meanwhile a southwest gale thundered up the English Channel, and the wind howled in Newhaven.
Crowhurst fumed and paced the floor of a waterfront bar.

Already he was into the first week of October. The race deadline was
only three weeks away. He should have been in Teignmouth long before
attending to dozens of large and small modifications. Certainly all his
stores, tools, radios, and electronic gear should have been on board.
Crowhurst should have been chasing the contestants who were far south
in the Atlantic, and in particular Knox-Johnston, who was already in the
Indian Ocean.

Finally the new crew members arrived, but the foul weather raged
for another two days. It then took an additional forty-eight hours to sail
50 miles to the Isle of Wight, where the new crewmen promptly quit. It
was here that Crowhurst met Alex Carozzo, the Italian who was in the
race. Both men had the parallel problems of feverish, almost hopeless,
preparation difficulties. They commiserated with each other and inspected each other's yachts.

Their meeting was a bit like Alain Gerbault and Harry Pidgeon, two
early world-circling small-boat sailors, who in 1925 met each other in
Panama. There, in steaming Balboa, on the shore of the Pacific, each
man looked at the other's vessel with interest and curiosity but returned
to his own yacht, which he much preferred above the other.

Crowhurst managed to recruit an expert local sailor and began bashing into the westerly winds again. After thirty-six hours, the wind direction finally changed and the trimaran soon finished the remaining 80
miles to Teignmouth, sometimes reaching 12 knots.

It was now October 15th. The three-day delivery had taken an unbelievable thirteen days. Instead of a planned average of 108 miles per
day, the average had dropped to 25! Not a good portent.

Crowhurst hoped that his problems would be over once he got to
Teignmouth and back to the resources of his family, friends, home, and
business. Hallworth's fund-raising had lagged (only £250 so far toward
the goal of £1,500), but his publicity was good and had attracted some
encouraging support among the leaders of the community. However,

there was an element of skepticism and mocking doubt among the waterfront locals who always laughed at anything new and different.

The boatyard pulled *Teignmouth Electron* out of the water, and carpenters started to work on a number of projects that either had not been completed or needed changes. Unlike Tetley's Victress trimaran, whose cockpit was covered by an enclosed wheelhouse, Crowhurst's cockpit was open. During normal ocean sailing, a good deal of water flew around, and the cockpit got spray from time to time plus an occasional wave top. A leak in Crowhurst's cockpit was particularly bad because the precious electric generator was underneath; if the generator failed, there would be no power for lights, radios, and the electronic devices.

Crowhurst had hoped to use radios that he built himself, but there was no time for proper certification, so he had to purchase commercial radio equipment. The installation of the antennas and groundplates was complicated and required specialists. Lists of food stores for 300 days plus emergency rations for another 120 days had to be drawn up and bought. Many of the food items were difficult to find in the half-closed summer resort area. Crowhurst's requirements included tools and parts for the electronic equipment, which hadn't been constructed yet. With time so short he intended to take along all the components and to build what he needed while under way. Every morning there were long shopping lists; people rushed off in all directions to stores and supply houses.

Crowhurst needed drill bits, solder, shackles, spare line, sail needles, rubber sheeting, gasoline cans, water jugs, oilskin patching kits, bedding compound, and signaling flags. He sent people to buy charts, navigation tables, nautical almanacs, light lists, logbooks, tidal tables, pilot books, and pencils. He bought underwear, woolen clothing, sea boots, watch caps, and warm gloves. The lists included copper tubing, plumbing fittings, hacksaw blades, black tape, bottles of aspirin, and toothbrushes. Yet it seemed that for every item bought and crossed off the shopping lists, two more things were added.

Workmen bolted a brace to the self-steering gear to strengthen its mounting, which had been plagued by vibration troubles at high speed. The special masthead buoyancy bag (deflated) was lashed aloft.

Crowhurst's efforts were newsworthy, so reporters scurried around town interviewing people and asking a lot of nosy questions. Television cameramen filmed the beamy, white-hulled *Teignmouth Electron*, while workers and technicians sawed, filed, welded, pounded, and painted. The cameras whirred and the BBC interviewers asked Crowhurst leading questions. At first Crowhurst cooperated and even delighted in giving cocky, exaggerated responses.

> Talking to yourself is very important [he said]. When one has been awake for a couple days, soaking wet and perhaps hadn't had enough to eat . . . you can restore a sense of urgency by telling yourself what the consequences of your lack of attention are. . . . This is a tremendous help because the very process of speaking, forming the words, helps to crystallise one's thoughts in a way that no mere process of thought can ever do.

Donald Kerr, the BBC announcer, asked Crowhurst whether he had ever been in a situation in which he thought he was going to drown.

> There was an occasion on the South Coast [said Crowhurst]. I was sailing with a following wind . . . blowing about force seven [a moderate gale with winds of 28–33 knots]. The boat was set up for self-steering and I must have been about twenty miles from shore. There were no guard rails, and I didn't have a safety harness—and I fell overboard. I thought, as the boat sailed on that I was either going to drown or else I was in for a very long swim. I realised of course that it was entirely my own fault and I didn't waste any time blaming myself. I just made a mental note that this sort of practice had to be avoided in the future and got on with the thinking about what one had to do about it. I was very lucky on that occasion because my boat, in point of fact, came up into the wind. My self-steering arrangements had in fact relied on a little manual assistance from myself from time to time. . . . But she did sail on something like a quarter of a mile before coming up into the wind and it was quite long enough to give me a fright.

This incident was, of course, pure fantasy. Fortunately there was little time for such grandiose interviews. Crowhurst's time was short, and there was a lot to do. Expert small-boat sailors know that before a race or a sailing deadline, the captain must be at the yard every minute and be in charge of everything. He must see that the important jobs are completed, vital parts are installed, and that all systems (engine, sails, pumps, stoves, generators, etc.) are tested. The captain can do this only by enlisting the cooperation of everyone. When the men in a boatyard work *with* such a person and are on his side, good progress is possible. Otherwise, the situation is all downhill.

All hell broke out during those two weeks he was here [said some of the shipyard workers]. Everyone was trying to help, but nobody rightly knew what to do. As for Crowhurst, he didn't look the man to go at all. He hadn't an inkling where anything was, or what was happening. He didn't test nothing. He didn't stay with his boat, as a skipper ought to. He'd suddenly clear off for something, and we'd be wandering around trying to find him. If it wasn't some mysterious drive up to London, it was a wine-and-cheese publicity party up the Royal. That's no way to start off round the world.

You couldn't tell what was going on inside of him. He just wasn't integrated with us, if you know what that means. He was in a daze. We'd have admired him much more if he'd simply said, "I've lost me nerve. Let's drop the whole business." Obviously he was in a blind panic and didn't have the guts to call it off. So what if it made him bankrupt and penniless? Life is very sweet, brother, even without money, and even looking a fool.

And that boat of his! It was just bloody ridiculous. A right load of plywood it was. The attitude here was he couldn't get further than Brixham.

One man thought him determined, confident, and eager, but a bit disorganized. Another said that he was cheery and raring to go.

Crowhurst was "strange, not all there," recalled a third friend. "He had gone peculiarly quiet. It worried me. It was a mood I had never seen before. I knew Donald's explosive fits of temper, and I would have welcomed a familiar outburst or two; that would have meant he was trying to get things done. But in those last few days he seemed absolutely subdued, as if his mind was paralyzed."

A fourth man told him not to go. "You won't be ready in time," he said. Crowhurst replied: "It's too late. I can't turn back now."

During the sixteen days that Crowhurst was at Teignmouth, he grew increasingly tense, confused, and forgetful. He wasted time on trifles and neglected important jobs. He continued to write letters, for example, soliciting money when there was no chance of replies in time. One day his wife noticed that water was running out of one of the trimaran's floats when it was out of the water. This might have indicated a dangerous leak. The captain shrugged off the warning.

Crowhurst took *Teignmouth Electron* out for a few hours to try out new sails and to work out his downwind running arrangements. A BBC photographer and interviewer went along. Crowhurst seemed slow and clumsy and was exasperated when various pieces of hardware and hatch bedding proved unsatisfactory. The afternoon was a disappointment for everyone.

Two days later when the BBC people looked over the yacht again, nothing much had changed. The vessel still needed a great deal of fitting out. Stores and equipment were piled haphazardly on the decks. Mrs. Crowhurst—who had cracked one of her ribs when Donald had accidentally fallen against her—was varnishing eggs in a nearby shed. The BBC man no longer saw a news story about a challenging sporting event. The reporter detected signs of trouble and quietly changed his story line.

A water-filled float in a trimaran is particularly dangerous because it can lead to a loss of stability and perhaps cause a capsize. With three hulls, however, the big bilge-pumping arrangements are complicated. Generally a series of separate watertight compartments are built with a suction hose from each compartment leading to a selector valve, which is then connected to a pump. By changing the selector valve setting, each compartment can be pumped out in turn. In a trimaran the pumping system is often split into two halves, each served by a separate pump. *Teignmouth Electron* had two Henderson hand bilge pumps but lacked a vital connecting hose. After urgent calls, the manufacturer flew a piece of special noncollapsible hose to an airport near Teignmouth. In all the confusion, the hose never reached the yacht, although Crowhurst thought it had been put on board.

In addition, a great pile of important parts either got off-loaded from the trimaran, or was left behind on the slipway by mistake, or the parts may have been thrown out as rubbish. Mrs. Crowhurst put a bag of personal gifts for Donald on his bunk. The bag was later found on the slipway.

Finally, with only twenty-four hours to the race deadline, the BBC crew took pity on Crowhurst, stopped filming and recording, and began to help him directly. The newsmen hurried out to buy flares and life jackets. In the late afternoon, the BBC men dragged an exhausted and trembling Crowhurst to a restaurant for something to eat. "It's no good. It's no good," he kept mumbling.

Why didn't someone object to this nightmare scene and cry stop? Why didn't Crowhurst's sponsor tell Donald to give up? Why didn't a group of Crowhurst's friends take him aside? Why didn't Mrs. Crowhurst refuse to let her husband go? And finally, what about the race officials at *The Sunday Times?* Where were they? Or was their intention only to sell more newspapers? It's hard to believe that the executives of the newspaper could have been so misinformed or cynical.

Crowhurst seems to have been caught up in a great Ferris wheel of publicity. The wheel was turning, but no one had enough sense to throw the brake lever. Crowhurst certainly lacked proper sailing experience. His vessel was clearly untried and not ready. It was late in the year and bad weather might come at any time. The race was hazardous and intended mainly for professional seamen, a class of men that certainly did not include Donald Crowhurst.

Of the nine entrants in the race, five were professional sailors. Four were not, and it's perhaps predictable that those four were not strong contenders. It was the old salts who kept plugging away to the bitter end. In the future, the rules for solo distance sailing races would be drastically changed to require long qualifying trips in the intended vessel far in advance of the starting date. The vessel herself would have to adhere to safety rules and would be inspected closely. But in 1968, when such single-handed competitions were unknown, the sponsors had a free and easy attitude. If an entrant was foolhardy he had only himself to blame.

True to form, the competition was designed to sell newspapers by promoting an unusual race, a circulation scheme that was decades old. Recall the wager of Phileas Fogg in *Around the World in Eighty Days*. The zanier the race, the better. Within gentlemen's limits of course. But what were the limits? Who set the calipers?

Crowhurst had accepted sponsorship and press exposure. At his elbow he had a professional journalist pounding the drums of publicity and telling the world that his man would win. Perhaps Crowhurst was too proud and too much of a show-off to admit that he was foolish and stupid.

An Argentine once described a famous sailor from his country, a person with unbounded egotism, as "a man with a touch of vanity." This certainly applied to Crowhurst, who wasn't a bit shy when it came to claims for himself. Publicity acting upon vanity translates to acid dripping on thin metal. It takes an uncommonly strong man to combine the two elements, to hold up the resistance of common sense, the barrier of silent reserves, the reassurance of laughing at oneself. Crowhurst had none of these defenses.

His biographers talked at length with Mrs. Crowhurst about the last night in the hotel. It had been another endless, frustrating day. The Crowhursts didn't get to bed until two in the morning.

Donald lay silent beside Clare. After struggling for the right words, he finally said, in a very quiet voice: "Darling, I'm very disappointed in the boat. She's not right. I'm not prepared. If I leave with things in this hopeless state will you go out of your mind with worry?" Clare, in her turn, could only reply with another question. "If you give up now," she said, "will you be unhappy for the rest of your life?"

Donald did not answer, but started to cry. He wept until morning. During that last night he had less than five minutes' sleep. "I was such a fool!" says Clare Crowhurst now. "Such a stupid fool! With all the evidence in front of me, I still didn't realise Don was telling me he'd failed, and wanted me to stop him."

Late the next afternoon—October 31st—after a false start because the masthead buoyancy bag had been lashed over the sail halyards, which made it impossible to raise the sails—Donald Crowhurst waved good-bye to forty friends and the BBC on three motor vessels that accompanied the trimaran to the starting line. The gun was fired at 1652, and the captain of *Teignmouth Electron* steered out to sea, tacking into a wind from the south. He was soon out of sight with 30,000 miles to go.

ON THE SAME DAY, Alex Carozzo also left England. The last two months had been a marathon for the cocky Italian, but he had accomplished wonders. The Medina Yacht Company had somehow built Carozzo's huge 66-foot ketch in an incredible forty-nine days, and *Gancia Americano*, as she had been named, was launched on October 8th.

The giant two-master was flush-decked with a bold sheer, and chine-built of marine plywood sheathed with fiberglass. Carozzo had transplanted the sails and rigging from his catamaran, which he had put up for sale. The new yacht had two steel rudders, one for self-steering and the second for minor course corrections. Her most startling feature was a 36-inch centerboard in front of the vessel's 8-foot keel to help keep the ship on course while running before giant seas. A small cockpit served as the control center. The builder, Terry Compton, couldn't quite believe that his company had produced the enormous yacht in only seven weeks. Seven months would have been a more usual time.

"It's a bloody miracle," said Compton. "I don't know how we managed to do it. She's built like a battleship and is certainly as strong as any other boat in the race. It's unlikely now that she'll catch up all the others, but she should take the prize for the fastest time."

Carozzo, supremely confident, calculated that *Gancia Americano* could sail twice as fast as the other entries and would soon zip past the leaders. However, the exhausted Italian still faced the thorny problem of outfitting his jumbo entry for a voyage of six months or more and check-

ing that everything was installed properly and worked. He had made remarkable progress, but the October 31st deadline for leaving had finally
caught up with him.

The plucky sailor from Venice asked the race committee for permission to sail a few days late. The committee turned down his request, so
the Italian captain put all his sailing supplies and food on board *Gancia
Americano*. On October 31st he officially departed on the race, but
anchored a few hundred feet off Cowes, where he had a long sleep before beginning to sort and stow and check everything prior to his real
departure.

For better or worse, all the contestants had left England.

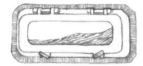

7~
What Do They Do All Day?

A SAILING YACHT IS DESIGNED TO BE STEERED BY A HUMAN hand, a hand that makes continuous small corrections as the wind shifts slightly and the vessel is pushed from side to side by wave action and water movements. If the helmsman lifts his hand from the tiller, and a reasonable balance of sails is set, a properly designed yacht will always head into the wind and stop. This design measure—weather helm—is important to safety in case the helmsman lets go of the tiller for any reason. The man on watch might need to deal with the sails during a squall. Or he might fall over the side. Then the tendency of the yacht to head into the wind and stop might save the helmsman's life.

Usually a yacht can be made to sail herself to windward if the tiller is pulled a little toward the wind and tied off. Self-steering across the wind or with the wind is more complicated, especially if the wind is strong and substantial seas are running. While it is possible to set downwind twin running sails and to lead the controlling lines—the sheets—to the tiller, these systems are cumbersome and require a good deal of trial and error and fine-tuning. A yacht with two masts and a number of separate sails has more potential self-steering adjustments.

The owners of model yachts sailing on a pond in a park have long been able to control their vessels by linking an air rudder—a sort of pivoting weather vane—to the ship's rudder. By adjustments to this wind blade, any course can be sailed. When this system is scaled up to an ocean-sailing yacht, however, it's soon apparent that a very large wind blade is needed in order to have sufficient force to steer a full-sized vessel. An obvious improvement was to design a device that would mechanically amplify the turning action on a small wind blade into a force with enough muscle to steer a 40- or 50-foot yacht.

A number of sailors worked on this problem in the 1950s and 1960s, led by a clever inventor named H. G. "Blondie" Hasler. Four of the entrants in the round-the-world race used Hasler self-steering devices. The other five sailors also had mechanical self-steering units, some made professionally and some cobbled together a few days before departure. Most of the units—then and now—relied to some extent on Hasler's brilliant invention, which has greatly expanded the sport of single-handed sailing.

This is not the place to describe the intricacies of self-steering devices, which involve shafts, paddles, linkages, pivots, bearings, blades, and so forth. What interests us is their *effect* on shorthanded sailing. A good unit means that the captain generally doesn't have to sit and steer his vessel at all. Once the gear is working properly, it will respond to every shift of wind. If the breeze is steady, the course will be steady too. The wind pilot functions on all points of sailing in both gales and zephyrs, in darkness and sunshine, in snow and clear weather. A good self-steering device seems almost human in its operation—except that it doesn't require coffee and sandwiches, periodic rests in bed, and aspirins during a storm.

Life at sea is a good deal more tolerable and pleasant when the captain is not the slave of the tiller; indeed, many of the owners of these mechanical helmsmen get so attached to their automatic friends that they give them pet names—Alfred, Columbus, George, Frankenstein, Picasso, and so on. Of course a lone sailor on board a yacht with a self-steering mechanism must be careful not to fall overboard because the vessel will continue to sail onward, with no one to bring her back to the man in the water.

A self-steering gear can guide a yacht all the way across the Pacific Ocean or the Bay of Biscay. Such a device can also steer a yacht directly into the shore, a sandbank, a reef, a lighthouse, or another vessel if the captain fails to keep a lookout and to adjust the mechanism from time to time. Around land and in shipping lanes the solo sailor must keep his eyes on the compass, other vessels, distant land forms, and lights and buoys every ten minutes or so. Out at sea and far from land and shipping, a single-hander can relax somewhat—enough to nap for an hour. Even with a self-steering gear, however, a person by himself has plenty to do.

"But what happens at night?"

Strangers to long-distance sailing can readily understand that a person can sail and cook and navigate during the day. However people who are unused to ocean sailing have trouble understanding what goes on at night. Many people think that a yacht stops at sunset each evening, the sails are lowered, an anchor is dropped, and the crew has dinner and goes to bed.

Not quite! If a vessel is to get anywhere in reasonable time, the yacht must be run on a twenty-four-hour basis. Sometimes one of these small ships is stopped in case of a severe storm, but this is unusual. Often during storms the wind is fair, which enables the yacht to make excellent mileage toward her goal.

In reality, sailing vessels—including all the romantic ships of history—are very slow movers. A 200-mile daily run was quite respectable for a clipper ship in the old days, a distance that modern passenger jet aircraft can do in less than twenty-five minutes. An average day for a 35-foot yacht at sea in all sorts of weather is much slower—say 95 to 110 or 120 nautical miles in twenty-four hours. An exceptional run might be 150, but there are also 50-mile days.

Knots (rate of speed per hour)	Nautical Miles per Day
2 knots × 24 equals	48
3	72
4	96
5	120
6	144
7	168
8	192

A second question people ask is: "What do those solitary seamen do out there all by themselves? How do they fight boredom? How do they pass the time?" Let's run through a typical twenty-four-hour period for a lone sailor far out at sea. Let's see what such a person actually does.

Midnight: Up to check around the horizon to make sure that the vane is steering OK. The yacht is some 15 degrees off course, so the captain changes the steering vane control line slightly and then watches the compass for ten minutes or so to verify the new setting. He then sits at the chart table for a few minutes and studies the course ruled on his chart. This suggests that he will pass about 35 miles to windward of an island to his south. The captain climbs up in the main hatchway and stands looking to the south, staring into the blackness of night, trying to see the island. He listens carefully for surf. He neither sees nor hears anything, so after a careful look in all directions he climbs down into the cabin and goes back to sleep.

0200: Up to look around again. The course is good and the wind is about the same—15 knots from the northeast. The barometer has dropped a little. The captain notes these things in the ship's logbook. He's hungry, so he primes the kerosene Primus stove with alcohol while he pumps a little water into the teakettle. This week the captain is on an herb tea kick, so after the kettle boils he makes tea and has a few crackers with strawberry jam. He switches on the radio receiver and listens to a woman announcer on one of the English language broadcasts from Radio Moscow. The woman is lambasting Australia on some obscure political issue. The captain concludes that government political broadcasts of all nations would be far more successful if they would play more music and lay off the hard political stuff.

The weather is a little cooler and the captain is glad to climb into his bunk again, where it's warm. Wait a minute! Back up again to turn on the 100-fathom depth sounder, which might show something in case the yacht is near one of the shallow banks around the island. Nothing shows on the depth sounder so back to the bunk and sleep.

0400: An easy night so far. The captain is about slept out, but the bunk is warm and pleasant. He bestirs himself and climbs up into the companionway. Hello, what's that? A light ahead and to the right, maybe 4 or 5 miles away. Probably a fishing boat from the island rising up and down on the ocean swells. He takes a compass bearing of the light (167 degrees) and writes it down. He should leave it well to starboard.

Soon it will be dawn. It's a good time for a round of star sights, but there's about 50 percent cloud cover so the captain decides to skip the morning stars and rely on sun sights later in the day, especially since there is plenty of sea room ahead. Our solo sailor walks around the deck and checks the sails and running rigging for chafe, shining a flashlight up and down as he walks with one hand sliding along a lifeline.

Hello, what's this? The lanyard from the cockpit bucket has fallen across one of the self-steering lines, gotten drawn into a small turning block, and half-sawed the vane line in two. The captain hunts up a piece of spare small line to replace the chafed line. While he is busy with the line, the yacht comes head to wind and the sails flap noisily. The sailor secures the new vane line, pulls the tiller hard over, and starts the vessel going again. It takes a few minutes to get back on course. The captain stuffs the bucket into a cockpit locker and resolves to keep odd lines away from the steering vane. It's incredible how two lines can rub each other to destruction in a few hours.

0600: Daylight and pink clouds in the east ahead. The wind is a bit fresher (northeast, 22 knots) and the yacht is overpowered a bit and would probably go just as fast with fewer sails. Is it worth the effort to change down further (there's one reef in the mainsail already) or should he wait? Maybe the wind will ease off. Might as well wait. The next sail change will be to the number three jib. Where is it? Under the saloon table or is it in the forepeak?

Time for a good breakfast in any case. Bacon and eggs, toast, and fresh coffee. Toast? No! The bread is covered with mold, so he'll have hot cereal instead. The captain lights the Primus stove, opens a can of Hungarian bacon, and peels off five slices. "I wonder what a pig farmer outside of Budapest would think if he saw his bacon being cooked here," muses the captain. While the bacon is frying, he looks out at the dawn and sees Venus low in the sky to the northeast. A good chance for a navigational fix if he combines it with a later sun shot.

The captain changes the course to the south a little, away from the wind so there won't be so much spray across the decks. He gets out his sextant and works his way along the port side deck to a spot clear of the shrouds. To overcome the up-and-down motion of the yacht as she rides over the ocean swells he wedges himself between a lifeline stanchion and the coachroof so that he'll be secure enough to use both hands for the sextant. The captain holds the sextant up to his eye and quickly adjusts the micrometer screw. When the shiny reflection of the planet just touches the horizon line on the lower mirror he glances at his watch, which is set to Greenwich time.

As he goes below and puts the instrument in its box he smells bacon. His frying pan has upset, and the bacon, grease, and eggs are all over the galley floor. What a mess! It never fails when he tries to do two jobs at the same time. At least he got a good shot of Venus. He writes the time and angle in the navigation workbook. He wipes up the galley floor with a piece of newspaper and starts breakfast all over again.

0800: Overcast and a steely look to the sea. No sun observations this morning. A little more wind. Oilskins and boots on. Number three jib to the foredeck. Number two down, unhanked, into a bag, and tossed below. Number three hanked on. One hank refuses to open; back to the cockpit shelf for pliers and the oil can. Finally the sail is up and drawing. A few storm petrels are nearby and dancing around above the water. It's marvelous to watch the tiny gray birds flitting just above the wake of the yacht. What can such delicate birds find to eat way out here? The yacht is going well and the motion is a bit easier now, so below and oil-skins off.

1000: The captain is at the chart table working out the observation of Venus. He takes a few figures from the *Nautical Almanac* and the navigation tables and makes some calculations. Then working from the 39th parallel of south latitude he draws a position line on the chart that comes out 7 miles from his dead-reckoning position. Not too bad, but he needs a second position line so he can cross the first and get a definite position fix. Maybe the sun will break through the clouds later.

Back to the current repair project, which is to overhaul the distance recording log. The problem is that both ball bearing assemblies on the revolving shaft are shot. There are some old spares, but they're corroded and rough. Maybe he can use one of the old bearings that's not too bad and combine it with the better of the new ones still in place. Plus lots of grease pushed in around the tiny balls. What a rotten bit of engineering to use plain steel instead of stainless steel. Too bad he didn't bring new bearings. Finally the distance recording log is back together. The captain attaches it to its bracket outside the port cockpit coaming and eases its little propeller over the side. Marvelous, it works. But for how long? The yacht is going at $5\frac{1}{2}$ knots according to the instrument. Enough tinkering for a while.

Then to his bunk and a book called *In the Company of Eagles* by Ernest K. Gann. Fascinating stuff about World War I flying. Richtofen and all that. The captain wonders how the Red Baron would have made out in a single-handed yacht at sea. Probably OK, but maybe not enough glory and medals and combat for him. There's plenty of open-cockpit flying in a yacht at sea though.

1200: Today is the captain's forty-fourth birthday. Out with a bottle of wine carefully saved and sheltered from breakage. The damned cork disintegrates when pulled. Cork fragments fly all over the galley. Cursed corks! The bottle was kept on its side so the cork was wet but it still came apart. The standards of everything are going down. Oh well, the wine is delicious. An ambitious spaghetti sauce simmers and fills the yacht with an aroma worthy of Naples. The sauce is excellent over spaghetti cooked so it's just chewy. A second helping empties both pots and fills the captain's stomach nicely.

Still no sun for a latitude shot. The skipper washes the dishes, pumping salt water into the galley sink and scrubbing the pots as the yacht bashes her way across the wrinkled surface of the sea. It's amazing how these small yachts can take such pounding day after day. No sense thinking about it because worrying won't help. The captain decides to have a good wash; he heats a little water, strips down, and has a sponge bath, spilling only half the water as the boat rolls. Talcum powder and fresh clothes feel great and are good for morale. The oilskins go back on, however, in case a boarding sea slops across the decks when he's outside. He can't afford to get his clean clothes wet with salt water on the first day.

1400: A small crisis. All the sleeping and eating and washing should have been a tip-off that things were too easy. The captain notices water on the cabin sole and pulls up a floorboard. The bilge is full of water! He immediately lays into one of the hand pumps and soon empties the bilge area. Where's the water coming in? From forward somewhere. The captain lifts up all the floorboards as he works his way toward the bow. The water is trickling in from the chain locker. The sailor hurries out on deck and goes forward.

Hooray! The leak is solved. The wooden plug that closes the access hole for the anchor cable has somehow come out and vanished. Every few minutes the foredeck is sprayed with water and some of this was finding its way below into the chain locker. It takes the captain half an hour to whittle a new tapered plug from a scrap of soft pine. He greases the plug and tamps it in place with a hammer. What a relief! Now the captain is all wet with sweat and spray.

1600: Oilskins off and into the bunk for a sleep. The hell with everything.

2000: Barometer up. The wind is lighter and now out of the north-northeast. Broken clouds and a bit of moonlight. The Southern Cross and Scorpius are just visible between the clouds, which periodically open and close. Gorgeous constellations. The compass course is terrible because the wind has changed and the vane has followed it around. The first thing is to decide the strength of the wind. Judging by the feel on the captain's face and the small whitecaps it is blowing about 17 knots. With a fair wind, however, the apparent wind will be less, say 12. The captain will have to change to the running rig. He takes over the helm, gets back on course, and adjusts the self-steering vane to the new wind.

He then shakes out the reef in the mainsail, eases the mainsheet, and ties the boom forward with a preventer line to the stem. Then he unhooks the spinnaker pole, adjusts its inboard end to shoulder height on the mast, and passes the jib sheet through the outer end of the pole. Back in the cockpit he eases the port jib sheet and takes in on the starboard sheet. Little by little the sail comes around to starboard side and fills with wind. Now both the eased mainsail and the poled-out jib are drawing nicely and the course is good.

The captain shines a flashlight on the sails and notices that the main-sail is rubbing on the port shrouds. He gets a small tackle out of the cockpit locker, walks forward on the port side, and hooks it between a deck fitting and the main boom. He pulls on the hauling part of the tackle, and the boom moves lower little by little, taking the sail away from the shrouds.

A large bird is flying behind the yacht, but it's too dark to identify the creature. The fair wind should be warmer, but it's definitely cooler. Where's the long underwear? Time for a few notes in the logbook.

2200: The compass course is still good to the east-southeast. The kerosene cabin lights are out and need filling. The captain gets a jug of kerosene from the bilge and tops up both the lamps and the Primus cooking stove.

Isn't it marvelous how the yacht goes on day after day? The important things seem to be to have a goal—something to look forward to, food to eat (not fancy, but wholesome, hot, and sufficient), and sleep (naps are OK, but they must add up to six to eight hours). One can get used to the interruptions.

Plus something to occupy the mind. It's best to read books about things other than sailing. Greek history is good, but those Greek names are impossible and the Greek heroes are always murdering one another. Was there a Greek mafia? James Bond is good but too fanciful and he has read all those books anyway. The captain goes to a wooden box in the forepeak and pulls out a silvery sphere. It's a thick-skinned orange wrapped in aluminum foil. The sailor strips off the foil, peels the orange, and slowly eats the juicy sections while he stands in the hatchway and looks out at the sea and stars. In spite of all the small problems of ocean voyaging, the captain knows no greater satisfaction and pleasure than taking his own vessel across the seas of the world. He takes a deep breath. The tiny yacht knifes her way through the long night.

We've gone through twenty-four hours. It's a new day!

8

Capsize

WHILE ALEX CAROZZO AND DONALD CROWHURST WERE STILL in England and frantically working to get away before the October 31st deadline, the leader in the race was far south in the Atlantic. On Robin Knox-Johnston's eighty-fourth day at sea, he was 700 miles southwest of the Cape of Good Hope, the southern tip of Africa. He had just crossed the 40th parallel of south latitude and had entered the Southern Ocean, that vast globe-circling expanse of cold water, strong and difficult wind systems, and circling albatrosses that lies north of the ice shelf of Antarctica.

Knox-Johnston planned to sail eastward along the 40th parallel all the way to Australia, but his north-south position depended entirely on the winds that he encountered. Since there was unlimited sea room, all he had to do was to keep his vessel going roughly eastward. On day eighty-four, *Suhaili* was at 42 degrees south, and she hurried along on an easterly heading under full sail with a fresh wind from the north.

Knox-Johnston had had good weather for the past few days. The barometer had begun to fall, however, and he knew that bad weather was coming, especially when he saw thin veiled clouds—mare's tails—high in the sky. Although he realized that it was crazy, Robin half wished for the first storm to appear. He wondered how he would get along in the enormity of the Southern Ocean, which reached right around the world south of Africa, Asia, Australia, and South America. He reckoned he would be in the Southern Ocean for four months or longer.

On September 5th, a shower of cold hail rattled on *Suhaili*'s deck, announcing the first storm. As the cold front overtook the yacht, the reading on the barometer suddenly rose 2 millibars; the wind shifted abruptly from the north to the west-southwest and increased to gale force. Knox-Johnston hurried on deck and made a drastic sail change.

He put three reefs in *Suhaili*'s mainsail, two reefs in the mizzen, and hoisted the storm jib in place of the working jib. After an adjustment for the new wind, the Admiral—Knox-Johnston's pet name for his self-steering gear—kept the yacht on an eastward course.

When wind blows across a stretch of ocean for many hours, seas build up and continue for a long time even if the wind dies away. The stronger the wind and the longer it blows, the bigger the seas—up to a point. If the wind is steady and, say, Force 5 (17 to 21 knots), the seas grow reasonably even and not too big, 2 meters or less in height. When a new weather system appears, however, the wind often switches around and blows from a different direction. The new wind begins to build up its own wave pattern, which interacts with the leftover wave train from the old wind. The new waves and the old waves generally slide into one another with some spray and slop and a bit of curling white water. As the old wave train dies out and the new train takes over, a regular pattern of seas from one direction becomes dominant.

With moderate winds, the interaction of overlapping swells is not too severe. The problem occurs when a strong wind from one direction is replaced by a fast-moving gale-force wind from a new direction. Then the old and new wave trains—both of which can be powerful—meet and intermingle over the course of many hours. This interaction occasionally results in large breaking waves from unexpected directions. Complicating this can be swells from a distant storm in a third direction, just enough to upset the first two. All old sailors know this game. You lie in your bunk listening to the big ones breaking out there and wondering if the next one has your name on it. You can go along for hours. Then suddenly a cross-sea or two or three can rise up and hammer the boat with cruel blows.

This is what happened to *Suhaili* on September 6th in the middle of the night. The wind switched from north to west-southwest and doubled in strength.

> The next thing I remember is being jerked awake by a mass of heavy objects falling on me and the knowledge that my world had turned on its side [wrote Knox-Johnston]. I lay for a moment trying to gather my wits to see what was wrong, but as it was pitch black outside and the lantern . . . had gone out, I had to rely on my senses to tell me what had happened. I started to try to climb out of my bunk, but the canvas which I had pulled over me for warmth was so weighted down that this was far from easy.
>
> As I got clear, *Suhaili* lurched upright and I was thrown off

balance and cannoned over to the other side of the cabin, accompanied by a mass of boxes, tools, tins and clothing which seemed to
think it was their duty to stay close to me. I got up again and climbed
through the debris and out onto the deck, half expecting that the masts
would be missing and that I should have to spend the rest of the night
fighting to keep the boat afloat. So convinced was I that this would be
the case that I had to look twice before I could believe that the masts
were still in place. It was then that I came across the first serious damage. The Admiral's port vane had been forced right over, so far in fact
that when I tried to move it I found that the stanchion was completely
buckled and the $\frac{5}{8}$-inch marine plywood of the vane had been split
down about 10 inches on the mizzen cap shroud. The whole thing was
completely jammed. Fortunately I was using the starboard vane at the
time, because I could not hope to try and effect repairs until I could
see, and the time was 2.50 a.m. It would not be light for another four
hours. *Suhaili* was back on course and seemed to be comfortable and I
could not make out anything else wrong; however, I worked my way
carefully forward, feeling for each piece of rigging and checking it
was still there and tight. I had almost gone completely round the boat
when another wave came smashing in and I had to hang on for my
life whilst the water boiled over me. This is what must have happened
before. Although the whole surface of the sea was confused as a result
of the cross-sea, now and again a larger than ordinary wave would
break through and knock my poor little boat right over. I decided to
alter course slightly so that the seas would be coming from each quarter and we would no longer have one coming in from the side, and
went aft to adjust the Admiral accordingly.

Having checked round the deck and rigging, and set *Suhaili* steering more comfortably, I went below and lit the lantern again. The
cabin was in an indescribable mess. Almost the entire contents of the
two starboard bunks had been thrown across onto the port side and the
deck was hidden by stores that had fallen back when the boat came
upright. Water seemed to be everywhere. I was sloshing around in it
between the galley and the radio as I surveyed the mess and I could
hear it crashing around in the engine room each time *Suhaili* rolled.
That seemed to give me my first job and I rigged up the pump and
pumped out the bilges. Over forty gallons had found its way into the
engine room and about fifteen more were in the main bilge, although
how it had all got in I did not know at the time. Doing a familiar and
necessary job helped to settle me again. Ever since I had got up I had
been in that nervous state when you never know if in the next minute

you are going to be hit hard for a second time. I could not really believe that the boat was still in one piece and, as far as I could see, undamaged. It's rather similar to when you uncover an ant nest. The exposed ants immediately wash their faces and this familiar task reassures them and prevents them panicking. Pumping the bilges was a familiar task to me and when it was completed I felt that I had the situation under control and set about tidying up quite calmly. The only real decision I had to make was where to start. I couldn't shift everything out of the cabin as there was nowhere else to put things, so I had to search for some large object amongst the mess, stow it away and then use the space vacated as a base. It was two hours before my bunk was cleared. I found books, films, stationery, clothes, fruit and tools all expertly mixed with my medical stores, and for days afterwards odd items kept appearing in the most out of the way places.

While straightening up, Knox-Johnston saw water dripping on the chart table in the after part of the cabin. He traced the path of the water and found cracks along the edge of the cabin, cracks that extended around the entire coachroof. Every time that water fell on deck, some of it ran into the cabin. Additionally, the captain soon discovered that the cabin bulkheads had been slightly shifted by the capsize.

The sight of this [wrote Knox-Johnston], and the realization that if we took many more waves over the boat the weakened cabin top might be washed away, gave me a sick feeling in the pit of my stomach. If the cabin top went it would leave a gaping hole 6 feet by 12 in the deck; I was 700 miles southwest of Cape Town and the Southern Ocean is no place for what would virtually be an open boat.

Some people would have sent out an SOS or Mayday and headed for land. Knox-Johnston was made of sterner stuff; he decided to see what he could do. After organizing the cabin stowage a bit, he looked into the engine room and found that the ship's batteries had broken away from their mountings during the capsize. He lashed the batteries in place, took a tot of whiskey, and turned in to sleep until daylight.

The next morning the gale was a little less strong and the seas more even. After a bowl of hot porridge, a cup of steaming coffee, and a cigarette, Knox-Johnston felt better. He got out his box of nuts and screws and managed to put some fastenings between the sides of the coachroof and the deck to strengthen the cabin somewhat and to close the cracks that were letting in water.

Traditional wooden boats with a cabin above the deck are often weak where the coachroof structure meets the deck. This is because the continuous athwartship deck beams are cut away to give headroom in the cabin below. To deal with this problem, naval architects call for vertical reinforcing rods down through the cabin sides, and horizontal rods to go between the outer edge of the deck and the bottoms of cabin sides. These bronze or stainless steel fastenings lock the whole deck and cabin structure together. Unfortunately, these rods are difficult and costly to install and are often omitted by builders ("we'll do it later") in spite of the designers' specifications. It was unfortunate that *Suhaili* lacked these reinforcements when she was capsized by a big wave.

Sometimes the frustrations of the voyage were small things but still maddening.

> I had just opened a new bottle of brandy for my evening drink [wrote Knox-Johnston], and having poured out a good measure I put the bottle on the spare bunk, jammed by the sextant box. About an hour later a strong smell of brandy began to invade the cabin and I eventually traced it to the newly opened bottle. The bottle was sealed by one of those metal screw caps, and as the boat rolled in the sea, the movement had slowly loosened the top until the contents could escape. I was furious about this. As my allowance was half a bottle of spirits a week I had lost two weeks' supply, but I consoled myself with the thought that I had at least taken that day's ration from it!

The men in the race often exhibited remarkable cleverness. One day Knox-Johnston needed to adjust the electric contact points on the magneto of his battery charger. He had no feeler gauge so he counted the pages of his diary. There were 200 to the inch so one page equaled $\frac{5}{1,000}$ or 0.005. Three pages equaled 0.015, the required gap.

Two days later the storm eased enough so that Knox-Johnston could repair his self-steering apparatus. Unlike the other contestants, *Suhaili*'s gear was divided into two parts, each identical and each located outboard of the cockpit on a spindly metal frame, one unit to port and the other to starboard. Each half could steer the yacht independently, depending on the wind. During the capsize, the port blade had split and the supporting framework had buckled. The captain had a spare stanchion for the vane and managed to mount it and to get the port steering gear into operation again.

Suhaili was lashed by five gales in ten days. It would have been easy to have stopped the vessel and waited for the disturbances to pass, but

Knox-Johnston wanted to keep going. Besides, the wind was fair and blew him toward Australia and New Zealand. The problem was a delicate balance between reducing sail too much and pressing on to the danger point. Going too fast risked a possible broach and capsize. Going too slow meant that he'd run out of supplies and never finish the race.

The motion in the 32-foot yacht was incredibly rough during the gales.

> I slept fully clothed, usually rolled up in the canvas on top of the polythene containers in the cabin [wrote the English captain]. As I would quickly get cramp in that position, I would then try sleeping sitting up. This would be all right for a bit, but sooner or later the boat would give a lurch and I would be picked up and thrown across the cabin. If I tried wedging myself in the bunk I could not get out so quickly in an emergency, and if the boat received a really big bang I would get thrown out of the bunk and across the cabin anyway.

Sometimes *Suhaili*'s master philosophized a bit. Why, he wondered, had he come on this voyage?

> The future does not look particularly bright [wrote Knox-Johnston], but sitting here being thrown about for the next 150 days . . . is not an exciting prospect. After four gales my hands are worn and cut about badly and . . . I have bruises all over from being thrown about. My skin itches from constant chafing with wet clothes, and I forget when I last had a proper wash. . . .I feel altogether mentally and physically exhausted and I've been in the Southern Ocean only a week. It seems years since I gybed to turn east and yet it was only last Tuesday night, not six days, and I have another 150 days of it yet. I shall be a Zombie in that time. I feel that I have had enough of sailing for the time being; it's about time I made a port, had a long hot bath, a steak with eggs, peas and new potatoes, followed by lemon meringue pie, coffee, Drambuie and a cigar and then a nice long uninterrupted sleep, although, come to think of it, to round it off properly. . . . Why couldn't I be satisfied with big ships? The life may be monotonous but at least one gets into port occasionally which provides some variety. A prisoner at Dartmoor doesn't get hard labour like this; the public wouldn't stand for it and he has company, however uncongenial. In addition he gets dry clothing and undisturbed sleep. I wonder how the crime rate would be affected if people were sentenced to sail round the world alone, instead of going to prison. It's ten months solitary confinement with hard labour.

In spite of Knox-Johnston's grumbling he was making excellent time. In one two-day burst he logged 314 miles, but the rapid pace was hard on the captain, and the banging about was beginning to wear down the ship's equipment, especially the self-steering gear, which needed a good deal of repairing. Would the ship hold together for the rest of the trip?

9

Oysters and Pheasant

Far to the north near the canary islands off the northwest coast of Africa, Nigel Tetley adjusted the volume of a Schubert aria sung by Rita Streich on the yacht's music system. The big blue trimaran *Victress* sped southward before a fair wind from the northeast. Tetley had just finished a superb meal of roast goose, peas, and beans washed down with half a bottle of wine. He felt fit and rested although it was hellishly hot in the tropics. After two weeks at sea, he finally had things under control.

Since his departure from England on September 16th, Tetley had had a succession of broken gear and annoying problems, some small and some not so small. During a sail change on the first day, one of the wooden spinnaker poles had splintered, and a second pole had somehow unhooked itself and been lost overboard. That night one of the rigging wires that supported the mast came loose. The mast bent alarmingly, and when Tetley looked aloft the next morning his heart froze.

By noon, the wind had eased to about 10 knots so the captain climbed the mast to find out what had happened. A diamond stay wire terminal fitting had cracked and the wire had pulled out. The movement of the yacht on the lumpy ocean made work up the mast difficult because the increased height aggravated the motion. Tetley felt seasick, but he managed to tie himself to the mast so that he could use both hands and to repair the rigging with wire clamps from his emergency kit. His prompt work saved the mast.

The speedometer and distance recording device had stopped on the first day. Either the cable to the instrument was broken or the tiny propeller under the hull was fouled. Tetley changed to a mechanical speedometer driven by a propeller towed behind the yacht at the end of a 50-foot line. On the second day, however, when Tetley pulled in the propeller to clear it of weed, the propeller and line slipped from his wet fingers, fell into the sea, and were lost. The captain had a twice-weekly radio schedule with England for the first part of the trip, but transmissions from the yacht were bad. Tetley traced the fault to the aerial tapping against the metal rigging wires during high winds.

During a calm period one day, Tetley tied a line around his waist and dived into the sea to inspect the speedometer propeller under the hull. The little propeller was undamaged, so the fault had to be in the cable connection somewhere in the hull. Later Tetley climbed the mast to clear two fouled halyards. He fashioned a new spinnaker pole from a long oar. And so it went. Fix. Fix. Fix. Repair this. Change that. Modify this. No wind. Too much wind. Take down the small sails. Put up the big ones. Then do it all over again. No wonder Tetley was weary.

Not only was there the effort of keeping *Victress* going so he could try to win the bloody race, but he had to recover from the hard work and nervous strain of getting the yacht ready, the publicity, and the departure. It was not enough to be an expert sailor. The captain needed to be a business executive to deal with all the commercial details. Romance aside, single-handing a big yacht was hard work!

Fortunately, Eve, Tetley's wife, had done a thorough job of provisioning the vessel before the race.

> I started a grand reading session, studying everything I could lay my hands on to do with diet, nutrition, and vitamin deficiencies, etc. [Eve wrote]. The thought of Nigel having to eat only tinned or dried foods for up to ten months and still remain healthy, kept me most evenings reading and re-reading until I had a grand list of "thou shalt haves." . . . [My goal was] to make all the food as attractive and tempting as [possible]. Anyone who has had to eat often alone, knows how miserable it can become, and how jaded one's appetite is, even if half an hour previously one felt starving. The newspapers swooped joyfully on to the "luxury" angle of the food. They didn't want to know about the bully beef and baked beans, but wrote up the pheasants, octopus, oysters, venison, etc. lyrically!

Tetley even had an electric mixer, with which he was able to concoct milk shakes from full-cream dried milk provided by Nestlé. Cutty Sark had given him two cases of whiskey. The Bass brewery had chipped in with 72 bottles of beer and 72 half-bottles of wine. "It's cheaper to heat the body than the boat," Tetley had joked to a reporter before he left.

Eve's hard work was all worthwhile, as Nigel found out early on his voyage. "The long weeks of preparation had taken more out of me than I supposed," wrote Tetley. "The sea no doubt would toughen me in time, but what I needed most just then was food to give me energy. I waded into an enormous roast chicken which Eve had provided and, sitting back listening to Handel's 'Water Music,' soon felt better."

By the end of the first eight days Tetley had logged 510 miles and was only 60 miles from the Atlantic coast of Spain. The captain joked to himself about stopping. "An impish thought crossed my mind. What about a run ashore in Corunna?" he mused. "Who would know?" He satisfied his wandering spirit by opening a bottle of wine and selecting a roast duck for supper.

A continuing hazard for small-boat sailors is the chance of being run down by big ships. In theory all vessels have lookouts, but in practice the lookouts often relax at sea or scan the horizon only occasionally. During the last thirty years the number of trading ships has doubled, the average length has increased by 40 percent, and there has been a significant increase in speed. In spite of these changes, the crews of big ships are proportionally smaller than in former years and more automatic devices are in use. Small-boat sailors sometimes see large ships hurrying along at sea on straight and undeviating courses with apparently no one on watch except the autopilot. Fishing vessels aggravate the problem because they also use autopilots and often make frequent and unexpected course changes. There's much talk of radar, but a yacht's radar reflector is worthless if no one is watching the receiving scope on the larger vessel.

Fortunately, the paths of cargo ships and oil tankers are well charted because big vessels usually take the shortest and most direct routes to save time and fuel. It behooves small-ship captains to cross shipping lanes quickly and at right angles if possible.

John Letcher, a professional mathematician and widely experienced sailor, has calculated that in the 2,500 miles between California and Hawaii the chances of a small vessel being run down by a big ship are one in a thousand, assuming no lookouts on either vessel. If daylight hours are reckoned safe and if 90 percent of the large vessels are in charted shipping lanes, the collision risk drops to one in twenty thousand. Dr. Letcher's numbers are only statistical odds, however, and in the waters he analyzed he was run down twice, once by a cargo ship and once by a fishing vessel. Dr. Letcher was lucky to have escaped with his life.

In spite of mathematical odds and the vastness of the oceans, a collision is a nagging worry to the captains of small vessels. These little boats are completely helpless before the towering bulk of a big ship that may be a thousand times (or ten thousand times) the tonnage of a yacht. Not only is a small sailing vessel dwarfed by a modern cargo ship or oil tanker, but these gigantic battering rams steam along at 15 knots or more.

On *Victress*, Tetley tried to minimize his time near shipping lanes. He set his alarm clock to remind him to check around the horizon. Usually the skyline was empty, but a few times he saw the distant silhouette of a ship during the day or the lights of a fishing boat at night. One morning Tetley looked out on a tunnyman, rolling heavily, that had run down to check on the sailing yacht. The fishing boat sheered off when her captain saw Tetley waving cheerfully. "A single-hander has to come to terms with the chance of being run down and learn to relax," wrote Tetley. Yet he was hard put to follow his own advice. He worried a good deal when he was near shipping lanes or fishing grounds. Fortunately, most of the round-the-world course was well clear of shipping, especially the long route in the Southern Ocean.

By October 6th Tetley had entered the zone of the northeast trade wind, which meant that since he was traveling southeast he had a fair and steady wind behind him. On the second night, the trade wind increased to 19 knots and *Victress* surfed for long stretches on wave crests.

> I had a long inward debate over the wisdom of leaving the mainsail set all night as well as the twins, a total of some 900 square feet of canvas [wrote Tetley]. It would have been a different matter with a crew and someone on watch all the time. The prudent course usually makes good seamanship, but in this case, banking on the constancy of the trade wind, I left everything up. All the same, sleep did not come easily with the yacht careening along.

The next day when Tetley calculated his position, he found that he had logged 156 miles in the last twenty-four hours, his best run so far. He might win the race yet! Certainly the trimaran was sailing faster, because each day Tetley was consuming about 10 pounds of food and fuel.

Yet the trimaran had persistent leaks and the captain repeatedly found water in the forward compartments of the outer hulls. Fortunately, before he had left England, Tetley had rigged up an inside bilge-pumping position in the main cabin where he could pump out seawater from the bow sections of the outer hulls. The trimaran leaked because the vessel was still grossly overladen with food, supplies, and equipment. The overloading caused flexing and pounding as the thin plywood hulls sped across the rough waters of the ocean. Tetley thought that the water got in along the joints between the outer hulls and the crosswings of the trimaran. He had covered these joints with copper sheeting before he left, but the leaks continued, which made him nervous.

Sometimes the whole sailing venture seemed too difficult and bizarre. Who in his right mind would try such a stunt? Sailing across a lake or an ocean might be explained away, but around the whole world nonstop? Alone and without human companionship? It was madness. Certainly all nine men in the race felt the strangeness of the undertaking at one time or another. The longer one went, the worse it got. Could one ever adjust to a state of tranquillity and balance? The sailing and the cooking and the navigation and the repairs were possible. But mental stability and ease of mind were something else. Maybe a Buddhist monk would make the ideal single-handed sailor. After all, a spiritualist was a sort of mental hermit.

"Thoughts of packing it in came into my mind for the first time today, brought on I think by too much of my own company," wrote Tetley on his sixteenth day at sea.

> It would be so easy to put into port and say that the boat was unsuitable or not strong enough for the voyage [Tetley wrote in his logbook]. What was really upsetting me was the psychological effect that seven or possibly twelve months of this might have. Would I be the same person on return? This aspect I knew worried Eve too. I nearly put through a radio call to talk over the question in guarded terms, then realized that although Eve would straightway accept the reason and agree to my stopping, say at Cape Town, we would feel that we had let ourselves down, both in our own eyes and those of our friends, backers, and well-wishers. It was just a touch of the blues, nothing more, due to the yacht's slow rate of progress.

Tetley began to find small flying fish on his deck rounds in the mornings. "I started reading for the first time on the voyage," he wrote. "An old *Sunday Times* colour supplement on motherhood—a husband with his wife at the moment of birth. Personally I think I would funk it."

Tetley frequently spoke with London on his radio although he was beginning to get out of range and would soon transfer to Cape Town. The news included a message from Eve that cheered Tetley greatly. Loïck Fougeron, the French entrant on *Captain Browne*, had been sighted off the Cape Verde Islands. Bernard Moitessier in *Joshua* had not been seen since September 1st. Bill King aboard *Galway Blazer II* was out of radio contact but was believed to be across the equator. Robin Knox-Johnston in *Suhaili* was making good time across the Indian Ocean.

To get electrical power for his radio and lights, Tetley ran a small gasoline battery charger every few days. But on the third week of the voyage, the ignition coil failed, and the charger was suddenly useless. Fortunately, Tetley was also able to charge his batteries by running the main engine, which had a generator. However, one morning Tetley discovered water sloshing over the floorboards and salt water above the level of the starter motor of the main engine.

Disaster! The captain traced the trouble to a corroded through-hull skin fitting and quickly pounded a cork into the leaky pipe to stop water running into the yacht. He then pumped out the bilges and poured fresh water over the starter motor and tried to dry it out. But the unit no longer worked. Without a starter, the main engine was finished. Tetley began to overhaul the starter, but this job would take a few days. In the meantime he relied on a second, small portable charging engine that he had brought along just in case.

While he was passing the Cape Verde Islands off the African coast on October 11th, the wind suddenly increased to 30 knots and the following seas grew big and nasty. Tetley steered by hand to help the vessel because he was afraid the yacht would turn sideways and get into trouble. All at once the wheel went dead. Fortunately, *Victress* handled the situation perfectly on her own and kept zipping along downwind. Hardly daring to breathe, Tetley hurried belowdecks to investigate the steering problem. The control wires had crumbled to powder inside their plastic sheaths. The captain quickly fitted new steering wires while the loudspeakers purred with the sound of Nielsen's violin concerto.

Tetley the sailor had turned into Tetley the mechanic.

In order to replenish drinking water, all the yachts in the race had water catchment systems, which ranged from a flat spot on the deck drained by a hose led to a water tank to the simple expedient of a bucket hung under the forward corner of a sail. Sometimes a downpour lasted an hour or more. The first few minutes rinsed the sail and bucket. Afterward the captain could pour buckets of clean fresh water into the tanks and dump a few buckets over himself.

One afternoon the wind was light. *Victress* ghosted along quietly, and a shoal of porpoises surfaced around the yacht and splashed alongside for an hour. "When tired of playing at the bows they would fan out on either side and flush the flying fish like gundogs working a field of game," said Tetley.

With good runs in the northeast trade wind, his average mileage increased to 125 miles per day. Tetley was lucky to find a steady easterly wind instead of calms in the doldrums. He crossed effortlessly from one trade wind zone to the other while he baked bread and listened to the music of Saint-Saëns. On October 22nd he slipped across the equator and continued southward.

BY THE THIRD WEEK in September, Loïck Fougeron was near the Cape Verde Islands. The master of *Captain Browne* had one big problem: his Moroccan cat, Roulis. This wild, globe-trotting cat was more trouble than all the other problems of the voyage combined. Fougeron had taken the cat for companionship, but at times it seemed that she was in charge and the captain was merely a servant whose work it was to clean up after the animal.

The little black cat had more energy than a box of exploding dynamite. On one of the early days of the voyage she had devoured the captain's dinner, "a beautiful cold roast of pork," that he had accidentally left uncovered.

A few days later he wrote: "Towards one in the morning, I switch on my radio. It remains silent. Without the radio, I have no time signal, no precise time for navigation, and I am worried. Before, the radio was working perfectly. Quickly I discover the reason for the breakdown. Roulis had played with the antenna wire and unhooked it!"

ROULIS, THE WILD CAT ABOARD THE *CAPTAIN BROWNE* [THE SUNDAY TIMES]

One night the wind shifted slightly. Fougeron made his way to the back of the cockpit to adjust the steering gear. In order to see, he held a small flashlight between his teeth. While he was working, he felt a gentle tug on his trousers. It was Roulis. As Fougeron began to talk to the cat, the flashlight fell from the captain's mouth and went overboard. "Still alight it glided slowly in the wake and I watched with regret as the little luminous light disappeared. I tried to imagine the astonishment of the fish."

With the cat stalking the yacht, any food left out was as good as gone. Even protected food was at risk. One night the captain was asleep when a curious noise woke him. The cat was up in the forepeak, where she had chewed open a bag of powdered eggs. The black cat was as yellow as a canary and seemed rather proud of herself. When Fougeron shouted at the cat, she fled to the oilskin locker, scattering egg powder everywhere.

Although Roulis exasperated Fougeron by her tricks, he liked the cat a lot. When the captain was asleep, she would sleep in the hollow of his shoulder. "Sometimes when Roulis thought I had slept long enough, she would wake me with gentle taps on my nose from her paws, with her claws withdrawn."

In spite of the cat's gentle side, Roulis continued her tricks. One day she dragged a can of corned beef into the captain's bunk, crumbled up the meat, and spread it in the bedding. Another time the cat upset a can of condensed milk, which ran under the floor of the galley and made an awful mess.

To his horror, Fougeron discovered that Roulis had fleas. Would these pests spread to his bedding and clothes? Would the fleas bite him and cause rashes and terrible illnesses and fevers? It was unthinkable.

> Even worse, Roulis had worms [wrote Fougeron]. In place of worm powder, I made her consume pellets of corned beef stuffed with garlic, an old wives' remedy, but this was not my worst worry. My cat, a female, was filling out, and I recalled the beautiful tomcat that patrolled the quay at Plymouth and who had looked so lovingly at her.
>
> Perplexed, I imagined six or eight wild kittens spreading panic during ten months at sea aboard my boat. The situation was impossible! What to do? Drown all her progeny? I could not dream of it. I confess to having thought for a moment of abandoning Roulis on a miniature raft furnished with food to windward of an island, but this idea revolted me.

Fougeron decided to pass his cat to a fishing boat. On September 8th he sailed close to La Palma in the Canary Islands, but it was Sunday and all the boats were in port. Fougeron decided to keep Roulis until he reached the Cape Verde Islands, 810 miles to the southwest.

LOÏCK FOUGERON

By September 15th he had reached the islands. He sailed between Santo Antão and São Vicente and stopped outside the port of Mindelo, where he signaled the local pilot boat, which came close alongside. The French captain passed across a special heavy plastic envelope marked "Press—Urgent" in four languages. It contained his report to *The Sunday Times* plus mail and films. Then he tossed over the cardboard box with Roulis inside. Fougeron had put a big flying fish inside the box for the cat. To the outside of the box he glued a carton of cigarettes and attached a £10 sterling note (all he had) for the pilot boat and to pay for the transport of Roulis.

The mail and the cat were quickly delivered to the British consul in the Cape Verde Islands. When Mr. Foulde, the consul, received the parcel and the cat, he kept the cat and forwarded the mail. A few days later, however, he cabled *The Sunday Times* and asked to be relieved of the cat because she was wrecking his house. The newspaper arranged to send Roulis to a friend of Fougeron who lived in Belgium. "Not to my home in Casablanca," said the captain. "Roulis might get eaten by the dogs out there."

Fougeron reported that the solitude of the voyage hadn't weighed him down—at least not yet. The French sailor had experienced no hallucinations; in fact, he had not seen as much as a single siren swimming around his vessel.

"It is hot, 28 degrees [Celsius] inside," he wrote in his report to *The Sunday Times*. "I live like Adam and am brown as a Kanaka. Some tan and perhaps also some dirt. Water is rare and precious. I have only shaved once since I left Plymouth. I am going to do it again because I see a tramp staring out of the mirror at me.

"I use two litres of water daily," he continued. "The wine is getting bitter. I will have to drink it quickly." The master of *Captain Browne* reported an international menu. Breakfast was porridge with powdered milk followed by Swedish bread with New Zealand butter, Dutch jam, and English tea. Lunch of mashed potatoes made from dried potatoes and powdered eggs diluted with a little milk. Dinner of English dried peas, Argentine corned beef, French cheese, and Moroccan wine.

"The automatic steering works perfectly," said Fougeron. "I have had no trouble since leaving Plymouth. . . . Fishing last night, caught six fish. I will eat them tonight with the rest of the potatoes."

The weather was settled for the next few days, and *Captain Browne* was sailing well. The cursed Roulis was gone at last, but the soft-hearted French captain missed her terribly.

> I now experienced the enormous weight of solitude from which I suffered frightfully [wrote Fougeron]. Yes, solitude exists and there is no need to run across the oceans of the world to encounter it. But on a boat, alone between the sky and the sea, it can reach crushing proportions. To my knowledge, few singlehanded sailors have dared to speak of it, no doubt by modesty. But I can assure you that man has need of contact with his fellow men.

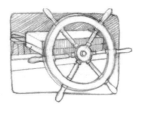

10

Collision at Cape Agulhas

ACH MORNING THE SUN TINGES THE LITTLE CLOUDS WITH PINK
AND mauve as they drift along like snowflakes [wrote Moitessier].
Then the sun begins to climb, a clear light in the pale blue sky—the
trade wind sky of the South Atlantic, where the weather is constant,
without squalls or calms. The wind breathes into my sails the life of
the open sea; it runs murmuring through the whole boat, to blend with
the rustling of water parted by the bow. . . . I listen to the sound of
water along the side, and the wind in the rigging. By turns, I read The
Roots of Heaven and Wind, Sand and Stars, in little sips. I spend long
moments on deck, watching the flecks of foam rising in the wake.
There are so many things in the flecks of foam and the water that runs
along the side. I could not ask for more; I have it all.

The sun rises, peaks, and sets, and one day gracefully makes way
for the next. I have only been gone a month; my boat and I could have
been sailing forever. Time stopped long ago. I have the feeling nothing will ever change; the sea will stay the same luminous blue, the
wind will never die, *Joshua* will always carve her wake for the pleasure of giving life to sheafs of spray, for the simple joy of sailing the
sea under the sun and the stars.

Joshua had averaged 159 miles a day for a week since finding the
southeast trade wind on September 17th. Such runs were phenomenal
for a single-hander on a 39½-foot ketch that measured a little over 34
feet on the waterline. Moitessier felt much better to be out of the calms
and frustrating winds of the equatorial doldrums, which had widened for
him to a 900-mile zone of rain squalls, heat, and discouragement. He

had figured on 600 miles. Sometimes the doldrums measured 1,000 miles from north to south; sometimes only 1 mile. Predicting the width was like trying to forecast earthquakes or the mood of a woman on her birthday. He was glad that the doldrums were behind him.

Moitessier was a little concerned about his health. He had problems with an ulcer and had to be careful. "I have to fill out a little," he said. "I did not have much fat to start, and there isn't any left. My inner barometer has been rising rapidly since last night, though. This morning I downed a huge mess of oatmeal and three mugs of Ovaltine with renewed appetite."

On September 29th, Moitessier called at Ilha da Trindade, a remote 3-mile-long Brazilian island that lies 600 miles east of the mainland of South America and 1,230 miles south of the equator. There was a tiny settlement on the high and jagged volcanic island where Moitessier hoped to leave a package of films and a note to be forwarded to *The Sunday Times* in London. But when Moitessier stopped 300 yards from the beach and blew his horn and waved, the untutored villagers were mystified by the red-hulled ketch. The Brazilians had no boats, so no one was able to come out. Moitessier had no dinghy, and in any case he was not allowed to go ashore under the rules of the race. After jilling around for a while and uncertain what to do, he reluctantly sailed away.

A little south of Trindade, *Joshua* ran out of the steady southeast trade wind and began to encounter the poky breezes of the horse latitudes. The French captain had done well—some 1,500 miles in two weeks—since he had entered the trade wind 240 miles north of the equator. Now south of Trindade and away from the southeast headwind, he changed direction abruptly from his south-southwest close-hauled course (about 65 degrees off the wind) to east-southeast toward South Africa and the Cape of Good Hope.

Moitessier wanted to get through the horse latitudes quickly and into the steady westerlies, but the winds he found were often feeble and false. One day *Joshua* covered only 23 miles. Since he was essentially becalmed, it was a good chance to inspect the hull. Moitessier pulled on his wetsuit and went over the side to give the hull a scrub below the water and to scrape off the gooseneck barnacles that had collected on a few places. The smoother the hull, the better she would sail. Once back on board, the captain checked the sky for signs of changing weather that would signal wind and better progress.

Four main belts of wind circle the globe and affect sailing vessels. The boundaries of these wind areas are somewhat imprecise and are influenced by seasonal changes, local disturbances, and unusual weather.

JOSHUA

As a general guide, however, the four wind zones are reasonably predictable.

1. In the high latitudes—both north and south—are the *westerlies*,
   which prevail roughly from the 40th parallel of latitude toward the
   polar regions.
2. The *trade winds* are the twin zones of constant, steady winds that

sailors like and dream of and which run from near the equator to very roughly 25 degrees north or south. The trade wind north of the equator blows from the northeast; south of the equator, the trade wind comes from the southeast.

3. The *doldrums* are equatorial calms between the two trade wind zones.

4. The *horse latitudes* (or variables) are the zones of uncertain winds between the trades and the westerlies.

In the old days, sailing commerce was well organized to take advantage of the trade winds and the westerlies, and the ships made long runs to the east or west in these wind zones. Conversely, the square-rigged ships tried to slip through the doldrums and horse latitudes as quickly as possible. Captains often took the long way around if they could stay within a favorable wind area because over time their passages were faster and easier on the ship and the crew. The contestants in the round-the-world race planned similarly.

As Moitessier sailed farther south and east and got closer to the tip of Africa and the Cape of Good Hope, the wind began to come from the west. The weather grew colder. The captain put on sneakers and woolen trousers and began to pack away his light-weather sails. He changed the regular mainsail and mizzen for smaller and heavier sails with extra reinforcing over the areas of potential hard wear.

Moitessier was a heavy smoker and often puffed away on a Gauloise cigarette while he worked. "There was a little gale yesterday, like a first brush with the high latitudes," he wrote on October 10th. "Mostly force seven or eight, always from the SW; the low was therefore far to the SE. Very manageable sea, and very beautiful; a little surfing, just to make sure everything is all right. The bow lifts like a feather."

Two days later there was another moderate gale, but under severely reduced sail *Joshua* continued at 7 knots and logged two twenty-four-hour runs of 182 and 173 miles with the help of some east-setting current.

Food has picked up in the last two weeks [wrote Moitessier], and I feel great. [I am] willing to take a reef, willing to shake one out, depending on the sky and the weather. Night and day, I sleep with one eye open, but I sleep well.

Last week we covered 1,112 miles, despite two short runs of 128 and 122 miles. The temperature falls to 55° when the wind is SW and climbs to around 60° when it is from the NW. I don't usually like cold weather, but I feel brisk when the temperature drops, because I am well bundled up and the SW winds blow in a fair weather sky, even when they are strong.

In addition to the ton of excess weight removed before the race, Moitessier decided to jettison 375 pounds more. Over the side went a mass of extra food, 25 bottles of wine, kerosene, alcohol, a box of batteries, and a big coil of valuable ¾-inch-diameter nylon line. The captain reasoned that emptying *Joshua*'s forward and aft compartments would make her faster in light airs, require less sail in fresh winds, and help the yacht to be more stable and responsive. Discarding hundreds of dollars' worth of food and supplies was a drastic step, but it made the Frenchman feel better.

On October 19th, the fifty-ninth day of the trip, *Joshua* was 40 miles southwest of Cape Agulhas, the extreme tip of South Africa. Moitessier had decided to try to pass his film and messages for *The Sunday Times* to a fisherman on the Agulhas bank. He photographed his log twice, page by page, and put the two films in separate watertight packages together with other films of the trip so far. He was also anxious for news of the other eight contestants in the round-the-world race.

> I can see Françoise's joy as she realizes all's well aboard [wrote Moitessier], that I have not lost weight (she will not know that I have—none of her business). I can just see my children's excitement, shouting all through the house, "*Joshua* is rounding Good Hope!"
>
> Yet it is a hard card to play, this need I feel to reassure family and friends, to give them news, pictures, life—to bestow that infinitely precious thing, the little invisible plant called hope. Logic shouts at me to play the game alone, without burdening myself with the others. Logic would have me run SE, far from land, far from ships, back to the realm of the westerlies where everything is simple if not easy, leaving well to the north the dangerous area of [converging currents and gales].
>
> But for many days another voice has been insisting, "You are alone, yet not alone. The others need you, and you need them. Without them, you would not get anywhere, and nothing would be true."

Moitessier made his landfall near the lighthouse at Cape Agulhas right on schedule and then sailed slowly along the South African coast. He hoped to find a fishing boat or a yacht, but it was Sunday and the fishing boats were in port. A gale was forecast, so the yachtsmen wouldn't be out either. All at once Moitessier noticed a small black freighter coming up behind him. He watched it carefully as it began to pass about 25 yards to *Joshua*'s right. When the ship, a Greek vessel named *Orient Transporter*, was even with him, Moitessier waved a package of film. The man at the helm waved back and put his wheel over to kick the freighter's stern toward *Joshua*. Moitessier tossed both of his packages on the freighter's deck. Success! But look out!

> *Joshua* begins to pull clear, but not fast enough [wrote Moitessier]. By a hair, the stern's overhang snags the mainmast. There is a horrible noise, and a shower of black paint falls on the deck; the masthead shroud is ripped loose, then the upper spreader shroud. My guts twist into knots. The push on the mast makes *Joshua* heel, she luffs up toward the freighter . . . and wham!—the bowsprit is twisted 20° or 25° to port. I am stunned.
>
> It is all over. The black monster is past. I gybe quickly and heave-to* on the port tack, drifting away from the coast. That is the main thing right now, so I can repair the shrouds without hurrying.

But the trouble wasn't over yet. Moitessier glanced toward the freighter. She was returning! He frantically waved that everything was OK. If the big ship came back to help, she would sink the yacht for sure!

It would have been far better for Moitessier to have accepted a battery and a low-powered radio from *The Sunday Times* for occasional short-range transmissions than to have tried to communicate directly with ships. Twice he had attempted to pass messages, and twice he had been threatened with destruction. Now he was aghast at what had happened.

"The beautiful trip is over," were words he tried not to say. "You can never continue non-stop with such damage . . . I have played and lost, that's all . . . later perhaps, it will hurt. But later is far away."

Nevertheless, Moitessier got out his tools to see what he could do. He repaired the two starboard shrouds whose cable clamps had only slipped. The spreaders were still OK thanks to their flexible mountings. "For the mast I feel nothing but admiration," he said. "At the moment of

---

*To heave-to is a maneuver designed to stop or slow forward way on a vessel. Generally a yacht is headed into the wind with a small headsail backed to force the bow to leeward (away from the wind). This action is balanced by putting the tiller to leeward, which tends to head the vessel up into the wind. The drag of the rudder and the backed headsail roughly balance each other, and the vessel is almost stopped. Most long-keel yachts heave-to from 50 to 70 degrees off the wind and jog along at a knot or two while making a lot of leeway (losing ground downwind).

impact it looked like a fishing rod bent by a big tuna. It confirms the trust I had instinctively felt for the good old telephone pole. All in all, I have had a lot of luck in my misfortune."

The problem was that the bowsprit—almost 7 feet long and made of a piece of reinforced 3-inch-diameter thick-walled steel pipe—was bent downward and twisted to port. To straighten it was a shipyard job.

Moitessier rested and pondered his next move. After a day of thinking, the captain decided to try to lever the bowsprit back into position with a boom-and-purchase arrangement. He took a spare mizzen boom and shackled one end of the 10-foot pole to a place on deck near the after end of the bowsprit. He then led the other end of the pole forward over the bow and held it above and a little to starboard of the bent bowsprit with a halyard coming down from the mast. Next Moitessier ran a four-part block and tackle from the forward end of the pole back along the starboard deck to *Joshua*'s cockpit. Finally, he fitted a piece of chain between the end of the twisted bowsprit and the forward end of the pole.

Now came the big moment. The Frenchman led the hauling part of the four-part tackle to a winch and started cranking in the line. As the powerful tackle began to pull, the forward end of the pole was forced upward and to starboard. Since the end of the pole was chained to the end of the bowsprit, the pole forced the bowsprit upward and to starboard too. Little by little the steel bowsprit began to point toward the horizon and to move to starboard. It was marvelous! Moitessier was practically dancing with pleasure.

"I feel I am going to start crying. It's so beautiful . . . the bowsprit begins to straighten out, very, very slowly. I am wild with joy!"

By the end of the day, *Joshua* was fully operational. The bowsprit rigging had stretched during the collision, so Moitessier clipped off a few links from the side and bottom chains and reshackled the stays. He straightened out the mangled pulpit and lifelines. "Worn out by fatigue and emotion I fall into bed after swallowing a can of soup for dinner."

Joshua was able to go on. Wow! What a day!

"I am tremendously tired, yet I feel crammed with dynamite, ready to level the whole world and forgive it everything," said Moitessier. "Today I played and won. My beautiful boat is there, as beautiful as ever."

On October 24th, *Joshua* crossed the longitude of Cape Agulhas near the southern tip of Africa and headed into the Indian Ocean. This was an area of turbulent waters, and Moitessier steered south-southeast to get away from the African coast.

The problem was that gales and storm-force winds from southerly directions often slammed into the Agulhas Current that runs southward along the east coast of Africa. When this 4-knot current collides with an opposing storm, it creates terrible breaking seas that turn into maelstroms of colossal size and fury. Even in 1968, there were many documented instances of large naval warships and supertankers laden with oil rising high on huge seas and then plunging deeply into the resultant "holes in the ocean." Some of these enormous, strongly built steel ships suffered severe damage; others broke in two and—except for pathetic, fleeting radio messages—disappeared forever.

It was no place for a small sailing boat.

11

A View of Death

SIX DAYS AFTER *JOSHUA* SAILED INTO THE INDIAN OCEAN, Loïck Fougeron, the second French entrant in the race, saw the 2,010-meter volcanic cone of Tristan da Cunha rise above the horizon.

Tristan da Cunha is one of an isolated group of five small islands in the mid–South Atlantic, a little over 1,500 miles from either South America or the southern tip of South Africa. These remote specks of land belong to Britain and are populated by three hundred people whose families came mostly in the nineteenth century and who today live by potato farming and fishing. When Fougeron passed this lonely outpost on October 30th, it meant that *Captain Browne*—his 30-foot steel cutter—was three weeks (at 100 miles a day) behind Moitessier, who had reached the Cape of Good Hope by a more direct route from the north.

At 37 degrees south latitude, Tristan da Cunha is midway between the horse latitudes and the westerlies. In such a zone, you might expect the weather to be moderate, yet the islands are often ravaged by west-moving gales that dart up from the south.

For several days, Fougeron had been running south toward the Roaring Forties with strong winds behind him. "A pale, dismal day breaks under a low sky, and the surface of the sea is streaked with zig-zagging white rays as the waves climb higher," he wrote. "They break against each other and chase us with their menacing crests. But *Captain Browne* spurts over each wave and pursues her route through the bubbling foam, safely guided by the self-steering device."

The French captain had made good progress, but he was worried by the strong winds and hardly dared to rest. "No question of sleep here as in the trade winds," he said. "One has to snatch an hour or a moment to rest without removing boots or oilskins—just in case."

Sometimes the barometer shot up to surprising heights after an east-moving weather depression passed *Captain Browne*. Then the wind would ease off or stop entirely. Fougeron would untie the reefs in the mainsail and put up bigger headsails. After a period of light weather, the winds would gradually become stronger and blow steadily for two or three days.

As Fougeron headed south into the Roaring Forties, the weather pattern changed abruptly. At 1300 hours on October 30th, on the little ship's sixty-ninth day from England, the barometer read 1,051 millibars (1,013 is normal), and the yacht rolled uneasily on a windless sea. At 1400, a light wind arrived; the captain soon had full sail up. But the wind kept blowing harder and harder. It was almost as if a genie had opened a door to a colossal wind machine. By 1500, the wind had become so strong that the French captain decided it was impossible to carry on, and he was busy clawing down the sails. By 1600, the intensity of the storm had doubled. At 1700, the conditions were simply ghastly.

From the shelter of *Captain Browne*'s cabin, Fougeron peered out uneasily. The wind flailed the tops off the waves and drove the spume across the water in horizontal streaks. As far as he could see, the ocean was entirely white.

"Never in my life have I seen the sea so high," wrote the captain. "Large albatrosses fly past at great speed, egged on by the wind."

Fougeron had unlocked the self-steering gear so the wind blade could feather into the wind. "I am scared it will be torn off," he said.

As night fell on the raging ocean east of Tristan da Cunha, the seas grew heavier and began to break dangerously. A heightened squall suddenly slammed down on the yacht and snapped the 1-inch-diameter stainless steel shaft of the steering device as if it were made of Swiss cheese. In a second, the blade disappeared downwind. What would go next?

> Night falls, a fierce wind rages in the rigging, and waves explode against the deck, accentuating the uproar [wrote Fougeron]. I am fearful that the revolving turret and hatches will be ruined, as they are made of plastic. How long can the sails hold out in this fury? . . . October 31st, 0200. The wind is at hurricane force. I . . . look at the sea, frightened and hypnotized at the same time. Clouds scudding across the bright moon make a Dantesque setting. . . . The sea is a gigantic cauldron. . . . I am not ashamed to admit my mounting fear.
>
> I get the impression that a single wave would suffice to crush us, like a nut under an elephant's foot. I am tired, cold, and should like to eat and drink something hot. Impossible to sleep. I curl up in the

cramped bunk and wait for the unbridled sea to win its victory
over me.

A few hours before dawn, while the yacht was lying beam-on to the
raging ocean, a huge wave roared out of the night, engulfed *Captain
Browne*, and rolled the yacht partway over. Fougeron thought his life
was finished.

> The boat lunges sideways, driven by a frightful force [he wrote].
> I am flattened violently against the side and then, in the middle of the
> bubbling waters, everything goes black. [There is] a cascade of
> kitchen materials, books, bottles, tins of jam, everything that isn't

CAPTAIN BROWNE

secured, and in the midst of this bewildering song-and-dance I am projected helter-skelter across the boat.

At this moment, I believe it is the end, that the sea will crush me, and prevent me from ever coming to the surface again. I will join the legions of sailors who have perished along this ancient route. In a flashing instant, I think of my family, my wife, and all those whom I love and will never see again.

Captain Browne's heavy ballast keel quickly rolled the yacht back upright. The steel hull was undamaged, but the mainsail had been ruined. The rigging was slack, and the mast vibrated and shook the whole boat.

> The tack of the staysail had been torn out [Fougeron wrote]. All the snap shackles had been sheared cleanly, and banged in the wind with the noise of scrap iron . . . almost all the stanchions [were] folded flat on deck. My poor . . . boat resembled a child's toy caught in the waves on a beach on a stormy day. . . . I put myself to work to save what I could rescue from the anger of the waves . . . I lowered the staysail, which hit me furiously; I felt the blood run into my mouth and, still today, I remember the strange hot taste, sugary and salty.

Worse than the chaos on board was the damage to Fougeron's confidence. He was terrified, completely and thoroughly. In a twinkling, the hurricane and resultant capsize had erased all his interest in the round-the-world race. The fury of the storm, the noise, the capsize, the mess in the cabin, and the cold were too much. He wanted out. He wanted land. He wanted a quiet harbor and a peaceful sunset. He was through. Absolutely and finally. Yet the French sailor continued his orgy of flamboyant writing.

> Each wave unfurls in spouting foam, reaching higher than the mast, while I am flung against the side [he wrote]. Blood runs down my face. Again I am almost thrust into the sea, but I clamber aboard, saved once more by the harness. The rigging must be secured immediately. My eyes burn, my teeth chatter—more from the diabolical sight of the enraged sea than from the unenviable situation in which I find myself.
>
> The sea is [a] moonlit landscape in a snowstorm. The waves rise up like cliffs. I am surrounded by buildings which collapse in order to stand up and fall down again.
>
> I loathe this sea, the sea that I love.

Below in the cabin a hundred precious things were churned together and ruined.

> I want to cry out at the sight of the shambles. Not a single book or utensil is in its place. Books on the bunk, condensed milk, onions, dried fruit in the pages of paperbacks, broken glass on the floor, a packet of cigarettes, mustard, pencils, a cask of wine. If I had been there, I would surely have been killed. Miraculously my alarm clock still ticks.

Fougeron was cold, tired, and filled with despair. He looked around and saw only the menacing waves and the powerless hand of a man about to be swallowed and crushed. His optimism and his will to win the race had been destroyed by the storm.

The tempest moved eastward and was gone in a day. Fortunately, the steel-hulled boat had survived the capsize without a leak and the mast was still in one piece. He had other sails and would be able to arrange something.

But Fougeron had had enough. He headed for Cape Town, 1,400 miles to the east. During the next two weeks, the weather was generally poor, with calms, headwinds, and gales. The French captain was thoroughly demoralized. The heart had gone out of him, and he sailed his vessel badly.

The essence of small-boat handling is to crack on sail in light airs and to reduce sail when it breezes up. But without proper food and rest, a sailor doesn't have the strength to handle sails or the wit to make reasonable decisions. Fougeron complained about losing weight. He said that he lived on cold coffee, sugar, alcohol, and vitamin C, hardly a reasonable diet, particularly for a Frenchman. Without spirit and strength, he tended to leave up his small sails and to wait for the next storm. His daily mileage dwindled. He lamented that he had lost several kilos in weight and had gained as many white hairs.

On November 3rd, another gale hit the *Captain Browne*, but this storm was minor and passed quickly.

After fifteen days, Fougeron gave up trying to get to Cape Town and changed his course for St. Helena, an island far to the north—only 960 miles from the equator. His new target meant that he was heading into the tropics again and would be able to run with the warm trade wind—the friendly following breeze. Now the going was easy.

On November 28th he arrived at St. Helena and anchored. "Eleven o'clock at night. I am lulled to sleep by a soft surge, under a sky studded with stars," he noted. "*Captain Browne* rocks gently at her anchor."

For Fougeron the race was over. To withdraw from such a marathon was no mark of cowardice; perhaps it was a sign of common sense. Maybe he had been unlucky or needed a larger boat. Or better preparations? Who knows?

Fougeron had never sailed south of 37 degrees south latitude, but he had peered into a window open to a view of death. He was the third man to withdraw from the round-the-world race.

Six were left.

NOT ONLY WAS Loïck Fougeron rolled over in the terrible storm near Tristan da Cunha, but a second contestant was caught as well. Bill King on *Galway Blazer* was about 380 miles east-southeast of Fougeron when the great storm came. Neither man realized that he was so near the other. Neither could have helped the other because in a severe storm at sea a man can survive only by withdrawing snail-like into the protective shell of his vessel.

During a big storm a sailor generally runs through a series of sail reductions and may drag a long line or drogue to slow his progress. However, unless he is holed or damaged, the last thing he wants to see is another vessel and be threatened with collision, dismasting, or sinking. Nevertheless, all sailors sometimes wonder about the other fellows out there.

At this very moment as you read this, a sailor on some far-off sea is being buffeted and thrown about by a storm. He is enduring the screeching of wind, the crash of noisy waves, and terrible rolling. Our man in the middle of a storm has difficulty doing anything constructive because he is half sick with lethargy. He is tired of the interminable waiting and the wasted time. It all seems so stupid and futile and crazy. Again the question: Why would anyone go to sea in a small vessel?

Yet a storm does end. Then hope and confidence snap back like the first brightening rays of a morning sun that suddenly click above the horizon after a dismal night. The blue sky returns, the sun warms everything, a reasonable wind blows, and the yacht goes along easily over seas that now seem friendly. The terrible battering from the storm is forgotten, when by rights the captain should carry a grudge against the tempest to his death and quit such a sorry business. The shiny truth, however, is that an hour of pleasant ocean sailing toward a goal somewhere makes the whole enterprise worthwhile.

Sailing on the sea is a mixture of black and white, of love streaked with hate, a confusion of good and bad, of rhapsody versus misery. Ocean sailing teaches self-reliance together with awe and respect for the sea. It tells a man to value his sense of humor and balance, and to laugh at himself once in a while. The life is one of simplicity, without pretense, a direct line to nature. Nothing else is so free and easy and pleasant and satisfying. Nothing else is so tedious, demanding, humbling, and difficult.

COMMANDER BILL KING had crossed the equator on September 30th and had run out of the southeast trade wind two weeks later. King knew that Knox-Johnston, who had left on the race seventy-one days earlier than *Galway Blazer*, was somewhere ahead. In addition, King had heard radio reports of Moitessier's fast progress, which was a bit demoralizing. However, like the contestants in any sport, King hoped to make better progress. Perhaps he would run into some good slants of wind so that *Galway Blazer*'s fine hull could make record runs and get him up with the leaders. The veteran sailor was wise enough to know that in any competition you can never tell when the leaders will stumble.

Now in his sixty-seventh day at sea—after more than nine weeks of sailing alone—King's thoughts of his place in the race were pushed from his head by an ominous development. He had become aware of a different feel to the sea; something big, something violent was coming. A few hours later King was deep into the worst storm he had experienced in half a lifetime spent at sea. He had watched storms from the tiny deck platforms of submarines and from sailing vessels all over the world. But nothing in his long background was like the wild ocean that now battered his graceful ocean cruiser.

> On Wednesday, the 30th of October, the barometer started to plummet downward [wrote King] . . . and as the wind's howl rose, I reefed down through gale to storm force. Finally I had just the peak of the foresail showing at about Force 10; but still the wind increased [with] huge slabs of foam skidding down the backs of the waves and the tops flying away. Night fell and every now and then the sky would clear. . . . A brilliant moon illuminated the scene which increased in grandeur and horror. I was now down to bare poles. Finally, a new note of scream came in the wind and, during each squall, the sea started to come right away in spindrift. The boat behaved beautifully, running down wind, with the vane steering. But this new hurricane speed defeated the vane; it could not steer, nor could the control work.

King, standing in the enclosed cockpit, took over the steering by hand and guided his vessel for the next twenty-four hours. There was no opportunity to eat, but he wasn't hungry and was spellbound by the storm raging around him.

> I stood up with my head in a Perspex dome, feeling remote and detached from the storm [King wrote]. . . . It was the most thrilling experience I have ever had. I estimated the waves at forty feet but, when the hurricane arrived, all pattern seemed lost in a confusion of tumbling hills. At one patch of moonlight as we came down off the top of a monster, I distinctly saw a petrel flying across my path way below me. . . .
>
> A sea top erupting into pointed mountain peaks would suddenly be pressed down into flatness, blown off by wind-scream, mercifully shutting out the grey-green light, so that only the immediate streaky shoulders of sea hills could be seen. The air might clear to reveal a quarter of a mile of racked, spume-laden ocean.

By 0500, the wind had eased a bit and King got the yacht to steer herself. But at 0930 the wind increased sharply again ("greater than before") and changed direction from the north to the west. King's barometer rose sharply. The center of the weather system to the south was moving southeastward of the yacht. Now came the worst problem of all. The old north wind had raised colossal seas that were running from the north. The new wind shrieking from the west began to send its gigantic seas slamming into the old seas from the north.

"Everything the sea had done until then was eclipsed by the fury and confusion of the two huge seas running across one another," said the slim captain of *Galway Blazer*.

King noticed that the top of his forward sail had started to come unfurled. He was afraid that the head of the sail might be destroyed by the wind, so he stopped running with the storm and lay ahull, broadside to the west wind. The vessel seemed to ride as well sideways to the wind as she had when she had run before the storm.

Toward evening—1700—on Halloween, the wind started to ease. King thought that the storm center had passed, so when the wind got down to 45 knots he took down his two hurricane hatches and went on deck to see about a problem with the self-steering gear. He then returned to the enclosed cockpit to get a piece of line to secure the loose foresail. He was sitting under the open hatches coiling the line when the unthinkable happened.

Galway Blazer rolled over to 90 degrees and was hurled forward on her side by a huge breaking wave. "She was using her side as a surfer would his board, to speed and accelerate down the face of the wave," said King. "The masts must still have been in the air, their proper element, and I had time to think, 'she will come back again; that great lead keel will swing her upright.' "

At that instant, a cross-sea erupted from the north. Instead of the yacht recovering, her masts were buried in the great cross-sea. The force of the water pushed on the masts, which acted as levers and started the mariner's most dreaded catastrophe: a complete rollover.

> I was on my shoulders pressed against the deckhead, which was normally above me [said King], my head pointing to the sea bottom, fifteen thousand feet below, looking at the green water pouring up through both hatches.
>
> Curiously, I felt no fear at that moment. There was nothing I could do, except cling on to my wedged-in position. I knew she would quickly right herself by the down-swing of the two-ton lead keel. The boat had been specifically designed to withstand a disaster of this nature, without hull damage. I felt, perhaps, a pained surprise that I should have been defeated by the aftermath of the tempest, after riding out its fury. I stared, perhaps stupidly, at the inrushing columns of water, and . . . then, with a mighty flick up she came.
>
> The cockpit was full of green water up to the top of the half door, perhaps three tons of it. My eyes flickered over the mess below deck and focused on the gymballed stove, hanging upside down.

King quickly closed the hatches. His first job was to pump out the water. When that was done, he hurried on deck to check the rig. What he saw almost made him scream. The foremast had snapped off about 12 feet up. The mainmast was still standing but was fractured and angled to starboard. The self-steering gear was a mass of twisted metal. His splendid yacht was a mess.

King realized that it was the end of the race for him.

The delicate unstayed wooden masts were adequate for ordinary ocean sailing if watched over by an expert seaman, but in the Roaring Forties their use was risky, perhaps even foolish. The trouble wasn't in the air but in the sea. Sooner or later, small vessels involved with really bad weather get into a severe roll, a broach, or a capsize situation, which means the masts get dipped into the water. If the vessel is going along at 4 or 5 knots, the flint-hard ocean yields only grudgingly. God knows it's risky enough with a time-proven rig whose masts are supported with a dozen strong wires, but without the help of the strengthening steel cables, unstayed masts that get pushed into water sometimes snap like toothpicks. An engineer would say: "It's an unfair strain in an incompressible medium."

Galway Blazer was at 39 degrees south latitude, about 1,000 miles southwest of Cape Town and 400 miles southeast of Tristan da Cunha. With one mast gone, the second mast damaged, and no engine, Bill King was in a tough spot.

Shortly after the rollover and dismasting, and still lying broadside to the storm, the yacht was knocked down again, fortunately to only 90 degrees. King managed to repair the self-steering gear and to straighten up his gear below. On November 1st, he sawed off the remains of the foremast. Then he gingerly tried a reefed sail on the mainmast and hoped the spar would hold. It seemed to be OK. The following day there was a storm and 60-knot winds. Again King lay broadside to the wind with no sail up and again was rolled to 90 degrees. On November 4th, he got under way and crept toward Cape Town at about 50 miles a day.

When *Galway Blazer* was designed, King had specified an emergency mast for the vessel. The spar was made in the form of an A-frame and was stored flat on deck with its arms along the side decks and its apex at the bow. Each arm was 18½ feet long and made of 4-inch-diameter aluminum pipe hinged on deck to a slider that ran in a 12-foot track, one on each side deck. The mast could be erected by sliding the arms forward in the deck tracks while someone hauled on the backstay. A short forestay completed the emergency mast, on which King hoisted an 85-square-foot storm jib.

On November 13th, King was sailing before a gale under the storm jib alone. He had been in radio contact with Cape Town and learned that a large South African yacht with a crew of seven was coming out to tow him the last 200 miles. On the following day the two yachts made contact and *Galway Blazer* was whisked into Cape Town.

Of the nine men who had started the round-the-world race, five were left.

12

The Impractical Sailor

OCTOBER 31ST WAS THE LAST DAY THAT ANYONE COULD start in the round-the-world race. On that date, Robin Knox-Johnston, in *Suhaili*, was far in the lead, halfway along the south coast of Australia near Melbourne and the Bass Strait area north of Tasmania. Bernard Moitessier had recovered from his collision with the freighter near the Cape of Good Hope, and *Joshua* was 900 miles east in the Indian Ocean. Nigel Tetley, on the blue trimaran *Victress*, was about to sight Ilha da Trindade in the tropical regions of the South Atlantic.

The final two starters in the race had barely left England. The Italian, Alex Carozzo, had anchored *Gancia Americano* off a south coast port while he sorted out his gear. Donald Crowhurst, aboard *Teignmouth Electron*, had just disappeared over the horizon toward the Bay of Biscay.

As we have seen, John Ridgway and Chay Blyth had retired earlier, largely because of unsuitable vessels. Both Loïck Fougeron and Bill King had been knocked out of the race by a particularly violent, fast-moving storm near Tristan da Cunha in the South Atlantic.

Of the nine starters, four had withdrawn. Knox-Johnston was in the lead, but he was battling to keep *Suhaili* from being knocked apart by the seas of the Southern Ocean. Moitessier's *Joshua* was in far better condition and was making the fastest runs of any of the entrants; nevertheless, the French captain was some 4,500 miles behind Knox-Johnston and had a lot of miles to make up. If Moitessier averaged 150 miles a day and Knox-Johnston did 100 miles every twenty-four hours, Moitessier would need ninety days—*three months*—to catch up.

It was a case of the tortoise and the hare, and the tortoise was going damn well. Observers of the race thought it would be impossible for Moitessier to maintain an average of 150 miles a day. Of course Knox-Johnston might fail to make 100 miles a day or he might even drop out.

The trimarans had been expected to make the fastest times of any of the yachts. The weight of their heavy stores, however, slowed them drastically and lopped off some 20 or 25 percent from their top speeds. As the captains ate into their food and used up fuel and various supplies, however, the trimarans began to sail faster. In the fresher trade winds, Tetley averaged 140 miles a day, much more than earlier in the race. Nevertheless, he was more than 7,000 miles behind Knox-Johnston.

All the men in the race wanted very much to know about the others—where they were, how they were doing, their problems and solutions, record runs—news of any kind, good or bad. Though the entrants were sometimes thousands of miles apart, each felt drawn to the others by the bond of the race and by the troublesome challenge of trying to sail a tiny vessel around the world nonstop. All the yachts had receivers and most had two-way radios. All listened, hoping for race information. When the news came, however, it was sparse, often rewritten by nonsailors, maddeningly incomplete, and most of the time there was none at all. Football, tennis, cricket, horse racing, road racing, golf, political news, stock prices, wool quotations, the inane chatter of radio announcers—there was everything except what the sailors wanted to hear.

The entrants with sponsors generally had scheduled radio calls, but even these were often poor and incomplete. The race lacked a dependable communication scheme, which tried the contestants' patience and sometimes kept them shadowboxing with invisible competitors. Before the race was over, the lack of reliable news and the absence of reasonable monitoring by the race sponsor would cause grievous problems.

At noon on November 3rd, Donald Crowhurst's sleek 40-foot trimaran, *Teignmouth Electron*, ran swiftly to the southwest before a fair wind. The yacht had left England three days earlier and now was well into the Atlantic off the northwest coast of France. The pretty white-and-blue multihull was one of the two Victress designs in the round-the-world race. The other was sailed by Nigel Tetley. Tetley's *Victress* had a high wheelhouse above a raised coachroof. This allowed a splendid accommodation arrangement below but rather spoiled the line of the vessel when viewed from the side. In addition, the raised coachroof and wheelhouse were structurally marginal and vulnerable to breaking waves.

On *Teignmouth Electron*, Crowhurst had eliminated the weight and

TEIGNMOUTH ELECTRON

windage of the raised coachroof and wheelhouse. For visibility ahead he had substituted a racy-looking blister with six small portlights facing forward. This modification saved a good deal of weight and made the yacht stronger but also reduced the living space and light below. *Teignmouth Electron*'s helmsman was somewhat exposed without a wheelhouse. However, the captain didn't plan to spend much time in the cockpit because he had a self-steering gear.

Crowhurst was nervous about getting away to sea after the long business of building the trimaran, sailing around the east and south coasts of England, and collecting and loading the stores for the 30,000-mile trip.

Fortunately, it wasn't all drudgery, as he had noted in his log the previous day.

> Earlier today porpoises came out to greet me. There were about 30 of them playing round the boat, accompanied by a mass of gulls. Sometimes as many as 6 pairs in a line (they seemed to prefer swimming in pairs) would jump on the starboard side and swim across the bows to port. All round the boat they were leaping around and inspecting me!

The first big problem on the voyage was the self-steering gear, which persisted in shedding screws because the high speed of the trimaran made the steering gear vibrate and shake out the fastenings. Crowhurst should have had spare screws, but he had forgotten to bring any. He was able to keep the gear working by switching a few fastenings, but obviously this practice could not go on. And he was just beginning the trip! On the delivery passage in England, Crowhurst had been advised to weld the screws in place, but in the rush to get away he had forgotten. He could have used lock washers, double nuts, a locking thread compound, cotter keys, or safety wire, or he could have mashed the thread ends with a hammer.

It was one of many jobs that needed attention, but just then Crowhurst was occupied with a boil on his forehead above his left eye. He decided to take vitamin pills. While fretting over his forehead, he went to work on the Racal radio receiver, which had stopped working. Since he was a radio expert he took the set apart and checked each component. It was only after some hours that he was embarrassed to discover that the problem was a blown fuse.

While Crowhurst ate his meals, he studied a large blue book titled *Ocean Passages for the World,* which outlined recommended sailing routes and discussed prevailing wind systems and currents. He felt a little like a clipper ship captain as he decided on his route southward in the Atlantic.

On Tuesday, November 5th, the second big problem appeared. Crowhurst saw bubbles coming out of the forward hatch on the port float of the trimaran. In addition, he could see that the float was low in the water. Could there be water inside? When he undid the twelve butterfly nuts and removed the circular hatch he found the compartment flooded to deck level. No wonder the float was low in the water! Unfortunately, just then the weather was nasty. According to Crowhurst the seas were running 15 feet high and almost as much water ran into the open compartment as the captain was able to bail out with a bucket. It took three hours to get the water out and to screw down the hatch on a new gasket.

> I cursed the people who'd been kind enough to help me stow ship, and I cursed myself for a fool [wrote Crowhurst]. I swore the boat was a toy fit only for the Broads or the pool at Earl's Court [the national boat show]. But when I'd got the job done, eaten some curry and rice with an apple and some tea, I experienced the great satisfaction that something I'd been fearing had happened and had been dealt with. Now I must do all the other hatches. I looked into the port main hatch, and things seemed OK. I got out my vitamin pills. A whaler, French or Spanish, said hullo.

November 5th was also the sixth birthday of Rachel, Crowhurst's youngest child. Her father, who was extremely fond of his four children, made both a radiotelephone call and sent a telegram to his daughter.

The wind had been blowing from the south, almost directly from the direction *Teignmouth Electron* had been trying to go. This forced Crowhurst to tack and to follow a zigzag course. From November 2nd to 6th, the yacht logged 538 miles, but in those four days she had made good only 290 miles—about 72 miles a day—toward her target. Finally, on the 6th, the wind changed to the west, and Crowhurst was able to head directly south at increased speed.

On the following day, sailing faster, the screws began to fall from the steering vane again. "That's four gone now—can't keep cannibalising from other spots forever!" said Crowhurst. "The thing will soon fall to bits."

The boil on the captain's forehead was better, apparently helped by the vitamins and penicillin pills that he had begun taking. Crowhurst complained of condensation and unpleasant smells in the small cabin; obviously the ventilation was bad and had never been properly thought out. The captain wrote that he had great luck making toast for supper over a Primus stove while the yacht bashed along in winds up to 39 knots.

Crowhurst's biographers—Nicholas Tomalin and Ron Hall—have pointed out that there were really two Donald Crowhursts. One was real and believable; the second was contrived and posturing. On a BBC tape, Crowhurst said the following:

> An involuntary gybe had hurtled my head against the cockpit side, and now I was conscious that my head hurt and my back hurt. I wondered if any serious damage had been done. Very tentatively I moved

one foot and one leg, and then the others. I lay there for a minute, thinking how careless I'd been, and then, very slowly sat up. I sat very quietly for about three minutes, and then very gingerly got up. Everything seemed to be all right. I didn't know then that it was going to be three days before I was able to move again. I gathered myself together, got to my feet, and finished making the attachment of the trisail to the boom, and continued my way eastwards.

This all sounded very heady and heroic. Unfortunately, the thoughts did not come from Crowhurst at all but were borrowed from Sir Francis Chichester's book *Gipsy Moth Circles the World* (page 195), which was on board *Teignmouth Electron*.

> . . . I was flung in a heap to the bottom of the far side of the cockpit [wrote Chichester]. I stayed motionless where I landed, wondering if my leg was broken. I relaxed everything while I wondered. For about a minute I made no movement at all, and then slowly uncurled myself. To my astonishment—and infinite relief—nothing seemed broken. . . . Picking myself up and collecting my wits, I carried on with my radio work. . . . During the night I had some difficulty in moving my ribs and ankle, and feared a bad stiffening. . . . I sailed out of the Forties that evening. . . . I tried to celebrate the event with a bottle of Veuve Cliquot, but it was a flop drinking by myself.

Not only did Crowhurst parrot the words of Sir Francis, but he preceded his message by drinking champagne from a bottle of Moët et Chandon. Clearly someone was in fantasyland.

By November 8th, the trimaran was west of Cape Finisterre, the northwest corner of Spain. Though he was in the shipping lanes, Crowhurst decided to take a long sleep and lowered the mainsail and mizzen. When he got up at 1100 and saw a big liner near him he began to hoist the sails. He found, however, that the mizzen halyard had gotten loose and had run partway up the mast. Before he climbed the mast to retrieve the halyard, Crowhurst carefully streamed a safety line astern in case he slipped and fell overboard. He went up the mast, captured the loose halyard, and soon had all the sails hoisted. While he was up the mast, he noticed that the rubber buoyancy bag at the top of the spar was loose and that the inflation hose was not attached to the bag.

Teignmouth Electron's progress got slower and slower because Crowhurst began to lower the mainsail at dusk. This made it easy to stay on course, but it ruined his daily progress. Crowhurst became depressed and sluggish. His celestial navigation wasn't working properly. One day he lost his temper at the spar-maker back in England when he noticed that a screw had fallen from the mizzen mast. On November 12th he was too weary (or lazy?) to change course after a wind shift at 0200 and sailed north—in the wrong direction—for seven hours. He bestirred himself with a warning in the log: "If I did that every day it would take over a year to finish. *I must not allow myself to be lazy.*"

On the next day—November 13th—a new disaster materialized. First Crowhurst had had trouble with loose screws in the steering gear. His second problem had been water in the floats. Now he found that salt water was running inside the yacht because of a faulty hatch in the cockpit floor.

> Today has had a sinister significance all right [he said]. Plugging away to westward in a southerly gale the cockpit hatch has been leaking and has flooded the engine compartment, electrics and Onan [the generating plant]. Unless I can get the Onan to work, I will have to think very seriously about the continuation of the project. With so much wrong with the boat in so many respects—it would perhaps be foolish . . . to continue. I will try to get the generator working, and think about the alternatives open to me.

Crowhurst wrote that 75 gallons of seawater had leaked through the floor of the cockpit in a single night. What could be done? Without electricity, none of his beloved electrical devices could function. His radios wouldn't work. How could he talk to England? His children? His sponsor? His press agent?

The captain of the *Teignmouth Electron* began a long written analysis of his problems. Not only did he have serious leaks, fastening problems with the steering vane, and doubtful electricity, but he had found that both the main and mizzen sails were cut far too full (too baggy) and chafed severely on the mast shrouds much of the time.

Without electricity, Crowhurst wouldn't have radios, which meant no way to send messages to his wife. It meant no electric lights and no radio time signals for accurate longitude. He had found that the steering gear didn't work properly at high speeds and was liable to cause wild broaches that might be disastrous in the big seas of the Southern Ocean,

He had brought along twin headsails for possible use when running before the wind. This rig might enable the yacht to steer herself, but the sails and gear had never been tried, and there was no telling what problems would develop. The masthead buoyancy bag scheme for self-righting the trimaran in case of a capsize wasn't completed and in truth was an experimental technique that might not work at all.

Worst of all was his seasonal timing. Because of the many delays and problems, *Teignmouth Electron* was scheduled to arrive at Cape Horn in the middle of autumn, which Crowhurst feared was too close to winter. He reckoned his chances of survival at fifty-fifty and shuddered when he thought of the odds.

Crowhurst's logbook discussion of these problems covered nine pages of closely spaced print. These private notes to himself were quite logical and realistic. His analysis should have convinced him to steer for the nearest port. Unfortunately, he didn't.

He was worried about humiliating himself by quitting and was concerned about the reaction of his family, his press agent, and the people of Teignmouth who had helped him. In particular he was anxious about losing face with his sponsor, Stanley Best, who might exercise the contract option that required Crowhurst to buy back the trimaran if the voyage was not completed.

Crowhurst had vague plans about stopping in Cape Town or Australia. He had fanciful notions about starting the race again the following year. As fast as he thought up one scheme, however, he would discredit it and come up with an even more bizarre idea. Would the other contestants drop out and leave the Golden Globe and the £5,000 to Crowhurst? If the others dropped out he had plan A, if not he was ready with plan B, and so on. Maybe he could market his company's navigation instruments in Australia. Maybe he could sell the yacht. It was maybe, maybe, maybe . . .

In reading all this, one cries out for the earthiness, the practicality, and the common sense of a Knox-Johnston, a Moitessier, or a Joshua Slocum, people who simply did things without a lot of frenzied thinking and planning. You begin to wonder whether Crowhurst could have sharpened a pencil without a prepared outline. Yet in reading over his writings, it's impossible not to be impressed by Crowhurst's intelligence.

Though he was a fledgling sailor, he had come a long way during the past year. He had started in the race only twenty weeks after handing the plans of his yacht to the builder. How many people could top that? His schemes to deal with *Teignmouth Electron*'s problems were reasonable. He would seal the leaky cockpit hatch and cut an access opening into the compartment from below. He would deal with the loose screws on the steering vane by tapping each screw head and putting in a small locking screw. The general pumping arrangements were a mess, but he would think of something. Maybe he could find the missing hose . . .

But at the end of it all, Crowhurst was a man who was impractical, unrealistic, and stubborn. He tried to solve ordinary difficulties by overkill. His solutions were too complicated and fancy. He was simply a visionary engineer full of top-heavy ideas who repeatedly boxed himself into impossible corners because of indecision and vanity.

It's no sin to admit failure born of ordinary human frailty. The sin is to not be strong enough to admit defeat. If the vessel was unsuitable and his resolve was faltering, he should have quit. A simple act. In 1968, a single-handed voyage from England to Madeira was impressive. A trip to Cape Town or Australia was extraordinary. Yet after a tortured session of self-analysis that clearly indicated he should give up, he couldn't bring himself to quit. Maybe later. He would try to get his sponsor, Mr. Best, on the radiotelephone and sound him out . . . cagily of course.

Meanwhile, by November 15th, *Teignmouth Electron* had logged about 1,300 miles and was near 40 degrees north latitude, about midway along the Portuguese coast. Much of this sailing—especially since November 8th—had been indirect and meandering. Along his direct route of 30,000 miles, Crowhurst had made good only 800 miles, or 2.6 percent. All the other contestants had done better. At this rate, it would take him seventy-five weeks, or almost a year and a half, to get around the world.

The next day *Teignmouth Electron* made good time to the southwest. Crowhurst had bailed out the generator compartment and managed to start the machine after stripping and drying the magneto. Again he had electricity for the radio, so he called Rodney Hallworth, his press agent, and told him that he was "going on towards Madeira," which was really 200 miles farther south. That night with the radio playing and milder weather he felt better, especially after a hearty supper of paella.

On November 17th, Crowhurst searched the yacht for the missing bilge pump hose, but it wasn't on board. On the following day he looked into the forward compartment of the starboard float and found it flooded. His instant coffee had been stored in this area, and the coffee-seawater mix had become an unholy mess. Crowhurst climbed into the float naked and bailed out the compartment, emerging covered with comical splotches of brown coffee stains that made him look like "something terrible from the deep" until he washed himself. He also bailed out 70 gallons from the main hull. He worried a lot about the leaks in all three hulls and the lack of a proper pumping system, something Nigel Tetley had anticipated and made provision for aboard his trimaran. Obviously, in bad weather it was dangerous to unscrew a hatch because a wave might flood the open compartment. How could he possibly take such an ill-prepared vessel to the Southern Ocean?

Crowhurst made a careful list of crucial points to discuss with his wife and Mr. Best, but when he got them on the radio on November 18th he lost his nerve and said nothing of substance. The next day he heard on the radio that Knox-Johnston has passed New Zealand. By now *Teignmouth Electron* was going around in a slow circle north of Madeira in bad weather. In seven days the captain had made only 180 miles to the south. He thought of putting in at Funchal, Madeira, and spent hours reading about the port and making a sketch chart. Again he called Mr. Best. Crowhurst wanted to talk about abandoning the race, but he was only able to bring himself to discuss pumping difficulties.

On November 22, he replaced a broken servo blade on the self-steering gear. The weather improved. *Teignmouth Electron* was almost into the northeast trade wind zone, which meant 1,000 miles of fair and warm winds. Crowhurst's spirits improved and he headed southwest again at 100 miles a day. He went up the mast to clear a problem with the jib halyard. His remarks were almost jaunty: "This mast climbing is good exercise—I feel exhausted. 'I'll take my constitutional now,' says he, disappearing up the mast twice daily!"

On November 26th, Crowhurst started a new type of logbook entry. Though he had ample logbooks, he began to conserve them by doubling up on his writing lines, which enabled him to squeeze a thousand words on a single page. He wrote with a new and chatty style: "Chicken Capri is quite nice with a fresh onion, extra dried peas and cheese added."

He began to drop bottles with messages into the ocean. The idea was for publicity, of course. The Teignmouth city officials had given him printed forms that read:

FROM DONALD CROWHURST, SAILING

ALONE, NON-STOP AROUND THE WORLD

The bottle containing this message was placed

in the sea at . . . . . hours on . . . . . 196 . .

my position being . . . . . . and my log reading

. . . . . . miles.

Signed . . . . . .

The finder of this message will be rewarded

if he sends it to Mr. D. H. Sharpe.

Bitton House, Teignmouth, England

Crowhurst was full of ideas for publicity, for new devices on the yacht, and for improved ways to sail his boat. Unfortunately, his bright mind was faster than his ability to put the ideas into practice. With

Crowhurst the difficulty wasn't the idea, the concept, or the notion. His problem was how to execute and apply his new strategy, his ideal scheme, or his perfect solution. He should have been employed in an idea factory or a think tank. If something didn't work or go according to plan there had to be a way around the difficulty" "Let's see now . . ."

AS WE HAVE SEEN, Alex Carozzo had officially sailed on October 31st, the last possible day to leave on the race. He wasn't quite ready, but he headed out anyway. He anchored his giant ketch, *Gancia Americano*, at Cowes off the Isle of Wight in southern England for a week in order to rest, to sort out his gear, and to hoist and check his various sails. Although he hadn't gone anywhere, he was technically at sea.

After the Italian sailor had satisfied himself that everything was in order aboard his 66-foot vessel, he headed west down the English Channel and into the Bay of Biscay. He soon encountered his first gale and was busy reefing the sails. "The roaring forties are not only in the Southern Ocean," he reported in a radiotelephone call to *The Sunday Times*.

The big ketch handled the heavy weather with ease, and Carozzo sometimes touched 9 knots as the racing machine knifed through the seas. On November 14th, he radioed that he was at 44 degrees 25 minutes north and 12 degrees 10 minutes west, or about 190 miles west-northwest of La Coruña, Spain. He was making excellent progress.

The cold weather and gales were behind him, but the Italian complained about heavy rain and low clouds. "What I need is some sun," said Carozzo. "The tomatoes on board are going bad. Unless the sun shines, mold will start growing on me too."

The captain of the shiny new ketch found that he was able to sail his enormous vessel very well in spite of the doubts of many people. As far as Carozzo knew, no single-hander had ever tackled such a large vessel before. *Gancia Americano*'s motion was much easier than his earlier smaller yachts, and Carozzo hoped to be able to log 200-plus-mile days when things settled down and he found steady winds.

The Italian sailor's big problem was not sailing or handling his giant entry, but terrible stomach pains. He had been vomiting blood, and with a history of ulcer problems, his prospects were grim. It seemed such a pity when the new yacht was going so well.

The Sunday Times quickly summoned a doctor to advise Carozzo by radiotelephone. After a consultation on November 14th, the doctor duly recorded that his seaborne patient had a record of ulcer trouble. "The symptoms indicate that it has blown up again," said the doctor. "I advised him to follow a strict simple diet and to take any alkali medicines

GANCIA AMERICANO

that he had. I told him that if he was still bleeding, he should give up. There's always the risk of an enormous haemorrhage." The doctor added that the bleeding had stopped, however, and that Carozzo was feeling better after keeping to a simple diet and drinking no alcohol.

Though the ulcer diagnosis was not good, Carozzo stubbornly refused to give up. "I'll sail on," he declared on November 17th.

Six days later, however, in spite of his determination and hoped-for improvement, Carozzo's condition had worsened. The desperate captain was limping toward Lisbon for emergency medical treatment. The Portuguese Air Force sent up a P2V5 rescue plane to try to find him.

"I do not know if we will be able to do much for the sailor," said Brigadier General Fernando de Oliveira, the Secretary of State for Air, "but the sight of a plane searching for him should cheer him up and make him aware that help is at hand."

Carozzo was determined to sail in by himself, but when the plane located him becalmed 15 miles from the coast, he signaled for assistance. A pilot launch from Oporto darted out and towed *Gancia Americano*, her mizzen and staysail still hoisted, into the Portuguese seaport. It was all desperately tragic.

"When you are alone at sea in a big yacht and the weather is poor, then it is bad enough. But when you are ill it is terrible," said a pale and exhausted Carozzo to a reporter from his bed in the English hospital in Oporto. "When the seas were rough in the Bay of Biscay all I wanted to do was sleep and be sick. I was vomiting blood and felt terrible. I was very weak, but I had to keep control of the yacht. No one can understand what it was like for me.

"To make things worse the thought kept pounding through my head that I would have to retire," he continued. "All the preparations that I and so many other people had made would be wasted. I greatly admire mountaineers and the men who are crossing the Arctic at the moment but they always have companions. Out at sea, I had no one to help me, no one to talk with me."

Carozzo's undertaking had been extraordinary. Not only had he dealt with the design and financial aspects of his big vessel, but he had supervised the rushed construction. Every day he had been obliged to solve a hundred large and small problems. Finally, when the big boat was launched, he skipped sea trials entirely and left immediately on the race.

But the slim, lion-hearted man from Venice had undertaken too much. The strong and powerful yacht didn't fail; it was Carozzo's health that collapsed. He explained that while at sea, he had begun to feel a little better, but he knew that he was seriously ill and needed an operation. Worse yet, he had used up all his injections. Fortunately he was near land instead of being out in the middle of the Atlantic. "I decided I must retire and make for port," he said.

Now four were left: Knox-Johnston, Moitessier, Tetley, and Crowhurst.

13

"Come On God"

ON ROBIN KNOX-JOHNSTON'S ONE HUNDREDTH DAY FROM England, he was 1,400 miles east of the Cape of Good Hope. He was far out in the Indian Ocean, a little more than a quarter of the way between the tip of Africa and the west coast of Australia. *Suhaili* hurried eastward near the 40th parallel of south latitude, with both the current and westerly winds pushing the yacht along.

The mileages between land masses in the Southern Ocean are enormous. From Africa to Australia is 4,660 miles of ocean, a forty- or fifty-day sailing proposition for a small vessel.

The weather had been wretched, with gale after gale. Now, however, Knox-Johnston was west of the turbulent area around the tip of Africa, and for a few days he found lighter winds and even sunshine. Soon *Suhaili* looked like a floating laundry with pants, shirts, sweaters, towels, underwear, and even a sleeping bag flapping in the drying wind.

Knox-Johnston had plenty to do. The self-steering gear had given him endless trouble. The problem was simply that the device wasn't strong enough for the hard sailing conditions in the Southern Ocean. Robin had two choices: either reduce *Suhaili*'s speed (in a race?) or strengthen the gear somehow. Otherwise the pipes and arms and brackets and auxiliary rudders were going to be bashed to pieces.

Even in a shipyard such repairs would have been awkward because they were of a "cut and try" variety. Machinists and welders could have added braces and strengthened various parts, but the nature of such changes means removal, modifications, and sea trials—often many trials. Out on the ocean any changes are extremely tedious and perhaps impossible. Just drilling a single hole in a piece of metal is a big deal with the vessel rolling all over the place. And such jobs—even if you have the tools and materials—must be fitted in between eating and sleeping and watch keeping. Fortunately most small-boat sailors are persevering types. Knox-Johnston combined the talents of an engineer and a metal worker and managed to put his wobbly self-steering back together.

> The repairs took me three days [he wrote]. The old rudder blade was hopelessly split, so I made a new one out of one of the teak bunkboards. The bar had broken by the middle of the blade, and to re-join it I cut the handle of a pipe wrench and then filed it down until it fitted inside the bar, like an internal splint. I put the two broken ends of the bar together and then drilled through the bar and wrench handle, riveting them together with pieces of a 6-inch nail, heated on the primus stove. The final job looked pretty strong, but to make sure of it, I bound it with glass fibre.

So far on the voyage, Knox-Johnston had taken his drinking and cooking water from plastic jugs that he had brought from England. He had managed to refill these at various times from rainfall in the tropics and hadn't touched the 86 gallons in his main tanks at all. Now he was into his fourth month at sea and had eaten deeply into his food stores. In addition he had used up a good deal of gasoline in his battery-charging engine and had thrown various bits of unwanted junk over the side. *Suhaili* was a bit out of trim—down in the bow—so the captain began to pump drinking water from the forward tank to shift a little weight. The water that flowed from the hand pump was brown and foul-smelling. When Knox-Johnston slid aside the tank inspection plate, he found that all the water was contaminated and undrinkable. The after tank was the same. All 86 gallons were useless.

This was a dreadful discovery. Robin still had 10 gallons in the plastic jugs, enough for forty days if he was careful. In addition, he had 300 cans of fruit juice and beer. By an end-of-the-world effort he could distill fresh water from salt by making a still and using his kerosene stove. A more practical and easier way was to continue to catch rain—there was often plenty with the gales—and to overlook no chance to fill the water containers. In any case he would keep going to Australia and see how things looked.

One day the captain stood in the cabin repairing his blue spinnaker. He was sewing rope around the edges of the sail, and he braced himself against the motion of the yacht with one hand while he sewed with the other. His technique was to stretch a light rope between two points—say

6 feet apart—fold the edge of the sail over the rope, and then sew the material to the rope. Knox-Johnston was making good progress, but after a while he ran out of thread.

In order to tie a new length of thread to the old, he used his fingers and teeth. When he started to stand up he felt a terrible pain in his upper lip. The more he moved, the more his mustache hurt. He had somehow tied his mustache to the spinnaker rope! He groped for the near end of the rope to untie it, but he was too far away. He grabbed for his knife. It was just out of reach. What to do? In desperation he jerked his head back and ripped off part of his mustache.

"It hurt like hell and tears filled my eyes, but it soon passed off and at least, as I rushed to the mirror to reassure myself, the symmetry of the moustache was not badly upset," he said.

Suhaili's radio transmissions were a problem. Knox-Johnston was able to hear Port Elizabeth in South Africa, but the station had difficulty receiving *Suhaili*'s signals. The ship's batteries were low, so one night the captain made a determined effort to re-power them by running the charger for hours. During the night Knox-Johnston went into the engine room to check the batteries with a hydrometer. As he leaned over the batteries, the yacht broached before a wave and the sudden roll knocked acid from the hydrometer into the captain's left eye. Knox-Johnston rushed on deck and splashed water in the eye, which started to throb and ache.

The poor captain was terrified. It was a disaster. Would he lose his eye? He put in antiseptic eyedrops but the throbbing continued. Should he turn back for Durban? Would it be worth an eye to carry on? Where were the other contestants? What should he do? After a harried debate with himself, Knox-Johnston continued toward Australia. At the end of a week the eye was OK.

> September 22nd. . . . Awoke to find us heading north so got up and gybed [he wrote]. I banged my elbow badly during the night and what with that, numerous other bruises and an eye that throbbed, I felt as if I had just gone through ten rounds [of boxing]. As the wind was down I let out some sail and then went back to bed. It's warm and reasonably dry there and I feel very tired. I awoke at 1400 to another gale building up, this time from the S.W. so I had to start taking in sail again. Reefing is no longer an easy business. My hands are very sore and covered with blisters and whirling the handle is sheer hell. I noticed today over seven sail slides loose or missing on the mainsail so there's the first job when the wind goes down. I got up at 2000 and

made a risotto which I followed with a tin of fruit . . . then I turned in again. This may seem very lazy, but I wanted to rest my eye as much as possible; also to give some idea of how tired I have become, each time I turned in I fell asleep at once and it was the alarm that woke me.

By September 30th, *Suhaili* had logged more than 3,000 miles in the Southern Ocean. The South African radio stations gradually faded out. Knox-Johnston tried to speak to Perth in Western Australia, but *Suhaili*'s transmitter had stopped working when the yacht broached. The captain tried repairs, but nothing had any effect. Not only was the radio transmitter dead, but *Suhaili*'s main engine would not turn over and appeared to be frozen up from corrosion. This was disappointing because Knox-Johnston had 100 gallons of diesel fuel on board. He had planned to generate electricity for the radios and to power through the doldrums in the Atlantic on his way home to England, when the bottom of the yacht would be especially foul with weed and marine organisms. (This was allowed by the rules of the race.)

Again and again the twenty-nine-year-old captain watched the seabirds, as do all sailors. The small dark-gray Wilson's storm petrels (wingspan 1 foot or less) flitted around the yacht in bad weather, their delicate, pattering legs nearly touching the water. The storm petrels were so frail looking that they seemed to have no business at all on a stormy ocean, yet they always appeared during gales—from where, nobody knows.

There are two kinds of albatrosses, both large and formidable. The black-browed albatross has wings that span 6 feet. The wandering albatross, *Diomedea exulans*, the largest of all ocean birds, possesses magical wings that stretch to 12 feet or more. Up close the albatrosses are comical-looking birds with squat, pear-shaped bodies that appear quite incapable of flight. It is only when you watch the perpetual soaring and gliding and wheeling of these incredible birds from a distance that you begin to consider the legend of motion that never stops.

The way the long, narrow, grayish white wings support these aerial wizards in their sweeping circles around a vessel at sea is forever a marvel. Certainly the wings—those slender high-aspect knife blades that are dark on top and white on the bottom with black leading edges—are the passports to magic. When an albatross flies around a vessel at sea, the bird's circles are large and leisurely, with scarcely a flap of the long wings. The bird usually climbs in a slanting direction against the wind, turns slowly across the wind, and finally rushes rapidly downwind before heading again into the wind. Additionally, the troughs and crests of the waves on the irregular surface of the waves appear to produce small air currents that the bird uses in some fashion. The albatross often flies very low and sometimes completely disappears behind a swell. A viewer is sure that the bird's wings have touched the water and that the creature has crashed and toppled into the sea, but in fact this never happens. The bird always appears a few moments later flying at high speed, circling around and around with great banking and wheeling motions, a creature that has hypnotized sailors for centuries and seems a true perpetual motion machine.

Sometimes a dozen dolphins raced alongside *Suhaili* and rolled and splashed under the bowsprit for a quarter of an hour. Occasionally a blowing whale passed the small white ketch.

"I always felt a little lonely when the whales left," said Knox-Johnston. "Even if we could not communicate, I felt that we shared the same difficulties."

At 0130 on October 6th, the main gooseneck—the metal pivot holding the main boom to the mast—broke with a loud bang. The foot of the mainsail sagged, and the roller reefing mechanism was no longer usable. The weary captain managed to lash the boom to the mast and once again got out his tools. Robin spent two days drilling and filing out the broken jaw, which he hoped to reuse by putting in a new bolt that he would secure to the two mast jaws. The only suitable large-diameter bolt was too short, however, so the captain compromised by fastening the gooseneck jaw to a single mast jaw, which he hoped would be strong enough.

While he was dealing with these repairs, another Force 10 gale swept down on *Suhaili*. Fifty-knot winds turned the sea all white. The air temperature was 38°F, but because of the wind, it seemed much colder to the captain, who nipped from a bottle of brandy to keep warm and to build up his resolve a little. As the wind increased, the triple-reefed mainsail began to come apart. Added to all this was a vicious cross-sea. Knox-Johnston took down all the sails except a tiny storm jib and streamed eight lines astern to slow and steady the yacht before the storm.

During the morning of October 8th, the barometer began to rise rapidly. While Knox-Johnston was eating breakfast, a cross-sea rolled the ketch to 90 degrees for a few moments. There was nothing to do except to wait out the storm, so Robin crawled into his sleeping bag and tried to doze. By midday the wind had eased to 30 knots. Knox-Johnston pulled in the warps, hoisted the staysail and the reefed mizzen, and was on his way westward again. He sewed the torn mainsail, but while hoisting it, the halyard winch brake failed, and he got a frightful blow on his right wrist from the wildly spinning handle. Fortunately the wrist bone did not break.

> On the 13th I thought we'd had it [he wrote]. The wind was blow-
> ing a good Force 10 and we were running under the storm jib when
> really big waves started to come up from the south and hit *Suhaili*
> with stunning force. This was by far the worst weather I had ever en-
> countered and the terrifying shudders and cracks every time a wave
> hit the hull convinced me that the boat would not last long. I did not
> see how anything could stand up to this sort of continual punishment.
> Water was coming into the boat as if out of a tap from leaks all round
> the coachhouse I had never known before.

Knox-Johnston panicked a bit and thought of getting out his life raft and a few supplies, abandoning his yacht, and drifting to Australia. He came to his senses, however, and climbed on deck and began looking at the ocean to see if he could do something to minimize the beating that the waves were giving *Suhaili*.

There was a huge swell from the southwest plus a system of dying swells from the south. The ketch was lying beam-on to the large south-west swell. If the captain could get the yacht to present her stern to the southwest swell instead of her side, she would perhaps stop taking such a terrible pounding and ride better. After some trial and error, Knox-Johnston found that when he streamed a very long floating line—600 feet of $5/8$-inch-diameter three-strand rope—in a U-shaped bight over the stern, the line held *Suhaili*'s stern nicely up into the wind. The ketch yawed back and forth a bit and snapped the storm jib from one side to the other, but the captain stopped this by centering the jib and pulling the sheets very tight. The sail steadied the little ship. The result was that even in the sustained Force 10 storm, the foredeck was sometimes dry.

The self-steering began to get stiff and unresponsive, so Robin did a little hand steering to help out. "We were about 500 miles from Australia by this time," he wrote. "Although the weather had been rough and un-comfortable, progress had been excellent, and I was beginning to pick up local radio stations in Western Australia. This kept me abreast of the news and the Albany wool sales; every time I tuned in, it seemed, I picked up the latest market report, and after a few days I could have given anyone a full run down on every aspect of them."

A few days later the self-steering gear broke again and various parts were lost in the sea. Knox-Johnston managed another marginal repair, but this was clearly the last because there were simply no more parts. On

October 25th, *Suhaili* sighted the Australian ship *Kooringa* of Melbourne and hoisted signal flags requesting that she send a radio signal to England. Captain Joseph Scott recognized the white double-ended ketch from newspaper publicity. He gave her a whistle blast and acknowledged the flag signals with an answering pennant. Knox-Johnston was overjoyed.

The weather in the southern spring improved and became quite balmy as *Suhaili* slowly sailed eastward toward Bass Strait, the 125-mile-wide waterway that separates Australia and Tasmania. Though the yacht was 60 miles south of the coast, a large butterfly fluttered on board and fascinated Knox-Johnston. The weather was pleasant, and the captain thought about his suntan. Meanwhile, poor *Suhaili* continued to fall apart. On November 2nd, the tiller head sheared off where it entered the rudder. Knox-Johnston managed to get the broken tiller head off and fitted the spare, but he was afraid to drive it on properly because the rudder bearings were worn and loose and any hammer blows might have weakened them further. He put lashings on the rudder to take some of the load from the bearings. The next day a key part of the self-steering gear sheared off, and the important underwater parts disappeared into the sea.

What next? The engine was ruined by corrosion. The self-steering gear was gone. The water tanks were foul. The rudder didn't look too good. A jury gooseneck rig held the main boom to the mast and might go at any time. The cursed halyard winch brakes were so dangerous that the captain had to tie the handles in place. Already two sails were worn out. The radio transmitter was dead. Only half of his stove worked. In heavy weather the yacht leaked everywhere. Not only was the captain bruised and scarred from the voyage, but he was exhausted and fed up. Even his sea boots were falling to pieces. And ahead lay 6,000 miles more of the Southern Ocean with Cape Horn at the end!

"Come on God," he wrote in his diary, "give me a bloody break, it's been nothing but calms or gales for weeks; how about some steady winds for a change."

Suhaili had already set a record for the smallest yacht to have traveled so far without stopping. With the vessel in such abysmal condition Knox-Johnston certainly would have been justified in stopping at Melbourne. Besides, the thought of a soft, unmoving bed, a hot bath, a large steak, humans to talk to . . .

But no! *Suhaili* was leading the race. Maybe she could make it all the way around the world nonstop. Wouldn't that be something! He was already halfway to his goal and still ahead of Moitessier. Why stop now?

He'd never forgive himself if he did. The big problem was the self-steering. With the mechanical gear sprinkled across the bottom of the Southern Ocean, the only way to make her steer herself was to somehow contrive a balance between the rudder and the various sails. Or if that wasn't possible, he could steer for sixteen hours a day and then stop the yacht while he slept—like the Argentine sailor Vito Dumas a quarter of a century earlier. Self-steering would be easier and infinitely less boring, however, so Robin began to experiment with the sails.

A little before midnight on November 6th, Knox-Johnston made his landfall on southeastern Australia when he picked up the lighthouse signal on Cape Otway, 75 miles southwest of Port Phillip Heads, the entrance to Melbourne. Just after lunchtime on the following day, *Suhaili* arrived at Port Phillip Heads and sailed up close to the pilot vessel *Wyuna*.

"I'm nonstop from the U.K.," shouted Knox-Johnston to a startled man on the bridge. "Will you please take my mail?"

The pilot vessel lowered a launch and the coxswain hurried to *Suhaili*. After 147 days on his own, Knox-Johnston passed a waterproof box with mail, films, track charts, and various writings to the coxswain. He also handed across a radio message for his family and friends in England. At ten minutes past four in the afternoon he waved good-bye to the pilot vessel, hardened in the sheets, and began tacking into the southwest wind to get back out into Bass Strait before night fell.

He was not quitting.

14

South from Trindade

O<small>N NOVEMBER 7TH, THE SAME DAY THAT ROBIN KNOX-</small>
Johnston watched the dark land mass of Australia gradually recede behind *Suhaili*'s port quarter, Nigel Tetley hurried toward the Cape of Good Hope in the South Atlantic on his big blue-and-white trimaran.

Three days earlier, Tetley had photographed himself on *Victress*'s port foredeck with the rocky mass of Ilha da Trindade only a mile or so in the distance. Moitessier had slipped past the same island thirty-five days earlier and was far ahead in the Indian Ocean. Tetley was sailing a little faster now, however, and began to make up time on the leaders because the trimaran was getting lighter and more responsive to weight changes.

The passage through the 1,400 miles of the southeast trades north of Ilha da Trindade had taken ten days. During that time, *Victress* had headed a little west of due south, close-hauled on the port tack. The winds had been remarkably steady between 12 and 15 knots. The yacht sailed well, but Tetley worried about the water that he had found in the forward compartments of the trimaran's port and starboard floats. Thirty gallons in one two-day period was not good. The captain was able to pump out the water quickly enough, but there should have been no leaks at all in these easy waters. After the radio stations in England had faded out, Tetley tried to speak to Cape Town, but although he tried a dozen times he couldn't make contact. He eased his uncertainties by listening to music—Irish ballads, Boccherini, Delius, and Beethoven's *Eroica*.

In Chapter Nine, I mentioned that a through-hull fitting on *Victress* had corroded away and caused partial flooding of the main engine. Tetley bunged the hole with a cork and pumped out the water. He then managed to dry out the starter and get the engine working, but he noticed something wrong with the stern gear or propeller. One calm afternoon Tetley dived over the side into the tropical water and found that both the propeller and the bracket for the propeller shaft were broken. While he nervously watched for sharks, he removed the stern bracket and damaged propeller and fitted a spare propeller, a big job at sea. Without a bracket to support the propeller shaft, the engine could only be used marginally at low revolutions. In truth, Tetley knew that the engine was finished.

Machinery at sea is troublesome to maintain on a long voyage. The constant enemies are corrosion from salt air and salt water and long periods of inattention. Almost no marine engine on a sailing yacht ever wears out; its innards get destroyed by corrosion. King and Moitessier—the old sea dogs in the race—preferred to sail with no engines at all. Knox-Johnston and Tetley had nothing but trouble and might as well not have had engines considering the amount of annoyance and complication. In addition, the machinery was extremely heavy, took up space, and cost a lot in the first place. The drag of the propeller was another factor. Knox-Johnston and Tetley would have been better off to have taken their engines apart piece by piece and tossed the scraps over the side.

Three of the contestants—Knox-Johnston, Tetley, and Crowhurst—needed to generate electricity for their big radios. Knox-Johnston and Tetley carried small air-cooled gasoline generators; Crowhurst had a large inboard diesel generator that suffered greatly from salt water. Moitessier, as we have seen, had no engine and no radio transmitter.

Now, on November 8th, Tetley was in the southern horse latitudes, or variables, which lay between 23 and 40 degrees south. Both the variables and the doldrums are difficult for sailors because the wind often blows from one direction for a few hours, dies away, and then starts up from a new point on the compass. You get the vessel going nicely, spend half an hour trimming the sails and adjusting the steering vane, and make good time toward your target for two hours. Then the wind collapses to a whisper and stops. The next morning the wind is blowing from the opposite direction with whitecaps on the water. Seas begin to build up. By the time you reef and get going again, the wind has faded away to a breeze that barely ruffles the water.

Sailors find that the variables and the doldrums are two whirlpools of frustration. (The French expression for the doldrums is *pot au noir*—the black pitch pot, or more loosely, the black hole.)

Tetley was 2,000 miles west-northwest of the southern tip of Africa. A fresh wind from the north pushed *Victress* directly toward Cape Town. The next day the wind dropped, rain fell, and the wind swung around to the southwest. Then came calms, followed by light airs from the

southeast. His daily run on November 11th was a miserable 24 miles—
and not all in the right direction. By evening, however, a fair wind was
pushing hard against Tetley's sails.

> I ate the last of the apples [wrote the captain]. The stock had kept
> very well considering the heat in the tropics; only two or three had
> gone rotten. The oranges have ripened nicely and are now in perfect
> condition. Eggs are down to half a dozen, but there are sufficient fresh
> onions for a month.

On November 16th, Tetley had been at sea for two months—sixty
days of solitude. Except for radio problems, he was in good spirits and
generally pleased, particularly after three days of fair winds during
which he logged 500 miles toward the tip of Africa. In the evening the
wind died. It was suddenly calm again. Tetley was in a reflective mood.

> Two months at sea [he wrote in the ship's logbook]! I now feel I
> have settled down, if that is the word, and [have] become conditioned
> to a solitary existence. This way of life no longer strikes me as novel
> or strange; the days go by more or less on a framework of routine. . . .
> Victress has traveled 6,100 miles along the clipper route, less than a
> quarter of the total distance, so far. But having reached the region of
> stronger winds, and the yacht being that much lighter, I anticipate a
> significant improvement in the average daily run. Working to a target
> of 120 miles a day, the trimaran is twelve days behind at this point;
> but barring some misfortune, I believe most of this can be made up
> over the next three months. Victress herself has given me little cause
> for worry. Bits [of trim] have dropped off her, it is true, leaks have
> developed, a mast stay has parted, but such minor troubles are to be
> expected. She is an excellent sea-boat; the self-steering works effec-
> tively and, from the sailing point of view, she is a very easy craft to
> handle.

The next day Tetley checked the bilges in the floats. The center section of the port float had 10 gallons of seawater in it—not too bad—but
the starboard float had 70 gallons! Victress was carrying almost 700
pounds of extra weight!

Tetley worried a lot about the continual leaks and decided to do
something. While the wind was light and the sea calm, he cleared the
stored gear from the floats and cut limber holes in the various compartments so all the water would drain to a central place in each float. He

then ran a bilge hose from the center section of each float into the main hull and to the pumps. Now he could handle any bilge water from a convenient, protected position. Installing this new plumbing was a tedious job at sea, but the captain felt that he had made a major improvement to safety. With the stormy Southern Ocean and the Roaring Forties ahead, who knew when there would be another chance to do such work?

In his spare time, Tetley read a book called *Lord of the Flies* by William Golding, a somewhat morbid best seller (1962) about the savage behavior of a gang of young boys on a remote island. "Whether or not . . . my emotions have grown more responsive through solitude, they have been well and truly wrung by this tale," he wrote.

During the afternoons when the wind was light and *Victress* slowly glided along, the captain often sat on deck in the sun, listening to the tinkling piano refrains of Chopin and watching the birds. Now on the fringes of 40 degrees south, there was usually an albatross and a petrel or two circling the trimaran. The black-and-white-checked pintado petrel (or cape pigeon) had a wingspan of 2 feet or so—long narrow wings with pointed tips. It was a fast flyer that went around the yacht quickly in small circles, sometimes coming in close for a look or occasionally landing on the water alongside.

On November 19th, Tetley finally made radio contact with Cape Town on 17 megacycles. He was immensely relieved to send a message to his wife and the newspapers. He was concerned that his long radio silence might have caused fears in England. When people expected you to call on schedule and you weren't heard from, there was a nagging uncertainty all around. In many ways it was easier on everyone not to have a radio and demanding schedules on such ventures.

The weather grew cooler. Tetley began to put on warmer clothing and to think of sweaters and long underwear. The main battery charger had given out weeks before. Tetley had been using a spare, but now it developed problems as well. Fortunately, the captain was able to get the spare charger working again. He had some anxious moments, however, because no battery power meant no radio communication and no electric lights.

Tetley became aware of increased activity in the cooler ocean. One morning he found two 12-inch squid on deck. There were more seabirds and he sighted two sperm whales. In a radio exchange with Cape Town on November 21st, Tetley learned that Bill King had been rolled over in a severe storm near Gough Island and was out of the race. Robin Knox-Johnston was reported to be in some sort of trouble off New Zealand. What would happen next? Who was left?

As Tetley neared the Cape of Good Hope, the winds continued light and fitful—even in the same area where Knox-Johnston had met his big storm. When it rained, the temperature sometimes dropped surprisingly, and the captain began to wear his polar suit. He felt quite mellow and content. On November 22nd he wrote: "While in the trade winds I had often towed a fishing line and spoon astern hoping for a tuna or bonito. Now, when I saw a small tuna jump near by, I left the fishing line in its box: I felt too much at peace with all God's creatures."

Because of the north-flowing current up the west coast of Africa, Tetley was careful to aim not for the continent itself but a little to the south. When possible, therefore, he steered south or southeast. The winds remained erratic; the sea was mostly calm with some fog and light drizzle. If the sun appeared, Tetley hurried out on deck with his sextant for a celestial observation.

He had plenty of sail drill in the fluky winds. One day he broke a spinnaker pole when lowering a poled-out jib. He was anxious not to use his two 300-square-foot headsails for running in the Southern Ocean because he found these large sails unmanageable in strong winds. Nevertheless, in winds under 15 knots he needed both these sails and more. The problem was running in light winds that increased rapidly. "Leaving a lot of sail up is like playing with dynamite," said Tetley. "And yet, I will have to learn to do just that to get anywhere in the race."

The captain of *Victress* began to get moody and depressed and didn't feel well. "The further I go, the madder this race seems," he wrote on November 27th. "An almost overwhelming temptation to retire and head for Cape Town is growing inside me. The cold finger of reason points constantly in that direction."

Tetley thought that his melancholy outlook might be due to missing nutrients in his diet. He looked at Eve's food recommendation sheet and made a daily drink from dried milk, dried cream, vitamins, yeast, and fruit juice. He reported that he felt better and wrote that his depression vanished in a few days. Nigel learned from Cape Town radio that Alex Carozzo had been forced into Lisbon by illness. Moitessier was making the best time and was three weeks ahead of *Victress*. Tetley decided to drive his vessel a lot harder.

Though the trimaran was almost even with the Cape of Good Hope, the winds were still light and sporadic. The barometer began to fall, however, and there was an ominous ring of heavy cirrus clouds around the sun that suggested a storm was coming. While it was still calm, the resourceful Tetley made a replacement spinnaker pole from a spare aluminum tube he had on board. Being a sailor in such a race wasn't enough; one needed to be an inventor, an engineer, a mechanic, and a squirrel who kept endless spare parts hidden in a burrow somewhere.

On December 1st, the following day, Tetley's sun sights and calculations confirmed that he was east of the tip of Africa, which lay 300 miles to the north. Now it was the Indian Ocean and the Roaring Forties. Sure enough, by the next morning the first gale shrieked out of the northwest.

15

Across the Indian Ocean

L̲ONG-DISTANCE SAILORS WITH AN EYE ON HIGH ADVEN-
TURE often speak of the Southern Ocean, but today you seldom find
mention of this great sea in encyclopedias. Indeed it's rare to discover
the Southern Ocean on a map or in a world atlas at all. Yet the boundaries are simplicity itself: the Southern Ocean is the great world of water
below 40 degrees south latitude that runs around the planet south of the
continents of Africa, Australia, and South America. The southern
boundary is the ice cap of Antarctica.

The Southern Ocean includes the following:

The South Atlantic—85° of longitude, or 3,619 miles from Cape Horn
 to the Cape of Good Hope (measured along 45° S.)
The Indian Ocean—120° of longitude, or 6,034 miles from the Cape
 of Good Hope to Tasmania (measured along 39° S.)
The South Pacific—146° of longitude, or 5,652 miles from Tasmania
 to Cape Horn (measured along 50° S.)
The islands of Bouvet, Kerguelen, McDonald, Heard, Macquarie,
 Auckland, Campbell, Diego Ramírez, South Georgia, South Sandwich, and so forth—all remote scraps of land that few people have
 ever heard of and which are inhabited mostly by birds, penguins,
 and seals

The Southern Ocean is really an anachronism. It's a term that dates
from the days of square-rigged sailing ships, when captains ran down

their easting in the high latitudes, where the west winds and east-setting currents were strong, and where the distance around the earth was shorter. In the days of the wind ships, the Southern Ocean was the fastest and most direct way to move valuable cargoes around the world. The weather was often severe, and floating ice was a hazard; celestial navigation was chancy with overcast skies and uncertain chronometers. The ships were sometimes leaky and short of supplies, but the men pushed on anyway and usually made it back home, where they laughed about it all. Now 100 to 150 years later, the big wind ships are long gone. Yet the Southern Ocean remains the same treacherous place, patrolled only by birds and whales.

OCTOBER 24TH WAS Bernard Moitessier's sixty-third day at sea, and he headed south-southwest to get away from the dangerous swells stirred up by the wind and converging currents near the Cape of Good Hope. As Africa fell astern, the French sailor calculated that he had logged 7,882 miles from Plymouth, England, a little more than a quarter of the 30,000-mile race. Roughly 23,000 miles still lay ahead as he headed into the Indian Ocean.

The flow of water around the southern tip of Africa at the Cape of Good Hope is complicated. The warm Agulhas Current, which runs up to 5 knots, flows roughly southwest along the west coast of Africa. The cold Benguela Current, whose source is in Antarctica, flows northward up the east coast. The Agulhas and Benguela meet at the southern tip of Africa, but their confluence is further confused by the weaker east-flowing, round-the-world current of the Southern Ocean.

The meeting of these huge masses of water of different temperatures, salinities, speeds, and directions sometimes results in slow-moving meanders and countercurrents. But more often, the ocean near the southern tip of Africa is a vast area of brutal and confused seas, particularly when strong winds are blowing. The best thing for large and small vessels is to get away from the southern tip of Africa as quickly as possible.

Moitessier was still mentally and physically weary from the strain of sailing past Africa after the terrible collision with the freighter and the bent bowsprit. In truth, it was a miracle that *Joshua* was still in one piece and fit to continue in the race. At the moment, the steel ketch was fully reefed and plowing along at 6 knots before a fresh westerly wind. Moitessier could have changed up to larger headsails from the tiny jib and staysail and picked up another 15 percent in speed. He was exhausted, however, and realized that he needed food and rest.

> My motions were clumsy and inefficient last night, [he wrote]. It took me three times longer than usual to secure gaskets and reef points. And my reflexes were dangerously slow: somehow I got caught with water up to my knees at the end of the bowsprit, without having seen it coming. The mounting fatigue and under-nourishment of these last days may be to blame.

In the evening the wind eased off. The captain hoisted more sail, and *Joshua* hurried through the night. By noon the next day, Moitessier had logged 164 miles and reached the latitude of 40 degrees south, 70 miles into the iceberg zone. Now he was well away from the Cape of Good Hope and had clear sailing all the way to Australia. The French sailor worried about ice dangers, however, so he steered northwest to stay out of trouble. His general strategy was to sail roughly eastward, but because of the current and the ice, Moitessier elected zigzag tactics.

The sky was decorated with fair-weather cumulus clouds that alternated with patches of blue. The pointer on the barometer hadn't moved for hours, and the wind stayed at about 25 knots from the west-northwest. Big seas rolled up past *Joshua* in a steady procession. Moitessier had spent most of the last two nights in the cockpit drinking coffee and smoking cigarettes. On the first night he worried about sea conditions; on the second was the danger of icebergs, which was marked on the pilot chart by an ominous dotted red line. In spite of his tiredness, the captain was exhilarated.

> I wonder [wrote Moitessier] if my apparent lack of fatigue could be a kind of hypnotic trance born of contact with this great sea, giving off so many pure forces, rustling with the ghosts of all the beautiful sailing ships that died around here and now escort us? I am full of life, like the sea I contemplate so intensely. I feel it watching me as well, and that we are friends.

A lone sailor at sea needs to be as cautious as a cat crossing an alley patrolled by fierce dogs. Danger is on every side, yet the path down the middle is safe. But if he lets down his guard or becomes careless he's liable to get into trouble that lurks only an eyelash away.

A seaman's best defense is routine, *the ship's routine*—the same way of doing each action, practiced until the behavior is almost automatic. He hoists a sail from a certain position. He belays a reefing pendant on a special cleat. He ties a bowline, a clove hitch, a reef knot, or a sheet bend with the same practiced motions. He holds onto a lifeline or a grab rail with one hand as he goes forward. He coils lines clockwise and puts each coil away in an orderly manner. His oilskins hang on the same hook. The winch handle is stored in a favorite place. His hand closes easily around his knife in a certain pocket. The sailor uses the same line for the same job week after week and becomes friendly with that certain well-worn three-strand line with the blue thread. The hauling part of the main halyard goes on the starboard side of the mast; the jib halyard lives to port. And so on. His routine, his practiced certainty, is the sailor's protection from danger. His actions all have a marvelous, essential simplicity.

The sailor is intensely conservative. He will change from his practiced routine, but only if the new way can be demonstrated to be better—infallibly better. He has a preferred way of doing each thing. If something fails he has a second scheme, and then a third, each carried out in methodical order. The seaman checks and rechecks in a patient, logical manner—probing, trying, testing. He is not perfect, of course, but the best sailors are orderly and deliberate. Sloppiness has no place on board.

Each seagoing vessel is different; nevertheless, the sail and anchor handling are standardized to a surprising degree, and a seaman can move easily from one yacht to another.

Sometimes when a sailor is tired he tries to deviate from the routine he's established. This almost never works. Moitessier took a noon sight of the sun. Instead of stowing his sextant in its box below in the usual place, he thought he could save a trip, so he put the boxed sextant in the cockpit for a few moments while he adjusted the sails. Just then a large sea broke on board, filled the cockpit, and almost washed the sextant overboard. Moitessier managed to grab the sextant before it floated away, but he was obliged to spend hours cleaning and drying the precious instrument and its box. So much for departing from a well-established routine!

After the sextant episode, an enormous breaking sea hammered into *Joshua*'s port side and rolled the yacht far over to starboard; the yacht was knocked flat for a few moments before her ballast keel rolled her back upright. From the impact of the sea and the crashing noise, Moitessier thought that all the portlights on the starboard side had been smashed when the *Joshua* was slammed downward.*

---

*As Adlard Coles and many others have pointed out, the damage is seldom on the side of the breaking sea but on the downside—the lee side—where the water is as solid and unyielding as a concrete blockhouse.

Fortunately the portlights were OK. In half a minute the vessel wound up headed into the wind with her sails flapping and the wind vane blade broken. Moitessier got back on course, fitted a spare wind blade, and replaced the mizzen boom preventer line.*

During the big roll, the poor sextant—still drying out—was hurled from the port berth to the starboard berth. "Poor little pal," said Moitessier. "If this hasn't done you in, there really is a guardian angel for sextants, and morons too. First I leave it in the cockpit, then on the *windward* berth. . . . It took an eight-foot free fall through the cabin when *Joshua* went over."

An hour later *Joshua* was knocked down again. The wind had moderated to 20 knots or so. "The sea had become strange, with peaceful areas where it was very heavy, yet regular, with no dangerous breaking waves," wrote Moitessier. "In those areas I could have walked blindfolded twenty times around the deck. Then, without any transition, it would turn jerky and rough; high cross-seas overlapped to provoke sometimes very powerful breaking waves. It was probably one of these cross-seas that hit us earlier. Then *Joshua* would again find herself in a quiet area for ten minutes or more, followed by another rough one."

Once again—in only 25 knots of wind—*Joshua* was knocked down and her mast and sails and spreaders shoved into the sea by a high overtaking wave. This one didn't break but picked up the steel ketch and scooted her forward and down. It was almost as if a giant's thumb had pushed on her coachroof and had pressed the yacht down into the water for four or five seconds. The mast and sails and rigging held. Moitessier saw the wave coming and embraced the chart table with a death grip until the yacht righted herself.

Finally, on October 26th, *Joshua* slipped away from the upset seas, and the Indian Ocean weather turned fair. The captain relaxed, cooked himself enormous meals (fish soup with rice and butter), and slept and slept. The daily runs totaled 117 miles and then 68 in calms and light airs. It was time for sail sewing and dealing with worn places on the staysail and mizzen halyards. While the yacht drifted eastward, she was festooned with damp sweaters and trousers and blankets drying in the sun. (Moitessier claimed that flapping and furious shaking and brushing

---

*A preventer is a line from the end of a boom taken forward to a strong point on deck to keep the boom under control (particularly when running before the wind). Holding a boom down and forward with various lines reduces sail chafe on the standing rigging. In Joshua's case, the preventer line on the mizzen boom kept the boom from striking the steering vane blade when the yacht gybed or if the yacht was rolling about in light airs.

loosens and drives out the salt crystals of garments washed in salt water.) The wind came back on October 28th and the ketch made a marvelous noon-to-noon run of 188 miles.

Moitessier considered the enormity of the challenge of trying to sail around the world alone. It was madness, impossible, much too much for one person. You had to work into it little by little. Perhaps it was like when he had built *Joshua*. In the beginning the project was too big to even think about. He had put the whole building job out of his mind and had concentrated only on an immediate detail—one frame, one steel plate, one deck fitting. A single step at a time. The rest would follow. Sailing around the world was the same. No one could do it at the start but had to work into the project with faith, hope, and lots and lots of patience.

The first gale came on October 30th. The wind rose to a little less than 40 knots, but the storm blew up from the southeast and was hardly worth slamming into. Moitessier hove-to under reduced sail. By the following morning the wind had veered to the northeast and finally to the northwest before dropping away to nothing. First the seas were steep, then white-streaked and choppy as the sky cleared and the barometer climbed. The Frenchman rested and read in his bunk. He often thought of his sailing friends with affection and wondered about the other people in the race. He was disappointed that neither Radio Cape Town nor the BBC had any news.

Was Loïck Fougeron growing his seeds in the plastic saucers the two sailors had bought together in Plymouth?

> Very easy: you take seven saucers, punch a few holes in them, and line them with cloth [wrote Moitessier]. Fill with wheat grains, soybeans, and watercress seeds. Stack them one on top of the other, and moisten with a little water. After a few days, the sprouts are long enough. Remove the bottom saucer, and boil the sprouts or make a salad. Refill the saucer with fresh seeds, put it on top of the pile and sprinkle; next day, remove the bottom saucer, eat the sprouts, refill with seeds, put it on top, sprinkle, etc. you have perpetual motion! . . .
>
> Nigel [Tetley] laughed at our germination experiments. He thought we were going to a lot of trouble for nothing, and he was probably right. Where is Nigel? How far will he get with his trimaran? And Bill King, where is he? Perhaps far ahead, perhaps behind if he got hung up in the doldrums. . . . It is surprising that I did not hear about anyone on the BBC or elsewhere, since Bill and Nigel have

weekly radio contact with their sponsoring newspapers. Maybe they just chucked it . . . transmitter, batteries, heave-ho!—the whole bloody lot overboard, for a little peace and quiet.

Soon a quarter of the Indian Ocean lay behind *Joshua*. The birds fascinated Moitessier. Not solitary fliers or half a dozen, but *hundreds* of birds. There were the two albatrosses: the colossal wandering albatross with its 12-foot wingspan, thick downy covering, and commanding performance; and the 6-foot black-browed albatross. ("All display an attractive almond-shaped pattern around the eye, like a vamp's make-up.") Next came the small black-and-white-checked cape pigeon or pintado petrel. The French captain watched chocolate-brown shearwaters that glided along in teams of eight to fifteen with hardly a flap of their slender, high-aspect wings. There were the diminutive, scampering, butterfly-like black and white storm petrels. And hundreds of unidentified tiny birds the size of robins with silvery plumage, white undersides, dark-gray tails, and a big "W" on top of the wings (perhaps Wilson's storm petrels, a second variety of petrel).

Fresh water was a nagging problem for the round-the-world sailors. Moitessier needed 2 liters of water a day. His tank held 400 liters and was still half full, so he had enough for more than three months. One night rain fell steadily and rinsed the sails. Moitessier added 40 liters to the tank, a bit of a relief because *Joshua* had sailed through very little rain since the Canary Islands two months earlier.

The French captain felt tired. He had lost a few pounds and was a bit underweight, so he began taking vitamin B complex tablets. He made an effort to cook better meals and began to exercise regularly.

He went onward across the Indian Ocean, taking in reefs, shaking them out, and pulling them down again, as the winds from the west rose and fell with the passage of the east-going weather systems. As he crossed the Indian Ocean, the French captain thought of the beautiful tropical islands far to the north. He recalled the three years he had spent on Mauritius and all his friends there. Was he mad not to head north at once and to forget the race, this stupid chase around the world?

During the first seventeen days of November, *Joshua* logged 2,114 miles, an average of 124 miles every twenty-four hours. But the average masked a phenomenal run of 183 miles on November 14th and nothing at all on the tenth and eleventh, when Moitessier hove-to because of adverse winds. Now *Joshua* was nearly halfway between the Cape of Good Hope and Tasmania. The captain drew a long line on the little world globe he carried to mark his progress.

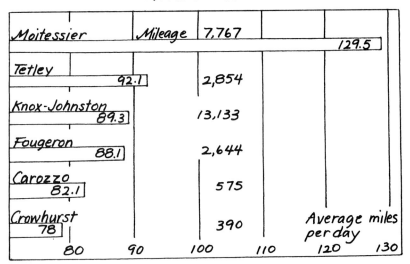

Mileages
November 17th

Moitessier	*Mileage*	7,767			129.5
Tetley 92.1		2,854			
Knox-Johnston 89.3		13,133			
Fougeron 88.1		2,644			
Carozzo 82.1		575			
Crowhurst 78		390		Average miles per day	
80	90	100	110	120	130

On November 17th he ate the last of the one hundred grapefruit he had put aboard in England. In three months, only five or six had gone bad. The garlic was keeping perfectly, and the lemons—each wrapped in paper—were good too. The little purple Morocco onions were in excellent shape; a few had sprouted so Moitessier plucked off the sprouts and put them in his rice. The big white onions were all rotten, however, and he heaved the whole bag into the sea.

Now, like Vito Dumas, the Argentine single-hander who had come this way in *Lehg II* in 1942—twenty-six years earlier—Moitessier was becalmed. *Joshua* drifted slowly eastward in the grip of the current of the Southern Ocean. When you sail on the sea during a brisk wind the surface is upset by waves and swells. The world beneath is totally lost. It's only during calms that you begin to get an idea of the teeming life under the surface.

> Absolutely flat calm [wrote Moitessier]. Sunshine everywhere, above and below. Filling a bucket with water for the dishes, I noticed that the sea is covered with plankton. It is made up of tiny animals smaller than pinheads, zig-zagging along the calm water. Scooped along the surface, the bucket harvests a good hundred of the living mites; a foot or so deeper it only brings up three or four.
>
> There is also a carpet of pretty, flat jellyfish the size of a penny,

that I do not recognize, and a few Portuguese men-o'-war, lovely in the sunlight. They look like blue-tinted oval balloons.

The calm and quiet gave the French captain time to rest and to reflect on his early days: "When I was a child, my mother told me God had painted the sky blue because blue is the color of hope," he wrote. "God must have painted the sea blue for the same reason."

The wind finally returned; *Joshua* was soon sailing fast on a flat sea. Moitessier added sail after sail and eventually flew eight sails that totaled 1,075 square feet.

> I gaze at my boat from the top of the mainmast [he wrote]. Her strength, her beauty, her white sails well set on a well found boat. The foam, the wake, the eleven porpoises on either side of the bowsprit. They are black and white porpoises, the most beautiful I know. They breathe on the fly, almost without breaking the surface, without wavering from the course, towing *Joshua* at nearly 8 knots by invisible bonds. Climbing down to fetch the Beaulieu [movie camera] is out of the question. I would lose everything, and what they give me is too precious; a lens would spoil it all. They leave without my touching them, but the bonds remain.

The albatrosses, malamocks, and shearwaters flew round and round *Joshua* as she surged eastward with the new wind. Light rain alternated with a hot sun. Each time it rained, the captain bucketed a few gallons of water into the tank. He listened to the radio in vain for news of the round-the-world race.

Moitessier had been born in Saigon of a French colonial family, and now as he twisted the radio dial he turned to programs from Vietnam. After twenty years away from his native land, however, he was barely able to understand the language that he had spoken flawlessly as a child and a young man. He thought of the native junks he had once sailed and the 15 to 25 tons of rice he had taken from Cochin China to Cambodia; then back to Rach Gia with a load of wood or palm sugar. The boats were lug-rigged with stayed masts that held fan-shaped sails of woven palm fronds. But the chafe on the rig was terrible, and the sails and sheets were forever sawing themselves to bits.

From November 17th to 24th, *Joshua* logged another 1,064 miles, an excellent run. If we surmise that the east-running current ran at $1\frac{1}{4}$ knots, then 210 of those miles, or about 20 percent of the total, were due to natural causes in the Southern Ocean. During the week, Moitessier collected another 64 liters of fresh water. Then as he neared the edge of an atmospheric high-pressure area that reached west and south from Australia, the wind dwindled and stopped. *Joshua* drifted slowly toward the southwest corner of Australia while shearwaters landed around the red ketch. A dozen, then more. Soon there were sixty birds. Moitessier fed them cheese, butter, and pâté, which they relished, scrapped over, and deviously stole from one another. The French captain watched the birds closely. They became almost tame, and Moitessier felt a great kinship with these wild, feathered sailors of the Southern Ocean.

The wind returned and blew steadily again. *Joshua* crossed the 113th meridian of east longitude. Now the French boat was south of Cape Leeuwin at the southwest corner of Australia. The plan was to sail south of this great land mass that measures 1,680 miles from top to bottom and 2,160 miles from west to east.

Moitessier wanted to give word of his progress to a fisherman or a ship in Bass Strait, a 110-mile-wide waterway between the southeast part of Australia and Tasmania, the island to the south. But the truth was that the French sailor was leery of another encounter with a ship after his disastrous collision off the Cape of Good Hope. How could he let his family and friends know that all was well? During the long calm, Moitessier had built two little model sailboats. Now he put letters on board and launched them.*

The wind remained fair, and in six days *Joshua* made runs that averaged 146 miles a day. The sky was full of signs of weather disturbances, but they didn't come. The southwest swell remained constant. Moitessier thought of his early sailing days.

> When I was sailing with the fishermen of the Gulf of Siam during my childhood in Indochina [he wrote], the taïcong would tell me, for example, "Keep the swell two fingers off the quarter, and you should always feel the wind behind your left ear, looking forward. When the moon is one big hand plus a small hand from the horizon, or when that star is one arm from the other side (in case the moon is hidden by a cloud) then the sea will become a little more phosphorescent, and we will almost be in the lee of the island to set the first lines."
>
> There were no compasses on the Gulf of Siam junks, and I did not

---

*Both models were found more than a year later. One on a beach in Tasmania and the other in New Zealand. The letters arrived intact.

want it used during my sailing school cruises in the Mediterranean. Instead of bearing 110° from France to Corsica, my crew had to steer with the *mistral* swell slightly off the port quarter. At night, it was the Pole Star one small hand abaft the port beam. And if there was neither distinct swell, nor star, we made do with whatever we had. I wanted it that way, because concentrating on a magnetized needle prevents one from participating in the real universe, seen and unseen, where a sailboat moves.

In the beginning [my students] could not understand my insistence on getting away from the compass, that god of the West. But in exchange, they began to hear the sky and sea talking with the boat. And when blue-tinted land appeared on the horizon, looking as it did to the mariners of old, all nimbed with mystery, a few of them felt that our rigorous techniques should leave a door open to those gods which the modern world tries so hard to exclude.

Cape Leeuwin lay far astern. Bass Strait was ahead in the distance, but the area was full of rocks and problems. The French captain decided to skip Bass Strait entirely and to go south of Tasmania. On the night when *Joshua* started her fifth month at sea, it began to rain. Bernard soon collected enough drinking water to last until the Atlantic doldrums.

He reached the mouth of the D'Entrecasteaux Channel in Tasmania before dawn one week before Christmas. The weather was squally. There was a new moon, but the sliver of light was scarcely enough to illuminate the dark sea. The Frenchman slowed his ketch by backing the staysail. In the morning he spotted a fishing boat in the distance and signaled to her with a mirror. The boat motored alongside and stopped 30 yards off. In it were Varley Wisby and his two sons from Launceston, Tasmania.

Moitessier passed his films and letters to Wisby, who said he would give them to the commodore of the Hobart yacht club. Did the Wisbys have any news of the round-the-world solo race? Had any of the sailors passed this way? One of the men had heard something about an English yachtsman who had rounded New Zealand without stopping. The fisherman was uncertain, however, of the man's name or the date. The crews of the two vessels chatted for a few minutes and then parted, one resuming fishing and the other an endless course eastward.

Tasmania and the sea around it seemed colored an enameled green to Moitessier. Everything was green. The land, the sea, and the wake of the ship all reflected a marvelous, incredible green. Only little by little as the land slipped astern did the green fade and turn to the familiar blue. Ahead lay the mighty Pacific and a whole new book of sailing.

When news of Moitessier reached England, excitement rippled through sporting circles and the yachting press. Knox-Johnston had told his sponsor that he expected to round Cape Horn during the first week in January. This would put him back in England about April 10th. However, Moitessier was picking up 30 miles a day on the Englishman.

It began to look like a close contest.

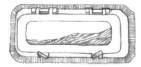

16

The Documented Liar

O<small>F THE FOUR MEN STILL IN THE RACE, DONALD CROW-</small>HURST was in last place. On December 10th, after forty-one days at sea, his Victress trimaran, *Teignmouth Electron,* was 240 miles south of the Cape Verde Islands off the bulge of West Africa, roughly 2,800 miles from England. Unfortunately, he had been averaging only about 68 miles per day, a long way from the 220 miles he had once hoped to achieve on a daily basis.

Crowhurst had been sailing fairly well in a southerly direction with the steady northeast trade wind behind him. However, instead of concentrating on sailing, navigation, keeping the yacht in order, eating, and resting, as a solo sailor should, he decided to win by another way.

On December 10th, he sent a telegram to his press agent, Rodney Hallworth:

PRESSE—DEVONNEWS EXETER

HURTLED SOUTH   FRIDAY 172   BROKE JIB POLE

SATURDAY 109   SUNDAY 243   NEW RECORD

SINGLE HANDER   MONDAY 174   TUESDAY 145

NORTH EAST TRADE FINISHED

The startling claim of 243 miles in twenty-four hours was a new mileage record for single-handed sailors. "Crowhurst Speed World Record?" headlined *The Sunday Times* for December 15th. In the article, the reporter quoted a radio message from *Teignmouth Electron* on December 12th: "I was on watch for the full 24 hours," said Crowhurst. "It took a pretty strong nerve. I have never sailed so fast in my life and I could only manage speeds of up to 15 knots because the sea was never higher than 10 feet. If I get the chance again and the seas run any higher I doubt if I will take it because it might prove too dangerous."

Both Sir Francis Chichester (the chairman of the race) and Captain Craig Rich (the navigational consultant) were surprised at such a fast daily run. The average mileage of the other contestants had been remarkably consistent and generally varied by only 20 or 25 miles a day unless the yacht encountered calms. Crowhurst's daily runs, by contrast, were wildly erratic and suggested problems other than weather. One day 60 miles, then 110, followed by 170. What on earth was going on aboard *Teignmouth Electron?*

Crowhurst was apparently ashamed of his progress, so he decided to give a boost to his ego and reassure his backers by showing that he could sail fast and still had a chance to win the race. His actual course was roughly south with the northeast trade wind blowing across his port quarter. Maybe he could improve things a little by claiming that he was going faster than he really was. Certainly a small addition to his speed wouldn't be noticed. After all, a single-hander can do or say anything he wants; who is out there to contradict him? No one, absolutely no one. In early December, Crowhurst began to prepare a series of bogus positions to authenticate a faster daily speed. In order to do this and keep an accurate series of navigational fixes on noon positions in his logbook, he had to invent a series of fake sun sights.

In the days before satellite navigation, which is only about twenty-five years old, ships at sea and planes in the air found their way by celestial navigation (the global positioning system—GPS—is even more recent). A celestial navigator works from the sextant angle of the sun (or stars, planets, or moon) at a certain moment of Greenwich time. He enters the figures in the *Nautical Almanac* and navigational tables to arrive at a *calculated* sextant angle (based on time), which he compares with his *observed* sextant angle (based on his actual angular measurement of the sun). He then compares one with the other and establishes his location somewhere along a position line toward or away from the sun (or other heavenly body). The navigator then makes a second observation (either later or of another heavenly body at a different angle). The ship's position is where the two position lines intersect.

Crowhurst, however, had to work *backward*. That is, from a bogus position he worked out a phony dead reckoning latitude and longitude, an ersatz intercept, false calculated and true sextant angles, and all the rest. Doing this sort of mental hocus-pocus while rolling around at sea is extremely difficult, yet the brainy Crowhurst worked it all out and wrote down the final figures in his falsified logbook.

He knew that the previous record for a twenty-four-hour run by a single-hander was 220 miles, so he exceeded it by just 23 miles. He added various details to round out the deception. On Friday, December 6th, for example, he wrote: "Boom guy parted, and jib pole folded up on shrouds."

Small-boat experts familiar with ocean sailing know that if a boom guy parts when running before the wind, the pole will go forward and bang against the headstay. It's possible—though unlikely—that the pole will break because only the forward portion of the pole will hit the headstay wire. Certainly this has nothing to do with the shrouds—the wires at the side of the mast.

Either Crowhurst made a mistake and wrote the word "shrouds" when he meant "headstay," or he was already fantasizing and writing fiction in the ship's logbook. From this and other clues you begin to get the feeling that Crowhurst was a character in a novel that had come to life. A fictional deception that had burst onto a nonfiction scene. A piece of brass in an iron world.

We know that in a seaman's day almost every moment is documented. Crowhurst was a fraud who now invented his own documentation. Henceforth his whole existence became one of tragic make-believe. The truth was somehow unfair for Donald; therefore the nasty truth had to be bypassed.

The trouble with lying is that once you begin a deception you create a monster that can hardly be stopped without destroying yourself. In order to protect himself, a liar must constantly compound his falsehoods. He needs a phenomenal memory. Eventually he becomes so involved in deceit that his false tower crashes to the ground. The only uncertainties are how high the tower will climb and how long it will stand. Few people have compassion for liars; the pity is reserved for the innocent who are caught up and victimized.

Yet the round-the-world race was so unique, the sailing demands so unusual, and the physical and mental requirements so daunting that no one dreamed that any of the contestants would cheat. The men out there had so much to do that there was no time for deceit. Or was there?

On Thursday, December 12th, Crowhurst began to keep a new logbook of his actual progress. He used a large blue exercise book, into which he entered his courses, the winds, mileages, sail changes, and so on. In case he were to continue with his fraudulent logbook he would need a *true* logbook—a genuine center of reality—from which to work.

Crowhurst's biographers point out that faking a one-day speed record is very different from faking an entire round-the-world voyage. It had taken Crowhurst hours to falsify his logbook when he claimed the one-day record run on December 8th. If he were to counterfeit his entire voyage, he would need the creative abilities of a Tolstoy plus the navigational background of a Sir Francis Chichester.

How could Crowhurst possibly know the weather off the Cape of Good Hope or New Zealand or Cape Horn at some date in the future? How would he explain his failure to be sighted? Or worse yet, suppose after radioing a spurious position he was seen and reported elsewhere by a ship? What if he—a monstrous thought grew in his brain—what if he returned to England before the others after marking time in the solitary backwaters of the South Atlantic? Suppose, just suppose, he sent false messages from time to time to suggest that he had rounded South Africa, that he was near Australia, and that he was passing Cape Horn? In each case he could arrange his progress to indicate that he was gaining on the leaders and finally had passed into the lead. He would arrive home ahead of the others and be declared the winner!

Could he pull off the radio and television interviews, the speeches at the banquets, and the yarning with other sailors without tripping himself up? He would need the skill of a Shakespeare repertory actor and the factual grasp of an encyclopedia editor.

To phony up a logbook was one thing. To be a false national hero was quite another. The humiliation of exposure could be disastrous. What would his friends say? How could he face his wife and his children? He would be denounced as a hoax and a fraud and a humbug. Yet the scheme was unique and had a certain fascination.

Crowhurst was full of indecision. He was like a child inching back and forth on a teeter-totter, not sure which way to go. He had three choices:

1. *Total falsification.* The round-the-world deception was tempting and a possible way out, but the problems were horrendous.
2. *Quit the race.* He could simply withdraw. By doing this he would admit failure. His sponsor, Mr. Best, had the right to demand that Crowhurst buy back the yacht, which would mean bankruptcy. This might not happen, but it could.
3. *Follow the rules and go on.* He could continue in the race and get down to the business of the necessary repairs and honest sailing. If he were the last to finish, at least he would complete the competition honorably.

But instead of making a choice, Crowhurst tried to juggle all three options. He postponed what should have been a simple decision of right and wrong. As a man he was weak, indecisive, timid, and afraid.

On an Admiralty planning chart he began to sketch a schedule for the false voyage:

Date	False Position	True Position
December 18th	3° south of the equator	2°N
December 22nd	10°S; off NE Brazil	2°S
December 24th	15°S; NE of Rio de Janeiro	6°S
January 5th	35°S; between Buenos Aires and Capetown.	17°S
January 15th	42°S, 12°W; SE of Gough Island in the Roaring Forties	22°S, 33°W

Crowhurst studied the pilot book for Brazil in case he decided to withdraw from the race. He made a detailed sketch chart for Rio de Janeiro just as he had earlier for Funchal, Madeira. If he continued around the world he needed to make a number of repairs. Therefore Crowhurst wrote out a list of sixteen projects, including repairs to the self-steering gear, which had become damaged, the masthead buoyancy bag arrangement that had never been completed, and work on the generator to make it less susceptible to saltwater damage.

While he was considering his three choices, Crowhurst kept sending misleading telegrams to Rodney Hallworth, his press agent, who was doing his best to present his client favorably. On December 17th, Crowhurst tapped out a message in Morse code that read:

THROUGH DOLDRUMS   OVER EQUATOR   SAILING FAST AGAIN

At this time he was really 180 miles north of the equator, still in the doldrums, and was scarcely making any progress at all. On December 20th, he radioed that he was off Brazil and averaging 170 miles daily. On this day he actually covered only 13 miles—his slowest twenty-four hours so far—and was only a little south of the equator at 30 degrees west, a position about 390 miles from the Brazilian coast.

Although he was leaning toward the false round-the-world voyage, Crowhurst still hadn't made up his mind. He continued to draw up lists of work necessary to get the trimaran into shape for going on. He was also still thinking of putting into Rio de Janeiro. On December 21st, Crowhurst received a new blow when he discovered that some of the plywood on his starboard float had begun to split. This discouraged him further.

Three days later he sent a telegram to Hallworth claiming that he was near Ilha da Trindade. In truth *Teignmouth Electron* was at 6 degrees south and 33 degrees west: a little east of Natal, Brazil, where the shoulder of the South American continent pushes farthest east into the Atlantic. Ilha da Trindade lay 900 miles away to the south-southeast!

The deceit was growing. Crowhurst's real world was falling apart. The repairs were beyond him, and he was afraid to put into Rio de Janeiro.

The decision had been made.

17

A Hell of a Prospect

WHEN ROBIN KNOX-JOHNSTON HAD A BIG JOB AHEAD OF HIM he always liked to split it in two and make the first part as difficult as possible. He was then able to reward himself with an easier second half. For the round-the-world trip, the logical halfway point was Melbourne, at the southeast corner of Australia. From this point on, Knox-Johnston marked his daily log "Homeward Bound" (underscored several times). As his personal halfway mark, however, he chose the international date line—which is east of New Zealand—a goal that he was not to cross for another three weeks.

From Bass Strait, *Suhaili* sailed southeast and passed the northeast corner of Tasmania via Banks Strait. The early November spring weather was calm and sunny, a good time for sail repairs. There was scarcely any swell and Knox-Johnston got lots of sleep. *Suhaili*'s course lay to the east-southeast to pass south of New Zealand, a distance of 960 miles. By now Knox-Johnston had broken Francis Chichester's nonstop sailing record of 15,517 miles.

Since the mechanical self-steering devices aboard *Suhaili* had fallen to pieces and there was nothing more on board from which to make parts, Knox-Johnston began to experiment with the sails to see if he could get the 32-foot wooden ketch to steer herself. This is a tricky business because the wind seldom blows steadily from the same point of the compass, and usually changes slightly in force and direction from time to time. In addition, a vessel at sea is pushed from side to side by the waves and swells of the ocean, which tend to disturb a ship's balance and heading. Also, an arrangement that is working well can be upset by all sorts of things—more wind, less wind, bigger seas, momentary calms, reefing the sails, and so forth. An effective self-steering arrangement needs to be dynamic; that is, you need something based on wind direction that will exert a positive, course-correcting force. The muscles for this can come from some part of the running rigging, from the wind pressure on a sail, centerboard balance, or a servo blade in the water.*

As *Suhaili* headed toward New Zealand, the wind was from ahead and the yacht steered herself close-hauled. On the third day, however, the wind changed to a fair breeze from the northwest—behind the vessel's port quarter. Knox-Johnston tried easing all the sheets, putting the sails on the starboard side, and lashing the tiller. The vessel kept swinging into the wind. The captain then lashed the tiller a little to port to give more corrective weather helm. This resulted in keeping the ship from turning into the wind. Now, though, she began to swing the other way and gybe—that is, to turn the stern of the yacht through the eye of the wind so that the wind blew on the other side of the sails. So far, the self-steering efforts were largely a failure.

Knox-Johnston kept adjusting the tiller, moving it a fraction of an inch at a time. The wind picked up, however, and obliged him to shorten sail, which made the vessel easier to steer. Obviously the self-steering problems were not going to be solved on the first day.

One night the wind increased and the yacht gybed. When the captain started to put his ship back on course, the tiller broke off at the rudder head. While Knox-Johnston was lashing the shortened tiller back on the rudder, he dropped the mainsail and most of the mizzen. To his surprise, with a jib set forward, *Suhaili* tended to run off before the wind right along on course. Knox-Johnston eventually found that if he sailed with the full mizzen and three reefs in the mainsail, his vessel would go along nicely at 5 knots. (Evidently the yacht was set up to run with lee helm and, if she bore off, the jib would be partially blanketed by the mainsail and the mizzen would push her back on course by increasing weather helm—the force that heads a vessel into the wind.)

With *Suhaili* now steering reasonably well, Knox-Johnston was heartened. His spirits went up and he began to think that maybe he would get across the Pacific yet. At one time, he had considered steering by hand for sixteen hours a day and then stopping for eight hours to eat and sleep. The actual work this involved did not bother him; what oppressed him was the boredom of months of sixteen-hour steering watches.

On Sunday, November 17th, at 2100, Knox-Johnston switched on his radio to get the weather report from New Zealand. The weather had been good for several days and the captain hoped it would continue until

---

*Small electric autopilots that use the output from a fluxgate compass to drive a reversible electric motor hooked to the rudder were not sufficiently developed in 1968.

he got through Foveaux Strait, a 15-mile-wide passage that lies between New Zealand's main South Island and smaller Stewart Island to the south. The weather forecast mentioned unsettled conditions for the next twenty-four hours and a deep low-pressure area forming south of Tasmania, which could mean a gale from the west. At the end of the forecast, the announcer read a special message that took Knox-Johnston's breath away:

> MASTER, *SUHAILI*. IMPERATIVE WE RENDEZVOUS OUTSIDE BLUFF HARBOUR IN DAYLIGHT. SIGNATURE: BRUCE MAXWELL.

Suhaili's master was overjoyed. Obviously his mail and messages from Australia had gotten through. He looked forward to news from home and a chance to find out how the race was going. The New Zealand radio station thought that he might be listening and had read the message for *Suhaili* with each broadcast.

Bluff Harbour was on the north side of Foveaux Strait, about 160 miles from *Suhaili*'s position. The ketch was running at 5 knots before a fair wind under a large jib and the mizzen. When Knox-Johnston awoke at 0500 the next morning, he saw South Island to the north and tiny Solander Island away to the east, which gave him his position. Bluff was still 90 miles away, too far to make it by sunset, so Knox-Johnston hove-to near Solander Island, 72 miles from Bluff, to use up a little time. He wanted to sail the remaining miles during the night so he would arrive at Bluff in the early-morning hours. Then he could see what he was doing and would have some extra daylight hours available in case of delays or problems in sailing and maneuvering.

One is seldom ahead of time in a small vessel.

The barometer had fallen, and the wind freshened. The sea grew rougher and Knox-Johnston had to steer by hand because the ketch was being tossed about too much for her to manage by herself. The predicted weather low had moved quickly to the east; obviously the front was not far away.

The situation was ominous and reads almost like the prelude to a shipwreck. Because he wanted to keep the rendezvous at Bluff, Knox-Johnston found himself sailing toward a lee shore in a gale. Foveaux Strait appeared to be a trap—a narrow passage impeded with islands and shoals and unknown currents and tidal streams. The visibility was rapidly growing worse. The yacht was in poor condition. The one-man crew was tired; Robin had only limited reserves of energy. All told, the prospects were grim.

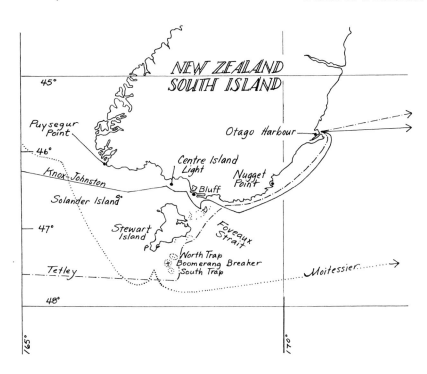

The prudent course would have been to have sailed southeast and left all the land to the north. Now, however, it was too late because *Suhaili* was already into the strait. The vessel was committed and running eastward with a tiny storm jib and a double-reefed mainsail. The only thing to do was to press on and try to avoid the hazards of the land and somehow get through. Knox-Johnston cleared his vessel for action.

He went below and switched on the evening weather report. He felt like a prisoner before a judge who was delivering a sentence. The words came in calm, methodical, passionless phrases.

> The cold front is 80 miles away and is moving at 40 knots. Winds of Force 9 are expected. The gale will increase to Force 10, with very heavy rain and poor visibility.

Knox-Johnston listened to his special rendezvous message read out again and wished that he had never heard it. If he hadn't slowed down he would have been clear of the strait and islands by now.

In the early evening of November 18th, he sighted the Centre Island lighthouse ahead. This gave him a course to steer. Shortly afterward, however, the lighthouse disappeared when the wind changed from north-northwest to west and freshened appreciably. Rain began to pour down. Knox-Johnston streamed a warp and sea anchor to slow his progress as much as possible.

By 0230 the wind was shrieking at gale force. The captain gulped a little brandy, handed the mizzen, and sheeted the storm jib amidships. The visibility was appalling. Clouds of spray from the wind-lashed waves streamed into the air and shattered into horizontal streaks of needlelike hail. Knox-Johnston climbed above the cockpit on the remnants of the self-steering gear and looked for the Centre Island light. It was bitterly cold and his hands grew numb. After what seemed an eternity he spotted a whitish glow with the time interval of the Centre Island light, so he adjusted his course 30 degrees to the south to clear some rocks southeast of the lighthouse. He watched for breakers until he was past the rocks and went below for an Irish coffee and a cigarette.

In the early dawn, the visibility was still abysmal because of the wind-driven spray. Knox-Johnston changed his course back to the east. He was worried that he might run past Bluff and onto a mass of shoals and small islands. Finally at 0730 a dim outline ahead straightened into land. *Suhaili* was being set directly down on it. There was no recourse except to set the main and reefed mizzen quickly and to take in the sea anchor and the 720-foot warp.

The sails went up OK, and *Suhaili* started to head up, but the warp and sea anchor were hopelessly tangled, and pulling in the mess was a frightful job. Knox-Johnston wondered if this was going to be the end of his voyage. With a strength born of desperation, he somehow hauled all the lines aboard. Waves battered the ship. Water flew everywhere as *Suhaili* labored to claw up to windward a little. She inched past the land.

It had been a near miss. Suddenly Robin realized how cold, wet, and tired he was. His hands were red and raw from the cold and the exertion of heaving on lines. And the day was only beginning! He managed to thaw out his aching hands around a cup of coffee. The barometer had begun to rise and although the wind was still a full gale, the seas were smoother in the strait.

At 0900 an island appeared. Then a second. Knox-Johnston tacked around the second island and headed north toward where he thought Bluff might be. A little later a local ferry, the *Wairua*, appeared, madly rolling. The people on board seemed to recognize *Suhaili* and called to Knox-Johnston that Bluff was 9 miles north.

At 1030 Bluff showed up ahead, but the tidal stream was pouring out of the channel into the harbor. *Suhaili* was now out of the protection of Stewart Island and was rapidly being shoved to leeward by the force of the storm. The water was shoaling so Knox-Johnston turned downwind again, streamed his various warps to slow the vessel, and went forward to drop the mainsail. When he threw the winch brake and the sail did not come down, his heart sank. The main halyard had somehow jumped off the masthead sheave and had jammed alongside. The sail could be neither hoisted nor lowered. What a time for this to happen!

The resourceful Knox-Johnston slacked off the reefed sail by unrolling three turns off the boom. He then topped the boom up and lashed the sail to the mast and boom. The job was not perfect by any means, but it was better than nothing because the wind was shrieking at more than 50 knots. By 1300, however, it had eased a little. By this time, *Suhaili* was north of all the small islands that lay across Foveaux Strait. The captain continued his watch until dusk, when he spotted the light signal on Nugget Point, which meant that he was well clear of danger. He went below and collapsed.

The next morning the wind was only 20 knots. *Suhaili* was alone on the ocean with no land in sight. Knox-Johnston took a number of celestial observations to establish his position and set a course for Otago, on the southeast coast of New Zealand's South Island. Land appeared in the early afternoon and the wind dropped off. With the jammed main halyard, however, only the reefed mainsail could be set, which was inadequate for the light weather.

Knox-Johnston finally slipped around the cliffs of Tairoa Heads at 1840. The wind had fallen still lighter, was fluky, and a strong tidal stream ran out of the harbor against *Suhaili*. He didn't have the proper chart of Otago Harbour and attempted to tack along the shore, where the strength of the tidal stream was less. While maneuvering in a little bay near Tairoa Heads, he ran aground on a sandy bottom.

Since the tide was dropping, the only thing to do was to carry out an anchor to deeper water and wait for the flood tide to float *Suhaili*. When Knox-Johnston took out the anchor and turned to swim back to his vessel, he got quite a shock. His home for the past five months looked ghastly. No longer were *Suhaili*'s topsides white and glistening. She was tousled and dirty. Ugly brown rust stains ran down from various pieces of ironwork along the hull and masts. The once-white Dacron mainsail was streaked and stretched. The yacht needed a big refit, but this was impossible now.

A voice shouted down from the cliffs above *Suhaili*. Knox-Johnston asked the caller to please contact Bruce Maxwell in Otago. The captain declined any help, however, because he was afraid of being disqualified from the race. He thought he could get off by himself.

A launch and the crayfishing boat *Anna Dee* came to see him and offer assistance. Knox-Johnston politely rejected help but was overjoyed to talk to people after having been alone for 159 days. While the talk continued and various people came and left, Knox-Johnston hoisted himself aloft and dealt with the jammed masthead sheave. While he worked, he kept talking to his visitors. It was lovely and peaceful in the little bay, a contrast to the day before, when *Suhaili* and the captain had been in a desperate fight for survival.

About an hour before midnight on November 20th, *Suhaili* began to lift on the rising flood tide. Bruce Maxwell, the chief reporter of the *Sunday Mirror* in England, finally arrived from Bluff. Knox-Johnston was keen for mail and news from home. However, the rules of the race had been changed and no material assistance of any kind was now allowed. Maxwell had decided this included mail, so he had brought none. This infuriated Knox-Johnston, who thought this was a petty and childish restriction.

Nevertheless, Maxwell quickly told his eager listener that his family was well and gave him the news about Fougeron, Moitessier, and King. The English sailor was disappointed to hear that King's *Galway Blazer II* had been forced out of the race with broken masts.

"If only [King] had had a conventional rig," lamented Knox-Johnston. "A junk rig may be easiest to handle, but junks have huge masts and even then [they] are constantly breaking. . . . The whip on a mast in a small, pitching boat is terrific, and this has to be restrained by shrouds [and stays]."

Knox-Johnston heard about Tetley and Crowhurst and Carozzo. He learned that the race authorities predicted a close finish between him and Moitessier if both kept going at the same rate. This news excited *Suhaili*'s captain and made him more determined than ever to win the race.

A little after midnight, a dangerous northwest wind began to blow into the anchorage. Knox-Johnston decided to leave. He hoisted the mainsail and mizzen. Then he went forward and set the jib. When *Suhaili* swung on to the port tack, the captain pulled in the sheets from the cockpit. As the ketch picked up speed she headed for the rocks along Tairoa Heads to the north. Knox-Johnston tacked quickly, rushed forward as *Suhaili* sailed over her anchor, and picked up the anchor and some of the line. He tacked again, cleared the rocks, set the staysail, and hauled the anchor aboard. It was a tricky maneuver for a single-hander to sail out the anchor by himself.

The *Anna Dee* had stood by just in case, and now Knox-Johnston threw across a completed diary, some letters, and charts to be sent to England. The Pacific and Cape Horn lay ahead.

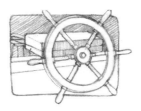

18~

"Nasty Hissing Seas"

NIGEL TETLEY WAS THE THIRD MAN IN THE RACE TO SAIL across the Indian Ocean. Though the weather was sharp and overpowering at times, he managed to keep his trimaran rushing eastward in pursuit of the leaders. Each day Tetley ate into his stores and used up various supplies a little more. Because she was lighter, the multihull sailed a bit faster, and the bearded naval commander nursed a faint hope that he would slip ahead of the leaders. At least he was getting closer.

In the meantime, every twenty-four hours was a small battle in itself. Tetley had heard so much about the Roaring Forties and the great westerly winds that he presumed he would have constant winds behind him as soon as he turned east in the Southern Ocean. In truth what he found was a never-ending series of east-moving weather depressions—some to his north and some to his south—whose winds boxed the compass as they overtook *Victress*. This meant endless sail drill to keep the vessel going at her fastest. Yet Tetley had to be careful not to put up too much sail or else he would overpower his vessel and drive her to destruction.

The advantage of multihulls is speed, which exercises an almost hypnotic fascination for some men. Tetley had already logged almost 200 miles in a single day and in theory could go a good deal faster. A monohull with a displacement hull, by contrast, has its maximum speed dictated by its waterline length. The monohull *Joshua*, for example, had a maximum hull speed of 8 knots or so, which could not be exceeded under any circumstances except when running before big waves that might sweep the vessel forward for a few seconds.

In theory the multihulls could go faster and easily win the race *if* they weren't capsized and *if* the three hulls could be made to stay together. In a short race in England, a multihull sailor named Bill Howell had pushed his catamaran *Golden Cockerell* up to 22 knots. She had capsized, however, and finished the race with her spars pointing downward before being towed into port. Unfortunately, there were neither friendly ports nor helpful rescue crews in the Indian Ocean where *Victress* was heading.

"The multihull sailor must be more skilful, more vigilant, and must work harder than his singlehull rival," wrote *The Sunday Times* reporter Murray Sayle in a high-flying story on November 24th. Unlike other reporters, Sayle had actually accompanied another man on an Atlantic crossing in a multihull. "The nervous strain is tremendous. The compensation is speed. Tetley now has before him 14,000 miles of a multihull sailor's paradise, with the relentless following winds of the Roaring Forties, all the way to the Horn," he continued, repeating the myths and fantasies about the Southern Ocean and its steady following winds.

> If his nerves hold out, 200 or 250 miles a day is possible [Sayle wrote]. . . . Sailing the Atlantic . . . this summer, we did 1,000 miles in four and a half days, but we found the self-steering wildly erratic. . . . A couple of hours at the wheel at speeds of 16 or 18 knots, wildly skating down waves and pulling up with the bows buried in a smother of foam, was like riding the Wall of Death. No one really knows whether a singlehander can keep a boat like *Victress* under control from [the Cape of] Good Hope to [Cape] Horn because Tetley is the first man to try it. His attempt has given the race a new fascination.

Certainly it took great talent and determination to keep a light and powerful vessel going at high speeds week after week. Already Tetley had sailed a solo trimaran much farther than anyone else and had set a record for long-distance multihull travel. A monohull with its heavy ballast keel is infinitely safer and easier to sail because the hull design is stable and forgiving. Except for an extreme design or unless she is holed, a monohull with a fixed lead or iron keel will always return to an upright, stable position. A multihull that is upset and flips upside down will stay upside down.

No one knew this better than Tetley. When the wind began to moan and the rigging began to hum, he did one of three things:

1. Quickly reduced sail.
2. Ran the yacht dead downwind with a small jib sheeted flat amidships.
3. Took down all the sails and allowed the yacht to drift before the storm and prayed that a breaking wave didn't capsize the vessel.

During the first two weeks of Tetley's run from the Cape of Good Hope to New Zealand, he experienced four gales, three near gales, and one spectacular broach. Another day *Victress* heeled so much that all the dishes on the sink drain crashed to the cabin sole (for the first time on the voyage). Yet there were times when the wind was so light that the seabirds gave up flying and the yacht was set backward by the west-setting meanders in the ocean current. There were moments when Nigel was lyrical about the sunsets on the Indian Ocean. "This evening's was no exception," he wrote on December 4th. "A beautiful matrix of indigo, blood red, bright gold, and cerulean blue."

Tetley's major problem was how long to hang onto his big sails when the wind increased. He needed large sails for speed, but in strong winds they were a risky business. The basic running sails were two 300-square-foot triangular jibs, each hanked to the headstay and held at the outer lower points—the clews—with long spinnaker poles that were angled slightly forward. One sail was poled out to port and the other to starboard. *Victress* went fast with these big running jibs and steered herself perfectly.

When the wind increased quickly, however, it was a hair-raising game for one person to get the big sails and long poles safely down on deck. On a crewed ocean racer, it took three or four men to deal with such a running rig.

Tetley was a clever and resourceful master mariner and managed by himself, but the job was scary. He wanted *Victress* to go as fast as possible, yet if he waited too long he was liable to get into trouble unhooking the unwieldy poles and lowering them. Once the poles were lashed on deck, he still had to take the halyards off the winches and do a dance to capture the slippery jibs, which were full of wind.

With gale- or near-gale-force winds coming from astern, Tetley used tiny 40-square-foot storm jibs without bearing-out poles. With this arrangement, however, the yacht did not steer herself downwind. In order for the yacht to run unattended, Nigel had to change course so the wind was on the quarter. This scheme was good in theory but did not work out because the sails were too small and flogged terribly when the yacht swung from side to side. Tetley happened to read an excerpt from Joshua Slocum's book *Sailing Alone Around the World,* in which the shrewd Nova Scotian had successfully run before a frightful storm on the west side of Tierra del Fuego by sheeting a jib amidships. Tetley tried this scheme, which worked so well that he adopted it at once.

During the night of December 14th, Tetley hung onto full sail before a 22-knot northwest wind. When he worked out his position the next day he was delighted to find that he had run 202 miles noon to noon, a new

VICTRESS

record for him. But in the afternoon the wind dropped to 5 knots. *Victress* glided slowly along while the captain played classical music, cooked his evening meal, and used a bit of extra fresh water for a bath. The calm weather lasted three days.

Tetley decided to make a larger rudder for his self-steering unit. He managed to cut one from some high-density laminate that he had on board. Meanwhile, albatrosses paddled up to *Victress* on the quiet sea. Tetley fed them bits of homemade bread that he baked once a week. He thought of Samuel Taylor Coleridge's poem "The Rime of the Ancient Mariner" as he fed a big bird:

> It ate the food it ne'er had eat . . .
> And every day, for food or play,
> Came to the mariner's hollo!

On December 17th, the project of the day was to repair a sheet winch that had seized up. Tetley had tried hammers, wedges, penetrating oil, and even a blowtorch, but the recalcitrant winch drum wouldn't budge. Finally he got the idea of drilling and tapping two holes in the top of the drum. He then bolted on a long piece of wood and with the leverage of length managed to twist the frozen drum off the winch base. The grease had evidently failed. Nigel resolved to use oil to lubricate his winches henceforth.

The wind returned on December 18th, and by the following noon *Victress* had run 183 miles. On the next day Tetley managed a marginal radio contact with Cape Town and was pleased to receive Christmas greetings from his family, his Music for Pleasure sponsors, and *The Sunday Times*. On December 20th, a mizzen shroud parted—"Over-strong wire for the job too, and the sail was not even hoisted at the time. Metal fatigue."

Three squid landed on board during the night and went into the pot for breakfast. The wind died away in the afternoon, so Tetley inflated his rubber dinghy, put it in the water, and began to scrape away a crop of fat, speed-robbing goose barnacles that he had noticed along the waterline of the boat. As Tetley worked around the hull he looked into the water and saw a 7-foot shark beneath him. When he finished with the barnacles and climbed back on board he baited a giant shark hook with a can of corned beef and hoisted the shark on board. Tetley kept the tail, which he decided to display on the bow of *Victress* if she should complete her trip around the world. To finish the day the captain repaired the broken mizzen shroud.

On December 22nd, the wind rose to 25 knots but dropped to 14 knots the next morning. At noon, Tetley discovered that the steering wires had broken again. He had put on new wire near the Cape Verde Islands—8,000 miles ago—and now fitted more new wire, this time a bit heavier. He sometimes wondered whether he could keep ahead of the problems that appeared each day and whether his spare parts and ingenuity would triumph over the deterioration and breakage.

"The wind continued to increase and I lowered the second jib and sheeted the other fore and aft," wrote Tetley the next day. "Before long it was blowing Force 8–9 [about 40 knots] with snarling crests flinging themselves at *Victress*'s stern—trying to slew her round. These conditions are typical of the Roaring Forties and I will have to learn to live with them. Towards dusk, when the sea had grown longer, though higher, she seemed a lot happier."

On Christmas Eve the wind blew hard all day but eased off at nightfall. Tetley had decided on a mushroom sauce to go with his Christmas bird, so he marinated some first-quality dried mushrooms in red wine. He made bread, tidied up the cabin, and got out the Christmas presents that had been put on board before he left England.

Tetley started Christmas Day by playing carols from Guildford Cathedral. When he opened his presents, he found a handsome pewter tankard from his wife Eve, a stainless steel comb from his son Mark, and a dictionary from his son Philip. Tetley had only seabirds for company, so he made up an offering of bread and tinned fish for his flying friends. The wind settled down in the afternoon, and the yacht steered herself nicely while the captain had a few glasses of sherry and prepared his holiday meal.

"The dinner table was made as attractive as possible with the last of the oranges, the only surviving packet of nuts, and raisins and sweets displayed," wrote Tetley. "The pheasant, on the verge of falling to pieces, was carved with due solemnity; and . . . [I toasted] the family with a bottle of champagne. . . . I felt very festive for a time with my favourite music playing—afterwards very lonely . . . then fortunately I fell asleep."

Tetley took several photographs of himself seated before his Christmas dinner in the cabin. Eventually—as we shall see—the films were tossed on the deck of a fishing vessel, flown to England, and developed.

Of all the photographs to come out of the round-the-world race, none is more poignant than the sight of Nigel Tetley raising his new pewter tankard to the camera while his elaborate Christmas dinner and bottle of champagne and loaf of bread sit on the table in front of him. The photograph demonstrates the paradox of the single-hander: the battle to prove his strength of purpose and resourcefulness and his need to be with his friends and loved ones.

Tetley's carefully arranged picture and his salute to the camera with his brimming tankard suggest a terrible loneliness and a longing for his wife and sons. We see a plucky naval officer on a tour of duty that turned out to be a hundred times more demanding than any military maneuvers. We look at a remarkable man on a voyage that hadn't been tried before. We watch a man in a naked moment of uncertainty mixed with hope, of doubt combined with striving, of longing twisted around enjoyment.

The picture was so strong and powerful that even the flint-hearted editor of *The Sunday Times*, a man used to news of a thousand crises, horror stories, and troubles, immediately printed the photograph in an eight-column cut across a full page so that his 1,413,847 weekly readers and their families would see and understand. Tetley had the champagne

NIGEL TETLEY ON CHRISTMAS DAY [THE SUNDAY TIMES]

and pheasant, but he had no one with whom to share it. What could be worse? It was the dedicated hermit writhing on a bed of loneliness.

Of course, trying to generalize about single-handed sailors is like trying to generalize about the human race. Each of the four men still in the round-the-world competition was as different from one another as a butterfly is different from a bluebird. The dogged and persevering Knox-Johnston was busy worrying about defeating the French and winning the race to uphold the honor of the British. He was also occupied trying to keep his small vessel together. Moitessier, with the best boat in the race by far and the most sailing experience, was completely happy communing with nature and the sea and recharging his spiritual batteries. Crowhurst was a pathetic mental case. Tetley couldn't wait to finish the wretched race and to be done with it. In the meantime he was perfecting his wine sauces and listening to Beethoven.

By January 1st, *Victress* had passed tiny Amsterdam and St. Paul islands in the south Indian Ocean, where Tetley listened to some "nasty hissing seas." He had done more sail sewing (after first gluing on patches) and had gone through yet another gale. The captain had eaten his last orange and had ceremoniously sacrificed the final onion for a special spaghetti sauce. During calms, whales swam past the trimaran while Tetley worked on his lifeless main engine, which had developed its fifth major defect since England and apparently had gone to sleep for good. On January 2nd, Tetley spoke on the radio to Australian operators who were surprised at the strength of *Victress*'s transmission.

During the afternoon of January 5th, the wind shifted to south by east. Rain thundered down, and Tetley collected several gallons of drinking water from the runoff on the wheelhouse roof. In the evening the wind veered south and increased to gale force. After two hours of sail shortening, Tetley finally put all the sails down and lay beam-on to the storm. The wind blew 50 knots, the rain continued, and the temperature plummeted to 40°F. There was a steep cross swell and several waves banged hard against the yacht. Water worked into the wheelhouse and even squirted past the usually impenetrable cabin skylight. Tetley finally got tired of the storm and tried sailing with one of the tiny storm jibs. But when the yacht got hit by a big wave and knocked half over, he quickly returned to lying-to before the storm without any sails at all. By the evening of January 6th, the wind had eased off and on the next morning was only 8 knots from the west. Tetley spent the day opening up and drying out the trimaran and his wet clothes and bedding, a sailor's usual move after a nasty storm.

On his January 7th call to Australia, Tetley learned that Moitessier had been sighted off Tasmania on January 2nd (the actual date was December 19th). Knox-Johnston's last known position was along the east coast of New Zealand's South Island on November 21st, six weeks earlier. Knox-Johnston's radio was out of order, so no one knew where he was at that moment. Donald Crowhurst's radio was also silent, but the race watchers postulated that on the basis of 100 miles a day (Crowhurst's reported average), *Teignmouth Electron* should be in the Indian Ocean.

During the next three days the wind blew at gale force, although not steadily. *Victress*'s course was erratic until the captain discovered that a control line had come off the self-steering unit. Tetley experimented with a small sail set on the centerline behind the mast (a sort of small trysail) for more speed but took it down at once when the trimaran started to run downwind at high speed with a wild, corkscrewing motion.

Two days later, three blowing whales startled Tetley while he was on the foredeck hoisting a sail. The captain wondered if the whales mistook his three-hulled vessel for three other whales. The daily celestial observations put *Victress* 400 miles south of Cape Leeuwin, Australia's southwest corner, so Tetley—ever the epicure—celebrated passing the second of the great southern capes with a roast duck and a bottle of sherry.

As Sunday, January 12th, began, the wind blew hard from the north. *Victress* steered herself until 0200, when Tetley took over. He managed a southeast course until 0400, when all he could do was to run south—downwind. By dawn the wind was shrieking at 50 knots. Tetley took down all sails.

"As the front passed at noon, the storm culminated in a very heavy squall which blotted out all visibility. It was followed by a wind shift to the northwest," he wrote, "and I plucked up courage to get underway again. The wind had moderated to Force 8, but there were periodic squalls, making it unwise to carry more sail than a single jib sheeted flat. My opinion of the Southern Ocean stood at zero, and I tried to forget that there were 7,000 miles more of it still to cross."

At midnight another gale started up, this time from the west. Tetley raced before the storm until 0330, when he took down his single sail. Most of the bronze hanks had been torn off the luff of the jib, and the captain had trouble throttling the sail and getting the flapping mess down on deck. At 0500 a large sea slammed on board.

"A battering ram," said Tetley. Cold water shot into the wheelhouse, cascaded below into the cabin, and poured over Tetley, who was drinking a cup of coffee. The force of the sea knocked the mainsail boom loose from its crutch and bashed in the side curtain and coaming board of the wheelhouse. Loose gear rocketed across the cabin. By 0700 the wind had risen to Force 11 (56 to 63 knots) and the entire sea was covered with white foam. Tetley watched nervously as an army of huge waves advanced relentlessly toward *Victress*. Was the enemy force going to batter him to death and march right over him? The bearded naval commander concluded that this was his last battle, that he was losing, and that his end was near.

> The sea, covered entirely in foam, seethed round . . . *[Victress]*
> and yet she remained undismayed, bobbing here, curtsying there, but
> always eluding the massive crests [wrote Tetley]. Repeated squalls of
> hurricane force only helped her slip sideways out of their reach. And
> despite my doubts, so it continued, with only an occasional wave hit-
> ting the side. The barometer, which had fallen half an inch, steadied at
> noon and began to rise. The wind continued at Force 11 all afternoon.
> Then [the weather] gradually started to ease.

The next morning Tetley decided to give up the race and head for Albany, Australia, 450 miles to the north. He had been shaken to the roots by the storm. "Had God first shown me his strength and then spared my life for some special purpose?" he wondered. "To warn other yachtsmen not to be such fools? . . . Then I realized that such conditions can be regarded as relatively commonplace in the Southern Ocean. . . . When I got under way at sunrise I headed her bows eastwards once more. I would endeavor to get as far as New Zealand."

Tetley sorted out the damage. The battery charger had been flooded and would need attention. A breaking wave had smashed the glass shade of the hurricane lamp. He began repairs to the wheelhouse coamings and side curtains.

By the next day, January 15th, the wind had worked around to the west. The terrible seas had eased off. Tetley set a small jib sheeted flat along the centerline and once more sped eastward at 6 knots. His sole source of electricity was the flooded battery charger. If it failed there would be no radio, no lights, no power tools, and no instruments. He would not be able to listen to his beloved music. . . . Tetley held his breath while he worked on the charger. To his delight, it began to work.

The next day the barometer began another weary plunge, and the wind switched to the north. Nigel stopped *Victress* for a few hours until the wind moved to the northwest, when he got going again. "The seas were steeper than usual and gave me some anxious moments," he said. "*Victress* plummeted down the faces of the waves, her stern cocked high in the air." Toward evening more storm clouds hove into sight and some wretched-looking seas began to slide up behind the dark blue trimaran.

The gales and frightening seas continued on and off for the next three days. The trimaran ran hard and at times turned sideways to the seas and rolled wildly. Once, the captain feared that she was burying her bows and about to somersault. Finally, on Sunday, January 19th, the waves began to hiss less loudly and the pointer of the barometer moved to the right. In an effort to keep the bows from plunging, Tetley tried setting a small lifting sail forward of the jib as a kind of spinnaker. This seemed to help. In the meantime Nigel was doing more sewing on sails that were getting thinner and thinner. He was certainly trying hard.

At two o'clock in the morning of January 22nd, the yacht rolled heavily in a violent rain squall. The captain rushed on deck to reef the mainsail. The wind was shifting so Tetley stayed on watch, kept company by the music of Boccherini and Delius. By the end of the day, the weather front had passed and *Victress* ran eastward under full sail while Nigel repaired a corroded navigation light. Tetley was now south of Tasmania and not far from Hobart, the capital, so his sponsor chartered an airplane and tried to locate the trimaran. The captain tidied up his vessel for photographs, but the plane wasn't able to find the yacht.

During the following week the weather alternated between black and white. On favorable days Tetley washed clothes and attempted to get his corroded main engine to run. On stormy days Nigel grimly hung on to his small sails and tried to make as much mileage as possible. By January 26th, the 132nd day from Plymouth, Tetley had logged 14,250 miles, the halfway mark of the round-the-world voyage.

Sometimes the motion of the yacht reminded him of a carnival ride. ("The trimaran made good speed close-hauled under mizzen and jib but did everything but loop the loop.") Nigel noticed that additional pieces of molding had been torn off the starboard side of the hull by the battering of the waves.

Finally, on January 30th, as *Victress* hurried along a little below 47 degrees south latitude, the yacht drew even with 168 degrees east longitude, the meridian of New Zealand (see map on page XXX). Tetley decided to head a little north to see if he could drop off mail and films with a fisherman. On February 1st he passed close to Stewart Island and was thrilled to glide along close to land that reminded him of Scotland.

He sailed near Waikawa Harbour, Long Point, and Newhaven Harbour on the southeast coast of New Zealand's South Island. Then, on February 2nd, as Knox-Johnston had done on November 20th—seventy-four days earlier—he headed into Otago Harbour. It was Sunday, and Tetley found a fishing launch whose owner, Keith Reid, motored alongside the multihull and took off films, a journal, tape recordings, and a letter for Tetley's wife. Reid offered Tetley some crayfish, but he declined because of the rules of the race. Tetley then tacked out of the harbor against an adverse wind. Once at sea he set a course eastward toward Cape Horn.

Since the start, Tetley had picked up twenty days on Knox-Johnston, which was not unexpected because *Victress* was longer and faster. Tetley had also gone farther south where the mileage was less but the weather was stronger. What was surprising was how well Knox-Johnston was doing in his smaller vessel.

In six weeks, the tail of the shark that Tetley had caught had shrunk to half its original size. The captain wondered whether he'd get a chance to display the tail on the bow of *Victress* in the Atlantic or whether the tail would find its way into the sea earlier.

19~
A Slice of His Soul

ON CHRISTMAS DAY, DONALD CROWHURST SAILED SOUTH-
WARD along the Brazilian coast near the great reef that forms the harbor
of the old city of Recife. The tropical weather was hot and sultry, and a
weak southeast trade wind blew lightly across *Teignmouth Electron*'s
baggy sails as the trimaran loped along close-hauled on the port tack.
The sleek, streamlined, two-masted white yacht with light-blue decks
was only three months old and her paint still had the shiny gloss of Eastwoods shipyard, where she had been built. An officer on a passing ship
might have sighed at her sight and wished that he, too, could have possessed such a fine yacht and a chance to sail on a warm and calm sea.
After all, to be the captain of a new boat and to sail on tropical oceans
was the dream of many men.

Teignmouth Electron had a few problems, it is true, but the main difficulty was the troubled mental state of her captain. Crowhurst had
started late with a new and untried vessel of radical design. He had exaggerated his sailing experience. He had bragged about the electronic
miracles he was going to perform. Once in the race, however, Crowhurst
should have knuckled down to business and solved his technical problems as the rest of the contestants did. He should have chased and overtaken the other yachts as he had boasted he would. Instead Crowhurst
effectively withdrew into a pathetic and hopeless inner shell and did
nothing constructive at all.

A fiendish plot—a fraud that was breathtaking in its dimensions—
had hatched in his troubled mind. Instead of sailing south of the Cape
of Good Hope, Australia's Cape Leeuwin, and Cape Horn as the rules
of the race dictated, Crowhurst's scheme was to mark time in the South
Atlantic.

He would send out a few vague radio messages and complain of electrical problems that might stop further transmissions. His sponsor, his press agent, *The Sunday Times* newspaper, and presumably the public would assume that during his radio silence he was crossing the Indian Ocean and making for Cape Horn. After a suitable interval he would reappear in the South Atlantic near the leaders. His radio—somehow repaired—would again issue position reports and terse bulletins from the intrepid Crowhurst. Finally, he would pull ahead into first place. He would return to England triumphantly, collect his prizes, write his book, and be acclaimed as his country's (and the world's) newest hero. He would do all this if he could stay out of sight and fake his logbook entries for three or four months in a way clever enough to defy detection.

DONALD CROWHURST

In order to fill out his fraudulent logbooks, Crowhurst began to fake detailed notes from marine radio broadcasts. He wrote down thousands of words of weather reports, routine messages to and from ships, accident summaries, requests for tugs and pilots, military traffic—any and all bits of miscellaneous information that he might be able to enter in his fictional logbooks. Weather forecasts from along the course of the round-the-world race were especially important, and Crowhurst carefully underlined all of his longhand transcriptions of weather data for Tristan da Cunha, Cape Town, the Indian Ocean, and elsewhere.

Crowhurst's messages to England were hard to compose. He wanted to send something concrete but not to give away his true position. His precise location, however, was exactly what his contacts in England wanted and asked for again and again. What could he do? It was similar to the lost sailor's game of stopping a fishing boat or other vessel along an unknown coast and trying to find out where he was without humiliating himself by admitting that he was lost.

On January 8th, Crowhurst tapped out a Morse code message to his agent, Rodney Hallworth:

STRICKEN GOUT FOLLOWING NEWYEAR SHERRY PARTY   NOW EQUAL
FOOTING MERMAIDS STOP   ALMOST INTO FORTIES

The message was jaunty but said nothing of substance. Hallworth radioed back the positions of the three leaders. He mentioned that *The Sunday Times* reckoned the winner to be home April 9th and suggested this date as a target for Crowhurst. A second cable pleaded for weekly positions and mileage. How could Hallworth possibly write stories with no information?

On January 19th, Crowhurst sent the following:

SOUTHEAST GOUGH   1086 GENERATOR HATCH SEALED
TRANSMISSIONS WHEN POSSIBLE ESPECIALLY 80 EAST 140 WEST

This cryptic, confusing message might have been composed by a crafty courtroom lawyer, and to make any sense out of it, Hallworth had to make some guesses and to think hard. We know that when he sent it, Crowhurst was in the shadow of South America. Yet he claimed the following:

1. He was far to the south and east, near Gough Island in the South Atlantic. (Gough is 1,400 miles west-southwest of Cape Town, South Africa.) In truth, at that moment *Teignmouth Electron* was only 640 miles east of Rio de Janeiro, Brazil. Crowhurst's false position was 1,670 miles from his true position.
2. He was sailing 1,086 miles a week, or 155 miles every twenty-four hours. (He was actually poking along the Brazilian coast.)
3. Crowhurst said earlier that his generator compartment was leaking. Now he said he had sealed it, which presumably closed down his generator and radio transmitter. Yet he spoke of possible future transmissions.
4. To encourage people to look for him farther east he suggested that coastal radio stations tune their receiving aerials to between 80 degrees east longitude and 140 degrees west longitude. These meridians of longitude lay between the middle of the Indian Ocean and the central Pacific, thousands of miles farther along on the route of

the race. Yet how Crowhurst would transmit if his generator was not working is not clear. Did he plan to unseal the generator compartment in the future, deal with repairs, and begin generating electricity? If that was possible, why didn't he make the repairs now, *before* he reached the Southern Ocean?

On January 19th Crowhurst also sent a cable to his sponsor in which he exaggerated the problems from the split plywood on the starboard float. He asked for release from the buyback scheme. Mr. Best replied that any decision to withdraw was Crowhurst's business. And in a generous gesture, Best offered to cancel the repurchase clause.

Crowhurst prepared other complicated and bizarre radio messages, but he did not send them. Even in the transmissions that did not go out, Crowhurst pleaded with other people to make up his mind for him. It was clear that in any conditions of strain, Crowhurst's will simply collapsed. After the cable to Mr. Best, Crowhurst closed down his transmitter for the next three months. He continued to receive messages perfectly.

In the meantime Hallworth tried to write bulletins for *The Sunday Times* based on the sparse information in the January cables and on a radiotelephone call between Crowhurst and his wife on Christmas Eve, when the captain vaguely mentioned Cape Town. "Almost into Forties" became "in Roaring Forties" in Hallworth's story. In the January 12th issue of *The Sunday Times* this was changed to an actual position: "Latest reports put him 200 miles southwest of Cape Town."

On the following weekend *The Sunday Times* speculated further: "If Donald Crowhurst has kept up his recent record-breaking runs in his revolutionary trimaran *Teignmouth Electron* he should now be well into the Indian Ocean and sailing hard for Australia."

If Crowhurst wasn't moving at a suitable rate, it was easy for the newspapers to speed him up. Hallworth looked over part of one of Crowhurst's January 19th cables that read "generator hatch sealed" and decided to provide a reason. The January 26th issue of *The Sunday Times* brazenly stated on page 2: "A giant wave smashed over the stern of his trimaran *Teignmouth Electron*, damaging the cockpit and causing splits in the superstructure. He was delayed for three days repairing the rear cockpit compartment."

Not only were the newspaper people inflating Crowhurst's progress and daily mileages, but they were inventing problems, solutions, and parts of the trimaran ("the superstructure") that did not in fact exist.

Crowhurst's January 3rd cable had an error in transmission in which

"GOUGH" was changed to "TOUGH." Hallworth assumed that his client was having a *tough* time near Cape Town, which advanced even Crowhurst's fanciful position by an additional 1,400 miles. Not only was Crowhurst moved bodily east to near Cape Town, but he was presumably averaging 1,086 miles per week, or 155 miles every twenty-four hours. Henceforth the newspaper calculations used this figure. The published estimates of Crowhurst's weekly position became more and more exaggerated. *Teignmouth Electron* was said to be zipping along eastward far out in the Indian Ocean toward Australia when in truth she was marking time near Brazil.

The word *extrapolation* means to infer or estimate unknown information by extending or projecting known information. Crowhurst's biographers wryly suggest that the newspapermen were "extrapolating on the extrapolations." Certainly the reporters did not allow any common sense or journalistic skepticism to temper their optimistic stories and bizarre calculations.

During Crowhurst's long and meandering sojourn in the southwestern Atlantic he spent days and days at his radio taking notes and working on his logbooks. During these months he sailed slowly without pushing the yacht very hard. *Teignmouth Electron* was in the trade wind zone off the Brazilian coast, where the winds are light, warm, and steady, which meant that the trimaran didn't require much attention, especially under reduced sail.

To fill his days Crowhurst played his mouth organ (badly) for his BBC tape recorder, wrote poetry (poor to appalling), and tried his hand at creative writing (no better). He showed a surprising talent for shooting motion pictures of himself with the 16mm camera the BBC had given him. Crowhurst clamped the camera to various strong points around the yacht and used a self-timer on the shutter release to shoot sequences of his sailing and living duties. Because of his mathematical interest, Donald studied a book called *Relativity* by Albert Einstein. Crowhurst spent hours watching fish and birds that appeared around the boat. He often drew pictures of these creatures, gave them childish names, and constructed complex stories in which his characters generally met violent ends, something that a psychiatrist would have noted.

The deceptions that Crowhurst was trying to invent seemed to parallel the collapse of the confidence and breezy self-esteem that he had shown in England before the start of the race. He began to cultivate pity for himself based on feelings that he was brighter than other men. The general mass of society somehow didn't appreciate him. This was unfair because *he* represented the true light, the spirit alone, the difficult way. Nevertheless, he was rejected and pushed aside. He was a misfit.

At some level, however, he realized that he was guilty of a grievous deception in the race, and that a penalty in one degree or another would be sliced from his soul as recompense. It was the old Anglo-Saxon guilt complex: you get what you give.

Crowhurst's confused mental state took a morbid turn. In one story that he wrote, he compared himself to a stray land bird lost out on the ocean, a bird "destined like the spirit of many of his human counterparts to die alone and anonymously, unseen by any of his species, yet accepting that one chance in a million of knowing things unknown."

In spite of this, Crowhurst still had a streak of common sense. He somehow managed to put aside all his mental turmoil and confusion and began to concentrate on a real-life problem that demanded attention.

The split in the plywood on the outboard side of the starboard float was getting worse. Already the split was 3 feet long. In addition, a frame on the inside of the float had pulled away from the plywood. Crowhurst tried to sail on the starboard tack as much as possible to keep the float out of the water, but heading south in the southeast trade wind meant that he was on the port tack. This pushed the damaged starboard float into the water and flooded it, which in turn lowered the float even further and made the problem worse. Something had to be done.

What Crowhurst needed were sheets of plywood and screws and nails. He could fix a patch or two in place at sea if the wind and ocean were calm. What Donald had in mind, however, was a quiet place ashore because he had neglected to take the plywood and necessary fastenings with him. Where could he go? If he selected a large city like Salvador or Rio de Janeiro or Santos or Buenos Aires, he would be discovered in short order. These cities had yacht clubs and boating enthusiasts and nosy reporters and officials with forms to be filled out. What Crowhurst didn't want above all were people with questions. He needed an out-of-the-way place where he could beach the trimaran for several days. A quick repair and then back to sea.

Crowhurst made his usual thorough study before doing anything. After a long session with the Admiralty sailing directions for the east coast of South America, he decided to go to a place called Bahía Samborombón. It was located in Argentina near the southern entrance to the great estuary of the Río de la Plata, about 80 miles southeast of Buenos Aires. The landing place had a small stream called Río Salado with a shallow bar at the entrance.

After Crowhurst had made his choice, he sailed slowly southward along the Brazilian coast and into the waters of Argentina. He used up the month of February working on his logbooks and various creative pursuits while he poked along toward Bahía Samborombón. When the weather was bad he sometimes took down all his sails (like Nigel Tetley) and drifted before the wind and sea.

On March 2nd, he was close to his target and spotted the various landmarks mentioned in the *Pilot*. For some reason he sailed back out to sea again and returned four days later. On the morning of March 6th he headed in toward Río Salado, where he promptly ran aground in the coffee-colored, silt-laden waters of the Río de la Plata.

The tiny settlement that Crowhurst saw in front of him didn't amount to much. There was a scattering of houses and crude buildings on low land along the coast, which was marked by trees and shrubs and tall grasses. A single dirt road led to the world beyond. The area was too rough for cattle or farming. A few hunters sometimes came to shoot deer, ostriches, or wild pigs, but in reality people seldom came to Río Salado or even knew that it existed. The place didn't even have a telephone.

A fifty-five-year-old fisherman named Nelson Messina ran out from his house and saw *Teignmouth Electron* aground. It was certainly a strange-looking vessel. Messina went next door to the three-man outpost of the Prefectura Nacional Marítima de Argentina (the Argentine Coast Guard), where he rounded up Senior Petty Officer Santiago Franchessi and a young conscript. The three men jumped into Messina's fishing boat *Favorito de Cambaceras*, motored out, and pulled the trimaran into the channel and up the river to the coast guard wharf.

The three Argentines were surprised that only one man was on the yacht. He was extremely thin and had a scraggly beard. Franchessi spoke to him in the local harsh dialect of Spanish. Crowhurst answered in English, then French, and finally in sign language. The Englishman made the trio understand that he was in a race of some kind. He stopped because he couldn't continue until he had repaired the damage to the right-hand float on his boat. Crowhurst showed the men the split plywood and used gestures to explain what he proposed to do. He also wanted some electrical parts. The men had difficulty understanding the technical details so they loaded Crowhurst into the coast guard jeep and drove 17 miles to a store where a former French army sergeant named Hector Salvati lived with his family.

Crowhurst spoke excellent French and explained to Salvati what he wanted. He also said that he had rounded Cape Horn as part of a five-month sailing race from England. Crowhurst would be back in England in a month or so if only he could get his yacht repaired. He accompanied his explanations with three quick sketches that he made on wrapping paper (these sketches are still in existence).

Salvati translated Crowhurst's information to Petty Officer Franchessi. Salvati and his wife noticed that Crowhurst was extremely thin and that his trousers were floppy and loose. When Franchessi went to telephone his superiors for instructions, Crowhurst grew upset and began to talk loudly and irrationally. He needn't have worried. Franchessi spoke to a junior midshipman in La Plata who decided the problem was a trifling matter. The young officer told Franchessi to give Crowhurst what he wanted and to send him on his way.

While Franchessi was on the telephone, Crowhurst kept talking to Salvati and his wife in an exaggerated, bizarre manner. Crowhurst repeated over and over, "Il faut vivre la vie" (life should be lived). The Salvatis didn't know what to make of such a strange person. "He laughed a lot, as though he were making fun of us," said Rose Salvati. "We thought that something was wrong, that he might be a smuggler."

The coast guard men and Crowhurst returned to Río Salado in the jeep. Crowhurst—who had no money at all—was given what he needed. He quickly made two small plywood patches, which he screwed in place and painted white to match the rest of the float. That evening Crowhurst shaved off his beard and ate beefsteaks with the two unmarried military men who lived at the outpost. Because of the language problem there wasn't much talk during dinner. Crowhurst again slept on board his trimaran.

The next morning Nelson Messina was asked to tow the trimaran out to sea. Once again the towline was attached and *Favorito de Cambaceras* pulled the strange ship with the three hulls down the Río Salado and across the bar. Crowhurst's mission had been accomplished. He had repaired his vessel. But when Franchessi had stepped on board to secure the towline on the day that Crowhurst had arrived, the Argentine's action had disqualified the Englishman from the race. The only catch was that no one connected with the race knew about the unscheduled stop in Argentina.

20

On to Cape Horn

Robin Knox-Johnston was the first man in the race to sail into the Pacific, and he ran into a terrible problem right away. Instead of strong westerly winds to push *Suhaili* toward Cape Horn, the English captain found easterly winds that forced him to tack back and forth. Since he no longer had his mechanical self-steering gear, each tack and each change of wind required complicated sail balancing to get *Suhaili* to steer herself.

The wind often blew from the southeast, which favored the starboard tack. The best that *Suhaili* could do on starboard, however, was a northeast heading, which meant that Knox-Johnston was aimed toward Alaska instead of Cape Horn. The captain wept with frustration at the persistent adverse winds and the constant upset seas that slapped at *Suhaili*'s hull. Sometimes the seas were quite short from crest to crest and caused *Suhaili* to pitch up and down. Then she scarcely logged any miles at all.

"A few extra feet in length would make all the difference," wrote Knox-Johnston. He gritted his teeth as the yacht hobbyhorsed and went almost nowhere.

When the wooden ketch had left New Zealand on November 21st she had been at 47 degrees 30 minutes south latitude. During the next three weeks, *Suhaili* slammed into easterly winds on all but one day. By December 12th, the captain was half out of his mind. He figured that the easterly winds had delayed him at least a week, and he feared that Moitessier would overtake him for sure. By this time, Knox-Johnston had slogged northward to 37 degrees south. The yacht seemed to be out of the westerlies and into the zone of variables, so the captain tacked to the south and determined to hang on until he found the westerlies—icebergs or no icebergs.

"After three days of heading slightly west of south I ran into [the westerlies] again," he wrote, "but I had lost about ten days, and I seriously wondered if this had [cost] me any chance of winning the race."

Knox-Johnston's radio transmitter had not worked for a long time, so he began taking it to pieces. He discovered a broken wire, which he resoldered. Although *Suhaili* was 900 miles east of New Zealand, the English merchant marine officer managed a faint radio contact and was pleased to know that his radio was in order. Farther east he was out of range and had trouble getting radio time signals, which were the only way to update his chronometer error. Although there were regular time signals broadcast from Hawaii, Argentina, Australia, various BBC repeater stations, and elsewhere, Knox-Johnston had no luck receiving them and was obliged to rely on his chronometer for longitude sights for the next four weeks.

Robin dreamed a lot on his Pacific crossing. Many dreams concerned the race, hot baths, and spectacular meals. ("The cook immediately took a huge steak with fried eggs, mushrooms, peas and chips and threw it overside. This outrage woke me up.")

Sometimes Knox-Johnston dreamed of people he had not seen in years. He was amazed at the recall powers of the mind, and he marveled at the capacity of the brain to store astonishing amounts of obscure information. Perhaps people should take dreams more seriously. Modern society is so busy and materialistic that it forgets to look at dreams and their meanings. In many rural societies in Africa and Asia, men often meet and talk about their dreams and what they represent. Knox-Johnston's more abstract dreams seldom made sense, but he continued to recall long-forgotten people and to speculate on the remarkable contents and depth of a person's mind.

Suhaili had found westerly winds, but the lack of a self-steering gear was a problem. In order to sleep, Knox-Johnston often shortened sail to achieve a steering balance. The reduced sail drive meant slower daily averages, which were disappointing. The bottom of the yacht was getting foul, but the weather and frigid ocean prevented any in-the-water scraping. Nevertheless, the captain leaned over the side and used his kitchen spatula to clean off the stringy weed that grew along the waterline.

This was only one problem. There were lots more. The truth was that after six months of continuous hard sailing, much of the gear and equipment was wearing out. Knox-Johnston was forced to spend two or three hours a day on repairs and upkeep just to stay even. Some of the running rigging began to look ragged and frayed. And more frequently, the captain had to lower a sail and run a row of hand stitches along a seam be-

SUHAILI SAILING TO THE LEFT

tween two Dacron panels or slap a patch over a weak place. Maintenance was a never-ending task; fortunately, Knox-Johnston was a quick
thinker and handy with tools.

Suhaili had been going poorly, and the vision of Moitessier speeding
into the lead was a nagging worry. To make up time, Robin decided to
chance the danger of ice and to sail farther south where the west-to-east
distances were shorter and the winds might be steadier and more westerly. However, this introduced two new problems: (1) the difficulty of
living with freezing cold, and (2) the difficulty of navigating near lethal
ice. The latter was especially troublesome for a single-hander who had
to sail blind in order to sleep. Knox-Johnston discovered that the advice
in his Admiralty *Pilot* differed from the information on his Admiralty
chart. The warning on the chart showed the ice a bit farther south, so he
decided to favor the chart over the book. He realized his action was not
prudent, but he was desperate to get east.

By December 19th, *Suhaili* was at 44 degrees 30 minutes south latitude and 137 degrees west longitude. In twenty-eight days, she had

made good about 2,209 miles, or 41 percent of the 5,340-mile run from Otago, New Zealand, to Cape Horn. (The great-circle distance from Otago, New Zealand, to Cape Horn is 3,990 nautical miles, but if that route were followed, it would put the vessel into pack ice in the south. The rhumb line distance is 4,604 miles. If you step the distance off on charts, it comes out to about 5,340 miles, which is closer to what a sailor faces.) The yacht's daily average from New Zealand had been only 78.8 miles per day because of the easterly winds and all the tacking. Farther south, the winds became somewhat more favorable and steady, and *Suhaili*'s twenty-four-hour runs increased a bit.

Sometimes while Knox-Johnston fixed something or steered during changing weather, he sang songs or recited poetry. He wondered whether the long solo voyage had changed him. Robin felt sure of himself and he thought that his powers and faculties were as good as ever. However, a few times he used his tape recorder to check his speech delivery. He especially enjoyed learning new stanzas of poetry and decided that the mental discipline was good for him.

Severe squalls often swept down on *Suhaili* and heeled the little vessel as if a giant hand were pushing on the sails. The captain learned to watch the clouds to windward and to shorten sails whenever he saw a low line of dark nimbus clouds advancing toward him—especially clouds with ragged bottoms.

For several days Knox-Johnston's eyes itched. He immediately thought back to the mishap he had had with the battery acid months earlier. Now, however, both eyes bothered him. He eventually traced the problem to a can of disinfectant that had leaked into the bilges.

Robin immediately tossed the defective can overboard, poured buckets of seawater into the bilges, and pumped out the water to flush away the horrible chemical. The fumes began to ease, and the captain opened both hatches to air out the cabin. Unfortunately, at that moment a large wave bounced on board and water cascaded below into the cabin. Robin immediately closed up the yacht and began pumping out the water. In twenty minutes he had the bilges emptied, but his clothes, the galley, the charts, and his radio were soaked. In his entire voyage, only three waves broke on board, and this had to be one of the times!

Knox-Johnston's clothes and bedding had been damp for a long time, but he had managed to keep them reasonably dry by airing them when he could and letting the warmth from his body help dry his things. To wash his clothes, Robin soaked them in seawater and detergent and then dragged them astern on a bit of line for a rinse.

If he were lucky, there would be rain to rinse his clothes; otherwise he wrung out the seawater and hung the clothes next to the heater. Unfortunately, clothes with salt in them never really get dry because salt is hygroscopic and absorbs moisture from the atmosphere. (As we saw in Chapter Sixteen, Moitessier had different ideas.)

In addition, any water that fell on the captain and ran underneath his oilskins while he was working on deck made things worse. After a while the clothes became so salty that a soak in seawater was an improvement. When Knox-Johnston slept, he generally stripped off his damp clothes, took a slug of brandy, and climbed into his damp sleeping bag, which gradually warmed up from the heat of his body. He longed for the warm freshwater rains of the tropics.

Forty-eight hours after the wave broke on board, *Suhaili* sailed into dense fog. She was at 47 degrees south latitude and some 2,000 miles from Cape Horn. Knox-Johnston immediately thought of ice and took the air and sea temperatures, which were colder than he had expected. The sudden cold could have been caused by an upwelling of water from the depths or by ice.

The water was blue and devoid of plankton and fish, and there was no bird life around *Suhaili*. Upwelling water is often greenish and full of plankton and small and large fish, with bird life overhead. Robin concluded that since the sea was blue, the cold was caused by ice. He climbed into the cockpit and kept watch, with naps when the fog cleared somewhat. After forty-eight hours the sun appeared again. The captain hurried below, climbed into his sleeping bag, and sacked out for eighteen hours.

On Christmas Eve, Knox-Johnston thought of his family back in England. He felt lonely, so he poured himself a few glasses of whiskey, climbed on deck, and sang all the Christmas carols he knew. His solo vocal performance managed to cheer him up, but on Christmas morning, *Suhaili*'s captain woke up with a wretched hangover. Nevertheless, he made a big effort for his holiday meal: stewed steak, potatoes, peas, a special currant duff, and a bottle of wine that his brother had sent along. He drank a toast to the queen of England and solemnly hoped that he—a Briton—would be the first man to complete the race. He also had the wisdom and sense to admit that he was thoroughly enjoying himself.

During the next few days the winds turned easterly again and soon *Suhaili* was banging along on a south-southeasterly course. The fat ketch did not sail well in lumpy head seas and when the course made good fell to due south (180 degrees), he tacked but could only make north-northeast (020 degrees). The wind kept its easterly component day after day. Sometimes he managed northeast or southeast, but when the yacht pounded into head seas the captain felt that he had to steer by hand to ease the vessel through the waves. Years before, in the Arabian Sea, when *Suhaili* was on her first long voyage, a seam in the hull had opened up and the three men on board had bailed for their lives for thirty hours. Knox-Johnston had no wish to duplicate that experience. Steering by hand near the ice zone was a cold business, however, and the captain's hands soon grew numb.

The easterly winds continued. Knox-Johnston got madder and madder. "I'm not the sort of person that takes adverse conditions calmly and my mood at present is murderous," he wrote. Seas swept over *Suhaili* until the captain felt that he had to bear off to ease the pounding. When the wind shifted and the English sailor tacked, he was left with the slop from the old sea. The wind rose and fell; the rain turned to hail; the barometer rose and fell again. In the meantime, Robin sewed split seams on the sails that weren't in use.

Even in midsummer at 48 degrees latitude in the Southern Ocean, the weather was bitterly cold. During gales *Suhaili* pitched and rolled. Knox-Johnston wondered whether his home afloat could withstand the swirling tempests around him. Sometimes the only recourse was to hoist the tiny storm jib, stream the long warp over the transom, drink a hot whiskey and water, and turn in.

Finally, on January 1st, the easterlies—the winds that did not blow according to the pilot charts—shifted to the west. The messy leftover seas hindered *Suhaili* at first, but soon the wooden ketch was hurrying toward the tip of South America. The English captain knew that he was nearing Cape Horn, so he looked over his vessel with an eye to extra-severe weather. He had already gone through so much, however, that he was reasonably prepared. The only thing he did was to hack off the remains of the iron self-steering vane structure and toss it over the side. He feared the legs of the framework might tear up the deck or endanger the mizzen mast.

At 0430 on January 10th, Knox-Johnston felt *Suhaili* head into the wind and straighten up. He looked out and saw that the mainsail had split in two. He furled the remains and went back to sleep. Later in the morning, while preparing breakfast, he spilled boiling porridge on his wrist when the yacht took an unexpected jump. A burned wrist on a hand in constant use was awkward, and it was only a short time until the cuff of his oilskin jacket broke the blisters. Robin took down the torn mainsail and bent on his old one, which surprised him by its relatively good condition. The torn mainsail had deteriorated so gradually that he hadn't realized how worn it had become.

The next day Robin had a fair wind so he steered by hand for twelve hours and made excellent mileage. In the evening he tried various radio transmissions but received no response. He had been gradually changing course to the southeast to reach the latitude of Cape Horn, which was at 56 degrees south. January 12th was relatively clear, and the sextant sights showed 480 miles to go. The weather was squally with a high sea and swell. The captain had trouble steering and was obliged to shorten sail. His burned wrist hurt a lot. He was short of matches and cigarettes and began to ration both items.

At noon on January 13th, he discovered that *Suhaili*'s jibstay wire had three broken strands and was unraveling. There were still sixteen strands left, but the broken wires were a bad sign. Knox-Johnston clipped on his safety harness for the first time in three and a half months and crawled out on the pitching bowsprit to tie the wire out of the way until he could prepare a new stay.

He surveyed his liquor stock and found that he had ten bottles left. So far he had drunk thirteen bottles and spilled one. He was drinking one bottle every two weeks.

Robin was extremely tired because of the long watches and never-ending repairs. His trials weren't over, however, because on January 14th the gooseneck on the main boom broke again. This time the brass casting sheared in two. Poor Knox-Johnston had been plagued with junky yacht hardware ever since the race began. The two worst items by far were the wire halyard winches and the main boom gooseneck, both of which had apparently been designed by dumbbells for a fool's market.

> So, now, there is no jibstay, the jib is damaged, the main goose-neck has gone and the new mainsail which has rope at its reefing points, is split [wrote Knox-Johnston]. Not to fuss, I've put the kettle on, and I shall settle down and try and work out a way of fixing up a jury gooseneck.

All throughout the race, Knox-Johnston exhibited marvelous patience and dogged perseverance to go on in spite of a marginal yacht and one frustration after another. To repair the broken gooseneck, he took a long piece of metal from the remains of the self-steering apparatus and cut a slot to fit the metal piece down the middle of the forward end of the wooden main boom. Next he bolted three-quarters of the long dimension of the metal piece into the slot. He then bolted the metal that stuck out of the end of the boom to the remains of the fitting on the mast.

Robin put fiberglass material over the metal plate boom joint and followed this with two strong rope seizings. The repair took two days. In the meantime Knox-Johnston set the spare mizzen as a loose-footed mainsail and logged another 90 miles.

The barometer took a mighty plunge, the wind increased, and Robin reefed the mizzen he had set in place of the damaged mainsail. Dreaded Cape Horn was only 200 miles away. "I don't mind admitting I feel a bit scared tonight," wrote the captain as he thought about the evil reputation of his approaching goal.

During the night, the cold front advanced from the west. Soon it was blowing 50 knots. *Suhaili*'s master dropped the sails, streamed his long warp over the stern, and turned in. By the middle of the next morning—January 16th—the weather was easing as the barometer began its usual dance upward. Robin soon had the yacht plowing along eastward with more sail up. Later in the day, *Suhaili* was bombarded with hail, which rattled on deck like stones falling on a snare drum. In the squally weather, Knox-Johnston had to shorten sail, but now every change was a special problem because of the raw and painful burned place on his right wrist.

An hour after midnight the captain tried to steer through a squall, but part of a wave broke over him from the port side. As *Suhaili* rolled, the remainder of the wave sluiced over the helmsman from the starboard side. Knox-Johnston was soaked. Between squalls the weather was reasonable, and except for the biting wind and the painful burn on his wrist, Robin thought it was "enjoyable on deck." Although he was still taking a dollop of whiskey now and then, he began to prefer hot coffee and cocoa, which he found warmed him more.

On the morning of January 17th, the visibility was excellent. At 0500 he saw the tiny islets of Diego Ramírez—60 miles southwest of Cape Horn—bearing south of his vessel. During the day the wind eased off. Knox-Johnston hoisted more and more sail. *Suhaili* ghosted along in 5 knots of wind while her captain watched heavy clouds rolling up in the west. Rain was falling on the land in the distance.

Knox-Johnston sat in the cockpit almost holding his breath while he looked at the marvelous scene before him. It was almost a make-believe dream. Was that long island really Tierra del Fuego? Were those mountains the southern end of the mighty Andes? Somewhere in that maze of geography lay the Strait of Magellan. A rain shower to the north moved away, and as the air cleared, Knox-Johnston could plainly see steep cliffs at the southern end of a small island. It was Cape Horn at last.

A little after seven o'clock in the evening the stern black islet was abeam. The long crossing from New Zealand was over. Knox-Johnston drank a bit of whiskey and broke open a fruitcake that his aunt had sent along for this moment. In his logbook he wrote "YIPPEE!!!"

21~

The Gentle Philosopher

Bernard Moitessier had left the Indian Ocean and Tasmania behind him and had sailed into the Pacific on December 19th, twenty-nine days before Knox-Johnston reached Cape Horn. Neither man had any idea where the other was, although each thought about his fellow competitor from time to time. Both men knew that *Joshua* was faster and more suitable for the race. Both also knew that Knox-Johnston had started the race sixty-eight days before the French sailor and that the Englishman was fiercely determined to be first.

Moitessier started off well, logging 642 miles during his first five days into the Pacific, and he looked forward to celebrating Christmas east of New Zealand. On December 24th, however, after a brief gale from the southeast, the wind fell away to nothing. A warm sun beamed down and *Joshua* rode easily on gentle swells in the Southern Ocean near the southern tip of New Zealand's South Island. Moitessier watched small seals swimming around his red ketch. "These seal families sleeping in the sun will be my Christmas present; especially the little ones—they're so much nicer than electric trains. If their parents let them, I wouldn't be surprised if they tried to climb aboard. . . . We could all have Christmas dinner together."

For Christmas, the French captain unwrapped a specially prepared York ham given to him by friends in England.

> The ham is perfect, without a trace of mould after four months in a humid atmosphere [he wrote]. Hey! What's happening to me? I suddenly start drooling like a dog with a choice bone under his nose. I

must have had a long-standing ham deficiency. . . . I snap up a piece of fat the size of my wrist; it melts in my mouth. . . .

For lunch, I fix a sumptuous meal. I pour a two-pound can of hearts of lettuce, well rinsed in seawater, into a pot where a piece of ham has been simmering with three sliced onions, three cloves of garlic, a little can of tomato sauce, and two pieces of sugar. Jean Gau was the one who explained that you should always add a little sugar to neutralize the tomatoes' acidity. Then I take a quarter of a canned camembert, cut it into little cubes, and sprinkle it over the hearts of lettuce, along with a big piece of butter. The aroma wafts all through the cabin as the pot simmers very gently on the asbestos plate. Cook it very, very slowly, because of the cheese. That is another secret.

As the red ketch crept ahead, the mountains of New Zealand—50 miles to the northeast—rose above the horizon and cut dark-blue notches in the sky. The Christmas sun set, the flimsy breeze died, and *Joshua* floated quietly on the silent ocean. The only light was from pinpricks of white from the stars far above the quiet sea.

Moitessier had given up listening to the radio because he was sick of the endless commercialism of Christmas. He hated the sleazy huckstering and the radio advertisements, which in essence chanted that if you didn't buy buy buy you would go to hell hell hell. Where in the Bible is it written that a person has to spend money with merchants at Christmas? Did God require you to buy expensive presents? "How could we so lose our sense of the divine and the meaning of life?" the French sailor wondered.

The wind returned the next day, and *Joshua* again made a white furrow eastward. The first problem was to get past the tip of Stewart Island, a 40-mile-long bit of hilly land that extended southwest from South Island, the more southerly of the two main islands of New Zealand. Besides Stewart Island itself, just south of the island were three nasty breaking ledges: North Trap, Boomerang Breaker, and South Trap (see the map on page XXX).

The day was overcast, which made it hard to catch the sun with the sextant. Nevertheless, Moitessier waited patiently on deck and followed the bright places in the clouds where the sun was trying to peek through. Suddenly the sun appeared for a few moments. The captain quickly raised the sextant to his eye and adjusted the micrometer screw to bring the reflected image of the sun down to the horizon. Then he glanced at his watch, wrote down the time and sextant angle, and hurried below to work out the calculations. Hooray! The job was done.

Joshua was 40 miles west of Puysegur Point, the southwest corner of South Island. Moitessier steered south to give Stewart Island and the rocks as wide a berth as possible.

By noon the next day *Joshua* had logged another 100 miles and was 32 miles southwest of Stewart Island; South Trap lay ahead to the east. While a good sailing breeze strengthened from the southwest and then west, Moitessier navigated carefully. Once South Trap was abeam, the ocean was clear for more than 4,000 miles—all the way to Cape Horn.

BERNARD MOITESSIER

All at once the captain heard familiar whistling and squeaking sounds. Dolphins! Moitessier hurried on deck to find a hundred dolphins swimming alongside. They were rushing around and around in tight formations like ballet dancers, splashing, cutting from port to starboard and back again, whipping the water white, then submerging and zigzagging upward. It was a wild exhibition of exuberance and power. Moitessier had seen thousands of similar creatures during his years at sea, but these dolphins seemed different and were nervous and agitated beyond normal. They jumped and beat the water with their flat tails and kept making massed turns to the right.

Moitessier glanced at the compass and froze. The west wind had shifted to the south, and the yacht—under the guidance of the steering vane—had obediently followed the shift. With the sea so smooth and the sky overcast, the French captain had not realized what had happened. *Joshua* was running straight toward Stewart Island and South Trap at 7 knots! How long had this been going on?

The captain immediately dropped the mizzen staysail, hardened in on the sheets, and adjusted the vane for a close-hauled course to the southeast to get away from the land and rocks. After the course change, Moitessier again watched the dolphins. Now their movements were different: more subdued, with the customary rapid swimming at the bow. The dolphins rushed along from port to starboard and back again, but their violent antics had stopped. An exception was one big black-and-white porpoise that leaped entirely clear of the water and rolled over and over. Had these creatures been trying to tell *Joshua* that she was headed for trouble? Or were these nautical acrobats merely crossing the sea and showing off? Or had the captain imagined the whole thing?

The porpoises stayed with the yacht for five hours instead of the usual ten or fifteen minutes. Moitessier was struck with wonder. He was tempted to go back on the course toward South Trap to see if the porpoises would resume their violent behavior, but his better judgment told him to keep headed away from danger.

Initially *Joshua* experienced light winds from the west. The mileages of the daily runs were irregular—80, 20, 63, 55, 130, 140—but the red ketch kept going in the right direction. Even at 48 degrees south latitude the days were mild and sunny. Where were the gales and the terrible seas?

And the icebergs? Icebergs? Moitessier knew almost nothing about the hazards of ice. Today's pilot books have little to say on the subject because all big ships carry radar. As part of his preparations for the voyage, therefore, Moitessier had written personal letters to fifteen French captains who had rounded Cape Horn under sail in the old days. Were there any ways to predict icebergs other than by visual sightings? Which routes across the Southern Ocean were the most dangerous? Had any of the captains encountered ice near the Falkland Islands after rounding Cape Horn?

Captain François Le Bourdais said not to worry. Icebergs exist and can be fatal but are usually not seen at all. The other captains agreed. In fact only three of the Cape Horn veterans had ever seen icebergs along the route. Captain Georges Aubin had come upon ice east of the Falklands in the South Atlantic but not elsewhere. Captain Francisque Le Goff and Pierre Stéphan had sailed near icebergs in the Southern Ocean only twice in eighteen voyages.

Le Goff wrote that the ice was clearly visible. Once, in a fogbank, his crew had seen little floes. A short time later his men sighted icebergs ahead. Captain Stéphan's sole sighting was a stranded berg on Falkland bank, south of the islands. This berg was enormous, some 240 feet high and 2,500 to 2,700 feet long, a colossus of flinty ice. The men on board had felt no temperature change when they passed the ice.

In truth, the letters did not give Moitessier much specific advice. Nevertheless, they were full of comradeship, hope, and encouragement. The retired master mariners may have been old and feeble (some were in their eighties; one was almost blind), but their spirits and memories were as sharp as brisk winter breezes.

The stars blazed in the night sky, and *Joshua*'s weather continued clear, even at 48 degrees south, near the broken red ice line on the chart. After passing New Zealand, Moitessier had planned to head up to 40 degrees for easier weather. However, as the sea and the wind continued fair where he was, he stayed 8 degrees farther south and logged daily runs of 130, 146, 148, 149, and 148 miles. He was almost to the middle of the Pacific and still the hatch was open. Scarcely any spray had fallen on the decks. "[I] breathe peacefully and thank heaven for its gifts," wrote the Frenchman.

Of the nine men who started the race, Moitessier was by far the most experienced in sailing small vessels across oceans. In previous voyages he had sailed tens of thousands of miles through the Indian Ocean, the South Atlantic, the Mediterranean, and the Pacific. He had left the bones of two yachts on remote shores, but he had learned much and had become a master mariner.

Three years earlier he had taken *Joshua* from Tahiti to Spain via Cape Horn on a trip with his wife. Although not a fancy yacht by any means, *Joshua* was strong, fast, and sailed to the limit by the French captain, who put up lots of canvas and drove his vessel as hard by himself as an ordinary captain would have done with a crew of five or six.

The lofty ketch rig could carry clouds of sails, and when the weather was light Moitessier hoisted maximum sail at once, not only the ordinary working sails but two or three extra sails. Depending on the wind and its steadiness, he chose from among a mizzen staysail, a watersail slung beneath the main boom, and an extra jib to fill the space to leeward behind the eased mainsail when running with a poled-out headsail. Sometimes he put up a bonnet or extension to the foot of the largest genoa or a lightweight storm jib hauled up as a second main-staysail. Such a collection of sails and their halyards and sheets was mind-boggling for a single-hander. In light weather, however, the rig picked up the slightest breeze.

When the wind strengthened, the sails were arranged so they could be easily shortened. They came down one at a time or were reefed to smaller and smaller sizes. Through the years, Moitessier had perfected his handling techniques so that it was easy for him to have the right sail area for the corresponding wind. Coupled with a fast hull, whose underwater parts he endeavored to keep clean by occasional scrubbing, he often chalked up 160 to 170 miles a day, astonishing runs by a single-hander in a vessel just under 40 feet in length.

Now with moderate winds in the Southern Ocean, he averaged 144 miles a day for the next six days. The good weather continued. On his earlier voyage from Tahiti to Cape Horn, Moitessier and his wife had had to close the companionway hatch when they passed 40 degrees south. They had not only closed the hatch but had been obliged to gasket the hatch with a heavy towel to keep the icy water from gushing in. On that trip Moitessier seldom went on deck without a safety line around his waist. Then it was double-thick woolen socks and sea boots and mittens and gloves and heavy sweaters and fishermen's trousers and oilskins just to survive.

On this voyage so far, however, except for a long southwest swell, the sea stayed relatively calm. At dawn the temperature of the unheated cabin was 55°F; at noon, 75°F. The captain seldom dressed during the day and he was as tanned as he had been in the tropics. Sunbathing at 48 degrees south? It was positively immoral!

The Frenchman had plenty of food on board. Enough for a year in case of dismasting or being stranded on an isolated island. The only thing the captain lacked, he complained, was talent as a chef. "Cooking reminds me of beautiful music: I can appreciate it, delight in it, but not produce it."

Before the start of the voyage, Dr. Jean Rivolier, the chief doctor of the French Polar Expeditions and a man who knew much about short-handed enterprises, had counseled varied and appetizing meals. He said not to eat the same things too often, cooked the same way, or not cooked at all. Michael Richey, another prominent single-handed sailor echoed a similar thought: "It seems important to eat well, to prepare the food with care, and even to serve it properly: one could be reduced to gnawing in one's bunk."

Finally, the needle on the barometer began to creep to the left. Five miles up in the sky a high-altitude wind was shredding feathery cirrus clouds into mares' tails. Heavy weather was on its way. Moitessier changed sails: a 54-square-foot storm jib, a reef in the staysail, two reefs in the small mainsail, and a close-reefed mizzen. He put up a half-size steering vane blade in place of the regular blade and set the steering to head east-northeast to get away from the approaching weather depression and possible icebergs.

When the storm came, it turned the sea white with spray and foam. Moitessier dropped his reefed mainsail entirely and then the mizzen. *Joshua* raced along under two tiny headsails. The captain had the yacht under careful control. His mind, however, raced far ahead and pondered incredible decisions.

The French sailor enjoyed a wonderful communication with the sea. The link was almost a spiritual thing, a semireligious appreciation of the sun and wind and clouds. He was attuned to the creatures of the sea and sky, and he came close to talking to the seals and dolphins. He treated the albatrosses and petrels as welcome friends. He loved the cloud forms and was fascinated by the changing moon.

At an earlier date, a friend and his friend's wife had noticed that the frantic pace of ordinary life in Europe was making them nervous and tired. Modern civilization was too demanding and hectic. The friend and his wife turned to yoga, which helped them regain their equilibrium. Before the race, Moitessier showed the same symptoms of being upset and frantic, so the friend sent Moitessier a book on yoga. At first he set the book aside, but in the Indian Ocean, Moitessier began to look at it. His ulcer pained him, and he suffered from lumbago. Both his energy and spirits were low.

> When I first leafed through the book in the Indian ocean [said Moitessier], I felt it emanating all the values of my native Asia, all the wisdom of the old East, and I found a few little exercises I had always done instinctively when I was tired. My ulcer stopped bothering me, and I no longer suffered from lumbago. But above all, I found something more. A kind of undefinable state of grace.

What Moitessier had discovered in his long solitary hermitage of the sea was a philosophy of peace, a mystical, oceanic experience that seemed better than all else. Land and people were foreign and alien. The sea was his friend. Once he was on the ocean, Bernard's mind and spirit were at ease, and he was filled with a marvelous tranquillity. After almost five months, his hair had grown to shoulder length, and with an enormous beard he looked like a Hindu swami. As his solitary sailing continued, he became so spiritually close to the sea that he found it hard to imagine any other life.

When this gentle man thought of Europe and all the people and business and commerce and automobiles and industrial smoke, he recoiled. When he remembered the noise of machinery and screaming children and bank payments and scheming attorneys and parades with booming bass drums and growling helicopters and shrieking jet airplanes, he wanted to put his hands over his ears. He just couldn't return to Europe. "Man has been turned into a money-making machine to satisfy false needs, false joys," he wrote.

He would not go back. Any life other than the present one was a desecration. He knew he would eventually have to stop his marathon voyage because of supplies and food; nevertheless, there was plenty of stuff on board for a long time yet. He thought of the seals and their friendly simplicity. Yes, he would sail back to the Galápagos Islands off the coast of Ecuador, where the seals were the friendliest anywhere. Or return to French Polynesia, where the dark-haired people accepted you simply and wholeheartedly.

To get to the Galápagos all he had to do was to turn gently to the left and head north. He could be there in a few weeks. A run north in the beautiful southeast trade wind.

Yet in spite of these thoughts he had to round Cape Horn first. He still had bridges to cross in his soul. "If I hold on, if *Joshua* holds on, then we will try to go further. Round [the Cape of] Good Hope again, round Tasmania again, across the whole Pacific again . . . and reach the Galápagos to add things up." Moitessier was determined to ignore Europe. He would "forget the world [and] its merciless rhythm of life. Back there, if a businessman could put out the stars to make his billboards look better at night, he just might do it."

The storm passed over in one day. Soon he hoisted the bigger sails again. Moitessier washed out his heavy woolen socks with rainwater. Now he wore heavier clothing because it was cold. The sea felt icy, and he seemed to have slipped into a zone of real Cape Horn weather. Another gale passed going eastward, and the sea rumbled continuously. He had days of 152, 166, 158, 147, 162, and 169 miles—a thousand miles a week. Neither Moitessier nor Knox-Johnston knew it, but *Joshua* was gaining steadily on *Suhaili.*

Now the cabin hatch was shut. Rain and low clouds swept across stormy skies. Cross-seas slammed on board. On these days, when Moitessier dealt with sails, he kept himself tied to his vessel with a safety harness snapped to a $3/16$-inch-diameter wire that stretched along each side deck from bow to stern. The harness clip slid along the wire and the captain was able to do deck work with both hands. He kept a bucket under the main boom to collect rainwater and so far in the Pacific had added 19 gallons to his tank, only a little less than he had used (he needed $2\frac{1}{2}$ quarts a day). During the fifty-six-day Indian Ocean crossing he had collected 40 gallons and used 35.

After four peaceful days (130, 111, 147, and 142 miles), more sunbathing, and a lot of drying and airing of bedding, all the signs pointed to another big gale: a wind shift, heavy swell, and a falling barometer. *Joshua* was dropping down toward Cape Horn; she crossed 50 degrees south as the French captain angled her toward the bottom of South America. The wind rose to 30 knots and then eased. The sky cleared partially, the heavy northwest swell lessened, and the barometer steadied. There was no gale.

Moitessier took stock of himself and felt that he was working within the limits of his strength. Compared with his first Cape Horn trip, he was ahead, both in miles covered and in energy saved. This was mostly because he flew small sails with lots of reefs that were easy to handle. On the first voyage, he had had no winches; now he owned excellent winches that made pulling down a reef a cinch. Every action—trimming, reefing, unreefing, or dealing with halyards—had to be easy; otherwise it would be dreaded and avoided.

This French philosopher of the sea savored the magic moments. It was the spirit of Melville and Ahab, the white whale and the eternal quest.

> A moonbeam bounces off a cloud far to the south, becoming a slender spire of softly glowing light rising straight up in the sky [wrote Moitessier]. I am wonderstruck. How did the moon pull off such a lovely trick?
>
> The spire widens, glows very brightly. It looks like a huge spotlight searching among the stars. . . . A chill comes over me. It isn't the moon playing with a cloud, but something uncanny I don't know about. Could it be the white arch of Cape Horn, that terrifying thing Slocum mentions, the sign of a big gale? The stars shine with a hard glint and the sea looks menacing beneath the icy moon.
>
> A second spire rises next to the first. Then a third. Soon there are a dozen, like a huge bouquet of super-natural light. And now I understand . . . it is an aurora australis, the first I have ever seen, perhaps this voyage's most precious gift to me.

Later *Joshua* sliced through thin banks of fog. Four small sails and a 30-knot wind drove her at hull speed. The Southern Ocean scarcely rumbled; perhaps the closeness of land to the east had eased the discontent of the ocean. Now the hazards were growing closer; sextant work was critical. Too far south risked ice; too far north meant the peril of land.

Moitessier wanted no surprises while he was asleep. *Joshua* hurried ever eastward and a bit south under her little sails, scudding and surfing while the captain stalked the elusive sun with his sextant. Sometimes the sun appeared for a few moments. On other days the cloud cover was too heavy, and he had to make do with dead reckoning—advancing his compass course and recorded mileage.

Now he was up at night, watching and looking ahead, trying to drive *Joshua* past Cape Horn before a new gale erupted from the west. In the darkness the sea sparkled with bits of blue-green. "The lower part of the staysail is full of living pearls," he wrote. "They reach almost a third of the way up, then run off along the bunt of the reef. They come from the phosphorescent foam picked up by the bow and shattered by the whisker stay."

The wind increased a little, so Moitessier put the third reef in the mainsail, which meant its area was only 65 square feet. *Joshua* logged 48 miles in six hours. The captain stood by the mainmast, hypnotized by the speed and the rushing water. He thought of dropping the mainsail altogether. But no! *Joshua* was going too well to be disturbed, surfing forward on each overtaking wave in a swelling whoosh of white. . . .

Down went a sail, another pot of coffee, a wind drop, a reef out, a nap, a noon sight (171 miles), a heavy sea, and 45 knots of wind. Then it was a hunt for the tiny islets of Diego Ramírez (the western outpost of Cape Horn), sunset, less wind, a clear night, and twinkling stars. Finally another sleep (dreams of youth and adventure), an alarm clock that rang but was not heard, and moonlight through a portlight on the captain's face. Up again. Less wind. A careful look in the moonlight. A black hillock that climbed over the sea and did not move. It was Cape Horn. The date was February 5th.

Joshua had crossed the Pacific.

22

The Battered Trimaran

AFTER THE DETOUR TO OTAGO HARBOUR IN NEW ZEALAND ON February 2nd to hand across his films and letters, Nigel Tetley steered his big blue-and-white trimaran eastward. The radio crackled with reports of Hurricane Carrie whirling closer and closer to New Zealand from the north, crushing and demolishing everything in sight. Down at the south end of New Zealand, Tetley hurried east to get as far away from the land and storm as he could. The wind drove the yacht so hard that he finally pulled down the sails and stopped in order to get something to eat and to rest.

By the afternoon of February 3rd, the wind had lessened, so he got under way again, but during the first few hours some nasty waves slammed into *Victress* and heeled her alarmingly. It was a hell of a way to start across the Pacific.

Tetley soon neared 180 degrees east longitude—the international date line—where his clock read twelve hours more than Greenwich time. Going eastward, this meant that he would have two days with the same date. Two February 5ths. He toyed with the idea of delaying the time change for three days—to February 8th—his birthday and the date of his official retirement from the Royal Navy after twenty-seven years of service. If there were two February 8ths, would there be two birthdays and two retirements? It sounded like a children's game of riddles, so the captain settled the problem by writing two February 5ths in the log and officially changing from east to west longitude.

Tetley continued regular radio talks with New Zealand as he sped onward. He was delighted to receive birthday greetings from Eve and his two sons. For his birthday lunch he baked white bread, uncorked a bottle of special wine, and served himself prawns and octopus pilaf. He might have been behind the others in the race, but he certainly ate well and was the undisputed gourmet of the solo round-the-world fleet. He had also become quite a music lover. While Tetley cooked and ate and washed the dishes, he played symphonies and choral music and concertos on his music system. Already the tapes seemed old, however, and he wished he had brought twice as many.

On the evening of his birthday, the wind settled in the northwest, where it stayed for the next four days. The bearded lieutenant-commander kept plenty of sail up, but during gusts and squally periods he took the helm to hold her steady while the trimaran planed ahead. Tetley wondered where the other contestants were, especially Moitessier, and hoped that *Victress* was pulling ahead in the race. A whale blew alongside and then blew again a little in front of the yacht before making off. Later the wind dropped to 8 knots, so Tetley checked the port float and pumped it free of water.

He switched to a full bottle of cooking gas for the galley and made efforts to caulk the skylight and cabin portlights with sealing compound. The leaks were so persistent, however, that to be sure he rigged a drip can inside the cabin over his bunk at the worst spot. He read a bit, but he had been through all the books and wished for something new in which to lose himself.

On the tenth day from New Zealand another gale developed. Tetley

NIGEL TETLEY

took down everything except two small headsails as the weather front passed. The battery charger needed new brushes. He had none, but after a lot of head-scratching and looking at everything electrical on board, he managed to rob the useless engine generator of one of its brushes, which he filed down to fit. Radios and charging plants certainly added to the complexity of a long voyage.

From February 14th to 19th the wind blew lightly from the south and east. "One day when the surface wind blew gently, I noticed several spiral-like cloud formations first gathering and then whirling away at great speed, as if marshalled by some unseen hand," he wrote. "I had an uneasy feeling."

When Tetley next spoke with New Zealand he learned that Moitessier's red-hulled two-master had been sighted off the Falkland Islands on February 10th. This meant that the Frenchman was two weeks ahead of *Victress*, which was a disappointment. There was no news of Donald Crowhurst or Robin Knox-Johnston.

On the afternoon of February 20th, *Victress* lay becalmed under a sunny sky on a quiet sea. "The ocean was almost asleep: even the swell had subsided," wrote Tetley. "An intense feeling of loneliness swept over me. Time . . . seemed of no account and mortal man [was] a brash intruder. Mid-ocean blues and pre-Horn nerves no doubt!"

To cheer himself up Tetley fired up his stove and cooked a spectacular meal of rice, runner beans, and mushrooms, together with a crab-and-mackerel dish with a tomato sauce.

The next day the west wind was back and *Victress* hurried eastward. The wind didn't rise above 25 knots, but he felt uneasy. "A heavy swell made me shorten sail after several alarmingly prolonged wave rides," he said.

Tetley had begun to play his tape recorder in the wheelhouse because the acoustics were better than in the cabin. One evening at sunset he listened to a guitar virtuoso softly plucking the strings of his instrument while the colors of the sky shifted from whites to reds to grays. "The world seems to pause and catch its breath," he wrote.

On February 24th, the yacht seemed to fly along, but when Nigel figured out his position, it was only a disappointing 156 miles. That evening the wave patterns were a mess, and the swells banged into one another from three directions. During the next morning, while the English captain ate a lumberjack's breakfast (to the strains of Bruch's violin concerto in G minor), the breeze picked up again.

Tetley's problem over and over again was that when the wind increased, it often rose too fast and overpowered the trimaran. Then sails had to come down and quickly. If not, they blew away or threatened the three-hulled yacht's stability. This happened on the morning of February 25th, when the wind split the jib from luff to leech as the gale escalated to 45 knots. Tetley stopped his vessel, but on three occasions, the yacht was knocked completely around to face the storm. A sea slammed into the wheelhouse and swept a 5-gallon jug of water into the cabin. The main engine was flooded again; this time Tetley gave up on it.

In the night the wind dropped to 35 knots. The captain doggedly hoisted the spare jib and sped eastward again. By noon the wind was a little less, and he had a second small headsail flying. The trimaran did well until the evening, when a breaking wave zoomed in from astern. "*Victress* all but capsized," he wrote. "I felt her teeter at an angle of about 50 degrees in a half cartwheel; then she slowly righted. One of the self-steering lines had parted, the cabin was a shambles, and as usual I received a soaking. Later I discovered that a heavy steel box of tools in the after cabin had been turned on end."

Tetley reviewed the incident:

> The yacht had accelerated on the slope of the wave, had broached, and had then been slammed over by the crest. A cross-swell had been running at the time. Was the boat or poor seamanship to blame? If the boat, then I should head north out of the Roaring Forties immediately. I came to the conclusion that it was the trimaran's great stability that had saved me. The extra weight in the stern had probably averted disaster.
>
> I harbored few illusions about . . . righting *Victress* if she did capsize—though I had of course made some provision. Firstly, I always carried at my waist a well-honed knife with which to slash a way out through the side curtain. Stowed ready to hand in the wheelhouse lay a zipper bag containing a frogman's suit and face mask. My plan was to take this with me and, from the upturned side of the yacht, pull out the life raft and other survival gear. . . . Dressed in the rubber suit, I would deliberately flood one of the floats by boring holes in it; then launch the big RFD life raft on the other side and, pulling on one of the masthead halyards, try to lever the trimaran upright. That all this would need calm weather and more than a little luck needs no emphasis.

It was a brave declaration, but would it work? The lieutenant-commander hoped it would succeed. He also hoped that he would never have to try to right his capsized trimaran in the cold and troublesome Southern Ocean. Or any ocean for that matter.

At noon on February 27th, Tetley was at 47 degrees south latitude and 115 degrees west longitude. Cape Horn lay 1,860 miles away on a course of 107 degrees true, a little south of east. Everything continued smoothly until the afternoon of Sunday, March 2nd.

> The wind increased to storm force [48 to 55 knots], [he wrote]. I hove-to for a couple of hours until I thought the worst had passed. But within an hour of getting under way it came on worse than before, and after experiencing a wild ride on a giant breaker, I hove-to once more. I particularly noticed one large overhanging crest as it broke near *Victress:* if she had been underneath, it would have smashed her open like an egg box.
>
> At 0300 . . . a sea climbed into the wheelhouse before I could straighten out the course. Constant hand-steering was needed, and I hove-to for breakfast and to pump out the floats. . . . During the night, conditions worsened. However the waves though powerful were still relatively low, and I was quite happy to let the trimaran surf. As a breaker passed beneath, *Victress* would bounce rapidly up and down. On one occasion this was accompanied by the sound of wood cracking below. A long piece of joinery had sprung away from the cabin side. . . .
>
> I was in the cabin clear of the window when the wave struck. There was a roar and the six-foot-wide starboard window gave way. Simultaneously the clear panel on the wheelhouse side curtain was punched out, and I heard the familiar sound of water coming in. Jagged pieces of perspex swept across the cabin; full paraffin containers were lifted from the deck on to the settee; practically everything else found its way into the bilges. There was no quick recoil this time, just a solid wham, and the sea was in.

Tetley's life was suddenly filled with problems. He needed hose clamps for the hand bilge pump. Rice from the galley clogged the electric pump. A ton of salt water rolled back and forth in the bilges with his clothes floating around here and there. All his precious music tapes had been submerged and soaked. The lieutenant-commander bailed with a bucket and somehow managed to board up the enormous hole where the cabin portlight had been.

The waves roaring past seemed enormous and irregular and often collided with heavy cross-seas, which caused acres of foam and several near misses. Each time the force of the falling water was like an avalanche of giant boulders. He felt the ocean tremble—or was that his heart?

The wave that had burst against the cabin had been focused on a small area, and when Tetley later inspected the starboard float, he found two split frames and the deck edging sprung. That night—March 4th, still summertime in the Southern Ocean—was long, miserable, and wet. At dawn the wind blew a little under 40 knots across a sea that looked gray and dismal.

> The cabin top had given way at deck level, posing a tricky repair problem [he wrote]. I could only hope to patch it up at best. My high regard for *Victress* as a sea boat remained unshaken. On the other hand . . . she was insufficiently robust for the Southern ocean. One thing was certain. I had to find better weather. . . . [He decided to sail northward.] I went forward to hoist the jib. While undoing a sail tie I was suddenly jerked off my feet and slammed into the safety net. I lay sprawled face downwards staring into the cold and restless water. If confirmation were still needed this was it. The sea was the victor. I would retire from the race, make for Valparaiso, put the trimaran up for sale, and fly home.

But in spite of his gloom about the voyage and his thoughts of quitting, the resourceful naval officer started repairs. He bolted various supports to the broken portlight area and covered part of the damage with a sheet of plywood. By the evening, the cabin was reasonably watertight again. He had performed another miracle of reconstruction.

While he was working, the storm moderated. Tetley set a reefed headsail and headed north, fed up with the Southern Ocean and the cursed race.

On the next morning—March 6th—he spun the wheel to the right and headed east-southeast for Cape Horn again. "Sheer obstinacy," he said. In fact Tetley felt groggy and staggered about with a headache. He had been drinking salt water that had leaked into his two rear tanks. He switched to a forward tank that was full of good water. The English sailor—exhausted by all the extra work and nervous tension—uncharacteristically gobbled down food when he could.

The next day he spent repairing his jib, which had two long rips. The spare jib was a terminal case; he had to fix the original because a jib was vital if he were to sail anywhere. His sewing wasn't over, however, because on the following day the mizzen split in two places. A little later several mainsail seams let go. Things were going to hell fast. Fortunately, while Tetley stitched, he was cheered by music from a Chilean radio station.

On March 9th he repaired the curtain in the wheelhouse and pumped out the main bilges, which he was surprised to find held 60 gallons of seawater. The cabin was a mess. The flooding had ruined a lot of food and gear. Nigel's prospects were grim and unnerving.

> I was determined to keep *Victress* going at full tilt [he wrote] and had the mainsail and reefed jib set when, in the evening, with a heavier sea running, water began to spurt into the cabin from under the starboard wing [the part connecting the main hull with the outer floats]. The side buckled each time she hit a large wave and slivers of wood dropped from the stringers. Fatigue had produced in me a terrible mood of pigheadedness and—even faced with this evidence—I might well have continued until the whole boat was in pieces, had not common sense finally prevailed and I lowered the mainsail. Both yacht and man were near the end of their tethers. Only the closeness of Cape Horn and the prospect of kinder weather beyond kept me going.

Fortunately during the next few days, the winds were less. Nigel had a chance to rest and to eat reasonable meals. He screwed a board over the center of the undamaged cabin window on the port side to break the force of any future waves "rejecting the idea of strengthening the window itself, as the whole cabin side might then go." The sails continued to fall apart and demanded daily sewing sessions.

Early on March 12th, Tetley dropped the mainsail because of rain and squally weather. He moved the radio batteries to a drier place because salt water coming in under the wings made the batteries fume and smoke (chlorine?). Later he hoisted the mainsail and sewed the mizzen. The next day he contacted Buenos Aires on the radio. On Friday, he dreamed that *Victress* was an airplane; he awoke and rushed out to drop the genoa as squalls swept in from the west.

Now he steered directly southeast for Cape Horn. The mainsail was in appalling condition, so he dragged the spare on deck and exchanged one for the other as he had done earlier. (How long could this go on?) The captain baked bread for the first time in two weeks. On March 16th, a spinnaker pole fitting sheared. While he limped along with another sail, Tetley did a midnight repair in the wheelhouse by the light of a flashlight. He then set the twin headsails again.

On March 17th, thick clouds made sun observations doubtful, but the veteran naval officer waited patiently and finally got useful sights. That night he kept a careful watch. The wind faded and then sprang up from the south—a bone-chilling breeze that seemed straight from the South Pole. Tetley sat huddled in thermal underwear, a polar suit, and sweaters. In addition he had a sleeping bag draped around his shoulders. Nevertheless, he still shook from the cold.

In the early morning, Nigel passed several islets to port that confirmed his position and gave him time for a nap. At noon he was close-reaching to the east under 1,000 square feet of sail. At 1300 he saw land ahead, and an hour later Cape Horn hove into view. The weary officer's spirits revived. He cooked a fancy celebration dinner and opened a bottle of wine. Tetley and the battered trimaran had rounded Cape Horn. It was the first time for Tetley, and the first time that a trimaran had sailed across the Southern Ocean. Both were damned lucky to have made it past Cape Stiff, the sailors' name for Cape Horn.

23

Back to the South Atlantic

IT WAS STILL ANYBODY'S RACE. ROBIN KNOX-JOHNSTON SOMEhow hung on to the lead, but his margin was slipping, and almost the

entire South and North Atlantic lay between Cape Horn and the finish line at Falmouth, England. According to Admiralty chart #5309, the distance between these two places is 8,260 miles. But by the time the mileage penalties for headwinds and storms are factored in, a vessel will usually log 9,000 miles or more.

Knox-Johnston used all his talents to try to keep his 32-foot vessel going at 4 knots. *Suhaili*'s wooden hull seemed reasonably sound and only leaked a little. However, the coachroof had shifted, some of the rigging had given way, the self-steering had crumbled before the force of the sea, and corrosion had ruined the engine. Not only was the roller reefing gear for the mainsail useless, but the main boom gooseneck had broken twice, and the wire halyard winches could only be used by tying the handles in place. *Suhaili*'s tiller was secured to the rudder with rope lashings, and the sails needed daily attention with a needle and thread. The list of defects went on and on. Fortunately, the English merchant marine officer was a good mechanic, and he attacked each problem with skill and gusto. He was determined to win the race.

At Cape Horn, the third mark of the competition and the turning point for the final dash to England, Bernard Moitessier seemed certain to win. He had already shaved forty-nine days from the sixty-eight-day lead of Knox-Johnston and was sailing about 20 percent faster than his English opponent. Could Moitessier continue to average 120 miles each day? With calms and poor winds, this meant he would need days of 150 and 160 miles. He was sailing *Joshua* all by himself and doing as well as with a racing crew; his yacht was in excellent order, and except for the collision incident near South Africa and a few minor repairs, he'd had no equipment difficulties at all.

Moitessier was a master mariner with lots of sailing experience. He was also a visionary whose yacht was his magic carpet to a kind of heaven-on-earth, and as the round-the-world race continued, he seemed increasingly unwilling to return to Europe.

During the previous August in England, he had seemed reasonably happy and full of confidence. He had shared his sailing knowledge with Nigel Tetley and had given him a special leak-stopping compound made of cement and plaster of Paris. Moitessier had been on the friendliest terms with his pal Loïck Fougeron and had even become acquainted with the patrician Bill King. But now the race seemed to be receding in importance; the Frenchman was muttering about withdrawing and sailing on to the Pacific. Could the effects of almost six months of solitude and the demands of twenty-four-hour-a-day sailing have influenced his judgment?

Nigel Tetley had rounded Cape Horn on March 18th, forty-one days after Moitessier and two months after Knox-Johnston. Tetley was a hearty man who liked good food and drink and who loved classical music. All three of these graces were firmly on board his experimental three-hulled yacht until the big wave of March 4th had flooded out his music system. Unfortunately, his chances of winning seemed small; his vessel was in poor condition and getting worse.

However, in a long race one could never tell. . . . The leaders might be dismasted or suffer collisions with floating wreckage or other vessels. Those ahead might get sick, decide to give up, or have their important sails blown out. Anything was possible. In a competition of this nature, you were honor bound to do your best, and an English naval officer would certainly do his utmost. There was no doubt that Tetley drove his vessel as hard as he dared. In any case, no one had ever sailed a trimaran around the world nonstop before. Tetley was well on his way to a new record, whether he won the race or not.

Donald Crowhurst was the fourth man still in the race, a shadowy figure lurking along the remote edges of the South Atlantic. He had left Río Salado in Argentina on March 8th after patching the starboard float of *Teignmouth Electron.* It was hard to believe that no one had noticed his illegal stop except for a few locals who had labeled him a harmless eccentric.

After his visit to Argentina in early March, Crowhurst zigzagged southward in the South Atlantic toward the Falkland Islands, which lay 450 miles northeast of Cape Horn. As he got farther south and away from the radio shadow of South America he was able to monitor the distant New Zealand radio channels for information and weather reports for his false logbook. He thought of trying to make transmissions to Wellington.

Crowhurst also wanted to sail in the Southern Ocean so his descriptions would have reality and substance; a few filmed sequences with his BBC motion picture camera would verify that he had actually been in the Roaring Forties. A few days north of the Falklands, *Teignmouth Electron* sailed into heavy weather and was blown more than 100 miles to the west-northwest. Crowhurst had found the gale he sought. He also felt safer in these southern waters because if he were seen and reported by a ship it would be better to be close to Cape Horn.

Crowhurst arrived at the Falkland Islands—the southernmost point of his journey—on March 29th. He didn't stop at Port Stanley, the main settlement, but merely jilled around for a day a little offshore before turning northeast toward England. By now, he had been aboard his white-hulled ketch for 150 days. He figured enough time had elapsed so that it was safe to head for home.

The distance from Gough Island in the South Atlantic—which he had radioed he was near on January 15th—to Cape Horn via South Africa, Australia, and the Pacific is roughly 13,500 miles. Crowhurst planned to emerge from radio silence on April 15th—ninety days after he wrote the Gough Island telegram. He hoped that people in the outside world would believe his announcement that he had averaged 150 miles a day during his supposed crossing of the Southern Ocean. An average of 150 was perhaps high and might be thought suspicious after his abysmal runs early in the race. If he used a lower figure, however, he would have to mark time in the South Atlantic even longer, and all the other contestants would be back in England. His idea was to slip in just before the other three and scoop up the prizes. Maybe even a knighthood!

In early April, while sailing northward, Crowhurst began to compose veiled messages for the commercial radio stations in New Zealand and Cape Town. He wanted to announce his presence and infer that he was *west of Cape Horn in the Pacific* without giving away his true position *east of Cape Horn in the Atlantic*. He tried to send "TR" messages, which are telegrams sent by ships to long-range radiotelegraphy stations that keep track of ships' positions and destinations. Of course the first question the radio operators asked was "Where are you? What is your latitude and longitude? [QTH in Morse code]"

Even the clever Crowhurst had trouble being evasive. Finally, on April 9th, he sent a regular telegram to his agent, Rodney Hallworth:

DEVONNEWS EXETER=HEADING DIGGER RAMREZ   LOG KAPUT
17697 28TH   WHATS NEW OCEANBASHINGWISE

Hallworth received the message on the morning of April 10th and immediately telephoned Crowhurst's wife. Then he began to try to puzzle out the cryptic telegram, which was studiously imprecise as always. What the hell was Donald trying to say? "Digger Ramrez" must be Diego Ramírez, the outpost islands a little west and south of Cape Horn. *Teignmouth Electron*'s mileage log had stopped working on March 28th, when it read 17,697. And Crowhurst asked for news of other contestants.

Hallworth calculated that if Crowhurst could maintain his speed he might win the race for the fastest time. Again, there was no position given. Just where in the hell was Crowhurst anyway? Sailing around Cape Horn was certainly newsworthy, but a press agent needed facts and information.

Hallworth was desperate for details of storms and equipment breakdowns. How was Crowhurst feeling? What he was eating? How was the trimaran holding up? Anecdotes. Color. Something to work with. Anything! Crowhurst's vague generalities, clever words, pointless questions, and too-short messages were useless.

Hallworth patiently reread all the old telegrams, did a lot of figuring of mileages, gazed into his crystal ball, and finally decided that Crowhurst had accidentally left out the information that he was 300 miles from Cape Horn when he had sent his last message. By now (April 10th) he should have been well around the tip of South America. Hallworth rushed to his typewriter, and the English newspapers for April 11th carried stories that *Teignmouth Electron* had weathered Cape Horn and was now speeding northeast toward England.

The news reports worked faster than Crowhurst had planned. Everything was a week ahead of schedule. The trimaran's time was really too fast for credibility, but in the usual press confusion this was overlooked. Only Sir Francis Chichester, the old fox of small-ship voyaging, was convinced that something was wrong. He reported his doubts to the race committee.

Crowhurst's wife, Clare, dutifully tried to explain her husband's inconsistent radio messages: "Donald has a great sense of humor and would think it a big joke to suddenly appear out of nowhere and surprise everyone," she told a reporter.

WHO AMONG US doesn't long for moments of quietness and solitude? Time to be alone with our private thoughts, our innermost hopes, our secret longings. Time for thoughts on the blue edge of consciousness. Time to reflect on dreams so personal that we hardly dare open the door to them. Who doesn't need time to think about what we've done (or not done), time to consider what we'll do next week, time to make peace with our souls?

We all have these moments, but most of us also have spells when we want to be with someone, to ask advice, to talk about a problem. Often we like to share a special experience with a loved one or just to laugh and be with friends. A person's mental health is usually a shifting balance between aloneness and gregariousness. Yet we vary hugely in our appetites for other people. Some individuals cherish a solitary walk; others want a party every night.

The nine men who sailed from England on the solo round-the-world race changed suddenly from living in an ordinary society with people, to a life with only one person. Each of the solitary mariners had to run his vessel, draw courses on his charts, keep an eye on the compass, and try to catch a fish once in a while.

Each man diagnosed his ills and remedies and made up his mind about the strength of the wind. He decided on his daily menu, the number of meals, and when he would eat. He had to determine when to sleep, for how long, and how to pace himself—that is, how to schedule his daily jobs so he didn't get too tired. Should he fill a kerosene lamp now or later? Should he climb out of his comfortable bunk to check around the horizon for ships? Should he do some extra navigation to be doubly safe or was it unnecessary? If he grew exhausted, his mind wouldn't work properly, so he was careful to take frequent naps and not overtax himself. Each decision was his alone, and every day he made dozens of large and small judgments. His self-reliance was complete, but he needed to be a strong and resourceful individual.

The solo sailor operates without other people. He practices his sport far from shore, far from cheering fans. Single-handed yacht racing doesn't have the excited watchers of the boxing ring or the baseball diamond. We all know that the tennis champion, the football quarterback, the ace cricket batsman, and the Olympic swimmer have enthusiastic flag-waving spectators who urge their heroes to greater efforts. The solo sailor has none of this. He functions in intense isolation. If he has any fans, they are generally a few close friends or admirers who see him at the beginning or the end. When the single-hander completes a race he sometimes even has to take his own finishing time ("If anybody cares," said the self-effacing Blondie Hasler after a faultless Atlantic crossing).

The whole sport has an aura of remoteness and isolation. The participants are a special brand of sportsmen who speak with a strange vocabulary and who get their kicks from competence in maneuvers that keep their vessels using the winds to the best advantage. All this is done in utter isolation—far from the land and other people. The whole zany business is a bit like stagecoach driving in the rain, hunting with falcons, or hot-air balloon ascensions in South Dakota. Yet solitary sailing—like mountaineering or soaring high in the sky in gliders—takes its practitioners into the great outdoors, gives them wonderful peace and tranquillity, and gets them supremely close to nature. Except for the few dabblers—who don't count—the commitment to single-handed sailing is usually total and complete. The solitary sailors treasure their special life.

The contestants in this round-the-world competition were all avowed sailors, but instead of a twenty-day passage between the Azores and Barbados, for example, this race went on and on. There were times when the nine men got sick of the endless competition and craved something different.

This test, this rivalry, was too big, too long, without limit. At the slow speed of a yacht, you logged 100 or 125 miles each day. The whole distance was 30,000 miles, more or less, which meant 300 days, or ten months, of sailing. That's 300 dawns and dusks, 300 noons and midnights, 900 solitary meals. No wonder most of the nine spoke of quitting at one time or another.

Five of the entrants—Blyth, Carozzo, Fougeron, King, and Ridgway—stayed in the race from twenty-six to ninety-eight days.

Ridgway pulled out because of a structural failure on his boat. Blyth panicked when salt water contaminated his gasoline supply, which in turn threatened his radio transmissions. These two men knew their vessels were small and ill-suited for the race; worse yet, both entrants were novice sailors and lacked the seasoning and cunning of a Francis Chichester.

Alex Carozzo withdrew because of bleeding stomach ulcers. A particularly nasty storm near the island of Tristan da Cunha knocked out Fougeron and King. Commander Bill King wanted to continue, but during the capsize, one mast had sheared off and disappeared; the second mast was cracked and looked ready to fall.

Loïck Fougeron was shocked by the severity of the storms off South Africa. He seemed quite pleased to retire from the awful seas and to head north into tropical waters. On November 27th (his ninety-eighth day), Fougeron wrote: "I am less than 100 miles from St. Helena. . . . At 1800 hours I drop anchor. . . . Eleven o'clock at night. I am lulled to sleep by a soft surge, under a sky studded with stars. *Captain Browne* rocks gently at anchor."

These five men got along with themselves fairly well. The other four sailors stayed in the race for much longer periods—seven to ten months. On November 1st, in the Indian Ocean, Moitessier wrote: "I find myself taking a long look at Mauritius, not very far north of here." The next day Knox-Johnston, nearing southeast Australia, echoed the same sentiments: "I think I'll give up at Melbourne. I've had enough. I'm tired, exhausted would be nearer the truth, frustrated because nothing I do seems to make any difference to the course, and scared to think what will break next." Tetley was far behind and nearing South Africa, but on November 27th he wrote: "An almost overpowering temptation to retire and head for Cape Town is growing inside me." We know that Donald Crowhurst never wanted to leave on the race in the first place and ever afterward schemed how to withdraw without losing face.

Five of the nine were out. The four who were left—grumbling and fussing now and then—sailed hard for England.

All four wanted to win.

24~
Homeward Bound

Ⅰт took Knox-Johnston six days to sail the 450 miles between Cape Horn and Port Stanley in the Falkland Islands. The English captain kept trying to make radio contact with someone in Punta Arenas (Chile) or Port Stanley. His receiver worked perfectly, and he could hear lots of Spanish and English voices on the commercial frequencies. But nobody answered.

Evidently *Suhaili*'s transmitter did not work. Knox-Johnston headed for Port Stanley to make himself known, but on January 20th the wind began to blow hard from the northeast—the direction of the port. With the foul bottom of *Suhaili* and his blown-out sails, about the best Knox-Johnston could head was either east-southeast (away from England) or north-northwest. The captain chose the eastward tack because he feared running into the south coast of the Falklands, especially if the wind switched to the southeast. Unfortunately, this put *Suhaili* within an area of the chart marked "extreme limit of pack ice" (in red).

The fickle northeast wind began to blow harder and harder, and by midafternoon it shrieked at 50 knots. As the wind increased, Knox-Johnston stripped off the sails. The freezing spray and rain blasted the captain's face and hands, and both were soon numb. The spray also ripped off the scab on the sensitive burn on his right hand. It had been ten days since he had spilled boiling porridge on his right wrist and hand, and now the healing process would have to start all over again.

In spite of the bitter cold, Knox-Johnston felt he had to keep an ice watch because of the danger of icebergs and loose ice. By evening the wind had eased, so the captain hoisted the mainsail again. He kept falling asleep in the hatchway and dimly realized that since the wind was down and the ketch was not going very fast the danger from ice was slight. He gave up and turned into his sleeping bag, wet clothes and all.

For the next few days the wind continued to blow mostly from the northeast, so Knox-Johnston abandoned his call at the Falklands. He didn't feel well; he was sick to his stomach and his head began to hurt so badly that he took two codeine tablets to ease the pain. Nevertheless, he managed to repair several chafed lines and did his daily sewing on the sails. On January 23rd, the wind finally settled in the west, which gave *Suhaili* a free wind on her port quarter.

The captain finally discovered that he had been drinking contaminated water from one of the ship's tanks. When he switched to rainwater from a plastic jug he began to feel better. Wonderful! A few days later he managed to catch 5 gallons of rainwater that he reckoned would last a month.

One day before sunset, *Suhaili*'s captain noticed patches of royal blue on the slate gray sea. "Ice!" was his first thought. As he looked closer he saw that the blue color was caused by hundreds of fast-moving tadpole-like creatures about 6 inches long. The tadpoles were on the surface and appeared to have long silver tongues. Incredible. Could they be the larval stage of something? Knox-Johnston leafed through his fish book for an identifying clue but found nothing. What could they be? He had no idea.

After lunch on January 26th the jib halyard carried away, and the headsail fell into the sea. Knox-Johnston pulled the wet sail on deck and began trying to climb the mast to reeve a new halyard. He made three attempts; all failed, and he was lucky not to have injured himself. The problem was the yacht swinging into the wind after he had gone partway up the mast. With the yacht heading into the wind she pitched forward and backward into the head seas. And the higher Robin climbed, the worse the motion grew. A person hauling himself aloft on a four-part tackle and a bosun's chair is liable to start swinging back and forth like a marble on a thread and to crash into the mast with bone-smashing results. (Oh, for a friendly hand at the tiller to run the boat off away from the swells.) After his third failure, Knox-Johnston decided to disconnect the topping lift from the main boom and to hoist the headsail on the topping lift. He would have to get along without the main boom lift until he found smoother waters.

Both Moitessier and Knox-Johnston were heavy smokers. North of the Falklands, Knox-Johnston accidentally dropped his last cigarette over the side. Now he would have to quit. A good thing. He stopped smoking for a whole day. The next evening, while drinking a cup of coffee, he craved a cigarette. Wait a minute! Hadn't he hidden twenty packs at the bottom of his clothing bag? He wasn't sure. Maybe. . . . "No mole ever dug as furiously as I did into my large clothing bag," he wrote. "Arms, head and shoulders disappeared as I scrabbled to the bottom, and emerged clutching a precious 400 fags. In my diary I promised 'I'll keep to 4 a day,' and then added more realistically 'or thereabouts.' "

On February 3rd, *Suhaili* crossed 40 degrees south latitude and left the Southern Ocean behind. She headed into the variables, the zone of uncertain winds between the westerlies of the high latitudes and the trade wind of the tropics. As the wooden ketch plowed northward, each day grew a little warmer. The sea was still too cold for swimming, so Knox-Johnston washed in a bucket of seawater he heated on his Primus stove. The captain spent a lot of time trying to coax his engine into life, but the only result was two cracked cylinders. As the weather warmed up he washed and dried all his damp clothing, scrubbed and aired the settee cushions, and wiped out and cleaned the interior.

On some days *Suhaili* looked like a floating laundry. Knox-Johnston began to check his stores and he threw out almost a hundred cans of food that had been corroded and pierced by salt water. Warm air poured in through the open hatches and filled the interior of the yacht. The damp woodwork dried out and the jammed locker doors began to work smoothly. Instead of sweaters and oilskins the captain now went without a shirt and wore only trousers. The warm weather was wonderful!

One day Robin shot two 7-foot nurse sharks that he heard scraping against the hull and knocking off antifouling paint. The next day he took his first cautious swim. The cool water refreshed him and he discovered three pilot fish keeping station with *Suhaili*. During various swims Knox-Johnston checked the hull and the worn rudder fittings. He scraped off underwater growth as best he could, particularly the gooseneck barnacles, some of which were bloated and 6 inches long.

Suhaili reached the latitude of Buenos Aires on February 9th. In this region of the South Atlantic east of the Argentine and southern Brazilian coasts, the yacht managed only 70 miles a day because of vicious line squalls called pamperos. These fierce winds demanded quick sail reductions and upset all normal progress.

Between these squalls the sun burned down on the Englishman. The cabin temperature rose to 95°F. Robin suffered a lot from the heat because his one-month transition from the coldness of the Southern Ocean to the broiling sun of the tropics had been too short. Now instead of sentences about a frozen face and numb fingers, the log spoke of mild sunstroke, headaches, and weakness caused by the heat. Robin sewed a sun hat from old canvas.

Knox-Johnston did everything he could to get northward, but his tubby vessel sailed poorly in the light airs. What he needed were moderate seas and brisk, steady winds on the beam. Light headwinds were hopeless. At night he steered by the stars because the compass light had given out long before and his last flashlight had stopped working.

He had to concern himself with catching drinking water. The water business was no joke because the British sailor had only 7 gallons of water on board. There was no engine and no radio, he had abysmal winds, and the yacht and her sails were in poor condition. In the scorching heat a person had to drink a fair amount of fluids each day just to stay alive. Robin still had plenty of food, however, and wrote in his log that he had finally perfected a cheese sauce to pep up some of his dishes.

On February 19th he logged 40 miles; on the 20th, he did 36; on the 21st, *Suhaili* made only a pathetic 18 miles noon to noon. At 0330 on February 22nd, the captain got up to look around and noticed a squall coming. He was ready when it arrived, but he was unsure of his course because the rain had obscured the stars and he couldn't see to steer properly. Nevertheless, he collected 4 gallons of water from the bucket hanging on the gooseneck of the mizzen boom. At 0630 he got another 2 gallons of water from a second squall. At 0825 1 more gallon, and at 1005, 2 more. Now Knox-Johnston had a total of 16 gallons of water, almost a two-month supply if he rationed himself. On this day he logged 87 miles and slipped into the southeast trade wind, which meant a steady 12 to 14 knots of wind across *Suhaili*'s starboard beam or quarter for the next 1,500 miles—from 24 degrees south latitude to roughly the equator.

> Now that we were moving again my spirits shot up, [wrote Knox-Johnston]. Like most sailors I immediately began calculating when I would reach my destination using the best day's run achieved so far; a totally unrealistic calculation, of course, but tremendously exciting.

On February 24th, *Suhaili* passed 140 miles east of Ilha da Trindade, which lies 600 miles east of the Brazilian coast. The captain began to think of England and home and tried to smarten up his vessel a little. He worked on some new rope netting beneath the bowsprit and splashed a bit of paint here and there. In truth the ketch looked terrible. The paint on her white topsides and cabin was dull and chalked and in places blistered and peeling. Various iron fastenings and the chainplates bled ugly streaks of rust. Her waterline showed grass, bits of marine growth, and traces of the captain's efforts at scraping off barnacles. The rudder fittings—once tight and efficient—had worn until there was a quarter inch of play in them. Long ago Knox-Johnston had put lashings on the rudder head to take some of the pressure off the fittings, but at times the loose rudder made frightful thumping noises. He hoped the worn gudgeons and pintles would last until the end of the voyage.

In spite of his problems, the captain kept the sails carefully trimmed. By now he was an expert at making his small ketch steer herself by adjusting the sails, and *Suhaili* glided along smoothly before the trade wind. The sailing was delightful. Knox-Johnston enjoyed it immensely and his spirits soared. The wind blew steadily, but not too strongly. There were no storms. The sun shone brightly, and the trade wind clouds made distinctive patterns in the sky. The wind reduced the temperature to a comfortable degree, and the sea sparkled and glittered as the sun bounced off the ocean swells that rolled along in an even rhythm.

Suhaili averaged almost 120 miles a day in the trade wind and took only twelve days to reach the equator. Robin continued to spruce up his vessel and somehow managed to give himself a haircut and beard trim (he had planned to shave, but he had forgotten razor blades). *Suhaili* neared the major shipping lanes, where Knox-Johnston hoped to get a message off to England by means of a merchant vessel.

By March 6th, he had finished all his cigarettes. Now he developed terrible stomach pains, a medical problem that turned into the most harrowing episode of the entire voyage. The sea can usually be dealt with in some fashion or another, but illness cannot. Knox-Johnston pulled out the *Ship Captains' Medical Guide* and began to read about possible problems based on his symptoms. The more he read the more alarmed he became. The possible troubles ranged from appendicitis to ulcers. As recommended, he commenced a soft diet of spaghetti, cheese, and rice puddings, but when the location of his stomach pains moved, he really got upset. It was appendicitis for sure!

The nearest port was Belém at the mouth of the Amazon, 1,000 miles or ten days away. He had no antibiotics on board, and in ten days he would be dead. A few days later he sighted a ship and tried to get help, but after a flicker of recognition the ship steamed away. Two other ships came close during the next days, but they also failed to answer *Suhaili*'s signals, which included flashing light signals and powerful flares. After a few more days Knox-Johnston's stomach pains eased; he began to think that his problem had been a bad can of corned beef plus chronic indigestion and acute imagination. Never give a layman a medical book!

While Knox-Johnston struggled northward in total isolation from the outside world, the newspapers back in England speculated at length about his location and whether he was even still alive. He had last been seen leaving New Zealand on November 21st, when he reported that his radio transmitter out of order. Now it was the middle of March, sixteen weeks later. Had he struck an iceberg? Had the Southern Ocean swallowed up *Suhaili?* Had Knox-Johnston's sails and running gear simply worn out? Was he somewhere at sea floating around helplessly? Moitessier had been sighted off Port Stanley in the Falkland Islands on February 9th, but no one had seen Knox-Johnston. Who was ahead? Who was behind? Indeed, who was alive?

The *Sunday Mirror* newspaper, always alert for headlines, attempted to launch a giant search for Knox-Johnston, who was presumed to be near the Azores if he had kept up his 90- to 100-mile daily average. By chance, a thirty-ship NATO naval fleet was on maneuvers in the area. The newspaper asked the navy captains to keep an eye out for a small weather-beaten ketch. The United States Air Force base at Terceira in the Azores agreed to watch for Knox-Johnston on its daily patrol flights. The *Sunday Mirror* also broadcast a notice to residents and fishermen in the Azores.

Meanwhile *Suhaili* had left the southeast trade wind, slipped through the narrow doldrums, and entered the northeast trade wind. The wooden ketch continued to make good runs—up to 125 miles a day. On March 17th, Knox-Johnston celebrated his thirtieth birthday. One week later, at 18 degrees north, he sailed out of the northeast trade wind and into the northern zone of variable winds. As usual, he was soon fed up with fickle winds and regarded any light winds from bad directions as personal insults.

The only way he could let off steam was to swim until he was exhausted and then to lose himself in some bit of maintenance. On March 23rd, he did 67 miles with headwinds; two days later he ran before a south-southeast gale until the sea conditions obliged him to reef and slow down. Then it was more variable winds. Unfortunately, the captain often had to steer by hand in the variables because the winds were so changeable.

In the Sargasso Sea he saw clumps of gulfweed. Robin pulled some on board and was fascinated with the tiny brownish yellow shrimps and crabs that fell on deck when he shook the weed. Once, a 5-inch eel or snake shot out of a clump of gulfweed and startled the amateur biologist.

On April 2nd, a Norwegian cargo vessel passed *Suhaili* at a distance of 150 yards. Knox-Johnston signaled frantically and even fired five shots from his rifle into the air but got no response. Other ships also paid no attention. Finally, on April 6th, a little west of the Azores near 39 de-

grees north latitude, he made contact with the British Petroleum tanker
Mobil Acme and sent the following message by flashing lamp signal:

> *Sent:* British *Suhaili*. Round the world non-stop.
> *Received:* Please repeat name.
> *Sent: Suhaili.* Please report me to Lloyd's.
> *Received:* Will do. Good luck.
> *Sent:* E.T.A. Falmouth two weeks.
> *Received:* R[oger].

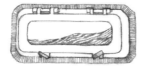

25

A Separate Peace

THE FOUR MEN STILL IN THE RACE DESPERATELY CRAVED NEWS of their fellow contestants. Where were the others? Was the competition still on? Were the other men ahead or behind? What sort of hair-raising adventures had they been through? Had there been any mishaps? Record daily runs? How could anyone make plans or decide what risks to take or even feel settled if he had no news of the race in general?

Every sports participant needs a milepost, a stopwatch gauge, a glance at his competitors' scores, or a glimpse of the other people on the race-track to reassure himself. He can relax a bit if he's ahead, or redouble his efforts if he is lagging behind. A person's mind is liable to wander without some idea of his progress and standing and a thought of the goal ahead. He may think he's far ahead and has won, or he may decide that he's failed miserably. His mind may rejoice in aggrandizement, or he may sulk because he's depressed and discouraged.

The solo round-the-world race required a tough nut to survive it physically. It was even more demanding on a mental level. Imagine sailing by yourself for ten months! Twenty-four hours a day, in all seas and in all sorts of weather. Consider having to deal with large and small problems every day for three hundred consecutive days and nights. Some of the yachts had been back in port for months, and the news had not been made known to those who were still at sea. Moitessier had rounded Cape Horn in February, but he was quite unaware that Bill King and Loïck Fougeron had been knocked out of the race the previous November.

The comradeship between the nine men who started the race was a thin link, but it was palpable and real. Some of the sailors were close friends; others hadn't even met. Yet they were all bound together in this marathon, and they struggled with the common problems of morale, endurance, determination, and resourcefulness. While each man hoped to win or at least to finish honorably, each wished the others good sailing and good fortune. Even Donald Crowhurst had begun with good intentions.

One would think that *The Sunday Times*, a giant newspaper in the communications business, would have arranged twice monthly (or whatever) briefings for all the contestants. This could have been done by long-range radio broadcasts at certain hours. The participants could have been given low-powered radios to make contact with shore stations in, say, the Azores, Cape Town, Kerguelen Island, Perth, Hobart, Christchurch, Hao, Juan Fernández, Punta Arenas, Port Stanley, and Salvador. Low-powered radios have only a short range, but their size, complications, and power requirements are modest, and a kite or balloon aerial put up on a calm day can increase their range enormously.

A contestant within range of one of the shore stations could have been read a prepared message or could have listened to a taped commentary of the race up to that moment. A few high-powered transmitters in key places might have extended the usefulness of the low-powered receivers on the boats. A ham radio link might have been arranged. Or pilot boats at various key ports could have been alerted to deliver an information bulletin when they made sightings of the yachts.

If the communication or visual sighting link had been two-way and obligatory, it would have given the newspaper up-to-the-minute information about each contestant and enabled the reporters to have written longer and better stories. And with a continuing look at each man, it would have kept the race honest and up to date.

The Sunday Times relied on long-distance radio communication that required expensive, delicate, bulky equipment with high electrical demands, which meant noisy, smelly generators and gasoline or diesel fuel. Long-distance equipment also needed special antennas, a certain amount of expertise, and radio schedules made out months in advance. No wonder some of the contestants balked at burdening their vessels and themselves with such gear and complications.

Let's be honest. *The Sunday Times* didn't sponsor the competition to encourage long-distance yacht racing because of feelings of goodwill toward men. The paper underwrote the race to generate exciting, ongoing stories that would sell newspapers. If the contestants had a bit of minor trouble now and then, well, all the better. The readers would eat it up, and the circulation and profits of the paper would increase. Newspapers have been putting on stunts and contests with prize money for decades. When I was a boy I read the English translation of Jules Verne's novel *Around the World in 80 Days*. I was enthralled by Phileas

Fogg and Passepartout and their adventures. Would they make it back to London in time to claim the prize of £20,000? I was so excited I could hardly put the book down when my mother called me for supper.

When reporter Murray Sayle and his boss Ron Hall of *The Sunday Times* made up the rules of the Golden Globe and set up the round-the-world yacht race, it never occurred to them to establish a way to keep the contestants informed about the progress of the race. This was a decisive blunder, but perhaps an understandable one since no one had ever run a contest of this nature before.

Certainly the sponsor of a competition that sent people out on the remote oceans of the world had a moral responsibility to keep everyone informed of what was going on. What the effect of occasional briefings would have had on the contestants is hard to judge, but a few paragraphs of authoritative information would have reassured everyone and eased the mental load on the men at sea.

Bernard Moitessier's behavior might have been strikingly different. He hadn't heard about anyone in the race for five and a half months even though he listened carefully to the BBC, which occasionally reported yachting news. On February 5th—only nineteen days behind Knox-Johnston—the bearded Frenchman was speeding past Cape Horn.

Four days later Moitessier's red ketch, *Joshua*, lay hove-to in a stiff north wind at Cape Pembroke at the eastern extremity of the Falkland Islands. It was a Sunday and no one replied to Moitessier's mirror signals that he flashed at the lighthouse, a black iron tower ringed by a white horizontal stripe. Port Stanley lay out of sight to the west. A sail to the settlement meant a hazardous detour to the far end of a complex bay. It meant night sailing in constricted waters littered with rocks and kelp and beset with strong tidal streams and hard squalls.

The French captain was extremely tired. He didn't have the right chart, and he lacked local knowledge. Yet he wanted very much to let his family and friends know that he was OK. In the end he refused to tackle the approach to Port Stanley. He had made it safely around the three great capes of the world, and he decided that he was not going to be wrecked in an insignificant sound on a mission that might not be successful.

Reluctantly, he sailed onward. His first order of business was to get out of the ice zone, so he headed northeast. His second requirement was to recover his strength. The rounding of Cape Horn and the Falkland Island episode had drained away every bit of vitality and zip from him. He began to sleep a lot and to prepare his meals with care. He read a little and climbed to the masthead three or four times a day to look for icebergs. He took long naps and did yoga exercises. Gradually he grew stronger and forgot about the gale south of the Falklands, the difficult landfall, and the disappointment at the Cape Pembroke light.

Sometimes Moitessier dreamed about the other men in the race and sailors he had known from earlier voyages. Bill King and Loïck Fougeron were in his dreams a few times but not Nigel Tetley. Moitessier believed that it was impossible to dream about a dead person. "Nigel is the one I think of most often, yet I have never seen him in my dreams. Good Lord! I hope nothing has happened to Nigel."

The surface of the Southern Ocean is usually turbulent and upset because of the heavy westerlies and the ground swell that sweep around the world. In the lee of the east coast of South America, however, this great ocean is often quite smooth by comparison.

As *Joshua* pushed northeastward and crossed 40 degrees south latitude, the ice danger receded and the sea warmed up little by little. One day during a calm, Moitessier dropped his headsails, sheeted the mainsail and mizzen flat to ease the rolling, and put on his wetsuit. He checked around for sharks and dropped over the side with a scraper to peel off the barnacles on the hull. In half an hour he was done; *Joshua* was on her way again. During another calm, the French captain did a little restitching on the mainsail and replaced a few luff slides.

Soon *Joshua* was halfway between Cape Horn and the Cape of Good Hope. On March 8th, the red ketch crossed her outbound track from England and completed her circumnavigation of the world. But the captain was strangely unexcited. Unlike Tetley, he opened no bottle of champagne nor cooked any special dinners.

> She [has] sailed round the world . . . but what does that mean, since the horizon is eternal? [he wrote in a strange philosophical outburst]. Round the world goes further than the ends of the earth, as far as life itself, perhaps further still.

IN LATE FEBRUARY, on his way east-northeast from the Falkland Islands, Moitessier made the boldest decision of his life. For several weeks he had been arguing with himself as he approached the southern tip of Africa, a place marked by the Cape of Good Hope, which was a major turning point for ocean travelers. To the north lay the Atlantic and Europe. To the east were the Indian Ocean, Australia, New Zealand, and the Pacific. It was the Pacific that included Bernard's favorite places in all the world: Tahiti and the Galápagos Islands.

Moitessier thought he had a good chance of winning the Golden Globe. He had the fastest yacht, and his average daily runs were the best in the race. If he won the competition he would collect the prize money, receive awards from England and France (perhaps the Légion d'Honneur), and have a chance to make a handsome sum of money from a book. He could endorse equipment and arrange personal appearances. When he was in Europe he could see his wife and children and his mother. He would have a good rest, re-equip *Joshua*, and then sail off to the Pacific. Certainly it was the sensible thing to do.

Unfortunately for the race sponsors, Bernard hated cities, noise, and business complications. He was a gentle person who had strong feelings of love for the earth, woods, and water.

Moitessier wrote that he "felt sick at the thought of going back to Europe, back to the snakepit." Why should he debase himself by sailing to France and England? Europe was a business hell, a place where men brutalized one another for false gods. It was all a senseless game to make money for pointless purposes: to buy a new car when the old one was perfectly good; to acquire stylish clothes when last year's were still OK; to pay a ransom to moor a yacht in a fancy marina. And so on.

Why did he need money? He already had *Joshua* and good sails and plenty of food. Why seek more when he already possessed everything? Why lose his peace and self-respect? He was happy and content.

Yes, he would keep circling the globe until he passed Good Hope, the Indian Ocean, Australia, and New Zealand. In the Pacific he would head north a little, pick up the gentle southeast trade wind, and sail to Tahiti, where he had friends. Or he would travel farther east to the Galápagos Islands, where he could see the marvelous seals that were so friendly and genuine. Yes, he was done with the stupid yacht race. It was over. Finished. Kaput. Terminated.

Moitessier reflected on his childhood and youth in Indochina, where he was born and where the value structure was more sensible.

> All at once I see my Chinese nurse again, teaching me, as a child,
> to lie face down on the ground when I had worn myself out, or been
> bad [he wrote]. And when I was bigger, she told me that the earth
> gives her strength and peace to those who love her.

He remembered his native land, where people still greeted one another by joining palms in front of their chests, which means, "I greet the God in you"—exactly as one addresses a divinity.

Bernard had made up his mind. On March 18th *Joshua* sailed into the harbor at Cape Town, a little north and west of the Cape of Good Hope. There the captain tossed a 3-gallon plastic jerrican to a sailor on a ship chandler's launch. In the can were movie films, tape cassettes, and still films, some of which included photographs of *Joshua*'s logbook entries. On the same day Moitessier fired a slingshot message on board the British oil tanker *Argosy*, which was anchored in the bay. The cable that was radioed to *The Sunday Times* read:

> I am happy at sea and perhaps I want to save my soul [he wrote]. I do not feel like going back to Europe. . . . my intention is to continue the voyage, still non-stop, towards the Pacific islands, where there is plenty of sun and more peace than in Europe.

When Moitessier's wife in Paris heard the news from Cape Town, she made a quick diagnosis and said that seven months of solo sailing had temporarily unbalanced her husband.

> I can't think what has made Bernard do this [she said]. It can only be some sort of *cafard* [fit of the blues] after seven months alone at sea. . . . But Bernard always has his own way, and if he's taken this decision, he'll stick to it.

Even Sir Francis Chichester, the shrewd adventurer who was the chairman of the race committee, found Moitessier's decision incredible. Sir Francis searched into his own great experience of solo voyaging for a theory that would account for Frenchman's action.

> Moitessier is a very unusual man and a yachtsman of exceptional experience [said Sir Francis] But the trouble is that on these long voyages you develop a sort of rhythm of life with the boat and the sea, and you are very loath to break that rhythm. When I was pulling towards Britain on my own round-the-world voyage I had the very strong feeling that instead of heading to Plymouth, I'd prefer to go on sailing for ever.

Moitessier realized that the world would think him deranged, so by way of explanation he wrote the following:

> Why am I playing a trick like this? Imagine yourself in the forest of the Amazon, looking for something new, because you wanted to feel the earth, trees, nature. You suddenly come across a small temple

of an ancient, lost civilisation. You are not simply going to come back
and say: "Well I found a temple, a civilisation nobody knows." You
would stay there, try to understand it, try to decipher it . . . and then
you would discover that 100 kilometres further on is another temple,
only the main temple this time. Would you return?

So on March 18th, the favorite in the race withdrew with a spectacular bow. It was an incredible exit and hard to believe. This able French
seaman had had no sailing or equipment problems. The race was his. Yet
for personal reasons that sometimes seemed hard to understand he had
opened his hand and let the white bird of victory fly away. Whether he
had won his own personal race, the reader must judge.

Now there were three men left in the Golden Globe. All were in the
Atlantic and charging hard for Plymouth.

Moitessier has sailed out of our story, but he continued to go around
the world a second time. The French sailor finally entered the lagoon at
Papeete, Tahiti, in French Polynesia on June 21st, 1969, after complet-
ing a ten-month nonstop voyage of 37,455 miles. I hope he found his
salvation, his nirvana, his peace of mind. He deserved it.

26~
Meeting with Himself

 I N EARLY APRIL, AFTER A SHIP NEAR THE AZORES REPORTED HIM, all odds were on Robin Knox-Johnston to win the race and collect the Golden Globe trophy for the first man to circle the world single-handed. However, the £5,000 for the fastest solo circumnavigation was a different matter. It looked as if one of the other two sailors in the race would scoop up the big cash prize. Remember that thirty-five years ago, £5,000 was a lot of money.

As we have seen, after nearly three months of radio silence Donald Crowhurst sent his April 9th telegram to England. The next day Crowhurst's press agent, Rodney Hallworth, announced that his man had rounded Cape Horn and was rushing toward Plymouth.

"Donald is proving to be one of the greatest sporting sailors of our time," crowed Hallworth. An analysis of Crowhurst's mileages since his departure the previous October showed incredible irregularities. He had started out badly, claimed a record run, mentioned a few place-names in his later telegrams, lapsed into silence, and now was again claiming sensational times.

The men at *The Sunday Times* kept correcting their old figures and revising their estimates of *Teignmouth Electron*'s arrival in England. First it had been November and then September 30th (after "the record run"). Later revisions put the date at September 8th (following the telegram sent—supposedly—from near Tristan da Cunha). The reporters then wrote August 19th (when Crowhurst was "in the Indian Ocean"). After the latest barrage of misinformation the new arrival date was posted at July 8th or before. One set of bizarre calculations put *Teignmouth Electron*'s speed at 188.6 miles a day for 13,000 miles.

Evidently the sleek blue-and-white trimaran had grown wings as she sped around the world. Some people theorized that as Crowhurst had

settled down and learned how to sail his craft and had worked into his
stores and provisions, his speeds had naturally increased. Additionally,
his admirers said, in the Roaring Forties of the Southern Ocean a vessel
would make better time. Of course these arguments applied to all the
yachts. . . .

According to the reporters' calculations, Crowhurst's time was fourteen days ahead of Tetley's time up to Cape Horn. Tetley, who had
started the race forty-five days before Crowhurst, had been speeding
northward in the Atlantic since March 18th, but it appeared that Crowhurst was sailing faster. None of Crowhurst's figures would have stood
up to scrutiny, but no one dreamed of foul play and there was no expert
inquiry except in the mind of Sir Francis Chichester, who had made no
public statement. All the newspapers meekly accepted Hallworth's numbers or calculated their own.

It began to look like a possible racehorse finish between the captains
of the two Victress-class trimarans. One man was a veteran naval officer;
the other was a brash young challenger who was proving to be a formidable threat. The staff at *The Sunday Times* was chuckling with satisfaction and planned full coverage; the picture department was checking
into hiring airplanes and fast launches for its best photographers when
the multihulls appeared near England. The editors envisioned front-page
stories plus inside feature articles about each man as he crossed the finish line.

On April 12th, Crowhurst received a message from Hallworth:

> YOURE ONLY TWO WEEKS BEHIND TETLEY   PHOTO FINISH WILL MAKE
> GREAT NEWS STOP   ROBIN DUE ONE TO TWO WEEKS==RODNEY

Crowhurst knew that his plan to win the race by staying in the Atlantic hadn't been detected. Also, his illegal stopover in Argentina
hadn't been exposed. So far, so good. All he had to do was to complete
the false logbook and start back to England. He had been sailing steadily
northward from the Falklands. On April 18th he answered a direct radio
call from England querying whether he had received Hallworth's recent
message. Crowhurst gossiped in Morse code with the Portishead operator and found out Tetley's position and learned that Moitessier was out
of the race. Now the captain of *Teignmouth Electron* knew about his
competitors; it was time for his big move.

The problem was how to coordinate his fake positions with his real
positions. He needed to advance his fraudulent daily location closer and
closer to his actual location so that the false Donald Crowhurst could fi-

nally meet the true Donald Crowhurst. Once he met himself he could use his actual daily positions. Then his life would be simpler because farther north he would certainly be reported by ships that would authenticate his latitude and longitude and expose any irregularities.

Instead of sailing north as fast as he could to implement his master plan, however, Crowhurst hesitated, almost on purpose it seemed. Once again he was guilty of indecision and delay. To anyone who examines the records it appeared that Donald almost wanted to lose. He would work out a scheme to do something and then be reluctant to act, as if he hoped someone else would make up his mind for him or push him this way or that. Even in the beginning Crowhurst was not a strong captain, and his resolve appeared to be growing weaker and weaker.

By now he was roughly 700 miles east of Buenos Aires and within easy radio range of the Argentine capital. He repeatedly tried to arrange a direct land-link telephone call to his wife, Clare, in England via New York. It was easy to speak to the Argentine radio operators, but the South American overseas telephone facilities were primitive. Crowhurst prepared telegrams to Clare asking her to wait for his call. He tried again and again, but the telephone connections did not succeed. It seemed that Crowhurst wanted to speak to his wife directly without going through the ears of the English radio technicians who by this time had become interested in the race and who might not respect his privacy. By routing his call via local Spanish-speaking operators and New York, where he was not known, he thought he could talk without the radio people in England monitoring his words.

Donald Crowhurst was a lonely and thoroughly confused thirty-seven-year-old man who had been caught in a complex spiderweb of his own making. He desperately wanted to quit the race, to somehow back out of this sailing marathon, to get away from an endurance contest that stretched on and on like the hard blue line of the horizon. He wanted to confide in someone and perhaps confess his deception. He wanted help from a human being he could trust, who would advise him and tell him what to do. The world was certainly an unjust place; it was not fair to him when he had so many important things on his mind.

Was this situation unique for Crowhurst? Had he ever deceived people before? What was his background?

Donald Crowhurst was born in India in 1932, where his father was a railroad superintendent. His childhood and youth reveal a sensitive, intelligent, sharp-tongued, gutsy young man who was clever at fixing things. He left school in England at sixteen and spent the next six years in the Royal Air Force, where he learned to be a pilot. He purchased an old sports car and liked to rush from place to place. His mind moved quickly, and when he was out with his fellow pilots he was usually a brash show-off. "Let's paint a telephone box yellow," he would shout. . . . "Who can drink the most gin backwards from a beer glass?" . . . "I hear that sniffing mothballs increases potency, let's try!" and so on. Eventually his outrageous behavior caught up with him and he was thrown out of the Royal Air Force.

He promptly enlisted in the army, was again commissioned, and took a course in electronic control equipment. Again he led his fellow officers on merry evenings and barroom high jinks. He smashed his car into a bus, was caught several times driving without insurance, lost his license, and yet kept driving. One night during a beery escapade he tried to steal a car and was arrested and fined; the local police sent his photograph to the criminal records office of Scotland Yard. Again he was asked to resign his commission.

At twenty-four, Crowhurst began work at the Reading University laboratories, where he was soon considered both an intellectual and a rather dashing figure. He met Clare in 1957 and after a flamboyant courtship married her the same year. It wasn't long until the first of four children arrived. He impressed everyone by being an excellent, devoted father.

Crowhurst began work as an equipment salesman for a prominent electronics company but left after a year because of trouble following a car accident. In his mid-twenties now, he had already blown three budding careers. He dabbled with several other companies but finally decided that he must work for himself as an electronics engineer and salesman. He would get rich by inventing new electronic gadgets and marketing them. His first successful product was a clever radio direction-finding device he called a Navicator. Though not brilliant or especially original, it was a useful and salable device and he set up a small factory with six employees.

Crowhurst lived in a village named Nether Stowey near Bridgwater in Somerset in southwest England. He was a typical small-town intellectual, somewhat loud-mouthed, and after a time got elected as a Liberal councillor, not by his record but by an image he somehow projected of himself as a skillful executive who would solve all of Bridgwater's industrial difficulties. He generally shouted down any opposition with a series of intricate questions that had only one answer: Donald Crowhurst.

About the time he began his political efforts he bought a new Jaguar sports car. The same dreary pattern repeated itself. He drove too fast and in six months had another mishap. This time the car flipped and Crowhurst received a nasty smash on his head.

Clare said that his personality was different after the accident. Donald grew more introspective, often sulked, and sometimes became infuriated. He would lose his temper and throw and smash things. All this reminds me of the Argentine small-boat sailor Vito Dumas, who underwent a marked personality change after a blow on the head. In the case of Dumas, it happened when he accidentally dove into an empty swimming pool.

When Crowhurst's able biographers reconstructed his story they found two Donald Crowhursts. One was an unpleasant bore, a braggadocio whose swaggering manner was so blatant that after an amusing minute or two his cockiness began to disgust people. This was the military Crowhurst who led his young officer friends from the bright lights and clamor of one noisy bar to another. This was the fast-driving Crowhurst who roared across the English countryside and wrecked car after car. This was the yachtsman Crowhurst speaking on radio interviews and BBC tapes, where he was the hale and hearty, tough, two-fisted, jocular, unforgiving sea captain who liked to mock his opponents and the world.

> Oh tis 'orrible to be out matey. Mountainous seas eighteen inches high an' horrible great black clouds, roll upon roll of them matey, stretching away as far as the eye can see. Now I will cast me optic on the wind recorder. Me gawd six knots . . . Oh I have been in some tight spots on the voyage matey, but this is diabolically tight matey.

To meet the second Donald Crowhurst we must walk through a door into a darkened room. The man ahead of us is a quiet, introspective, moody individual without the vaudeville posturing and pathetic attempts at humor that we've seen earlier. The lonely professor at the desk is a serious Donald, the ultimate intellectual, who is seeking revolutionary answers to engineering mysteries and arcane electronic problems. As he probes his private, specialized world, he makes us think of an explorer walking toward a range of high, uncharted mountains.

According to Crowhurst, all mankind over its whole course of history is a blank and meaningless void. Donald's mind and the entire system of the universe are really rival mathematical computers. He speculated on the interplay between economics, politics, and religion. The Englishman spent enormous effort in writing, scratching out, and correcting pages of gloomy and morbid paragraphs that were all mixed up with God, mathematics, and his childhood.

Instead of sailing his yacht and concentrating on his great deception, which, after all, was a fiendishly clever scheme, Crowhurst exhausted himself in a foggy world of mental fantasy.

Crowhurst thought of himself as an engineer and a mathematician. There were no novels, light humor, or travel books for him. He needed heavy stuff. Books with muscle. One of the volumes he had with him was *Relativity: The Special and the General Theory* by Albert Einstein, a book the great scientist had written to explain his work to popular audiences. Crowhurst studied the book day after day.

Donald read into Einstein all sorts of mystical meanings and interpretations the renowned physicist certainly never intended. Crowhurst made notes on the margins of the book, wrote a critical commentary, and prepared a confused and puzzling essay on Einstein's book. What Einstein considered mere mathematical and logical explanations, Crowhurst turned into cosmic meaning and Godlike associations. The amateur sailor saw great things in $E = mc^2$, a mathematical statement that according to Crowhurst was the same as the Christian formula "God is love."

The English sailor wrote at length about his childhood and how he had learned about God and man. He did his writing with difficulty and his pages were filled with deletions and changes. The content made some sense, but it was a confused and melancholy business and certainly not done by a person in control of himself.

> One night while looking at the stars and wondering about God I thought I detected a pattern in the stars resembling the head of Christ with a crown of thorns [he recollected]. I turned to my companion and tried to point it out, but she could not see it. Nor could I. I had been brought up on miracles, and decided that this was a miracle. . . .
>
> One day soon afterwards I noticed a fruitcake in the pantry and ran to my mother to thank her for obtaining my favourite food. "I bought no fruitcake," said my mother. "Yes you have!" "No I haven't." I was worried. What could the explanation be? You see, it never occurred to me that my mother could be lying. "But I have just seen it in the pantry." "Oh," said my mother, "I bought it as a surprise." My mother had lied to me! I reeled under the mental blow.

ALL THESE DEPRESSING and unhealthy mutterings were drops of corrosive acid on the thin cord that connected Crowhurst to the real world. Donald's personality was crashing about him in ruins. It was the pressure of his loneliness, the incomplete work at the boatyard when the trimaran was built, the supplies that he left behind on the dock, the other competitors who were honest and winning—all these things hammered on his muddled brain.

There were further blows. He had stubbornly refused to give up the race. He had made the illegal stop in Argentina. He had spent months of cowardly hiding in the Atlantic. Finally there was the falsified logbook, a written document that was to damn him for all time.

These separate pressures and deceptions converged and steadily drove him toward madness. After five and a half months at sea, Crowhurst was a nutcase.

27 ~
Valiant to the End

LIEUTENANT-COMMANDER NIGEL TETLEY ROUNDED CAPE HORN on March 18th and immediately shaped a course to the northeast in the South Atlantic. Knox-Johnston had slipped past Cape Horn sixty days earlier, but Tetley was sailing faster and gradually gaining on the leader. At least he thought he was. Who knew what the final outcome would be? Tetley wondered where Crowhurst and the others were, and as the question pulsed through his mind, he turned and looked around the horizon for a sail although he realized there was only a million to one chance of spotting anyone.

Tetley always had plenty to do aboard *Victress*. The day after he had rounded Cape Horn he noticed his yacht was not keeping her course properly. When he went aft to check the self-steering he discovered that both the special stainless steel shaft and the self-steering rudder had fallen off. This was presumably impossible because they were secured to their metal frame with a washer and a stout cotter pin that could not wriggle loose. Yet somehow the cursed cotter pin had sheared off and allowed the vital parts to drop into the sea. Damn!

Tetley steered by hand for several hours while he considered alternatives. He tried a combination of small sails that did not work at all; at one point the storm jib began to flog so violently that its sheets whipped back and forth and lashed Tetley's face hard enough to close one of his eyes for several hours. He was too tired to think properly. He hove-to and slept.

The next day Tetley managed to get *Victress* to steer herself by carefully adjusting her larger sails. Meanwhile he was busy thinking about how to make proper self-steering replacement parts from odds and ends on board. On March 23rd, he passed Port Stanley in the Falkland Islands. During the afternoon *Victress*'s main steering wires broke again.

Tetley fitted new wires. So far he had been reasonably successful in getting the trimaran to steer herself by adjusting the sails. He hesitated to rebuild the mechanical self-steering, which meant a lot of work.

Victress was now north of the Falklands, clear of ice danger, and sailing quite fast. On March 26th, Tetley gave himself a haircut; the next morning he spoke to his English newspaper contact in Buenos Aires on the radio and was amazed to learn that Bernard Moitessier had dropped out of the race. Tetley reckoned that only he, Knox-Johnston, and Crowhurst were left. This was certainly a strange race; two-thirds of the starters had withdrawn. Fortunately all were safe.

The day had been squally, but the air and sea were gradually warming up. Tetley brought up new food stocks from the bilges, including twenty-four cans of beer he had been saving for the tropics. On March 30th it rained heavily. Nigel was pleased to see water gurgling into his tanks from the wheelhouse roof scuppers.

As the days passed, Tetley broke and repaired a spinnaker pole, fitted a new compass light, sewed sails, and read in Palgrave's *Golden Treasury*. To his delight he managed to find a corroded fuse on the rectifier of his radio transmitter; a new fuse restored the unit to full power. Tetley was not pleased at all, however, with water that was running into the trimaran's floats and the main hull from beneath the connecting wings. The leaks were bad signs.

By April 7th *Victress* was level with Rio de Janeiro and bumping and slatting through the variables. This meant a lot of sail drill, hand steering, and frustrations. One day Tetley tuned in to an American religious station that played classical music. He thought it was wonderful. During a calm on April 9th, he checked the structural damage under the wings of the trimaran and considered going for a swim when a nasty-looking shark suddenly reared up out of the water.

For the next week *Victress* ghosted slowly before light winds from the south. On April 16th, Tetley sat on deck eating his supper, a large bowl of stew. As the wind died, his vessel gradually came to a stop. The radio played native Brazilian music, which alternated with commercials in Portuguese. One commercial was repeated over and over by a hard-driving announcer who seemed to delight in his job. Tetley was curious about the commercial, so he looked up a few key words in his dictionary and discovered that the advertisement was extolling a patent medicine for tapeworms.

On April 17th, Tetley received a new radio message from Buenos Aires. Robin Knox-Johnston had been seen near the Azores. Donald Crowhurst was reported to be in the eastern Pacific. "What a relief to hear that both were still afloat," said Tetley who figured that Robin's arrival in England would siphon off most of the race publicity.

> Crowhurst's challenge to me from the rear was a different matter [he wrote]. . . . I still wanted to win; or put another way, I didn't want anyone to beat me . . . least of all in a similar type of boat.

Sometimes Tetley thought about the long trip he had made.

> While traversing the Pacific I had had the absurd notion that I was under judgement by the "spirit" of the Southern Ocean. It would, I knew, be touch and go whether he allowed me through. In so many ways, I was wanting. That I would have to undergo a period of trial and some ultimate penance I realized only too well, But because of my love for the seabirds I believed that he might spare my life.
>
> Bernard, the only competitor who knew exactly what to expect, refused to regard the voyage as a race. "It will be a question of survival," he had said, "everyone who gets round will have won." How right he was! I now understand why there was a complete absence of rivalry in his make-up.

On April 18th, Tetley inspected his trimaran again. It was a grim survey. The starboard float had four cracked frames. The fastenings on most of the inner beams were in bad condition. In addition there was all the cabin damage from the Pacific storm. "The old girl will see me home, but . . . she is a write-off," he concluded. Almost as if to counter this bad news, a steady 8-knot wind began to blow, and with 1,000 square feet of sail, *Victress* pressed onward, her three hulls furrowing the smooth sea.

At noon the next day the trimaran was only 100 hundred miles from crossing the track of her outbound voyage. Tetley was anxious to hang up his shark's tail at the bow, the sign of a successful circumnavigation. At 0300 on April 20th the wind freshened. Keen to outpace Crowhurst, Tetley kept his big sails flying. *Victress* raced ahead at high speed. An hour later the genoa tack fitting—held with only wood screws—pulled out, something else to fix. The tack fitting was small stuff, however, compared with what happened next.

As dawn rose over the tropical sea Tetley heard the sound of water splashing forward. When he rushed into the bow section of the main hull, he was horrified to see daylight coming through the access section to the port wing. The whole forward part of the port wing back to the crossarm (which would correspond to the left shoulder of a bird) had come away—beams, plywood, braces, doublers, fiberglass sheathing, and all.

Tetley hurried out to the bow of the port float, where he found split and holed plywood, the deck sprung, and five ruined frames. "Squatting in the narrow hull, knee deep in water, I could feel the sides moving in and out like a concertina," he wrote. "It looked as if the voyage were over . . . and with the gods' true gift for irony, sixty tantalizing miles short of circling the world."

He quickly pulled down all the sails and scanned his charts for the nearest port. It was Recife, on the easternmost bulge of Brazil, where John Ridgway had gone the previous July when he had withdrawn from the race. "The yacht is too badly damaged to make the West Indies," Tetley scribbled in his log. "I will patch up the worst of the holes and steer for Recife."

Tetley sawed away the wing decking over the damaged area and put a piece of plywood over the hole in the main hull. He began to fit strengthening crossbeams to the broken frames in the port float, but he was unsure how to fasten the new bracing. He started to saw wooden battens, which he planned to bolt to the float sides. Once the battens were in place he would fasten the new crossbeams to the battens. Partway through sawing the battens, however, he remembered that he had some stainless steel straps with predrilled holes. He decided to bend the metal straps into brackets that he would fasten between the beams and the hull of the float. Tetley worked throughout the day and the following night, pausing only to pump and eat. The repairs seemed stronger than mere patches. Nigel began to think about continuing toward England. After a long sleep on Sunday night he went on with his carpentry and metal bending; by late Monday afternoon he had fastened the last beam and metal bracket in place.

It was impossible to make the forepeak of the port float watertight because of all the cracks and the delaminated plywood. When Tetley put up the sails, got under way, and looked in, the forepeak was like a shower bath. Since the forward compartment was sealed off from the rest of the float, however, Tetley drilled several holes below the waterline to let the water out as fast as it came in from above.

The work was makeshift. No doubt a shipwright would have fainted away. Yet *Victress* was sailing again. By the evening of April 22nd the battered trimaran had crossed her outbound track. In 179 days she had logged 20,500 miles and averaged 114.5 miles a day. Tetley raised his glass: "To Miss *Vicky*. Much abused yet great-hearted to the end."

The next day the wind increased to 25 knots. The captain watched gravely as the port bow crashed into wave after wave. Everything seemed to be holding, so on he went. At 1300 on April 26th, *Victress* crossed the equator and neared the doldrums between the two trade wind zones. Tetley sat on deck and toasted Father Neptune with his last two cans of beer. In the evening the fickle winds of the doldrums blew first one way then another. Sheet lightning crackled from towering banks of purplish cumulonimbus clouds. The moon seemed to float beneath a halo. The following day the temperature soared into the nineties and Tetley had to steer by hand to keep going at all.

> I was beginning to feel the strain when, towards evening, squall clouds brought a spanking wind [wrote the captain]. By this time I no longer cared if the port bow should drop off. I decided to keep her going at full tilt as long as the wind lasted.

Three days later *Victress* picked up the northeast trade wind and logged 150 miles.

> I screwed back the hatch over the port bow—an unnecessary precaution in view of the space's self-draining qualities [he wrote]. What I might have found going on down there, as *Victress* bashed to windward on the starboard tack, must have been secretly worrying me. I could not afford to waste any more time in repairs. Even if the whole section came away it shouldn't matter too much—the space retained little buoyancy anyway. I was quite prepared to bring *Victress* home minus one bow.

On Friday, May 2nd, Tetley discovered that most of the fiberglass sheathing had peeled off the port float. Now bare plywood showed. During the night the wind freshened and the vessel assumed an alarming angle of heel to port. Tetley, dreading to look, figured that the center section of the port float had filled with seawater. The next morning, sure enough, when he peered into the float he found the compartment full. He quickly routed a suction line to the compartment so that he could pump out the area from the bilge pump in the main hull. The center compartment of the port float had always been watertight before, but now was taking water beneath the wings in the same way as the starboard float. None of the frames of the port center compartment were damaged, but the plywood sides bellied in and out as waves passed. To ease the strain Tetley emptied the compartment of all stores and supplies, some of which he tossed over the side.

While he worked on the float compartment, *Victress* charged northward. On May 8th, she was at 23 degrees north latitude and 34 degrees west longitude, almost out of the northeast trade wind. Two days later Tetley spoke to *The Sunday Times* on his radio. The yacht continued to sail well. By now the hard-driving, resourceful Tetley had the knack of adjusting the sails to keep his vessel sailing herself at good speed. One evening at dusk a small merchant ship steamed close by and asked if the yacht needed any supplies or assistance, which cheered the captain a good deal. Another night Tetley's radio picked up some splendid Spanish music from the Canary Islands.

By May 16th *Victress* was about 800 miles west of Portugal and close to the Azores. The islands had six radio beacons that helped Tetley determine his position. During the day he saw two westbound cargo ships. The wind blew at 18 knots on the beam of *Victress*, and she raced along in great form and covered 100 miles during daylight hours. At dusk the wind increased. Tetley took down some sails before he turned in.

Tuesday morning, May 20th, marked *Victress*'s 245th day at sea. The wind whistled at 30 knots. Tetley reefed the mainsail, but the yacht continued at speed. The seas kept increasing. Tetley knew he was in for a gale. He substituted the mizzen for the mainsail; later he lowered even that small sail. That evening the wind shrieked at 45 knots; large seas with dense streaks of foam rumbled past the trimaran. Tetley dropped all sails and drifted in front of the storm. Before he went to sleep he drew a line on his chart to Plymouth. The distance to go was exactly 1,100 miles. Only a few more days.

At midnight Nigel woke up. He heard a strange scraping sound and knew at once that the port bow had come adrift. He rushed on deck and looked. The damage was far worse than he had imagined. Not only had the bow of the port float come off, but it had slammed into the main hull and holed it. *Victress* was filling with water. By the time the captain had returned to the cabin the water was 6 inches deep. Her roll and light motion had become sluggish and ponderous from the weight of water pouring into the yacht; even if she did not sink she would be prey for every sea now. Tetley picked up his radiotelephone micro-phone and transmitted a Mayday call. He received an immediate response from a Dutch ship, which alerted the ships in the area.

Tetley collected his life raft and survival gear. The boat continued to sink, so the captain heaved the raft into the sea, inflated it, and tossed in some warm clothing along with his camera, films, binoculars, sextant, chronometer, and logbook. He climbed aboard.

> I could easily get sentimental over the moment of parting [he cried as he pushed off into the dark night]. The yacht had become a person to me during the long voyage. I would often talk to her—call her all the names under the sun sometimes, though always in jest. . . . Give over, *Vicky*, I have to leave you.

From a downwind position he looked back and saw the lights of *Victress* blink out. She was gone.

Tetley's life-raft equipment included an emergency hand-cranked transmitter. By mid-morning he had contacted a four-engined Hercules aircraft from the United States Air Force 57th Rescue Squadron in the Azores. The plane was soon circling overhead and directed a commercial ship to the tiny life raft. A little after 1700 hours Tetley was aboard the MT *Pampero*, Italian owned and manned, on charter to British Petroleum, and bound for Trinidad.

Tetley went to the mate's cabin for a change into dry clothes and a tot, and then to see Captain Diego de Portada, who gave the castaway a slap on the back and a big welcome.

It was all over. Finished. The bitter end. Everything had happened so fast. *Victress* was gone. Part of Tetley's life was gone too. Maybe it was all a dream, a hazy, smoke-filled dream that would stop when he woke up. Certainly *Victress* was still beneath him. He could almost sense the familiar handholds, his bunk, the galley, the chart table, the compass, and the cleat for the long mainsheet. Of course everything was still there; England was not far now. Soon the powerful lighthouse beacons and the pretty green hills would appear. He was still ahead of Crowhurst, of course, of course. . . .

But as Tetley saw the big ship around him, sensed the throbbing engine, and felt the comradeship of the kind Italian officers, he knew the rescue had been real. His sailing, the great race, and his three-hulled yacht were all through. The seventh man to start was no longer in the race.

Only two were left.

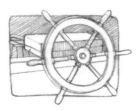

28

The Winner

WHEN THE BRITISH PETROLEUM TANKER *MOBIL ACME* ACknowledged Knox-Johnston's signal on April 5th he was overjoyed. Finally! It was the first time he had contacted anyone in four and a half months. No doubt his family, friends, and sponsors had been thinking the worst. Now everyone would know where *Suhaili* was and that he was safe.

That night Knox-Johnston tuned to the BBC hoping that he might be mentioned on the evening news. He heard nothing, however. Robin thought that perhaps Moitessier had already crossed the finish line and that the race was over.

The *Mobil Acme* had in fact radioed London at once. Shortly afterward, Lloyds telephoned Knox-Johnston's family. The officer on *Mobil Acme* who had received the flashing lamp signal from *Suhaili* had added to the message: "Standard of signaling excellent." This told everyone that the captain was still in good form and in control of things.

The next day, huge banner headlines in the *Sunday Mirror* read:

Robin Is Safe
They Thought He Was Dead

When *Suhaili* had met the *Mobil Acme,* the yacht was in the zone of westerlies, which meant fair winds across the ketch's port quarter. Knox-Johnston had calculated his arrival date on the basis of these winds. But the wind veered perversely to the north, a turn that reduced the next two days' runs to 89 and 79 miles. Knox-Johnston did not feel well and had a severe headache. "Probably due to food poisoning," he said.

The following day *Suhaili* ran before brisk southwest winds that gradually fell away to nothing. "We are completely becalmed and there are ships all around so I dare not sleep—not that I could with the booms banging as they are," he wrote. "I feel completely licked. I don't think, even in the Variables, I have felt so low the whole voyage."

On April 12th, Knox-Johnston signaled to a French ship, *Mungo* of Le Havre, and found that he was able to use his radio to talk to the captain. The astonishing news was that Moitessier was continuing around the world and that *Suhaili* was "Le Premier." The following day Robin logged 98 miles. In the evening he heard a high-frequency commercial station in England and idly tried a call. To his surprise the Baldock operator answered at once and even patched through a connection to Knox-Johnston's family. After months of no news at all, *Suhaili's* master now seemed to be getting daily reports. It was all amazing.

Knox-Johnston's brother confirmed that Moitessier was in the Indian Ocean for the second time and that only three British contestants remained in the race. The two trimarans were in the South Atlantic somewhere off Brazil.

On April 16th, Knox-Johnston spoke to the *Sunday Mirror* newspaper, which by now had run dozens of stories about him. The editors realized that Robin was about to become a national hero and were desperate for exclusive material. Fortunately the paper had worked out a code before the race; henceforth the captain was to radio his positions, arrival times, and all details in cipher.

Some of Robin's family and friends were planning to meet *Suhaili* in a private launch named *Fathomer*. The other newspaper reporters and photographers were certain that Robin would radio his position to the launch and were already shadowing *Fathomer* as if she were a pot of gold. Robin began to feel like a spy in a cloak-and-dagger scheme. It was all good fun.

The wind dropped again, and *Suhaili's* battery charger stopped working, which meant there was no way to charge the batteries for the radio. Knox-Johnston started to overhaul the charger. However, he had all his big sails up and had to abandon the battery charger so he could steer the boat.

At noon on April 18th, *Suhaili* had 280 miles to go to Falmouth, the port in England from which she had started. The *Sunday Mirror* radioed that it was sending a plane—Beechcraft G-ASDO—for photographs and that the other newspapers were still shadowing the launch that be-

ROBIN KNOX-JOHNSTON REEFING THE MIZZEN

longed to Knox-Johnston's friend. More cloak-and-dagger stuff. Maybe Robin should have been wearing a mask.

In the evening a small gray bird with a slender beak suddenly appeared next to the captain, who was sitting in the cabin reading *Timon of Athens*. A bit later, ships' lights began to appear around the horizon and the captain prepared for a sleepless night by drinking coffee fortified with whiskey. Two vessels, one small and one large, worked up close to *Suhaili*. At first Robin was wary until he realized that people were shouting his name. The first vessel had Knox-Johnston's parents on board; the second had a group of his friends and there was a lot of shouting back and forth. However, the wind and sea increased and Knox-Johnston had to reduce sail and get some sleep. The next morning when he looked out on the ocean he was alone.

At noon he worked out his latitude and radioed it to the escorts, but the wind had become contrary and up to gale force. He stopped *Suhaili* and napped for a bit in the afternoon until the powerboats found him.

The wind continued from the southeast and blew *Suhaili* northward toward the Bristol Channel. Knox-Johnston wanted to sail east up the English Channel, so he tacked to the south until the following morning, when he tacked again and headed for Land's End, 150 miles away. In the evening, with a cup of cocoa in one hand, he began to work through a fleet of French fishing boats. A little before noon the next day, the Bishop's Rock lighthouse hove into view.

> I suppose that seeing the slim silhouette of the Bishop on the horizon should have been an emotional moment [he wrote]. Over the centuries it has been the last and first sight of Britain for generations of seamen, but my recollection is that I noted the sighting in the log simply as a navigational mark. My emotions, more prosaically, were concerned with a pint of beer, a steak, a hot bath, and clean white sheets.

During the afternoon the two escort vessels continued to sail along with *Suhaili*. Now helicopters, a military patrol plane, and a naval minesweeper joined the little flotilla. Knox-Johnston snatched sleep and food when he could. Meanwhile the escorts darted back and forth to land to refuel. By Tuesday morning, April 22nd, *Suhaili*'s accompanying fleet had been increased by the Falmouth lifeboat, the tug *St. Mawes*, and a handful of private yachts. Light aircraft buzzed overhead, and helicopters, with press photographers leaning out dangerously, fluttered here and there. The little flotilla had swelled into a parade.

The wind swung around to the north-northwest and freshened, which obliged Robin to tack back and forth under shortened sail. But *Suhaili* was now in the lee of the land, and the water was smoother. Slowly, ever so slowly, she gained on her goal. By now there were large and small vessels everywhere on the sea. As he neared Falmouth, Knox-Johnston saw lines of parked cars; the waterfront was black with throngs of spectators. People and flags waved from all sides.

Suhaili crossed the finish line at 1525. A cannon echoed across the waterfront, and thousands of people cheered a new popular hero. The tiny, wooden, rust-streaked, tubby white ketch and her modest captain had sailed all the way around the world without stopping. The first contestant to complete the race had returned. Robin Knox-Johnston and *Suhaili* had made it back to the port from which they had started 313 days earlier. During the long voyage the vessel logged 30,123 miles, which translates to a little over 96 miles per day, or just over 4 knots.

Knox-Johnston was the first sailor to go around the world under *The Sunday Times*' rules, which were essentially to sail from England to England south of the three great continental headlands of Good Hope, Leeuwin, and Cape Horn. During the race two other entrants also circumnavigated. Bernard Moitessier crossed his outbound track on March

8th, more than a month before Knox-Johnston. Strictly speaking, therefore, Moitessier should get credit for the first solo circumnavigation.
Nigel Tetley touched his earlier wake on April 22nd, the third man
around. Depending on your definition of solo sailing you can take your
choice. Maybe the best answer was from Moitessier, when he said (page
XXX): "Everyone who gets round will have won."

They were all heroes.

29

The Loser

O<small>N APRIL 22ND, THE DAY THAT KNOX-JOHNSTON CROSSED</small>
THE finish line in England, Donald Crowhurst was slowly sailing northward about 700 miles east of northern Argentina. Nigel Tetley, whose *Victress* was not to sink until May 21st, was approximately 2,000 miles to the north-northeast, off the easternmost bulge of northern Brazil.

In his usual deceptive message to Rodney Hallworth, Crowhurst claimed that he was near the Falkland Islands and sailing well. In a separate cable to the BBC, he congratulated Knox-Johnston but pointed out that although the Golden Globe had now been won, the overall prize (of fastest voyage) was far from decided, and that he, Donald Crowhurst, was certainly going to try to win the £5,000. When these two messages had been transmitted, Crowhurst was back in the race. He had decided to join his false and true positions on May 4th. It seemed as if everything was set for the final dash up the Atlantic to England.

Although Tetley was some 2,000 miles ahead of Crowhurst, we must remember that Crowhurst had started the race forty-five days after Tetley. Crowhurst's alleged position on April 30th was at the Falkland Islands, another 1,000 miles to the south, or roughly 3,000 miles behind Tetley.

By May 4th Crowhurst had begun to sail northward with determination. He advanced rapidly before strong following winds and made some first-class runs. Two days later he logged only a little less than the 243-mile record he had falsely claimed months earlier. This fast run clearly demonstrated that Crowhurst and his trimaran had plenty of potential. The captain scarcely mentioned this remarkable mileage, however, because he had too many other things on his mind. A few days later the strong southerly winds died out when *Teignmouth Electron* entered the variables. Soon fickle headwinds slowed the progress of the blue-

and-white multihull to a crawl. Crowhurst tacked to the east, looking for the southeast trade wind.

Whenever he could, Crowhurst worked on his grand scheme of deception. He sent a cable to England explaining that his direct connection to Portishead radio had been an isolated stroke of luck. He recorded long excuses on his BBC tape recorder concerning his lapses in radio communication. He invented complicated lies and all sorts of fanciful stories.

Hallworth and Crowhurst exchanged cable after cable. Hallworth knew that elapsed-time victories mean little to the general public and urged Crowhurst to cross the finish line in a neck-and-neck duel with Tetley. Crowhurst's wife and friends began to send adulatory messages that said how proud they were of him.

On May 16th Hallworth cabled:

TEIGNMOUTH AGOG AT YOUR WONDERS   WHOLE TOWN PLANNING HUGE
WELCOME—RODNEY

Although Crowhurst made efforts to perfect his fraudulent log and to account for the lapses in his radio messages, his efforts weren't wholly sincere. Again and again he procrastinated and failed to follow up his scheme to win. The other men in the race had used every bit of their skill and energy to keep their yachts going as fast as possible. Knox-Johnston, Tetley, Moitessier, and Bill King were hard drivers. Crowhurst, by contrast, was weak, vacillating, and irresolute. He failed to press on regardless, as the others had. He treated the actual sailing as if it was a peripheral task, not his main business, which by now had become the saving of Donald Crowhurst.

On some level, Crowhurst wanted to lose to Tetley. If that happened, no one would care a fig about the fake logbooks. Maybe the best thing would be to lose to Tetley at the last minute. This approach would still get a lot of publicity for *Teignmouth Electron*, for Crowhurst's sponsor, Mr. Best, and for Crowhurst himself. After the middle of May, *Teignmouth Electron*'s daily average slumped to 70 miles. *The Sunday Times* again calculated his estimated arrival date and added one week. Admittedly he was in the zone of variable winds, but he simply wasn't paying attention to sailing.

Now came the most ironic twist of the entire race. On May 21st, as we have seen, *Victress* fell apart and was abandoned. The plucky captain took to his life raft and was rescued. Tetley's three-hulled yacht had disintegrated because he had driven the old trimaran too hard and had subjected her to trials that her California designer, Arthur Piver, had never dreamed of when he had drawn the plans in Mill Valley, California, years earlier.

Tetley was desperately keen to win. He had received message after message that Crowhurst was gaining, so he drove *Victress* harder and harder when she was getting weaker and weaker and beginning to splinter to pieces. If Tetley had nursed and coddled *Victress* and continued to patch her, he might have limped into Plymouth and won the £5,000. Fame, fortune, and perhaps a title would have been his. Crowhurst could have come home just behind Tetley and would have nailed down a respectable place in sailing history. Crowhurst could then have retired to Nether Stowey and his electronics business with his logbooks unexamined.

When Tetley's *Victress* disintegrated, however, and Tetley was suddenly out of the race, it meant a whole new cave of horrors for Crowhurst. Now he would win the race for the fastest time and the £5,000 for sure. He would become famous and respected. He would receive money and prestige. Or would he? What about the fiddled logbooks? What about the interviews with the damned reporters and their endless, prying questions? A magnifying glass would be focused on his every action. Could he keep up such a folly and lie with certainty?

Would that ace navigator, that damned old fox Sir Francis Chichester, be there with a devastating inquiry into Crowhurst's uneven daily runs and his peculiar radio silences? One slip and Crowhurst's whole world of Let's Pretend would come crashing down. He would be humiliated and scorned. His family and friends would be horrified and shamed.

It was a grim prospect. Crowhurst must have felt remorse, and regretted that he had ever started in the race. The only escape was to let Knox-Johnston win the £5,000; that would require Crowhurst to stall around for months, something not possible because now everyone knew where he was.

What could he do? Exactly what he had done during the long months when he had hidden on the fringes of the South Atlantic while the others had sailed around the world. He would abandon the sailing of *Teignmouth Electron* and start a solo voyage into the depths of his mind.

How do we know all this? From a mass of radio transmissions, tape recordings, and motion pictures that Crowhurst made while he doddered in the Atlantic. Crowhurst's expert biographers sifted through all this material and patiently unwound the captain's mental foibles. Taken piece by piece, up to the time of his final collapse, each bit seems normal—perhaps a little strange but within the bounds of credulity. Taken altogether, however, as the sum of a thousand morbid fragments, the evidence points a hard finger toward explaining the shattering of Crowhurst's personality.

On May 23rd, Crowhurst radioed his condolences to Tetley regarding the abandonment of *Victress*. A week later *Teignmouth Electron* was well north into the tropics. But instead of speedy daily runs in the trade winds, the captain often didn't even bother to set his mainsail and poked along at 3 or 4 knots. He still had to bail out the floats with a bucket, and his mechanical self-steering hadn't worked for a long time.

He began to run low on certain supplies; his food became dull and monotonous. Not only was he short of gasoline for the electric generator, but there was a new crisis. His radio transmitter, his all-important connection with the outside world and a vital tool in his efforts at deception, failed. When this happened, Crowhurst abandoned everything and started working sixteen hours a day soldering wires and parts together in a frenzied attempt to get back on the air. Meanwhile he kept talking into the BBC tape recorder: "The tea's gone off. Something's happened to it . . . I think it's gone mouldy or something, but it makes me ill."

By now the trimaran was north of the equator and jogging along under jib and mizzen in the northeast trade wind. Meanwhile Crowhurst, the expert electronics engineer, was determined to repair his radio transmitter. He soon found that he was unable to fix his big Marconi Kestrel set, so he undertook to modify a small Shannon radiotelephone. The Shannon was designed for short-range work on medium wavelengths. Crowhurst decided to modify the Shannon for long-range transmission on the shortwave band.

This was a major project, which meant redesigning and rebuilding various circuits and adding parts from other radios. The captain needed books on design, and test equipment to check his work as he went along. Undaunted, he started work at once while the trimaran bounced along on the trade wind waves and the equatorial sun burned down from overhead. While he soldered and tinkered he listened to his receiver. On June 18th the BBC sent a long telegram, the first of a series:

CONGRATULATIONS ON PROGRESS   HAVE NETWORK TELEVISION PRO-
GRAMME FOR DAY OF RETURN   YOUR FILM URGENTLY WANTED   CAN
YOU PREPARE FILM AND TAPES INFORMATION   ANY SUGGESTION PLEASE
ON GETTING IT BACK AT LEAST FOUR DAYS BEFORE TEIGNMOUTH ARRIVAL
CAN ARRANGE BOAT OR HELICOPTER HOW CLOSE AZORES BRITTANY OR
SCILLIES   REPLY URGENTLY=DONALD KERR

TEIGNMOUTH ELECTRON

In response to the telegram, Crowhurst shot new 16mm film of himself doing various jobs: shaving, baking bread, using the sextant, working at the chart table, and so forth. All these scenes were done by clamping the camera and using a self-timer on the shutter, a tedious and time-consuming job for a single-hander who was involved in radio design and reconstruction.

Finally, on June 22nd, after some remarkable effort, Crowhurst got his rebuilt transmitter working. Donald immediately fired off messages in Morse code to the BBC, Hallworth, and his wife. He still hoped to speak directly to his wife, Clare, however, so he took the transmitter to pieces again and tried to modify it for long-range voice transmission. In spite of all his skill and determination, he didn't succeed.

On June 24th, a few days into the northern summer, Crowhurst's mind made an abrupt spiral turn downward. He started on something entirely new—a long, complex, hard-to-follow religious-philosophic essay. During the next week he scribbled 25,000 words while *Teignmouth Electron* drifted slowly along in the calms of the Sargasso Sea north of the northeast trade wind zone.

According to Crowhurst, each word that he wrote was of supreme significance. He had a great message, and his contribution to mankind had to be committed to paper within seven days. By now he had forgotten about the race, the sailing, and the radio modifications. Donald had retreated into a private, arcane world whose dimensions only he could fathom and appreciate. He had given up housekeeping on his fine yacht—still less than a year old—and the cabin was filthy and smelly. His bedding lay unwashed. Radio parts were scattered everywhere. The sink was stacked high with dirty dishes.

Again Crowhurst turned to Einstein's book. Donald thought the great physicist could somehow help him solve the nightmare he faced. But instead of Einstein's writing clarifying Donald's thoughts and improving his behavior, Crowhurst's writings became increasingly rambling, ill directed, and incoherent.

> Man is a lever whose ultimate length and strength he must determine for himself [wrote Crowhurst]. . . . The first shattering application of the idea that $E = mc^2$ is a good example o $\sqrt{-1}$—I refer to the bombing of Hiroshima. . . . I introduce this idea   because [it] leads directly to the dark tunnel of the space–time continuum, and once technology emerges from this tunnel the "world" will "end."

Crowhurst spoke of mathematics as the language of God. He talked of an Antichrist. He rambled on and on and concluded that the next change in human society would be the liberation of the mind from the body so that the mind could soar to an abstract existence. The moment for this move was at hand, and Crowhurst—Crowhurst himself—was to present this message to the world. Those who made this leap, this total jump, became like a God. "*If* creative abstraction is to act as a vehicle for the new entity . . . <u>it lies within the power of creative abstraction to</u> <u>produce the phenomenon!!!!!!!!!!!!!!!!!!</u>" He became so excited as he wrote that he almost pressed his pencil through the paper.

Crowhurst claimed that he had reached a state so elevated that he could free his mind from his body and float away—and leave *Teignmouth Electron*—whenever he desired. Now he could escape from his predicament. Forget the cheating and lying. Forget the radios and the schemes for money. Forget the fools in England. Forget all the earthly impedimenta. Not only could Crowhurst obtain salvation, he could become God.

All these words were a jumble of prophesy, scientific double-talk, mathematics, religion, and nonsense. This self-taught engineer-cum-sailor suffered from a psychiatric complaint called paranoid grandiosity. Crowhurst showed all the symptoms, and his delusions revolved around complex, highly organized beliefs that he was a great prophet and scientist.

He was insane.

WHILE DONALD CONTINUED to agonize about himself, back in England great preparations were going on for a colossal reception for the speedy trimaran and her captain. In Teignmouth the Crowhurst Welcome Home Sub-Committee met and outlined every minute of the hero's grand entry. The *Teignmouth Electron* would be escorted into the harbor by a naval minesweeper. At a suitable moment the yacht club would fire its cannon. Then the trimaran would be towed along the seafront of the resort town so the thousands of cheering visitors and townspeople could catch a glimpse of the world hero.

During the time when the helicopters with the press buzzed overhead, Crowhurst would be formally presented to the town council. There would be a press conference at the theater and receptions at the hotels. Enormous "TEIGNMOUTH WELCOMES CROWHURST" banners would be draped all over town, particularly along the seafront.

Rodney Hallworth had become respected and important in Teignmouth. The early civic doubters had come round, and the pubs and inns rang with praise for Hallworth's astute handling of Crowhurst. The companies that had donated equipment and supplies for the trimaran relished the publicity prospects; a sculptor proposed a special trophy to commemorate the arrival.

Crowhurst was scheduled to present awards for Prince Philip, and the post office readied a special franking mark. Hallworth had ten thousand postcards printed with Crowhurst's picture, and the press agent wrote fawning copy for a welcoming edition of the local newspaper. He even arranged for Crowhurst's wife to prepare a lachrymose article titled "My Life as an Ocean Widow."

Meanwhile, on board *Teignmouth Electron*, still thousands of miles to the south, Crowhurst continued to write furiously. By now he had worked back to the actions of cavemen who in the past had shocked society into change. As he wrote he got so excited that he could scarcely put down the words. He'd had a great revelation, but it needed to be handled with care.

> When we decide to act we must be careful not to rush things [he wrote]. Like nuclear chain reactions in the matter system, our whole system of creative abstraction can be brought to the point of "take off."

On June 26th, Crowhurst worked hard on the linked ideas of escape from his body. Words poured onto the paper.

> Mathematicians and engineers used to the techniques of system analysis will skim through my complete work in less than an hour [he continued]. At the end of that time, problems that have beset humanity for thousands of years will have been solved for them. . . . Do we go on clinging to the idea that "God made us", or realise that it lies within our power to make GOD? The system IS SHRIEKING OUT THIS MESSAGE AT THE TOP OF ITS VOICE why does no one listen I am listening anyway.

Crowhurst had become so deeply involved in his theories that he was unable to treat them as abstract ideas. Now whatever he wrote about he *became*. At one time he thought of abstract intelligence as a conceptual idea. Now his mind went through the actual change. Once it had been a game; now it was the actual, palpable truth.

As his dream world blurred into his real world, time had begun to be important to Crowhurst. A defective chronometer was not simply a clock that had gone wrong. It was not a symbol of his own condition. It *was* his own condition. *Crowhurst was the clock.* "God's clock is not the same as our clock," he wrote. "He has an infinite amount of 'our' time. Ours has nearly run out."

Crowhurst's verbal outbursts grew increasingly morbid. He wrote of his dead father, of his mother's religious ties, about secrets of his past, and about the idea of himself as a new God. It was all a demented, pathetic jumble. He hinted increasingly of death. He wrote: "Christ . . . had arrived at the truth. . . . People witnessed the manner of his death. I must consider whether to . . ."

The sentences blathered on and on. Thousands of tortured words. He talked of apes, revolutionaries, Julius Caesar, and problems of the world. Crowhurst's only real problem, of course, was how to get out of his faked sailing trip. His answer was a tormented, roundabout view of his own death. He was so far gone, however, that you wonder whether the demented captain understood what he was writing.

Donald began a discussion with himself about the false voyage. Should he confess? Or should he destroy all the evidence? If he pitched everything into the sea it would be contrary to the principle of always telling the truth and would keep mankind from Crowhurst's great revelation. He wrote about three levels of pain. Again he spoke of time. He raged against the devil who had tricked him unfairly. He wrote slogans: "IT IS THE MYSTERY OF FREEWILL."

Crowhurst was now so far gone that he had decided he would be a better god than God himself. He spoke directly to cosmic beings. The faults with his voyage were really the faults of the gods because they should have made his voyage and the forging of his logbooks easier. Donald was beyond human morality. "The truth was that there was no good or evil, only truth," he said. Later he spoke of death, "a swift death, and translation into the world of Gods."

In the motion pictures that Crowhurst took of himself with a self-timer during this period, the man we see is not the smooth-faced Englishman who had joked and laughed with his friends and the BBC reporters before the voyage. Instead we see a sailor whose face is hardened and aged and puckered with wrinkles and lines of anxiety. In only eight months his eyes had grown dark, sunken, and strained. The unruffled, boyish look was gone and replaced by haggard middle age. He was thirty-seven years old.

By June 30th, Crowhurst had lost all track of time. His watches and chronometer had run down. He used the *Nautical Almanac* and the moon to establish the date and time. It was really 1000 hours, July 1st, but he no longer cared about anything. His writing had become even more confused and rambling. Death and negativism had become paramount. He decided to leave the evidence of his wrongdoing so that anyone who found *Teignmouth Electron* would be able to understand what he had done. "There can only be one perfect beauty that is the great beauty of truth," he wrote. A little later that morning the weary captain penciled these words:

I will only resign this game
if you will agree that [on]
the next occasion that this game
is played it will be played
according to the
rules that are devised by
my great god who has
revealed at last to his son
not only the exact nature
of the reason for games but
has also revealed the truth of
the way of the ending of the
next game that

It is finished—

It is finished

IT IS THE MERCY

A little later he added the words:

I will resign the game [at] 11 20 40

Clutching his chronometer, Crowhurst climbed to the stern of *Teign-mouth Electron*. When the time reached 11 20 40 he jumped into the sea. His long race was over.

30~

The Last Word

O<small>N JULY 10, 1969, THE ROYAL MAIL VESSEL</small> *PICARDY*, <small>OUT-</small>
<small>BOUND</small> from London for the Caribbean, came upon *Teignmouth Electron*
gliding slowly along on the smooth Atlantic about 525 miles southwest
of Ilha das Flores in the Azores. The trimaran had only her mizzen sail
set. Captain Richard Box blew his foghorn three times and maneuvered
to pass close astern of the multihulled craft. There was no sign of life, so
the captain stopped his ship, lowered a boat, and sent an officer and
three men to have a look.

The inspecting crew found no one on board. There was no trace of
anyone in the water and no small boat or life raft to be seen. The last
entry in the vessel's three logbooks was a notation in the radio log for
June 29th, eleven days earlier. Captain Box had a derrick rigged on the
Picardy and hoisted *Teignmouth Electron* on board. In the meantime he
alerted his London owners, who immediately called the Royal Navy,
which flashed the United States Air Force unit in the Azores and requested an aerial search. Both the United States Air Force and the *Picardy* crisscrossed the area but found nothing. It appeared that Donald
Crowhurst, the single-handed captain, had fallen overboard. A regrettable accident.

Back in England, sympathy poured into the Crowhurst home. On
July 12th *The Sunday Times* started a fund drive for the Crowhurst family with £5,000. Because of Crowhurst's death, Knox-Johnston—the
only entrant to complete the race—would receive the £5,000 race prize,
but in a noble gesture he donated the entire amount to the fund. No one
dreamed of duplicity or foul play.

Meanwhile on board the *Picardy*, which was steaming steadily toward the Caribbean, Captain Box studied Crowhurst's logbooks. Most
of the entries seemed routine enough, but in the last log there was a good

deal of disorganized and peculiar writing that suggested psychological unrest and mental disorder. Captain Box continued reading.

The story of Crowhurst's disappearance could not be investigated without the logbooks. All the newspapers coveted Crowhurst's records and asked for a look. Rodney Hallworth, who worked at the speed of light whenever he detected the glimmer of money, naturally arranged an auction among the various British newspapers. *The Sunday Times* won with a bid of £4,000.

Hallworth, along with reporter Nicholas Tomalin and photographer Frank Herrmann from *The Sunday Times*, flew to Santo Domingo to take charge of the logbooks and inspect the trimaran. On July 16th, when the *Picardy* came into port, the three journalists met Captain Box, who took Hallworth aside and showed him the log entries that contemplated suicide. At Box's suggestion, Hallworth ripped out these pages to spare the Crowhurst family. Hallworth held the pages aside. He planned to show them to the editor of *The Sunday Times* privately.

Meanwhile Hallworth started going through the logbooks and soon discovered that Crowhurst had never sailed farther than the Atlantic Ocean! Incredible! Even these hardboiled British journalists must have wondered how to handle the story. It was obvious that the abbreviated voyage and the death of Crowhurst were somehow connected. Hallworth realized that he couldn't keep back the secret of Crowhurst's death, so he replaced the log pages he had ripped out.

The three journalists hurried back to London and huddled with the paper's senior editors. What to do? The Crowhurst story was sensational copy, but its unfolding might cause a lot of bruises. There was the negative effect on the Crowhurst family, still reeling from the shock of Crowhurst's death. *The Sunday Times* itself, the sponsor of the race, would not look too good when the truth of its incredibly sloppy race administration spilled out. But feelings and egos aside, the story had to be printed. A confidential warning was passed to the BBC, which was busy working up a triumphant version of the Crowhurst circumnavigation based on the films and tape recordings. The editors of *The Sunday Times* did a lot of teeth-gnashing and decided to publish the full account after a review by Mrs. Crowhurst and Hallworth.

On the weekend of July 27th, 1969, the story came out. It was an immediate national sensation as front-page news. Every newspaper in the land picked up the story and amplified the bizarre tale of Donald Crowhurst's faked trip around the world, his mental failure, and his final suicide. The story spread to the foreign press, and newspaper wire services telegraphed details to the corners of the world. The cunning twists of the story intrigued radio and television news editors everywhere, and enormous pressure poured into London from abroad for more details.

French and American news magazines prepared special coverage, and Italian and Polish readers looked at photographs of Crowhurst. A herd of reporters from all over the globe stalked Mrs. Crowhurst for a month. Her telephone rang day and night. What did she think of it all? What did his vessel look like? What was a trimaran? What kind of a stupid race was this anyway? Captain Box was asked to repeat the details of finding *Teignmouth Electron* over and over. A dozen fanciful rumors of Crowhurst's reappearance were published, speculated upon, and finally quashed as the story ran its course. The mighty *Sunday Times* itself came in for plenty of criticism for sponsoring circus stunts without adequate supervision. The overall feeling, however, was that the fault was the mental collapse of a weak man rather than an overzealous and careless sponsor.

In future races of this type, the yachts would be inspected for design suitability and seaworthiness. The contestants would need to demonstrate their sailing proficiency in qualifying trials in the actual vessels to be used. The trials would be obligatory well in advance of the starting date to prevent a rush of last-minute building and qualifying. The entries would depart from one place at the same time. Radio communication—vastly improved since 1968—would assist safety, help rule compliance, and foster general race information. As early as 1982 the boats would carry tiny satellite automatic-position-reporting transponders that would keep race headquarters advised of the exact position of each contestant.

But if these rules had been announced in 1968 before *The Sunday Times* race, there would probably have been no competition at all. The two Frenchmen would have objected to the radio rule, Carozzo and Crowhurst wouldn't have been ready, and Blyth and Ridgway might not have qualified. With only Tetley, King, and Knox-Johnston—all ship officers—there wouldn't have been enough entrants.

BECAUSE OF CROWHURST'S DEATH, the Teignmouth town council hastily canceled its huge civic homecoming, and the great victory dinner of the Golden Globe race was postponed. The town elders of Teignmouth summoned Hallworth to task, but the loquacious press agent pointed out that although it was regrettable that Crowhurst was dead, the resort town had received millions of pounds' worth of publicity. Eventually the Publicity Committee commended him for "the terrific publicity reaped from the Donald Crowhurst saga."

What happened to the other entrants in the race? John Ridgway and Chay Blyth had both tried to substitute determination and toughness for what they lacked in sailing experience. Everyone agreed that their small yachts were inadequate for the task. Yet both men liked their taste of deep sea-adventuring. Quite separately, they continued ocean racing in various sponsored yachts. In 1970–71, Blyth soloed west-about around the world via the Southern Ocean in a 58-foot ketch named *British Steel*. Ridgway started a school for physical fitness and adventure training in Ardmore, Scotland, and later sailed around the world as well.

Bill King, the retired submarine commander, who was among the first to suggest a solo round-the-world voyage, shipped his sleek *Galway Blazer II* back to England from Cape Town after the yacht was dismasted. Following several setbacks he eventually sailed south and east again. However, his vessel was struck and seriously damaged by a whale in the Southern Ocean near southwest Australia. King, always the clever old sea dog, managed emergency repairs and struggled into Fremantle for assistance. He eventually continued eastward, rounded Cape Horn, and returned to England in May 1973 and fulfilled his dream.

The spirited Italian, Alex Carozzo, disappeared from the yacht racing scene after Lisbon and has left no further wake.

Loïck Fougeron made a trip around the world via the Southern Ocean in 1972–73 with a female friend but was forced to divert to the Panama Canal when he ran into terrible weather 900 miles west of Cape Horn. In late 1975, the determined Fougeron left France by himself, passed through the Panama Canal, and again set out for his nemesis, Cape Horn, which he finally rounded early the next year.

Bernard Moitessier sailed to French Polynesia, where he lived for eleven years. He wrote a splendid book *(The Long Way)* about the race. He met a French woman named Iléana; a year later they had a son named Stephan. Bernard sailed among the French islands and attempted to introduce farming on Ahe atoll in the Tuamotu Archipelago. He began a plan to get the mayors of all the towns in France to cooperate in a project to plant fruit trees along city streets and in public parks. In 1980 he sailed to California, where I got acquainted with this gentle man and had a good look at his famous yacht with the tall masts. Bernard lectured a little with a 16mm film he made during the Golden Globe race, but he was not a businessman and had limited success. He died in 1994.

Robin Knox-Johnston became well known after his return to England, where he was lionized and feted as he deserved. The British Empire and her military heroes were mostly gone; now the sporting heroes of soccer, football, and sailing took the place of the intrepid admirals and gallant generals of old. The round-the-world race was a tough sporting event. Not everyone understood the race or why it was held, but

Knox-Johnston was quite a fellow and the English reward their heroes well. Both Francis Chichester and Alex Rose had been knighted for their sailing trips around the world. Knox-Johnston received a CBE (Commander of the British Empire), a great honor for a thirty-year-old man. Later he was knighted by Queen Elizabeth.

A week after he docked, a newspaper reporter wrote: "Accompanied by four friends and 20 dozen cans of beer, Robin Knox-Johnston sailed for London on the *Suhaili* yesterday, after four days of skilful tacking through business negotiations which could bring him £100,000 in the next year."

During his long solo trip Robin had plenty of time to reflect on his life up to that time. He decided to have a new look at his earlier marriage, which had broken up in India. Shortly after he returned to England, Knox-Johnston remarried his former wife, Sue. It was a nice step. He wrote a best-selling book about his circumnavigation titled *A World of My Own*. Robin has continued to make outstanding voyages under sail, to write about sailing, to explore the coast of Greenland, and to collect medals and honors.

I met Robin and became friends with him in 1986 when he was the director for the BOC Challenge round-the-world single-handed race. I found him modest, unassuming, and a hands-on sailor who was always willing to pitch in and help.

We have now accounted for eight of the nine contestants, all except Nigel Tetley, the tall, handsome, retired naval commander whose voyage in an experimental yacht had been so exemplary. Tetley—more than any other—was sorely victimized by the machinations of Crowhurst and maybe by fate herself. Certainly Tetley deserved to win the £5,000 and some share of the accolades that had cascaded on Knox-Johnston's shoulders. Perhaps to atone for its bungling and to try to achieve a sense of fair dealing, *The Sunday Times* awarded Tetley £1,000 as a consolation prize. This was a nice gesture, but somehow it seemed trifling. Knox-Johnston had become a national hero. Tetley remained an obscure mariner.

Nigel had put everything he had into the race. Yet all he received was gall and bitter lemons. Of the nine boats that had entered the round-the-world competition, only his vessel had been lost. Tetley wrote a good book about his part in the great race, but its sales were poor. Meanwhile everyone in the UK was reading Knox-Johnston's account.

Tetley discussed multihull construction and safety aspects with other sailors. He started to build a new yacht for upcoming voyages, but he had trouble getting on with the project. When *Victress* had broken up during that stormy night in the North Atlantic, part of Tetley had gone down with his ship. He tried to recoup and to start again, but his stout heart wasn't in it. On February 5th, 1972, thirty-three months after *Victress* sank, Tetley committed suicide by hanging himself. Like Crowhurst, Tetley's long race had ended.

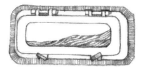

Bibliography

Blyth, Chay, and Maureen Blyth. *Innocent Aboard*. Lymington, England: Nautical Publishing Co., 1970.

Fougeron, Loïck. *Si pres du Cap Horn*. Paris: Éditions du Pen Duick, 1974.

Gliksman, Alain. *La voile en solitaire: de Slocum à la Transatlantique*. Paris: Éditions maritimes et d'outre-mer/Denoël, 1976.

Hasler, H. G. "There and Back—Singlehanded." *Roving Commissions* 5 (1965): 130.

Heaton, Peter. *The Singlehanders*. London: Joseph, 1976.

Journal of Navigation. January 1969: 134.

King, William Donald Aelian. *Adventure in Depth*. New York: Putnam, 1975.

———. *Capsize*. Lymington, England: Nautical Publishing Co.; London: Harrap, 1969.

Knox-Johnston, Robin. *A World of My Own: The Single-Handed, Non-Stop Circumnavigation of the World in 'Suhaili.'* London: Cassell, 1969.

Letcher, John S. Jr. *Self-Steering for Sailing Craft*. Camden, ME: International Marine, 1974.

Moitessier, Bernard. *Cape Horn: The Logical Route*. Translated by Inge Moore. London: Adlard Coles, 1969. (Originally published as *Cap Horn à la voile*. Paris: Arthaud, 1967.)

———. *The Long Way*. Translated by William Rodarmor. London: Adlard Coles, 1974. (Originally published as *La longue route: Seul entre mers et ciels*. Paris: Arthaud, 1971.)

———. *Sailing to the Reefs*. Translated by René Hague. London:

Hollis & Carter, 1971. (Originally published as *Un vagabond des mers du sud*. Paris: Flammarion, 1960.)

————. *Tamata and the Alliance*. Translated by René Hague. Dobbs Ferry, NY: Sheridan House, 1995. (Originally published as *Tamata et l'alliance*. Paris: Arthaud: 1993.)

Pidgeon, Harry. *Around the World Single-Handed: The Cruise of the "Islander."* London: Rupert Hart-Davis, 1950.

Ridgway, John. *Journey to Ardmore*. London: Hodder & Stoughton, 1971.

Ridgway, John, and Marie Christine Ridgway. *Round the World with Ridgway*. New York: Holt, Rinehart, and Winston, 1978.

Tetley, Nigel. *Trimaran Solo: The Story of Victress' Circumnavigation and Last Voyage*. Lymington, England: Nautical Publishing Co., 1970.

Tomalin, Nicholas, and Ron Hall. *The Strange Last Voyage of Donald Crowhurst*. New York: Stein & Day, 1970.

Issues of *The Sunday Times, Daily Express,* and *Sunday Mirror* between 11 January 1968 and 24 February 1972.

Interview with Bobby Uriburu regarding Vito Dumas, whom Bobby knew well.